LET'S

■ PAGES PACKED WITH ESSENTIAL INFORMATION

"Value-packed, unbeatable, accurate, and comprehensive."

—*The Los Angeles Times*

"The guides are aimed not only at young budget travelers but at the independent traveler; a sort of streetwise cookbook for traveling alone."

—*The New York Times*

"Unbeatable; good sight-seeing advice; up-to-date info on restaurants, hotels, and inns; a commitment to money-saving travel; and a wry style that brightens nearly every page."

—*The Washington Post*

■ THE BEST TRAVEL BARGAINS IN YOUR BUDGET

"All the dirt, dirt cheap."

—*People*

"Let's Go follows the creed that you don't have to toss your life's savings to the wind to travel—unless you want to."

—*The Salt Lake Tribune*

■ REAL ADVICE FOR REAL EXPERIENCES

"The writers seem to have experienced every rooster-packed bus and lunar-surfaced mattress about which they write."

—*The New York Times*

"[Let's Go's] devoted updaters really walk the walk (and thumb the ride, and trek the trail). Learn how to fish, haggle, find work—anywhere."

—*Food & Wine*

"A world-wise traveling companion—always ready with friendly advice and helpful hints, all sprinkled with a bit of wit."

—*The Philadelphia Inquirer*

■ A GUIDE WITH A SPIRIT AND A SOCIAL CONSCIENCE

"Lighthearted and sophisticated, informative and fun to read. [Let's Go] helps the novice traveler navigate like a knowledgeable old hand."

—*Atlanta Journal-Constitution*

"The serious mission at the book's core reveals itself in exhortations to respect the culture and the environment—and, if possible, to visit as a volunteer, a student, or a teacher rather than a tourist."

—*San Francisco Chronicle*

LET'S GO PUBLICATIONS

TRAVEL GUIDES

Australia 9th edition
Austria & Switzerland 12th edition
Brazil 1st edition
Britain 2007
California 10th edition
Central America 9th edition
Chile 2nd edition
China 5th edition
Costa Rica 3rd edition
Eastern Europe 12th edition
Ecuador 1st edition
Egypt 2nd edition
Europe 2007
France 2007
Germany 13th edition
Greece 8th edition
Hawaii 4th edition
India & Nepal 8th edition
Ireland 12th edition
Israel 4th edition
Italy 2007
Japan 1st edition
Mexico 21st edition
Middle East 4th edition
New Zealand 7th edition
Peru 1st edition
Puerto Rico 2nd edition
South Africa 5th edition
Southeast Asia 9th edition
Spain & Portugal 2007
Thailand 3rd edition
Turkey 5th edition
USA 23rd edition
Vietnam 2nd edition
Western Europe 2007

ROADTRIP GUIDE

Roadtripping USA 2nd edition

ADVENTURE GUIDES

Alaska 1st edition
Pacific Northwest 1st edition
Southwest USA 3rd edition

CITY GUIDES

Amsterdam 4th edition
Barcelona 3rd edition
Boston 4th edition
London 15th edition
New York City 16th edition
Paris 14th edition
Rome 12th edition
San Francisco 4th edition
Washington, D.C. 13th edition

POCKET CITY GUIDES

Amsterdam
Berlin
Boston
Chicago
London
New York City
Paris
San Francisco
Venice
Washington, D.C.

LET'S GO

HAWAII

Sara Joy Culver Editor
Michael E. Steinhaus Associate Editor

Researcher-Writers
Akash Goel
Paul Hamm
Jake C. Levine
Summer Montacute

Clifford S. Emmanuel Map Editor
Anna A. Mattson-DiCecca Managing Editor

St. Martin's Press New York

HELPING LET'S GO. If you want to share your discoveries, suggestions, or corrections, please drop us a line. We read every piece of correspondence, whether a postcard, a 10-page email, or a coconut. **Address mail to:**

Let's Go: Hawaii
67 Mount Auburn St.
Cambridge, MA 02138
USA

Visit Let's Go at **http://www.letsgo.com,** or send email to:

feedback@letsgo.com
Subject: "Let's Go: Hawaii"

In addition to the invaluable travel advice our readers share with us, many are kind enough to offer their services as researchers or editors. Unfortunately, our charter enables us to employ only currently enrolled Harvard students.

Distributed outside the USA and Canada by Macmillan.

ISBN-13: 978-0-312-36090-0
ISBN-10: 0-312-36090-8
Fourth edition
10 9 8 7 6 5 4 3 2 1

Let's Go: Hawaii is written by Let's Go Publications, 67 Mount Auburn St., Cambridge, MA 02138, USA.

CONTENTS

DISCOVER HAWAII 1
When to Go 1
What to Do 2
Suggested Itineraries 5

LIFE AND TIMES 11
Land 11
People 21
The "Other" Islands 22
Culture 25

ESSENTIALS 36
Planning Your Trip 36
Safety and Health 44
Getting to Hawaii 49
Getting Around Hawaii 52
Keeping in Touch 56
Accommodations 58
Specific Concerns 60
Other Resources 64

BEYOND TOURISM 66
A Philosophy for Travelers 66
Volunteering 67
Studying 69
Working 71

THE GREAT OUTDOORS 75
Camping in Hawaii 75
Wilderness Safety 81
Outdoor Activities 84
Useful Publications and Resources 86
Organized Adventure Trips 87

OAHU 88
HONOLULU 90
WAIKIKI 117
CENTRAL OAHU 133
SOUTHEAST OAHU 137
Waimanalo 140
WINDWARD COAST 143
Kailua 143
Kaneohe and the Windward Coast 150
NORTH SHORE 156
Waimea and Sunset Beach 157
Haleiwa 161
Waialua and Mokuleia 168
LEEWARD COAST 171

THE BIG ISLAND 179
KAILUA-KONA 181
SOUTH KONA 192
KAU AND KA LAE 199
HAWAII VOLCANOES NATIONAL PARK 203
PUNA 214
Volcano 214
Pahoa 217
HILO 221
SADDLE ROAD 230
Mauna Kea 231
Mauna Loa 234
HAMAKUA COAST 235
Honokaa 236
Waipio Valley 239
Waimea 241
NORTH KOHALA INCLUDING HAWI AND KAPAAU 246
SOUTH KOHALA 252

MAUI 256
WEST MAUI 258
Lahaina 259
Kaanapali 269
Honokowai, Kahana, and Napili 270
Kapalua and Beyond 272
CENTRAL MAUI 274
Kahului and Wailuku 274
SOUTH MAUI 282
Maalaea 282
Kihei 283
Wailea 290
Makena and Beyond 291
NORTH SHORE 293
Paia 296
Haiku 299

Hana 302
Kipahulu and Oheo Gulch (Haleakala National Park) 306
The Road from Hana 307
UPCOUNTRY MAUI 307
Kula 308
Polipoli Spring State Recreation Area 310
Haleakala National Park 311
Pukalani 316
Makawao 317

MOLOKAI 322
Kaunakakai 325
CENTRAL MOLOKAI 331
Kalaupapa Peninsula 331
Kamakou Preserve 334
Kalae and Kualapuu 336
Hoolehua 338
EAST OF KAUNAKAKAI 339
WESTERN MOLOKAI 345

LANAI 349
Lanai City 351

KAUAI 360
EAST SHORE 360
Lihue 362
Wailua 370
Waipouli 373
Kapaa 375
NORTH SHORE 378
Kilauea 379
Princeville 382
Hanalei 385
Haena 389
NA PALI COAST 392
Kalalau Trail 393
West of Kalalau 396
SOUTH SHORE 397
Poipu 397
Koloa 404
WEST SHORE 406
Kalaheo 406
Kalaheo to Waimea 408
Waimea 411
Waimea Canyon State Park 414
Kokee State Park 415
Kekaha 420
Polihale State Park 421

GLOSSARY 423

INDEX 426

MAP INDEX 434

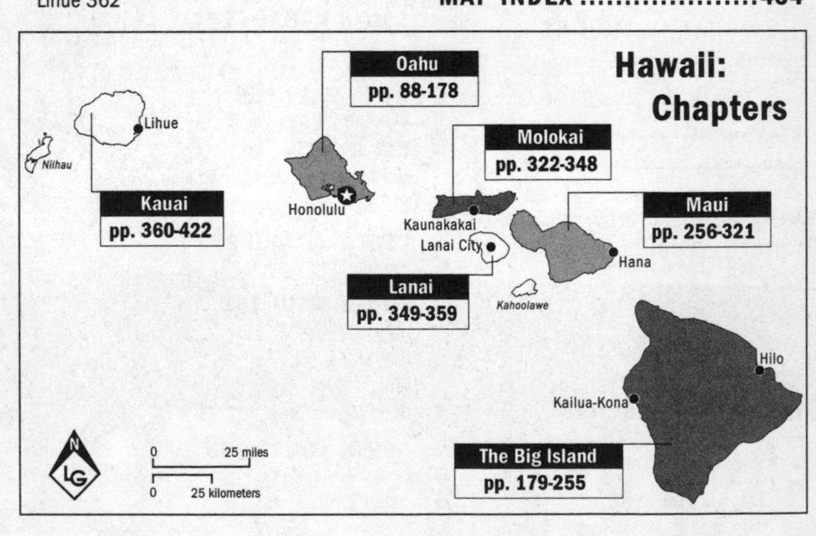

1 2 3 4 5

PRICE RANGES>>HAWAII

Our researchers list establishments in order of value from best to worst; our favorites are denoted by the Let's Go thumbs-up (☒). Since the best value is not always the cheapest price, we have also incorporated a system of price ranges, based on a rough expectation of what you'll spend. For **accommodations,** we base our range on the cheapest price for which a single traveler can stay for one night. For **restaurants** and other dining establishments, we estimate the average amount a traveler will spend. The table tells you what you'll *typically* find in Hawaii at the corresponding price range; keep in mind that no system can allow for every individual establishment's quirks. In other words: expect anything.

ACCOMMODATIONS	RANGE	WHAT YOU'RE *LIKELY* TO FIND
❶	under $25	Camping; most dorm rooms, such as hostels or university dorm rooms. Expect bunk beds and a communal bath; you may have to provide or rent towels and sheets.
❷	$25-65	Upper-end hostels or small hotels. You may have a private bathroom or a sink in your room.
❸	$66-110	A small room with a private bath. Should have decent amenities, such as phone and TV. Breakfast may be included. Many B&Bs are in this range.
❹	$111-150	Similar to ❸, but may have more amenities or be closer to the beach.
❺	$151 and up	Resorts, large hotels, or upscale chains; almost always near the beach.

FOOD	RANGE	WHAT YOU'RE *LIKELY* TO FIND
❶	under $7	Mostly street-corner stands, pizza places, or plate lunch joints. Rarely a sit-down meal.
❷	$7-10	Sandwiches, appetizers at a bar, or low-priced entrees. You may have the option of sitting down or getting takeout.
❸	$11-15	Mid-priced entrees, possibly coming with a soup or salad. Expect the tip to add a couple dollars, since you'll probably have a waiter or waitress.
❹	$16-20	A somewhat fancier restaurant or a steakhouse. Either way, you'll have a special knife.
❺	$21 and up	Food with foreign names and a decent wine list. Wear your best aloha shirt and don't order PB&J.

ABOUT LET'S GO

NOT YOUR PARENTS' TRAVEL GUIDE

At Let's Go, we see every trip as the chance of a lifetime. If your dream is to grab a machete and forge through the jungles of Brazil, we can take you there. If you'd rather bask in the Riviera sun at a beachside cafe, we'll set you a table. We write for readers who know that there's more to travel than sharing double deckers with tourists and who believe that travel can change both themselves and the world—whether they plan to spend six days in London or six months in Latin America. We'll show you just how far your money can go, and prove that the greatest limitation on your adventures is not your wallet, but your imagination.

BEYOND THE TOURIST EXPERIENCE

To help you gain a deeper connection with the places you travel, our fearless researchers scour the globe to give you the heads-up on both world-renowned and off-the-beaten-track attractions, sights, and destinations. They engage with the local culture, only to emerge with the freshest insights on everything from local festivals to regional cuisine. We've also opened our pages to respected writers and scholars to hear their takes on the countries and regions we cover, and asked travelers who have worked, studied, or volunteered abroad to contribute first-person accounts of their experiences. In addition, we've increased our coverage of responsible travel and expanded each guide's Beyond Tourism chapter to share more ideas about how to give back while on the road.

FORTY-SEVEN YEARS OF WISDOM

Let's Go got its start in 1960, when a group of creative and well-traveled students compiled their experience and advice into a 20 page mimeographed pamphlet, which they gave to travelers on charter flights to Europe. Four and a half decades later, we've expanded to cover six continents and all kinds of travel—while retaining our founders' adventurous attitude toward the world. Laced with witty prose and total candor, our guides are still researched and written entirely by students on shoestring budgets, experienced travelers who know that train strikes, stolen luggage, food poisoning, and marriage proposals are all part of a day's work.

THE LET'S GO COMMUNITY

More than just a travel guide company, Let's Go is a community. Our small staff comes together because of our shared passion for travel and our desire to help other travelers see the world the way it was meant to be seen. We love it when our readers become part of the Let's Go community as well—when you travel, drop us a postcard (67 Mt. Auburn St., Cambridge, MA 02138, USA), send us an e-mail (feedback@letsgo.com), or post on our forum (http://www.letsgo.com/connect/forum) to tell us about your adventures and discoveries.

For more information, visit us online: www.letsgo.com.

Hawaii

N
LG

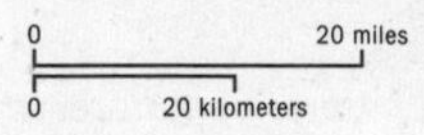
0
20 miles
0
20 kilometers

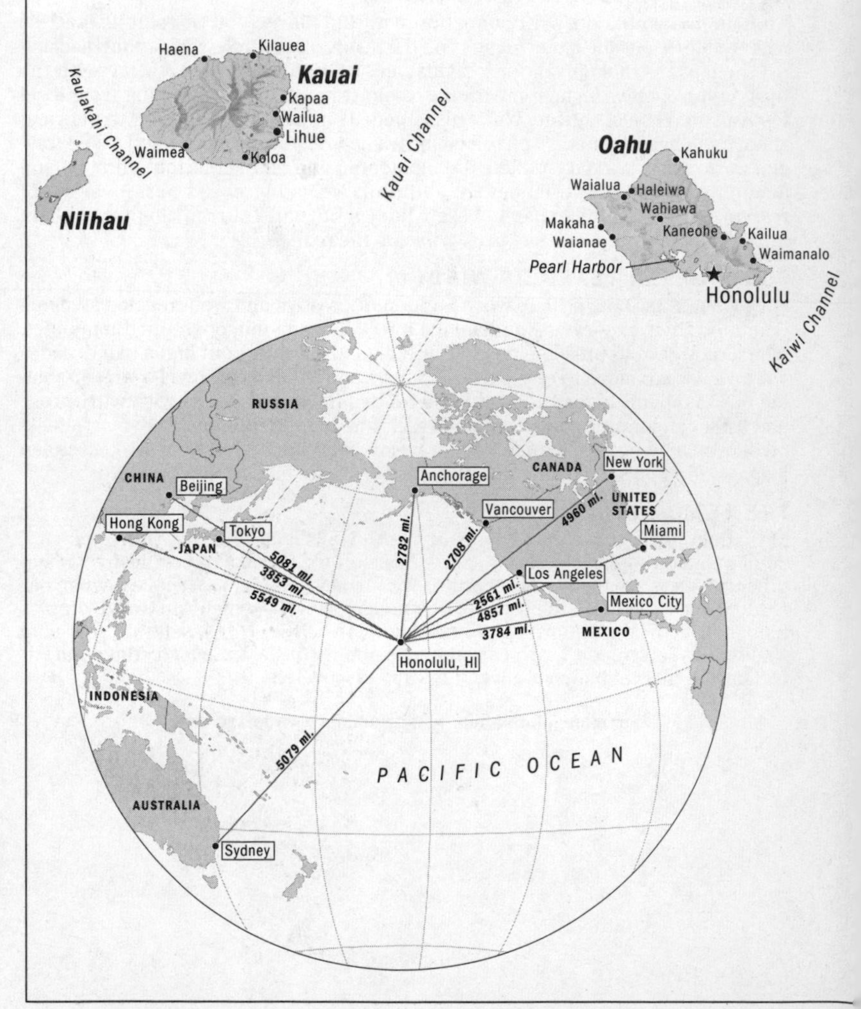
PACIFIC OCEAN
Haena
Kilauea
Kauai
Kapaa
Wailua
Lihue
Waimea
Koloa
Kaulakahi Channel
Niihau
Kauai Channel
Oahu
Kahuku
Waialua
Haleiwa
Wahiawa
Makaha
Waianae
Kaneohe
Kailua
Waimanalo
Pearl Harbor
Honolulu
Kaiwi Channel
RUSSIA
CHINA
Beijing
Hong Kong
Tokyo
JAPAN
Anchorage
CANADA
New York
UNITED STATES
Vancouver
Miami
Los Angeles
Mexico City
MEXICO
5081 mi.
3853 mi.
5549 mi.
2782 mi.
2708 mi.
4960 mi.
2561 mi.
4857 mi.
3784 mi.
Honolulu, HI
INDONESIA
5079 mi.
PACIFIC OCEAN
AUSTRALIA
Sydney

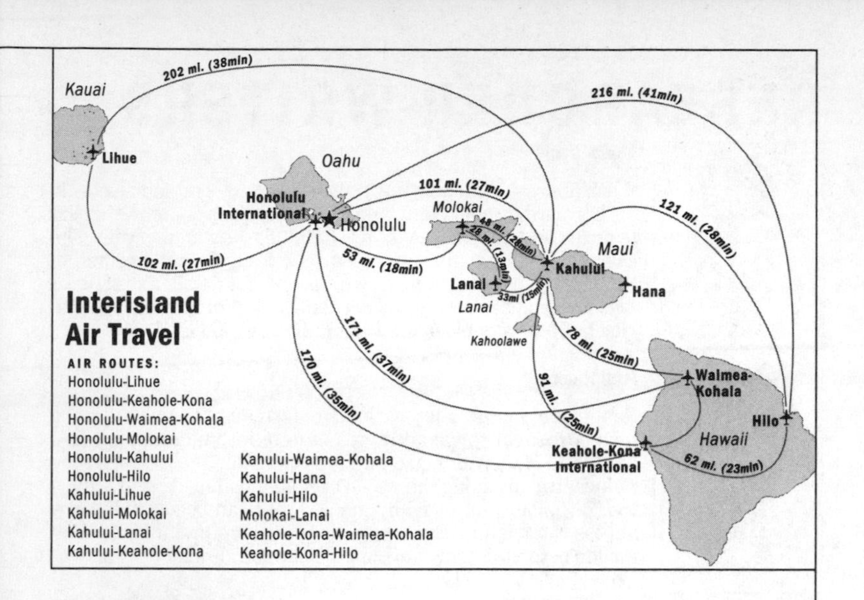
Kauai
202 mi. (38min)
216 mi. (41min)
Lihue
Oahu
Honolulu International
Honolulu
101 mi. (27min)
Molokai
121 mi. (28min)
48 mi. (28min)
28 mi. (13min)
Maui
Kahului
102 mi. (27min)
53 mi. (18min)
Lanai
33mi (15min)
Hana
Lanai
Kahoolawe
171 mi. (37min)
78 mi. (25min)
170 mi. (35min)
91 mi. (25min)
Waimea-Kohala
Hilo
Hawaii
Keahole-Kona International
62 mi. (23min)
Interisland Air Travel
AIR ROUTES:
Honolulu-Lihue
Honolulu-Keahole-Kona
Honolulu-Waimea-Kohala
Honolulu-Molokai
Honolulu-Kahului
Honolulu-Hilo
Kahului-Lihue
Kahului-Molokai
Kahului-Lanai
Kahului-Keahole-Kona
Kahului-Waimea-Kohala
Kahului-Hana
Kahului-Hilo
Molokai-Lanai
Keahole-Kona-Waimea-Kohala
Keahole-Kona-Hilo

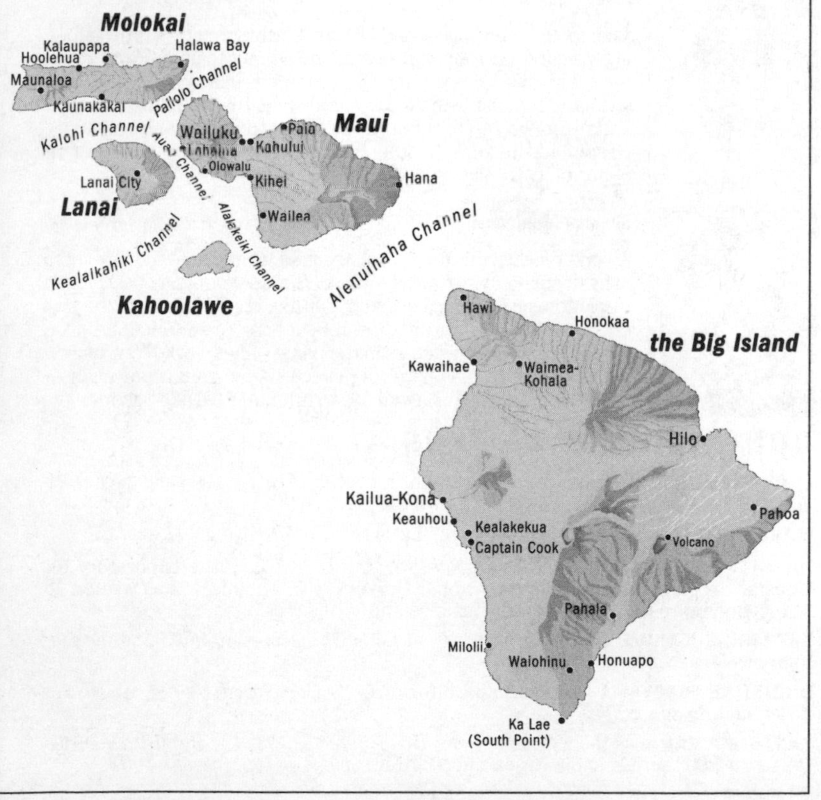
Molokai
Kalaupapa
Hoolehua
Halawa Bay
Maunaloa
Pailolo Channel
Kaunakakai
Maui
Wailuku
Paia
Kalohi Channel
Kahului
Lahaina
Auau Channel
Olowalu
Kihei
Lanai City
Hana
Lanai
Wailea
Kealaikahiki Channel
Alalakeiki Channel
Alenuihaha Channel
Kahoolawe
Hawi
Honokaa
the Big Island
Kawaihae
Waimea-Kohala
Hilo
Kailua-Kona
Keauhou
Kealakekua
Captain Cook
Pahoa
Volcano
Pahala
Milolii
Waiohinu
Honuapo
Ka Lae
(South Point)

RESEARCHER-WRITERS

Akash Goel *Oahu*

When he wasn't tracking down the cast of *Lost* or double-checking lifeguarding hours on Waikiki Beach, Akash composed stellar features and informative copy. Reliably outstanding, this Chicago native threw himself into researching the bustling hub of Honolulu. A pre-med student with an eye for detail, Akash never failed to send back accurate facts and stylish prose, truly embodying both sides of research-writing. Thanks, Akashie!

Paul Hamm *Lanai/Maui*

Paul made our job a joy with his entertaining anecdotes and a hearty respect for deadlines. Ukulele in hand, he explored Lanai and Maui with equal enthusiasm, gathering a close group of local friends along the way. Originally hailing from Washington, D.C., Paul embraced his rugged route and camped his way across the islands. Even an ancient laptop and a lost wallet couldn't stop this truly amazing researcher. Rock on, Paul!

Jake C. Levine *The Big Island/Oahu*

Jake took the Big Island and Oahu's North Shore by storm, gathering insight on surfing, kava bars, and so much more. From swimming with sharks to playing third base for Sharky's Steelers, Jake spent the summer living it up, island-style. His enthusiastic writing and thorough researching never failed to amaze and amuse us. Despite his hectic schedule, he never missed a deadline—or an opportunity to chat up a friendly local. Much love, Jake!

Summer Montacute *Kauai/Molokai*

Always reliable, this recent college grad went above and beyond to meet deadlines with flawless prose. Summer courageously braved rural Molokai and rugged Kauai, battling impeding injury, the brutal Hawaiian sun, and its harsh beaches. Ms. Montacute even fended off Hawaiian suitors in the name of her work. Traveling off the beaten path, this researcher succeeded in uncovering many of the hidden gems that Hawaii has to offer. *MAHALO*, Summer!

CONTRIBUTING WRITERS

LUCY EBERSOLD was a Researcher-Writer for *Let's Go: Hawaii 2004* and the Associate Editor for *Let's Go: Spain, Portugal, and Morocco 2003*.

MAREN LAU was a Researcher-Writer for *Let's Go: California 1997*.

DR. STEPHEN P. LEATHERMAN is a professor and Director of the Laboratory for Coastal Research at Florida International University in Miami. He has written 18 books and more than 200 scientific articles about beaches.

KATHERINE J. THOMPSON was the Editor of *Let's Go: Germany 2005* and the Cartography Manager for the 2006 series.

CHRISTINE YOKOYAMA was the Map Editor of *Let's Go: Hawaii 2004*, *Australia 2004*, and *Boston 2004*.

SARAH ROTMAN was the Editor of *Let's Go: Boston 2001*, the Publishing Director of the 2002 series, and a Researcher-Writer for *Let's Go: Hawaii 2003*.

ACKNOWLEDGMENTS

TEAM HAWAII THANKS: To Anna, for slow dancing and keeping us on schedule; to Cliff for love from Mapland; and to our RWs, who kept us entertained all summer. Thanks to 67 Mt. Auburn for **air-conditioning,** to Darwin's for sandwiches, and to the Decemberists for kick-ass working music.

SARA THANKS: Many thanks to Michael Stupidhead, for hours and hours of hard work and a great sense of humor—this book would not exist without your passion(fruit). Thanks to Anna, for being the most patient ME in the world. Love to the entire USA pod, my parents, and my **little sister.** Thanks to Mimi and Poppa for giving me a much-needed vacation! This summer would not have been possible without you all...and googlechat, **Dunkin' Donuts,** the P&P chair, and Big Love.

MICHAEL THANKS: Fearless **Sara** for her organization, playlists, and teaching me the subtleties of the passion fruit; insightful **Anna** for her morning visits and purple-covered pages; our RWs for giving me flawless copy and vicarious sun and sand all summer; and noble Falcor, the flying dog. Love to my housemates; to Betsy; to **Dan, Joel,** Anne, and Witchy for helping me live the dream; to G&P and B&B; and Papa, especially, whose love of Maui was a continual source of inspiration. Finally, to **Mom and Dad,** to whom I am forever indebted.

CLIFF THANKS: Thanks to Akash for brevity, Jake for variety, Summer for consistency, and Paul for the sweet map and epic Beirut game. Also thanks to my first-rate, always-on-time editors, Sara and Michael.

Editor
Sara Joy Culver
Associate Editor
Michael E. Steinhaus
Managing Editor
Anna A. Mattson-DiCecca
Map Editor
Clifford S. Emmanuel
Typesetter
Katherine J. Thompson

LET'S GO

Publishing Director
Alexandra C. Stanek
Editor-in-Chief
Laura E. Martin
Production Manager
Richard Chohaney Lonsdorf
Cartography Manager
Clifford S. Emmanuel
Editorial Managers
August Dietrich, Samantha Gelfand, Silvia Gonzalez Killingsworth
Financial Manager
Jenny Qiu Wong
Publicity Manager
Anna A. Mattson-DiCecca
Personnel Manager
Sergio Ibarra
Production Associate
Chase Mohney
IT Director
Patrick Carroll
Director of E-Commerce
Jana Lepon
Office Coordinators
Adrienne Taylor Gerken, Sarah Goodin

Director of Advertising Sales
Mohammed J. Herzallah
Senior Advertising Associates
Kedamai Fisseha, Roumiana Ivanova

President
Brian Feinstein
General Manager
Robert B. Rombauer

HOW TO USE THIS BOOK

INTRODUCTORY MATERIAL. The first chapter, **Discover Hawaii,** will introduce you to the Hawaiian islands and get you primed for an unforgettable adventure. Additionally, our brand-new **Suggested Itineraries** make planning your trip a no-brainer.

ESSENTIALS. All the practical information involved in traveling can get downright pesky. Flip here for a quick and easy guide to Hawaii, including advice on getting there, getting around, finding a place to stay, and staying safe.

LIFE AND TIMES. This chapter has the answer to all your burning questions. Why do so many Hawaiian words sound the same? Who was Kamehameha the Great? What's the deal with Spam? History, culture, music—you name it. It's all here.

GREAT OUTDOORS. Want to know how to cut through camping red tape, stay safe in the wilderness, or find out where the best beaches are for all your favorite activities? We're giving it to you, dear reader, in one convenient and practical location.

COVERAGE. A chapter is dedicated to each major Hawaiian island—Oahu, the Big Island, Maui, Molokai, Lanai, and Kauai. Info on the "Other Islands"— Kahoolawe, Niihau, and the NW Hawaiian Islands—is in the Life and Times chapter.

SCHOLARLY ARTICLES. We hired the experts to share their insight in the following articles: **"Ride the Wave: Surfing in Hawaii"** (p. 178), **"Hula: A Brief History"** (p. 321), and **"Dr. Beach on Hawaii's Beaches"** (p. 422).

SOLO TRAVELERS. All of our accommodations and transportation information is geared toward options for the solo traveler; we do report on accommodations for travelers in larger groups, but the default is one person. Transportation prices are for one-way travel unless otherwise noted.

GLOSSARY. The Hawaiian islands have a language all their own. In our Hawaiian glossary, we've included many common words and phrases to help you avoid looking and sounding like a tourist.

PRICE RANGES AND RANKINGS. Our researchers list establishments in order of value from best to worst. Our favorites have earned the Let's Go thumbs-up (☒). Since the best value may not mean the lowest price, we have incorporated a system of price ranges for food and accommodations into the guide on p. viii and inside the back cover. These are indicated by ❶❷❸❹❺ symbols in the text.

TIP BOXES. Tip boxes provide a wealth of information, from the smallest "didn't you know..." tip to pointers that can make or break your Hawaiian vacation (or at least part of it). Boxes with other icons contain warnings and further resources.

SIDEBAR FEATURES. Read up on recent news, hidden deals, big splurges, local interviews, festivals, regional cuisine, local lore, and researchers' stories from the road.

A NOTE TO OUR READERS. The information for this book was gathered by *Let's Go* researchers from May through August of 2006. Each listing is based on one researcher's opinion, formed during his or her visit at a particular time. Those traveling at other times may have different experiences since prices, dates, hours, and conditions are always subject to change. You are urged to check the facts presented in this book beforehand to avoid inconvenience and surprises.

DISCOVER HAWAII

A state unlike any other, Hawaii has been billed as the American tropical paradise since the 1950s. Half a century later, millions of people have discovered Hawaii—they've sunbathed on its spectacular white-, black-, golden-, green-, and red-sand beaches, become infatuated with Hawaiian culture and the forgivably tacky aloha shirts, felt the sublime allure of powerful Pacific waves and the inexplicable awesomeness of flowing lava and active volcanoes, and succumbed to the indelible charm of a laid-back Hawaiian lifestyle. Hawaii's six major islands have so many facets it is impossible to uncover them all in one trip.

The beauty of the trails, verdant wilderness, and cliffs of Kauai—the oldest and arguably most majestic island—is unrivaled. Maui unveils its elegance on the road to Hana, one of the most beautiful drives in the world, or from the lonely summit of Haleakala National Park. The Big Island brandishes its raw and rugged side at Hawaii Volcanoes National Park and the Waipio and Pololu Valleys. On Oahu, tan or learn to surf at Waikiki's wide beaches; at night, hit up the glamorous clubs and free beachside hulas and movies. Oahu's North Shore, the domain of professional surfers, serves as a pleasant escape from the touristy areas elsewhere on the island. Molokai and Lanai remain a Hawaii without stoplights or many paved roads, where street addresses are largely irrelevant and life is best taken slowly

Even without the historic temples and palaces to see, the legends to absorb, the waves to surf, the bays to snorkel in, and the whales to watch, the quintessence of Hawaii's appeal may still be that accessible, yet exotic, tropical paradise: part of the US, yet decidedly independent. You will come back for the beaches, for the lava, hula, hikes, and, above all, for the intangible allure that is Hawaii. Along every coast there is a more secluded stretch of sand, and beyond each stunning vista an even more breathtaking view. The diversity of land, people, and culture ensures that, in Hawaii, the journey never ends.

FACTS AND FIGURES

STATE POPULATION: 1,275,194.

LOWEST RECORDED TEMPERATURE: 56°F.

STATE MOTTO: *Ua mau ke ea o ka aina i ka pono.* (The life of the land is perpetuated in righteousness.)

STATE SPAM CONSUMPTION RATE: over 18,000 cans per day.

MAXIMUM WEIGHT OF A DOUBLE COCONUT: 50 lb.

UNOFFICIAL STATE FISH: *Humuhumunukunukuapuaa* (Hawaiian triggerfish).

WHEN TO GO

How soon can you leave? With year-round temperatures rarely straying far from 80°F, Hawaii's climate is always welcoming. Even the hotter summer months are cooled by trade winds, and the ocean averages a pleasant 75°F. Though wind and rainstorms are more common in winter, they usually pass through the

BEST ADVENTURES BY SEA

Your trip won't be complete without a day on the beach or time in the water: Hawaii has 750 mi. of coastline, coastal waters that contain 70% of the reefs in the US, and perfect conditions for a slew of watersports.

1. Maui: Snorkel in the **Fishbowl** (p. 292), located away from the crowds and 35min. off the beaten path, or at the **Aquarium** (p. 292), a larger cove.
2. Oahu: Kiteboard–or learn how to–on the gorgeous and windy **Kailua Bay** (p. 148).
3. The Big Island: Bodysurf at the often overlooked **Papalokea Green Sands Beach** (p. 202).
4. Maui: Windsurf off Paia at **Hookipa Beach** (p. 299).
5. Maui: Sail from Kihei out to **Molokini Crater** (p. 288) for unparalleled snorkeling.
6. Oahu: Surf on world-class waves at any one of several **North Shore beaches** (p. 159).
7. Kauai: Spelunk through the frigid water of the wet caves in **Haena State Park** (p. 392).
8. Oahu: Swim or snorkel next to hundreds of brightly colored fish in **Hanauma Bay** (p. 137).
9. Molokai: Kayak along the **North Shore Sea Cliffs** (p. 344), with untouched valleys and the longest ocean-terminating waterfall in the world.
10. Kauai: Marvel at the fiery sunset from blissfully remote **Polihale Beach** (p. 421).

islands quickly and without incident. Hawaii's mountainous regions and valleys are often rainy and damp, though weather is localized and beachgoers are almost always able to find sunny patches on the drier, leeward sides of the islands. Depending on the focus of your vacation, there may be specific times when you should travel. Winter is surf season, when hard-core board riders and their groupies make the pilgrimage to Oahu's North Shore for the biggest waves of the year. Families with young children should consider a summer vacation, when swimming conditions are generally safer and plenty of other kids are guaranteed to be playing in the surf. December through April is considered high season in Hawaii, with a second high season in the summer. Accommodations are generally cheaper in the fall and spring, but flights are consistently expensive. The relatively cheap tickets are usually available in September.

WHAT TO DO

It is far less difficult to find things to do in Hawaii than to find time in which to do them. Hundreds of miles of winding trails, deep valleys, canyons, swamps, windswept crater floors, and lava-desecrated land await. There's plenty of sand and surf to occupy the beach bum and more than enough frozen concoctions to fill the nights. If the Mai Tais aren't slowing you down, Hawaii's historical sights, tours, and museums might. Throughout the islands, Hawaii's local culture remains a vivid backdrop, wooing travelers with colorful tales, local island grinds, and a genuinely welcoming attitude.

ADVENTURE SPORTS

Hawaii takes sports to a new level. Across the islands, there are athletes and travelers toeing the edge and pushing the limits of what is possible. Yet, adventure sports aren't just for the future Ironman—for every grueling hike, there's a leisurely one, and for every big surf beach, there's a handful of "learning" beaches. Whatever your level of expertise, Hawaii has you covered.

On **Oahu,** surfing reigns supreme. Every year, countless people catch their first waves at **Baby Queen's** (p. 128) in Waikiki, while many others perfect their technique on innumerable others. The winter months bring mammoth waves to the **North Shore** (p. 156) and the Leeward Coast's **Makaha Beach** (p. 175), as well as the surf junkies who roam the globe in search of the perfect wave. The rest of the island is also not without appeal. **Kailua Beach** (p. 148), with its constant breeze, is a windsurfer's paradise, and on the eastern coast, **Sandy Beach** (p. 139) and **Makapuu** (p. 139) are to boogie boarding what the North Shore is to surfing.

The **Big Island** offers opportunities for on-land adventures, with mountain biking on **Mauna Kea** (p. 231), as well as biking, horseback riding, and ATVing in the **Waipio Valley** (p. 239). Snorkelers will delight in the underwater sights of **Kealakekua Bay** (p. 196) and **Lapakahi State Historical Park** (p. 249). The Big Island is also the site of the most extreme event of them all—the **Ironman Triathlon,** held annually in October.

Maui beckons adventurers. Helicopter tours run out of **Kahului** (p. 274), dolphin- and whale-watching cruises leave from **Maalaea** (p. 282), and snorkel trips to **Molokini** are popular in **Kihei** (p. 283). **Paia** beaches (p. 298) are prime surfing and windsurfing spots, and within **Haleakala National Park** (p. 311), several companies offer bike tours. The surf spot **Jaws** (p. 301) is known for its immense waves that are too big to tackle without motorized assistance—surfers have jet skis tow them in.

On **Kauai,** beginners can get an easy introduction to the art of surfing on **Hanalei's** (p. 385) gentle waves. Advanced kayakers navigate the **Na Pali Coast** (p. 392) and snorkelers drift happily among the native fish at **Tunnels Beach** (p. 391).

ALOHA SPIRIT

The evidence of Hawaii's storied past is everywhere—from the 25 million artifacts that are meticulously maintained in the Bishop Museum to petroglyphs etched into rock throughout the islands. Every landmark, be it valley, rock, mountain, or cave, has a story behind it. The *menehune* (legendary laborers) supposedly have had a hand in the creation of everything, and ancient Hawaiian kings had more stomping grounds and battlefields than we could possibly record.

Oahu is the site of the only Royal Palace on US soil, **Iolani Palace** (p. 107), built by King Kalakuala, and the **Aliiolai Hale** (p. 108), which housed the legislature and Supreme Court of the Hawaiian Kingdom. The **Polynesian Cultural Center** (p. 154) performers dance Tahitian hula and demonstrate Samoan fire-making skills.

Hilo, on the **Big Island** hosts the biggest and most prestigious hula festival, the **Merrie Monarch Hula Festival** (p. 228). The **Puuhonua O Honaunau National Historical Park** (p. 198) is a reconstructed 180-acre village that was the home of Kona's royal chiefs. **Mookini Luakini Heiau** (p. 250) is one of Hawaii's oldest and most sacred religious sites by the birthplace of Kamehameha I, where kings would pray and make human sacrifices to Ku, the god of war.

Maui's Iao Valley State Park (p. 280) is a battlefield where Kamehameha I won a victory over the rival king of Oahu, and its **Iao Needle** is named after the phallus of sea god Kanalou. **Maui Nei** (p. 266) leads a historical tour of downtown Lahaina from a Native Hawaiian perspective. The **Hana Cultural Center** (p. 306) preserves Hawaiian history and culture with unique quilts and woodcarvings.

Little **Molokai** was the birthplace of hula and celebrates it every year with the **Ka Hula Piko** (p. 347) festival. It also has the second-largest temple in Hawaii, **Iliiliopae Heaiu** (p. 341), whose flat stone surface rivals the size of a football field. **Lanai** has two well-preserved collections of petroglyphs at **Shipwreck Beach** (p. 357) and the **Luahiwa Petroglyphs** (p. 359) on the way to Manelele Bay. The rocky landscape of the **Garden of the Gods** (p. 356), or *Keahikawelo*, is steeped in legend.

Kauai is the location of the first American possession in Hawaii, the offshore **Mokuaeae Rock** (p. 382) that King Kalalakua lost in a poker game. **Polihale Cliff** (p. 421) was a "jumping point of souls" where the spirits of the dead would spring away from the earth into the blazing sun. See the index for a complete list of the *heiaus* (temples) covered.

LET'S GO PICKS

BEST PLACE TO HANG TEN: Learn to surf at **Waikiki Beach** (p. 127), where the gentle rollers make every wave a party wave.

BEST COLLECTION OF HAWAII'S HISTORY: The **Bishop Museum** (p. 110), in Honolulu, holds nearly 25 million works of art and artifacts from Hawaii's history.

BEST PLACE TO TEST YOUR METTLE: The **Ironman Triathlon,** a grueling three-part trial, held each year in Kailua-Kona.

BEST PLACE TO FEEL PELE'S FURY: The lava flows of **Kilauea,** the most active volcano in the world, on the Big Island (p. 208).

SWEETEST TESTAMENT TO A FRUIT: The **Dole Plantation Gardens** (p. 136), on Oahu, a shrine to that famed island fruit, the pineapple.

BEST PLACE TO WATCH THE SUN DISAPPEAR BENEATH THE WAVES: Reclining on the dunes of **Polihale State Park** (p. 421), on Kauai.

MAUI (1 WEEK)

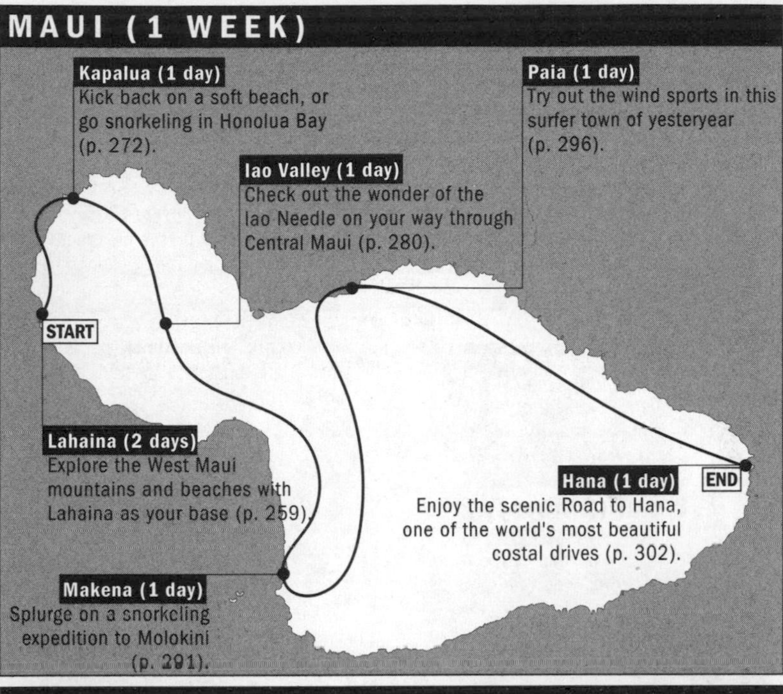
Kapalua (1 day)
Kick back on a soft beach, or go snorkeling in Honolua Bay (p. 272).
Paia (1 day)
Try out the wind sports in this surfer town of yesteryear (p. 296).
Iao Valley (1 day)
Check out the wonder of the Iao Needle on your way through Central Maui (p. 280).
START
Lahaina (2 days)
Explore the West Maui mountains and beaches with Lahaina as your base (p. 259).
Hana (1 day)
END
Enjoy the scenic Road to Hana, one of the world's most beautiful costal drives (p. 302).
Makena (1 day)
Splurge on a snorkeling expedition to Molokini (p. 291).

KAUAI (1 WEEK)

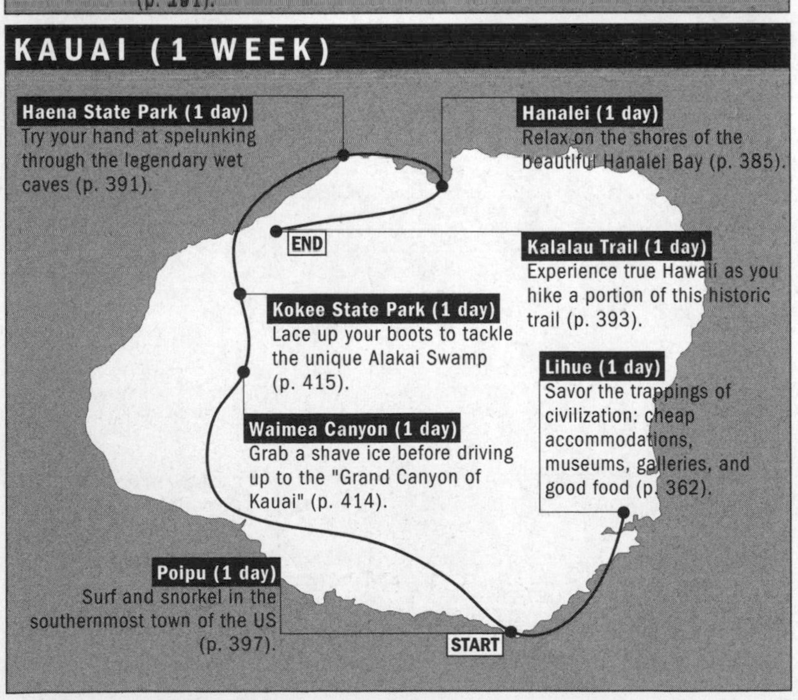
Haena State Park (1 day)
Try your hand at spelunking through the legendary wet caves (p. 391).
Hanalei (1 day)
Relax on the shores of the beautiful Hanalei Bay (p. 385).
END
Kalalau Trail (1 day)
Experience true Hawaii as you hike a portion of this historic trail (p. 393).
Kokee State Park (1 day)
Lace up your boots to tackle the unique Alakai Swamp (p. 415).
Lihue (1 day)
Savor the trappings of civilization: cheap accommodations, museums, galleries, and good food (p. 362).
Waimea Canyon (1 day)
Grab a shave ice before driving up to the "Grand Canyon of Kauai" (p. 414).
Poipu (1 day)
Surf and snorkel in the southernmost town of the US (p. 397).
START

OFF THE BEATEN PATH (2 WEEKS)

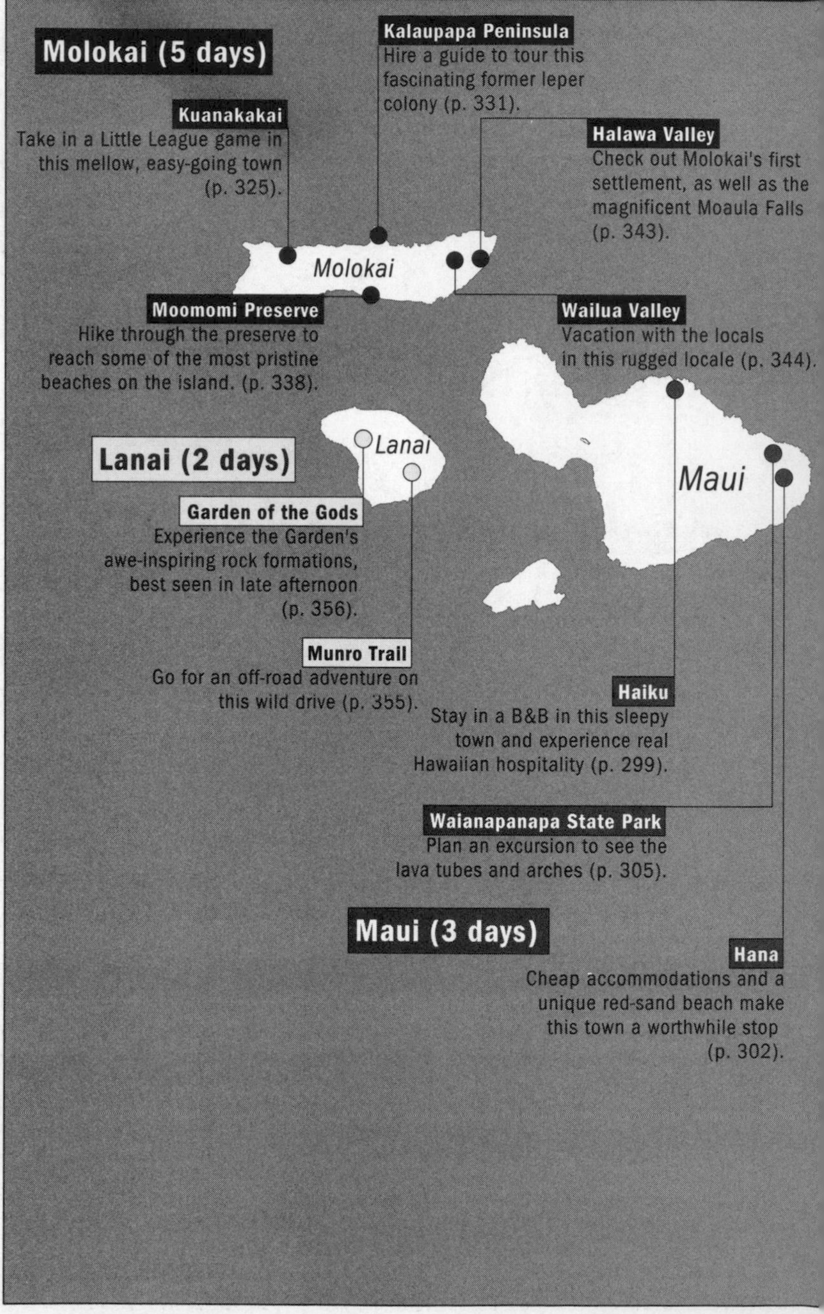

Molokai (5 days)

Kuanakakai
Take in a Little League game in this mellow, easy-going town (p. 325).

Kalaupapa Peninsula
Hire a guide to tour this fascinating former leper colony (p. 331).

Halawa Valley
Check out Molokai's first settlement, as well as the magnificent Moaula Falls (p. 343).

Molokai

Moomomi Preserve
Hike through the preserve to reach some of the most pristine beaches on the island. (p. 338).

Wailua Valley
Vacation with the locals in this rugged locale (p. 344).

Lanai (2 days)

Lanai

Garden of the Gods
Experience the Garden's awe-inspiring rock formations, best seen in late afternoon (p. 356).

Munro Trail
Go for an off-road adventure on this wild drive (p. 355).

Maui

Haiku
Stay in a B&B in this sleepy town and experience real Hawaiian hospitality (p. 299).

Waianapanapa State Park
Plan an excursion to see the lava tubes and arches (p. 305).

Maui (3 days)

Hana
Cheap accommodations and a unique red-sand beach make this town a worthwhile stop (p. 302).

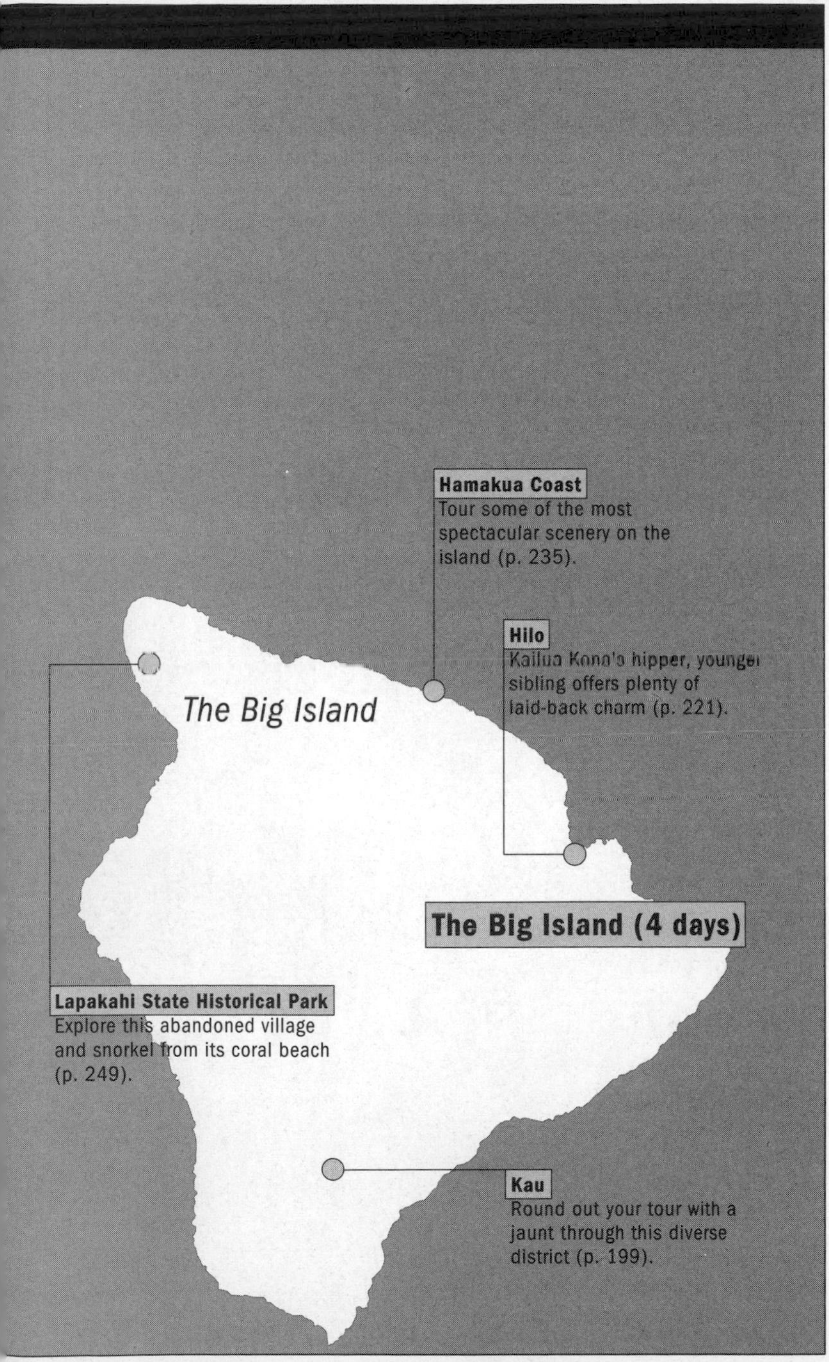

The Big Island

Hamakua Coast
Tour some of the most spectacular scenery on the island (p. 235).

Hilo
Kailua Kona's hipper, younger sibling offers plenty of laid-back charm (p. 221).

The Big Island (4 days)

Lapakahi State Historical Park
Explore this abandoned village and snorkel from its coral beach (p. 249).

Kau
Round out your tour with a jaunt through this diverse district (p. 199).

BACK TO NATURE (2 WEEKS)

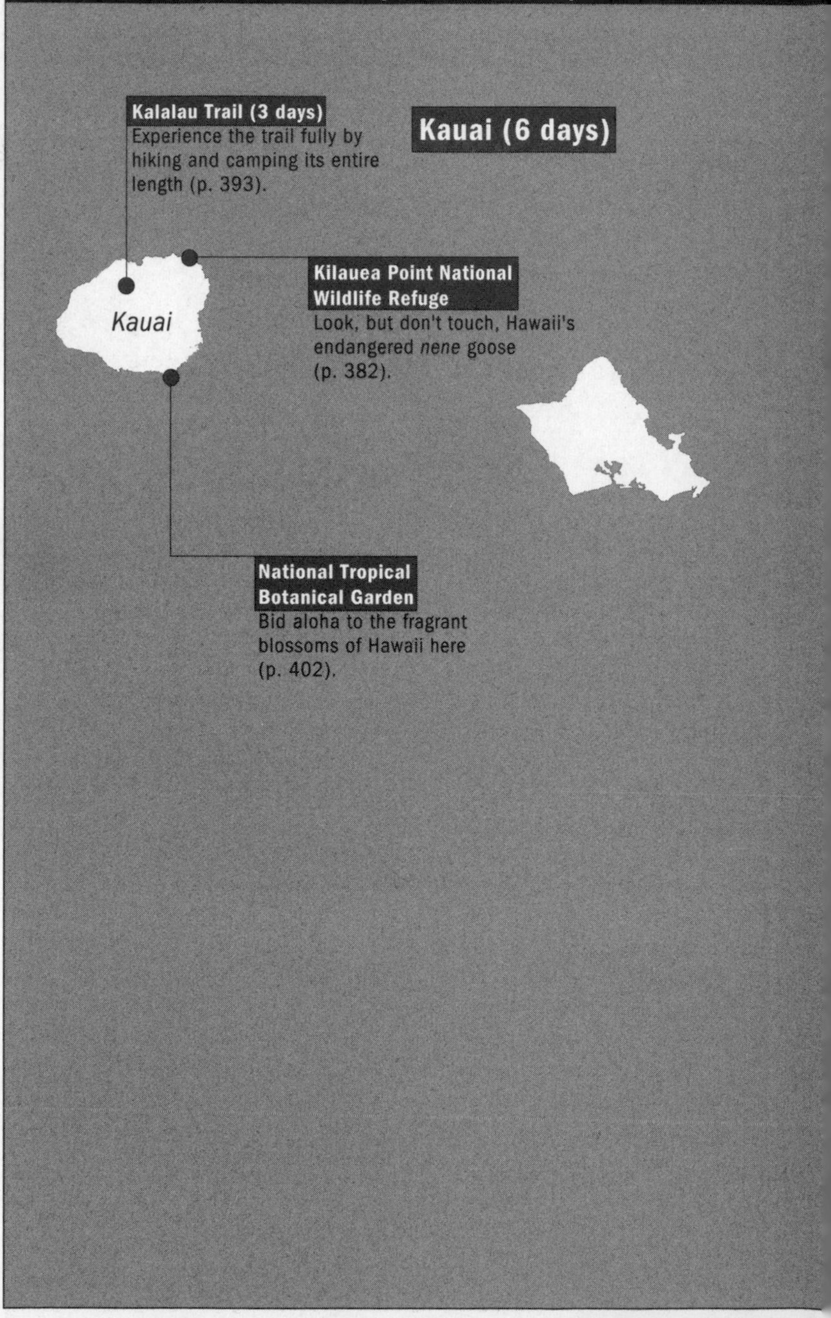

Kalalau Trail (3 days)
Experience the trail fully by hiking and camping its entire length (p. 393).

Kauai (6 days)

Kauai

Kilauea Point National Wildlife Refuge
Look, but don't touch, Hawaii's endangered *nene* goose (p. 382).

National Tropical Botanical Garden
Bid aloha to the fragrant blossoms of Hawaii here (p. 402).

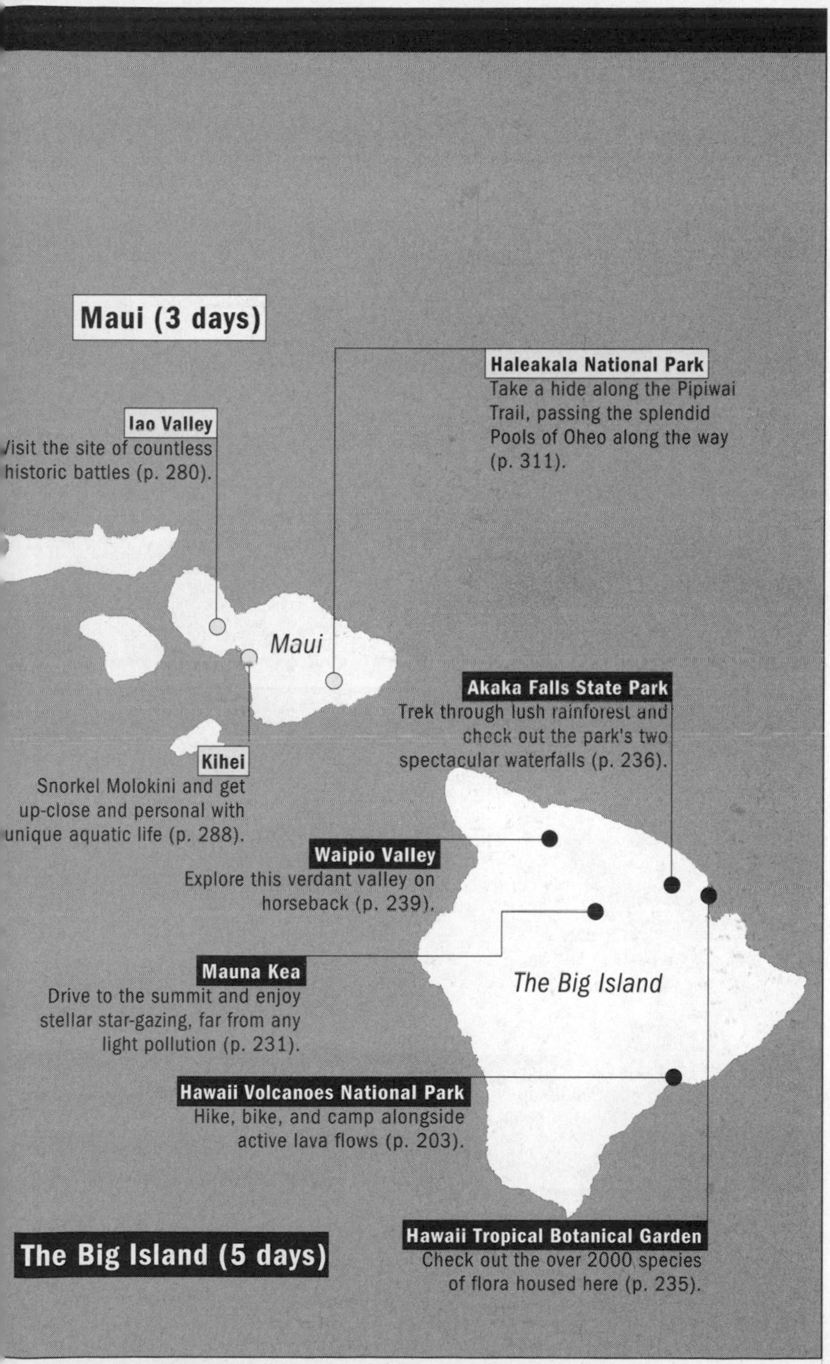

Maui (3 days)

Haleakala National Park
Take a hide along the Pipiwai Trail, passing the splendid Pools of Oheo along the way (p. 311).

Iao Valley
Visit the site of countless historic battles (p. 280).

Maui

Akaka Falls State Park
Trek through lush rainforest and check out the park's two spectacular waterfalls (p. 236).

Kihei
Snorkel Molokini and get up-close and personal with unique aquatic life (p. 288).

Waipio Valley
Explore this verdant valley on horseback (p. 239).

Mauna Kea
Drive to the summit and enjoy stellar star-gazing, far from any light pollution (p. 231).

The Big Island

Hawaii Volcanoes National Park
Hike, bike, and camp alongside active lava flows (p. 203).

The Big Island (5 days)

Hawaii Tropical Botanical Garden
Check out the over 2000 species of flora housed here (p. 235).

OAHU (1 WEEK)

END

North Shore (1 day)
Head up to Sunset Beach to check out the professional surfing on the Bonzai Pipeline (p. 156).

Honolulu (2 days)
Take a day or two to explore the museums and historical sights in downtown Honolulu and Chinatown (p. 90).

Waimanalo (1 day)
Get acquainted with aloha by wandering the streets of this small town, shave ice in hand. (p. 140).

Pearl Harbor (1 day)
Elbow aside the tourists and history buffs to tour the moving WWII memorials (p. 133).

START

Waikiki (1 day)
Kick your vacation up a notch with Waikiki's lively nightlife (p. 127).

Hanauma Bay (1 day)
Snorkel in the crystal-clear bay or kick off your shoes on Sandy Beach (p. 137).

THE BIG ISLAND (1 WEEK)

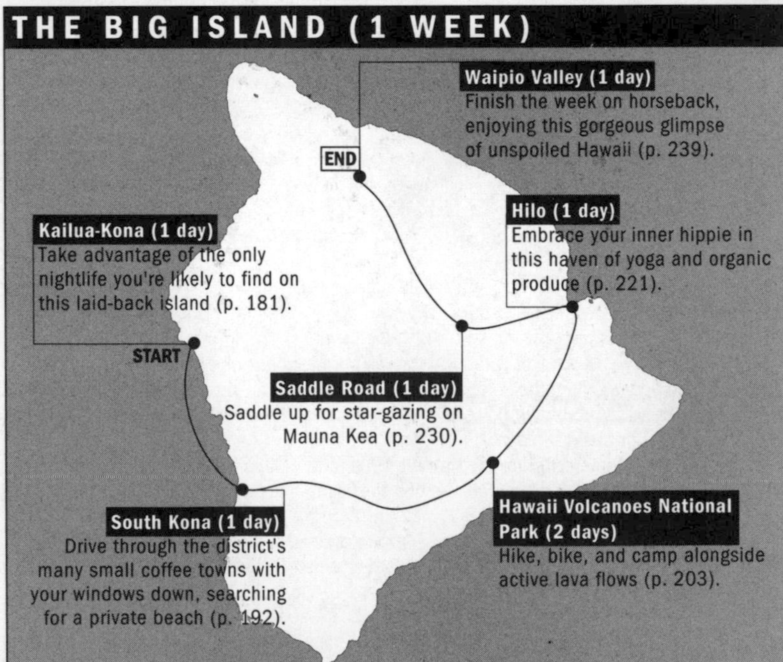
Waipio Valley (1 day)
Finish the week on horseback, enjoying this gorgeous glimpse of unspoiled Hawaii (p. 239).
END
Hilo (1 day)
Embrace your inner hippie in this haven of yoga and organic produce (p. 221).
Kailua-Kona (1 day)
Take advantage of the only nightlife you're likely to find on this laid-back island (p. 181).
START
Saddle Road (1 day)
Saddle up for star-gazing on Mauna Kea (p. 230).
South Kona (1 day)
Drive through the district's many small coffee towns with your windows down, searching for a private beach (p. 192).
Hawaii Volcanoes National Park (2 days)
Hike, bike, and camp alongside active lava flows (p. 203).

LIFE AND TIMES

LAND

Hawaii is located in the Pacific Ocean, about 2400 mi. (3900km) off the coast of the continental US. It is the most isolated populated landmass in the entire world. At approximately the same latitude as central Mexico, it is the southernmost state and the 4th smallest in area, spanning 6450 sq. mi. (16,706 sq. km). The average temperature in Hawaii is 85°F (29°C) in summer and 78°F (26°C) in winter. Hawaii stretches 1523 mi., making it the world's longest island chain, and it contains 132 islands and atolls, all of which are the result of volcanic activity. Only seven of the islands are inhabited, and with the exception of the large but uninhabited Kahoolawe, most of the rest are too small to make human occupancy viable.

Hawaii (or the **Big Island**), the youngest and largest of the Hawaiian islands, is home to three active volcanoes: Kilauea, Mauna Loa, and Hualalai. Kilauea has been erupting continuously since 1983, and visitors to the Hawaii Volcanoes National Park can observe her lava flows up close. Mauna Kea, a dormant volcano that last erupted 45,000 years ago, is the highest point in the state at an altitude of 13,796 ft. (4208m) above sea level. The high cliffs along the northern and southeastern coasts of the Big Island create several dramatic waterfalls. In addition to its natural wonders, the Big Island is known for being the world's leading producer of macadamia nuts and orchids.

LAVA ME TENDER. When Dr. Evil plotted to cover the Earth with "liquid hot magma" in 1999's smash *Austin Powers: The Spy Who Shagged Me,* the would-be world dictator erred in his geological calculations. When the volcanic substance made of liquid and solid rock remains below ground, it is known as **magma.** Once magma is exposed to the air, either through a volcanic eruption or a fissure in the earth, it becomes **lava.** The behavior of lava depends on its chemical composition. **Low silica lava,** which is common in Hawaii, flows and can travel for great distances. **High silica lava,** also called *pyroclastics,* explodes in ash or cinders when it leaves a volcano. In addition to having varying silica levels, Hawaiian lava generally comes in three forms:

Pahoehoe: Nearly all lava in Hawaii erupts as *pahoehoe.* Fast-flowing, it hardens into a smooth, ropy solid because the outermost lava of a lava channel cools before the lava inside does. Such a delay in solidification produces lava tubes; lava can flow within these tubes for long distances.

Pillow: A type of *pahoehoe* lava, pillow lava forms when lava flows into the ocean. When the lava makes contact with water, a solid crust forms immediately. As more lava flows beneath the crust, the crust cracks and oozes "pillows," or blobs, of lava.

Aa: Some attribute the name of this form of lava to an old tale about Captain Cook walking barefoot across the lava, screaming, "Ah! Ah!" Slow-moving *aa* lava is characterized by its rough and jagged appearance. Its flows are thicker than those of the other forms of lava and have been known to pile up (sometimes to heights over 100 ft.). *Pahoehoe* can become *aa* if it experiences an increase in viscosity, that is, if it cools or loses gas.

Maui is a "volcanic doublet"—it was formed by two separate volcanoes that overlapped. The East Maui volcano, sometimes referred to as Haleakala, is considered to be dormant; its last eruption was in 1790. The remains of the West Maui volcano are known as the West Maui Mountains. The fertile expanse between the two volcanoes is conducive to sugarcane cultivation, and much of eastern Maui is covered by tropical rainforest.

Molokai has three distinct geographic regions: the mountainous east, the arid west, and the verdant central plain. The island also contains some of the world's tallest sea cliffs, which soar up to 3000 ft. above the ocean.

Castle & Cooke Resorts owns 98% of **Lanai.** Historically a center for commercial pineapple production, Lanai is aptly nicknamed "the Pineapple Island." Lanai is the only Hawaiian island from which five of the other main islands are visible.

Considerable pineapple and sugar production also takes place on **Oahu,** in the central valley between the Koolau Mountain Range and the Waianae Range. One of the most famous sights on the island is Diamond Head, an extinct volcanic crater on the southeastern coast. At 760 ft. in height and 3520 ft. in diameter, it's impressive, but it hasn't erupted in 150,000 years. Oahu is also the home of Honolulu, the state capital, and Waikiki, a tourist hub.

Kauai is home to the rainiest spot on earth, Mount Waialeale, which averages 460 in. (1143cm) of rain per year. Such heavy rainfall has succeeded in eroding parts of the mountains of Kauai, generating a number of impressive canyons. The northernmost and geologically oldest of the Hawaiian islands, Kauai is often called "The Garden Island," a nod to its lush natural beauty.

FLORA AND FAUNA

Because Hawaii was never part of a larger landmass, none of the plants and animals that exist in Hawaii today originated there. Since the islands of Hawaii were formed from volcanoes on the Pacific floor, it was not until after the lava cooled that tides, winds, and birds carried seeds to the islands. Later, when Polynesian settlers arrived in canoes, bringing plant and animal species from their native lands, much of the flora and fauna on Hawaii developed special adaptations to their new home and evolved into new species. Today, about 90% of the plants and animals on Hawaii are endemic—they exist nowhere else in the world.

Since Hawaii's native plants and animals evolved in the absence of predators or competitors, they did not develop natural defenses like thorns or camouflage. As a result, many native species have been pushed to the brink of extinction by alien plants and animals that have been introduced to the islands in the past few hundred years. Considered the endangered species capital of the US, Hawaii is home to more endangered species per square mile than any other place on the planet.

PLANTS

There are more than 2500 species of native plants in Hawaii, as well as a considerable number of non-native species. One hundred and thirty-nine different types of **ferns** cover Hawaii, and these lush, green plants were some of the first to arrive on the islands, sprouting up on the cooled lava flows. Hawaii's most abundant native tree, the ***ohia lehua,*** is also among the first to spring up on fresh lava flows. Highly distinctive, the *ohia lehua* can be identified by its crooked branches and red, pom-pom-like flowers. It can survive in numerous environments, including elevations from 1000 to 9000 ft. above sea level.

Hawaii's second most prominent native tree is the ***koa,*** which, like the *ohia lehua*, is indigenous to the islands. Capable of growing up to 100 ft. tall, the *koa* has sickle-shaped leaves and yellow flowers clustered into puffballs. Ancient Hawaiians used the reddish wood of the *koa* tree to fashion canoes, surfboards, and weapons. The hard wood is highly sought-after today as a material for making household furniture. Cattle and other feral animals have destroyed thousands of acres of Hawaiian *koa*, but, fortunately, the tree is highly resilient and has thrived under recent reforestation programs.

The **Haleakala silversword,** a spherical flowering plant that grows close to the ground, nearly became extinct in the 1920s due to grazing by goats and cattle. The silversword is still very rare due to its limited range; the only place in the world it can be found is on the Haleakala volcano on Maui. However, protection programs within the Haleakala National Park have saved the species from extinction. Its thin, spiny leaves are covered with tiny silver hairs, and at the end of its 15- to 50-year life span it produces a tall stalk covered with maroon blossoms.

Ki, or ***ti,*** was a symbol of power in ancient Hawaii and was also used as a good-luck charm. Sacred to the fertility god Lono and the goddess of the hula, Laka, *ki* was introduced to Hawaii by Polynesian settlers. A member of the lily family, the *ti* plant has shiny green leaves, which were used as roof thatching, food wrappers, and decoration. The leaves are still used in religious ceremonies and in floral arrangements. *Ki* grows abundantly throughout Hawaii, thriving in areas of low elevation where moisture is plentiful.

Hawaii's state flower is the **yellow hibiscus** (*pua aloalo* or *mao hau hele*). Ubiquitous throughout the islands, there are five endemic species of hibiscus in Hawaii. These brightly colored tropical blossoms can measure up to a foot in diameter and have become a popular symbol of the state. **Orchids, plumeria, bougainvillea,** and **birds of paradise** are also commonly found in Hawaii.

Sugarcane, pineapples, guavas, mangoes, papayas, coconuts, avocados, bananas, limes, passion fruit, macadamia nuts, taro root, breadfruit, and ginger are all cultivated on Hawaii. The endangered **sandalwood** tree, famous for its aromatic oil, also grows on the islands.

ANIMALS

Hawaii has only two native mammals: the **Hawaiian monk seal** and the **hoary bat,** found on the Big Island and in Kokee State Park on Kauai. Unlike most seals, Hawaiian monk seals are solitary animals. They are a very old species; scientists believe that they have not evolved in 15 million years. They are primarily found in the remote regions of the Northwestern Hawaiian islands. Like many species native to Hawaii, they evolved in the absence of predators and have few defense mechanisms. Today, with a population of around 1300-1400, they are considered the most endangered marine mammal in the US. Because the survival of these gentle creatures remains precarious, it is important that visitors not disturb them—please stay a safe distance away.

Humpback whales were among the first species to discover the joy of wintering in Hawaii. Each autumn they travel 3000 mi. from their arctic feeding grounds to the tropical waters of Hawaii, where they mate and give birth. These baleen whales grow to over 50 ft. in length and weigh 30-50 tons. They are known for their spectacular acrobatics and their complex underwater mating songs. They are now an endangered species, as there are only between 15,000 and 20,000 humpbacks worldwide (15-20% of the original population). Maui is the best island from which to see humpback whales, particularly in the winter, from November to February.

Hawaii's state bird, the highly endangered ***nene,*** or Hawaiian goose, is the rarest goose in the world—fewer than 900 exist in the wild. As they tend to nest low to the ground, their low numbers are in part attributed to predation by mongooses, as well as destruction of nests by pigs and other feral animals. Capable of living up to 4000 ft. above sea level, most *nene* dwell on the slopes of volcanoes on the Big Island, though they can also be found on Maui and Kauai. Thought to be closely related to the Canadian goose, the *nene* developed long toes and reduced webbing on their feet for climbing on lava flows.

There are an estimated 700 different species of fish in Hawaiian waters, many of which exist nowhere else in the world. Impress your friends by telling them about Hawaii's unofficial state fish, the ***humuhumunukunukuapuaa*** (pronounced HOO-moo-HOO-moo-NEW-coo-NEW-coo-AH-poo-AH-ah), which is also known as the **reef triggerfish.** This tiny tropical fish is 8-9 in. long and has a trigger-shaped, blue-and-yellow dorsal fin. There are also about 40 different species of **shark** inhabiting Hawaiian waters. The most commonly seen are **tiger sharks** (considered the most dangerous), **reef sharks,** and **hammerheads** (see **Wilderness Safety,** p. 81).

The **mongoose** was introduced to Hawaii in the late 19th century in an attempt to exterminate the rats that were overrunning sugar plantations. Unfortunately, this solution was ineffective, since rats are nocturnal, while mongooses are diurnal. Today, mongooses abound on all of the islands except for Kauai, and they are considered pests because they prey on the eggs of ground-nesting birds, many of which are rare. For more information on the land, plants, and animals of Hawaii, see **Additional Resources,** p. 33.

HISTORY

EARLY HISTORY (AD 500-1778)

The original inhabitants of the Hawaiian islands are believed to have been the descendants of Asiatic peoples who migrated over land and water routes, eventually landing in the Central Pacific. **Polynesian voyagers** from the Marquesas were probably the first to discover the islands, landing near Ka Lae on the Big Island around AD 500-750.

500-750 AD Polynesians arrive from the Marquesas Islands.

1000-1200 AD Tahitian settlers arrive.

Tahitians were the next group of people to reach Hawaii, arriving between AD 1000-1200. These new arrivals are thought to have conquered and enslaved the Marquesans. The Tahitians have had a profound influence on Hawaiian history, bringing their language, customs, government, and religion to the islands. A Tahitian priest known as Paao founded the *kahuna nui* (high priest) line around 1175, initiating a new system of rule that lasted for several hundred years. One *alii nui*, the most powerful *alii* (royal) of the region, headed each island and distributed land to the chiefs below him in a feudal system. The *alii* were believed to have been chosen by the gods, and they served as a link between the people and the deities they worshipped. Below the *alii* and the priest class were the *makaainana* (commoners) and a third class of citizens known as *kaua*. The *kaua* were most often those who had broken *kapu* (taboo) and had neither rights nor property. These early Hawaiians used little writing and preserved most of their history in chants, known as *mele*, and legends. Much of Hawaiian history was lost with the deaths of *kahunas* and others whose duty it was to pass on the knowledge of the ancients.

REDISCOVERY AND WESTERN TRADE (1778-1872)

THE BRITISH ARE COMING

The first known European to arrive in the Hawaiian islands was **Captain James Cook,** who happened upon the islands in 1778 during his third and final quest for the Northwest Passage. After only a brief stop in Hawaii, which he dubbed the Sandwich Islands in honor of the English Earl of Sandwich, Cook sailed north. Cook and his crew are credited with bringing Western plants and animals to the islands, as well as (the somewhat less enchanting) venereal disease.

1778
Captain Cook "discovers" Hawaii and dubs it the Sandwich Islands.

About a year later, on his way back from Alaska, Cook once again spotted the Hawaiian islands, this time landing on the Big Island. Cook and his men were welcomed and allowed to trade with the islanders, departing after two weeks of festivities, only to meet fierce storms that severely damaged their vessels. After being at sea for a week, they returned to Kealakekua Bay, but their second welcome was not as warm as the first. The Native Hawaiians helped themselves to items from Cook's ships in exchange for the supplies and gifts that they had given the British sailors upon their previous arrival. Cook and a small party of his men went ashore to take the island chief hostage and demand the return of their goods (in particular, a small cutter) but the plan went awry; Cook and several of his men were killed in a skirmish with the Hawaiians on Valentine's Day in 1779. Some debate has arisen regarding the true manner of Cook's reception; see **Additional Resources** (p. 33) for further readings.

KAMEHAMEHA THE GREAT

At the time of Cook's discovery, the islands were under the rule of a number of warring kings. Eventually, in 1810, a royal from the Big Island, **Kamehameha,** succeeded in uniting the islands under his rule and reigned for nine peaceful years.

1810
Kamehameha the Great unites the islands into one kingdom.

During Kamehameha's reign, the export of highly prized **sandalwood** to China increased, facilitating trade with other nations, most notably the US and Britain. In 1819 the first whaling ships arrived in Kealakekua Bay. The **whaling industry** became profitable for the conveniently-placed Hawaiian economy, but Western influence was to prove detrimental to the islands. Even as Kamehameha was creating peace and a strong culture, *haoles* (foreigners) were quietly undermining his progress.

1813
Spanish explorers introduce the pineapple to Hawaii.

THE KAMEHAMEHA DYNASTY

With the death of Kamehameha in 1819, power passed to his son, **Kamehameha II,** also known as **Liholiho.** History suggests, however, that Kamehameha the Great's favorite wife, **Kaahumanu,** may have been the real force behind the throne. At Kaahumanu's behest, Liholiho overthrew the ancient *kapu* system by allowing men and women to eat at the same table and ordering the destruction of *heiaus* (temples) and idols. Rolling with the changes, Liholiho became the first Hawaiian king to venture off of the islands. In 1823, he and Queen Kamamalu made their first

1820
Missionaries arrive from Boston.

1822
First cockroach appears on Hawaii, species *Pycnoscelus surinamensis.*

and only official state visit to England, where they both contracted measles and died shortly thereafter.

After his death, Kamehameha's second son, **Kauikeaouli, Kamehameha III** (1813-1854), became king. Only nine years old when he received the crown, Kamehameha III was raised amidst the changing Hawaiian culture. His actions during his reign are emblematic of this cultural transformation. In 1839, Kamehameha III introduced the Declaration of Rights, which is regarded as the Hawaiian Magna Carta. The Declaration of Rights served as the preamble for the Constitution of 1840, which ended Hawaii's days as an absolute monarchy. Eight years later, in 1848, Kamehameha III enacted The Great *Mahele* (division), effectively ending the traditional feudal style of land ownership. True to its name, the edict divided land between the *alii* (royals) and the *makaaina* (commoners), and provided the first legal basis for private land ownership. The division opened the door for the purchase of land not only by previously disenfranchised Native Hawaiians, but also by *haoles* (Caucasians) and commercial investors.

EMERGING INDUSTRY (1840-1940)

SUGAR AND PINEAPPLES

1835
First sugar plantation emerges in Koloa, Kauai.

The release of land in Hawaii in 1848 coincided with the beginning of the decline of the whaling industry and a subsequent movement toward the development of agriculture. By the end of the 19th century, sugar and pineapple plantations run by American businessmen had overtaken much of Hawaii's land, and the crops were the two most important sources of revenue for the Hawaiian economy. The first sugar plantation in Hawaii, the **Koloa Plantation** on Kauai, was founded in 1835, initiating an explosion in the sugar industry; mills soon began to appear all over the islands. In 1850, the Hawaiian legislature approved the hiring of immigrant laborers from Japan, China, the Philippines, and Portugal to work in the booming sugar industry. The inhabitants of today's Hawaii reflect the diversity of these immigrant laborers.

1851
Hawaii's first permanent dentist, Dr. John Mott Smith, takes up residence on Oahu.

The massive Hawaiian pineapple industry began as a one-man operation, but today Hawaii produces one third of the world's commercial supply of pineapples. In 1901, James D. Dole built a pineapple cannery near Wahaiwa, on Oahu, marking the start of the **Hawaiian Pineapple Company.** In 1922, Dole purchased the island of Lanai for the purpose of large-scale production; by 1950, his was the largest pineapple company in the world. Dole was eventually bought out by the **Castle & Cooke** company, which still owns much of Lanai. Pineapples were the state's second-biggest industry until the mid-1940s.

ANNEXATION AND AMERICAN INFLUENCE (1875-1900)

THE END OF THE MONARCHY

David Kalakaua (1836-1891) was elected king in 1874. The "Merrie Monarch" began his reign with a tour of the United States in 1881, the first time a Hawaiian king had visited the mainland.

Kalakaua was proud of Hawaiian culture and promoted traditional Hawaiian customs and heritage at home and abroad. He reintroduced hula and wrote the lyrics for the Hawaiian national anthem, "*Hawaii Ponoi*," which is now the state song.

Under Kalakaua's reign the **Reciprocity Treaty of 1875** was passed, which foreshadowed the annexation of Hawaii. Under the treaty, Hawaiian sugar was admitted tax-free into the US, and in return a number of American products could enter Hawaii duty-free. The treaty gave Hawaiian sugar a favorable position in US markets, but it also consolidated American economic supremacy in Hawaiian trade and strengthened the influence of American sugar interests in the kingdom.

In 1887, Kalakaua signed the **Bayonet Constitution,** which revised Kamehameha V's Constitution of 1864. Kalakaua signed the constitution under threat of armed disturbance and much of his power was transferred to his cabinet. The new constitution granted Americans and other foreigners with at least one year of residency in Hawaii the right to vote if they paid taxes and pledged to honor the constitution. The act enfranchised foreign businessmen, cementing their increasing influence in the islands.

The controversy over the constitution and struggle for political power under Kalakaua carried over into the reign of his sister, **Queen Liliuokalani** (1838-1917). Hawaii's last monarch and only reigning queen ascended to the throne in 1891 following the death of her brother. In 1893, Liliuokalani recommended a new Hawaiian constitution, seeking to empower herself and Native Hawaiians. Queen Liliuokalani, slowed by ministers who feared a backlash from the white business community, failed to move quickly enough to ratify the proposals to expand suffrage to the common people. In the meantime, the **Annexation Club,** a group of white plantation owners, held a secret meeting to discuss the proceedings in government. The group formed a Committee of Public Safety that planned for troops to take control of Iolani Palace and other government buildings, set up a provisional government, and put forth a bid for US annexation.

AMERICAN RULE BEGINS

Queen Liliuokalani abdicated her throne to avoid bloodshed, and the provisional government gained power in 1893, due in large part to the force and manipulations of the Annexation Club. US President Grover Cleveland did not immediately ratify the annexation but instead sent **James Blount** to investigate the conditions of the overthrow of the monarchy. Blount's report indicated that the majority of Hawaiians had not favored the move, and that American plantation owners had incited the revolt in order to further their own business interests. Blount charged that the illegal overthrow of Liliuokalani resulted from pressure by revolutionary leaders and US Minister John L. Stevens.

The annexation advocates succeeded in establishing a provisional government headed by Sanford B. Dole in 1894, despite President Cleveland's subsequent attempts to restore Queen Liliuokalani to her throne. Liliuokalani was arrested and imprisoned for eight months in Iolani Palace in 1895 after she was accused of attempting a counterrevolution.

1881
Macadamia nuts are first introduced to Hawaii.

1889
Father Damien dies on the Kalaupapa Peninsula leper colony on Molokai. (p. 332)

1899
The first two automobiles arrive in Honolulu; the first car accident occurs a mere five months later.

1900
Honolulu's Chinatown burns to the ground after a disastrous attempt to stop an outbreak of bubonic plague.

Hawaii becomes a US territory.

1902
Cables connect Hawaii to the mainland, facilitating communication with the rest of the world.

1912
Duke Kahanamoku participates in the Olympics in Stockholm.

In 1898, under President Cleveland's successor, William McKinley, a joint resolution of the US Congress approved **official annexation** of Hawaii. Native Hawaiians protested the action silently by boycotting the ceremonies. The islands were made a **US territory** in 1900, with Dole as governor.

1913
The first Hollywood movies are filmed on location in Hawaii: *Hawaiian Love* and *The Shark God.*

WORLD WAR II (1941-1945)

A DAY THAT WILL LIVE IN INFAMY

In 1941, half a world away from Hawaii, European nations were caught in the horror of **WWII.** The US had yet to be drawn into the war, though their eventual participation seemed inevitable. The Japanese capitalized on Europe's preoccupation with war by making a bid for supremacy in Southeast Asia. One of the few obstacles left in their way was the sizable American fleet that lay within striking distance of the South Pacific—the fleet based at **Pearl Harbor,** Hawaii (p. 133).

1927
The world witnesses the first nonstop flight from the US mainland to Hawaii.

At 7:55am, on the morning of December 7, 1941, Japanese planes swooped through the still air of the military base at Pearl Harbor, initiating a surprise strike that would prove to be one of the single most destructive attacks in naval history. The Japanese targeted the seven US battleships moored in the harbor and aimed to cripple the American military strength in the Pacific as a whole. Of the seven battleships, the **USS Arizona** suffered the most severe damage. One of the bombs fell through the steel decks, detonating stored ammunition; the twisted hull of the ship lies as a poignant monument to the 1177 crewmen who lost their lives. In total, the attack took the lives of 2388 American military personnel and civilians and propelled the US into the conflict in both the Pacific and European theaters.

1930
Hawaii's first set of quadruplets are born; none survive longer than 24 hours.

1934
In Hawaii's first ever recorded bank robbery, $976 is stolen from the Bank of Hawaii. The culprits are apprehended hours later.

HAWAII'S ROLE IN THE PACIFIC THEATER

Following the attack at Pearl Harbor, Hawaii continued to serve as a base for military operations in the Pacific. The next notable clash in the Pacific islands was the **Battle of Midway** in June of 1942. The battle—a victory for the US—was a turning point for the American forces in the Pacific and marked Hawaii's transition from a combat zone to a military base.

1935
10,000 fans greet Shirley Temple when she visits Hawaii.

Hawaiian citizens stepped up to take part in the war effort. Some civilians participated in domestic defense and administration; island-born Japanese served as language interpreters for the military. Many others took up arms. Among these was a contingent of Japanese Americans who were discharged from the Hawaii Territorial Guard, most likely as a result of paranoia regarding those of Japanese descent. About 1400 of these Hawaiian men banded together to form the **100th battalion,** the most decorated battalion of the war. They fought valiantly in the European theater and suffered heavy casualties, earning the nickname the "Purple Heart Regiment."

1937
Spam is invented and quickly gains popularity on the islands.

War continued to rage in the Pacific for several months after the European theater ended on **V-E Day** (Victory in Europe), May 8, 1945. The Pacific theater closed with the Japanese surrender on **V-J Day,** September 1, 1945, following the bombing of Hiroshima and Nagasaki.

THE ALOHA STATE (1945-1970)

THE QUESTION OF STATEHOOD

The move to statehood had been considered since the overthrow of the monarchy, but for nearly 50 years, statehood proposals were defeated for a number of reasons, including opposition from southern states, the problem of distance, and concerns about the destruction of traditional Hawaiian ways of life. In the islands, the sugar industry and other businesses were concerned with the move to statehood, and doubts about the balance in representation between the islands' ethnic groups existed as well.

One proposal for Hawaiian statehood was presented as part of a combined bill for both Hawaiian and Alaskan statehood. The combination complicated the congressional political processes during the debate of the plan, and progress stalled. Hawaiians favored the move to statehood, and in 1954 over 110,000 islanders signed a petition urging Congress to act. Hawaii and Alaska were eventually put on separate bills, and in 1959 Hawaii became the **50th US state.**

THE GROWTH OF TOURISM

Advances in air travel and increased investment in the islands during WWII helped to expand Hawaii's tourism industry. Once Hawaii became a state, it was marketed on the mainland as the **"American Paradise,"** and tourists flocked to experience it. By the 1970s, tourism had a firm position as the state's top industry, surpassing the military.

1946
A devastating tsunami strikes Hilo on the Big Island.

1948
The islands witness the first Miss Hawaii contest.

1953
Beachgoers don bikinis for the first time at Waikiki.

1959
Hawaii becomes the 50th US state.

A HAWAIIAN RENAISSANCE (1970-1990)

HAWAIIAN HOMELANDS

In the early 1920s, **Prince Kuhio,** a member of the nobility and a Republican delegate to Congress, spearheaded the passage of the **Hawaiian Homes Commission Act.** The act, which became law in 1921, was meant to protect Native Hawaiians by releasing public lands for the purposes of agricultural development and homesteading, much of it on the island of Molokai. The act also set up a commission to administer the program. The success of the program itself was questionable, since much of the land was leased to corporations. It was, however, a part of the movement that gained particular significance in the wake of the tourism boom during the post-war years.

Hawaiian activism in the 1970s focused on *aloha aina*, or love for the land. The tiny island of Kahoolawe became a focal point for the movement. The US Navy seized the island at the start of WWII to use it as a training area, but failed to return it at the end of the war. The island lay littered with military wreckage until the formation of **Project Kahoolawe Ohana** in 1976. Kahoolawe Ohana challenged the Navy and the government by carrying out a series of occupations that brought national attention to the movement. Kahoolawe Ohana settled a federal suit against the Navy in 1980

1969
Hawaii Five-O debuts on TV.

with a Consent Decree that allowed access to the island for educational, scientific, and cultural purposes.

In 1993, the Hawaii State Legislature established the **Kahoolawe Island Reserve,** consisting of the island proper and all the waters around it in a 2 mi. radius. The area was preserved solely for Native Hawaiian cultural, spiritual, environmental, educational, and historical purposes; commercial usage is strictly prohibited. Congress also passed a law requiring the Navy both to return the island to the state and to conduct a cleanup and environmental restoration of the area. Under the bill, federal funding was allocated to the project through November 2003.

1975
First Hawaiian skateboarding fatality occurs.

HOKULEA

On May 1, 1976, a double-hulled canoe, a replica of the kind that brought the first Polynesians to Hawaii, departed from the islands to begin an overseas voyage re-creating the route of those ancient mariners. The vessel, the **Hokulea** ("star of gladness"), was named in honor of Hawaii's zenith star. The crew traversed the seas in 33 days using ancient navigational methods, relying only upon the stars and ocean currents as guides. When they arrived in Tahiti, more than 17,000 spectators were waiting to greet them.

1980
Magnum P.I. debuts on TV.

The voyage was not only a physical triumph, but a cultural one as well, creating a focal point for Hawaiian pride. After its successful journey, the vessel was taken to schools throughout Hawaii and used as an educational tool to promote knowledge of Hawaiian heritage. The boat capsized in a storm in 1978, but after raising the standards of preparation and safety to a new level, the boat has since sailed more than 100,000 mi. A second voyaging canoe, **Hawaiiloa,** was completed and launched in 1993. Both are a powerful testament to the efforts of Hawaiians to recover their native traditions.

1983
Kilauea volcano begins erupting on the Big Island and continues to erupt incessantly.

Hurricane Iniki hits Kauai.

HAWAII TODAY (1990-PRESENT)

TOO LITTLE, TOO LATE?

In the late 90s, there were perfunctory moves made to rectify the injustices of Hawaii's past. Both Dole's Iwilei pineapple cannery and the last sugar plantation on the Big Island closed in 1992 and 1995, respectively, ending more than a century of worker exploitation. In 1993, Congress passed the **"Apology Resolution,"** which formally apologized to Native Hawaiians for the overthrow of the monarchy in 1893 and for the deprivation of rights to self-determination.

1990
Census records show Hawaii is home to 136 centenarians.

1999
The Real World: Hawaii debuts on TV.

THE NEW MILLENNIUM

The US Supreme Court case of ***Rice v. Cayetano*** (2000) was another seminal event in the series of legislative moves regarding the rights of Native Hawaiians. The ruling declared that the restriction of eligible voters to Native Hawaiians in the Office of Hawaiian Affairs trustee elections violated the 15th Amendment. The issue of ethnicity regulations gained another dimension in 2002, when **Kamehameha Schools** admitted a non-Hawaiian student to their Maui campus. Heated debate erupted over the

2002
Hawaii passes a bill to become the first state to put a cap on gasoline prices.

First edition of *Let's Go Hawaii* begins production.

schools' admissions policies, which have traditionally limited the acceptance pool to students of Hawaiian blood. Many critics of the school's actions claim that the policies are an attempt to protect the school from claims of discrimination and, in turn, safeguard its tax-free status.

2004
Lost, filmed on Oahu's North Shore, debuts on TV.

Air travel suffered following the tragedy of **September 11, 2001,** and Hawaii saw a significant decline in tourism, since it is accessible primarily by plane. However, tourism in Hawaii has returned to regular levels, with 2005 seeing a record $11.5 billion in visitors' spending.

PEOPLE

DEMOGRAPHICS

The people of Hawaii are world-famous for their spirit of aloha. This attitude of friendly acceptance is characterized by a sense of warmth, kindness, generosity, humility, and patience.

The secret to Hawaiian harmony may lie in the fact that Hawaii is one of the few places in the US, and perhaps the world, where there is no racial or ethnic majority. The state population of 1.26 million (2004) is 25% white (*haole*), 10% Hawaiian, 41% Asian, 2% black, and 22% multiracial.

LANGUAGE

Oleo Hawaii, the Hawaiian language, belongs to a family of Polynesian languages which also includes Tahitian, Maori, Tumotuan, and Rarotongan. Hawaiian is distinctive for its reduplication, apparent in words like *wikiwiki* (fast), its application of glottal stops, and the prolific use of vowels. The key to speaking Hawaiian is to pronounce every vowel: the Likelike Hwy. is pronounced "LEE-kay-LEE-kay."

Oleo Hawaii was a strictly oral language until the arrival of Captain James Cook in 1778 and the Protestant missionaries who flocked to the island thereafter. The missionaries' primary goal was to teach the islanders to read the Bible, so they set about giving the Hawaiian language a written form. What emerged was a 12-letter alphabet that became the official **writing system** of the Hawaiian government.

When Hawaii was annexed by the US in 1898, **English** became the state's official language. Oleo Hawaii dwindled to near-extinction until the 1970s, when a Hawaiian cultural renaissance (p. 19) rekindled interest in the language. In 1978, Oleo Hawaii again became an official language of the state of Hawaii (along with English), and it remains the only Native American language that is officially used by a state government. By 1987, public schools were teaching the language, and the number of speakers continues to grow today.

Hawaii's unofficial language is **Hawaiian Creole** or **Pidgin.** A by-product of Hawaii's tremendous diversity, Pidgin developed as a means of communication for business transactions between people who spoke different languages. The dialect integrates elements from Hawaiian, English, Chinese, Japanese, and several other languages. Although it is primarily used by teenagers, Pidgin is incorporated in nearly every Hawaiian's daily conversations. While Native Hawaiians often appreciate attempts by visitors to speak Oleo Hawaii, it is inadvisable for visitors to try to speak Pidgin, as it is usually considered condescending.

RELIGION

Prior to contact with the West, life in Hawaii was governed by the system of ***kapu,*** or taboo, meaning literally, "obey or die." Every aspect of the early Hawaiians' daily life was regulated by this strict set of rules and customs. ***Kahunas*** (priests) wielded considerable power and were responsible for enforcing the *kapu.* Among their other responsibilities were healing, canoe building, and leading the islands' chiefs in elaborate religious ceremonies carried out in meticulous detail, since the slightest deviation from *aha* (perfection) would incur the wrath of the gods.

Hawaiians believed that all natural phenomena were controlled by the gods, whose aid and protection they sought through offerings and worship. Particularly in times of trouble, sacrifices—sometimes even human sacrifices—would be made in order to appease the gods and to encourage them to look upon the people with favor. Every home had a *kuaaha* (altar) where families worshipped their *aumaka* (guardian deities). *Akua* (greater gods) were worshipped in more complex ceremonies in ***heiaus*** (open-air temples), which were presided over by *kahunas.* Among the *akua* are: **Kane,** god of creation; **Ku,** god of war; **Lono,** god of peace, fertility, wind, rain, and sports; **Kanaloa,** god of the ocean; and **Pele,** goddess of fire, who lives in Kilauea Volcano.

After the death of Kamehameha around 1820, just before the arrival of missionaries from the West, the congregation of the ancient Hawaiians dissolved. *Heiaus* were destroyed, and the *kapu* was abolished, making way for the new religion—Christianity—that was soon to arrive. Elements of this earlier belief system persist in Hawaii today, however, and many people, locals and tourists alike, still make offerings to Pele and other deities in attempts to win their favor. Numerous stories remain that describe the adventures and exploits of the gods.

As one would expect, religion in Hawaii today is as varied as its colorful and diverse population. Christianity, Judaism, Buddhism, Hinduism, and a variety of other beliefs exist peacefully together. Travelers will have no difficulty finding services to meet their spiritual needs, regardless of their faith. For more reading on religion in Hawaii, see **Additional Resources,** p. 34.

THE "OTHER" ISLANDS

KAHOOLAWE

LAND. Kahoolawe is 6 mi. southwest of Maui and the smallest of Hawaii's eight major islands. Kahoolawe's sloping northern and western coasts were heavily populated by feral goats and sheep until 1988. Overgrazing by these animals destroyed the plant cover, causing massive soil erosion. The silt eroded into the water and killed much of the coral around its coast.

HISTORY. Early Hawaiians inhabited Kahoolawe 1000 years ago in fishing and farming settlements. Kahoolawe was a renowned training ground for *kahunas* (priests), and the island is still home to hundreds of *heiaus* (temples) and shrines.

Starting in 1778, criminals who had been exiled from Maui were sent to Kahoolawe, where they managed to subsist by raiding Maui and Lanai. The island's population dwindled, and it was the site of two failed sheep ranches.

The day after Pearl Harbor was attacked, the US Navy appropriated the entire island and began using it for bombing practice. Kahoolawe holds the distinction of being the most bombed island in the Pacific both during and after WWII. After the war, the island was supposed to be returned, but to maintain control over it, President Eisenhower signed an executive order placing the island under the authority of the Secretary of the Navy. The order mandated the island be restored to a habitable condition once it was no longer needed.

In 1976, Hawaiians formed the **Protect Kahoolawe Ohana**, which was dedicated to opposing the bombing of Kahoolawe and demanding its return to the Hawaiian people. In the early 1980s, the US offered allies use of Kahoolawe for bombing exercises, which prompted an outcry from groups in Great Britain, Australia, New Zealand, and Japan. The international media attention generated by protests and several occupations of Kahoolawe staged by the Ohana eventually led to a cessation of bombing. The Ohana also filed suit demanding the return of the island on environmental and religious grounds. The suit was settled in 1980, when the government allowed visitors to the island for cultural, educational, religious, or scientific purposes. Since then, the Ohana has brought over 5000 visitors to Kahoolawe, several trails have been cleared, and a few religious sites have been re-dedicated.

In 1990, Congress established the **Kahoolawe Island Conveyance Commission** to coordinate the return of the island to Hawaii. The commission held public hearings and conducted research, eventually outlining cleanup measures that would make Kahoolawe habitable. In November 1993, Congress prohibited all military activity on Kahoolawe and set aside $400 million for a 10-year cleanup. The same year, Hawaii established the **Kahoolawe Island Reserve,** declaring the island and the surrounding water closed to the public. In May 1994, the island was returned, and the Kahoolawe Island Reserve Commission was established to preserve the island's archaeological, historical, and environmental resources.

TODAY. The goals of the 10-year cleanup plan that expired November 11, 2003, proved too lofty. The Navy intended to clear all surface debris, make the land reasonably safe for human access, re-vegetate the island with native species, clear hiking trails, and construct camping and educational facilities. Although much of the island is reasonably safe for closely controlled visits by the Ohana and their guests, the vision of true public access remains out of reach. The Navy has hired a California firm to complete the cleanup. If you want to visit, contact the Protect Kahoolawe Ohana (www.kahoolawe.org) and ask about joining a monthly trip. The trips have a religious and cultural focus and are primarily for Hawaiian residents. For further reading on Kahoolawe, see **Additional Resources,** p. 33.

NIIHAU

LAND. Niihau, 18 mi. southwest of Kauai, is the smallest of the inhabited islands, and of the eight major islands, it is the westernmost. Niihau averages a mere 12 in. of rain per year, giving it a flat, arid landscape. This grassy lowland is well suited for the grazing herds of animals on the island, which outnumber the people.

HISTORY. Niihau was never conquered by Kamehameha I during his campaign to unite the islands, but in 1810 it joined his kingdom on its own volition. In 1863, a woman named Eliza Sinclair moved to Honolulu, where Kamehameha V offered to sell her land on Oahu stretching from Honolulu Hale to Diamond Head. Sinclair did not think it was suitable for grazing and instead purchased the island of Niihau along with all of its inhabitants for $10,000. There Sinclair established the Niihau Ranch, where she enlisted the island's residents and her family to raise livestock. After she died in 1892, her grandson, Aubrey Robinson, took over. The highly isolated island owes its nickname, **"The Forbidden Isle,"** to the fact that uninvited visitors have been prohibited since its purchase.

Niihau is famous for intricate hand-strung shell leis that Native Hawaiian women have made for hundreds of years from tiny *laiki*, *kehelelani*, and *momi* seashells that wash up on shore. Many of these beautiful necklaces have become treasured heirlooms and can fetch up to four figures.

TODAY. Niihau is still owned by the Robinson family, and descendants of Eliza Sinclair managed the ranch until its closure in 1999. With the unemployment rate close to 100%, the island was finally forced to open its doors to outsiders. Tourists can now visit the islands through a number of expensive excursions, from helicopter tours to hunting safaris.

Even today, the only electricity on the island is produced by privately owned generators. There are also no telephones, no paved roads, and only one school, which goes up to eighth grade. High school students must commute to Kauai or Oahu. Hawaiian is the primary language on Niihau, and the inhabitants are committed to preserving traditional Hawaiian culture. Residents are known for their insularity, widespread rejection of modern conveniences, and staunch opposition to Western ways. Residents are free to come and go as they please, though most stay on the island.

NORTHWEST HAWAIIAN ISLANDS

LAND. The Northwest Hawaiian Islands are an archipelago of small islands and coral atolls that stretch a thousand miles across the Pacific, starting 150 mi. northwest of Kauai. The islands and the surrounding water constitute the **Northwest Hawaiian Islands Coral Reef Ecosystem Reserve,** the largest protected area in the US, covering 131,800 sq. mi. The fragile ecosystem of the Northwest Hawaiian Islands contains over 70% of the coral reef in US waters and 7000 marine species, half of which are unique to the island chain. The Hawaiian monk seal, loggerhead turtle, hawk bill turtle, leatherback sea turtle, and green sea turtle are among the endangered species that have habitats here.

About 1400 monk seals live on the islands; the largest breeding colony is on French Frigate Shoals, or Mokupapapa Island. Necker Island, or Mokumanamana Island, is the top of the oldest-known active volcano in the chain. Numerous *heiaus* (temples) indicate that it was once frequented by Native Hawaiians. Laysan Island, or Kauo, is notable for its nesting birds and salty lagoon. Kure Atoll, or Kanemilohai, named after Pele's brother, is the most distant island. Next to it are the Midway Islands, or Pihemnau, the best-known island group.

HISTORY. Evidence of a human presence exists on the islands from ancient times. In 1885, King Kalakaua had a wooden house built and stocked with provisions on the distant Kure Atoll for anyone who became stranded. In 1903, part of the trans-Pacific cable was laid on Midway, drawing people to the island to manage the station. Midway became a national defense area in 1941 and served as a naval base through WWII. One of the most decisive battles of WWII's Pacific Theater, the Battle of Midway, in June 1942, took place there. It was a victory for US forces that turned the tide of war in their favor, (p. 18). Midway remained a naval base until it was made a National Wildlife Refuge by the US Fish and Wildlife Service in 1996.

TODAY. The National Oceanic and Atmospheric Administration's (NOAA) National Ocean Service manages the Coral Reef Reserve, conducting scientific research for fisheries and protected species and documenting and removing marine debris from the islands and reefs. Meanwhile, the US Fish and Wildlife Service manages and protects the two wildlife refuges of the islands. These organizations, together with the State of Hawaii Department of Land and Natural Resources, US National Park Service, University of Hawaii, Bishop Museum, and the Hawaii Maritime Center, among others, have participated in multiple and wide-ranging research projects on and around the islands. Learn about their projects at www.hawaiianatolls.org. The Midway Islands housed an ecotourism resort until 2002, when it closed due to lack of profit. For more info, contact the **Midway Atoll National Wildlife Refuge,** P.O. Box 50167, Honolulu 96850 (☎674-8237; http://midway.fws.gov).

CULTURE

FOOD

Food. Hawaiian culture. The two are inseparable. In many ways, the confluence of backgrounds and ethnicities that make up Hawaii's unique population is most evident in local culinary offerings. Most popular dishes combine elements of several cultures and incorporate unique island ingredients. Much like Hawaii residents, island fare is unpretentious and low-key; anything that isn't beach-friendly is immediately suspect.

The epitome of local cuisine is the **plate lunch.** It's practically sacrilegious to leave the islands without trying this meal. Plate lunches are available almost everywhere, from roadside stands to fast-food chains. The meal is a descendant of the Japanese plantation worker's **bento,** a bucket lunch of rice, meat, and pickled vegetables. A typical plate lunch is a combination of two scoops of white rice, one scoop of macaroni salad, and an entree. For the entree, most places offer an overwhelming array of choices. At the very least, expect Japanese teriyaki or *katsu*, Korean short ribs, Filipino adobo, Chinese soy sauce chicken, hamburgers, and chili. Quantity often trumps quality in this island comfort food—most plate lunches can feed two people.

Many other local favorites have been taken from outside cultures and adapted over the years. **Saimin,** Japanese noodle soup that is often confused with Ramen, is so common that even McDonald's offers a fast-food version. Locals turn the packaged noodles into a stew of vegetables, tofu, leftover meat, or dumplings—whatever is handy. **Crack seed,** residents' preferred snack, is a generic term that refers to a type of preserved fruit that was brought to Hawaii by Chinese plantation workers. Many generations of Hawaiian children have flocked to neighborhood crack seed shops for after school snacks. The little stores are packed with island delicacies—Japanese rice crackers (*arare*), coconut candy, and dried squid—in addition to the huge glass jars filled with varieties of crack seed.

Some other local treats are Hawaiian to the core. Japanese immigrants supposedly brought **shave ice** to the islands during the plantation era, and it has been an island favorite every since. According to legend, the treat was created by an ancient Japanese *shogun* (general) who liked to snack on snow from Mt. Fiji. Modern toppings include the basic flavored syrups as well as fancier options such as ice cream, condensed milk, shaved *li hing mui* (salty plum), and *azuki* beans. **Spam,** the lovable spiced ham in a can, rounds out any true Hawaiian's diet. After the US military introduced Spam during WWII, islanders quickly incorporated the food into their cooking. Despite mainland conceptions of Spam as pedestrian and unappealing, islanders are addicted. Hawaii now boasts the highest Spam consumption in the world (over 18,000 cans daily). **Spam musubi,** sticky rice topped by Spam and wrapped in dried seaweed, is one of the most popular forms of the food's preparation. **Poi** is another unique island dish. Made out of pounded taro root, poi is a thick, purplish-gray paste. Lacking a strong flavor, poi's unfamiliar consistency and appearance make it an acquired taste. Locals swear by it, however, and some even rave about its semi-magical healing powers.

In recent years, Hawaii-based chefs have developed a style of cooking they call **Hawaii Regional Cuisine.** Led by **Sam Choy, Alan Wong,** and **Roy Yamaguchi,** the chefs have taken advantage of Hawaii's unique ingredients to create a type of cuisine that honors Hawaii's diverse culture while meeting the highest culinary standards.

LUAUS

Luaus began nearly 200 years ago with the flaunting of tradition. Under *kanawai*, the ancient Hawaiian system of laws, certain things were *kapu*, or forbidden. *Kapu* dictated that women eat separately from the men; in addition, women were prohibited from eating many island delicacies. However, in 1819, King Kamehameha II held a huge feast, during which he ate with women. With that event, the ancient religious traditions died and the **luau** was born.

The luau takes its name from a dish prepared with young taro root leaves and coconut milk. Originally a celebration giving thanks to the gods, the luau has become one of the most well-known aspects of Hawaiian culture. Birthdays, anniversaries, and other significant events are marked by these feasts. The tourism industry has capitalized on the marketability of the luau, and almost every major hotel and restaurant offers some version.

Historically, luau guests sat on woven mats laid on the floor and used their fingers to devour the feast. Many modern-day luaus are still held on the grass, though bigger celebrations might have tents and picnic tables. There is almost always some form of musical entertainment, whether it is a cousin strumming a guitar or an entire group complete with ukulele, steel guitar, and bass. The main focus of any luau is the traditionally prepared kalua pig. The meat is covered in *ti* or banana leaves and roasted in an *imu* (underground oven). The meat is supplemented by other island dishes, such as poi, *poke* (raw, seasoned sashimi), and *lomi* salmon (salted salmon with tomatoes and Maui onions). The meal is often finished with a dessert of *haupia* (coconut pudding), pineapple, and coconut cake.

HAWAIIAN DRESS

On any given day, locals look beach-ready. The preferred style of dress often incorporates one or more of the following: slippers (plastic flip-flops), board shorts, other surf-inspired clothing, and anything aloha print. One of the most popular elements of Hawaiian dress, the **aloha shirt,** actually owes its inspiration to both Western and Asian cultures. Supposedly a descendant of the thick "thousand-mile" shirt worn by pioneers and missionaries, the aloha shirt came into its familiar form in the late 1920s at the hands of Waikiki tailor Ellery J. Chun. The style became common after Herbert Briner began mass-manufacturing the shirts in the late 1930s. During the 1950s, the aloha shirt craze spread to the mainland when audiences saw icons like Elvis Presley, John Wayne, and Frank Sinatra wearing them in feature films. In response to the widespread mimicking of the aloha shirt, the Hawaii Chamber of Commerce ruled in the 1960s that a true aloha shirt must be made in Hawaii. Currently, the only company to design and produce shirts entirely in Hawaii is Reyn Spooner.

CUSTOMS AND ETIQUETTE

Hawaii residents place so much stock in the **aloha spirit** that there is an actual law in the Hawaii Revised Statutes (section 5-7.5) that requires residents to abide by the spirit of ancient Hawaiians. And, for the most part, locals do. Smiles abound and islanders are quick to wave hello, usually in the form of **shaka,** a greeting made by extending the pinkie and thumb and curling up the middle three fingers of the right hand. It is especially popular with young people in Hawaii; the gesture is a way of saying, "hang loose" or "relax." The word **aloha** is also used extensively throughout the islands. Don't be afraid to use it to say hello; it's not regarded as corny. The **lei,** a garland of flowers, shells, leaves, or even candy, is a traditional Hawaiian symbol of love or friendship. Visitors entering and leaving Hawaii are often gifted with the fragrant necklaces. Leis are also given to mark special occasions like anniversaries, birthdays, and graduations.

While Hawaii is extremely laid-back, there are a few things that travelers should keep in mind. Hawaii is inhabited by an exceptionally diverse group of people, but the only people who are referred to as **Hawaiian** are those of Hawaiian blood. Except for Caucasians, anyone born in the islands is a **local.** The term ***haole*** for Caucasians is not necessarily offensive. Residents who were born outside of Hawaii but have lived in the state for a long time are known as ***kama aina.***

Respect is a key word in Hawaiian culture. It is especially important to treat sacred sites, such as *heiaus* (temples), with appropriate consideration. On a more casual level, it is polite to remove your shoes when entering someone's home.

THE ARTS

ARCHITECTURE

Hawaii's architecture reflects its varied past. ***Heiaus*** (temples) are a remnant of ancient Hawaiian religion. These simple structures were built as temples to the gods and typically consist of altars and taboo houses enclosed by lava or limestone walls. Many still stand today, albeit in varying stages of disrepair, and there have been initiatives to restore them to their original states.

Plantation-style houses are another throwback to Hawaii's past. Built to house immigrant workers from China, Japan, and the Philippines, the houses were grouped in villages. They stood on lava rock foundations and featured single-wall construction and cedar shingle roofs. The plantation-style commercial structures of this era were much more elaborate, often consisting of multiple buildings grouped around a courtyard. The main building would sometimes be modeled in mainland-style, with wide canopies extending over the sidewalk. The **Honolulu Hale** and the **Hawaii State Public Library** are prominent examples of this design.

Along with Christianity, missionaries also brought a more ostentatious style of architecture. Neoclassical edifices like the **Iolani Palace** and Gothic structures like the **Cathedral of Saint Andrew's** were built in the late 19th century and strongly reflect Western influences. The 1990s saw the construction of Hawaii's first true skyscrapers, including **First Hawaiian Center,** Hawaii's tallest building.

Most residential houses in Hawaii have been built with regard to the islands' tropical climate. They are typically low, airy structures that were built with an eye to the cooling trade winds.

VISUAL ARTS

Although it may never rival New York City or Paris, Hawaii has a healthy art community. Along with numerous private galleries, Oahu has two notable art museums. The **Honolulu Academy of the Arts** will soon celebrate its 80th birthday, and the museum houses a permanent stock of over 35,000 pieces, including a celebrated collection of Asian art. The less conventional **Contemporary Museum** has two locations on Oahu (p. 109). Part of the organization's mission dictates that a significant portion of its exhibits must focus on art created in Hawaii. Maui too has a strong coalition of artists and art lovers. Each spring, the island hosts **Art Maui,** a prestigious exhibit of about 100 new works by Maui County artists.

Hawaii has inspired a number of extraordinary artists. Although prominent oil painter **John Young** died in 1999, he is remembered by a museum within the University of Hawaii. Prior to settling down in Honolulu, Paris-born **Jean Charlot** (1898-1979) worked as Diego Rivera's assistant in Mexico. During his time in Hawaii, Charlot applied the techniques he learned with Rivera to a number of fresco murals that can be seen in various Oahu locations, including the University of Hawaii at Manoa. **Madge Tennent** (1889-1972) concentrated on capturing the beauty she saw in the Hawaiian people. She is best known for her oil paintings of Hawaiian women, many of which hang prominently in buildings around Honolulu. Other notable Hawaiian artists include watercolor artist **Hon-Chew Hee,** painter and printmaker **Yvonne Cheng,** and potter and watercolor artist **Charles Higa.**

Art takes on a practical form in the distinctive **Hawaiian quilts.** After learning quilting techniques from New England missionaries, Hawaiian women translated the images from their daily lives onto fabric. The quilts, with their flower, leaf, and vine designs, are still popular today.

LITERATURE

Early in his career, **Mark Twain** journeyed from San Francisco to Hawaii for a four-month stay that eventually helped him achieve his mammoth literary stature. Chronicles of his trip were published in the *Sacramento Union* and scholars hold that it was in Hawaii that Twain first began to develop his singular descriptive and interpretive style. Twain later compiled his personal and professional writings from this period into *Roughing It.* Intrigued by the islands and people of the Pacific, **Robert Louis Stevenson** explored the area extensively and lived the last years of his life in Samoa. Much of his writing from that period is compiled in *Travels in Hawaii.* One of the most well-known novels about Hawaii is **James Michener's** 1036-page epic titled, simply, *Hawaii.* A combination of fact and fiction, the book begins with the creation of the islands and follows their growth until the year 1955.

Nurtured by local organizations, such as *Bamboo Ridge,* the journal of Hawaiian literature and arts, local writers are gaining exposure and critical acclaim. The leader of this generation of authors is Hawaiian-born novelist **Lois-Ann Yamanaka,** who tackles the themes of Asian-American families and local culture in Hawaii. Yamanaka's work addresses the reality of living in paradise; she eschews flowery word painting, aiming instead for authentic Pidgin dialogue between her characters. Other authors who are a part of this reinvention of Hawaiian literature include **Milton Murayama, Darrell Lum, Sylvia Watanabe, Kathleen Tyau,** and **Nora Okja Keller.**

MUSIC

Traditional musicians record songs almost entirely in Hawaiian and use the **ukulele, steel guitar,** and **slack key guitar** extensively. Legends hold that the ukulele was introduced to Hawaii in 1879 by a Portuguese immigrant named **Joao Fernandes.** The islanders dubbed Fernandes's *braguinha* (a type of guitar) a ukulele (literally, "jumping flea") because of the way the musician's fingers jumped across the strings of the instrument. The ukulele quickly gained popularity; even Hawaiian royalty became proficient. The ukulele became a symbol of Hawaiian beach culture during the 1920s and 30s, thanks to the **Waikiki Beachboys,** who serenaded locals and tourists with their ukuleles. The Beachboys included such renowned Hawaiian musicians as **Squeeze Kamana** and **Chick Daniels.**

The steel guitar was developed on Oahu by local **Joseph Kekuku** in the late 19th century. Kekuku's instrument was able to achieve a previously unthinkable range of sound and to this day remains a centerpiece of Hawaiian music. Hawaiian musicians round out the distinctive island sound with a guitar technique called slack key, or ***ki hoal.*** Literally, "loosen the key," this method of playing consists of relaxing the strings of an acoustic guitar and picking them with the fingers. The guitar is reputed to have come to the islands via early 19th-century cowboys. However, Hawaiians developed the unique slack-key sound themselves.

With the Hawaiian renaissance of the 1970s, traditional artists, such as **Israel "IZ" Kamakawiwoole** (1959-1997), the **Sons of Hawaii,** and **Kealii Reichel,** all experienced a boost in their popularity. Pop artist and surfer **Jack Johnson** also hails from Oahu, and the influence of laid-back North Shore culture permeates his recent album, *On and On*, recorded in Hawaii.

DANCE

The **hula** has long been a symbol of Hawaiian culture. The dances and chants of ancient hula were an integral part of the Hawaiians' oral tradition; through them, elders ensured that their traditions, customs, and history would live on in a younger generation. For a short period in the early 19th century, Christian missionaries convinced the reigning monarchs to outlaw the dance. However, in 1874, **King David Kalakaua** ascended to the throne. The new king, nicknamed the "Merrie Monarch," became hula's greatest patron, and during his rule, the dance flourished. The ukulele and the steel guitar were used to accompany dancers, who began wearing *ti* leaf skirts for the first time. Kalakaua is remembered each Easter in the **Merrie Monarch Festival,** which showcases both ancient hula and the more modern versions that have developed.

FILM

Despite the difficulty of transporting film-making equipment, movie producers have never been able to resist Hawaii's allure. The islands are reputed to have made their on screen debut as early as 1898, when a film crew shot footage of the tropical paradise during an 18hr. layover. Early Hawaiian films, such as *Honolulu Street Scene*, were simple, silent films showing local life. In the early 1900s, Hawaii was used in numerous silent films, including *Hawaiian Love* and *The Shark God*, both made in 1913. The advent of "talkies" added a new dimension to Hawaiian-set films. In 1937, Bing Crosby starred in *Waikiki Wedding*, playing a crooning press agent for a pineapple cannery. The film's hit song, "Sweet Leilani" garnered an Oscar and earned Crosby his first gold record.

Although WWII put filmmaking in Hawaii on hold for a few years, it also provided the industry with its most enduring subject: war. *From Here to Eternity* (1953) chronicled the days leading up to the Pearl Harbor attack, but it is probably best remembered for Burt Lancaster and Deborah Kerr's passionate embrace on the sand (and in the water) of Halona Cove. Kauai was used to film the musical *South Pacific* (1958), in which Mitzi Gaynor plays a love-struck Army nurse who tries, unsuccessfully, to wash a captivating man out of her hair. Elvis Presley gratified his adoring fans on Hawaii when he starred in 1961's *Blue Hawaii.* As an island boy back from the war, Presley spends much of the movie strumming the ukulele and wooing beach bunnies with his signature dance moves. The film yielded several musical hits, including "Can't Help Falling In Love."

Filmmakers switched gears in 1976, when Hawaii was featured in the blockbuster *King Kong.* Following the movie's release, Hawaii increasingly became the filming site of action-packed blockbusters. In 1980, George Lucas and Steven Spielberg joined forces to produce the first of the Indiana Jones series,

Raiders of the Lost Ark, filmed partly in Kauai. Spielberg continued his blockbuster trend with *Jurassic Park* (1992), also filmed in Hawaii. The 1997 dino-sequel, *The Lost World,* features gorgeous shots of Kauai's lush scenery and boasted an opening weekend gross of over $92 million. Other crowd-pleasers filmed in Hawaii include *George of the Jungle* (1997) and *6 Days, 7 Nights* (1998).

Filmmaking in Hawaii shows no signs of stopping in the new millennium. In 2001, producer Jerry Bruckheimer let loose his biggest (and longest) film yet, the epic *Pearl Harbor.* The Hawaii Visitor's and Convention Bureau joined forces with Disney to market *Lilo & Stitch* (2002), a widely appreciated film about a young girl and an extraterrestrial fugitive set in the islands. The surfing flick *Blue Crush* (2002) features Kate Bosworth tackling Oahu's famous Bonzai Pipeline (see p. 159) and scoring points for female surfers everywhere. The same island plays host to Adam Sandler and a forgetful Drew Barrymore in 2004's *50 First Dates,* a romantic comedy whose sound track features several Hawaiian artists.

Hawaii hosts a few film festivals each year. The **Hawaii International Film Festival** began at the University of Hawaii (Manoa) in 1981 as a means of cultural exchange between North America, Asia, and the Pacific. It is now a state-wide event, with screenings on the six major Hawaiian islands. The **Maui Film Festival** is still in its infancy—it began in 2000—but it seems as if the event is around to stay.

TV SERIES

Hawaii has a long, successful history on television, beginning with the popular **Hawaii Five-O.** The show, filmed almost exclusively on Hawaii from 1968 to 1980, was one of the longest-running series on television. A daytime variety show featuring a local performer, **The Don Ho Show,** aired from 1976-1977. During the 80s, Tom Selleck charmed viewers across the nation as a dashing Hawaii-based private investigator in **Magnum, P.I.** The **Baywatch** cast packed up its itty-bitty wardrobe and suntan oil in 1999 to relocate from California to Hawaii. The new series, **Baywatch Hawaii,** lasted only two seasons. MTV's **The Real World: Hawaii** (1999) was the first in a series of reality TV shows to choose Hawaii as a backdrop. Soon to follow were **The Bachelor** (2002) and **Average Joe: Hawaii** (2004). Most recently, the first two seasons of ABC's smash hit, **Lost,** were filmed on Oahu's North Shore. The 2hr. pilot for the series was one of the most expensive in television history, costing over $10 million.

SPORTS AND RECREATION

Watersports reign in Hawaii—some of the world's best surfing and windsurfing spots can be found here. Golf is the chosen sport of many tourists, and manicured greens are spread across the islands. Other popular activities include paddling, kayaking, snorkeling, surfing, scuba diving, swimming, boogie boarding, bodysurfing, hiking, and biking.

COLLEGE SPORTS AND FOOTBALL

Water polo, volleyball, and sailing are among the most popular high school and college competitive sports in Hawaii. The **University of Hawaii at Manoa** Warriors boast a nationally ranked sailing program, and the 2002 men's volleyball team were national champions. Since 1997, the **Hula Bowl All-Star Football Classic** has been held each year on Maui, and the islands have long been home to the NFL's **Pro Bowl.** In addition, the fairly new NCAA **Hawaii Bowl** is played each year in Honolulu on Christmas Eve or Christmas Day.

THE DIFFERENCE BETWEEN BOOGIE AND BODY BOARDS. We'll let you in on a secret: they're the same thing. In Hawaii everyone calls the good old mainland "boogie board" a "body board," and that's what you'll always hear on your visit to the islands. In this book we refer to them as boogie boards because that's what *we* call them, and unless you're from Hawaii, we figure you do, too. That said, it's kind of derogatory to refer to them as boogie boards: boogie board has the connotation of little kids splashing around in half-foot waves that the serious and more hard-core body board avoids. It is considered pretty touristy to exclaim, "Let's go boogie boarding, dude!" as opposed to saying, "Ho brah seen that barrel I wen get on my body board? Brah, was nuts."

GOING THE DISTANCE

Laid-back lifestyle aside, Hawaii is home to hundreds of running events and triathlons, from 1 mi. fun-runs to a 100 mi. ultra marathon on the Big Island. Among these is one of the world's most bad-ass multi-sport events—the **Ironman Triathlon.** Held each October in Kailua-Kona on the Big Island, the event draws 50,000 hopefuls from all 50 US states and over 50 countries, of whom 1500 are selected to compete in the grueling race. Competitors start with a 2.4 mi. ocean swim, followed by a 112 mi. bike race, and cap the whole thing off with a full 26.2 mi. marathon. The course is open for 17 hours; the record (8:04:08) was set by Luc Van Lierde in 1996. Over five million viewers world-wide tune in to witness the event each year.

Hawaii also has several official **marathons.** The Honolulu Marathon, held each December, is the 6th-largest marathon in the world. The Maui Marathon, held in March, is the oldest continuously held running event in Hawaii. Other marathons are the Kilauea Volcano Marathon in July, the Kona Marathon in August, and the Big Island International Marathon in October.

PADDLING

Outrigger canoe paddling is popular throughout Hawaii. The outrigger canoe differs from a regular canoe in that it has a rig, known as an outrigger, extending from one or both sides of the vessel. The outrigger acts to balance the hull of the boat. Early Hawaiians used the outrigger canoes extensively in their daily lives, and paddling eventually became a means of recreation.

Encouraged by King Kalakaua, paddling enthusiasts formed the first official outrigger club in 1908. **The Outrigger Canoe Club of Hawaii** was followed shortly after by Hui Nalu; there are now over 60 outrigger clubs throughout the islands. Canoe racing began in 1910, and formal regattas began in the 1940s. Paddlers are typically grouped into divisions by age. There is a separate junior season in late winter to ensure that younger athletes get as much attention as possible. Though paddling had previously been dominated by males, the number of women competing in the sport has increased steadily since the 1980s.

Sailing canoes are a variation on the outrigger canoes. Although not nearly as common as paddling, sailing canoe races have been gaining popularity. Each May, participants race the 75 mi. between Maui and Oahu in canoe sailing's most well-known competition, the **Steinlager Hoomanao Sailing Canoe Race.**

SURFING

Surfing was born in Hawaii, and the sport stays true to its homeland. There is no impeding continental shelf surrounding the islands to slow incoming waves, so they arrive huge and powerful on Hawaiian shores, creating magnificent, world-renowned surf. There are two surf seasons which differ with respect to wind and storm patterns. Summer surf (May-Aug.) is generated by storms in the South Pacific and occurs on the southern shores of the islands. In the winter (Sept.-Apr.), storms in the northern Pacific create surf on the northern shores of the islands. The seasons' overlap allows for nearly year-round surfing.

The so-called "sport of kings" began as the ancient sport of *hee nalu* (wave-sliding) and was later perfected by the kings of Hawaii. The revival of interest in surfing in the early 20th century is attributed to Hawaii's **Duke Kahanamoku.** Kahanamoku, also known as "The Big Kahuna," was a talented swimmer, representing the United States at four Olympic Games between 1912 and 1924, winning three gold medals and two silvers to become Hawaii's first Olympic medalist. His first love was surfing, however, and he organized one of the first amateur surfing clubs in 1908.

Since then, the evolution of **board design** and material has made major changes to surfing, both as an activity and as a culture. The first boards were made of wood; their weight and lack of maneuverability was part of what limited the sport to certain physiques. The first big breakthrough in board design came in 1958 when construction changed to lightweight foam and fiberglass. A bottom fin also helped stabilize the new boards. These lighter, steadier boards made surfing more accessible to the general public. When surfing was introduced to California it quickly gained popularity as both a sport and a culture, inspiring fashion, music, and movies in the 1950s and 60s.

Today, surfers use one of two types of boards: **long boards** (a traditional style that can be as long as 10-12 ft.) and **short boards.** Short boards are less than 9 ft. in length, are faster, and have better maneuverability. Although beginning surfers generally start off on long boards, most surfers use short boards as well, as they are better for riding larger waves. Surfboards often have two to three fins, called **thrusters,** which provide greater maneuverability. The addition of a **leash,** attached at the ankle, improved both the safety of surfing and its style. Before leashes were added, lost boards would collide with reefs and rocks as well, resulting in significant damage. With leashes, surfers can ride waves near rocks and reefs and try radical tricks with greater security.

A SURFING STATE OF MIND. For many locals, surfing is not just an activity but a way of life. Surfers range from the hard-core professionals, to local *bruddahs,* to 9-5ers who keep a board on the roof of their car to catch a post-work wave. While tourists are welcome to pick up a board and try their hand on a curl, don't expect to be inducted into surfer culture fresh off your first wave. Surfers are secretive about the best spots, have their own slang, and abide by their own code. A few tips on surfer etiquette for novice wave riders: never "drop in" on a wave. The surfer closest to the curl (the breaking part of the wave) has the right of way on that wave, and all other surfers should back up out of it (failure to do so is dropping in). Be careful of boogie boarders and other surfers—collisions can cause serious injuries.

HOLIDAYS AND FESTIVALS

Late Jan.: Pacific Islands Arts Festival. In Waikiki. Highlights include local culinary favorites, "make 'n' takes" for kids, and demonstrations by local artists.

Jan.-Feb.: Chinese New Year. This celebration is best seen on Oahu, in Chinatown, where you'll be treated to a lion dance, fireworks, and an abundance of Chinese food.

Early Mar.: Honolulu Festival. Music, dance, and parades throughout the city.

Mar. 26: Prince Kuhio Day. In celebration of the birthday of Prince Jonah Kuhio Kalanianaole, one of Hawaii's first delegates to Congress.

Apr. 15: Father Damien DeVeusteur Day. In celebration of Father Damien DeVeusteur, the highly regarded Christian missionary to the Kalaupapa Peninsula leper colony.

Late Apr.: Merrie Monarch Festival. In Hilo. A week of cultural events culminating in Hawaii's most prestigious hula competition.

May 1: Lei Day. More fun than May Day. Also, more floral.

Late May: Kauai Polynesian Festival. Food, entertainment, and crafts from Polynesian islands.

June 11: King Kamehameha Day. See p. 15 for information on Kamehameha the Great.

Mid-June: Maui Film Festival. In Wailea. Mainstream and indie film premieres under the stars, as well as culinary events.

Late June: Taste of Honolulu. An outdoor wine, food, and entertainment charity benefit.

July: Parker Ranch Rodeo. On the Big Island. Food, activities, and of course, rodeo events.

Third Friday in Aug.: Statehood Day. See p. 19 for the history of Hawaii-US relations.

Sept.-Oct.: Aloha Festival. Hawaii's largest cultural festival, spanning 2 months and featuring events on all the major islands.

Late Oct.: Macadamia Nut Festival. In Hilo. Macadamia nut concoctions, plus local music and entertainment.

Late Oct.-early Nov.: Kona Coffee Festival. A 10-day celebration of caffeination.

Oct. 31: Halloween in Lahaina. Trick-or-treat with over 30,000 revelers on Front Street.

Nov.: Hawaiian International Film Festival. State-wide. Screenings of (mostly) Pacific Rim films in various locations.

ADDITIONAL RESOURCES

HISTORY

A Concise History of the Hawaiian Islands. Phil Barnes (Petroglyph Ltd., 1999).

Ancient Hawaii. Herb Kane (Kawainui Press, 1998).

The Apotheosis of Captain Cook. Gananath Obeyesekere (Princeton UP, 1992).

The Betrayal of Liliuokalani: Last Queen of Hawaii 1838-1917. Helena Allen (Mutual Publishing, 1991).

Day of Infamy: The Classic Account of the Bombing of Pearl Harbor. Walter Lord (Owl Books, 2001).

Niihau: The Last Hawaiian Island. Ruth Tabrah (Booklines Hawaii Ltd., 1987).

Kahoolawe Na Leo o Kanaloa: Chants and Stories of Kahoolawe. Wayne Levin and Rowland B. Reeve, eds. (Al Pohaku Press, 1995).

Paradise Remade: The Politics of Culture and History in Hawaii. Elizabeth Buck (Temple UP, 1994).

To Steal a Kingdom. Michael Dougherty (Island Style Press, 2000).

THE GREAT OUTDOORS

A Field Guide to the Birds of Hawaii and the Tropical Pacific. Douglas Pratt (Princeton UP, 1987).

Hawaii's Best Beaches. John R. K. Clark (University of Hawaii Press, 1999).

Hawaii's Best Hiking Trails. Robert Smith and Kevin Chard (Hawaiian Outdoor Adventure, 2004).

Plants and Flowers of Hawaii. Seymour H. Sohmer (University of Hawaii Press, 1994).

Remains of a Rainbow: Rare Plants and Animals of Hawaii. David Littschwager, et al. (National Geographic Society, 2003).

SPORTS

The Big Drop: Classic Big Wave Surfing Stories. John Long, ed. (Falcon Publishing, 1999).

Eddie Would Go: The Story of Eddie Aikau, Hawaiian Hero. Stuart Coleman (St. Martin's Griffin, 2004).

Girl in the Curl: A Century of Women's Surfing. Andrea Gabbard (Seal Press, 2000).

The Great Hawaii Sports Journal. Kirk Lee Aeder (Island Heritage Publishing, 2003).

North Shore Chronicles: Big Wave Surfing in Hawaii. Bruce Jenkins (North Atlantic Books, 2005).

Sleeping in the Shorebreak and Other Hairy Surfing Stories. Don Wolf (Waverider Publications, 1999).

Becoming an Ironman. Kara Douglass Thom (Breakaway Books, 2002).

CULTURE

The Aloha Shirt: Spirit of the Island. Dale Hope (Thames and Hudson Ltd., 2002).

The Food of Paradise: Exploring Hawaii's Culinary Heritage. Rachel Laudan (University of Hawaii Press, 1996).

Ethnic Foods of Hawaii. Ann Kondo Corum (Bess Press, 2000).

Hawaiian Magic & Spirituality. Scott Cunningham (Llewellyn Publications, 2002).

Hawaiian Mythology. Martha Warren Beckwith (University of Hawaii Press, 1977).

Illustrated Hawaiian Dictionary. Kahikahealani Wight (Bess Press, 2005).

The Kahuna. Likeke R. McBride (Petroglyph Press, 2000).

The Legends and Myths of Hawaii: The Fables and Folk-Lore of a Strange People. David Kalakaua (Tuttle Publishing, 1972).

FICTION AND TRAVEL NARRATIVES

A Hawaii Anthology. Joseph Stanton, ed. (University of Hawaii Press, 1997).

Blu's Hanging. Lois-Ann Yamanaka (Harper Perennial, 1998).

Comfort Woman. Nora Okja Keller (Penguin Books, 1998).

da word. Lee Tonouchi (Bamboo Ridge Press, 2001).

Growing Up Local: An Anthology of Poetry and Prose from Hawaii. Eric Chock, ed., et al. (Bamboo Ridge Press, 1999).

Hawaii. James A. Michener (Random House, 1973).

Hawaii One Summer. Maxine Hong Kingston (University of Hawaii Press, 1998).

The House of Pride and Other Tales of Hawaii. Jack London (Classic Publishers, 1919).

Roughing It. Mark Twain (Signet Classics, 1994).

Song of the Exile. Kiana Davenport (Ballatine, 2000).

Travels in Hawaii. Robert Louis Stevenson (University of Hawaii Press, 1991).

The Trembling of a Leaf. W. Somerset Maugham (Dixon-Price, 2002).
Wild Meat and the Bully Burgers. Lois-Ann Yamanaka (Harvest Books, 1997).

FILM

50 First Dates. (Dir. Peter Segal. Columbia Pictures, 2004.)
Blue Crush. (Dir. John Stockwell. Universal Studios, 2002.)
Blue Hawaii. (Dir. Norman Tauroq. 20th Century Fox, 1961.)
The Endless Summer. (Dir. Bruce Brown. Bruce Brown Films, 1966.)
From Here to Eternity. (Dir. Fred Zinneman. Columbia TriStar, 1953.)
Gidget Goes Hawaiian. (Dir. Paul Wendkos. Columbia TriStar, 1961.)
Hawaii. (Dir. George Roy Hill. MGM, 1966.)
Lilo and Stitch. (Dir. David DeBlois and Chris Sanders. Disney, 2002.)
Molokai: The Story of Father Damien. (Dir. Paul Cox. Unapix, 1999.)
Pearl Harbor. (Dir. Michael Bay. Buena Vista, 2001.)
Step into Liquid. (Dir. Dana Brown. Lionsgate/Fox, 2003.)
Tora! Tora! Tora! (Dir. Fleischer, Fukasaku, Masuda. 20th Century Fox, 1970.)
Waikiki Wedding. (Dir. Frank Tuttle. Paramount, 1937.)

ESSENTIALS

PLANNING YOUR TRIP

ENTRANCE REQUIREMENTS

Passport (p. 37). Required for citizens of all foreign countries.

Visa (p. 38). A visa is usually required to visit the US, but can be waived.

Work Permit (p. 38). Required of all foreigners planning to work in the US.

International Driving Permit (p. 55) Required of all those planning to drive.

EMBASSIES AND CONSULATES

US CONSULAR SERVICES ABROAD

US EMBASSIES

Australia: Moonah Pl., Yarralumla, Canberra ACT 2600 (☎61 2 6214 5600; http://usembassy-australia.state.gov/index.html).

Canada: 490 Sussex Dr., Ottawa, ON K1N 1G8 (☎613-238-5335; www.usembassycanada.gov).

Ireland: 42 Elgin Rd., Ballsbridge, Dublin 4 (☎353 1 668 8777; http://dublin.usembassy.gov).

New Zealand: 29 Fitzherbert Terr., Thorndon, Wellington, Mailing Address: P.O. Box 1190, Wellington (☎64 4 462 6000; http://usembassy.org.nz).

UK: 24 Grosvenor Sq., London W1A 1AE (☎44 020 7499 9000; www.usembassy.org.uk).

US CONSULATES

Australia: 553 St. Kilda Rd., **Melbourne** VIC 3004 (☎61 3 9526 5900, fax 9510 4646); 16 St. George's Terr., 13th fl., **Perth** WA 6000 (☎61 8 9202 1224, fax 9231 9444); MLC Centre, Level 10, 19-29 Martin Pl., **Sydney** NSW 2000 (☎61 2 9373 9200, fax 9373 9125).

Canada: 615 Macleod Trail SE, Ste. 1000, **Calgary,** AB T2G 4T8 (☎403-266-8962, fax 264-6630); Ste. 904, Purdy's Wharf Tower II, 1969 Upper Water St., **Halifax,** NS B3J 3R7, Mailing Address: P.O. Box 2130, CRO, Halifax, NS B3J 3B7 (☎902-429-2480, fax 423-6861); 1155 rue St.-Alexandre, **Montréal,** QC H3B 1Z1, Mailing Address: P.O. Box 65, Station Desjardins, Montréal, QC H5B 1G1 (☎514-398-9695, fax 398-0702); 2 Pl. Terrasse Dufferin, **Québec City,** QC G1R 4T9, Mailing Address: B.P. 939, Québec City, QC G1R 4T9 (☎418-692-2095, fax 692-4640); 360 University Ave., **Toronto,** ON M5G 1S4 (☎416-595-1700, fax 595-5466); 1075 W. Pender St., **Vancouver,** BC V6E 2M6, Mailing Address: P.O. Box 5002, Point Roberts, WA 98281 (☎604-685-4311, fax 685-7175).

New Zealand: Citibank Building, 3rd fl., 23 Customs St., **Auckland,** Mailing Address: Private Bag 92022, Auckland (☎64 9 303 2724, fax 366 0870).

UK: Danesfort House, 223 Stranmillis Rd., **Belfast,** N. Ireland BT9 5GR (☎44 028 9038 6100, fax 9068 1301); 3 Regent Terr., **Edinburgh,** Scotland EH7 5BW (☎44 0131 556 8315, fax 557 6023).

CONSULAR SERVICES IN THE US

IN WASHINGTON, D.C.

Australia, 1601 Massachusetts Ave. NW, 20036 (☎202-797-3000; www.austemb.org). **Canada,** 501 Pennsylvania Ave. NW, 20001 (☎202-682-1740; www.canadianembassy.org). **Ireland,** 2234 Massachusetts Ave. NW, 20008 (☎202-462-3939; www.irelandemb.org). **New Zealand,** 37 Observatory Circle NW, 20008 (☎202-328-4800; www.nzemb.org). **UK,** 3100 Massachusetts Ave., 20008 (☎202-588-7800; www.britainusa.com/consular/embassy).

IN HONOLULU, HI

Australia, 1000 Bishop St., Penthouse, 96813 (☎808-524-5050; www.dfat.gov.au/missions/countries/usha.html). **New Zealand,** 900 Richards St. #414, 96813 (☎808-543-7900; plewis@hei.com).

TOURIST OFFICES

The **Hawaii Visitors & Convention Bureau** (HVCB) oversees tourism and will provide brochures and facilitate orientation in Hawaii. The main office is located at 2270 Kalakaua Ave., Honolulu, 96815 (☎800-464-2924; www.gohawaii.com).

Australia: Level 3, 11-17 Swanson Plaza, Belconnen ACT 2616 (☎61 2 6228 6100; www.tra.australia.com). Open M-F 9am-5:30pm.

Canada: Four Bentall Centre, Ste. 1400, 1055 Dunsmuir St., Box 49230, Vancouver, BC, V7 1L5 (☎604-638-8300; www.travelcanada/ca). Open M-F 9am-5pm.

New Zealand: Richwhite Building, 17th fl., 151 Queen St., Auckland 1 (☎64 (0)800 700 741; www.visitbritain.com/nz). Open M-F 10am-6pm.

United Kingdom: Thames Tower, Blacks Road, London, W6 9EL (☎020 8846 9000; www.visitbritain.com).

DOCUMENTS AND FORMALITIES

PASSPORTS

REQUIREMENTS

Starting January 1, 2008, citizens of all countries other than the US need valid passports to enter the US. Passports must be valid for at least six months beyond the intended stay. Returning home with an expired passport is usually illegal and may result in a fine, or it may not be possible at all. Your passport, however, is the most convenient method of identification.

NEW PASSPORTS

Citizens of Australia, Canada, Ireland, New Zealand, the UK, and the US can apply for a passport at any passport office or at selected post offices and courts of law. Citizens of these countries may also download passport applications from the official website of their country's government or passport office. Any new passport or renewal applications must be filed well in advance of the departure date, though most passport offices offer rush services for a very steep fee, typically $60-200. Note, however, that "rushed" passports still take up to two weeks to arrive.

PASSPORT MAINTENANCE

Photocopy the page of your passport with your photo. Carry one copy in a safe place, apart from the original, and leave a copy at home. Consulates recommend that you carry an expired passport or an official copy of your birth certificate in a part of your baggage separate from other documents.

If you lose your passport, immediately notify the local police and the nearest embassy or consulate of your home government. To expedite its replacement, you will need to know all info previously recorded and show ID and proof of citizenship, as well as pay a fee and include a police report. Replacements take approximately 10 days to process, but some consulates offer three-day rush service for an additional fee. A replacement may be valid only a limited time. Any visas stamped in your old passport will be irretrievably lost. In an emergency, some consulates provide immediate temporary traveling papers that will permit you to re-enter your home country.

VISAS AND WORK PERMITS

VISAS

Citizens of some non-English speaking countries need a visa—a stamp, sticker, or insert in your passport specifying the purpose of your travel and the permitted duration of your stay—in addition to a valid passport to enter the US. Canadian citizens do not need to obtain a visa for admission; citizens of Australia, New Zealand, and most European countries (including the UK and Ireland) can waive US visas through the **Visa Waiver Program (VWP).** Visitors qualify if they are traveling only for business or pleasure (not work or study), are staying for fewer than 90 days, have proof of intent to leave (e.g., a return plane ticket), possess an I-94W form (arrival/departure certificate issued upon arrival), are traveling on particular air or sea carriers (most major carriers qualify—contact the carrier for details), and have no visa ineligiblities.

As of October 2004, visitors in the VWP must possess a **machine-readable passport** to be admitted to the US without a visa, although most countries in the VWP have been issuing such passports for some time and many travelers will not need new passports. **Children** from these countries who normally travel on a parent's passport will also need to obtain their own machine-readable passports. Additionally, as of June 2005, the following requirements are in place for the use of **biometric** identifiers as visa waivers: passports issued before October 26, 2005 do not require biometric identifiers, passports issued between October 26, 2005 and October 25, 2006 require either a digital photograph or an integrated data chip, and passports issued after October 26, 2006 require an integrated data chip. See http://travel.state.gov/visa or contact your consulate for a list of countries participating in the VWP as well as the latest info on biometric deadlines.

For stays of longer than 90 days in the US, all foreign travelers (except Canadians) must obtain a visa. Travelers eligible to waive their visas who wish to stay for more than 90 days must receive a visa before entering the US.

WORK PERMITS

Admission as a visitor does not include the right to work, which is authorized only by a work permit. Entering the US to study requires a special visa. Be prepared for long processing times for work permits especially. For more information, see **Beyond Tourism** (p. 66).

IDENTIFICATION

When you travel, always carry at least two forms of identification on your person, including a photo ID; a passport and a driver's license or birth certificate are usually an adequate combination. Never carry all of your IDs together; split them up in case of theft or loss, and keep photocopies of all of them in your luggage and at home.

STUDENT, TEACHER, AND YOUTH IDENTIFICATION

The **International Student Identity Card (ISIC),** the most widely accepted form of student ID, provides discounts on some sights, accommodations, food, and transportation; access to a 24hr. emergency helpline; and insurance benefits for US cardholders (see **Insurance,** p. 46). For example, in Honolulu, this card will earn a 20% room rate discount at the Central YMCA at Waikiki or enable the purchase of two tickets for the price of one on the Waikiki Trolley. Applicants must be full-time secondary or post-secondary school students at least 12 years of age. Because of the proliferation of fake ISICs, some services (particularly airlines) require additional proof of student identity.

The **International Teacher Identity Card (ITIC)** offers teachers the same insurance coverage as the ISIC and similar but limited discounts. For travelers who are under 26 years old but are not students, the **International Youth Travel Card (IYTC)** also offers many of the same benefits as the ISIC.

Each of these identity cards costs US$22. ISICs, ITICs, and IYTCs are valid for one year from the date of issue. To learn more about ISICs, ITICs, and IYTCs, try www.myisic.com. Many student travel agencies (p. 50) issue the cards; for a list of issuing agencies or more information, see the **International Student Travel Confederation (ISTC)** website (www.istc.org).

The **International Student Exchange Card (ISE Card)** is a similar identification card available to students, faculty, and youths aged 12 to 26. The card provides discounts, medical benefits, access to a 24hr. emergency helpline, and the ability to purchase student airfares. An ISE Card costs US$25; call ☎800-255-8000 for more info, or visit www.isecard.com.

ESSENTIALS

CUSTOMS

Upon entering the US, you must declare certain items from abroad and pay a duty on the value of those articles if they exceed the allowance established by the local customs service. Note that goods and gifts purchased at **duty-free** shops abroad are not exempt from duty or sales tax; "duty-free" means that you need not pay a tax in the country of purchase. Upon returning home, you must declare all articles acquired abroad and pay a duty on the value of articles in excess of your home country's allowance. To expedite your return, make a list of any valuables brought from home and register them with customs before traveling abroad; be sure to keep receipts for all goods acquired abroad.

MONEY

CURRENCY AND EXCHANGE

The currency chart below is based on August 2006 exchange rates between US dollars (US$) and Australian dollars (AUS$), Canadian dollars (CDN$), European Union euros (EUR€), New Zealand dollars (NZ$), and British pounds (UK£). Check the latest exchange rates in a large newspaper, or try a currency converter on websites like www.xe.com or www.bloomberg.com.

CURRENCY ($)		
	AUS$ = US$0.76	US$ = AUS$1.31
	CDN$ = US$0.89	US$ = CDN$1.12
	EUR€ = US$1.28	US$ = EUR€0.78
	NZ$ = US$0.63	US$ = NZ$1.58
	UK£ = US$1.90	US$ = UK£$0.53
	SAR= US$0.15	US$ = SAR6.86

As a general rule, it's cheaper to convert money in the US than at home. While currency exchange will probably be available in your arrival airport, it's wise to bring enough foreign currency to last for the first 24 to 72 hours of your trip.

When changing money abroad, try to go only to banks that have at most a 5% margin between their buy and sell prices. Since you lose money with every transaction, **convert large sums** (unless the currency is depreciating rapidly), but **no more than you'll need.**

If you use traveler's checks or bills, carry some in small denominations (the equivalent of US$50 or less) for times when you are forced to exchange money at disadvantageous rates, but bring a range of denominations since charges may be levied per check cashed. Store your money in a variety of forms; ideally, at any given time you will be carrying some cash, some traveler's checks, and an ATM and/or credit card.

TRAVELER'S CHECKS

Traveler's checks are one of the safest and least troublesome means of carrying funds. American Express and Visa are the most-recognized brands. Many banks and agencies sell them for a small commission. Check issuers provide refunds if the checks are lost or stolen, and many provide additional services, such as toll-free refund hotlines abroad, emergency message services, and assistance with lost and stolen credit cards or passports. Traveler's checks are readily accepted in Hawaii. Ask about toll-free refund hotlines and the location of refund centers when purchasing checks, and always carry emergency cash.

American Express: Checks available with commission at select banks, at all AmEx offices, and online (www.americanexpress.com; US residents only). American Express cardholders can also purchase checks by phone (☎800-528-4800). Checks available in Australian, British, Canadian, European, Japanese, and US currencies, among others. American Express also offers the Travelers Cheque Card, a prepaid reloadable card. Cheques for Two can be signed by either of two people traveling together. For purchase locations or more information, contact AmEx's service centers: in Australia ☎800 688 022, in New Zealand 050 855 5358, in the UK 0800 587 6023, in the US and Canada 800-221-7282; elsewhere, call the US collect at 801-964-6665.

Travelex: Thomas Cook MasterCard and Interpayment Visa traveler's checks available. For information about Thomas Cook MasterCard in Canada and the US call ☎800-223-7373, in the UK 0800 622 101; elsewhere call the UK collect at +44 1733 318 950. For information about Interpayment Visa in the US and Canada call ☎800-732-1322, in the UK 0800 515 884; elsewhere call the UK collect at +44 1733 318 949. For more information, visit www.travelex.com.

Visa: Checks available (generally with commission) at banks worldwide. For the location of the nearest office, call the Visa Travelers Cheque Global Refund and Assistance Center: in the UK ☎0800 895 078, in the US 800-227-6811; elsewhere, call the UK collect at +44 2079 378 091. Checks available in British, Canadian, European, Japanese, and US currencies, among others. Visa also offers TravelMoney, a prepaid debit card that can be reloaded online or by phone. For more information on Visa travel services, see http://usa.visa.com/personal/using_visa/travel_with_visa.html.

CREDIT, DEBIT, AND ATM CARDS

Where they are accepted, credit cards often offer superior exchange rates—up to 5% better than the retail rate used by banks and other currency exchange establishments. Credit cards may also offer services such as insurance or emergency help, and are sometimes required to reserve hotel rooms or rental cars. **MasterCard** and **Visa** are the most frequently accepted; **American Express** cards work at some ATMs and at AmEx offices and major airports.

The use of ATM cards is widespread in the US. Depending on the system that your home bank uses, you can most likely access your personal bank account from abroad. ATMs get the same wholesale exchange rate as credit cards, but there is often a limit on the amount of money you can withdraw per day (usually around US$500). There is typically also a surcharge of US$1-5 per withdrawal.

Debit cards are as convenient as credit cards but have a more immediate impact on your funds. A debit card can be used wherever its associated credit card company (usually MasterCard or Visa) is accepted, yet the money is withdrawn directly from the holder's checking account. Debit cards often also function as ATM cards and can be used to withdraw cash from associated banks and ATMs throughout the US.

The two major international money networks are **MasterCard/Maestro/Cirrus** (for ATM locations ☎800-424-7787 or www.mastercard.com) and **Visa/PLUS** (for ATM locations ☎800-847-2911 or www.visa.com). Most ATMs charge a transaction fee that is paid to the bank that owns the ATM.

GETTING MONEY FROM HOME

If you run out of money while traveling, the easiest and cheapest solution is to have someone back home make a deposit to your bank account. Failing that, consider one of the following options.

WIRING MONEY

It is possible to arrange a **bank money transfer,** which means asking a bank back home to wire money to a bank in the US. This is the cheapest way to transfer cash, but it's also the slowest, usually taking several days or more. Note that some banks may only release your funds in local currency, potentially sticking you with a poor exchange rate; inquire about this in advance. Money transfer services like **Western Union** are faster and more convenient than bank transfers—but also much pricier. Western Union has many locations worldwide. To find one, visit www.westernunion.com, or call in Australia ☎1800 173 833, in Canada and the US 800-325-6000, in the UK 0800 833 833. To wire money using a credit card (Discover, MasterCard, Visa), call in the US and Canada ☎800-225-5227, in the UK ☎0800 833 833. Money transfer services are also available to **American Express** cardholders and **Thomas Cook** offices.

COSTS

The cost of your trip will vary considerably, depending on where you go, how you travel, and where you stay. The most significant expenses will probably be your round-trip **airfare** to Hawaii (see **Getting to Hawaii: By Plane,** p. 49), although for travelers planning on driving, the costs of renting a car can quickly escalate. Before you go, spend some time calculating a reasonable daily **budget.**

STAYING ON A BUDGET

To give you a general idea, a bare-bones day in Hawaii (camping or sleeping in hostels/guesthouses, buying food at supermarkets) would cost about $25-30; a slightly more comfortable day (sleeping in hostels/guesthouses and the occasional budget hotel, eating one meal per day at a restaurant, going out at night) would cost $50-65; and for a luxurious day, the sky's the limit. Don't forget to factor in emergency reserve funds (at least US$200) when planning how much money you'll need. Be aware of the local availability of budget accommodations; while some exist, in some towns the cheapest room might go for $90. Transportation costs will only increase the above figures.

HAWAII ON ZERO DOLLARS A DAY

Everyone's told you that Hawaii is an expensive place to take a vacation. We've devoted this guide to proving exactly the opposite. Below is the créme de la créme of our labor—the best free things in the islands.

1. All Islands: **Go to the beach.** You can go to the beach for free anywhere, but Hawaiian beaches are so much better.

2. Oahu: A free show at the **Honolulu Zoo** (p. 129) features new live entertainment every Wednesday.

3. Molokai: Take a free tour of **Purdy's Macadamia Nut Farm** (p. 337) and enjoy the free samples after you crack your first nut.

4. The Big Island: Attend a free nightly stargazing at the **Onizuka Center** (p. 232) on the slopes of Mauna Kea.

5. Kauai: Stroll the streets during **Art Walk,** when art galleries stay open late and offer free gallery showings and food.

6. Maui: Try the Maui Blush at **Tedeschi Vineyard's** free wine tasting (p. 310).

7. Oahu: **Sunset on the Beach** (p. 130). Stay put for a free movie after a free hula show and torch-lighting ceremony.

8. Maui: Take a free self-guided **historical tour** (p. 266) through Lahaina's whaling past.

9. Oahu: The 1st W and 3rd Su at the **Honolulu Academy of Arts** (p. 105) are free explorations into cross-cultural connections in art.

10. Oahu: Experience the moving **Arizona Memorial** (p. 133).

TIPS FOR SAVING MONEY

Some simple ways include searching out opportunities for free entertainment, splitting accommodation and food costs with trustworthy fellow travelers, and buying food in supermarkets rather than eating out. **Camping** (p. 75) is often a good way to save money, as is doing your laundry in the sink (unless this is explicitly prohibited). If you are eligible, consider getting an ISIC or an IYTC; many sights and museums offer reduced admission to students and youths. For getting around quickly, bikes are the most economical option. Renting a bike is cheaper than renting a moped or scooter. Don't forget about walking, though; you can learn a lot about a city by seeing it on foot. Drinking at bars and clubs quickly becomes expensive. It's cheaper to buy alcohol at a supermarket and imbibe before going out. That said, don't go overboard. Though staying within your budget is important, don't do so at the expense of your health or a great travel experience.

TIPPING AND BARGAINING

In the US, it is customary to tip waitstaff and cab drivers 15% (though especially poor or good service warrants tipping from 10-20%). Tips are usually not included in restaurant bills unless you are in a large party of six or more, and a restaurant will tell you if gratuity is included. At the airport and in hotels, porters expect at least a $2 per bag tip to carry your luggage. Except at flea markets or other informal settings, bargaining is generally frowned upon and fruitless in Hawaii.

TAXES

In Hawaii, the state general excise tax is 4%, which in most situations is effectively identical to a sales tax and is levied on groceries as well. Usually this tax is not included in the prices of items. A transient accommodations tax of 7.25% applies to all rooms that are let for fewer than 180 consecutive days; this tax is on top of the state general excise tax for a total of 11.25%. A somewhat arcane tax on rental cars is automatically factored into the price of a rental.

PACKING

Pack lightly: Lay out only what you absolutely need, then take half the clothes and twice the money. The Travelite FAQ (www.travelite.org) is a good resource for tips on traveling light. The online **Universal Packing List** (http://upl.codeq.info) will generate a customized list of suggested items based on your trip length, the expected climate, your planned activities, and other factors. If you plan to do a lot of hiking, also consult **The Great Outdoors,** p. 60. Some frequent travelers keep a bag packed with all the essentials: passport, money belt, hat, socks, etc. Then, when they decide to leave, they know they haven't forgotten anything.

Luggage: If you plan to cover most of your itinerary by foot, a sturdy **frame backpack** is unbeatable. (For the basics on buying a pack, see p. 75.) Toting a **suitcase** or **trunk** is fine if you plan to live in one or two cities and explore from there, but not a great idea if you plan to move around frequently. In addition to your main piece of luggage, a **daypack** (a small backpack or courier bag) is useful.

Clothing: Dress in Hawaii is like the Hawaiian lifestyle—casual and laid-back. Almost everyone, from grandparents to preschoolers, swears by plastic flip-flops. Shorts and light T-shirts or tank tops will do for almost any occasion. Although, if you're planning a trip to Haleakala on Maui, bringing warmer clothing is advisable. It is also always a good idea to bring a light rain jacket. If you're hiking, sturdy shoes or hiking boots are a must. You may also want one nicer outfit—such as a sundress for women and khakis and an aloha shirt for men—for going out, eating at an upscale restaurant, or attending a religious site.

Sleepsack: Some hostels require that you either provide your own linen or rent sheets from them. Save cash by making your own sleepsack: fold a full-size sheet in half the long way, then sew it closed along the long side and one of the short sides.

Converters and Adapters: In Hawaii, as in the rest of the US, electrical appliances are designed for 120V. Canadians who use 120V at home will be able to use electrical appliances in the US without problem. Visitors from the UK, Ireland, Australia, and New Zealand (who use 230V) will need to purchase a converter to step up the lower American voltage to the higher voltage required for most foreign appliances. Certain electrical devices accept both 230V and 120V so a converter may not always be necessary. Also, an adapter (around $5) is always needed to make other plug types compatible with the 3-prong outlet found in the US. For more on all things adaptable, check out http://kropla.com/electric.htm.

Toiletries: Condoms, deodorant, razors, tampons, and toothbrushes are readily available.

First-Aid Kit: For a basic first-aid kit, pack bandages, a pain reliever, antibiotic cream, a thermometer, a multifunction pocketknife, tweezers, moleskin, decongestant, motion-sickness remedy, diarrhea or upset-stomach medication (Pepto Bismol® or Imodium®), an antihistamine, sunscreen, insect repellent, and burn ointment.

Film: Less serious photographers may want to bring a disposable camera or two. Despite disclaimers, airport security X-rays can fog film, so buy a lead-lined pouch at a camera store or ask security to hand-inspect it. Always pack film in your carry-on luggage, since higher-intensity X-rays are used on checked luggage.

Other Useful Items: For safety purposes, you should bring a **money belt** and a small **padlock.** Basic **outdoors equipment** (plastic water bottle, compass, waterproof matches, pocketknife, sunglasses, sunscreen, hat) may also prove useful. **Quick repairs** of torn garments can be done on the road with a needle and thread; also consider bringing electrical tape for patching tears. If you want to do laundry by hand, bring detergent, a small rubber ball to stop up the sink, and string for a makeshift clothes line. Other things you're liable to forget include: an umbrella, sealable **plastic bags** (for damp clothes, soap, food, shampoo, and other spillables), an **alarm clock,** safety pins, rubber bands, a flashlight, earplugs, garbage bags, and a small calculator. A **cell phone** can be a lifesaver (literally) on the road; see p. 56 for information on acquiring one that will work in Hawaii.

Important Documents: Don't forget your passport, traveler's checks, ATM and/or credit cards, adequate ID, and photocopies of all of the aforementioned in case these documents are lost or stolen (p. 37). Also check that you have any of the following that might apply to you: a hosteling membership card (p. 58); driver's license (p. 38); travel insurance forms (p. 46); and an ISIC card (p. 39).

SAFETY AND HEALTH

GENERAL ADVICE

In any type of crisis situation, the most important thing to do is **stay calm.** Your country's embassy abroad (p. 37) is usually your best resource when things go wrong; registering with that embassy upon arrival in the country is often a good idea. The government offices listed in the **Travel Advisories** box (p. 45) can provide information on the services they offer their citizens in case of emergencies abroad.

LOCAL LAWS AND POLICE

DRUGS AND ALCOHOL

As in the continental US, the drinking age in Hawaii is a strictly enforced 21. Young people should expect to be asked to show government-issued identification when purchasing any alcoholic beverage. Drinking and driving is prohibited everywhere, and it is illegal to have an open container of alcohol inside a car, even if you are not the driver and even if you are not drinking it. Those caught drinking and driving face fines, a suspended license, imprisonment, or all three.

Marijuana and narcotics such as heroin, cocaine and methamphetamines are illegal in the US, and possession carries extremely harsh sentences. If you carry prescription drugs while you travel, it is important that you keep a copy of the prescription with you.

SPECIFIC CONCERNS

TERRORISM

In light of the September 11, 2001 terrorist attacks in the eastern US, the US government frequently puts the nation, and its territories, on an elevated terrorism alert. Hawaii has not had any attacks, or threats of attacks, but like the rest of the US the islands have taken necessary precautions. Allow extra time for airport security and do not pack sharp objects in your carry-on luggage, as they will be confiscated. Monitor developments in the news and stay on top of any local, state, or federal terrorist warnings, but do not let fear of terrorism prevent you from enjoying your vacation. The box on **travel advisories** lists offices to contact and webpages to visit to get the most updated list of your home country's government's advisories about travel.

PERSONAL SAFETY

EXPLORING AND TRAVELING

To avoid unwanted attention, try to blend in as much as possible. Respecting local customs (in many cases, dressing more conservatively than you would at home) may placate would-be hecklers. Familiarize yourself with your surroundings before setting out, and carry yourself with confidence. Check maps in shops and restaurants rather than on the street. If you are traveling alone, be sure someone at

TRAVEL ADVISORIES. The following government offices provide travel information and advisories by telephone, by fax, or via the web:

Australian Department of Foreign Affairs and Trade: ☎6 12 6261 1111; www.dfat.gov.au.

Canadian Department of Foreign Affairs and International Trade (DFAIT): ☎800-267-8376; www.dfait-maeci.gc.ca. Call for their free booklet, *Bon Voyage...But.*

New Zealand Ministry of Foreign Affairs: ☎044 398 000; www.mfat.govt.nz.

United Kingdom Foreign and Commonwealth Office: ☎020 7008 1500; www.fco.gov.uk.

US Department of State: ☎888-407-4747; http://travel.state.gov. Visit the website for the booklet *A Safe Trip Abroad.*

home knows your itinerary, and never tell anyone you meet that you're by yourself. When walking at night, stick to busy, well-lit streets and avoid dark alleyways. If you ever feel uncomfortable, leave the area as quickly and directly as you can.

There is no sure-fire way to avoid all the threatening situations you might encounter while traveling, but a good **self-defense course** will give you concrete ways to react to unwanted advances. **Impact, Prepare,** and **Model Mugging** can refer you to local self-defense courses in the US. Visit the website at www.modelmugging.org for a list of nearby chapters. Workshops (2-4hr.) start at US$50; full courses (20hr.) run US$350-500.

If you are using a **car,** learn local driving signals and wear a seatbelt. Children under 40 lbs. should ride only in specially-designed carseats, available for a small fee from most car rental agencies. Study route maps before you hit the road, and if you plan on spending a lot of time driving, consider bringing spare parts. For long drives in desolate areas, invest in a cellular phone and a roadside assistance program (p. 54). Park your vehicle in a garage or well-traveled area, and use a steering wheel locking device in larger cities. If renting, 4WD is advisable, since many of the roads in Hawaii can be rough to drive on. **Sleeping in your car** is the most dangerous way to get your rest. For info on the perils of **hitchhiking,** see p. 55.

POSSESSIONS AND VALUABLES

Never leave your belongings unattended; crime occurs in even the most safe-looking hostel or hotel. Bring your own padlock for hostel lockers, and don't ever store valuables in a locker. Be particularly careful on **buses** and **trains;** horror stories abound about determined thieves who wait for travelers to fall asleep. Carry your bag or purse in front of you where you can see it. When traveling with others, sleep in alternate shifts. When alone, use good judgment in selecting a train compartment: never stay in an empty one, and use a lock to secure your pack to the luggage rack. Use extra caution if traveling at night or on overnight trains. Try to sleep on top bunks with your luggage stored above you (if not in bed with you), and keep important documents and other valuables on you at all times.

There are a few steps you can take to minimize the financial risk associated with traveling. First, **bring as little with you as possible.** Second, buy a few combination **padlocks** to secure your belongings either in your pack or in a hostel or train station locker. Third, **carry as little cash as possible.** Keep your traveler's checks and ATM/credit cards in a **money belt**—not a "fanny pack"—along with your passport and ID cards. Fourth, **keep a small cash reserve separate from your primary stash.** This should be about US$50 sewn into or stored in the depths of your pack, along with your traveler's check numbers and photocopies of your passport, your birth certificate, and other important documents.

In large cities **con artists** often work in groups and may involve children. Beware of certain classics: sob stories that require money, rolls of bills "found" on the street, mustard spilled (or saliva spit) onto your shoulder to distract you while they snatch your bag. **Never let your passport and your bags out of your sight.** Hostel workers will sometimes stand at bus and train station arrival points to try to recruit tired and disoriented travelers to their hostel; never believe strangers who tell you that theirs is the only hostel open. Beware of **pickpockets** in city crowds, especially on public transportation. Also, be alert in public telephone booths: If you must say your calling card number, do so very quietly; if you punch it in, make sure no one can look over your shoulder.

If you will be traveling with electronic devices, such as a laptop computer or a PDA, check whether your homeowner's insurance covers loss, theft, or damage when you travel. If not, you might consider purchasing a low-cost separate insurance policy. **Safeware** (☎800-800-1492; www.safeware.com) specializes in covering computers and charges $90 for 90-day comprehensive international travel coverage up to $4000.

PRE-DEPARTURE HEALTH

In your **passport,** write the names of any people you wish to be contacted in case of a medical emergency, and list any allergies or medical conditions. Matching a prescription to a foreign equivalent is not always easy, safe, or possible, so if you take prescription drugs, consider carrying up-to-date prescriptions or a statement from your doctor stating the medication's trade name, manufacturer, chemical name, and dosage. While traveling, be sure to keep all medication with you in your carry-on luggage. For tips on packing a **first-aid kit** and other health essentials, see p. 43.

IMMUNIZATIONS AND PRECAUTIONS

Travelers over two years old should make sure that the following vaccines are up to date: MMR (for measles, mumps, and rubella); DTaP or Td (for diphtheria, tetanus, and pertussis); IPV (for polio); Hib (for *haemophilus* influenza B); and HepB (for Hepatitis B). For recommendations on immunizations and prophylaxis, consult the Centers for Disease Control and Prevention (CDC) in the US or the equivalent in your home country, and check with a doctor for guidance.

INSURANCE

Travel insurance covers four basic areas: medical/health problems, property loss, trip cancellation/interruption, and emergency evacuation. Though regular insurance policies may well extend to travel-related accidents, you may consider purchasing separate travel insurance if the cost of potential trip cancellation, interruption, or emergency medical evacuation is greater than you can absorb. Prices for travel insurance purchased separately generally run about US$50 per week for full coverage, while trip cancellation/interruption may be purchased separately at a rate of US$3-5 per day depending on length of stay.

Medical insurance (especially university policies) often covers costs incurred abroad; check with your provider. **Canadian** provincial health insurance plans increasingly do not cover foreign travel; check with the provincial Ministry of Health or Health Plan Headquarters for details. **Homeowners' insurance** (or your family's coverage) often covers theft during travel and loss of travel documents (passport, plane ticket, railpass, etc.) up to $500.

ISIC and **ITIC** (see p. 38) provide basic insurance benefits to US cardholders, including US$100 per day of in-hospital sickness for up to 100 days and US$10,000 of accident-related medical reimbursement (see www.isicus.com for details). Cardholders have access to a toll-free 24hr. helpline for medical, legal, and financial emergencies overseas. **American Express** (☎800-338-1670) grants most cardholders automatic collision and theft car rental insurance on rentals made with the card.

USEFUL ORGANIZATIONS AND PUBLICATIONS

The American **Centers for Disease Control and Prevention** (**CDC;** ☎877-FYI-TRIP; www.cdc.gov/travel) maintains an international travelers' hotline and an informative website. Consult the appropriate government agency of your home country for consular information sheets on health, entry requirements, and other issues for various countries (see the listings in the box on **Travel Advisories,** p. 45). For quick information on health and other travel warnings, call the **Overseas Citizens Services** (M-F 8am-8pm from US ☎888-407-4747, from overseas 202-501-4444), or contact a passport agency, embassy, or consulate abroad. For information on medical evacuation services and travel insurance firms, see the US government's website at http://travel.state.gov/travel/abroad_health.html or the **British Foreign and Commonwealth Office** (www.fco.gov.uk). For general health info, contact the **American Red Cross** (☎202-303-4498; www.redcross.org).

STAYING HEALTHY IN HAWAII

Common sense is the simplest prescription for good health while you travel. Drink lots of fluids to prevent dehydration and constipation, and wear sturdy, broken-in shoes and clean socks.

ONCE IN HAWAII

ENVIRONMENTAL HAZARDS

Heat exhaustion and dehydration: Heat exhaustion leads to nausea, excessive thirst, headaches, and dizziness. Avoid it by drinking plenty of fluids, eating salty foods (e.g., crackers), abstaining from dehydrating beverages (e.g., alcohol and caffeinated beverages), and wearing sunscreen. Continuous heat stress can eventually lead to heatstroke, characterized by a rising temperature, severe headache, delirium, and cessation of sweating. Victims should be cooled off with wet towels and taken to a doctor.

Sunburn: Always wear sunscreen (SPF 30 or higher) when spending excessive amounts of time outdoors. If you get sunburned, drink more fluids than usual and apply an aloe-based lotion. Severe sunburns can lead to sun poisoning, a condition that can cause fever, chills, nausea, and vomiting. Sun poisoning should always be treated by a doctor.

INSECT-BORNE DISEASES

Many diseases are transmitted by insects—mainly mosquitoes, fleas, ticks, and lice. Be aware of insects in wet or forested areas, especially while hiking and camping; wear long pants and long sleeves, tuck your pants into your socks, and use a mosquito net. Use insect repellent such as DEET and soak or spray your gear with permethrin (licensed in the US only for use on clothing). **Mosquitoes**—responsible for malaria, dengue fever, and yellow fever—can be particularly abundant in wet, swampy, or wooded areas, such as those on Kauai, Maui, Oahu, and the Big Island. **Ticks**—which can carry Lyme and other diseases—can be particularly dangerous in rural and forested regions, found throughout the islands.

Dengue fever: An "urban viral infection" transmitted by *Aedes* mosquitoes, which bite during the day rather than at night. The incubation period can be 3-14 days, but is usually 4-7 days. Early symptoms include a high fever, severe headaches, swollen lymph nodes, and muscle aches. Many patients also suffer from nausea, vomiting, and a pink rash. If you experience these symptoms, see a doctor immediately, drink plenty of liquids, and take fever-reducing medication such as acetaminophen (Tylenol). *Never take aspirin to treat dengue fever.* There is no vaccine available for dengue fever.

Tick-borne encephalitis: A viral infection of the central nervous system transmitted during the summer by tick bites (primarily in wooded areas) or by consumption of unpasteurized dairy products. The risk of contracting the disease is relatively low, especially if precautions are taken against tick bites.

Lyme disease: A bacterial infection carried by ticks and marked by a circular bull's-eye rash of 2 in. or more. Later symptoms include fever, headache, fatigue, and aches and pains. Antibiotics are effective if administered early. Left untreated, Lyme can cause problems in joints, the heart, and the nervous system. If you find a tick attached to your skin, grasp the head with tweezers as close to your skin as possible and apply slow, steady traction. Removing a tick within 24 hours greatly reduces the risk of infection. Do not try to remove ticks with petroleum jelly, nail polish remover, or a hot match. Ticks usually inhabit moist, shaded environments and heavily wooded areas. If you are going to be hiking in these areas, wear long clothes and DEET.

FOOD- AND WATER-BORNE DISEASES

While drinking water is generally safe in Hawaii, travelers should exercise caution around natural bodies of water, which can harbor dangerous bacteria.

Leptospirosis: A bacterial disease caused by exposure to fresh water or soil contaminated by the urine of infected animals. Able to enter the human body through cut skin, mucus membranes, and through ingestion, it is most common in tropical climates, and can be found in fresh water streams and ponds throughout Hawaii. Symptoms include a high fever, chills, nausea, and vomiting. If not treated it can lead to liver failure and meningitis. There is no vaccine; consult a doctor for treatment.

OTHER INFECTIOUS DISEASES

The following diseases exist in every part of the world. Travelers should know how to recoginize them and what to do if they suspect they have been infected.

AIDS and HIV: For detailed information on Acquired Immune Deficiency Syndrome (AIDS) in Hawaii, call the US Centers for Disease Control's 24hr. hotline at ☎800-342-2437, or contact the Joint United Nations Programme on HIV/AIDS (UNAIDS), 20, Ave. Appia, CH-1211 Geneva 27, Switzerland (☎41 22 791 3666; www.unaids.org). According to US law, people who are HIV positive may not legally enter the US unless they obtain special permission from the US embassy before traveling. Contact the US consulate for information.

Sexually transmitted infections (STIs): Gonorrhea, chlamydia, genital warts, syphilis, herpes, and other STIs are easier to catch than HIV and can be just as serious. Though condoms may protect you from some STIs, oral or even tactile contact can lead to transmission. If you think you may have contracted an STI, see a doctor immediately.

OTHER HEALTH CONCERNS

MEDICAL CARE ON THE ROAD

Medical services in Hawaii are accessible 24hr. at hospitals throughout the islands. Some more rural towns may be a short drive away from the nearest hospital, but for the most part, medical care is readily available. In an emergency, dial ☎**911** from any phone, and an operator will send out paramedics. Alternatively, if there is an emergency room near by, go directly there for immediate service. Almost all cities and towns have standard pharmacies.

If you are concerned about obtaining medical assistance while traveling, you may wish to employ special support services. The *MedPass* from **GlobalCare, Inc.**, 6875 Shiloh Rd. East, Alpharetta, GA 30005, USA (☎800-860-1111; www.globalcare.net), provides 24hr. international medical assistance, support, and medical evacuation resources. The **International Association for Medical Assistance to Travelers** (**IAMAT;** US ☎716-754-4883, Canada 519-836-0102; www.iamat.org) has free membership, lists English-speaking doctors worldwide, and offers detailed info on immunization requirements and sanitation. If your regular **insurance** policy does not cover travel abroad, you may wish to purchase additional coverage (p. 46).

Those with medical conditions (such as diabetes, allergies to antibiotics, epilepsy, or heart conditions) may want to obtain a **MedicAlert** membership (first year US$35, annually thereafter $20), which includes among other things a stainless steel ID tag and a 24hr. collect-call number. Contact the MedicAlert Foundation, 2323 Colorado Ave., Turlock, CA 95382, USA (☎888-633-4298, outside US 209-668-3333; www.medicalert.org).

WOMEN'S HEALTH

Women traveling in unsanitary conditions are vulnerable to **urinary tract (including bladder and kidney) infections.** Over-the-counter medicines can sometimes alleviate symptoms, but if they persist, see a doctor. **Vaginal yeast infections** may flare up in hot and humid climates. Wearing loosely fitting trousers or a skirt and cotton underwear will help, as will over-the-counter remedies like Monostat or Gynelotrimin. Bring supplies from home if you are prone to infection, as they may be difficult to find on the road. **Tampons, pads,** and **contraceptive devices** are widely available, though your favorite brand may not be stocked—bring extras of anything you can't live without. **Abortion** is legal in the US, and information is available through Planned Parenthood of Hawaii (☎589-1156; www.plannedparenthood.org).

GETTING TO HAWAII

BY PLANE

When it comes to airfare, a little effort can save you a bundle. If your plans are flexible enough to deal with the restrictions, courier fares are the cheapest. Tickets bought from consolidators and standby seating are also good deals, but last-minute specials, airfare wars, and charter flights often beat these fares. The key is to hunt around, to be flexible, and to ask persistently about discounts. Students, seniors, and those under 26 should never pay full price for a ticket.

AIRFARES

Airfares to Hawaii are consistently high throughout the year. Holidays and the winter months are particularly expensive. It is slightly cheaper to travel in the fall and spring. Midweek (M-Th morning) round-trip flights run US$40-50 cheaper than weekend flights, but they are generally more crowded and less likely to permit frequent-flier upgrades. Taking flights with long layovers or multiple stops can significantly reduce the price of your fare. Not fixing a return date ("open return") or arriving in and departing from different cities ("open-jaw") can be pricier than standard round-trip flights. Patching one-way flights together is the most expensive way to travel. Flights into Honolulu are most common and will almost always be less expensive than flights into cities on other islands.

When traveling from North America, flights to the Big Island, Maui, and Kauai are anywhere from $25-75 more than a comparable flight to Oahu. It's usually a toss-up between American, Continental, Delta, Northwest, or United as to which airline can offer the cheapest fare on a particular date. Smaller airlines like Hawaiian Airlines, ATA, America West, Alaska Airlines, and others may occasionally be able to offer a significantly lower price, but for the most part their fares are comparable with the major carriers.

Fares for round-trip flights to Hawaii from the US or Canadian East Coast range from $560-1000 depending on when your flight is and how early you book it; from the US or Canadian West Coast, prices range $300-1000 with the average cost around $600; from the UK £750-1000; from Australia AUS$1500-4000, although Hawaiian Airlines offers flights from around AUS$800; from New Zealand NZ$1500-4500.

If Hawaii is only one stop on a more extensive globe-hop, consider a round-the-world (RTW) ticket. Tickets usually include at least five stops and are valid for about a year; prices range $3000-5000. Try **Northwest Airlines/KLM** (US ☎800-447-4747; www.nwa.com) or **Star Alliance,** a consortium of 22 airlines including United Airlines (US ☎800-241-6522; www.staralliance.com).

BUDGET AND STUDENT TRAVEL AGENCIES

While knowledgeable agents specializing in flights to Hawaii can make your life easy and help you save, they may not spend the time to find you the lowest possible fare—they get paid on commission. Travelers holding **ISICs** and **IYTCs** (p. 39) qualify for big discounts from student travel agencies. Most flights from budget agencies are on major airlines, but in peak season some may sell seats on less reliable chartered aircraft.

STA Travel, 5900 Wilshire Blvd., Ste. 900, Los Angeles, CA 90036, USA (24hr. reservations and info ☎800-781-4040; www.statravel.com). A student and youth travel organization with over 150 offices worldwide (check their website for a listing of all their offices), including US offices in Boston, Chicago, L.A., New York, Seattle, San Francisco, and Washington, D.C. Ticket booking, travel insurance, railpasses, and more. Walk-in offices are located throughout Australia (☎03 9207 5900), New Zealand (☎09 309 9723), and the UK (☎08701 630 026).

Travel CUTS (Canadian Universities Travel Services Limited), 187 College St., Toronto, ON M5T 1P7, Canada (☎866-246-9762; www.travelcuts.com). Offices across Canada and the US including Los Angeles, New York, Seattle, and San Francisco.

USIT, 19-21 Aston Quay, Dublin 2, Ireland (☎01 602 1904; www.usit.ie), Ireland's leading student/budget travel agency has 20 offices throughout Northern Ireland and the Republic of Ireland. Offers programs to work, study, and volunteer worldwide.

COMMERCIAL AIRLINES

The commercial airlines' lowest regular offer is the **APEX** (Advance Purchase Excursion) fare, which provides confirmed reservations and allows "open-jaw" tickets. Generally, reservations must be made seven to 21 days ahead of departure, with seven- to 14-day minimum-stay and up to 90-day maximum-stay restrictions. These fares carry hefty cancellation and change penalties (fees rise in summer). Book peak-season APEX fares early. Use **Expedia** (www.expedia.com) or **Travelocity** (www.travelocity.com) to get an idea of the lowest published fares, then use the resources outlined here to try and beat those fares. For useful information on Hawaii's airports, including a list of airlines that fly into Hawaii, go to www.state.hi.us/dot/airports.

FLIGHT PLANNING ON THE INTERNET. The Internet may be the budget traveler's dream when it comes to finding and booking bargain fares, but the array of options can be overwhelming. Many airline sites offer special last-minute deals on the Web. Try **Aloha Airlines** (www.alohaair.com), **Hawaiian Airlines** (www.hawaiianair.com), or the new **go!** airline (www.iflygo.com). **STA** (www.statravel.com) and **StudentUniverse** (www.studentuniverse.com) provide quotes on student tickets, while **Orbitz** (www.orbitz.com), **Expedia** (www.expedia.com), and **Travelocity** (www.travelocity.com) offer full travel services. **Priceline** (www.priceline.com) lets you specify a price, and obligates you to buy any ticket that meets or beats it; **Hotwire** (www.hotwire.com) offers bargain fares, but won't reveal the airline or flight times until you buy. Other sites that compile deals include www.bestfares.com, www.flights.com, www.lowestfare.com, www.onetravel.com, and www.travelzoo.com. Increasingly, there are online tools available to help sift through multiple offers; **SideStep** (www.sidestep.com) and **Booking Buddy** (www.bookingbuddy.com) let you enter your trip information once and search multiple sites. An indispensable resource on the Internet is the **Air Traveler's Handbook** (www.faqs.org/faqs/travel/air/handbook), a comprehensive listing of links to everything you need to know before you board a plane.

STANDBY FLIGHTS

Traveling standby requires considerable flexibility in arrival and departure dates and cities. Companies dealing in standby flights sell vouchers rather than tickets, along with the promise to get you to your destination (or near your destination) within a certain window of time (typically 1-5 days). You call in before your specific window of time to hear your flight options and the probability that you will be able to board each flight. You can then decide which flights you want to try to make, show up at the appropriate airport at the appropriate time, and present your voucher. Vouchers can usually be bought for both one-way and round-trip travel. You may receive a monetary refund only if every available flight within your date range is full; if you opt not to take an available (but perhaps less convenient) flight, you can only get credit toward future travel. Carefully read agreements with any company offering standby flights as tricky fine print can leave you in the lurch. To check on a company's service record in the US, contact the Better Business Bureau (☎703-276-0100; www.bbb.org). It is difficult to receive refunds, and clients' vouchers will not be honored when an airline fails to receive payment in time.

TICKET CONSOLIDATORS

Ticket consolidators, or **"bucket shops,"** buy unsold tickets in bulk from commercial airlines and sell them at discounted rates. The best place to look is in the Sunday travel section of any major newspaper (such as *The New York Times*), where many bucket shops place tiny ads. Call quickly, as availability is typically extremely limited. Not all bucket shops are reliable, so insist on a receipt that gives full details of restrictions, refunds, and tickets, and pay by credit card (in spite of the 2-5% fee) so you can stop payment if you never receive your tickets. For more info, see www.travel-library.com/air-travel/consolidators.html.

TRAVELING FROM THE US AND CANADA

Some consolidators worth trying are **Rebel** (☎800-732-3588; www.rebeltours.com), **Cheap Tickets** (www.cheaptickets.com), **Flights.com** (www.flights.com), and **TravelHUB** (www.travelhub.com). But these are just suggestions to get you started in your research. Let's Go does not endorse any of these agencies. As always, be cautious, and research companies before you hand over your credit card number.

CHARTER FLIGHTS

Tour operators contract charter flights with airlines in order to fly extra loads of passengers during peak season. These flights are far from hassle free. They occur less frequently than major airlines, make refunds particularly difficult, and are almost always fully booked. Their scheduled times may change and they may be cancelled at the last moment (as late as 48 hours before the trip, and without a full refund). And check-in, boarding, and baggage claim for them are often much slower. They can be, however, much cheaper.

Discount clubs and fare brokers offer members savings on last-minute charter and tour deals. Study contracts closely; you don't want to end up with an unwanted overnight layover. Try **Travelers Advantage** (☎800-835-8747; www.travelersadvantage.com; $90 annual fee includes discounts and cheap flight directories).

GETTING AROUND HAWAII

BY PLANE

There are several interisland airlines, including **Hawaiian Airlines** (☎800-367-5320), **Aloha Airlines** (☎800-367-5250), and **Island Air** (☎800-323-3345). All offer competitive rates on interisland flights. One-way flights from Honolulu to the outer islands start around $40.

BY BUS

Public transportation on **Oahu** is generally safe, clean, and relatively convenient. With 93 routes criss-crossing the island and over 4200 bus stops, **TheBus,** 811 Middle St., Honolulu 96819 (☎848-5555, customer service 848-4500; www.thebus.org), can usually get you where you're going. Adult one-way fare is $2. Monthly passes ($40) can be purchased at various supermarkets and drugstores. The county of **Kauai** also maintains a decent bus system ($1.50). Schedules and other information are available at the **County of Kauai Transportation Office,** 3220 Hoolako St., Lihue, Kauai 96766 (☎241-6410). The **Big Island** has limited bus service. Contact the **County of Hawaii Mass Transit Office,** 630 E. Lanikaula St., Hilo 96720 (☎961-8744; www.hawaii-county.com/mass_transit/transit_main.htm). **Maui** offers only localized shuttle service through **Speedishuttle** (☎877-521-2085; www.speedishuttle.com). **Molokai** and **Lanai** have no form of public transportation.

BY CAR

Though car rental can be expensive, driving is the best and most efficient way to get around in Hawaii. "U.S." (as in "U.S. 1") refers to US highways, and "Rte." (as in "Rte. 7") refers to state and local highways.

RENTING

Depending on which island you plan to visit, the business of renting a car varies. **Molokai** and **Lanai** have only a few car rental agencies. In addition, some areas all but demand **4WD** (Lanai in particular). In general, cheaper cars tend to be less reliable and harder to handle on difficult terrain. Less expensive 4WD vehicles tend to be more top-heavy and are more dangerous when navigating bumpy roads.

RENTAL AGENCIES

Car rental agencies fall into two categories: national companies with hundreds of branches, and local agencies that serve only one city or region. National chains usually allow you to pick up a car in one city and drop it off in another for a hefty charge, sometimes in excess of $1000. Generally, airport branches have more expensive rates. To rent a car from most establishments in Hawaii, you need to be at least 21 years old and have a major credit card. Some agencies require renters to be 25, and most charge those ages 21-24 an additional insurance fee (around $15-25 a day). Policies and prices vary from agency to agency. Small local operations occasionally rent to people under 21, but be sure to ask about the insurance coverage and deductible, and always check the fine print.

You can generally make reservations before you leave by calling major international offices in your home country. However, occasionally the price and availability information they give doesn't jive with what the local offices in your country will tell you. Try checking with both numbers to make sure you get the best price and accurate information. Local desk numbers are included in town listings; for home-country numbers, call your toll-free directory.

NATIONAL AGENCIES

Alamo (☎800-462-5266; www.alamo.com) rents to under 25 with a major credit card for a surchage of about $25 per day. Locations on Oahu, Maui, Kauai, and the Big Island.

Budget (☎800-527-0700; www.budget.com) rents to under 25 with a surcharge that varies by location. Locations on Oahu, Maui, Kauai, the Big Island, and Molokai.

Dollar (☎800-800-4000; www.dollar.com) rents to under 25 with a variable surcharge. Locations on Oahu, Maui, Kauai, the Big Island, Lanai, and Molokai.

Enterprise (☎800-261-7331; www.enterprise.com) rents to under 25 with a variable surcharge. Locations on Oahu, Maui, and the Big Island.

Hertz (☎800-654-3131; www.hertz.com). Policy varies by city. Locations on Oahu, Maui, Kauai, and the Big Island.

Rent-A-Wreck (☎800-944-7501; www.rentawreck.com) specializes in supplying vehicles that are past their prime for lower-than-average prices; a bare-bones compact less than 8 years old rents for around $20-25 per day; cars 3-5 years old average under $30. The only Rent-a-Wreck location in Hawaii is Lihue, Kauai.

Thrifty (☎800-847-4389; www.thrifty.com) locations rent to under 25 for varying surcharges. Locations on Oahu, Maui, Kauai, and the Big Island.

LOCAL AGENCIES

Hawaii also has a number of locally owned rental services. Be aware that their selection of vehicles may be more limited than that of national chains. Local car rental agencies are listed in the **Transportation** section of towns and cities.

AA Aloha Cars-R-Us (☎800-655-7989; www.hawaiicarrental.com). Researches the lowest rates for cars from major rental agencies. Also offers special Hawaii promotions.

Aloha Rent a Car (☎877-452-5642; www.aloharentacar.com). Maui-based, airport pickup.

Car Rentals in Hawaii (☎888-292-3307; www.carrentalsinhawaii.com). Travelers can search available rentals online.

Harper Car and Truck Rental (☎800-852-9993; www.harpershawaii.com). Two locations on the Big Island. Rents motor homes as well.

Kihei Rent A Car (☎800-251-5288; www.kiheirentacar.com). Family-owned business located in Kihei, Maui. Also a certified travel agency.

COSTS AND INSURANCE

Rental car prices start at around $35 per day from local and national companies. Expect to pay more for larger cars and for 4WD. Many rental deals offer unlimited mileage, while others offer a limited number of miles per day with a surcharge per mile after that. Return the car with a full tank of gasoline to avoid high fuel charges. National chains often allow one-way rentals (picking up in one city and dropping off in another). There is usually a minimum hire period and sometimes an extra drop-off charge of several hundred dollars. Be sure to ask whether the price includes **insurance** against theft and collision. In Hawaii, remember that if you are driving a conventional rental vehicle on an **unpaved road,** you are almost never covered by insurance; ask about this before leaving the rental agency.

DRIVING PERMITS AND CAR INSURANCE

INTERNATIONAL DRIVING PERMIT (IDP)

If you plan to drive a car while in Hawaii, you must be over 18 and have a US driver's license or an International Driving Permit (IDP). Your IDP, valid for one year, must be issued in your own country before you depart. An application for an IDP usually requires one or two photos, a current local license, an additional form of identification, and a fee. To apply, contact your home country's automobile association. Be careful when purchasing an IDP online or anywhere other than your home automobile association. Many vendors sell permits of questionable legitimacy for higher prices.

CAR INSURANCE

Most credit cards cover standard insurance. If you rent, lease, or borrow a car, you will need a **Green Card,** or **International Insurance Certificate,** to certify that you have liability insurance and that it applies abroad. Green cards can be obtained at car rental agencies, car dealers (for those leasing cars), some travel agents, and some border crossings.

DRIVING PRECAUTIONS. When traveling in the summer or in the desert, bring substantial amounts of **water** (a suggested 5 liters of water per person per day) for drinking and for the radiator. For long drives to unpopulated areas, register with police before beginning the trek, and again upon arrival at the destination. Check with the local automobile club for details. When traveling for long distances, make sure tires are in good repair and have enough air, and get good maps. A **compass** and a **car manual** can also be very useful. You should always carry a **spare tire** and **jack, jumper cables, extra oil, flares,** a **flashlight,** and **heavy blankets** (in case your car breaks down at night or in the winter). If you don't know how to **change a tire,** learn before heading out, especially if you are planning on traveling in deserted areas. Blowouts on dirt roads are exceedingly common. If you do have a breakdown, **stay in your car;** if you wander off, there's less likelihood trackers will find you.

BY MOPED

Mopeds are a popular mode of transport in parts of Hawaii, especially Waikiki. Two major rental agencies are listed below.

A&B Moped Rental (☎808-669-0027), 3481 Lower Honoapiilani Hwy., Lahaina, Maui 96761.

The Moped Zone (☎808-732-3366), 750-A Kapahulu Ave., Honolulu, Oahu 96815.

BY THUMB

Let's Go never recommends hitchhiking as a safe means of transportation, and none of the information presented here is intended to do so.

Let's Go strongly urges you to consider the risks before you choose to hitchhike. Hitching means entrusting your life to a stranger and risking assault, sexual harassment, theft, and unsafe driving.

KEEPING IN TOUCH

BY EMAIL AND INTERNET

Though in some places it's possible to forge a remote link with your home server, in most cases this is a much slower (and thus more expensive) option than taking advantage of free **web-based email accounts** (e.g., www.hotmail.com and www.gmail.com). **Internet cafes** and the occasional free Internet terminal at a public library or university are listed in the **Practical Information** sections of major cities. For lists of additional cybercafes in Hawaii, check out www.world66.com/northamerica/unitedstates/hawaii.

Travelers find that taking their **laptop computers** on the road with them can be an increasingly convenient option for staying connected. Hawaii has many Internet cafes that allow laptop users to connect to the Internet, and travelers with wireless-enabled computers can take advantage of an increasing number of Internet "hotspots," where they can get online for free or for a small fee. Newer computers can detect these hotspots automatically; otherwise, websites like www.jiwire.com, www.wififreespot.com, and www.wi-fihotspotlist.com can help you find them.

BY TELEPHONE

CALLING HOME FROM HAWAII

You can make **direct international calls** from pay phones in Hawaii, but if you aren't using a phone card, you may need to drop your coins as quickly as your words. **Prepaid phone cards** are a common and relatively inexpensive means of calling abroad.

Placing a **collect call** through an international operator can be quite expensive, but may be necessary in case of an emergency. You can frequently call collect without even possessing a company's calling card just by calling its access number and following the instructions.

PLACING INTERNATIONAL CALLS. To call Hawaii from home or to call home from Hawaii, dial:

1. The **international dialing prefix.** To call from **Australia,** dial 0011; **Canada** or the **US,** 011; **Ireland, New Zealand,** or the **UK,** 00.
2. The **country code** of the country you want to call. To call **Australia,** dial 61; **Canada** or the **US,** 1; **Ireland,** 353; **New Zealand,** 64; the **UK,** 44.
3. The **city/area code.** The city/area code for all of Hawaii is **808.** When calling internationally, if the 1st digit is a zero (e.g., 020 for London), omit the zero when calling from abroad (e.g., dial 20 from Canada to reach London).
4. The **local number.**

CELLULAR PHONES

The international standard for cell phones is **Global System for Mobile Communication (GSM),** although GSM-compatible phones are not generally sold in the US. GSM users will have no trouble using their phones in Hawaii; however, all that is necessary to make and receive calls in Hawaii is a phone and a **SIM (Subscriber Identity Module) card,** a country-specific, thumbnail-sized chip that gives you a local phone number and plugs you into the local network. Some SIM cards are **prepaid,** meaning that they come with calling time included and you don't need to sign up for a monthly service plan. Incoming calls are frequently free. When you use up the prepaid time, you can buy additional cards or vouchers (usually available at convenience stores) to get more.

TIME DIFFERENCES

Hawaii has its own time zone—**Hawaii Standard Time (HST).** HST is 10hr. behind **Greenwich Mean Time (GMT).** It is 6hr. behind New York and Boston (5hr. behind during daylight saving time), 2hr. behind Vancouver and San Francisco, 3hr. ahead of Sydney, and 2hr. ahead of Auckland (NZ). **Hawaii does not observe daylight saving time.** The chart below gives the time in various cities around the world when it is midnight in Honolulu.

12AM	2AM	6AM	10AM	6PM	9PM
Honolulu	Vancouver Seattle San Francisco Los Angeles	Toronto Ottawa New York Boston	London (GMT)	China Hong Kong Manila Singapore	Sydney Canberra Melbourne

BY MAIL

SENDING MAIL HOME FROM HAWAII

Airmail is the best way to send mail home from Hawaii. These are standard rates for mail from Hawaii to:

Australia: Allow 4-7 days for regular airmail home. Letters up to 1 oz. cost $0.80; packages up to 0.5 lb. $7.50, up to 2 lb. $20.80.

Canada: Allow 4-7 days for regular airmail home. Letters up to 1 oz. cost $0.63; packages up to 0.5 lb. $2.50, up to 2 lb. $14.00.

Ireland: Allow 4-7 days for regular airmail home. Letters up to 1 oz. cost $0.84; packages up to 0.5 lb. $6.75, up to 2 lb. $20.05.

New Zealand: Allow 4-7 days for regular airmail home. Letters up to 1 oz. cost $0.84; packages up to 0.5 lb. $7.50, up to 2 lb. $16.85.

UK: Allow 4-7 days for regular airmail home. Letters up to 1 oz. cost $0.80; packages up to 0.5 lb. $6.40, up to 2 lb. $13.30.

SENDING MAIL TO HAWAII

There are several ways to arrange pickup of letters sent to you by friends and relatives while you are abroad. Mail can be sent via **General Delivery** to almost any city or town in Hawaii with a post office. Address General Delivery letters like so:

John RESIDENT

General Delivery

City, HI postal code

USA

The mail will go to a special desk in the central post office, unless you specify a post office by street address or postal code. It's best to use the largest post office, since mail may be sent there regardless. It is usually safer and quicker, though more expensive, to send mail express or registered. Bring your passport (or other photo ID) for pickup; there may be a small fee. If the clerks insist that there is nothing for you, have them check under your first name as well. *Let's Go Hawaii* lists post offices in the **Practical Information** section for each city and most towns.

ACCOMMODATIONS

HOSTELS

Many hostels are laid out dorm-style, often with large single-sex rooms and bunk beds, although private rooms that sleep two to four are becoming more common. They sometimes have kitchens and utensils for your use, bike or moped rentals, storage areas, transportation to airports, breakfast and other meals, laundry facilities, and Internet access. There can be drawbacks: some hostels close during certain daytime "lockout" hours, have a curfew, don't accept reservations, impose a maximum stay, or, less frequently, require that you do chores. In Hawaii, a dorm bed in a hostel will average around $20.

A HOSTELER'S BILL OF RIGHTS. There are certain standard features that we do not include in our hostel listings. Unless we state otherwise, you can expect that every hostel has no lockout, no curfew, free hot showers, some system of secure luggage storage, and no key deposit.

HOSTELLING INTERNATIONAL

Joining the youth hostel association in your own country (listed below) automatically grants you membership privileges in **Hostelling International (HI),** a federation of national hosteling associations. Non-HI members may be allowed to stay in some hostels, but will have to pay extra to do so. There are three HI hostels in Hawaii—one in Volcano on the Big Island, and two in Honolulu—all of which accept reservations via Hostelling International's website (www.hihostels.com).

Most HI hostels also honor **guest memberships**—you'll get a blank card with space for six validation stamps. Each night you'll pay a nonmember supplement (one-sixth the membership fee) and earn one guest stamp; get six stamps and you're a member. A new membership benefit is the FreeNites program, which allows hostelers to gain points toward free rooms. Most student travel agencies (p. 50) sell HI cards, as do all of the national hosteling organizations listed below. All prices listed below are valid for **one-year memberships** unless otherwise noted.

Australian Youth Hostels Association (AYHA), 422 Kent St., Sydney, NSW 200 (☎02 9261 1111; www.yha.com.au). AUS$52, under 18 AUS$19.

Hostelling International-Canada (HI-C), 205 Catherine St. #400, Ottawa, ON K2P 1C3 (☎613-237-7884; www.hihostels.ca). CDN$35, under 18 free.

An Óige (Irish Youth Hostel Association), 61 Mountjoy St., Dublin 7 (☎830 4555; www.irelandyha.org). EUR€20, under 18 EUR€10.

Hostelling International Northern Ireland (HINI), 22-32 Donegall Rd., Belfast BT12 5JN (☎02890 32 47 33; www.hini.org.uk). UK£13, under 18 UK£6.

Youth Hostels Association of New Zealand (YHANZ), Level 1, Moorhouse City, 166 Moorhouse Ave., P.O. Box 436, Christchurch (☎0800 278 299 (NZ only) or 03 379 9970; www.yha.org.nz). NZ$40, under 18 free.

Scottish Youth Hostels Association (SYHA), 7 Glebe Cres., Stirling FK8 2JA (☎01786 89 14 00; www.syha.org.uk). UK£6, under 17 £2.50.

Youth Hostels Association (England and Wales), Trevelyan House, Dimple Rd., Matlock, Derbyshire DE4 3YH (☎08707 708 868; www.yha.org.uk). UK£15.50, under 26 UK£10.

Hostelling International-USA, 8401 Colesville Rd., Ste. 600, Silver Spring, MD 20910 (☎301-495-1240; www.hiayh.org). US$28, under 18 free.

BOOKING HOSTELS ONLINE. One of the easiest ways to ensure you've got a bed for the night is by reserving online. Click to the **Hostelworld** booking engine through **www.letsgo.com,** and you'll have access to bargain accommodations from Argentina to Zimbabwe with no added commission.

OTHER TYPES OF ACCOMMODATIONS

YMCAS AND YWCAS

Young Men's Christian Association (YMCA) lodgings are usually cheaper than a hotel but more expensive than a hostel. Not all YMCA locations offer lodging; those that do are often located in urban downtowns. Many YMCAs accept women and families; some will not lodge those under 18 without parental permission. In Hawaii, there are YMCAs in Oahu and Maui and YWCAs in Oahu and Kauai.

YMCA of the USA, 101 North Wacker Dr., Chicago, IL 60606, USA (☎888-333-9622 or 800-872-9622; www.ymca.net). Provides a listing of the nearly 1000 Ys across the US and Canada. Offers info on prices, services, telephone numbers, and addresses.

YWCA of the USA, 1015 18th St. NW, Ste. 1100, Washington, DC 20036, USA (☎800-YWCA-US1; www.ywca.org). Provides a directory of YWCAs across the US.

HOTELS

Several major hotel chains have multiple locations within Hawaii. **Outrigger** (☎800-688-7444; www.outrigger.com) trumps the competition with its sheer number of offerings. Between its upscale resorts and the more moderately priced sister chain **Ohana Hotels** (☎800-464-6262; www.ohanahotels.com), there are dozens of Outrigger and Ohana options. The chain offers myriad specials and packages, including discounts for seniors and military personnel. Call to inquire about promotions or see their website. **Hilton** (☎800-774-1500; www.hilton.com) has a resort on Oahu and one on the Big Island. **Sheraton** (☎888-625-5144; www.sheraton.com), which includes the **Westin** and **W** hotel chains, has locations on each of Hawaii's islands. Sheraton rates range from high to higher, depending on the island and location. **Best Western** (☎800-780-7234; www.bestwestern.com) and **Marriott** (☎888-236-2427; www.marriott.com) also maintain a number of locations throughout Hawaii.

Hotel singles in Hawaii start around $65-90, depending on the island. If you make **reservations** in writing, indicate your night of arrival and the number of nights you plan to stay. The hotel will send you a confirmation and may request payment for the first night. Often it is easier to make reservations over the phone.

BED & BREAKFASTS (B&BS)

For a cozy alternative to impersonal hotel rooms, B&Bs (private homes with rooms available to travelers) range from acceptable to sublime. Rooms in B&Bs can run anywhere from $50-150 in Hawaii. Any number of websites provide listings for B&Bs; check out **Bed & Breakfast Inns Online** (www.bbonline.com), **InnFinder** (www.inncrawler.com), **InnSite** (www.innsite.com), **BedandBreakfast.com** (www.bedandbreakfast.com), **Pamela Lanier's Bed & Breakfast Guide Online** (www.lanierbb.com), or **BNBFinder.com** (www.bnbfinder.com).

CAMPING

Why stay near the beach when you can stay on the beach? Camping is an economical and fun way to tour Hawaii, with most campsites charging around $5 for a permit. Sites exist on every island (and in almost every town), and backcountry camping is possible as well. County-maintained campsites are generally safe and frequently gated. Some (especially on Oahu) have newly renovated facilities, and are quite modern and popular with families. For more information on camping, including safety tips and permit information, see **The Great Outdoors,** (p. 75).

SPECIFIC CONCERNS

SUSTAINABLE TRAVEL

As the number of travelers on the road continues to rise, the detrimental effect they can have on natural environments becomes an increasing concern. With this in mind, Let's Go promotes the philosophy of **sustainable travel.** Through a sensitivity to issues of ecology and sustainability, today's travelers can be a powerful force in preserving as well as restoring the places they visit.

Ecotourism, a rising trend in sustainable travel, focuses on the conservation of natural habitats and how to use them to build up the economy without exploitation or overdevelopment. Travelers can make a difference by doing research in advance and by supporting environmentally friendly organizations and establishments that pay attention to their impact on their natural surroundings.

For more local information about businesses that subscribe to and promote ecotourism see www.hawaiiecotourism.org and www.alternative-hawaii.com.

ECOTOURISM RESOURCES. For more information on environmentally responsible tourism, contact one of the organizations below:

Conservation International, 1919 M St. NW, Ste. 600, Washington, D.C. 20036, USA (☎800-406-2306 or 202-912-1000; www.conservation.org).

Green Globe 21 (☎61 2 6257 9102; www.greenglobe.com).

International Ecotourism Society, 733 15th St. NW, Ste. 1000, Washington, D.C. 20005, USA (☎202-347-9203; www.ecotourism.org).

United Nations Environment Program (UNEP), 39-43 Quai André Citroën, 75739 Paris Cedex 15, France (☎33 1 44 37 14 50; www.uneptie.org/pc/tourism).

RESPONSIBLE TRAVEL

The impact of tourist dollars on the destinations you visit should not be underestimated. The choices you make during your trip can have powerful effects on local communities—for better or for worse. Travelers who care about the destinations and environments they explore should make themselves aware of the social, cultural, and political implications of the choices they make when they travel. Simple decisions such as buying local products instead of globally available ones, paying fair prices for products or services, and attempting to say a few words in the local language can have a strong, positive effect on the community.

Hawaii has been a center of tourism for nearly a century, but that does not mean travelers should assume that they are welcome. In some areas, particularly the more rural districts, visitors would be well advised to keep a low profile. It is always important to show respect to everyone you encounter on your journeys through the islands; courtesy is paramount in Hawaiian culture.

Hawaii's unique ecosystem is often affected by tourism as well, both positively and negatively. Be advised that it is unwise (and often illegal) to get too close to some of the plants and animals, such as dolphins, sea turtles, and seals.

If you are interested in learning more about opportunities to help preserve all things Hawaii, check out **Beyond Tourism** (p. 66).

TRAVELING ALONE

There are many benefits to traveling alone, including independence and a greater opportunity to connect with locals. On the other hand, solo travelers are more vulnerable targets of harassment and street theft. If you are traveling alone, look confident, try not to stand out as a tourist, and be especially careful in deserted or very crowded areas. Stay away from areas that are not well lit. If questioned, never admit that you are traveling alone. Maintain regular contact with someone at home who knows your itinerary, and always research your destination before traveling. For more tips, pick up *Traveling Solo* by Eleanor Berman (Globe Pequot Press, US$18), visit www.travelaloneandloveit.com, or subscribe to **Connecting: Solo Travel Network,** 689 Park Rd., Unit 6, Gibsons, BC V0N 1V7, Canada (☎604-886-9099; www.cstn.org; membership US$30-48).

WOMEN TRAVELERS

Women exploring on their own inevitably face some additional safety concerns, but it's easy to be adventurous without taking undue risks. If you are concerned, consider staying in hostels which offer single rooms that lock from the inside or in religious organizations with single-sex rooms. Stick to centrally located accommodations and avoid solitary late-night treks or metro rides.

Always carry extra cash for a phone call, bus, or taxi. **Hitchhiking** is never safe for lone women, or even for two women traveling together. Look as if you know where you're going and approach older women or couples for directions if you're lost or uncomfortable.

Generally, the less you look like a tourist, the better off you'll be. Wearing a conspicuous **wedding band** sometimes helps to prevent unwanted advances.

Your best answer to verbal harassment is no answer at all; feigning deafness, sitting motionless, and staring straight ahead at nothing in particular will usually do the trick. The extremely persistent can sometimes be dissuaded by a firm, loud, and very public "Go away!" Don't hesitate to seek out a police officer or a passerby if you are being harassed. Memorize the emergency numbers in places you visit, and consider carrying a whistle on your keychain. A self-defense course will both prepare you for a potential attack and raise your level of awareness of your surroundings. Also be sure you are aware of the health concerns that women face when traveling (p. 49).

GLBT TRAVELERS

Hawaii is one of the most progressive states when it comes to gay, lesbian, bisexual, and transgendered (GLBT) travelers, though more so in cities than in rural areas. Listed below are contact organizations, mail-order catalogs, and publishers that offer materials addressing some specific concerns. **Out and**

About (www.planetout.com) offers a weekly newsletter addressing travel concerns and a comprehensive site addressing gay travel concerns. The online newspaper **365gay.com** also has a travel section (www.365gay.com/travel/travelchannel.htm).

Gay's the Word, 66 Marchmont St., London WC1N 1AB, UK (☎44 020 7278 7654; http://freespace.virgin.net/gays.theword/). The largest gay and lesbian bookshop in the UK, with both fiction and non-fiction titles. Mail-order service available.

Giovanni's Room, 345 South 12th St., Philadelphia, PA 19107, USA (☎215-923-2960; www.queerbooks.com). An international lesbian and gay bookstore with mail-order service (carries many of the publications listed below).

International Lesbian and Gay Association (ILGA), Avenue des Villas 34, 1060 Brussels, Belgium (☎32 2 502 2471; www.ilga.org). Provides political information, such as homosexuality laws of individual countries.

ADDITIONAL RESOURCES: GLBT

Spartacus 2005-2006: International Gay Guide. Bruno Gmunder Verlag.

Damron Men's Travel Guide, Damron Road Atlas, Damron Accommodations Guide, Damron City Guide, and *Damron Women's Traveller.* Damron Travel Guides. For info, call ☎800-462-6654 or visit www.damron.com.

The Gay Vacation Guide: The Best Trips and How to Plan Them, Mark Chesnut. Kensington Books.

Gayellow Pages USA/Canada, Frances Green. Gayellow Pages. They also publish smaller regional editions. Visit Gayellow pages online at www.gayellowpages.com.

TRAVELERS WITH DISABILITIES

In large Hawaiian cities, most hotels and restaurants are wheelchair accessible, though this may not be the case in smaller towns or rural areas. Wheelchair-accessible vans are available to rent in most places, as are wheelchairs. Those with disabilities should inform airlines and hotels of their disabilities when making reservations; some time may be needed to prepare special accommodations. Call ahead to restaurants, museums, and other facilities to find out if they are wheelchair accessible. **Guide dog owners** should inquire as to the quarantine policies of the US.

In the US, both Amtrak and major airlines will accommodate disabled passengers if notified in advance. Amtrak offers a discount to physically disabled travelers (☎800-872-7245; www.amtrak.com). Greyhound buses will provide a 50% discount for a companion if the ticket is purchased at least one day in advance. If you are without a fellow traveler, call Greyhound (☎800-752-4841) at least two days before you plan to leave, and they will make arrangements to assist you. For information on transportation availability in individual US cities, contact the local chapter of the **Easter Seal Society** (☎800-221-6827; www.easter-seals.org).

If you are planning to visit a national park or attraction in the US run by the National Park Service (☎888-467-2757; www.nationalparks.org), obtain a free **Golden Access Passport,** which is available at all park entrances and from federal offices whose functions relate to land, forests, or wildlife. The Passport entitles disabled travelers and their families to free park admission and provides a lifetime 50% discount on all campsite and parking fees.

USEFUL ORGANIZATIONS

Accessible Journeys, 35 West Sellers Ave., Ridley Park, PA 19078, USA (☎800-846-4537; www.disabilitytravel.com). Designs tours for wheelchair users and slow walkers. The site has tips and forums for all travelers.

Flying Wheels, 143 W. Bridge St., P.O. Box 382, Owatonna, MN 55060, USA (☎507-451-5005; www.flyingwheelstravel.com). Specializes in escorted trips to Europe for people with physical disabilities; plans custom trips worldwide.

The Guided Tour, Inc., 7900 Old York Rd., Ste. 114B, Elkins Park, PA 19027, USA (☎800-783-5841; www.guidedtour.com). Organizes travel programs in Canada, Hawaii, Ireland, Italy, Mexico, Spain, the UK, and the US for persons with developmental and physical challenges.

Mobility International USA (MIUSA), P.O. Box 10767, Eugene, OR 97440, USA (☎541-343-1284; www.miusa.org). Provides a variety of books and other publications containing information for travelers with disabilities.

Society for Accessible Travel and Hospitality (SATH), 347 Fifth Ave., Ste. 610, New York, NY 10016, USA (☎212-447-7284; www.sath.org). An advocacy group that publishes free online travel information and the travel magazine *OPEN WORLD* (annual subscription US$13, free for members). Annual membership US$45, students and seniors US$30.

MINORITY TRAVELERS

Hawaii is such a diverse place that no ethnic group stands out as an obvious minority. Caucasians may be uncomfortable with being called a *haole*, but in general, if you treat the island and its inhabitants with respect, the same respect will be afforded to you. While there are relatively few people of African descent on the islands, racial prejudice against blacks is extremely rare, especially in larger cities.

DIETARY CONCERNS

With a little extra research, vegetarians should be able to find places to eat. Many restaurants are Asian or Asian-inspired and use noodles, rice, and vegetables to prepare their dishes. The travel section of **The Vegetarian Resource Group's** website, at www.vrg.org/travel, has a comprehensive list of organizations and websites that are geared toward helping vegetarians and vegans traveling abroad. They also provide an online restaurant guide. For more information, visit your local bookstore or health food store, and consult *The Vegetarian Traveler: Where to Stay if You're Vegetarian, Vegan, Environmentally Sensitive*, by Jed and Susan Civic (Larson Publications). Vegetarians will also find numerous resources on the web; try www.vegdining.com, www.happycow.net, and www.vegetarians-abroad.com, for starters.

Travelers who keep kosher should contact synagogues in larger cities for information on kosher restaurants. Your own synagogue or college Hillel should have access to lists of Jewish institutions in Hawaii. If you are strict in your observance, you may have to prepare your own food on the road. A good resource is the *Jewish Travel Guide*, edited by Michael Zaidner (Vallentine Mitchell). Travelers looking for halal restaurants may find www.zabihah.com a useful resource.

OTHER RESOURCES

Let's Go tries to cover all aspects of budget travel, but we can't put *everything* in our guides. Listed below are books and websites that can serve as jumping-off points for your own research.

USEFUL PUBLICATIONS

Aloha from Hawaii (☎808-538-0330; www.aloha-hawaii.com). Online magazine including features on popular sights and a Hawaiian dictionary.

Hawaii Magazine (☎808-534-1515; www.hawaiimagazine.com). Monthly magazine with features on restaurants, events, and community happenings.

Honolulu Magazine (☎808-537-9500; www.honolulumagazine.com). Articles on community figures and events.

Islander Magazine (www.islander-magazine.com). A web magazine specializing in the Hawaiian islands. Information on Hawaiian cuisine, books, and history.

WORLD WIDE WEB

Almost every aspect of budget travel is accessible via the web. In 10min. at the keyboard, you can make a hostel reservation, get advice on travel hot spots from other travelers who have just returned from Hawaii, or find out how much a surfboard rental in Kauai costs.

Listed here are some regional and travel-related sites to start off your surfing; other relevant websites are listed throughout the book. Because website turnover is high, use search engines (such as www.google.com) to strike out on your own.

WWW.LETSGO.COM. Let's Go's website features a wealth of information and valuable advice at your fingertips. It offers excerpts from all our guides as well as monthly features on new hot spots in the most popular destinations. In addition to our online bookstore, we have great deals on everything from airfares to cell phones. Our resources section is full of information you'll need before you hit the road, and our forums are buzzing with advice from other travelers. Check back often to see constant updates, exciting new tips, and prize giveaways. See you soon!

THE ART OF TRAVEL

BootsnAll.com: www.bootsnall.com. Numerous resources for independent travelers, from planning your trip to reporting on it when you get back.

How to See the World: www.artoftravel.com. A compendium of great travel tips, from cheap flights to self defense to interacting with local culture.

Travel Intelligence: www.travelintelligence.net. A large collection of travel writing by distinguished travel writers.

Travel Library: www.travel-library.com. A fantastic set of links for general information and personal travelogues.

World Hum: www.worldhum.com. An independently produced collection of "travel dispatches from a shrinking planet."

INFORMATION ON HAWAII

Alternative-Hawaii: www.alternative-hawaii.com. "Your guide to the path less travelled." Self-described ecotourism site with links to accommodations and a section on Hawaii's special places.

Best Places Hawaii: www.bestplaceshawaii.com. An online travel planner with a virtual island tour and information on attractions.

DaKine: www.dakine.net. The local's guide to Hawaii. Reviews of Oahu plate lunch and shave ice establishments. Local humor!

Hawaii: www.hawaii.gov. Official website of the state of Hawaii.

Hawaii Surf Report: www.surf-news.com. Up-to-the-minute weather and surf information.

PlanetRider: www.planetrider.com. A subjective list of links to the "best" websites covering the culture and tourist attractions of Hawaii.

World Travel Guide: www.travel-guides.com. Helpful practical info.

BEYOND TOURISM

A PHILOSOPHY FOR TRAVELERS

HIGHLIGHTS OF BEYOND TOURISM IN HAWAII

DISH UP meals at the Honolulu Food Bank (p. 69).

GUIDE tourists on trails through Volcanoes National Park (p. 68).

RESEARCH and swim with spinner dolphins off the coast of Oahu (p. 69).

ENCOUNTER true Hawaiian life by au pairing for a local family (p. 71).

As a tourist, you are always a foreigner. While hostel-hopping and sightseeing can be great fun, you may want to consider going *beyond* tourism. Connecting with a foreign place through studying, volunteering, or working can help reduce that touristy stranger-in-a-strange-land feeling. Furthermore, travelers can make a positive impact on the natural and cultural environments they visit. With this Beyond Tourism chapter, Let's Go hopes to promote a better understanding of Hawaii and to provide suggestions for those who want more than a photo album out of their travels. The "Giving Back" sidebar features (p. 140, p. 234) also highlight regional Beyond Tourism possibilities.

From the sun-kissed sands of Waikiki to the awe-inspiring lava flows in Volcanoes National Park, Hawaii presents many unique opportunities for Beyond Tourism experiences. The tourism industry exploded during the past century; in 1927, there were about 17,000 people traveling to Hawaii, but by 2005, there were over 7.3 million. The dramatic rise in tourism created an interdependence among the economy, environment, and culture of Hawaii that is impossible to ignore. Since tourism has long since surpassed agriculture as the islands' preeminent economic force, it is important that travelers be aware and respectful of all that is unique to this small, remote island chain.

As a **volunteer** in Hawaii, you can participate in a number of exciting projects either on a short-term basis or as the main component of your trip. Such opportunities include helping to preserve Hawaiian biodiversity with the Sierra Club or researching geodesy in Volcanoes National Park. Participate in river cleanup and be rewarded with a kayak trip, or lead hikes through the park. Later in this chapter, *Let's Go Hawaii* recommends organizations that can help you find the opportunities that best suit your interests, whether you're looking to pitch in for a day or a year.

Studying at a college or language program is another option. Kilauea, the world's most active volcano, presents an unrivaled opportunity to study intensely all things geological, the University of Hawaii at Hilo is the only school in the country to offer a masters program in the study of indigenous languages, and the Pacific Island cultural studies and marine science are also strong programs in Hawaii.

Many travelers also structure their trips by the **work** that they can do along the way: either odd jobs as they go, or full-time stints in cities where they plan to stay for some time. Many hostels will exchange room and board for short-term work cleaning or helping at the reception desk (p. 72). In addition, Willing Workers on Organic Farms (WWOOF) has a long listing of organic farms that are looking for help. Given the high turnover rate, the tourism industry, Hawaii's largest source of jobs, will likely be an available source of employment.

Start your search at **www.beyondtourism.com,** Let's Go's brand-new searchable database of alternatives to tourism, where you can find exciting feature articles and program listings divided by country, continent, and program type.

VOLUNTEERING

WHY PAY MONEY TO VOLUNTEER? Many volunteers are surprised to learn that some organizations require large fees or "donations." While this may seem ridiculous at first glance, such fees often keep the organization afloat, in addition to covering airfare, room, board, and administrative expenses for the volunteers. If you're concerned about how a program spends its fees, request an annual report or finance account. A reputable organization won't refuse to inform you of how volunteer money is spent. Such programs might be a good idea for young travelers who are looking for more support and structure (such as pre-arranged transportation and housing), or anyone who would rather not deal with the uncertainty implicit in creating a volunteer experience from scratch.

Volunteering can be a very fulfilling experience, especially if you combine it with the thrill of traveling in a new place. Many volunteer programs focus on conserving the beauty of Hawaii's biodiversity and environment. There are also plenty of opportunities geared toward traditional community service, such as the chance to volunteer for PBS or at a yoga and wellness center.

Most people who volunteer in Hawaii do so on a short-term basis at organizations that make use of drop-in or once-a-week volunteers. The best way to find opportunities that match up with your interests and schedule may be to check with national databases, such as **Idealist** (www.idealist.org), **ServeNet** (www.servenet.org), and **VolunteerMatch** (www.volunteermatch.com). A local database is maintained at **Volunteer Zone** (www.volunteerzone.org) as well, and short-term volunteer work is common among the many environmental and wildlife conservation initiatives in Hawaii.

Those looking for longer, more intensive volunteer opportunities usually choose to go through a parent organization that takes care of logistical details and often provides a group environment and support system—for a fee. There are two main types of organizations (religious and non-sectarian) although there are rarely restrictions on participation for either.

ENVIRONMENTAL CONSERVATION

Department of Land and Natural Resources, Kalanimoku Bldg., 1151 Punchbowl St., Honolulu, HI 96813 (☎587-0400, State Parks 587-0307, Marine and Freshwater Wildlife 587-0099, Forestry and Wildlife 587-0061, Trails 587-0062, Natural Area Reserves 587-0063; www.hawaii.gov/dlnr/Volunteer.html). Manages all of Hawaii's natural and cultural resources in the state's public lands and waters. Join a group of 10 or more for a weekend activity, or work individually with a staff member for an extended period of time in the state parks, harbors, trails, or historic buildings.

Environment Hawaii, 72 Kapiolani St., Hilo, HI 96720 (☎934-0115 or 877-934-0130; www.environment-hawaii.org). The organization focuses on planting trees, eradicating alien species, cleaning beaches, and other activities. Volunteer locations are color-coded, sorted by island, and plotted on a map. Traditional groups are listed in addition to beaches that can be cleaned independently.

Global Volunteers, 375 E. Little Canada Rd., St. Paul, MN 55117 (☎800-487-1074; www.globalvolunteers.org/1main/hawaii/volunteer_hawaii.htm), runs "volunteer vacations," which are short-term service programs, to the Limahuli Gardens in the National Tropical Botanical Gardens and Kokee State Park, both on the island of Kauai. Their aim is to help preserve the natural Hawaiian ecosystem. Programs run 1-2 weeks, and are offered almost continuously throughout the year. $1300-1700, which includes meals, lodging, project expenses, and administrative costs, but not airfare.

Haleakala National Park, P.O. Box 369, Makawao, HI 96768 (☎572-4487; www.haleakala.national-park.com). Various volunteer positions available, including the **Student Conservation Association (SCA),** which provides meals and lodging. Apply for SCA positions at least 1 year in advance.

Hawaii Sierra Club, P.O. Box 2577, Honolulu, HI 96803 (☎538-6616; www.hi.sierraclub.org), seeks to improve natural resource management, clean up pollution, and protect biodiversity in Hawaii.

Hawaii Volcanoes National Park, P.O. Box 52, Hawaii National Park, HI 96718 (☎985-6000; www.nps.gov/havo). Various volunteer positions, including SCA positions available; some provide meals and dorm-style housing. A listing of all the volunteer positions offered by the park service in Hawaii can be found at www.volunteer.gov/gov/uisearch.cfm?states=hi.

Hawaii Youth Conservation Corps (YCC), 46-148 Kahuhipa St., Ste. 201, Kaneohe, HI 96744 (☎247-5753; www.hawaiiycc.com). Runs programs, from June to July, on the islands of Oahu, Maui, Molokai, Kauai, and Big Island for high school sophomores through college sophomores. Learn first-hand about conservation through field work and service learning projects. Participants receive a stipend and 3 college credits at the end of the program, if eligible.

Institute for Cultural Ecology, P.O. Box 991, Hilo, HI 96721 (☎866-230-8508; www.cultural-ecology.com), offers both experiential learning programs (a combination of internships and study that takes place in Hawaii, Fiji, Australia, Thailand, and Nepal) and a field studies program. Field studies run 6 weeks and provide exposure to Hawaiian culture, geology, ecology, and biodiversity. In-country/project expenses are $1850, which includes housing and academic credit fees. Up to 15 academic credits are available through UC Santa Barbara. Application fee $75.

Malama Hawaii, 923 Nuuanu Ave., Honolulu, HI 96817 (www.malamahawaii.org). Sponsors a number of programs to help the environment as well as a number of community-based initiatives. Be on the Maui County Frog Squad or watch over a mother monk seal and her pup. The website lists both volunteer and work opportunities.

USGS Hawaiian Volcano Observatory (HVO), US Dept. of the Interior, US Geological Survey, Menlo Park, CA (http://hvo.wr.usgs.gov/volunteer/), assigns each volunteer researcher a support group and HVO staff member. Opportunities include work in geochemistry, seismology, geology, geodesy, electronics, carpentry, and website or library support. If you can commit to 3 months of work, free lodging and transportation will be provided. Opportunities for housing are limited, so plan ahead.

WILDLIFE CONSERVATION

EarthTrust Windward Environmental Center, 1118 Maunawili Rd., Kailua, HI 96734 (☎261-5339; www.earthtrust.org), occasionally needs unpaid interns for 6 months or longer in its efforts to protect marine life from driftnets or to research dolphins.

Pacific Whale Foundation, 300 Maalaea Rd., Ste. 211, Wailuku, HI 96793 (☎249-8811; www.pacificwhale.org) is an organization on Maui dedicated to marine conservation. Conducts research on humpback whales, Lanai's wild dolphins, and Maui's threatened coral reefs. Inquire about the availability of volunteer and internship positions.

Wild Dolphin Foundation, 87-1286 Farrington Hwy., Waianae, HI 96792 (☎306-3968; http://wilddolphin.org/index.html), offers visitors the opportunity to work alongside marine biologists studying Oahu's spinner dolphins, whales, turtles, and coral reefs. There is no cost for the program, but it does not offer food, housing, or transportation.

COMMUNITY OUTREACH

Aloha United Way, 200 N. Vineyard Blvd., Ste. 700, Honolulu, HI 96817 (☎536-1951; www.auw.org). Umbrella organization for a variety of community-oriented programs.

American Red Cross, 4155 Diamond Head Rd., Honolulu, HI 96816 (☎734-2101; www.hawaiiredcross.org). Volunteer opportunities in disaster relief, instruction, and first aid, among others.

Catholic Charities Hawaii, 200 N. Vineyard St., Ste. 200, Honolulu, HI 96817 (☎536-1794; www.catholiccharitieshawaii.org). Provides a range of social services.

Goodwill Industries of Hawaii, 2610 Kilihau St., Honolulu, HI 96819 (☎836-0313; www.higoodwill.org). Goodwill expects a minimum commitment of a month of career development service with 16hr. per week of retail store support. The revenue they generate goes to helping people with disabilities (or other employment barriers) find jobs.

Hawaii Food Bank, 2611 Kilihau St., Honolulu, HI 96819 (☎836-3600; www.hawaiifoodbank.org). Volunteers are needed year-round for inspecting, data entry, and cleaning and sorting food, especially for the annual food drive in Apr.

Honolulu Habitat for Humanity, 1136 Union Mall, Ste. 510, Honolulu, HI 96701 (☎538-7070; www.habitat.org), is a non-denominational, non-profit group that builds affordable housing. There are affiliates on all of the other major islands as well.

Kalani Oceanside Retreat, RR2 Box 4500, Pahoa, HI 96778 (☎965-0468, volunteer coordinator ext. 117; www.kalani.com). This nonprofit organization offers several programs where visitors can volunteer for 2 weeks to 3 months.

PBS Hawaii, 2350 Dole St., Honolulu, HI 96822 (☎973-0289; http://pbshawaii.org/index_support/index_volunteer.html), tries to find activities that match your interests and skills, with opportunities for any type of commitment. Few options include receptionist and clerical duties, data entry, and special event support.

Volunteer Hawaii (☎539-1951, ask for the Volunteer Hawaii administrator; www.volunteerhawaii.org/index.php), maintains a listing of over 200 volunteer opportunities on the islands. Listings range from being an acupuncture assistant to helping with child literacy. Many organizations have low hourly commitments, but expect to spend 6 months to a year on a project.

Volunteer Legal Services Hawaii, 100 Honuakaha Bldg., 545 Queen St., Honolulu, HI 96813 (☎839-5200; www.vlsh.org), invites attorneys, law students, and others to volunteer and help tackle the unmet legal needs of Hawaii's less fortunate residents.

Volunteer Zone, 2021 Pauoa Rd., Honolulu, HI 96813 (☎524-9343; www.volunteerzone.org). An organization founded to facilitate volunteering in Hawaii. Provides a free, searchable catalogue of volunteer opportunities on the islands in a variety of fields.

STUDYING

Programs of study in Hawaii range from basic language and culture courses to college-level classes, graduate work, and technical training. Before choosing a program, do as much research as possible—determine costs and duration, what kind of students participate in the program, and what sort of accommodations are provided. Dorm life provides a better opportunity to mingle with fellow students, but there is less of a chance to experience the local scene. If you live

VISA INFORMATION. Foreign students who wish to study in the US must apply for either an M-1 visa (vocational studies) or an F-1 visa (for full-time students enrolled in an academic or language program). If English is not your native language, you will probably be required to take the **Test of English as a Foreign Language (TOEFL),** administered in many countries. Contact **TOEFL/TSE Publications,** P.O. Box 6151, Princeton, NJ 08541 (☎609-771-7100; www.toefl.org).

with a family, there is potential to build lifelong friendships with locals and to experience day-to-day life in more depth, but conditions can vary greatly from family to family.

UNIVERSITIES

The **University of Hawaii** (www.hawaii.edu) is composed of 10 independent university and community college campuses and five education centers throughout the islands. Students wishing to study in Hawaii may find it cheaper to enroll directly in one of the two major universities on Oahu and the Big Island (listed below), but check about obtaining college credit.

Hawaii Pacific University, 1164 Bishop St., Honolulu, HI 96813 (☎544-0200; www.hpu.edu), offers 10 different masters programs, as well as hundreds of courses over the summer for anyone wishing to take a few classes.

Maui Community College, 310 Kaahumanu Ave., Kahului, HI 96732 (☎984-3500; http://maui.hawaii.edu), has 2-year vocational and liberal arts degree and certificate programs in addition to 4-year programs. The Culinary Arts program and Maui Language Institute are particularly notable.

University of Hawaii at Manoa, 2500 Campus Rd., Honolulu, HI 96822 (☎956-8111; http://manoa.hawaii.edu). A research institution with close to 20,000 students has strengths in tropical agriculture, tropical medicine, oceanography, and Hawaiian, Pacific Island, and Asian studies and languages. Over 1000 graduate and undergraduate classes are offered over the summer. Airfare discounts are available. A program for high school students to earn college credit is also offered.

University of Hawaii at Hilo, 200 W. Kawili St., Hilo, HI 96720 (☎974-7414 or 800-897-4456; http://hilo.hawaii.edu), specializes in the study of indigenous languages, volcanoes, astronomy, and marine science, and offers undergraduate liberal arts, professional programs, and some graduate degrees. A summer session, including a Marine Science Summer Program, is offered.

LANGUAGE SCHOOLS

Language schools can be independently-run international or local organizations or divisions of foreign universities. They rarely offer college credit. They are a good alternative to university study, if you desire a deeper focus on the language or a slightly less rigorous courseload. These programs are also good for younger high school students who might not feel comfortable with older students in a university program. Some worthwhile programs include:

Academia Language School, 1600 Kapiolani Blvd., Ste. 1215, Honolulu, HI 96814 (☎946-5599; www.academiaschool.com). Offers English and TOEFL, TOEIC, and CLEP classes starting every week and ongoing classes in French, Japanese, and Spanish.

Hawaii English Language Program (HELP), 1395 Lower Campus Rd. MC 13-1, Honolulu, HI 96822 (☎956-6636; www.hawaii.edu/eslhelp/). Offers 4- or 8-week programs in English on the UH-Manoa campus and full-time TOEFL and TOEIC prep classes.

Institute of Intensive English, 2155 Kalakaua Ave., Ste. 700, Honolulu, HI 96815 (☎924-2117; www.studyenglishhawaii.com/index.html). Offers both intensive and short-term English programs, TOEFL and TOEIC prep courses, and other specifically-geared programs like "Business English" or "Travel English."

WORKING

VISA INFORMATION. A **work permit** (p. 38) is required for all foreigners planning to work in the US. Your employer must obtain this document, usually by demonstrating that you have skills that locals lack. It may be up to you, however, to apply for an **Employment Authorization Document** to prove that you may work in the US. Friends in the US can sometimes help expedite work permits or arrange work-for-stay exchanges. Obtaining a worker's visa may seem complex, but it's critical that you go through the proper channels. Visit the **Bureau of Citizenship and Immigration Services (BCIS)** website (www.immigration.gov) for more information on the process for acquiring a work permit.

As with volunteering, work opportunities tend to fall into two categories. Some travelers want long-term jobs that allow them to get to know another part of the world as a member of the community, while others seek out short-term jobs to finance the next leg of their travels. In the major tourist areas of Hawaii, work is often available on the staffs of hotels and resorts, or at local restaurants. Another possibility is to check with the national car rental agencies, which may have jobs on their lots that need to be filled. Consult the help wanted sections of local newspapers for more listings—*Honolulu Star Bulletin* and *Hawaii Tribune Herald* on Oahu, *The Garden Island* on Kauai, *The Maui News* on Maui, and *West Hawaii Today* on the Big Island are helpful sources. For links to Hawaii **job banks,** check out www.employmentspot.com/state/ha.htm, as well as the classified sections of the aforementioned publications.

LONG-TERM WORK

If you're planning on spending a substantial amount of time (more than three months) working in Hawaii, search for a job well in advance. International placement agencies are often the easiest way to find employment abroad, especially for those interested in teaching English. **Internships,** usually for college students, are a good segue into working abroad, and although they are often unpaid or poorly paid, many say the experience is well worth it. Be wary of advertisements for companies claiming the ability to get you a job abroad for a fee—often the same listings are available online or in newspapers. Reputable organizations include:

Council Exchanges, 3 Copley Pl., 2nd fl., Boston, MA 02116 (☎617-247-0350; www.councilexchanges.org) charges a $300-475 fee for arranging short-term working authorizations (generally valid for 3-6 months) and provides extensive information on different job opportunities in Hawaii.

AU PAIR WORK

Au pairs are typically young women who work as live-in nannies in foreign countries, caring for children and doing light housework in exchange for room, board, and a small spending allowance or stipend. Most former au pairs speak favorably of their experience. One perk of the job is that it allows you to get to know the country without the high expenses of traveling. Drawbacks, however, often include long hours of constant duty for somewhat mediocre pay (in Hawaii, this is usually between $120-200 per week, plus room and board). Much of the au pair experience really does depend on the family with whom you're placed. The agencies below are a good starting point for looking for employment as an au pair.

Au Pair in America, River Plaza, 9 West Broad St., Stamford, CT 06902 (☎800-928-7247 or 203-399-5000; www.aupairinamerica.com).

Childcare International, Ltd., Trafalgar House, Grenville Pl., London NW7 3SA (☎020 8906-3116; www.childint.co.uk).

InterExchange, 161 Sixth Ave., New York, NY 10013 (☎212-924-0446; www.interexchange.org).

SHORT-TERM WORK

Traveling for long periods of time can get expensive, so many travelers try their hands at odd jobs for a few weeks at a time to help finance another month or two of touring around. Short-term work in exchange for room and board can be found at farms and hostels across Hawaii. Organic farms are often looking for help, and another popular option is to work several hours a day at a hostel in exchange for free or discounted room and/or board. Most often, these short-term jobs are found by word of mouth or simply by talking to the owner of a hostel or restaurant. Due to the high turnover in the tourism industry, many places are eager for help, even if the work is only temporary. *Let's Go Hawaii* tries to list temporary jobs like these whenever possible; look in the practical information sections of larger cities or check out the list below for some of the available short-term jobs in popular destinations.

Evie's Natural Food, 79-7460 Mamalahoa Hwy. 11 (☎322-0739), in Mango Court south of Kainaliu on the Big Island. A bulletin board lists current short-term work possibilities provided by the nearby Kona coffee industry. There are often farm jobs available that trade room and board for labor.

Willing Workers On Organic Farms (WWOOF), 4429 Carlson Rd., Nelson, BC, Canada, VIL 6X3 (☎250-354-4417; www.wwoofhawaii.org), matches visitors with host farms. Program applicants are required to fill out a short form and pay a small fee ($20). They then receive a booklet of all the available hosts in their desired destination; travelers are expected to contact farms and arrange a situation with the host. Most volunteers stay at the farms for 1-3 weeks. There are WWOOF farms on 5 of Hawaii's islands: the Big Island, Kauai, Maui, Molokai, and Oahu.

HOSTELS

The following hostels offer the possibility of trading room and board for part-time work around the establishment in maintenance and housekeeping.

Banana Bungalow, 310 N. Market St., Wailuku, HI 96793 (☎800-846-7835; www.mauihostel.com). Call about the availability of short-term work.

Hostelling International Honolulu, 2323A Seaview Ave., Honolulu, HI 96822 (☎946-0591; www.hiayh.org). Contact Mrs. Akau Naki.

Koa-wood, 75-184 Ala Ona Ona St., Kailua-Kona, HI 96740 (☎326-7018; www.alternative-hawaii.com/affordable/kona.htm). Sometimes needs people to help run the inn.

Waikiki Beachside Hostel, 2556 Lemon Rd., Ste. B101, Honolulu, HI 96815 (☎923-9566; www.hokondo.com), offers short-term work in exchange for accommodations depending on availability and duration of stay. Longer stays preferred.

YMCA Camp Erdman, 69-385 Farrington Hwy., Waialua, HI 96791 (☎637-4615; www.camperdman.net). After completing a lengthy application process, travelers can work short-term in exchange for room and board.

FURTHER READING ON BEYOND TOURISM

Alternatives to the Peace Corps: A Directory of Third World and U.S. Volunteer Opportunities, by Jennifer S. Willsea. Food First Books, 2003.

Back Door Guide to Short-Term Job Adventures: Internships, Extraordinary Experiences, Seasonal Jobs, Volunteering, Working Abroad, by Michael Landes. Ten Speed Press, 2002.

Green Volunteers: The World Guide to Voluntary Work in Nature, by Ausenda and McCloskey. Universe, 2003.

How to Live Your Dream of Volunteering Overseas, by Collins, DeZerega, and Heckscher. Penguin Books, 2002.

International Directory of Voluntary Work, by Whetter and Pybus. Peterson's Guides and Vacation Work, 2000.

International Job Finder: Where the Jobs Are Worldwide, by Daniel Lauber. Planning Communications, 2002.

Invest Yourself: The Catalogue of Volunteer Opportunities, published by the Commission on Voluntary Service and Action (☎646-486-2446).

Live and Work Abroad: A Guide for Modern Nomads, by Francis and Callan. Vacation-Work Publications, 2001.

Overseas Summer Jobs 2002, by Collier and Woodworth. Peterson's Guides and Vacation Work, 2002.

Volunteer Vacations: Short-term Adventures That Will Benefit You and Others, by Cutchins and Geissinger. Chicago Review Press, 2003.

Work Abroad: The Complete Guide to Finding a Job Overseas, by Hubbs, Griffith, and Nolting. Transitions Abroad Publishing, 2002.

Work Your Way Around the World, by Susan Griffith. Vacation Work Publications, 2003.

A VOLATILE CLASSROOM

Studying in Hawaii Volcanoes National Park

Once you're away from it, it's hard to remember the intensity of the heat. You can tell people, "Oh yes, it was really hot. The lava was radiating about 900°F and the tropical sun was on our necks the entire time." But when you're out on the *pali* (cliffs), sweating, trapped between the sun and the hotter-than-asphalt-in-August *pahoehoe* lava, you can see the heat in waves that blur the Pacific and smell it in the melting rubber of tourists' flip-flops. You can taste the heat in the sulfur-filled air, and once you're close enough, you can hear it, too: the crackling of tiny hardened lava flakes as they chip off the front of the flow. It sounds almost like fire, though it's far hotter and flames only flare up if someone throws *ohelo* berries on the lava as an offering to Pele.

When a geologist steps on the flow to prove it won't hurt his shoe, he's wrong—the sole melts and flaps uselessly off his boot. We laugh at him and begin our hike back to the road where vans wait to take us back to the top of the volcano, our home for the next three weeks.

We sleep at the Kilauea military campground, 200 vertical feet from the barren summit crater, and we eat and take classes in a schoolhouse farther down the mountain. But we don't spend much time in the classroom; this is an intensive introduction to field methods in volcanism (Geology 471 at the University of Hawaii at Hilo, offered by the Center for the Study of Active Volcanoes), and we work on the mountain itself. Kilauea is one of the most active volcanoes in the world, and there is always something to measure, something to watch, and something to injure us. The University makes us sign forms saying we understand that working on a volcano is dangerous; this may seem obvious (it *is* obvious), but the release form lists more than 20 different ways people have been killed or seriously injured on the mountain, from the man who fell 30 feet into a newly-formed crevice to the Boy Scouts pulled out to sea by a tsunami.

Reading about these accidents on our first day, it is hard to believe that these are dangers we're actually going to face, but then we've all only read about volcanoes from the safety of our respective universities. Our group of 18 includes geology students from England, Australia, Germany, and the United States, as well as a high school teacher who wants to add volcanology to his curriculum. His students are lucky—not only will they find out how to analyze seismograms (the records of earth tremors) and to identify the precursors of an eruption, but they might also learn things like the fact that curious tourists tend to follow an official-looking reflective vest—which doesn't seem important until you're out on the *pali* looking for a clump of bushes to use as an emergency bathroom.

The subjects we learn about include seismology (recording earthquakes), physical volcanology (looking at landforms to understand past eruptions), deformation monitoring (measuring the movement of the volcano's flanks), and gas geochemistry (analyzing gases to map magma migration). To generate seismograms, we hike across the Halemaumau and Kilauea Iki craters, stopping in the middle of each to deploy a seismometer. Only a matter of years ago, each of these craters held a lava lake; the slabs of rough black rock we walk over are younger than many of us. We pass streams of tourists also hiking the Kilauea Iki trail and wonder how many of them realize how recently this whole area was molten. They get the same views we do; smell the same stifling gases; develop similar tank-top-and-shorts tan lines—but the things they don't know are endless and fascinating.

At one corner of Halemaumau we don gas masks and stand over glistening yellow crystals to collect sulfur emitted by one of the thousands of fumaroles that vent Kilauea's volcanic gasses. Even breathing through the masks, our mouths fill with the rotten egg taste of hydrogen sulfide. We love it, because we love the volcano. We love the early morning hikes, the tedious calibration of instruments that measure tilt to an accuracy of one part in a million, the state of being forever dirty with volcanic debris. We don't have the same fervor for the hours it takes to analyze our samples at the lab, but once we walk outside again into the green humidity we remember that we are in Hawaii, and getting course credit for it.

Katherine J. Thompson *attended the Field Methods in Volcanology course, through the Center for the Study of Active Volcanoes, in the summer of 2003. In three weeks she received an unparalleled crash course in volcano monitoring, several burns (sun, wind, and lava), and coral cuts on her feet. She loved every minute of it.*

THE GREAT OUTDOORS

You were warned about the jungle of Waikiki; about the overgrowth of hotels, the maze of restaurants, and herds of people; about the concrete tangle of high-rise resorts, upscale stores, and more free hula shows than you could shake a stick at. But you braved its whirlwind of glitter and light, and survived it. Nay, even dominated it. It's tested your mettle and found you worthy. Ready for a real adventure?

Hawaii has nearly 275,000 acres of national and state parks and hundreds of miles of trails along which you may be the only hiker. It has deserts where NASA astronauts trained for moon landings, lush rainforests, rolling grasslands, 51 mi. of coastal reef, and over 110 species of fish that are found nowhere else in the world. It is a stopping point in winter for migratory whales that play, breach, and spout in the water. Some of the best and biggest surf breaks in the world are found on the North Shore of Oahu and attract top-notch, world-famous surfers at the height of the winter surf season.

If this guidebook is your atlas, think of this section as your compass, map legend, and index rolled into one. We'll tell you how to cut through camping red tape, point out some of the best places to go when you want to hit the surf, and, above all, tell you how to keep safe while enjoying the outdoors.

CAMPING IN HAWAII

Oceanfront campsites afford travelers the opportunity to enjoy a million-dollar view at a fraction of the price of a hotel. Hawaii's temperate climate only adds to the appeal and ease of camping. Many county beach parks (p. 79) have areas set aside for camping, though some are better equipped than others. The number of campsites varies; some parks offer as few as four spots while others have up to 50. In addition, Hawaiian state parks (p. 78) are open year-round and issue permits for camping, lodging, and group day use for those who are at least 18. Contact the **Department of Land and Natural Resources, Division of State Parks,** P.O. Box 621, Honolulu 96809 (☎587-0300; www.hawaii.gov/dlnr/dsp/index.html), for permit availability and additional information. If you plan on camping, make sure to rent a car with a lockable compartment (not a soft-top Jeep) for your gear. Building a fire, where permitted, can be difficult due to lack of wood, so bring a **stove** for cooking and boiling water. Two excellent resources for travelers planning on camping or spending time in the outdoors are the **Great Outdoor Recreation Page** (www.gorp.com) and **Na Ala Hele** (www.hawaiitrails.com).

CAMPING AND HIKING EQUIPMENT

WHAT TO BUY

Good camping equipment is both sturdy and light. North American suppliers tend to offer the most competitive prices.

Sleeping Bags: Most sleeping bags are rated by season; "summer" means 30-40°F (around 0°C) at night; "four-season" or "winter" often means below 0°F (-17°C). Areas of high elevation in Hawaii tend to get chilly at night; all-season bags are a

LEAVE NO TRACE. Let's Go encourages travelers to embrace the "Leave No Trace" motto, minimizing impact on natural environments and protecting them for future generations. Trekkers and wilderness enthusiasts should set up camp on durable surfaces, use cook stoves instead of campfires, bury human waste away from water supplies, bag trash and carry it out with them, and respect wildlife and natural objects. For more detailed information, contact the **Leave No Trace Center for Outdoor Ethics,** P.O. Box 997, Boulder, CO 80306 (☎303-442-8222 or 800-332-4100; www.lnt.org).

safe bet to keep you cozy. Bags are made of **down** (warm and light, but expensive, and miserable when wet) or of **synthetic** material (heavy, durable, and warm when wet). Prices range $50-250 for a summer synthetic to $200-300 for a good down winter bag. **Sleeping bag pads** include foam pads ($10-30), air mattresses ($15-50), and self-inflating mats ($30-120). Bring a **stuff sack** to store your bag and keep it dry.

Tents: The best tents are freestanding (with their own frames and suspension systems), set up quickly, and don't generally require staking. Low-profile dome tents are the best all around. Worthy 2-person tents start at $100, 4-person start at $160. Make sure your tent has a rain fly, and seal its seams with waterproofer. Other useful items include a **battery-operated lantern,** a plastic **ground cloth,** and a nylon **tarp.**

Backpacks: Internal frame packs mold well to your back, have a lower center of gravity, and flex adequately to allow you to hike difficult trails, while **external frame packs** are more comfortable for long hikes over even terrain, as they carry weight higher and distribute it more evenly. Make sure your pack has a strong, padded hip belt to transfer weight to your legs. There are models designed specifically for women. Any serious backpacking requires a pack of at least 4000 $in.^3$ (16,000cc), plus 500 $in.^3$ for sleeping bags in internal frame packs. Sturdy backpacks cost anywhere from $125-420—your pack is an area where it doesn't pay to economize. On your hunt for the perfect pack, fill up a prospective model with something heavy, strap it on correctly, and walk around the store to get a sense of how the model distributes weight. Either buy a **rain cover** ($10-20) or store all of your belongings in plastic bags inside your pack.

Boots: Regular sneakers should be sufficient for all but the most hard-core hiking in Hawaii. If you buy boots, be sure to get ones with good **ankle support.** To spare yourself blisters, break in boots several weeks before you go.

Other Necessities: Synthetic layers, like those made of polypropylene or polyester, and a pile jacket will keep you warm even when wet. A **space blanket** ($5-15) will help you to retain body heat and doubles as a ground cloth. Plastic **water bottles** are vital; look for shatter- and leak-resistant models. Carry **water-purification tablets** for when you can't boil. Although some campgrounds provide campfire sites, you may want to bring a small **metal grate** or **grill.** For those places that forbid fires or the gathering of firewood, you'll need a **camp stove** (starting at around $50) and a propane-filled **fuel bottle** to operate it. Also bring a **first-aid kit, pocketknife, insect repellent,** and **waterproof matches** or a **lighter.**

WHERE TO BUY IT

The mail-order and online companies listed below offer lower prices than many retail stores. A visit to a local camping or outdoors store will give you a good sense of the look and weight of certain items.

Campmor, 400 Corporate Dr., P.O. Box 680, Mahwah, NJ 07430 (☎888-226-7667; www.campmor.com).

GREAT OUTDOORS

Discount Camping, 833 Main North Rd., Pooraka, South Australia 5095, Australia (☎08 8262 3399; www.discountcamping.com.au).

Eastern Mountain Sports (EMS), 1 Vose Farm Rd., Peterborough, NH 03458 (☎888-463-6367; www.ems.com).

L.L. Bean, Freeport, ME 04033 (US and Canada ☎800-441-5713, UK 0800 891 297; www.llbean.com).

Mountain Designs, P.O. Box 824, Nundah, Queensland 4012, Australia (☎07 3856 2344; www.mountaindesigns.com).

Recreational Equipment, Inc. (REI), Sumner, WA 98352 (US and Canada ☎800-426-4840, elsewhere 253-891-2500; www.rei.com).

NATIONAL PARKS

Hawaii has two national parks, **Haleakala National Park** (p. 306) on Maui, and **Hawaii Volcanoes National Park** (p. 203) on the Big Island. Haleakala is the site of Haleakala Volcano, whose majestic summit above the cloud line has become a popular peak for watching the magnificent sunrise. Rangers are actively engaged in the preservation of the park's fragile ecosystem, which includes the silversword and *nene* goose, two endangered species. Hawaii Volcanoes National Park encompasses the most active volcano in the world, Kilauea, and the most massive volcano in the world, Mauna Loa. There are miles of hikes through amazingly diverse ecosystems and the awesome trappings of 70 million years of volcanic activity; you can even walk up to the slow-flowing active lava in the eastern rift zone.

HALEAKALA. Prepare for mosquitoes, sun, rain, and—if you are camping on Haleakala—cold and wind. Haleakala has two drive-in campgrounds, two wilderness campgrounds, and three wilderness cabins. No permits, reservations, or registration are necessary for the drive-in campgrounds. Permits are required for the campsites that aren't accessible by road and are issued the day of the hike for free on a first-come, first-served basis at Park Headquarters (though they rarely run out). Permits are good for a maximum of three nights per month, with no more than two nights at any site. Cabin reservations are awarded by a monthly lottery. Apply three months in advance for the cabin lottery. See **Camping and Cabins,** p. 314, for more info.

HAWAII VOLCANOES. Volcanoes has two drive-in campgrounds, two backcountry tent sites, and three backcountry shelters with tent sites, pit toilets, and

TOP TEN LIST

BEST ADVENTURES ON LAND

Any exploration of the varied terrain of Hawaii, from off-road trails to majestic peaks, will bring you face-to-face with nature's peerless, awesome beauty.

1. Oahu: Trek to the top of **Diamond Head** (p. 129) for an uninterrupted view of city and sky.
2. Oahu: Tiptoe along the water through lowland coastal dunes and pass tide pools in **Kaena Point State Park** (p. 176).
3. The Big Island: Muddy your shoes in the rugged, amazingly lush **Waipio Valley** (p. 239) on the way to Hiilawe Falls, Hawaii's longest single-drop waterfall.
4. The Big Island: Feel the heat from flowing lava at **Hawaii Volcanoes National Park** (p. 230).
5. Maui: Catch the sun cresting over the ocean at **Haleakala National Park** (p. 311), or hike by cinder cones and *nene* geese.
6. Maui: Splash or swim in the pools at **Oheo Gulch** (p. 306).
7. Molokai: Hike through the **Moomomi Preserve** (p. 338), home to half a dozen plants found nowhere else on the planet.
8. Lanai: Take the **Munro Trail** (p. 355), where you can catch sight of the other islands.
9. Kauai: Scale down to the base of the **Waimea Canyon** (p. 414), Kauai's Grand Canyon, or skirt its edge on the Canyon Trail in **Kokee State Park** (p. 415).
10. Kauai: Take the multi-day **Kalalua Trail** (p. 393), which winds through valleys and hugs the edge of plunging cliffs.

water catchments. The drive-in campgrounds are free and no permits, reservations, or registration are required. Permits for the backcountry sites are free and can be easily obtained from the Visitors Center on a first-come, first-served basis. Stays are limited to seven days per month and no more than 30 days per year. Registration is required for backcountry camping.

STATE PARKS

Camping at a state park requires a permit from the Division of State Parks, which maintains offices on Oahu, Maui, the Big Island, Kauai, and Molokai. The same fees and restrictions apply on each island. A camping permit is $5 per night per campsite, with a maximum of 10 people per site for a maximum of five nights. You are only allowed one permit per park within a 30-day period. (One exception is Na Pali Cost, which is $10 per person per night and 3-night max. stay.) You can apply in writing, by phone, or in person no earlier than one year in advance, unless noted otherwise below. The permit will be held at the office for pickup, or you can include a self-addressed, stamped envelope to have it mailed to you. If you decide to mail your request, be sure to include your name, address, and phone number, specify the dates and the park where you wish to camp, and give the names and some form of ID number (driver's license, passport, or Social Security number) of all campers. For further information visit www.state.hi.us/dlnr/dsp/dsp.html or call ☎587-0400. All parks are open seven days a week with exceptions noted below. All offices are open M-F 8am-3:30pm.

OAHU. Mail requests to P.O. Box 621, Honolulu 96809, or call ☎587-0300. Pick up or apply for permits in person at 1151 Punchbowl St., Rm. 310, Honolulu. Parks are only open M-W and F-Su, and permit applications will be accepted no sooner than 30 days before the 1st day of camping. The Friends of Malaekahana (☎293-1736) manage cabins at Malaekahana; see p. 151 for more info.

PARK NAME	PAGE
Keaiwa Heiau State Recreation Area (4 10-person campsites)	p. 136
Malaekahana Campgrounds	p. 151

MAUI. Mail requests to 54 S. High St., Rm. 101, Wailuku 96793, or call ☎984-8109. Pick up or apply for permits in person at the same address. The cabins are $45 per night for one to four people, and $5 per night for each additional person.

PARK NAME	PAGE
Polipoli Spring State Recreation Area (also has a 6-person cabin)	p. 310
Waianapanapa State Park (also has 10-person cabins)	p. 303

THE BIG ISLAND. Mail requests to P.O. Box 936, Hilo 96721. Or call ☎974-6200. Pick up or apply for permits in person at 75 Aupuni St., Hilo. Reservations taken 8am-noon only. A-frame cabins are $20 per night. Six-person cabins are $45 per night for one to four people, and $5 per night for each additional person.

PARK NAME	PAGE
Kalopa State Recreation Area (also has cabins)	p. 237
Mackenzie State Recreation Area	p. 218
Mauna Kea State Recreation Area (4 6-person cabins)	p. 232

KAUAI. Mail requests to 3060 Eiwa St., Rm. 306, Lihue 96766, or call ☎274-3444. Pick up or apply for permits in person at the same address. It is the white building, behind the Big Save Market when seen from Hwy. 56. During summer, one-third of camping spaces for the Na Pali Coast are issued in person for a one-week period four weeks ahead of time. Other restrictions apply. Kokee State Park also has 12 cabins managed by Kokee Lodge (☎335-6061); see p. 415 for more info.

PARK NAME	PAGE
Kokee State Park	p. 415
Na Pali Coast State Park (3 campsites along the Kalalau Trail, 1 beyond it)	p. 392
Polihale State Park	p. 421

MOLOKAI. Call the Division of State Parks at ☎984-8109 (open M-F 8am-4:30pm), or go to the caretaker's office at the entrance to the park.

PARK NAME	PAGE
Palaau State Park	p. 337

COUNTY PARKS

HONOLULU COUNTY. Permits are free and available from the Department of Parks and Recreation on the ground floor of the Honolulu Municipal Building, 650 S. King St., Honolulu 96813. (Open M-F 8am-4pm.) They can also be picked up at any one of 10 satellite city halls. A conveniently located satellite is in the Ala Moana Shopping Center (p. 112). Camping is allowed from 8am Friday to 8am Wednesday. Some campsites are open only on weekends (see below). Permits must be obtained in person at least one week in advance but no more than two Fridays before your camping date. The permits are very popular so you should count on showing up early in the morning two Fridays before, or have alternate lodging arrangements. One permit allows up to 10 people and two tents. For more information call ☎523-4525 or visit http://www.co.honolulu.hi.us/parks/permits.htm.

PARK NAME	PAGE
Bellows Field Beach Park (50 campsites; weekends only)	p. 143
Hauula Beach Park (15 campsites)	p. 152
Kaiaka Beach Park (7 campsites)	p. 163
Kualoa Regional Park (30 campsites; extremely popular)	p. 152
Swanzy Beach Park (9 campsites; weekends only)	p. 152
Waimanalo Bay Recreation Area (10 campsites)	p. 142
Waimanalo Beach Park (22 campsites)	p. 142

MAUI COUNTY. Permits cost $3 per person per night ($0.50 per child) and are available from the Department of Parks and Recreation. They are good for a maximum of three consecutive nights. For Maui parks, mail a money order to 700 Halia Na Koa St., #2, Wailuku 96793. Pick up or apply for permits in person at the Permit Office in the War Memorial Gym next to Baldwin High School on Rte. 32 in Wailuku. (Open M-F 8am-4pm.) For more information call ☎270-7389. For Molokai parks (which are in Maui County and follow the same regulations) send a money order to 90 Aiona St., Kaunakakai 96748. Pick up or apply for permits in person at the same address, in the Mitchell Pauole Center (open M-F 8am-4pm). For more information call ☎553-3204.

PARK NAME	PAGE
Kanaha Beach Park (on Maui; closed Tu-W)	p. 278
One Alii Beach Park (on Molokai)	p. 328

PARK NAME	PAGE
Papalaua Wayside Park (on Maui; closed W-Th)	p. 262
Papohaku Beach (on Molokai)	p. 347

HAWAII COUNTY. Permits cost $5 per night, ages 13-17 $2, and 12 and under $1; they can be purchased no more than one year in advance. You can camp at each site for a maximum of seven nights total in summer and 14 nights in winter. Permits can be purchased online with a major credit card, or you can write to the Department of Parks and Recreation, 101 Pauahi St., Ste. 6, Hilo 96720. For more information call ☎961-8311 or visit www.hawaii-county.com.

PARK NAME	PAGE
Hookena Beach Park (22 campsites)	p. 196
Isaac Hale Beach Park (22 campsites)	p. 220
Kapaa Beach Park (22 campsites)	p. 248
Mahukona Beach Park (22 campsites)	p. 248
Milolii Beach Park (22 campsites)	p. 196
Punaluu Black Sand Beach (22 campsites)	p. 202

KAUAI COUNTY. Permits cost $3 per night and are free for those under 18 if accompanied by an adult. Each permit is good for a maximum of six consecutive nights and no more than 60 nights in a year-long period. Permits are issued M-F 8:15am-4pm. For more information call ☎241-4463 or visit www.kauaigov.org.

PARK NAME	PAGE
Anini Beach Park (closed Tu)	p. 381
Haena Beach Park (closed M)	p. 391
Hanamaulu Beach Park (closed W)	p. 366
Lucy Wright Beach Park (closed M)	p. 412
Salt Pond Beach Park (closed Tu)	p. 410

OTHER PLACES TO CAMP

FORESTRY AND WILDLIFE. Some campsites on Kauai and Molokai require a permit available from the Division of Forestry and Wildlife. On Kauai, call ☎274-3433. Permits are issued free of charge M-F 7:45am-4:30pm. On Molokai, you need to give one week advance notice. Call ☎984-8100.

PARK NAME	PAGE
Kawaikoi (on Kauai; max. 3 nights)	p. 419
Sugi Grove (on Kauai; max. 3 nights)	p. 416
Wiliwili Campground in Waimea Canyon (on Kauai; max. 4 nights)	p. 414
Waikolu Lookout (on Molokai; max. 2 nights)	p. 335

PRIVATE CAMPING. Many establishments will also allow you to pitch a tent.

NAME	PAGE
Arnott's Lodge (on the Big Island; $10 per person)	p. 225
Camp Mokuleia (on Oahu; $7 per person)	p. 169
Camp Pecusa (on Maui; $6 per person)	p. 262
Hoomaluhia Botanical Garden (on Oahu; free; F-Su only)	p. 153
Kalani Oceanside Retreat (on the Big Island; campsite $20)	p. 219
YMCA Camp Erdman (on Oahu; campsite $50; max. 10 people)	p. 169

NAME	PAGE
YMCA Camp Keanae (on Maui; $15 per person)	p. 297
YMCA Camp Naue (on Kauai; $10 per person)	p. 389
YMCA Camp Sloggett (on Kauai; $10 per person)	p. 416

WILDERNESS SAFETY

Staying **warm, dry,** and **well hydrated** is key to a happy and safe wilderness experience. For any hike, prepare yourself for an emergency by packing a first-aid kit, a reflector, a whistle, high-energy food, and extra water. The sun can be brutal, so take a hat, sunscreen, and sunglasses on any outdoor excursion.

Check **weather forecasts** often and pay attention to the sky when hiking, as weather patterns can change suddenly. Always let someone, either a friend, your hostel, a park ranger, or a local hiking organization, know when and where you are going hiking. Know your limits and do not attempt a hike beyond your ability. See **Safety and Health,** p. 44, for information on medical concerns.

DANGEROUS WILDLIFE

BOX JELLYFISH. Transparent box jellyfish swarm to Hawaii's leeward shores a week or so after the full moon. The box jellyfish, which measures 1-3 in. with tentacles of up to 2 ft. long, has a painful sting, which, in some cases, can cause anaphylactic shock. If you are stung by a box jellyfish, apply vinegar to the sting, pluck any tentacles out of the affected area using a towel or cloth (avoid using your hands), and apply a hot or cold pack.

PORTUGUESE MEN-OF-WAR. Not technically a jellyfish though it resembles one, the Portuguese Man-of-War is endemic to Hawaiian waters. Purplish-blue in color with tentacles up to 30 ft. long, the Portuguese Man-of-War also has a painful and potentially dangerous sting, which can cause anaphylactic shock, interference with heart and lung function, and even death. Do not apply vinegar to a sting from a Portuguese Man-of-War. Instead, rinse the sting with salt or fresh water and apply a cold or hot compress to the affected area. If pain persists or if breathing difficulty develops, consult a medical professional immediately.

SHARKS. About 40 species of sharks inhabit Hawaiian waters, ranging in size from the 8 in. pygmy shark to the whale shark, which can measure over 50 ft. in length. There are eight species that are commonly sighted near shore, most of which pose little threat to humans. The tiger shark, recognizable by its blunt snout and the vertical stripes on its sides, is the most dangerous species of shark found in Hawaiian waters and is known to attack humans. Shark attacks in Hawaii are actually quite rare—only two to three occur each year and few of these prove fatal. Surfers and spear fishers are at greatest risk of attack, and swimmers are advised to stay out of the water at dawn and dusk, when sharks move close to shore to feed. Experts also advise against wearing high-contrast clothing or shiny jewelry, and to avoid excessive splashing, all of which can attract sharks.

FOR MORE INFORMATION. Consult *Pests of Paradise*, by Susan Scott and Craig Thomas, M.D. (University of Hawaii Press; $20), and *How to Stay Alive in the Woods*, by Bradford Angier (Macmillan Press; $8).

ENVIRONMENTAL HAZARDS

HEAT EXHAUSTION AND DEHYDRATION. Heat exhaustion leads to nausea, excessive thirst, headaches, and dizziness. Avoid this condition by drinking plenty of fluids, eating salty foods (e.g., crackers), abstaining from dehydrating beverages (e.g., alcohol and caffeinated beverages), and wearing sunscreen. Continuous heat stress can eventually lead to heatstroke, characterized by a rising temperature, severe headache, delirium, and the cessation of sweating. Victims should be cooled with wet towels and taken to a doctor.

SUNBURN. The sunshine of paradise comes at a price if you're not careful. It is extremely easy to get sunburnt in Hawaii, even on a cloudy day. Be sure to apply sunscreen of SPF 15 or higher before you go out for the day and after swimming. If you are spending many consecutive hours in the sun, you should reapply sunscreen periodically—the trouble you take will be well worth avoiding the pain and discomfort of a persistent sunburn. A higher SPF is advisable at the start of your trip until you develop a tan. If you do get sunburnt, drink more fluids than usual and apply aloe. Severe sunburns can lead to sun poisoning, a condition that affects the entire body, causing fever, chills, nausea, and vomiting. Sun poisoning should always be treated by a doctor.

HIGH ALTITUDE. Allow your body a few days to adjust to lower oxygen levels before exerting yourself. Alcohol is more potent, and UV rays are stronger at high elevations. Pregnant women, young children, and people with respiratory and heart conditions should consult a doctor before traveling to high altitudes.

SURFING AND SWIMMING PRECAUTIONS. Hawaiian waves make for some of the world's best surf, but they can also be deadly. High surf brings strong currents and riptides, and each year lives are lost when surfers and swimmers fail to heed precautions. More people drown in Hawaii each year than anywhere else in the country. Know your limits, and use extra caution whenever you get into the water. The following are a few simple precautions:

Never swim alone.
Swim and surf only in lifeguarded areas.
Do not struggle against a riptide; swim parallel to the beach across it.
Signal for help if you are unable to swim out of a strong current.
Use a leash for surf and boogie boards.
Keep your distance from other surfers and swimmers–a loose board can deliver a lethal blow.
Familiarize yourself with beach and surf conditions as well as beach safety signs and symbols before you head out.

INSECT-BORNE DISEASES

Many diseases in Hawaii are transmitted by insects—mainly mosquitoes, fleas, and ticks. Beware of insects in wet or forested areas, especially while hiking and camping; wear long pants and long sleeves, and use a mosquito net. Use insect repellents with DEET and soak or spray your gear with permethrin (licensed in the US only for use on clothing). **Mosquitoes**—responsible for reported cases of dengue fever—are particularly prevalent in wet, wooded areas around hiking trails, such as those in East Maui, Kauai, and the Big Island.

DENGUE FEVER. An acute viral disease transmitted by day-biting mosquitoes, dengue fever has symptoms that include a high fever, severe headaches, swollen lymph nodes, and muscle aches. Many patients also suffer nausea, vomiting, and a pink rash. If you experience these symptoms, see a doctor immediately, drink plenty of liquids, and take acetaminophen (Tylenol). Never take aspirin to treat dengue fever. An outbreak of dengue fever occurred in 2001 with 119 confirmed cases, predominantly on Maui. The last locally transmitted case in Hawaii was in February 2002. Always use insect repellent when outside.

FOOD- AND WATER-BORNE DISEASES

Travelers in Hawaii experience food- and water-related illness much less often than in most parts of the world, thanks to good water-treatment facilities and fairly well-maintained restaurant standards. The tap water in Hawaii is treated to be safe for drinking. There are, however, a few campsites that require water treatment. Purify your own water by bringing it to a rolling boil or treating it with **iodine tablets.** Note, however, that some parasites have exteriors that resist iodine treatment, so boiling is more reliable.

LEPTOSPIROSIS. A bacterial disease caused by exposure to fresh water contaminated by the urine of infected animals, *leptospirosis* enters the body through cuts on the skin or through the mouth, nose, or eyes. Known exposure sites and all state and county parks that have freshwater streams or ponds are regularly posted with *leptospirosis* warning signs; never swim in fresh water if you have cuts. Symptoms include a high fever, chills, nausea, and vomiting. If not treated, it can lead to liver failure and meningitis. Consult a doctor for treatment.

NATURAL DISASTERS

EARTHQUAKES. Seismic activity on Hawaii is frequent due to its active volcanoes. The vast majority of earthquakes are too small to be felt, but about once a decade a stronger quake can cause real damage. The most destructive earthquakes in Hawaii were in 1868 and 1975. In the event of an earthquake, stay away from windows and from things that may fall, such as bookcases, tall furniture, or ceiling fixtures. Drop to the ground, try to find cover under a sturdy desk or against a wall, and protect your head and eyes.

HURRICANES. Hurricanes rarely hit Hawaii, but the state is not immune to these high-wind speed storms or the large waves they kick up. In the event that a hurricane or tropical storm watch or warning is issued, listen closely to the radio or TV for further updates and instructions from civil defense authorities. You should also prepare to cover all windows and doors; stock up on food, water, prescription medicine, and batteries; have an available supply of cash; and be ready to evacuate if told to do so.

TSUNAMIS. Tsunamis are caused by any displacement of a large mass of water—often an underwater earthquake—that creates a rapidly traveling wave that slows and gains height as it approaches the shoreline. The wave floods low-lying areas and can be incredibly destructive and cause a large loss of life; tsunamis have killed more people in Hawaii than all other natural disasters combined. Thirteen significant tsunamis have struck Hawaii in the last century; the most destructive were in 1946 and 1960. If a tsunami warning is issued, follow the evacuation procedures broadcast. Maps and more detailed information are in the front pages of a phone book. If you are at the beach and feel an earthquake, see a rapid withdrawal of the sea, or otherwise suspect that a tsunami is approaching, head to higher ground immediately. For more information see www.tsunami.org/faq.htm.

VOLCANOES. Hawaii's volcanoes are typically considered safe, given the relatively gentle, non-explosive outflow of lava that characterizes the eruptions. However, Kilauea erupted violently in 1790 and 1924 and will undoubtedly do so again. Mauna Loa erupted for three weeks in 1984, with lava flows coming within 4 mi. of Hilo. The volcanologists at Volcanoes National Park continually monitor volcanic activity—heed all warnings and instructions they give regarding an impending explosive eruption. Other, more dangerous hazards are commonplace in the park; be careful and follow the guidelines described at the park (p. 203).

OUTDOOR ACTIVITIES

Let's face it. While we may claim that there are a million reasons to come to Hawaii, only one stands out in your mind: the beaches. The glorious crescents of sand that see millions of sunbathers, snorkelers, surfers, boogie boarders, and swimmers each year are at the heart of any Hawaiian getaway. In this section, we'll give you a quick overview of where you can find your favorite activities. Beach is indicated by "B." and beach park by "B.P."

THE PRICE OF A WAVE. Surfboards usually rent for $10-20 per day and $70-100 per week, depending on the type of board. Short boards are generally cheaper but infinitely more difficult to learn on than long boards. Roof racks (to hold the board) typically cost an additional $5 per day or $15 per week. Boogie boards are much cheaper, renting at about $5 per day or $30 per week. Snorkel gear usually costs $5 per day or $15 per week.

SURFING

The best surfing is almost always in the winter, when the biggest waves roll in along the northern shores of the islands. The surfing spots we list here run the gamut from the easiest surf to breaks you'd have to train for years to tackle. Note that during the summer some of the beaches listed here may in fact be quite calm.

OAHU. Duke Kahanamoku B.P. (p. 126), Gray's B. (p. 127), Waikiki B. (p. 127), Baby Queen's (p. 128), Kuhio B. (p. 128), Diamond Head B. (p. 129), Sandy B. (p. 139), Makapuu B.P. (p. 139), Sunset B.P. to Ehukai B.P. (p. 159), Three Tables B. (p. 159), Waimea B.P. (p. 159), Haleiwa Alii B.P. (p. 165), Kawailoa B. (p. 166), Nanakuli B.P. (p. 175), Makaha B.P. (p. 175), Keawaula Bay (p. 176).

THE BIG ISLAND. Kahaluu B.P. (p. 188), Wawaloli B. (p. 188), Kekaha Kai B. (p. 188), Kealakekua Bay (p. 196), Milolii B.P. (p. 196), Waipio B. (p. 240), Pine Tree B. (p. 188).

MAUI. Maalaea Harbor (p. 282), Launiopoko Wayside Park (p. 263), Honolua Bay (p. 273), D.T. Fleming B.P. (p. 273), Hookipa B. (p. 299), Koki B. (p. 305), Hamoa B. (p. 305), Jaws (p. 301), Mokuleia Bay (p. 273).

MOLOKAI AND LANAI. Molokai: Rock Point (p. 342), Halawa Bay (p. 343), Make Horse B. (p. 348). **Lanai:** Lopa B. (p. 358).

KAUAI. Kalapaki B. (p. 366), Hanamaulu B.P. (p. 366), Kealia B. (p. 374), Donkey B. (p. 374), Secret B. (p. 380), Kahili Quary B. (p. 380), Kalihiwai B. (p. 381), Anini B.P. (p. 381), Waioli B.P. (p. 387), Kepuhi B. (p. 390), Haena B.P. (p. 391), Lawai B. (p. 400), Poipu/Kiahuna B. (p. 401), Poipu B.P. (p. 401), Shipwreck B. (p. 401), Pakala B. (p. 411).

SNORKELING

Many of the snorkeling spots are also good places to dive. If you plan to snorkel a lot, it might be more cost-effective to buy equipment instead of renting.

OAHU. Hanauma Bay (p. 137), Waimanalo B.P. (p. 142), Swanzy B.P. (p. 152), Pupukea B.P. (p. 159), Sharks Cove (p. 159), Three Tables B. (p. 159), Waimea B.P. (p. 159), Nanakuli B.P. (p. 175), Makaha B.P. (p. 175), Keaau B.P. (p. 176), Keawaula Bay (p. 176).

THE BIG ISLAND. Richardson Ocean Park (p. 228), Kapoho Bay (p. 221), Kahaluu Bay (p. 189), Kealakekua Bay (p. 196), Puuhonua O Honaunau Natl. Hist. Park (p. 198), Milolii B.P. (p. 196), Punaluu Black Sand B. (p. 202), Lapakali State Hist. Park (p. 249), Anaehoomalu B. (p. 254).

MAUI. Kamaole B.P. I, II, III (p. 288), Ulua B. (p. 288), Ahihi Bay (p. 292), La Pérouse Bay (p. 292), Keawakapu B. (p. 287), Mokapu B. (p. 290), Makena Landing (p. 291), Fishbowl (p. 292), Aquarium (p. 292), Kahekili B.P. (p. 270), Black Rock (p. 270), Kapalua B. (p. 272), Honolua Bay (p. 273), Canoe B. (p. 270), Mokuleia Bay (p. 273), Kaihalulu Red Sand B. (p. 305).

MOLOKAI AND LANAI. Molokai: Waialua B. (p. 342), Murphey's B. (p. 342). **Lanai:** Hulopoe B.P. (p. 358).

KAUAI. Queen's Bath (p. 384), Hideaways B. (p. 384), Puu Poa B. (p. 384), Waikoko B. (p. 388), Kepuhi B. (p. 390), Tunnels B. (p. 391), Kee B. (p. 391), PK's (p. 400), Koloa Landing (p. 401), Poipu B.P. (p. 401).

BOOGIE BOARDING

Many places listed as boogie boarding beaches may be great for bodysurfing, too.

OAHU. Queen's Surf (p. 128), Kuhio B. (p. 128), Sandy B. (p. 139), Makapuu B.P. (p. 139), Waimanalo Bay Rec. Area (p. 142), Kalama B. (p. 148), Nunakali B.P. (p. 175), Maili B.P. (p. 175), Keawaula Bay (p. 176).

THE BIG ISLAND. Kahaluu B.P. (p. 188), Richardson Ocean Park (p. 228), Hapuna B. (p. 254), White Sands B. (p. 188).

MAUI. Maalaea Harbor (p. 282), Little B. (p. 292), Puamana B. (p. 263), Kaanapali B. (p. 270), Oneloa B. (p. 273), D.T. Fleming B.P. (p. 273), Paia Bay (p. 298), Koki B. (p. 305), Hamoa B. (p. 305).

MOLOKAI. Halawa Bay (p. 343).

KAUAI. Kalapaki B. (p. 366), Hanamaulu B.P. (p. 366), Kealia B. (p. 374), Kalihiwai B. (p. 381), Hanalei Pavilion B.P. (p. 387), Lawai B. (p. 400), Poipu/Kiahuna B. (p. 401), Brennecke's B. (p. 401), Shipwreck B. (p. 401).

SCENIC AND STUNNING SUNSETS

OAHU. Ala Moana B.P. (p. 105), Sans Souci B. (p. 128), Kahe Point B.P. (p. 171), Makaha B.P. (p. 175).

THE BIG ISLAND. Makalawena (p. 188), Waialea B. (p. 254), Papakolea Green Sands B. (p. 202), Hapuna B. (p. 254).

MAUI. Little B. (p. 292), Dig Me B. (p. 270), Punalau B. (p. 273).

MOLOKAI AND LANAI. Molokai: Make Horse (p. 348), Halawa Bay (p. 343), Lauhue B. (p. 347). **Lanai:** Shipwreck B. (p. 357), Hulopoe B.P. (p. 358).

KAUAI. Moloaa B. (p. 374, Secret B. (p. 380), Black Pot B. (p. 387), Lumahai B. (p. 390), Tunnels B. (p. 391), Kee B. (p. 391), Lawai B. (p. 400), Polihale B. (p. 421).

EVERYTHING ELSE

ATV TOURS. Oahu: Kualoa Ranch (p. 155). **Maui:** Maui ATV (p. 309). **Lanai:** Adventure Lanai Ecocenter (p. 352).

HORSEBACK RIDING. Oahu: Kualoa Ranch (p. 155). **Maui:** Thompson Ranch (p. 309). **Molokai:** Puu O Hoku Ranch (p. 342). **The Big Island:** Waipio Naalapa Stables (p. 240), Waipio on Horseback (p. 240), Paniolo Riding Adventures (p. 245), Dahana Ranch (p. 245).

KITEBOARDING. Oahu: Kailua B. (p. 148), Mokuleia (p. 170). **Maui:** Kanaha B. (p. 279). **Kauai:** Kapaa B.P. (p. 377), Waioli B.P. (p. 387), Kepuhi B. (p. 390), Gillins' B. (p. 402).

DOLPHIN- OR WHALE-WATCHING. Oahu: Deep Ecology (p. 166). **Maui:** Pacific Whale Foundation (p. 289). **Molokai:** Molokai Action Adventures (p. 344). **The Big Island:** Dolphin Discoveries (p. 189).

WINDSURFING. Oahu: Diamond Head B. (p. 129), Kailua B. (p. 148). **Maui:** Kanaha B.P. (p. 279), North Kihei B. (p. 287), Hookipa B. (p. 299). **The Big Island:** Anuehoomalu B. (p. 254). **Kauai:** Anini B.P. (p. 381).

USEFUL PUBLICATIONS AND RESOURCES

A variety of publishing companies offer hiking guidebooks to meet the needs of novices or experts. For information about camping, hiking, and biking, write or call the organizations listed below.

Family Campers and RVers/National Campers and Hikers Association, Inc., 4804 Transit Rd., Bldg. #2, Depew, NY 14043, USA (☎800-245-9755; www.fcrv.org). Membership fee ($25) includes their publication, *Camping Today.*

Hawaii Trail and Mountain Club. Guests are welcome on their hikes (see schedule online at www.htmclub.org). Suggested $2 donation.

The Mountaineers Books, 1001 SW Klickitat Way, Ste. 201, Seattle, WA 98134, USA (☎206-223-6303; www.mountaineersbooks.org). Over 600 titles on hiking, biking, mountaineering, natural history, and conservation.

The Nature Conservancy of Hawaii, 923 Nuuanu Ave., Honolulu 96817 (☎537-4508; www.nature.org/wherewework/northamerica/states/hawaii).

Wilderness Press, 1200 5th St., Berkeley, CA 94710, USA (☎800-443-7227; www.wildernesspress.com). Carries over 100 hiking guides and maps for the western US.

Woodall Publications Corporation, 2575 Vista Del Mar Dr., Ventura, CA 93001, USA (☎877-680-6155; www.woodalls.com). Annually updates campground directories.

ORGANIZED ADVENTURE TRIPS

Organized adventure tours offer another way of exploring the wild. Activities include hiking, biking, canoeing, kayaking, and sailing. Tourism bureaus often can suggest parks, trails, and outfitters. Organizations that specialize in camping and outdoor equipment, like REI and EMS (p. 77), are also good sources of info.

Hawaii Activities, Aloha Tower 5th fl., 1 Aloha Tower Drive, Honolulu, HI 96813 (☎877-877-1222; www.hawaiiactivities.com). Service that books activities for tourists. Searchable website with links to different tour companies offering every kind of adventure/excursion/activity under the sun.

The Real Hawaii (☎877-597-7325; www.therealhawaii.com). Eco-cultural excursions led by Native Hawaiians.

Specialty Travel Index, P.O. Box 458, San Anselmo, CA 94979 (☎888-642-4030 or 415-455-1643; www.specialtytravel.com). Tours worldwide.

Wild Side Specialty Tours, 87-1286 Farrington Hwy., Waianae, HI 96792 (☎808-306-7273; www.sailhawaii.com). Sailing and kayaking adventures on Oahu.

OAHU

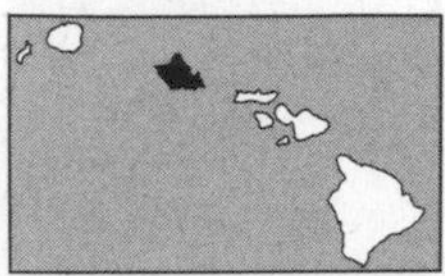

Oahu appropriately means "the gathering place"—not only is the island the seat of the state government and Hawaii's financial and business center, it is also the home of nearly three-quarters of the state's total population. Over half its residents are concentrated in Honolulu, Hawaii's state capital and premier city. This bustling metropolis is the nexus of Oahu, with all the glamor of a major urban center and tourist mecca. Waikiki, a magical mile of beachfront hotels, shops, restaurants, and endless entertainment in the southeastern quarter of the city, is one of the most famous destinations in the world.

Oahu's urban nature makes it a less scenic island than the others, but the commercial tourism does have its benefits. Visitors need look no further than Waikiki to get their fill of tropical kitsch and frenzied nightlife, and downtown Honolulu offers myriad opportunities to explore Hawaii's historical and cultural past. However, with little effort, visitors can venture beyond the gift shops and guided tours and uncover the island's subtler treasures. On the Windward Coast, a pleasant drive passes by rickety fruit stands and acres of pineapple fields on the way to the fabled North Shore, home to some of the world's best surf breaks. Drive 10 mi. up the Leeward Coast and both the scenery and the mood change dramatically; you're in rural Hawaii, where inhabitants embrace a slower, more traditional way of life. The luxuriant Manoa Valley overflows with fragrant blossoms and tropical fruit, and hikers have their pick of countless trails that lead to pockets of unspoiled Hawaiian rainforest.

On Oahu, visitors can discover the multifaceted appeal of Hawaii. Oahu offers the Big Island's hippie culture on the sands of the North Shore, Maui's beauty and opulence in the Windward Coast's resorts, Kauai's natural splendor in the lush interior valleys, and rustic Molokai in the streets of Waimanalo. Consider this your crash course in appreciation of these magnificent islands.

HIGHLIGHTS OF OAHU

PAY YOUR RESPECTS at the Pearl Harbor memorials (p. 133).

SNORKEL BESIDE TROPICAL FISH of all colors at Hanauma Bay (p. 137).

RELIVE THE GLORY of the Hawaiian monarchy at Iolani Palace (p. 107).

CATCH A WAVE at Waikiki Beach (p. 127), the perfect spot to learn to surf.

CLIFF JUMP into the crystalline waters of North Shore's Waimea Bay (p. 159).

INTERISLAND TRANSPORTATION

Honolulu International Airport (☎836-6413; www.honoluluairport.com) is off the Airport exit from H-1, 9 mi. west of Waikiki. The airport is also accessible via **Ala Moana Boulevard.** Take Ala Moana west until it becomes **Nimitz Highway** and continue west. Turn left into the airport just after the Roger's Blvd. intersection underneath H-1. TheBus #8, 19, and 20 make three stops: the Interisland Terminal, Lobby 4, and Lobby 7. TheBus #20 is the Waikiki bus; travelers coming from other parts of the island will have to change at the Nimitz Hwy. stop.

The only **ATM** before security is in the American Airlines office in the main terminal next to the H-2 baggage carousel on the ground level. **Currency exchange** services are available behind all international gates in the main terminal. Taxis and shuttles

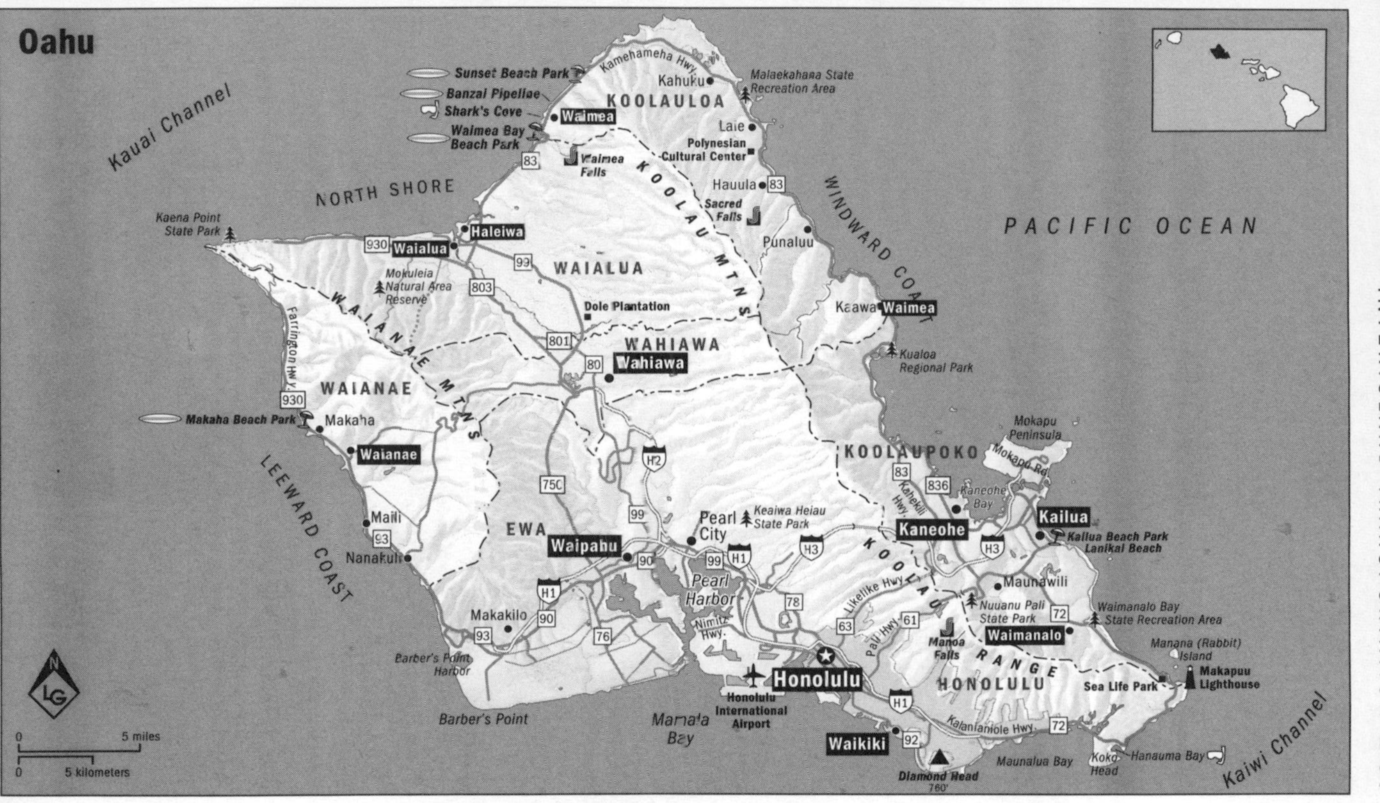

Oahu
PACIFIC OCEAN
Kauai Channel
Kaiwi Channel
NORTH SHORE
WINDWARD COAST
LEEWARD COAST
KOOLAULOA
KOOLAUPOKO
WAIALUA
WAHIAWA
WAIANAE
EWA
HONOLULU
KOOLAU MTNS
WAIANAE MTNS
KOOLAU RANGE
Sunset Beach Park
Banzai Pipeline
Shark's Cove
Waimea Bay Beach Park
Waimea
Waimea Falls
Kamehameha Hwy.
Kahuku
Malaekahana State Recreation Area
Laie
Polynesian Cultural Center
Hauula
Sacred Falls
Punaluu
Kaena Point State Park
Haleiwa
Waialua
Mokuleia Natural Area Reserve
Dole Plantation
Kaawa
Kualoa Regional Park
Wahiawa
Farrington Hwy.
Makaha Beach Park
Makaha
Waianae
Maili
Nanakuli
Makakilo
Barber's Point Harbor
Barber's Point
Waipahu
Pearl City
Keaiwa Heiau State Park
Pearl Harbor
Nimitz Hwy.
Honolulu
Honolulu International Airport
Mamala Bay
Waikiki
Diamond Head
760'
Mokapu Peninsula
Mokapu Rd.
Kaneohe Bay
Kahekili Hwy.
Kaneohe
Kailua
Kailua Beach Park
Lanikai Beach
Maunawili
Likelike Hwy.
Pali Hwy.
Nuuanu Pali State Park
Manoa Falls
Waimanalo
Waimanalo Bay State Recreation Area
Manana (Rabbit) Island
Makapuu Lighthouse
Sea Life Park
Kalanianaole Hwy.
Maunalua Bay
Koko Head
Hanauma Bay
0
5 miles
0
5 kilometers

OAHU

leave from the median strip outside the baggage claim. Taxis to Waikiki run around $25-30. A cheaper option is the **Reliable Shuttle** (☎924-9292), which runs between the airport and hotels in Waikiki and Honolulu, as well as the *USS Arizona* Memorial, for about $8. Make reservations by phone at least one day in advance. Shuttles run 24hr., most frequently between 6am and 10pm. See Interisland Transportation at the start of each chapter for info on flights between the islands.

FLIGHTS

Most of the incoming international, domestic, and interisland flights fly to or through Honolulu International Airport. See **Essentials,** p. 49, for more information. The following are a few major interisland carriers.

Aloha Airlines, 1001 Bishop St., Ste. 130 (☎484-1111 or 800-367-5250; www.alohaairlines.com), in downtown Honolulu, has ticket offices across Oahu. Bishop St. office open M-F 8:30am-4:30pm. Service from Burbank, Oakland, Orange County, Las Vegas, Sacramento, and Vancouver, Canada. Also operates interisland flights from Honolulu to: Hilo and Kona on the Big Island; Lihue on Kauai; and Kahului on Maui.

Hawaiian Airlines (☎838-1555; www.hawaiianair.com) has a ticket office inside Sears at Ala Moana Center. Service from: Las Vegas, Los Angeles, Phoenix, Portland, San Diego, Sacramento, San Francisco, and Seattle. Interisland service to Hilo and Kona on the Big Island, Maui, Kauai, Lanai, and Molokai. Ticket office open M-Sa 9:30am-5:45pm.

Island Air (☎484-2222; www.islandair.com) services many interisland flights in smaller turbo-prop planes that are usually more expensive than Hawaiian or Aloha Airlines.

HONOLULU

Hawaii's capital and largest city, Honolulu (pop. 377,260) is a commercial center, college town, and living landmark of Hawaiian history. Although downtown Honolulu is less of a tourist destination than Waikiki, its state buildings and sights within the civic center illuminate the complex history of Hawaii's modernization. Today's Hawaiians inherit a cosmopolitan city of almost 400,000 as their capital. On weekdays downtown bustles with businesspeople as they walk through palm tree-lined, skyscraper-filled streets in their finest aloha wear. Chinatown is crammed with daytime shoppers in search of a deal among its markets, gift shops, and restaurants. The mellow residential outskirts of Kaimuki and the University of Hawaii offset the fast pace of life in the city. Those who do live downtown kick back by slipping away to Manoa's tropical mountains, cruising Waikiki's gorgeous beaches, or barbecuing *ohana*-style at Ala Moana Beach Park.

LOCAL TRANSPORTATION

BY BUS. Oahu's public transit system, **TheBus** (☎848-4500; www.thebus.org) offers service across the island. Many people have expressed frustration that TheBus schedule is meaningless; indeed, the bus times we provide may not hold up, since buses are often stuck in traffic. Service is generally friendly, and if you are not sure of your bus route or stop, drivers are willing to help you find your way. Buses have the same number going in both directions, but the title of the bus changes depending on direction.

Routes and Fares: One-way fare $2; seniors, disabled, and children $1; free transfers are good for 2hr. and available upon request from bus driver. **The Oahu Discovery Passport,** available at ABC Stores, is good for 4 consecutive days of unlimited travel ($20). Monthly passes at 7-Eleven stores and select ABC stores $40, youth $20, seniors and disabled $5. **Route A,** the CityExpress, goes from Kalihi and Waipahu in the west, then

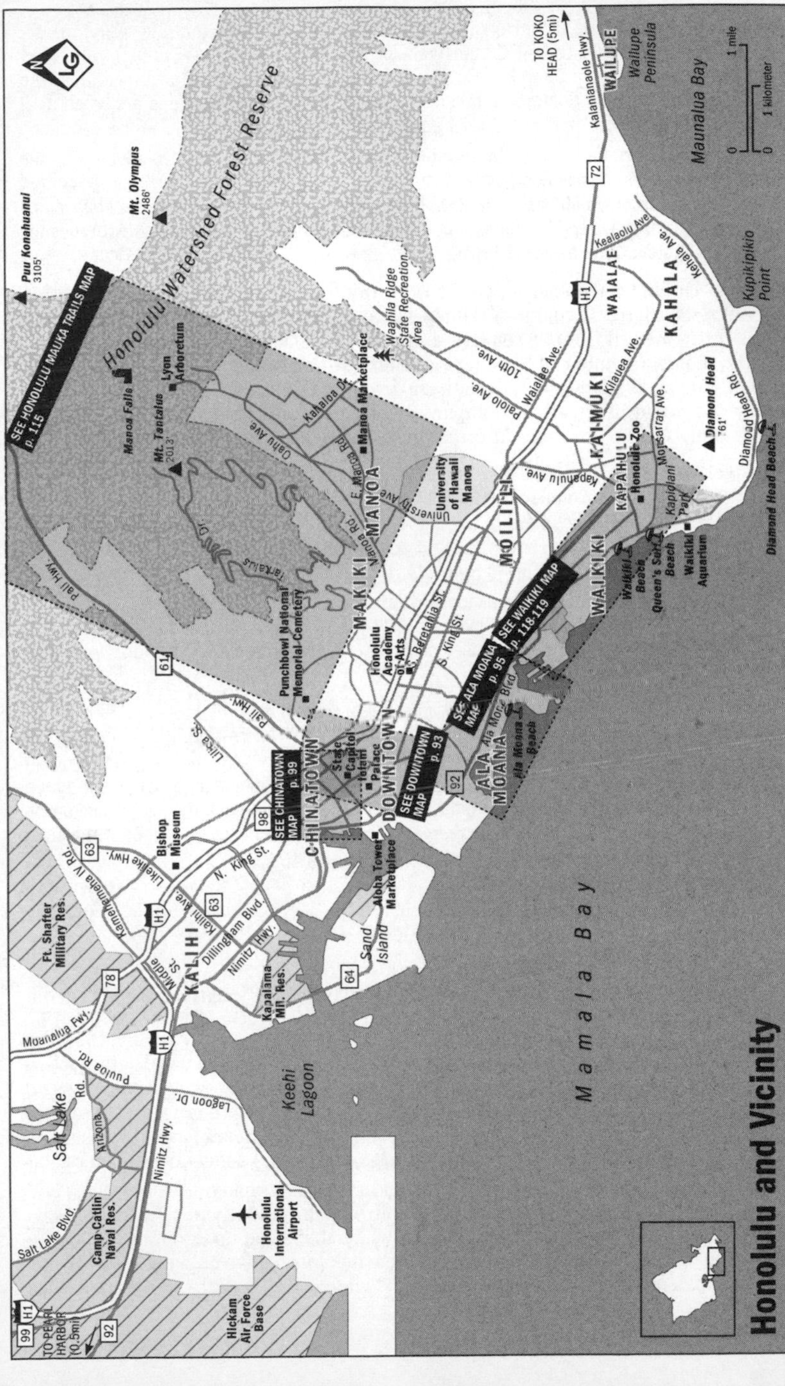

Honolulu and Vicinity

down King/Beretania to University Ave. and Manoa. **Route B,** the other CityExpress, runs from the Kalihi Transit Ctr. to Waikiki. **Route C,** the CountyExpress, runs from Makaha to Ala Moana Shopping Ctr. These are just a few of TheBus's many routes; see the website or call the information lines below for details. TheBus stops are listed near sights wherever applicable. Waikiki Transportation (p. 119) lists Waikiki-based routes.

Information Lines: Call **TheBus Information Service** (☎848-5555) with your location, time of departure, and destination points, and they will find the best route. The 24hr. **Recorded Information from Waikiki** (☎296-1818) hotline offers an automated directory of bus routes to sites across the island for routes that pick up from Kuhio Ave. TheBus also publishes the **TheBus System Map,** available for free in the Satellite City Hall in Ala Moana Center.

BY CAR. Driving is the easiest way to get around Oahu, despite traffic congestion and limited parking. The major national car rental chains have branches by the airport and in Waikiki; most require a credit card. Honolulu's tourism capital, Waikiki, holds a number of excellent smaller car and moped rental companies (p. 119). Rental costs fluctuate by season and availability; be sure to call in advance to reserve a vehicle and to check company websites for online deals and promotions. See **Essentials,** p. 36, for more information on traveling by car in Hawaii.

Budget (☎836-1700 or 800-527-7000; www.budget.com), at the airport and another location in Waikiki. Compacts from $34 per day, $210 per week. Unlimited mileage. 25+. Rentals can be returned to another location. CDW $23 per day, liability $14 per day. Open daily 4:30am-1am. Ask about special rates. AmEx/D/MC/V.

Dollar (☎831-2331 or 800-800-4000; www.dollar.com), at the airport and 3 other locations, including one at 2002 Kalakaua Ave., in Waikiki. Cars $30 per day, $210 per week, depending on season. Unlimited mileage. CDW $18 per day, liability $13 per day. 21+. Under-25 surcharge $25 per day. $20 charge to return car to Waikiki branch. Open daily 4:30am-midnight. AmEx/D/MC/V.

Hertz (☎831-3500; www.hertz.com), at the airport. Cars from around $39 per day. Unlimited mileage. Liability $23 per day. 25+. Ask about returning car to another location during reservation. Pickup and return service. Open 24hr. AmEx/D/MC/V.

National Car Rental (☎973-7200 or 800-227-7368; www.nationalcar.com), at the airport and one location in Waikiki. Cars from around $40 per day. Unlimited mileage. Full coverage $22 per day. 21+. Under-25 surcharge $25 per day. Returns can be made at the other Honolulu locations. Open daily 5:30am-midnight. AmEx/D/MC/V.

ORIENTATION

HIGHWAYS AND BYWAYS

Honolulu's main highway, **H-1,** runs east-west along the length of the city from Kaimuki to the southwest corner of Oahu, past the airport. Getting onto H-1 can be frustrating, as some streets only provide eastbound or westbound access. Freeway access is available via **Ala Moana Boulevard,** which stretches from Waikiki to the airport and turns into Nimitz Hwy. west of Nuuanu River, and **King Street,** which leaves H-1 north of Waikiki and splits into two one-way streets between University Ave. and the Aala Park edge of Chinatown. The one-way streets formed from the split of King St., **Beretania Street** (heading west) and **King Street** (heading east), are the backbone of downtown and Chinatown, and bear the brunt of intra-Honolulu traffic. Beretania and King St. also run near many of greater Honolulu's sights and activities. **TheBus** has several routes that ply their way down King St., which then head up Beretania St. for the return trip. **Kapiolani Boulevard** is a major two-way thoroughfare, slicing a northwest-southeast passage from Wailae Ave. to H-1 and intersecting Waikiki's **Kalakaua Avenue** on the way over to its western endpoint at King St. and the Civic Center. Streets that

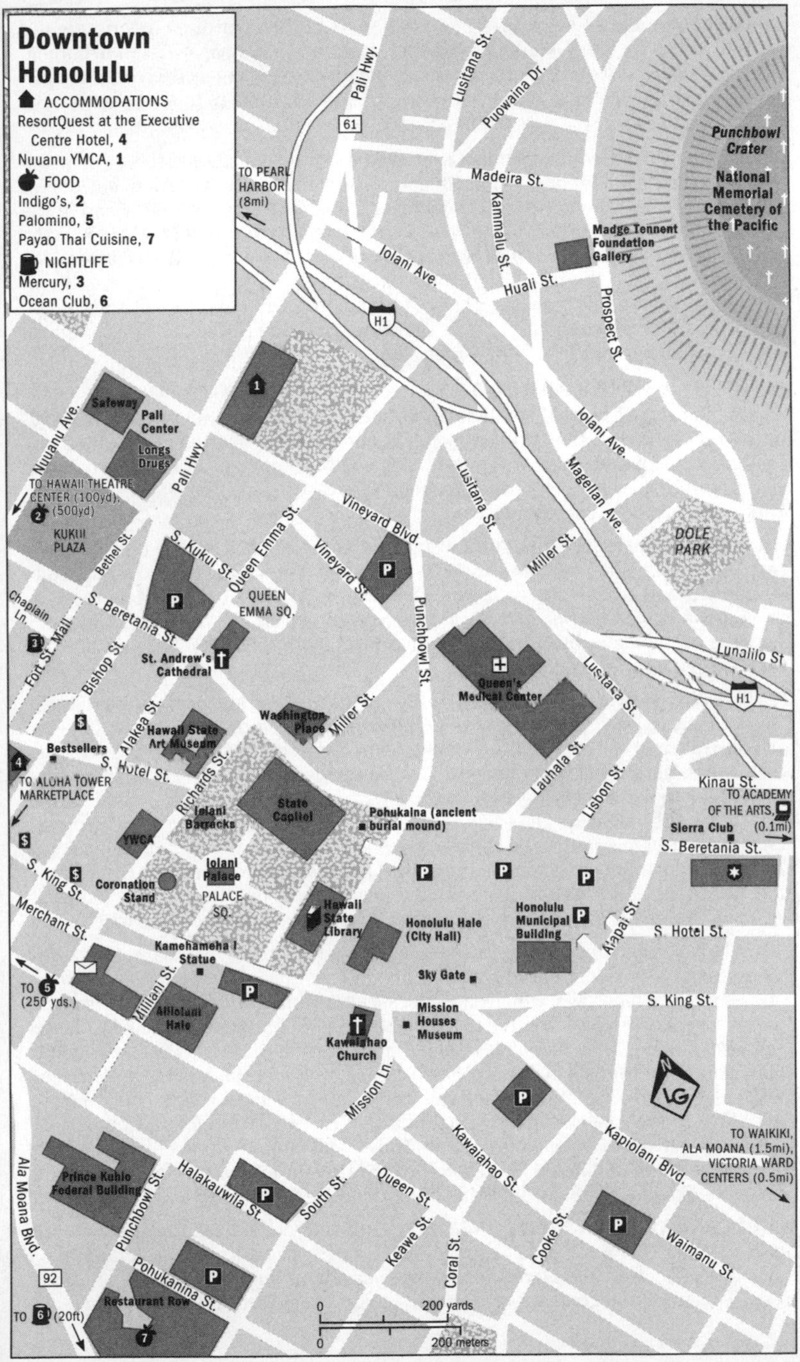

Downtown Honolulu

ACCOMMODATIONS
ResortQuest at the Executive Centre Hotel, **4**
Nuuanu YMCA, **1**

FOOD
Indigo's, **2**
Palomino, **5**
Payao Thai Cuisine, **7**

NIGHTLIFE
Mercury, **3**
Ocean Club, **6**

Pali Hwy.
61
Lusitana St.
Puowaina Dr.
Punchbowl Crater
National Memorial Cemetery of the Pacific
TO PEARL HARBOR (8mi)
Madeira St.
Kammalu St.
Madge Tennent Foundation Gallery
Iolani Ave.
Huali St.
Prospect St.
H1
Safeway
Pali Center
Longs Drugs
Nuuanu Ave.
TO HAWAII THEATRE CENTER (100yd), (500yd)
KUKUI PLAZA
Bethel St.
S. Kukui St.
Queen Emma St.
Vineyard Blvd.
Vineyard St.
Lusitana St.
Magellan Ave.
Miller St.
DOLE PARK
QUEEN EMMA SQ.
Chaplain Ln.
Fort St. Mall
S. Beretania St.
Punchbowl St.
Lunalilo St.
St. Andrew's Cathedral
Bishop St.
Queen's Medical Center
Lusitana St.
Washington Place
Miller St.
Alakea St.
Hawaii State Art Museum
Bestsellers
S. Hotel St.
Richards St.
Lauhala St.
Lisbon St.
TO ALOHA TOWER MARKETPLACE
Kinau St.
TO ACADEMY OF THE ARTS (0.1mi)
Iolani Barracks
State Capitol
Pohukaina (ancient burial mound)
Sierra Club
S. Beretania St.
YWCA
S. King St.
Coronation Stand
Iolani Palace
PALACE SQ.
Merchant St.
Hawaii State Library
Honolulu Hale (City Hall)
Honolulu Municipal Building
Alapai St.
S. Hotel St.
Kamehameha I Statue
Sky Gate
TO 5 (250 yds.)
Mililani St.
Aliiolani Hale
Mission Houses Museum
Kawaiahao Church
S. King St.
Mission Ln.
Kapiolani Blvd.
TO WAIKIKI, ALA MOANA (1.5mi), VICTORIA WARD CENTERS (0.5mi)
Kawaiahao St.
Prince Kuhio Federal Building
Halakauwila St.
South St.
Queen St.
Ala Moana Blvd.
Punchbowl St.
Keawe St.
Cooke St.
Waimanu St.
Coral St.
92
Pohukanina St.
Restaurant Row
TO 6 (20ft)
0 200 yards
0 200 meters

OAHU

intersect these east-west routes include Kapahulu Ave. (on the eastern edge of Waikiki), McCully (from Waikiki to the university and Manoa), Piikoi (northbound one-way from Ala Moana Beach), Pensacola (southbound one-way from around Makiki), and Ward Ave. (along the western edge of the Ward Centers in Ala Moana).

THE LEI OF THE LAND

Honolulu is an abused place-name: it is often used to refer to whatever (or wherever) is presently under discussion. To many, Honolulu means the urban and suburban sprawl that stretches along the south shore of Oahu, from Koko Head in the east to Kalihi and the airport in the west. Others consider Honolulu the small downtown area surrounded by the districts of **Chinatown** to the west, **Ala Moana** to the south, **Kaimuki** and the revitalized **Wailae** area to the east, and the University of Hawaii and **Manoa** valley neighborhoods to the north. Diamond Head Crater in the east provides some of the best views on Oahu while the Koolau Mountain Range forms a backdrop for the varying streetscapes.

HONOLULU NEIGHBORHOODS

Honolulu is a collection of small neighborhoods, but Ala Moana, downtown, Chinatown, Manoa and the University Area, and Waikiki are the major districts treated by this guide. For convenience, some listings appear under a certain district even though they technically lie outside the district's established boundaries. Waikiki is considered separately (p. 117).

ALA MOANA. Spanning Honolulu's waterfront along Ala Moana Blvd. from downtown to Waikiki, Ala Moana is a shopper's paradise. The area is dotted with a number of malls and complexes, including Aloha Tower Marketplace, Restaurant Row, the Victoria Ward Centers, and Ala Moana Shopping Center. Ala Moana Shopping Center is also a major bus terminal. Many routes stop in front of the mall at Kona St. or behind it on Ala Moana Blvd.

DOWNTOWN. Downtown Honolulu is Hawaii's financial and legislative district. The centrally located Bishop Square is Oahu's economic powerhouse and the Senate and House of Representatives sit nearby in the State Capitol. During weekday work hours, the streets are crowded with businesspeople, though at any other time of the week the area feels more like a ghost town. Downtown draws a small crowd with the historic sights of the Civic Center; yet few tourists venture into the financial district, where some of the city's best restaurants and public art are found. The downtown area, between Ala Moana and Chinatown, is bordered by the Fort St. Mall, South St., and Kakaako. To avoid the headache of one-way streets and parking, take TheBus #2, 13, or B CityExpress to Hotel St. and then explore on foot.

CHINATOWN. Chinatown assaults every sense with pungent fish markets, sizzling dishes, incense-shrouded shrines, and vocal street vendors. Honolulu is home to the nation's oldest Chinatown, which dates back to 1860 and was originally the red light district for sailors. Now it's home to a diverse Asian population, including Chinese, Japanese, Korean, Thai, Vietnamese, and Filipino communities and is consequently a destination for tourists in search of a cultural experience, shopping bargains, and inexpensive food. Chinatown is a small grid of a few square blocks, bordered by downtown to the east and Aala Triangle Park to the west. You'll find Chinatown's shops lining River St., Maunakea St., Smith St., and Nuuanu Ave. between Nimitz Hwy. to the south and Kukui St. to the north. Start your exploration at the intersection of Hotel and River St.; from Waikiki take TheBus #2, 13, or B CityExpress.

MANOA AND THE UNIVERSITY AREA. The University of Hawaii hangs its mortarboard in the pleasant Manoa Valley district, north of central Honolulu. Manoa itself is a peaceful valley overflowing with greenery, lava rock walls, and fruit trees. The streets become more tranquil as you tread farther up into the valley,

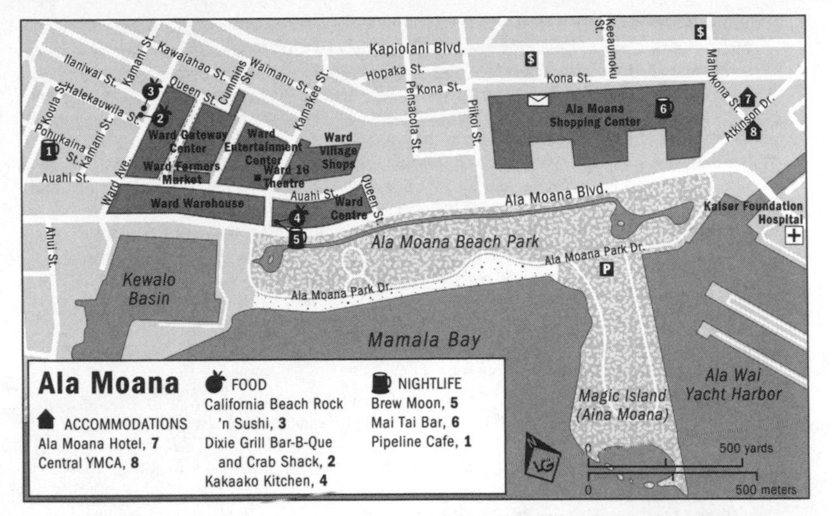

away from the city center and toward the Honolulu Watershed Forest Reserve. Two of Honolulu's main roads, University Ave. and Punahou St., become Oahu Ave. and Manoa Rd., respectively, once they hit Manoa. Past Punahou School, Manoa Rd. splits into E. Manoa Rd. and Manoa Rd. E. Manoa Rd. veers to the Manoa Marketplace; Manoa Rd. continues on to Lyon Arboretum and Manoa Falls. Strip malls radiate out from the intersection of King St. and University Ave., in the more densely populated base of Manoa Valley, known as Moiliili West of Manoa, between Punahou School and Punchbowl Crater north of H-1, is the high-rise-clogged neighborhood of Makiki. Excellent hiking and scenic drives are found at the extreme ends of Makiki Heights Dr., Round Top Dr., and Tantalus Dr.

TheBus #4 picks up on Kuhio Ave. in Waikiki and continues on University Ave. toward downtown. The #5, 6, and 18 all pick up at Ala Moana Shopping Center and head to Manoa. On school days from 6-7:30am, the #80A is an express from Hawaii Kai to lower Manoa and downtown on school days, going as far into Manoa as Dole St. and UH. In the afternoon, #80A runs from Punahou School at Punahou St. and Wilder Ave. back to Hawaii Kai.

KAIMUKI. Kapahulu/Waialae and the blocks adjacent to these avenues in the amiable Kaimuki area are the cradle of a revitalized neighborhood known for its wide range of unique restaurants and quiet residential areas, which are only a short walk or bus ride (TheBus #1) away from downtown Honolulu.

PRACTICAL INFORMATION

Many of Oahu's services are based in Honolulu, but most tourist services can also be found in Waikiki (see **Waikiki, Practical Information,** p. 121).

TOURIST AND FINANCIAL SERVICES

Tourist Information: Hawaii Visitors and Convention Bureau Information Office, 2270 Kalakaua Ave., Ste. 801 (☎923-1811 or 800-464-2924; www.gohawaii.com), at Waikiki Business Plaza. A friendly office with a room full of free tourist magazines, such as *Islands of Aloha Official Vacation Planner.* Open M-F 8am-4:30pm.

Beyond Tourism:

The Clean Air Team (☎948-3299) volunteers lead a 2 mi., 3hr. pleasant stroll through Kapiolani Park and along the Diamond Head Coast, ending at the Diamond Head Lighthouse. Leaves from the Gandhi statue near the Honolulu Zoo entrance, 151 Kapahulu Ave. 1st Sa of the mo., 1-4pm. Under 18 must be accompanied by an adult; groups of 5 or more must call ahead. Parking available at the Waikiki Shell. Free.

The Diamond Head Story (☎948-3299), a field-trip-like walking tour about the history of Diamond Head that ends at the beginning of a 2 mi. hike to the top of the crater. Leaves from the Gandhi statue (see above). 1st Sa of every mo., 9am. Under 18 must be accompanied by an adult; groups of 5 or more must call ahead. Parking available at the Waikiki Shell. Free.

The Program to Preserve Hawaiian Placenames, at the Liliha Public Library, 1515 Liliha St. Take H-1 west to School St. and take N. School St. west to Liliha St. Catch the free "Introduction to Hawaiian Words" lecture, the easiest and fastest (1½hr.) way to become acquainted with Hawaiian word structure. 1st W of every month, 7pm. No late arrivals.

Banks and Currency Exchange: With the exception of the Philippine National Bank, all banks have ATMs throughout Honolulu.

Bank of Hawaii, 111 S. King St. (☎538-4171 or 888-643-3888; open M-Th 7:30am-3pm, F 7:30am-4:30pm), and in Ala Moana Center, 1441 Kapiolani Blvd. (☎942-6111; open M-Th 8:30am-4pm, F 8:30am-6pm, Sa 9am-1pm).

Central Pacific, 220 S. King St. (☎544-0500). Open M-Th 7:30am-3pm, F 7:30am-4:30pm.

First Hawaiian Bank, 999 Bishop St. (☎525-6340), and in Chinatown, 2 N. King St. (☎525-6888). 24hr. customer service line ☎844-4444. Both open M-Th 8:30am-4pm, F 8:30am-6pm.

LOCAL SERVICES

Bookstores: Bestsellers, 1001 Bishop St., #138 (☎528-2378, fax 528-2389), on the corner of Hotel St. Open M-F 7:30am-5:30pm, Sa 9am-3pm. AmEx/MC/V.

Libraries: Hawaii State Library, 478 S. King St. (☎586-3500; www.librarieshawaii.org), east of Iolani Palace, in the Civic Center—look for the huge white pillars. Added to the State and National Register of Historical Places in 1975, the Hawaii State Library anchors the only state-wide library system in the United States, with over 560,000 catalogued books. Temporary library passes can be purchased here or at any state public library for use at all branches. 3-month visitor's card $10, 51-year nonresident pass $25. Open Tu and F-Sa 9am-5pm, M and W 10am-5pm, Th 9am-8pm. **McCully-Moiliili Public Library,** 2211 S. King St. (☎973-1099). Open Tu-W and F-Sa 10am-5pm, Th noon-7pm. **Manoa Public Library,** 2716 Woodlawn Dr. (☎988-0459). Open Tu 1pm-8pm, M and W-Sa 10am-5pm.

Outdoor Services:

Department of Parks and Recreation, 1000 Uluohia St., Ste. 309 (☎692-5585), in Kapolei, Oahu. **Camping permits** (☎523-4525) available at the Main Permits Office, 650 S. King St. Both offices open M-F 7:45am-4pm.

Hawaii Nature Center, 2131 Makiki Heights Dr. (☎955-0100; www.hawaiinaturecenter.org), in Makiki Valley. Hands-on programs, community events, and guided hikes. Schedule available online. Open daily 8am-4:30pm.

Hawaiian Trail and Mountain Club (☎674-1459; www.htmclub.org), hikes a different trail every weekend; visitors are welcome. Quarterly hike schedules available online. All hikes meet at Iolani Palace at 8am on Su and 9am on Sa. Under 18 must be accompanied by adult. $2 suggested donation.

Sierra Club, Beretania St. (☎538-6616), across from the police station. Hikes, outings, and service projects. Visitors and nonmembers welcome. Schedule available online. Unless otherwise noted, hikes leave at 8am from 2510 Bingham St., in Moiliili. Under 18 must be accompanied by adult. $5, Sierra Club members and under 14 $1.

EMERGENCY AND COMMUNICATIONS

Police: Honolulu Police Department, 801 S. Beretania St. (☎529-3111). **Downtown-Chinatown Substation,** 79 N. Hotel St. (☎529-3932), at the corner of Mauneakea St. **Airport Sheriff** (☎836-6606).

Crisis Lines: Sex Abuse Treatment Center (☎524-7273). Crisis Response Team (☎832-3100). Poison Center (☎800-222-1222). Missing Child Center (☎586-1449).

Fire Department: ☎723-7101.

Red Cross: Hawaii Chapter ☎734-2101.

24hr. Pharmacies: Longs Drugs, 1330 Pali Hwy. (☎536-7302 or 536-5542), on the corner of Pali Hwy. and Vineyard Blvd. Both pharmacy and drugstore open 24hr. Another branch at 2220 S. King St. (☎949-4781, pharmacy 947-2651), across from Honolulu Stadium State Recreation Area. AmEx/D/MC/V.

Hospital: Queen's Medical Center, 1301 Punchbowl St. (☎538-9011). An **Emergency Services Department** (☎547-4311) provides pre-hospital emergency medical care and ambulance services. Their referral line (☎537-7117) can help visitors find a doctor.

Medical Assistance: Urgent Care Clinic of Waikiki, 2155 Kalakaua Ave., Ste. 308 (☎432-2000). **Straub Clinic and Hospital,** 888 S. King St. (☎522-4000). See Waikiki, **Practical Information,** p. 121. **Planned Parenthood of Hawaii,** Honolulu Clinic: ☎589-1149.

Internet Access:

etopia, 1363 S. Beretania St. (☎593-0226), on the corner of Beretania and Keeaumoku St. Members get a better rate ($2 per hr.) and go to the front of waiting lists for the fast machines. Membership fee $10. Nonmember rate $4 per hr. 33 computers. Open M-Th and Su 9am-2am, F-Sa 9am-4am. Cash only.

Netstop (☎955-1020; www.netstopcafe.com), at the intersection of S. King St. and University Ave. in Manoa. Internet access $0.09 per min. B/W printing $0.10 per page, color printing $0.70 per page. Free scanning and CD-burning. Coffee $1. Open M-F 8:30am-midnight, Sa-Su 9:30am-midnight. AmEx/D/MC/V.

Post Offices:

Airport, 3600 Aolele St. (☎423-6029), offers the only General Delivery service in Honolulu. Open M-F 7:30am-8pm, Sa 8am-4pm.

Ala Moana, 1450 Ala Moana Blvd., Ste. 1006 (☎532-1987). Open M-F 8:30am-5pm, Sa 8:30am-4:15pm.

Downtown Honolulu, 335 Merchant St. (☎532-1987), west of Aliiolani Hale in the Civic Center. Open M-F 8am-4:30pm.

Postal Codes: 96819 (Airport); 96814 (Ala Moana); 96813 (downtown Honolulu); 96816 (Kaimuki); 96822 (Makiki); 96839 (Manoa); 96828 (Moiliili).

HONOLULU AND WAIKIKI INFORMATION LINES.

Oahu Surf Report: ☎973-4383.

US Weather Service Recording: ☎973-4380. Might as well be a broken record saying, "It's [82-86°F] and sunny."

Ocean Safety and Lifeguard Services: ☎922-3888. A daily message gives a safety report about current water hazards like box jellyfish or Portuguese Men-of-War and a surf and beach condition report.

Pacific Gateway Center (Foreign Language Translation Service): ☎845-3918

Honolulu Job Information: ☎523-5301.

Mayor's Office of Culture and the Arts (MOCA): ☎523-4674.

Parks and Recreation Department Information: ☎692-5561.

Camping Permits: ☎523-4527.

Fishing and hunting permits: ☎587-0072.

PUBLICATIONS

Honolulu Weekly (www.honoluluweekly.com) is a free community paper with events listings, incisive articles, and reviews available on street corners throughout Honolulu. **This Week Oahu** and **Oahu Gold** are free weekly coupon- and ad-laden brochure magazines ubiquitous in Oahu. Both publications include helpful maps of

Waikiki and Oahu. **Downtown Planet** (www.downtownplanet.com) is a free weekly published Mondays that lists events and activities in downtown Honolulu. Hawaii Pacific University puts out **Kalamalama,** its student newspaper, 12 times a year. Pick up the paper on magazine racks around campus and write (kalamalama@hpu.edu) if interested in writing about student or community issues. The **Honolulu Advertiser** (www.honoluluadvertiser.com) is Honolulu's most esteemed daily paper, covering national and international news, business, technology, entertainment, sports, and island life. It is available in grocery and convenience stores and street vending boxes (M-Sa $0.50, Su $1.75). **Weekend,** in the Friday edition of the Honolulu Advertiser, is Hawaii's best source for island entertainment listings and editorials.

ACCOMMODATIONS

You'll probably find the best deals in Waikiki, but options exist in other neighborhoods as well. These places usually cater more to locals and businesspeople; in general, expect either a more cozy atmosphere or unbeatable amenities.

BY PRICE

AM Ala Moana **DC** Downtown and Chinatown **G** Greater Honolulu **M** Manoa **W** Waikiki

UNDER $25 (❶)	
Hale Aloha Hostel (HI Waikiki) (123)	W
Hostelling International Honolulu (100)	M
Polynesian Beach Club Hostel (122)	W
Seaside Hawaiian Hostel (123)	W
Waikiki Beachside Hostel (122)	W
$25-65 (❷)	
Central YMCA (98)	AM
Nuuanu YMCA (99)	DC
$65-110 (❸)	
Hawaiian King (123)	W
Pacific Marina Inn (100)	G
Pagoda Hotel and Terrace (100)	G
Waikiki Gateway Hotel (124)	W
Waikiki Sand Villa (124)	W
$110-150 (❹)	
Aqua Marina Hotel (124)	W
Manoa Valley Inn (99)	M
ResortQuest Coconut Plaza Hotel (124)	W
Waikiki Grand Hotel (123)	W
$150 AND UP (❺)	
Ala Moana Hotel (98)	AM
Aqua Bamboo (123)	W
Ilima Hotel (124)	W
The Imperial of Waikiki (123)	W
ResortQuest at the Executive Centre Hotel (99)	DC
Waikiki Beachcomber Hotel (124)	W

BY LOCATION

ALA MOANA

Ala Moana Hotel, 410 Atkinson Dr. (☎955-4811; www.alamoanahotel.com), 2 blocks from Kapiolani Blvd. A great location within walking distance of the Ala Moana Shopping Center, TheBus routes, Ala Moana Beach Park, and Waikiki, this hotel is still isolated enough to duck the crowds. It also tops all but the best of Waikiki's hotels, with a business center, fitness room, heated pool, sun deck, 4 restaurants for both casual and fine dining, and Rumours nightclub. Parking $15 per day. Check-in 3pm. Check-out noon. Doubles $150-190. Call for discounted rates. AmEx/D/MC/V. ❹

Central YMCA, 401 Atkinson Dr. (☎941-3344), across the street from the Ala Moana Hotel. Catering to budget tourists with a fantastic location outside Waikiki, 1 block from Ala Moana Beach Park. College-style dorms with a twin bed, desk, chair, and storage closet. Limited A/C available. Amenities include use of the pool, fitness room, and free access to all exercise classes. Internet access in lobby ($1 per 10min.). Parking $5 per day. No reservations accepted. Check-out 10am. 18+ with photo ID. Single with shared bath (male only) $35, with private bath (male or female) $43; doubles $55. AmEx/MC/V. ❷

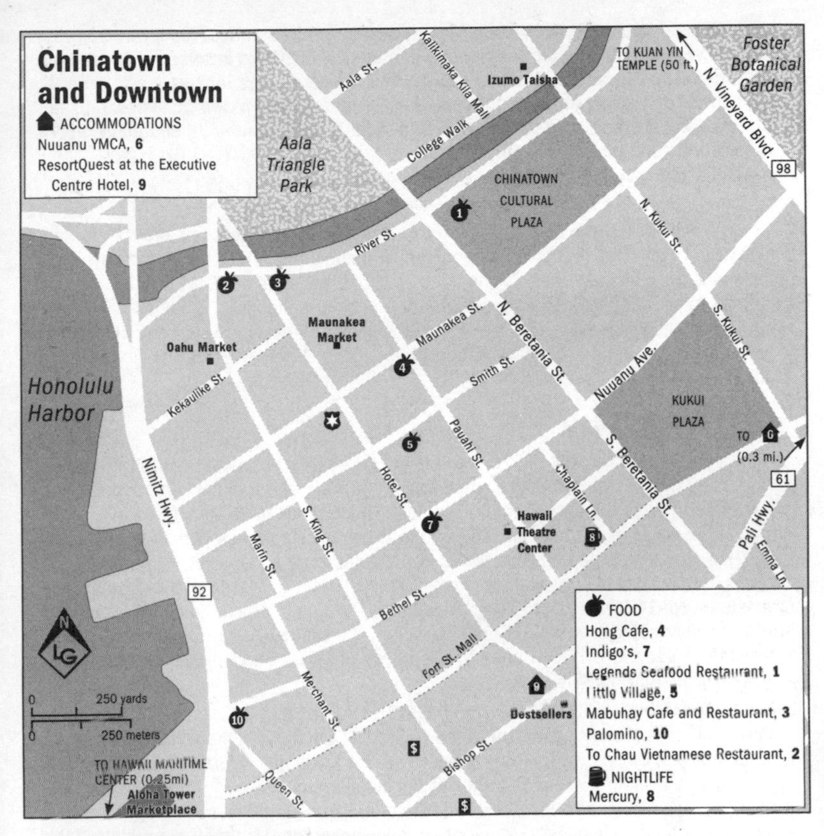

DOWNTOWN AND CHINATOWN

ResortQuest at the Executive Centre Hotel, 1088 Bishop St. (☎539-3000). Close to the Bishop Sq. banking center, on the corner of Hotel St. and Bishop. From H-1 East take Exit 21A and turn right onto Pali Hwy., which becomes Bishop. ResortQuest keeps this property gleaming and secure. All rooms come with full amenities, including same-day laundry and dry cleaning for a fee, free in-room Internet, 24hr. business center, outdoor whirlpool, and sun deck with a 20m lap pool. Guests can pay $7 per visit to use the gym at 24 Fitness across the street. Continental breakfast included. Check-in 3pm. Check-out noon. Business suite $220. 1-bedroom executive suites with full kitchen $280-295. AmEx/D/MC/V. ❺

Nuuanu YMCA, 1441 Pali Hwy. (☎536-3556), on the corner of Vineyard Blvd. and Pali Hwy. Guests have free access to local facilities including a lap pool and cardio room. Room phones with free incoming calls, hall phones with free outgoing local calls. No A/C. In-house **Sharon's Kitchen** ❶ (☎545-5554; plate lunch, wraps, soups $3-6; open M-F 6:15am-4pm, Sa 8am-4pm). Key deposit $5. Reception 24hr. Check-in 3pm. Check-out noon. No reservations accepted. Single rooms $32. Weekly rooms $175. AmEx/D/MC/V. ❷

MANOA AND THE UNIVERSITY AREA

Manoa Valley Inn, 2001 Vancouver Dr. (☎947-6019; www.manoavalleyinn.com). Take Kapiolani Blvd., S. King St., or H-1 to University Ave. *mauka* (toward the mountains) and turn left onto Vancouver. This cozy, Victorian-style inn is a perfect hideaway from the hurried pace of Honolulu. Complimentary continental breakfast is served each morning on the breezy veranda. Hot tub in the garden. Make reservations at least 1 mo. in advance. Free parking for compact cars. 2-night min. Check-in 3pm. Check-out 11am. Doubles with shared bath $125, private bath $150; cottage with A/C and fridge $170. Reduced rates in low season. MC/V. ❹

Hostelling International Honolulu, 2323A Seaview Ave. (☎946-0591; www.hiayh.org). Turn onto Seaview Ave. from University Ave.; the hostel is opposite the UH campus 4 blocks north of H-1. The best-kept hostel in Honolulu welcomes international travelers with tidy rooms and a calm atmosphere in a mellow residential neighborhood. Free lockers (bring padlock). Linen $2. Key deposit $5. Communal bath, full kitchen, coin-op laundry, and TV lounge. Reception 8am-noon and 4pm-midnight. 3-day max. for non-members, 7-day max. for members. Reserve 2 weeks in advance. Single-sex 6- or 7-bed dorms $16 for members, nonmembers $19; basic 2-person studio (bunk bed, no amenities) $42/48. AmEx/MC/V. ❶

GREATER HONOLULU

Pagoda Hotel and Terrace, 1525 Rycroft St. (☎941-6611; www.pagodahotel.com). From Waikiki, take Kapiolani Blvd. west from McCully St. and turn right onto Kaheka St.; take Kanunu St. to the parking lot on the right. Outstanding rates and promotions make up for a less-than-ideal location. The Pagoda Hotel has standard 4-person doubles and the Terrace building has studios and 1- and 2-bedroom suites with kitchenettes. All rooms have A/C, cable TV, Internet access ($2 per 10min.), and access to 2 pools. The restaurant (p. 104) is accessible by bridge over the water garden. Parking $5 per day. 24hr. reception. Check-in 3pm. Check-out noon. Doubles $102-112; studio $107-127; 1-bedroom $132-173; 2-bedroom $183. Check out "Hot Deal" promotional rates on their website. AmEx/D/MC/V. ❸

Pacific Marina Inn, 2628 Waiwai Loop (☎836-1131, fax 833-0851). Take the frontage road from Nimitz Hwy. outside the airport east to Lagoon Dr.; take a left onto Waiwai Loop, opposite Ualena St. The only place where it's worth paying extra to be so close to the airport and within walking distance of the beach. Pool, cable TV, and massage therapist (☎375-4199) who specializes in *shiatsu, lomilomi,* and foot reflexology to relieve your plane-cramped legs. Free transportation to the airport. Limited free parking. 24hr. reception. Check-in 3pm. Check-out noon. Doubles $79-129; 4- to 6-person suites $165. AmEx/D/MC/V. ❸

FOOD

BY TYPE

AM Ala Moana **C** Chinatown **D** Downtown **G** Greater Honolulu **K** Kaimuki **M** Manoa **W** Waikiki

ASIAN

California Beach Rock 'n Sushi (101)	AM ❸
Ezogiku Noodle Cafe (104)	M ❶
Hale Vietnam (104)	K ❷
Happy Day Restaurant (104)	K ❷
Hong Cafe (102)	C ❶
Indigo's (101)	D ❹
Keo's (126)	W ❸
Kit N Kitchen (103)	M ❸
Legends Seafood Restaurant (102)	C ❷
Little Village (102)	C ❸
Mabuhay Cafe and Restaurant (102)	C ❷
Maharani Cafe (103)	M ❸
Mekong Thai Restaurant (105)	G ❷
O-Bok Korean Restaurant (103)	M ❷
Payao Thai Cuisine (102)	D ❷
Siam Cafe	K ❶
Spices (103)	M ❸
To Chau Vietnamese Restaurant (102)	C ❶
Yabusoba (125)	W ❸

AMERICAN

Restaurant	Area	Price
Andy's Sandwiches and Smoothies (103)	M	1
Dixie Grill BBQ and Crab Shack (101)	AM	2
Pagoda Floating Restaurant (104)	G	4
Rainbow Drive-In (125)	W	1
Top of Waikiki (126)	W	5

ITALIAN

Restaurant	Area	Price
Arancino (125)	W	3
Auntie Pasto's (104)	G	2
C and C Pasta Company (104)	K	4
Palomino (102)	D	4
Petite Garlic (125)	W	3

CAFES AND BAKERIES

Restaurant	Area	Price
Bubbies (104)	M	1
Covenant Books and Coffee (104)	K	1
Leonard's Bakery (126)	W	1
Volcano Joe's Island Bistro and Coffee House (103)	M	1

LOCAL

Restaurant	Area	Price
Kakaako Kitchen (101)	AM	2
Ono Hawaiian Foods (125)	W	2
South Shore Grill (125)	W	1

OTHER

Restaurant	Area	Price
Cha Cha Cha (125)	W	2
Olive Tree (104)	K	2
The Pyramids (125)	W	3
Ruffage Natural Foods (126)	W	1

GROCERY STORES AND MARKETS

Daiei (124)	W
Down to Earth (103)	M
Food Pantry (124)	W
Maunakea Marketplace (102)	C
Manoa Marketplace (103)	M
Oahu Market (102)	C
People's Open Market Program (124)	W
Puck's Alley (103)	M
Safeway (103)	M

BY LOCATION

ALA MOANA

California Beach Rock 'n Sushi, 404 Ward Ave. (☎597-8000). This is *the* place to get authentic sushi. The specialty rolls like Stuntman ($12) and Crunchy Roll ($10) are especially popular. 3-course early-bird special 5-6:30pm $12. Lunch specials $6.50-17. Sake $3.50-12. Lunch M-F 11am-2pm. Dinner M-Th and Su 5-10pm, F-Sa 5-11pm. AmEx/D/MC/V. 3

Dixie Grill Bar-B-Que and Crab Shack, 404 Ward Ave. (☎596-8359). This open-air grill serves up Southern favorites like Dixie's Baby Back Ribs (half slab, $14) in a fun atmosphere. Fire-roasted crab and artichoke dip $9. The Big Pig Jig—1 lb. of smoked and hand-pulled pork—$13. Happy hour 3-6pm; domestic drafts $1, mixed drinks $2, house wine $3. Open M-F 11am-10:30pm, Sa-Su 8am-10:30pm. AmEx/D/MC/V. 2

Kakaako Kitchen, 1200 Ala Moana Blvd. (☎596-7488), at the Ward Center. The flavorful cooking at Kakaako Kitchen is worth the wait in line: plates include Mysoyaki wild salmon, a fire-roasted fillet with wasabi ailoi, $12. Madras curry chicken, served with mango chutney and toasted coconut, $9.25. Gourmet salads $8-10. Sandwiches $7-10. Open M-Th 7am-9pm, F-Sa 7am-10pm, Su 7am-5pm. AmEx/MC/V. 2

DOWNTOWN

The renovated **Restaurant Row,** 500 Ala Moana Blvd., between Punchbowl and South St., houses an assortment of restaurants, nightclubs, gift stores, and theaters. The modern, geometrically designed, open-air structure appeals to a medley of tastes—visitors can choose between 11 restaurants that range from Italian to Thai, and from drive-in to fine dining. From Waikiki head west on Ala Moana Blvd., turn right onto South St., and park in the covered garage.

Indigo's, 1121 Nuuanu Ave. (☎521-2900), next to the Hawaii Theater Center, amid fountains and trees. Indigo's cooks dishes and desserts in a delicious fusion of European and Asian flavors (grilled shrimp and Thai macadamia nut pesto, $24.50; Indonesian sumatra coffee bread pudding with creme anglaise sauce, $6.50). Lunch and dinner reservations recommended. Lunch Tu-F 11:30am-2pm. Dinner Tu-Th 6-9:30pm, F-Sa 6-10pm. D/MC/V. 4

Palomino, 66 Queen St. (☎528-2400), on the Harbor Court mezzanine. To park, drive west on Ala Moana Blvd. 1 block past Aloha Tower Marketplace. Turn right onto Bethel St.; parking's on the right. Palomino's beautiful staircase is just a hint of its impressive interior aesthetics. Affordable thin crust pizzas $9.50-13, dreamy desserts $5-7.50, and seafood paella $20-25. Wine $6-11. Their "First Seating" special (5-6pm) offers a 3-course dinner for under $20. Dinner reservations recommended F-Su. Happy hour daily 4-6pm. Lunch M-F 11am-2:30pm; dinner M-Th and Su 5-10pm, F-Sa 5-11pm. Bar open M-Th and Su until 11pm, F-Sa until 12:30am. AmEx/D/MC/V. ❹

Payao Thai Cuisine, 500 Ala Moana Blvd., #1E (☎521-3511), in Restaurant Row. Known as the "home of sticky rice," served extra-sticky in cute bamboo containers. Payao offers an assortment of affordable, appetizing selections (curries, $8.50-10.50; pad thai, $8.50-10.50), as well as a varied vegetarian menu (all entrees, $7.50). Try Payao's Evil Tofu. Lunch M-F 11am-2pm. Dinner daily 5-9:30pm. AmEx/D/MC/V. ❷

CHINATOWN

While this is the best place to get Chinese, the thrill of Chinatown is hunting through markets for other cheap and delicious ethnic specialties, such as giant bowls of Vietnamese *pho*, Filipino chicken *adobo*, and Korean *kimchee*. Most markets are along N. King St. and Hotel St. and are bounded by River St. and Maunakea St. For fruits and vegetables peruse the outdoor vendors along N. King St.; for fish and poultry, prepare yourself for jarringly fresh-cut meats hanging in the indoor stalls of **Oahu Market,** 145 N. King St., at the corner of Kekaulike St. (Most stalls open around 6am-4pm.) Connected to N. King St. by Kekaulike St., Hotel St. is also populated by fruit and vegetable stands and shops with extensive selections of sun-dried fruit. Inside Chinatown's primary shopping plaza, **Maunakea Marketplace,** 1120 Maunakea St., you'll find fish and poultry vendors, a food court with Chinese, Vietnamese, Thai, Korean, and Filipino fast food (most entrees under $7), and small shops that sell everything from aloha-print t-shirts (starting at 2 for $5) to bubble tea and Thai movies. (Most stalls open around M-Sa 7am-6pm, Su 7am-3pm.) Keep in mind that these are not typical malls and most shops do not accept credit cards. Many vendors sell the same thing so it helps to look around for the best deal.

Little Village, 1113 Smith St. (☎545-3008). Step into this soothing little bamboo village for exquisite, health-conscious Chinese food (no MSG). Signature dishes such as the *szechwan* spicy chicken ($8.25), sizzling scallops ($13.95), and eggplant with garlic sauce ($7.95) will restore your faith in Chinese restaurants. Open Su-Th 10:30am-10:30pm, F-Sa 10:30am-midnight. AmEx/D/MC/V. ❸

Legends Seafood Restaurant, 100 N. Beretania St., Ste. 108 (☎532-1868), in the Chinatown Cultural Plaza. Legends is probably the nicest restaurant in Chinatown, and thankfully, that elegance does not inflate its price. Appetizing dim sum is served the traditional way: from a train of circling carts. The dumplings come in small ($2.15), medium ($3), and large ($4). Open M-F 10:30am-2pm and 5:30-10pm, Sa-Su 8am-2pm and 5:30-10pm. AmEx/DC/MC/V. ❷

To Chau Vietnamese Restaurant, 1007 River St. (☎533-4549). Join the masses for the most unbelievable *pho* noodle soup you've ever had ($4-5.50). Get there early; sometimes a line forms by 9:45am. Open daily 8am-2:30pm. Cash only. ❶

Hong Cafe, 1145 Maunakea St. (☎538-0775). While it may be difficult to choose between several similar Vietnamese restaurants, rest assured Hong Cafe serves the freshest and most flavorful. Spicy stir-fried lemon grass chicken with rice ($6). Service is prompt and friendly. Cash only. ❶

Mabuhay Cafe and Restaurant, 1049 River St. (☎545-1956), next to Riverside Travel on the corner by N. Hotel St. This unassuming cafe/restaurant spices up Chinatown's culinary

OAHU

spectrum with top-notch Filipino food. The tender chicken *adobo* ($8.15), marinated in their special house sauce and served with a huge bowl of rice, makes a good meal for diners not quite ready their *dinuguan* specialty (pork with pig stomach, liver, and blood, $9.15). Open daily 10am-10pm. MC/V. ❷

MANOA AND THE UNIVERSITY AREA

To get to **Manoa Marketplace,** take University Ave. north from H-1 past the UH campus. Bear right to merge with Oahu Ave. and take a quick right onto E. Manoa Rd. The Manoa Marketplace parking lot is after Huapala St., the 4th street on the right. By bus, take Woodlawn Dr. #6 from Ala Moana Shopping Center. The marketplace is where Manoa residents run errands—a quiet area removed from the activity of downtown. The pink buildings are filled with small shops and inexpensive ethnic restaurants (choose among dim sum, sushi, plate lunch, and Korean barbecue). Most establishments don't take credit cards, but there is an ATM in Safeway and at the **Bank of Hawaii.** (Open M-Th 8:30am-4pm, F 8:30am-6pm, Sa 9am-1pm.)

Puck's Alley, at the intersection of University Ave. and King St., around the corner from the Moiliili Post Office, is a strip mall that perfects the collegiate triumvirate of cheap beer, cheap books, and cheap bites, all with appropriate hipness. The A CityExpress bus stops in front of Puck's, or take TheBus #1, 4, 6, or 18.

For groceries, try **Down to Earth,** 2525 S. King St., a reasonably priced health food store with a bakery full of good-for-you (or at least not-too-bad-for-you) goodies. (☎947-7678. Open daily 7:30am-10pm. AmEx/D/MC/V.) There is also a **Safeway,** 2855 E. Manoa Rd., to satisfy those more commercial cravings. (Open 24hr. AmEx/D/MC/V.)

Andy's Sandwiches and Smoothies, 2904 E. Manoa Rd. (☎988-6161), across from Manoa Marketplace. A trip to Oahu is not complete without visiting this 30-year-old Honolulu institution, loved for big sandwiches on fresh homemade bread (fresh roasted turkey sandwich, $4), vegetarian options (mushroom medley, $5), and fruit smoothies ($3.25-5). Open M-Th 7am-5:30pm, F 7am-4pm, Su 7am-2:30pm. AmEx/MC/V. ❶

Maharani Cafe, 2509 S. King St. (☎951-7447), next to Down to Earth. Indian cuisine in a casual atmosphere (an Indian film is always on the TV). The Shahi chicken korma ($10.50), marinated in yogurt and cooked in a creamy spice sauce, is delicious. A range of vegetarian options includes eggplant *tikka masala* ($11). Mango *lassi* $3. Open daily 5-10pm. AmEx/D/MC/V. ❸

Spices, 2671D S. King St. (☎949-2679), on the same block as Kokua Market. Spices dishes up southeast Asian fusion cuisine like the Budda's Delight (a stir-fry of baby vegetables, $13). Tapioca pudding with Okinawan sweet potato topping $4. Parking available behind restaurant. BYOB, $2.50 cork fee. Open Tu-Su 5:30-10pm. MC/V. ❸

Volcano Joe's Island Bistro and Coffee House, 1810 University Ave. (☎941-8449), across the street from the UH campus. This informal island bistro serves an affordable gourmet menu to the university crowd. Get your greens with a salad ($5-8). Sandwiches (chicken guacamole, turkey bacon club, portabella and roasted eggplant, $7-8) are served on baked focaccia bread with salad or fries. Coffeehouse and bakery next door. Day-old muffins and cookies half-price. **Free wireless Internet access.** Free parking behind restaurant. Bistro open daily 11am-10pm. Coffeehouse open M-F 6am-8pm, Sa-Su 7am-8pm. MC/V. ❶

Kit N Kitchen, 1010 University Ave. (☎942-7622), next to Varsity Theater. This offbeat East-meets-West fusion diner offers many types of spaghetti ($8), gratins ($11), pizzas, and specialties for the adventurous (volcano chicken roasted with flaming spicy marinara sauce, $12; ox tail udon, $11). Open daily 11am-2:30pm and 5-10pm. MC/V. ❸

O-Bok Korean Restaurant (☎988-7702), in the Manoa Marketplace. A simple setting to enjoy the barbecue beef short ribs in heaping portions ($8.50). The special plate allows you to sample *Kalbi*, chicken, *Man Du*, and *Na Mul* all at once (with rice, $6.30). Open Tu-Su 10am-8pm. AmEx/MC/V. ❷

Ezogiku Noodle Cafe, 1010 University Ave. (☎942-3608), next to Varsity Theater. Ezogiku has served enormous bowls of traditional ramen since 1968, with a *shoyu* ($5.25), *shio* ($5.50), or *miso* ($5.50) base. Open daily 11am-11pm. Cash only. ❶

Bubbies, 1010 University Ave. (☎949-8984), across Coyne St. behind Varsity Theater. Bubbies offers 16 heavenly homemade ice cream flavors (coconut delight, green tea, and rotating specials; 1 scoop, $2.50-3) and a long list of creative desserts. Try the "come here little girl" ice cream cake (thin mints and Baileys Irish Cream ice cream, $4.55). Mochi ice cream is always popular ($1; chocolate-dipped, $1.50). Full of college students on weekends during the school year. Open M-Th noon-midnight, F-Sa noon-1am, Su noon-11:30pm. Cash only. ❶

KAIMUKI

Olive Tree, 4614 Kilauea Ave. (☎737-0303). This hip and hidden Greek restaurant has an open kitchen and outdoor seating. Don't leave without trying their mussel ceviche appetizer with capers, lime, and herbs ($5) and the lamb souvlakia ($10) served with a Greek side salad. BYOB. Open M-Th 5-10pm, F-Su 11am-10pm. Cash only. ❷

Covenant Books and Coffee, 1142 12th Ave. (☎732-4600), serves a different soup each day, including creamy crab and asparagus, roasted garlic and potato, and lobster bisque ($3.50). Soup with a half salad $6. Open M-Sa 7am-5pm. ❶

Siam Cafe, 3404 Waialae Ave. (☎732-7433). Siam Cafe has probably the freshest and most flavorful Thai food in all of Oahu. Favorites include the calamari and spring roll appetizers ($6-8) and the pad siew, a chow-fun noodle with broccoli in a yellow-bean sauce. BYOB. Open daily 10am-9:30pm. ❶

C and C Pasta Company, 3605 Waialae Ave. (☎732-5999). The rustic dining room and delicious, rich food make the restaurant a cut above Honolulu's other Italian offerings. Sample the trio of bruschetta ($10.50), splurge for the signature *tagliatelle* with sausage ($19), or indulge in peach tiramisu ($7.50). Open for lunch Tu-F 11am-2pm and for dinner daily 5pm-9pm. MC/V. ❹

Hale Vietnam, 1140 12th Ave. (☎735-7581), near Waialae Ave. Locals go for quality Vietnamese food in a comfortable environment: incredible beef noodle soup, delectable appetizer rolls ($7-10), *pho* ($6-8), and entrees like tofu with eggplant and chicken sauteed with lemongrass ($10-11). Open daily 10am-10pm. AmEx/D/MC/V. ❷

Happy Day Restaurant, 3553 Waialae Ave. (☎738-8666). This bright, spacious restaurant serves everything from Chinese/American staples (lemon chicken, $7) to dim sum (around $3) and exotic delicacies (shark fin soup, $33). Most entrees under $10. Open daily 8am-10:30pm. AmEx/D/MC/V. ❷

GREATER HONOLULU

Auntie Pasto's, 1099 S. Beretania St. (☎523-8855), on the corner of Beretania and Pensacola St. Auntie's pasta ($8-11) is authentic enough for any Italian. Eggplant parmesan ($9.50) is a local favorite. Gourmet pizzas $11-13. Wine $3.50-10. Open M-Th 11am-10:30pm, F 11am-11pm, Sa 4-11pm, Su 4-10:30pm. MC/V. ❷

Pagoda Floating Restaurant, 1525 Rycroft St. (☎941-6611), at the Pagoda Hotel. An archipelago of pagoda-style huts connected by bamboo walkways to a central dining room, all "floating" over a *koi* pond. The acclaimed Su brunch buffet features an omelet station, crepes, french toast, and Belgian waffles (10am-2pm; $20). Salad bar and dessert table included with all buffets. Reservations recommended. Open M-Sa 6:30am-10am and for dinner daily 4:30-9:30pm. AmEx/D/MC/V. ❹

Mekong Thai Restaurant, 1295 S. Beretania St. (☎591-8841). Locals often debate the restaurant deserving of the Thai cuisine throne. After satisfying Thai food cravings for 30 years, Mekong is always one of the top contenders. Vegetarian entrees $8.50, green papaya salad $7, and yellow, red, green, and Panang curries $8-10.50. Open M-F 11am-2pm and 5:30-9:30pm, Sa-Su 5:30-9:30pm. AmEx/D/MC/V. ❷

BEACHES

As a rule, the closer you are to Waikiki, the more populated the sand will be. Ala Moana presents a peaceful, nearby option for avoiding the crowds.

ALA MOANA BEACH PARK. *(Open daily 5am-8pm. Lifeguards 9am-5pm.)* Ala Moana means "path to the sea," and the palm tree-dotted park does the name justice. A popular jogging circuit runs around Mamala Bay, which is perfect for an easy swim. The circuit then veers onto **Magic Island (Aina Moana),** a peninsula that juts out on the east side of the bay, separating the beach from the Ala Wai Yacht Harbor. Magic Island may be the best spot in the city to watch the sun dissolve into the sea and sky, casting translucent beams of light through the looming clouds that frequently roll over the mountains. The beach is in front of Ala Moana Shopping Center, on Ala Moana Park Dr. Access driveways are at the western end of the park just past Kamakee St. Or, take TheBus #8, 19, 20, 42, or 58 to the Ala Moana Center. Restrooms and outdoor showers are available.

SIGHTS

DOWNTOWN

HONOLULU ACADEMY OF ARTS. Over 30 galleries display the permanent collection and visiting exhibits of the Academy's classic and contemporary artwork from local and international artists amidst beautifully landscaped courtyards. Notable galleries include the James A. Michener Collection of Japanese *Ukiyo-e* wood-block prints, the Kress Collection of Italian Renaissance paintings, the East Meets West exploration of cross-cultural connections in art, and the impressive John Dominis and Patches Damon Holt Hawaiian art gallery. Works by Picasso, Monet, Matisse, Van Gogh, Gauguin, and Cezanne from their permanent collection are also on display. The **Doris Duke Theatre** (☎532-8768) screens experimental, contemporary, international, and revival films. Refuel at the **Pavilion Cafe** ❷ on the patio, shaded by an ancient monkeypod tree with views of the pavilion's gardens and waterfall. Reservations recommended. (☎532-8734. Feta tapenade and *hauula* tomato sandwich, $9.) **Free wireless Internet access** in the outdoor pavilion areas near the cafe. *(900 S. Beretania St., in front of Thomas Sq. From Waikiki, take TheBus #2 toward town on Beretania. If driving or going to the theater, enter on Kinau St. ☎532-8700; www.honoluluacademy.org. Museum open Tu-Sa 10am-4:30pm, Su 1-5pm. Cafe open Tu-Sa 11:30am-2pm. Parking $3 per 4hr. Guided tours Tu-Sa 11:30am-1:30pm and Su 1:15pm, free with admission. Call ☎532-8726 for group tour information. $7; seniors, students and military $6; children under 12 and members free.)*

ART AFTER DARK. The Academy of Arts hosts Art After Dark on the last Friday of the month. Galleries are open until 9pm with live music, catered food, and drinks. Gallery talks are also given by renowned lecturers. Admission $7.

THE HAWAII MARITIME CENTER. The Maritime Center has much to offer, including one of only five humpback whale skeletons in the world. The 45min. audio tour of the museum chronicles Hawaii's maritime history, from the outrigger ships of

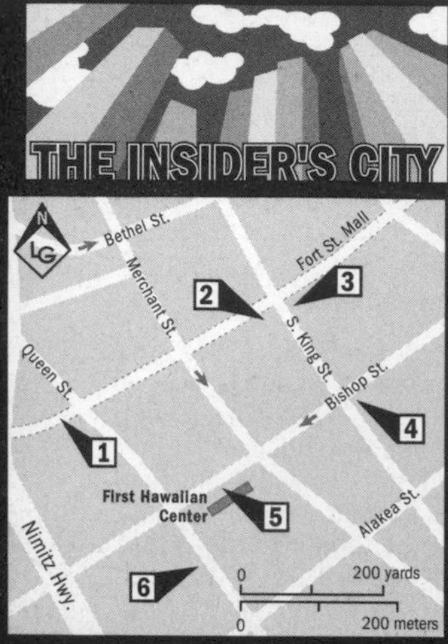

A DOWNTOWN PATH OF PUBLIC ART

The skyscrapers that line downtown Honolulu's Business District may seem bland compared to the rich cultural structures of Chinatown and the Civic Center. Although downtown was once accented with elements of early 20th-century beaux arts, a lot was lost in modern restructurings. Open, palm tree-shaded plazas host a variety of public art. The following path will take you through a selection of the area's modern sculptures. Allow 45min.

1 ***Puna,*** by Sean Browne, 1991. Between Ala Moana Blvd. and Queen St. at the base of the Fort St. Mall. This bronze, fountain-set sculpture was created in the memory of Una Craig Walker, an influential activist for the advancement of art and culture in Honolulu. Her family called her "Puna," short for *kapuna* (grandparent), which also means "spring"—the waters that sustain life.

ancient Polynesian explorers to the present. Admission includes passage aboard the *Falls of Clyde*, the last four-mast, fully-rigged ship in the world, and an exhibit on whaling. *(On Pier 7 at Honolulu Harbor, across from Aloha Tower Marketplace, off Nimitz Hwy. ☎536-6373. Open daily 8:30am-5pm. $7.50, seniors $6, ages 4-12 $4.50, under 4 free.)*

CIVIC CENTER

East of Honolulu's business district, skyscrapers give way to peaceful, open, grassy areas around the Civic Center's government buildings and historic sights. Parking can be tight, though there are metered spots in front of the downtown Post Office at Richards and Merchant St., along King, and on other side streets. Avoid the hassle of navigating and parking by taking TheBus #1, 2, 13, or B CityExpress to S. Beretania and Punchbowl St., at the corner of the State Capitol's grounds.

SAINT ANDREW'S CATHEDRAL. This beautiful French Gothic cathedral, built in stages between 1865 and 1958, sits serenely behind a fountain in which a 10 ft. bronze statue of apostle (and fisherman) St. Andrew stands surrounded by 10 water-spouting fish. The cathedral was named in honor of King Kamehameha IV, who died on St. Andrew's Day in November 1863, after inviting the Anglican Church to Hawaii and donating the land where the cathedral stands today. The magnificent stained-glass Great West Window depicts the life of Christ, the creation of the Anglican Church, and the story of the Church in Hawaii. In the afternoon, the sun casts a colorful shadow on the stone wall adjacent to the stained glass. Organ virtuoso Arlan Sunnarborg plays the enormous Aeolian-Skinner organ every Sunday at the 8 and 10am services. *(On the corner of Beretania and Alakea St., past the State Capitol in Queen Emma Sq. ☎524-2822; www.saintandrewscathedral.net. Mass Tu, Th, F 7am; Su 7, 8, 10am. Office open M-F 9am-5pm. Free historical tours are available after the Su 10am service. Call 1-2 wk. ahead to reserve. All are also welcome to attend services in Parke Chapel daily at 7am.)*

HAWAII STATE ART MUSEUM. In November 2002, the Hawaii State Art Museum opened its doors as the jewel of the Art in Public Places program, which began in 1967. The ongoing exhibit, "Enriched by Diversity: The Art of Hawaii," houses pieces by 284 Hawaiian artists, most of which date from the 1960s to the present. Along with temporary thematic exhibits, the collection has been hailed as one of the most sophisticated and powerful expressions of contemporary Hawaiian identity, often weaving social consciousness and daily experience. Much of the work combines Western aesthetics with traditional Hawaiian and Pacific art forms. Gallery highlights include Jean Charlot's *The Drummer* and Herb Kane's *Discovery of Hawaii.* The unique focus of the museum and the beautiful setting in an old Spanish mission-style YMCA building make this a must-see for all those interested in Hawaiian culture, tradition, and art. *(No. 1 Capitol District Building, 250 S. Hotel St., 2nd fl., west of the State Capitol building. ☎586-0900. Open Tu-Sa 10am-4pm. Tours Tu-Sa 1pm. Call to arrange group tours. Free.)*

HAWAII STATE CAPITOL. This unique building replaced Iolani Palace as Hawaii's capitol building in 1969 and is now the workplace of Hawaii's governor and legislators. The capitol's eccentric architecture supposedly reflects Hawaii's geography and culture: the structure's conical legislative chambers mimic volcanoes that symbolize the birth of the islands. Surrounding concrete pillars that rise like coconut trees represent the eight larger islands, and the encircling moat symbolizes the ocean. The open-air design signifies the openness of Hawaii and its people, welcoming the winds that blow from the sea and over the mountains while the center lies open to sun, sky, and stars.

Across Beretania St., stately **Washington Place** was the home of Hawaii's last reigning monarch, Queen Liliuokalani, and for many years after was the home of Hawaii's governors. Current Governor Linda Lingle is the first governor not to live there, but she still hosts dignitaries and ceremonies in the house. Call the Washington Place Foundation (☎586-0240) for reservations at least 48 hours in advance. *(On the corner of S. Beretania and Punchbowl St. ☎586-0178; www.hawaii.gov/sfca. Building open M-F 8am-5pm. Grounds open 24hr. Free 1hr. tours M, W, F 1:30pm, meet in rm. 415. Groups of 10 or more must reserve 2 wk. ahead.)*

IOLANI PALACE. Hawaii's latter monarchs resided in the "American-Florentine" style Iolani Palace, situated amidst lovely, coral-fenced grounds. Though not mentioned on the tour, Iolani Palace is an important symbol for some Hawaiian sovereigntists, who decry the overthrow of the Hawaiian kingdom for U.S. business interests. The palace was originally built in 1883 for only $360,000 as a show of strength and independence. As the official residence of Hawaii's last royal family, King Kalakaua and Queen Liliuokalani, Iolani Palace is the only state residence of royalty on US soil. After falling into disrepair as the capitol of the subsequent Republic, Territorial, and State governments, the palace has since been restored and maintained by the Friends of Iolani Palace. The building gleams as it did in the

2 ***Three Columns,*** by Arnaldo Pomodoro, 1970. At Fort St. Mall and S. King St. Three cryptic contemporary totem poles echo the verticality and confinement of the surrounding skyscrapers: the bronze and concrete "Colonna Intera Recisa," the bronze "Cilindro Construito," and the stainless steel "Mole Circolar."

3 ***Lt. Robert W. K. Wilcox,*** by Jan Gordon Fisher, 1993. King St. and Fort St. Mall, in Wilcox Park. A bronze sculpture of Lt. Wilcox, nicknamed "The Roaring Lion of the Pacific" for his dogged defense of the Hawaiian Monarchy's independence.

4 ***Upright Motive, No. 9,*** by Henry Moore, 1979. At Bishop St. and King St. in Tamarind Park. This Native-American-, Polynesian-, and Stonehenge-influenced sculpture emerges gracefully from a fountain pool.

5 ***Holualoa and Palani,*** by Deborah Butterfield, 1997. At Bishop St. in front of First Hawaiian Center. A full-size sculpture made from driftwood branches cast in bronze.

6 ***Mauka & Makai,*** by John Tanji Koga, 1995. Bishop St. and Queen St., in Grosvenor Center Plaza. Two taro plants and poi pounder stand in a garden on the Queen St. side of the plaza, representing *mauka* (inland). On the other side, two fish and a fishhook emerge from a bush garden, representing *makai* (ocean).

monarchy's early days; portraits of Hawaiian monarchs hang beside portraits of French, German, Russian, and British leaders. The palace contains one of Hawaii's first telephones, the royal crown jewels, and electric chandeliers, which Kalakaua had installed after meeting Thomas Edison. Still on the grounds is the ancient burial site, *Pohukaina*, which holds the sacred remains of *alii* (royalty). The **Royal Hawaiian Band** plays a free concert Fridays at noon.

The white-pillared building to the right of the palace is the **Hawaii State Library,** which holds the private book collections of several monarchs. *(Ticket office inside the Iolani Barracks, the white structure on the Richards St. side of the grounds. 364 S. King St. ☎538-1471, tour reservations 522-0832; www.iolanipalace.org. Open Tu-Sa 9am-2:15pm. 1½hr. grand tour $20, ages 5-17 $5; no children under 5. Tour leaves every 30min. 9am-2pm. Self-guided gallery tour $6, children under 17 $3, children under 5 $2. Gallery open Tu-Sa 8:30am-4pm, last admission 3:30pm. No cell phones, photos, video cameras, or food. MC/V.)*

ALIIOLANI HALE. Built in 1874, Aliiolani Hale once housed both the legislature and the Supreme Court of the Hawaiian kingdom, and it is the current seat of Hawaii's Supreme Court. Its name, Aliiolani ("Chief unto Heavens"), pays homage to King Kamehameha V, who initiated the planning and construction of the building as a symbol of the stability and prosperity of an independent Hawaiian nation. The **Judiciary History Center** contains a 1913 courtroom, movie theater with educational programming, and exhibits that detail 200 years of Hawaiian legal history, with a special focus on the *kapu* (forbidden) law system and evolution of the complex Hawaiian land structure. Stop in even if you're not a legal history buff; the friendly program coordinators are more than happy to help or just chat. You can't miss the building—one of Hawaii's most recognizable and beautiful landmarks, the **King Kamehameha Statue,** stands in front of it. The gleaming, golden-caped statue honors the man who established the Hawaiian kingdom and united the islands under one rule. *(417 S. King St. ☎539-4994. History center open for self-guided tours M-F 9am-4pm. Guided tours by reservation only. Free.)*

KAWAIAHAO CHURCH. The effort undertaken to construct Kawaiahao Church, the first Christian church in Hawaii, is perhaps the church's most remarkable characteristic. Hawaiians dove 10-20 ft. to chisel out 1000 lb. slabs of coral, 14,000 of which were hauled here for use as bricks in the foundation of the New England-style structure that was dedicated on July 21, 1842. The church gained its name from the sacred spring called *Kawaiahao* ("the water of Hao"), where Chieftess Hao bathed. The church is also home to 21 portraits of various *alii* (royalty) and the tomb of King Lunalilo, the first democratically elected Hawaiian monarch. *(957 Punchbowl St., at the corner of S. King St. ☎522-1333. Open M-F 8am-4pm. Services Su 9 and 11am; all are welcome.)*

MISSION HOUSES MUSEUM. These three 19th-century buildings once formed the headquarters of the Sandwich Island Mission. Various artifacts, including desks, four-post beds, and settees, can be found within the Boston-style houses. You'll also find a replica of the printing press that was the birthplace of the written Hawaiian language. Admission to the houses and to a rotating exhibit may be purchased from the Mission Houses Museum, which leads tours of the mission. *(531 S. King St., past Kawaiahao Church. ☎531-0481; www.missionhouses.org. Open Tu–Sa 10am-4pm, 45min. tours of the mission Tu-Sa 11am, 1pm, and 2:45pm. House tour $10, seniors $8, students $6, children under 5 free. Exhibit $5. Exhibit and tour $13. MC/V.)*

CHINATOWN

KUAN YIN TEMPLE. A strong sense of peace pervades this beautiful, single-room temple dedicated to Kuan Yin Boddhisattva, the personification of compassion and a disciple of Buddha. It is believed she returned to this world after attaining enlightenment in order to help end the suffering of others. *(170 N. Vineyard Blvd., next to the Foster Botanical Gardens. Drive west on Vineyard from H-1 W. to Exit 22 and turn right before Aala St. ☎533-6361. Open 8:30am-2pm. Donations recommended.)*

FOSTER BOTANICAL GARDEN. This beautiful garden is a 13-acre arrangement of tropical plants amassed from across the planet over the past 140 years. Twenty-six of Oahu's "exceptional trees," chosen for their outstanding rarity, age, size, beauty, location, endemic status, or historical and cultural significance, grow in the garden, including the garden's great *Bo* tree, which Hindus and Buddhists both consider sacred. Other notable attractions include the bronze Dhaibatsu statue and the plants in the Prehistoric Glen. *(50 N. Vineyard Blvd. Take H-1 W. or Ward Ave. north from Ala Moana Blvd. to Vineyard Blvd. Turn right into the parking lot after the Kuan Yin Temple, the last drive on the right before the river and Aala St. You can also take TheBus #4 from University to Nuuanu Ave. and Vineyard Blvd. and walk up the block, toward the river. The entrance and visitor parking are on the right past the temple. ☎ reservations 522-7066, info line 522-7065. Open daily 9am-4pm. 1½hr. guided tours included with admission. Tours given M-Sa 1pm or by phone request. $5, ages 6-12 $1, under 5 free. MC/V.)*

IZUMO TAISHA. A distinctive peaked roof and pillared entrance mark Izumo Taisha, a Japanese Shinto shrine. An important remnant of pre-WWII Japanese culture, the shrine is now the site of regular observances, usually on the 10th of the month at 7pm. Instructions for making a prayer and offering are posted at the shrine, or you could consult the Izumo Taishakyo Mission next door on the proper etiquette. *(215 Kukui St. ☎538-7778. Open daily 9am-4pm. Donations kindly accepted.)*

MANOA AND THE UNIVERSITY AREA

THE CONTEMPORARY MUSEUM. This modern, minimalist museum has a pleasant view of Honolulu from the base of Makiki Heights. Exhibits address contemporary visual, performance, and media art, with an educational bent. (A branch of the museum, dedicated solely to Hawaiian art, is in the First Hawaiian Center, downtown at 999 Bishop St.) Here you can see a seasonally rotating exhibit and David Hockney's haunting "*L'Enfant et les Sortileges,*" a permanent audio-visual display inspired by Maurice Ravel's opera about a naughty child's dreamworld. The 3½ acre grounds are interlaced with trails and tropical vegetation. *(2411 Makiki Heights Dr. Take Punahou St. past the YWCA at Vineyard toward Manoa Valley. Turn left on Nehoa St. and right on Mott Smith Dr. Drive until*

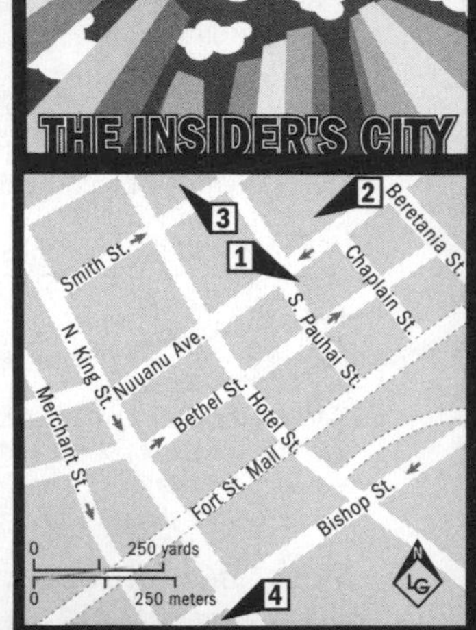

CHINATOWN GALLERIES

An official walk (the first Friday of the month 5-9pm) includes refreshments and entertainment. ☎521-2904; kim@artatmarks.com.

1. **The ARTS at Mark's Garage,** 1159 Nuuanu Ave. (☎521-2903). Offers workshops and exhibitions in theater, dance, sculpture, and painting. Open Tu-Sa 11am-6pm.
2. **The Pegge Hopper Gallery,** 1164 Nuuanu Ave. (☎524-1160). Collection of Pegge Hopper's renowned portraits of Polynesian women. Open Tu-F 11am-4pm, Sa 11am-3pm.
3. **Ramsay Gallery,** 1128 Smith St. (☎537-2787). Displays exquisitely detailed quill and ink drawings. Bring your own magnifying glass. Open M-F 10am-5pm, Sa 10am-4pm.
4. **The Contemporary Museum at First Hawaiian Center,** 999 Bishop St. (☎526-1322). This offshoot of the Contemporary Museum has rotating exhibits of Hawaiian art. Open M-Th 8:30am-4pm, F 8:30am-6pm.

you see the signs for the museum's driveway. Or take TheBus #15 to Makiki Heights Dr. ☎526-0232. Museum open Tu-Sa 10am-4pm, Su noon-4pm. $5, over 62 and students $3, 12 and under free. Guided tours Tu-Su 1:30pm. AmEx/D/MC/V.)

LYON ARBORETUM. The University of Hawaii's 194-acre refuge in the Koolau Mountains holds thousands of tropical plants, some of which have become extinct in their native habitats. Today, in addition to being a beautiful locale, the facility is highly regarded by horticulturalists, conservation biologists, and botanists. The park is open to exploration on a self-guided tour or on the weekly guided tours. A trail map and bird checklist are available at the visitors center. *(3860 Manoa Rd. Leaving Waikiki on McCully St., take the 1st left after the Ala Wai Canal onto Kapiolani Blvd.; turn right onto Kalakaua Ave., then right on King St. Take the 1st left onto Puou St. After Punahou St., Puou becomes Manoa Rd. Go left at the fork in the road, just after Kamehameha Ave. Or, take TheBus #5 to the last stop and walk the remaining ½ mi. up Manoa Rd. The Manoa Falls trailhead is accessible at the base of the hill that leads up to the Arboretum. ☎988-0456. All visitors must sign in at the Visitors Center next to the parking lot. Open M-F 9am-4pm. 1½hr. guided tours are available, call ☎988-0461 for schedule and reservations. Free. Suggested donation $7, students $5, seniors $4, children $3.)*

GREATER HONOLULU

PUNCHBOWL NATIONAL MEMORIAL CEMETERY OF THE PACIFIC. The cemetery lies within the 116-acre Puowaina Crater in northern Honolulu, known as the "Punchbowl" because of its shape. The site of secret *alii* (royal) burials, today it is the resting place of over 33,000 identified and unidentified soldiers from the Spanish-American War to the present. The monument includes a nonsectarian chapel, Courts of the Missing, battle scene tableaus, a dedication stone, and a 30-ft. sculpture of Lady Columbia, who symbolizes all grieving mothers. Anywhere from four to five million visitors pay their respects here each year. The path left of the memorial building leads to an overlook with an amazing view of Honolulu. *(2177 Puowaina Dr. From Kuhio Ave., take TheBus #2, 13, or B CityExpress away from Diamond Head to Beretania and Alapai St., in front of the Honolulu police headquarters. Walk toward the mountains 1 block to the bus stop on Alapai St., and transfer to the #15 Pacific Heights bus, which stops at the cemetery. 10-15min. walk to the memorial building. ☎532-3720. Open daily Oct.-Feb. 8am-5:30pm; Mar.-Sept. 8am-6:30pm. Free.)*

BISHOP MUSEUM. Founded in 1889, the Bishop Museum is the best place to learn about the history and culture of Hawaii. The hefty admission is justified by the spectacular collection of almost 25 million works of art and artifacts, including publications, photographs, films, audio recordings, manuscripts, and millions of animal and plant species, many of which are extinct. The Bishop Museum has the world's best collection of ancient Hawaiian artifacts as well as more contemporary subjects. The chill-inducing Kahili Room, which showcases the *kahili* (feather standards of Hawaiian royalty) and portraits of 19th-century Hawaiian monarchs is a must-see. A program of museum tours, garden tours, planetarium shows, and music, dance, and dramatic performances is included with admission; events take place every 30min. from 10am to 3:30pm. *(1525 Bernice St. From Kuhio Ave., heading away from Diamond Head, take the #2 School St./Middle St. bus to School St. and Kapalama Ave. Walk toward the ocean on Kapalama Ave. to Bernice St. ☎847-3511; www.bishopmuseum.org. 1 free return is allowed within 1 wk. of your ticket's purchase. $15, seniors and ages 4-12 $12.)*

HAWAII NATURE CENTER. The Hawaii Nature Center has a changing schedule of weekly programs for families and adults. Knowledgeable guides lead hikes, answer questions, and can give out a free trail map or a trail guide ($2) that pinpoints some of the plants along featured hikes. The center is also the trailhead of the popular Makiki Valley Loop trail. *(From Ala Moana Shopping Center take Keeaumoku St. beyond H-1 until Nehoa St., then turn right. Take the 1st left onto Makiki St. and bear left at the fork in the road onto Makiki Heights Dr. At the 1st hairpin turn, about ¼ mi. up Makiki Heights Dr., continue straight onto the narrow 1-lane road. Park along the side of the road. Or take TheBus #15 to Makiki Heights Dr. Turn left up the 1-lane road at the 5 mailboxes, walk through a green gate, and continue for approximately ¼ mi. ☎955-0100; www.hawaiinaturecenter.org. Open daily 8am-4:30pm. Free.)*

THE TENNENT FOUNDATION GALLERY. This charming gallery, one of Hawaii's registered historic sites, is dedicated to the artist Madge Tennent. Born in England and considered a child prodigy, Tennent moved to Hawaii in 1923, where she lived until her death in 1972. The large oils show the influence of Gauguin, as they glorify Hawaiian women as the embodiment of nature. Tennent is considered one of Hawaii's greatest artists, and some of her pieces are on permanent loan to the National Museum of Women, in Washington, D.C. *(203 Prospect St. Take Ward Ave. away from Ala Moana Blvd. to the base of Punchbowl Crater and turn left onto Prospect St.; bear right at the intersection, hugging the crater on the left between Huali and Madeira St. ☎531-1987. Open Tu-Sa 10am-noon, Su 2-4pm, or by appointment. Donations appreciated.)*

ARTS AND ENTERTAINMENT

THEATER, MUSIC, AND DANCE

THE KENNEDY THEATRE. On the University of Hawaii at Manoa campus, the Kennedy Theatre is known internationally for its English language presentations of Chinese, Japanese, and Southeast Asian theater and dance. Highlights include plays by local playwrights Lisa Matsumoto and Ed Sakamoto, Indonesian martial arts dance-drama, pidgin versions of Shakespeare's comedies, and the annual dance concert. *(1770 East-West Rd. Take H-1 to University Ave. From University Ave. turn right onto Dole St. and follow it to the corner of East-West Rd. Or, take the #6 Woodlawn Dr. bus from Ala Moana Shopping Center. ☎956-7677, box office 956-7655, fax 956-4234; www.hawaii.edu/theatre. Box office open M-F 10am-3pm, closed in summer. MC/V.)*

HAWAII THEATRE CENTER. Built and opened by Consolidated Theaters in 1922, the Hawaii Theatre Center is now the spearhead of the Honolulu Culture and Arts District, serving as a venue for theatrical, musical, dance, and multi-media performances. It also has an excellent volunteer-run gift shop. *(1130 Bethel St. ☎528-0506; www.hawaiitheatre.com. 1hr. guided tours on the theater's history, art, and architecture Tu 11am, show schedule permitting. Tours $5, reservations recommended. Open Tu-Sa 9am-5pm and 2hr. prior to performances. AmEx/D/MC/V.)*

HONOLULU SYMPHONY. Founded in 1900, the symphony is the oldest orchestra west of the Rocky Mountains. Performances are held at the Neil S. Blaisdell Hall and include performances of works by Tchaikovsky, Brahms, Gershwin, Mozart, and more. *(At the corner of King St. and Ward Ave., in Ala Moana. ☎792-2000; www.honolulusymphony.com. Box office open M-F 9am-5pm, or use TicketMaster ☎888-750-4400. Performances Sept.-May $21-75. AmEx/MC/V.)*

FILM

MOVIE MUSEUM. The museum screens classic, modern, and foreign films as they should be seen: on the big screen, from the comfort of one of the theater's 19 leather recliners. Bring your own concessions; alcohol is permitted but not encouraged. *(3566 Harding Ave. In Kaimuki, 1 block from Waialae's restaurants on 12th Ave. TheBus #1 or 3. ☎735-8771. Open M and Th-Su noon-8pm. 1 movie is screened 4 times daily. Ticket purchase recommended at least 1hr. in advance. $5, seniors $4. MC/V.)*

VARSITY THEATER. The art-house theater shows independent, foreign, and second-run movies. *(1106 University Ave., across from Puck's Alley in Manoa. ☎593-3000 or 973-5835. $8, ages 60+ and 2-12 $6. Matinees before 4pm $6. Cash only.)*

WARD 16 THEATRE. First-run movies show in the highest quality movie theater in town in the Ward Entertainment Center (p. 112). Ward is everything you've come to expect from multiplexes, including the steep price. Get discounts at many of the Victoria Ward Center establishments with a movie ticket stub. *(1044 Auahi St. ☎593-3000; www.victoriaward.com/movie. M-Th and Su $8; seniors and children $6. F-Sa and holidays 4-6pm $8, after 6pm $9; children $6. Before 4pm $6.75, ages 60+ and 2-12 $6. AmEx/MC/V.)*

SHOPPING

PEOPLE'S OPEN MARKETS. These markets provide the chance to buy inexpensive produce from local farmers and fishermen. There are markets in Waikiki's Queen Kapiolani Park (p. 112), Makiki District Park *(1527 Keeaumoku Ave., next to the Makiki Public Library 1 block north of H-1; take TheBus #17, 18, or 83; M 8:30-9:30am)*, City Hall Parking Lot Deck *(At Alapai and Beretania St. M 11:45am-12:30pm)*, Manoa Valley District Park *(2721 Kaaipu Ave., 2 blocks down Lowrey Ave. from the 5-way intersection of Manoa Rd. and Oahu Ave.; M 6:45-7:45am)*, and Old Stadium Park *(2237 S. King St.; W 8:15-9:15am)*. The program is run by the City and County of Honolulu *(www.co.honolulu.hi.us/parks/programs/pom/sked.htm)*.

ALA MOANA SHOPPING CENTER. A tri-level temple of commerce with approx. 1.8 million sq. ft., Ala Moana is the US's largest open-air shopping center. Over 200 of the world's best-known brand names intersect with more than 56 million of the world's sophisticated shoppers each year. Standard mall stores such as Gap and Abercrombie & Fitch stand alongside some of the glitziest names in fashion, including Burberry, Versace, Prada, and Chanel.

The **Honolulu Satellite City Hall,** Ste. 1286., on the first level, provides city job information, camping permits, motor vehicle permits and registration, and TheBus passes. (☎973-2600. Open M-Tu and Th-F 9am-5pm; W 9am-8:30pm; Sa 8:30am-4pm.) There's also a small **post office,** 1450 Ala Moana Blvd., Ste. 1006., on the first level of the mall. (☎532-1987. Open M-F 8:30am-5pm, Sa 8:30am-4:15pm. Last collection M-F 2:30pm. **Postal Code:** 96814.) The Ala Moana Center also has plentiful dining options, with over 25 fine and casual dining restaurants, over 20 specialty food shops, and Makai Market with over 20 international restaurants. *(1450 Ala Moana Blvd., between Ala Moana Blvd., Kapiolani St., Atkinson Dr., and Piikoi St. From Waikiki, take the #8, 19, 20, 42, or 58. The shopping center's private shuttle service—the Pink Line trolleys—runs every 8-10min. M-Sa 9:30am-9:00pm, Su 9:30am-7:30pm through 8 Waikiki stops; one-way $2. For shuttle info, call the Waikiki Trolley Hotline at ☎593-2822. The Customer Service Center, ☎955-9517, near the main escalator on the ground floor, has maps, guides, and shopping center magazines, free wheelchairs, and Ala Moana Gift Certificates. Open M-Sa 9:30am-9pm, Su 10am-7pm. Department stores and restaurants may have different hours.)*

VICTORIA WARD CENTERS. This four-block, seven-center complex mixes old-fashioned markets with modern shops, trying to sell visitors the true island experience in a setting that is decidedly less pretentious (and generally less pricey) than the Ala Moana Center. On the corner of Ward Ave. and Auahi St., **Ward Warehouse** is a bi-level, open-air mall that peddles Hawaiian souvenirs, clothes, and other items. Inside the Ward Warehouse, the helpful staff at the information desk will answer questions, call a taxi, or make restaurant reservations for you. **Ward Centre,** across Kamakee St. from Ward Warehouse, contains art galleries, specialty stores, bars, and restaurants. **Ward Farmers Market,** across Auahi St. from Ward Warehouse, is a quaint row of indoor markets where savvy shoppers can buy fresh produce, seafood, groceries, and various Asian and Hawaiian delicacies. (Markets generally open M-Sa 7am-5pm, Su 7am-1pm.) **Ward Gateway Center,** next to the Farmers Market along Ward Ave., houses several bargain stores across the street from the **Ward 404** restaurant complex. **Ward Entertainment Center,** on the corner of Auahi St. and Kamakee St. next to the Farmers Market, holds both cinemas and upscale shops. (☎597-1243. Open W-Su noon-9pm.) **Ward Village Shops,** across Kamakee St. from the Entertainment Center, has stores like Pier One Imports and Nordstrom Rack. *(Between Queen St., Ward Ave., and Ala Moana Blvd., 1 block west of Ala Moana Shopping Center. Free parking lots and garages have entrances on Auahi St., Kamakee St., and Ward Ave. Take the $2 Waikiki Trolley Yellow Line Shuttle, ☎593-2822, or TheBus #19, 20, or 42 from Kuhio Ave. in Waikiki, or the #6 from the University area. www.victoriaward.com. Shopping hours M-Sa 10am-9pm, Su 10am-5pm; restaurants open later. The Information Center, ☎591-8411, in Ward Warehouse, has free Ward Centers Magazines.)*

NIGHTLIFE

Honolulu has all the tried-and-true nightlife formulas, including laid-back budget dives, sports bars, swanky lounges, and live music venues. Fickle Honolulu crowds—including the surfer boys, socialites, and the ever-changing tourist hordes—ebb and flow from nightlife spots on a daily basis. Most bars close at 2am, though a few popular establishments stay open until 4am.

To keep up with the constantly evolving scene, visit http://quadmag.com for up-to-date event and venue listings and message board posts, or pick up a copy of *Honolulu Weekly* for nightly live music and party listings, free on street corners and stores. *DaKine* magazine, "the voice of Hawaii's Out Community," and *Odyssey* magazine (www.odysseyhawaii.com) frequently list gay-friendly events and nightlife. Both magazines are free and available in stores throughout Honolulu.

ALA MOANA

Pipeline Cafe, 805 Pohukaina St. (☎589-1999). The huge dance floor with a 2000-person capacity fills up fast, especially on Ultimate Tu, when Pipeline breaks out hip-hop and $1 drink specials. Arrive before midnight on Foreplay Fridaze (18+) to skip the lines for the $3 Sex on the Beach. Hip-hop until 4am. Pool tables, dart boards, and a foosball table in the bar upstairs. Happy hour M-F 4-9pm; drinks and *pupus* $2. Dress code for men Tu and F. 21+; F and Sa 18+. Cover $10, F and Sa $12; Ages 18-20 $15. Open M-Sa 4pm-4am. AmEx/D/MC/V.

Mai Tai Bar, 1450 Ala Moana Blvd. (☎947-2900), on the 3rd fl. of the Ala Moana Shopping Center. Mai Tai brings in droves of young, energetic bar-goers with a late-night Happy hour daily 8-11pm; pitchers $6-8, mixed drinks $3, and **Icy Lychee Mai Tais** $4. Live Hawaiian music daily 4-7pm and 9:30pm-12:30am. 21+. No cover. Food served until midnight. Open daily 11am-1am. AmEx/D/MC/V.

Brew Moon, 1200 Ala Moana Blvd. (☎593-0088), on the 2nd floor of the Ward Center. This restaurant and microbrewery (6 original beers on tap) hosts live entertainment during dinner. Tu-Th jazz 7-9pm. Hawaiian music F-Sa 7-9pm. Try one of their brewed beers during the Zero Gravity Happy hour (daily 3-6pm; pints and wine $3, *pupus* $5). Friday night dance party is 18+ after 9pm, cover $10. Open M-Th and Su 11am-11pm (bar until midnight), F-Sa 11am-8pm (bar until 2am). AmEx/MC/V.

MANOA AND THE UNIVERSITY AREA

Anna Banana's, 2440 S. Beretania St. (☎946-5190). This dim hole-in-the-wall is a love-worn Manoa and UH institution, having rocked live music for 35 yr. Excellent Happy hour daily 2-7pm; domestic drafts and bottles $2 and mixed drinks $2.50. Nightly drink specials. The biggest nights are M (open mic at 9pm) and F-Sa (live bands at 10pm). 21+. Cover generally $5. Open daily 2pm-2am. AmEx/D/MC/V. Credit card min. $10.

Magoo's, 1015 University Ave. (☎946-8830 or 949-5381), is a favorite nighttime UH student hangout due to the $1-2 drafts at the open-air bar. Magoo's also bakes a mean pizza ($9.50-30), big enough to justify another pitcher ($5 and up; try the Apricot Ale). 21+ after 9pm. Open daily 10:30am-2am (food until 1am). AmEx/MC/V.

DOWNTOWN

The Green Room and Opium Den at Indigo's, 1121 Nuuanu Ave. (☎521-2900). The party starts at Indigo's with **Martini Madness** (Tu-F 4-7pm; $2.75 martinis and a free mini-buffet of *pupus*). Its 2 bars—the French-themed Green Room and the Chinese-inspired Opium Den—are popular nightspots. DJs and special events Tu-Sa until 2am. Usually live bands on weekdays. Get Fresh! Friday has different visiting DJs and live music. Wine tasting Tu 6-8pm (reservations recommended, $20). Lunch Tu-F 11:30am-2pm. Dinner Tu-Sa 6-9:30pm. Lounges open nightly 4pm-2am. D/MC/V.

Ocean Club, 500 Ala Moana Blvd. (☎531-8444), inside Restaurant Row. Tu Ladies' Night; $2.50 drinks all night. Th Peddler's Night; 21+, wear aloha and skip the $5 cover, margaritas $2.50, Coronas $3. Tu-F 4:30-8pm and Sa 7-9pm, *pupus* half-priced. Dress is "island chic"—no shorts, torn or ripped jeans, or athletic attire for men, and no beach wear, rubber slippers, or athletic attire for women. Music is mostly hip-hop. 23+ every night but Th. After 8pm Tu-F and after 9pm Sa cover $5. Open Tu and F 4:30pm-2am, W-Th and Sa 4:30pm-4am. AmEx/D/MC/V.

Mercury, 1154 Fort St. Mall, Ste. 10 (☎521-2519). Enter on Chaplain Ln. This dimly lit, artsy bar brings in an eclectic crowd. The place is popular among locals, and you'll find the same regulars at the bar on any given night. Drum and Bass Nights (1st F and 2nd Sa) are especially fun. The bar also features local artists' work in rotating exhibits. Ask the bartender for information about displaying your work. Beer $3-4, mixed drinks $3. 21+. Open M-F 4pm-2am, Sa 8pm-2am. MC/V.

HIKING

The pedestrian-only rainforest trails of the **Honolulu Mauka Trail System** lead through a variety of climates within a small area, allowing many unique plants to grow. The most popular trails are the Manoa Falls Trail and the Makiki Valley Loop. The bugs can get aggravating; you may want to pack insect repellent in addition to water and sunscreen. Allow enough time to return with daylight to spare, never hike alone, and always **stay on the trail**—unmarked offshoots and access roads may be private and are not maintained as public recreation routes. Be careful of wild pig and goat hunters while hiking and always wear bright clothing. Drinking or washing in fresh water streams is not advised, as some areas may have *leptospirosis*. Never leave valuables in your car, and respect the land by taking out everything you took in. The trails usually receive cell phone coverage; if you get lost during a hike call the Hawaii Nature Center (☎955-0100; open daily 8am-4:30pm). For more information, go to www.hawaiitrails.org or www.backyardoahu.com.

MANOA FALLS TRAIL. *(¾ mi. one way. Elevation gain: 800 ft. Easy.)* This is one of Oahu's most popular trails, and for good reason. The well-marked path leads from the Manoa Falls parking area through eucalyptus and bamboo groves, over bubbling streams, and by old guava and mountain apple trees. Manoa Falls cascades down a stone face into a pool at the end of the trail. Small fissures in the rock wall contain stacks of rocks left by locals out of respect for

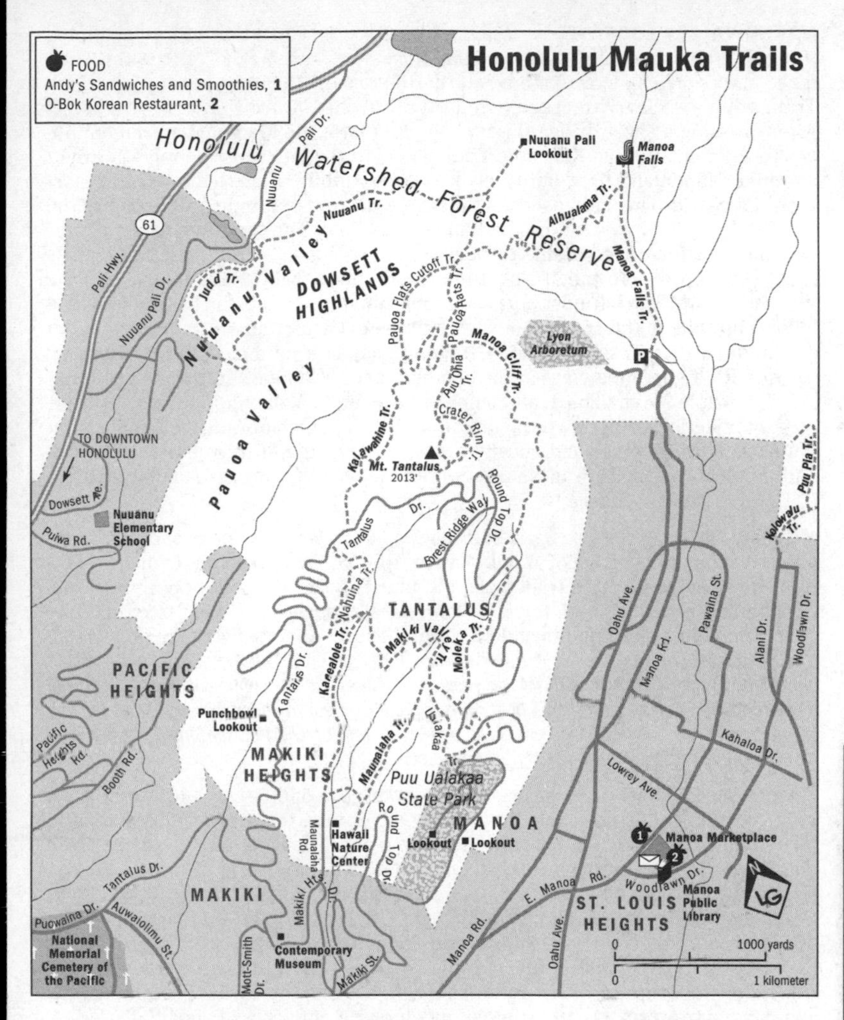

the *mana* (spirit) of the area. Heed the warnings about falling rocks at the falls. *(Do not leave valuables in your car. The trailhead is in the same place as the Lyon Arboretum. See p. 110 for directions. Currently $5 parking is available in a private and guarded lot at the base of the trail.)*

AIHUALAMA TRAIL. *(1½ mi. one way. Elevation gain: 1200 ft. Moderate.)* This trail takes more experienced hikers on a trek that starts 150 ft. before the end of the Manoa Falls Trail and climbs the west ridge of Manoa Valley. Aihualama features bamboo forests and attractive views of Honolulu, Diamond Head Crater, and the valley below. The trail also links the Manoa Valley hikes and the Tantalus area hikes. To get to the Tantalus trails, keep going 1 mi. after the lookout to **Pauoa Flats** and the **Puu Ohia Trail.** Otherwise, return the way you came. *(Follow the directions through the Manoa Falls Trail to the marker for Aihualama.)*

MAKIKI VALLEY LOOP. *(2½ mi. round-trip. Elevation gain: 760 ft. Moderate.)* Combining three Tantalus area hikes—**Maunalaha, Kanealole,** and **Makiki Valley**—this loop takes hikers on a spectacular adventure. Hikers start the loop on the Maunalaha Trail, which is clearly marked behind the Hawaii Nature Center (see p. 110). After crossing a short bridge the trail splits in two: the Maunalaha Trail continues to the right and the Kaneaole Trail begins to the left. Most people veer right and hike Maunalaha first, but to avoid a steep uphill climb, head left and start with Kanealole. This path ascends for three-quarters of a mile and becomes the Makiki Valley Trail just before the Kaneaole Stream. The trail then meets a four-way intersection after passing through a field of Job's Tears, a tall, thick grass that grows up to 5 ft. tall. To continue on the loop, take Maunalaha Trail, the rightmost path. The leftmost *mauka* (mountain) side trail is the **Moleka Trail** (see below) and the middle path (between Maunalaha Trail and a brief continuation of Maikiki Valley Trail) is **Ualakaa Trail,** an easy half-mile path under a canopy forest with a gorgeous view from Diamond Head. Ualakaa Trail ends at Round Top Dr., while Maunalaha Trail completes the Maiki Valley Loop from the four-way intersection back down the mountain through webs of difficult roots from immense Norfolk pines and eucalyptus trees. The steep three-quarter-mile trail ends back above the Hawaii Nature Center. *(See directions to the Hawaii Nature Center,* p. 110. *Area closes at 6:30pm.)*

MOLEKA TRAIL. *(¾ mi. one way. Elevation gain: 300 ft. Easy.)* A short one-way jaunt along the upper east edge of Makiki Valley, Moleka Trail stretches from the Makiki Valley Trail to its other trailhead on Round Top Dr. The path between the two endpoints plunges through thick, wet forest and passes by expansive outlooks over Honolulu's skyscrapers and Mt. Tantalus. *(To reach the Round Top Dr. trailhead, take Keeaumoku St. past the Makiki Public Library. Turn right on Wilder Ave. and take the 1st left onto Makiki St., keeping right at the Makiki Heights Dr. Y-intersection. Continue left at the next split in the road, up Round Top Dr. After about 4¼ mi., there will be a trailhead sign and small parking lot on the left; the trail begins in front of the parking lot and behind the sign. The other trailhead can be reached via the Makiki Valley Trail; see above.)*

MANOA CLIFF TRAIL. *(2½ mi. one way. Elevation gain: 500 ft. Easy.)* Known for its range of indigenous flora and amazing scenic points, this trail climbs gradually through a dense guava and swamp mahogany forest, emerging at an overlook with three waterfalls toward the back and a sweeping view of Manoa Valley. Near the end of the hike, the trail connects with Puu Ohia Trail and Pauoa Flats Trail (see below). If you stick with Manoa Cliff Trail, you'll find that it ends at a 3rd junction, this time with **Kalawahine Trail** (formerly considered part of the Manoa Cliff Trail). Kalawahine Trail delivers you to Tantalus Dr. via a 1½ mi. trek along the contours of Mt. Tantalus through a lush forest that has *koa*, guava, and banana trees, as well as scenic points looking out across Pauoa Valley.

Toward the end of Manoa Cliff Trail, the path intersects **Puu Ohia Trail** on the left. This simple path leads three-quarters of a mile to an overlook at the highest point of Tantalus Crater. Along the way, Puu Ohia passes night-blooming jasmine, wild ginger, Christmas berry, avocado trees, and inspiring views of Honolulu and Diamond Head. Past the Puu Ohia fork, Manoa Cliff Trail meets **Pauoa Flats Trail.** Heading inland, the three-quarter-mile Pauoa Flats Trail traverses through swamp mahogany, wild ginger, and eucalyptus trees before connecting with **Nuuanu Trail,** below. *(Follow the directions to the Moleka trailhead. The parking lot for Manoa Cliff is the same as the one for the Moleka Trail. The trail starts across the street from the parking lot. To reach Kalawahine Trail from the road, head toward the mountains on Tantalus Dr. There will be a sign for the trailhead on the left, next to a private road about 1½ mi. before the Manoa Cliff trailhead.)*

NUUANU TRAIL. *(1½ mi. one way. Elevation gain: 600 ft. Moderate.)* This trail can be reached from Kalawahine Trail or Manoa Cliff Trail. Climbing up the side of Pauoa Valley, Nuuanu Trail catches periodic views of Honolulu and intersects **Pauoa Flats Trail** on the valley side (see above) and the **Judd Trail** on the cliff side (see below). After peaking atop the ridge, the trail continues down to the Nuuanu Valley Floor.

JUDD TRAIL. *(¾ mi. one way. Elevation gain: 200 ft. Easy.)* This trail connects Nuuanu Pali Dr. with the Nuuanu Trail and can be reached from either. If you start from the road, Judd Trail crosses a stream and becomes a loop that takes hikers through damp valley vegetation. The rocks can be slick, so be careful keeping your balance. Midway through the path, the trail connects with **Nuuanu Trail.** *(Take Pali Hwy. away from town and turn right on Nuuanu Pali Dr. Continue approximately 1 mi. until you reach a concrete bridge. The trailhead is to the right, in the clearing. You can park here but be aware that it is a high-theft area.)*

PUU PIA TRAIL. *(1¼ mi. one way. Elevation gain: 400 ft. Easy.)* Gradually ascending through dense vegetation beneath a nearly opaque tree canopy, Puu Pia is a painless hike for almost anyone. The climb begins at the heel of Manoa Valley and reaches a small summit where hikers can survey Honolulu and the surrounding area before heading back down. *(Drive past the Manoa Marketplace on E. Manoa Rd., toward the mountains. Continue for 1 mi. to the end of the road and turn left on Alani Dr. Less than ¼ mi. later the road takes a sharp right and becomes Woodlawn Dr. From here, Alani Ln. continues straight. Park and walk down Alani Ln., past the houses and through a gate. A dirt road leads to the Forestry and Wildlife picnic shelter; the Puu Pia trailhead is on the left.)*

KOLOWALU TRAIL. *(1 mi. one way. Elevation gain: 1100 ft. Challenging.)* Kolowalu Trail is one of the area's most challenging hikes and is for experienced hikers only. The extremely steep trail rises 1100 ft. through dense forest to Waahila Ridge and intersects **Waahila Ridge Trail,** below. *(Follow the directions above until you get to the Puu Pia trailhead; the Kolowalu trailhead is on the right side of the Forestry and Wildlife picnic shelter.)*

WAAHILA RIDGE TRAIL. *(2½ mi. one way. Elevation gain: 500 ft. Moderate.)* Starting from the Waahila State Recreation Area, and skirting the Waahila Ridge above Manoa and Palolo Valleys, this trail passes amazing landscapes and views every turn. The hike is more demanding than others (it rises fairly quickly), though many people enjoy beautiful native plants like *koa* and *ohia lehua* along the way. At the end of the path, there is a junction with the **Kolowalu Trail,** above. *(Take Kapahulu Ave. away from Waikiki and turn right on Waialae. Take the 1st left onto St. Louis Dr. and follow it up the residential area before turning right on Peter Pl. At the cul-de-sac, turn left on Ruth Pl. into Waahila Ridge State Recreation Area.)*

WAIKIKI

From surf swells to sushi to beachside Mai Tais and vibrant nightlife, there's always something going on in Waikiki. Start out on the main drag along Waikiki Beach, Kalakaua Ave., where designer shops, restaurants, and beachside bars host spectacular people-watching. On your beach day, you can plan for boogie boarding and beach volleyball near Kapahulu Pier, surfing at Canoes break on Waikiki Beach, or a more relaxed lounge near the calmer Fort DeRussy and Duke Kahanamoku Beach. Waikiki offers idyllic sunsets, gorgeous weather, and plenty to do: something for every traveler.

The center of tourism in Hawaii's biggest city, Waikiki is less a site of local culture than a thoroughly commercial vacation destination, but the area has an electrifying allure nonetheless. If manufactured gimmicks do not fulfill your culture

Waikiki

ACCOMMODATIONS

- Aqua Bamboo, **1** *D1*
- Aqua Marina Hotel, **2** *A1*
- Aston Aloha Surf Hotel, **3** *D1*
- Celebrity Resorts, **4** *D1*
- Hale Aloha Hostel (Waikiki HI), **5** *D2*
- Hawaiian King, **6** *D1*
- Ilima Hotel, **7** *D1*
- Imperial of Waikiki, **8** *C2*
- Polynesian Beach Club Hostel, **9** *E2*
- ResortQuest Coconut Plaza Hotel, **10** *C1*
- Royal Grove Hotel, **11** *D1*
- Seaside Hawaiian Hostel, **12** *C1*
- Waikiki Beachcomber Hotel, **13** *C1*
- Waikiki Beachside Hostel, **14** *E2*
- Waikiki Gateway Hotel, **15** *B1*
- Waikiki Grand Hotel, **16** *E2*
- Waikiki Sand Villa, **17** *17*

FOOD

- Arancino, **18** *C2*
- Cha Cha Cha, **19** *C1*
- Keo's, **20** *B1*
- Leonard's Bakery, **21** *E1*
- Ono Hawaiian Foods, **22** *E1*
- Petite Garlic, **23** *C1*
- The Pyramlds, **24** *E1*
- Rainbow Drive-In, **25** *F1*
- Ruffage Natural Foods, **26** *D1*
- South Shore Grill, **27** *F2*
- Yabusoba, **28** *C2*

ACTIVITIES

- Aloha Beach Services, **29** *D2*
- Hans Hedemann Surf School, **30** *E2*
- Koa Board Sports, **31** *D2*
- Local Motion, **32** *B1*
- Outrigger Beach Services, **33** *D2*

NIGHTLIFE

- Angles, **34** *C1*
- Diamond Head Grill, **35** *E2*
- Duke's Canoe Club, **36** *D2*
- Fusion Waikiki, **37** *C1*
- Hula's Bar and Lei Stand, **38** *E2*
- Kelley O'Neil's, **39** *C1*
- Moose McGillycuddy's Pub and Cafe, **40** *C1*
- Nashville Waikiki, **41** *D1*
- Scruples, **42** *D1*
- Snappers, **43** *A2*
- Zanzabar, **44** *C1*

SHOPPING

- DFS Galleria, **45** *C1*
- Hyatt Shops, **46** *D2*
- The International Market Place, **47** *D1*
- Royal Hawaiian Shopping Center, **48** *C2*

craving, take an afternoon stroll down the offbeat Kapahulu Ave. on the east end of town, where you can explore a street full of mom-and-pop shops, antique stores, and authentic local eateries.

In 1922, Waikiki's water was diverted into the new Ala Wai Canal, turning the marshland into an epicenter of tourism. Waikiki Beach was built by importing sand onto the Waikiki wetlands, which were a former Hawaiian gathering place. With the completion of the beach, tourism gained an early foothold here, and as a result, a significant portion of today's residents are only temporary visitors. An international melange of travelers and tourists and a smaller contingent of locals consistently crowd the area's streets, shops, sights, sands, and dance floors. To put it simply, if Oahu is "the gathering place," Waikiki is where the party's at.

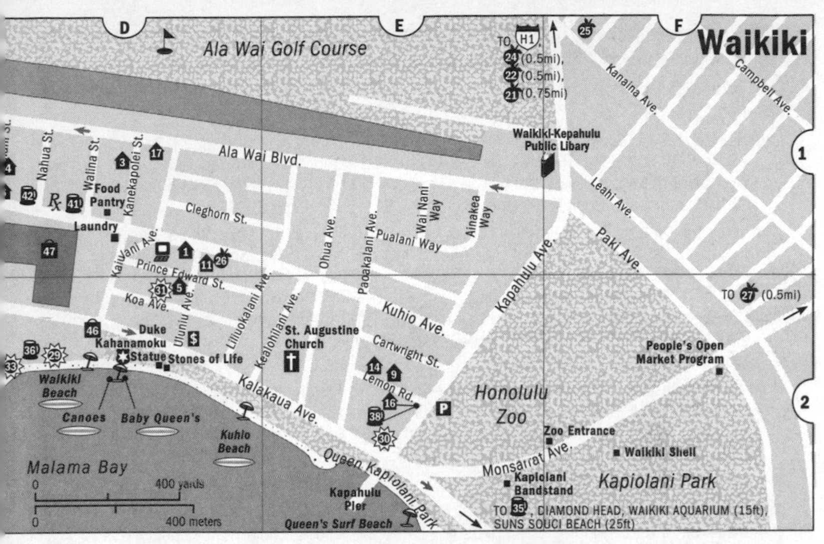

LOCAL TRANSPORTATION

Bus: For help on how to reach a specific destination, call ☎848-5555 5:30am-10pm. Listed below are a few convenient routes that leave from Waikiki. Consult a bus schedule or www.thebus.org for more information.

#2 goes up Kuhio and Kalakaua Ave. through the heart of town (and Chinatown) and back through Waikiki to Kapiolani Park.

#4 goes by the University of Hawaii in Manoa, west through Makiki, and up Nuuanu Ave. into Nuuanu Valley via downtown Honolulu.

#13 goes from the intersection at Kapahulu Ave. and Campbell Ave. up Kuhio and Kalakaua Ave., through downtown, and up Liliha St.

#8 begins its island voyage at Kalakaua Ave. and Monsarrat Ave., exits Waikiki at Kuhio Ave., and finishes at the Ala Moana Shopping Center.

#19 leaves Monsarrat Ave. and Kalakaua Ave. for Kapahulu Ave., Waikiki and the Ala Moana Shopping Center, downtown, and finally, the airport and Hickam AFB.

#20 follows the route of #19 to the airport, heading to Pearlridge Shopping Center, near the Pearl Harbor memorial and Aloha Stadium.

#22, known as the **Beachbus,** starts at the northwest end of Waikiki at Pau St. and Ala Wai Blvd., turns around at Niu St. onto Kalakaua Ave. and then Kuhio Ave. The Beachbus continues on to the intersection of Kapahulu and Paki Ave., up Diamond Head Rd., and by Kahala Mall. It then jumps on to the Kalanianaole Hwy. to Hanauma Bay, Sandy Beach, and Makapuu Beach, ending at Sea Life Park.

#42 leaves Waikiki via Ala Moana Blvd. and heads west through downtown to Waipahu and Ewa.

#58 leaves Ala Moana, goes through Waikiki east to Hawaii Kai and Sea Life Park, continues around through Waimanalo and Kailua, and then heads back to Ala Moana.

Trolley: Waikiki Trolley (☎593-2822; www.waikikitrolley.com) runs 3 lines: Red (Honolulu City Line), Blue (Ocean Coast Line), and Pink (Ala Moana Shopping Shuttle Line) from 8:55am-8:10pm. 1-day tickets: $25, children $1, seniors $18. Check online or call for up-to-date route schedules.

Taxis: Waikiki is small—a ride across the district is around $6. Taxis to the airport are expensive ($25-30); it is wise to arrange transportation through your hotel or hostel, or via the myriad airport shuttle services ($7). **Charley's Taxi & Limousine** (☎955-2211) has 24hr.

service to most of Oahu. Base $2.45, $2.80 per mi. **The Cab** (☎422-2222) offers 24hr. island-wide service. $2.75 for the first ¼ mi., $3 per mi.

Car Rentals: Keep in mind that rates can differ significantly based on season and branch location.

Enterprise, 1888 Kalakaua Ave., #C107 (☎979-2600; www.enterprise.com), or 445 Seaside Ave., Ste. 3C facing Nohohani St. (☎922-0090). Standard daily rates: compacts $55, mid-size $61, standard $65. Collision Damage Waiver (CDW) $17 per day. Free pick-up and drop-off. No under-25 surcharge. Open M-F 7am-6pm, Sa-Su 8am-5pm. AmEx/D/MC/V.

Paradise Rent-a-Car, 355 Royal Hawaiian Ave. (☎924-7777), 200 Lewers St. (☎924-2222), 151 Uluniu Ave. (☎926-7777), 1867 Kalakaua Ave. (☎946-7777), and 1843 Ala Moana Blvd (☎943-6877). Standard daily rates: compacts from $29, mid-size from $40, Jeeps $70, Mustangs $80. 3-day min. The Royal Hawaiian Ave., Lewers St., and Uluniu Ave. shops rent bikes ($15 per 24hr., $75 per week), mopeds ($35 per 24hr.), and motorcycles ($179 per 24hr.) as well. CDW $19 per day. Under-25 surcharge $10 per day; under-21 surcharge $20 per day. Open daily 8am-5pm. AmEx/D/MC/V.

VIP Car Rentals, 2463 Kuhio Ave. (☎924-6500), 234 Beachwalk (☎922-4605), and 1944 Kalakaua Ave. (☎946-7733). VIP rents older, less expensive cars. Standard daily rates: compacts from $30, mid-size from $54. 3-day rentals get $13 off the first day. CDW $14 per day. Open daily 7am-5pm. AmEx/MC/V.

Moped and Motorcycle Rentals:

Hawaiian Peddler, 2139 Kuhio Ave. (☎926-5099 or 382-9049 for reservations). Offers personal service and a wide selection of mopeds (8am-4:30pm $35, overnight $40) and Jeeps ($95 per day). Their pride and joy are the Harley-Davidsons (8am-4:30pm $140). They also rent bikes ($21 per 24hr.) and watersports equipment. Ask about promotions and special rates. Discounts for longer rentals. Open daily 8am-4:30pm. D/MC/V.

Moped Direct, 750A Kapahulu Ave. (☎732-3366), about ½ mi. outside of Waikiki past the Ala Wai Golf Course. Generally has the lowest rates and loans out helmets for free. Mopeds 8am-4pm $15-20, overnight $25-30, weekly $100. 18+. Open M-F 9am-6pm, Sa-Su 9am-5pm. Credit card or driver's license required. AmEx/D/MC/V.

ORIENTATION

Waikiki's boundary is defined on the north and west by the Ala Wai Canal, on the south by its beaches, and on the east by Diamond Head Crater. Three main thoroughfares run Waikiki's two-mile length from east to west: **Ala Wai Boulevard** runs parallel to the canal with one-way traffic going west; **Kalakaua Avenue** runs by the ritziest hotels and beaches with one-way traffic going east; **Kuhio Avenue** splits off Kalakaua Ave. at the western end of Waikiki and bears the brunt of the two-way traffic all the way to **Kapahulu Avenue** on the east end of town. The three main east-west streets intersect numerous one-way side streets, which are confusing when on the road—drivers should carry a good map.

The Ala Wai Canal is a scenic area that is popular with joggers and walkers, but its distance from major tourist areas makes it the least safe part of Waikiki at night. The district on the whole is safe, and the Waikiki Police Substation is located centrally near the **Duke Kahanamoku Statue** on Kalakaua Ave. It's safest around the intersection of Kalakaua Ave. and Kuhio Ave., which is noisy with unending traffic during the day and the occasional moped pack at night. Kalakaua Ave. is more for show than transportation: it has no bus traffic, loads of pedestrians, and all manner of street performers and vendors. The edges of Waikiki, up Kapahulu Ave. or along Kalakaua Ave. toward Diamond Head, may be less safe after dark.

To get to **H-1 West** from Kalakaua Ave. or Kuhio Ave., make a left onto Kapahulu Ave. Take Kapahulu past Kaimuki, under the H-1 overpass and left on Waialae Ave., following the signs to merge onto H-1. For **H-1 East** take Ala Moana Blvd. over the canal, leaving Waikiki, and turn right on Atkinson Dr., then right again on Kapiolani Blvd. toward H-1.

PRACTICAL INFORMATION

TOURIST AND FINANCIAL SERVICES

Tourist Information: Hawaii Visitors and Convention Bureau Information Office, 2270 Kalakaua Ave., Ste. 801 (☎923-1811; www.gohawaii.com), in the Waikiki Business Plaza. A friendly office with free tourist magazines. Open M-F 8am-4:30pm.

Tours: See **Honolulu, Practical Information,** p. 95.

Banks:

American Savings Bank, 321 Seaside Ave. (☎923-1102), in the Waikiki Business Plaza. Currency exchange fee 3%. Open M-Th 9am-4:30pm, F 9am-6pm.

Bank of Hawaii, 2228 Kalakaua Ave. (☎543-6900). Currency exchange fee $2 by 24hr. machine. Open M-Th 8:30am-4pm, F 8:30am-6pm.

First Hawaiian Bank, 2181 Kalakaua Ave. (☎844-4444). Currency exchange fee $3-5. **24hr. ATMs** outside. Open M-Th 8:30am-4pm, F 8:30am-6pm.

LOCAL SERVICES

Library: Waikiki-Kapahulu Public Library, 400 Kapahulu Ave. (☎733-8488), across from Leahi Ave., before the Ala Wai Golf Course. Internet access available with a 3-month visitor's card ($10). Open Tu-W and F-Sa 10am-5pm, Th noon-7pm. Printing $0.10 per page; color $0.20 per page. 3 internet terminals available; call to reserve.

Laundromats: Waikiki Laundromats (☎923-2057) operates numerous self-serve, coin-operated laundromats in Waikiki that are on hotel premises, but are open to the public. One is in the Ohana East, 150 Kaiulani Ave., at the corner of Kuhio and Kanikapolei. Wash $1.75; dry $1 per 20min. Open daily 6:30am-11pm.

Weather/Surf Conditions: See Honolulu and Waikiki Information Lines, p. 97.

EMERGENCY AND COMMUNICATIONS

Police: Waikiki Substation, 2425 Kalakaua Ave. (☎529-3801), in the Duke Paoa Kahanamoku Building on Waikiki Beach opposite the Hyatt Regency. Officers are on foot patrol throughout Waikiki to offer information. Open daily 10am-11pm.

Crisis Lines: Sex Abuse Treatment Center, 55 Merchant St., 22 fl. (☎524-7273). 24hr. crisis hotline, medical and legal exams, counseling and education.

Red Cross: American Red Cross, Hawaii Chapter (☎734-2101).

Medical Services: Urgent Care Clinic of Waikiki, 2155 Kalakaua Ave., Ste. 308 (☎924-3399), at Beachwalk above Planet Hollywood. Accepts walk-ins. Free ride to clinic; call for information. Open daily 8:30am-7pm, last patient 6pm. **Straub Doctors on Call Waikiki:** ☎971-6000.

Pharmacy: Prince Kuhio Pharmacy, 2330 Kuhio Ave. (☎923-4466, fax 922-1104). Open daily 7:30am-10pm. Prescription pickup M-F 9am-5pm, Sa 9:30am-4:30pm. AmEx/D/MC/V.

Internet Access: Internet Cafe and Beautiful Day Tours, 2161 Kalia Rd., Ste. 110 (☎922-0000), behind the Outrigger Shore Resort, offers high-speed Internet access. $2 for the first 10min., $1 each additional 10min., $6 per hr. Copies $0.25 per page. Fax $0.25 per page. Open M-Sa 8am-8pm, Su 8am-5pm. Cash only. **Wiki Wiki Cyber Cafe,** 2301 Kuhio Ave., Ste. 2 (☎923-9797), also has high-speed Internet access. $1 per 10min. Open daily 10am-10pm. MC/V.

Post Office: Waikiki Post Office, 330 Saratoga Rd. (☎973-7515). Open M-F 8am-4:30pm, Sa 9am-1pm. Last collection M-F 4:30pm, Sa 12:30pm.

Postal Code: 96815.

LARGER THAN LIFE

After 2000 years, it seemed impossible for an athlete of non-Japanese descent to win the grand championship sumo tournament and be promoted to the highest rank *(yokozuna)*. Hawaii native Chad Rowan achieved the impossible in 1993, becoming the first foreign born wrestler to be promoted to Sumo Grand Champion.

Rowan was convinced to try the sport by a recruiter looking for a Hawaiian wrestler. Previous success with Samoan and Tongan wrestlers suggested Hawaiians might possess the elusive sumo gene.

Although he was considered lanky for a wrestler, Rowan had a unique talent for proving people wrong if they thought he couldn't do something. Contrary to everyone's expectations, he won several tournaments in 1992 and was promoted to top rank after winning the title in 1993.

After Rowan's success as a wrestler, sumo became more popular in Hawaii. The islands have hosted several exhibition matches, and there is now a Hawaii Sumo Club for amateur wrestlers in Haula. The town of Waimanalo even commissioned and gave her a life-sized, bronze sculpture of her son to keep outside the store in the town center. Like Rowan himself, the statue is immense, both weighing in at close to 600 lb.

ACCOMMODATIONS

As Oahu's center of tourism, Waikiki is not short of places to stay. Hotels dominate the skyline, and some have quite inspiring views 30 floors above Waikiki. Travelers should ask to see rooms before paying extra for any view, be it ocean, mountain, or "city" (which can range from a lit-up, panoramic Honolulu landscape to the slightly less exhilarating ABC Store or parking garage across the street). Most hotels offer rotating promotions and discounts that can result in significant savings. The prices listed below are standard rates, but be sure to ask about current deals and Internet prices, which can be substantially lower than the prices listed here. Many hotels participate with Internet wholesalers like Priceline, Expedia, or Hotwire. Unless otherwise noted, all accommodations have A/C and 24hr. reception, check-in at 3pm, and check-out at noon.

HOSTELS

These establishments are "travelers only," so be prepared to show out-of-state identification and a departing ticket at check-in.

Waikiki Beachside Hostel, 2556 Lemon Rd. (☎923-9566; www.waikikibeachsidehostel.com). Follow Kalakaua Ave. east toward Diamond Head. Turn left on Kapahulu Ave. and take the 1st left onto Lemon Rd. Guests share animated night-time conversations on patios overlooking a parking lot-turned-courtyard (with a big-screen TV). The hostel also rents surfboards, boogie boards, and snorkel equipment (all $10 each) for the day. Continental breakfast included. Lockers $3. Coin-op laundry. Internet cafe on premises ($1 per 10min.). Parking $5 per night. 2-week advance reservations recommended. 30-day max. 8-bed dorm $23, $145 per week; 4-bed dorm $32/$205; semi-private rooms $68/$438. 7th consecutive night half-off in low season. Ask about long-term work. AmEx/D/MC/V. ❶

Polynesian Beach Club Hostel, 2584 Lemon Rd. (☎922-1340; http://hostelhawaii.com), near the Waikiki Beachside Hostel. The Polynesian Beach Club welcomes guests with a friendly, low-key atmosphere. Open-air common room with cable TV and several hammocks strung from the ceiling. Group activities include soccer, barbecues, cocktail parties, hikes to Diamond Head, and a sunset sail. Guests have free use of boogie boards, snorkel gear, safety deposit boxes, and storage. 10pm quiet hour. Continental breakfast included. Coin-op laundry. Internet access $1 per 10min., $5 per hr. Check-out 10am. 2-week max. 4-person dorms (all co-ed) $23; semi-private double $45-54; private studio with kitchenette $67. Ask about short-term work. MC/V. ❶

Seaside Hawaiian Hostel, 419 Seaside Ave. (☎924-3303; www.seasidehawaiianhostel.com). Turn left onto Seaside Ave. from Kalakaua Ave. Take Seaside past Kuhio Ave. and turn right down the alley just before Manukai St. Turn left at the end of the alley; Hawaiian Hostel is 50 ft. back. This hostel manages to survive among giants by offering cheap and clean basic accommodations to young travelers. Amenities include cable TV in the courtyard, free Internet access, and free use of boogie boards and snorkel equipment. Communal kitchen and breakfast included. $20 refundable deposit covers linens, a padlock, and key. Coin-op laundry. Reception daily 6am-10pm. Check-out 10am. Single-sex, 6-bed dorm with full bath $23; co-ed $20; semi-private single $39; private double $54. MC/V. ❶

Hale Aloha Hostel (HI Waikiki), 2417 Prince Edward St. (☎926-8313). Head up Kaiulani Ave. from Kalakaua Ave. and turn right onto Prince Edward St. Hale Aloha offers quiet, standard accommodations. Guests share a large and comfortable common room with a kitchen and cable TV. Hale Aloha also provides a $6 shuttle ride to the airport. Lockers in all rooms (provide your own padlock). Coin-op laundry. Internet access $1 per 10 min. Reception daily 7am-3am. 7-day max; extended stay possible depending on availability. Non-member prices: 6-bed dorm $23; private studio $54. Member prices are slightly discounted. AmEx/MC/V. ❶

HOTELS

Waikiki Grand Hotel, 134 Kapahulu Ave. (☎923-1814; www.waikikigrand.com). Turn left on Kapahulu from Kalakaua Ave.; the Waikiki Grand is on the left. The hotel rents out privately owned, recently renovated luxury vacation units; amenities include a swimming pool, coin-op laundry, and limited parking ($10-12 per night). Hula's bar is on the 2nd fl. Reservations recommended 1 month in advance. Studios for 2 start at $115; $700 per week. Rates sometimes drop to $85 per night during the low season. Suites for 4 start at $169, $1078 per week. AmEx/D/MC/V. ❹

Aqua Bamboo, 2425 Kuhio Ave. (☎922-7777; www.aquabamboo.com). The units and hallways in this boutique hotel are accented with a cool beige and black decor and a bamboo motif. The small pool is surrounded by a beautiful garden area, spa, and sauna. Guests receive discounts at Waikiki restaurants. "Bamboozled!" cocktail reception held on Th. Continental breakfast. 4-person studio with kitchenette $190; 4-person family suite with full kitchen $240. See website for discounts. AmEx/D/MC/V. ❺

The Imperial of Waikiki, 205 Lewers St. (☎923-1827; www.imperialofwaikiki.com). Take Lewers St. toward the beach from Kalakaua Ave. The Imperial is part timeshare and part hotel, with a sense of community and an approachable staff. 20th-floor roof-top sun deck with pool, hot tub, and ocean view. 3-day min. during high season. Check-in 4pm. 4-person studio $173-185; 6-person suite $205-218. Under 12 free without extra bed; extra bed $10. Check website for promotional rates. AmEx/D/MC/V. ❺

Waikiki Sand Villa, 2375 Ala Wai Blvd. (☎922-4744; www.waikikisandvillahotel.com). Take Kalakaua Ave. to Kanekapolei St. and turn left. The Waikiki Sand's newly renovated rooms, wrap-around lanais, large pool, and hot tub are almost enough to make guests forget the distance to the ocean. Friendly staff, on-site bar (open noon-4am), rental shop, and fitness center. Breakfast included. Parking $9 per night. Check-out 11am. Double with private lanai, cable TV, mini-fridge, and coffee maker $109-160; 4-person studio with full kitchen $190. Under 18 free without extra bed; each additional person $25. Check website for discounts. AmEx/D/MC/V. ❸

Hawaiian King, 417 Nohonani St. (☎922-3894). Drive down Ala Wai Blvd. and turn left on Nohonani. Amenities include pool, coin-op laundry, and wireless Internet access in lobby and pool-side. Guests also have access to the Waikiki Sand Villa, including the large swimming pool, jacuzzi, fitness center, and complimentary breakfast. Check-out 11am. Singles and doubles $105, weekly rate $95 per night. AmEx/D/MC/V. ❸

Waikiki Gateway Hotel, 2070 Kalakaua Ave. (☎955-3741; www.waikikigateway.com), on Kalakaua Ave. before Olohana St. just after the Kuhio Ave. split. The Waikiki Gateway offers standard hotel rooms close to Ft. DeRussy Park at reasonable prices. All rooms have cable TV and a fridge, and the lower floors have a private lanai. Breakfast included. Parking $9.50 per day. Check-in 3pm. Check-out 11am. Singles and doubles $65-105, with kitchenette $120-180. Under 12 free without extra bed; extra bed $15. Website discounts. AmEx/D/MC/V. ❸

Ilima Hotel, 445 Nohonani St. (☎923-1877; www.ilima.com). The Ilima is centrally located 1 block from the canal down Nohonani Pl. Paintings by Hawaiian artist Ralph Kagehiro complement the neat and well-kept lobby. Good-sized private lanais and unobstructed Ala Wai views outside of some rooms, and nothing but cleanliness within. All rooms have full kitchen and cable TV. Guests have access to the fitness room and swimming pool. Free parking and Internet access. Dec. 21-Mar 31. doubles $157-220; suites (sleep 4) $160-180. Apr.-Dec. 20 save $10 on studios, $20 on suites. Children under 17 free with parents at full rate and no extra bed. Each additional guest $10. Check website for promotions. AmEx/D/MC/V. ❺

Aqua Marina Hotel, 1700 Ala Moana Blvd. (☎942-7722; www.aquaresorts.com/marina). Turn right onto Ala Moana Blvd. from Kalakaua Ave. The low rates and beautiful view from the upper floors of this sleek high-rise make up for its distance (about a 15 min. walk) from Waikiki Beach. Amenities in the condo-style hotel include a large tennis court, swimming pool, and hot tub. All available daily 9am-9pm. Rooms have a cable TV, safe ($2 per day), high speed Internet and full kitchen. Parking $15 per 24hr. Reception daily 7am-8pm. Studios (sleep 2) $119-133. Roll-away $17. Check online or call for discounts based on occupancy and availability. AmEx/D/MC/V. ❹

ResortQuest Coconut Plaza Hotel, 450 Lewers St. (☎923-8828; www.resortquesthawaii.com), down Ala Wai Blvd. and an immediate left up the driveway after Lewers St. The spotless Coconut Plaza is a corporate chain hotel on the Ala Wai Canal with affordable rates, owing to its distance from central Waikiki. Standard rooms in this old-fashioned hotel have a private lanai with city view, microwave, cable TV, data port, and a pleasing floral motif. Swimming pool. Breakfast included. Valet parking $9 per day. Doubles $115; studio with kitchenette (sleeps 3) $135-145; junior suite with kitchenette (sleeps 5) $195. Rates depend on the season, and their website's rates are usually cheaper. AmEx/D/MC/V. ❹

Waikiki Beachcomber Hotel, 2300 Kalakaua Ave. (☎922-4646; www.waikikibeachcomber.com). The Waikiki Beachcomber is sandwiched between the International Marketplace and Duke's Lane, across from the Royal Hawaiian Shopping Center and Waikiki Beach. Location like this is pricey, but the Beachcomber rewards guests with an attentive staff and full entertainment agenda. The Don Ho, Magic of Polynesia, and Blue Hawaii (Elvis) shows take place several times each week. Swimming pool and hot tub. Standard singles and doubles from $230, but check online for discounts. 3rd person or roll-away bed $30 per day. Children under 17 stay free with parents and no extra bedding. AmEx/MC/V. ❺

FOOD

With everything from tempting tourist traps to hidden local eateries, Waikiki is full of good places to dine. If you're on a tight budget, stocking up at a grocery store and cooking in hostel kitchens or hotel kitchenettes is an inexpensive way to keep fortified and beach-ready. Head to **Daiei,** 801 Kaheka St. (☎973-4800), a cavernous Japanese supermarket with everything from imported Asian foods to home appliances and electronics. (Open daily 24hr. AmEx/D/MC/V.) **Food Pantry,** 2370 Kuhio Ave. (☎923-9831), has a much better selection and lower prices than the ubiquitous ABC stores. (Open daily 6am-1am. AmEx/D/MC/V.) Finally, the unique **People's Open Market Program** (☎522-7088), in Kapiolani Park at Monsarrat and Paki St., sells fresh produce from local farms. (Open W 10-11am. Cash only.)

RESTAURANTS

The Pyramids, 758-B Kapahulu Ave. (☎737-2900). Although Egypt isn't exactly at the crossroads of the Pacific, this place still mixes up excellent Egyptian and Mediterranean cuisine. Live belly dancers perform nightly at 7:30 and 8:30pm. Huge bowl of hummus $6. *Tabouleh* salad $5. All-you-can-eat lunch buffet $11 (daily 11am-2pm). Dinner reservations recommended F-Su. Lunch daily 11am-2pm; dinner M-Sa 5:30-10pm, Su 5-9pm. AmEx/D/MC/V. ❸

Petite Garlic, 2238 Lauula St., 2nd fl. (☎922-2221). Turn onto Royal Hawaiian Ave. from Kalakaua Ave., and make the 1st right onto Lauula. This small cafe/kitchen/wine bar is at once classy, chic, and chill, with a warm and intimate atmosphere. An exquisite experimental blend of Eurasian cuisine uses the freshest garlic and herbs. Entrees range from garlic rice ($12) to Kona lobster ($24). Salads $8-14. Desserts $5.50. Wine $6.25-8. Mixed drinks $5-6. Open daily 6pm-2am. AmEx/MC/V. ❸

South Shore Grill, 3114 Monsarrat Ave. (☎734-0229), ½ mi. stroll toward Diamond Head from Kapiolani Park. TheBus #13 or 22. This local diner serves up fresh and healthy dishes for a reasonable price. The barbecue chicken plate ($5.75) cooked Korean-style is generous enough for a day without breakfast. Other specialties are the grilled mahi mahi sandwich ($5.75) served on a giant ciabatta roll and the Caprese sandwich ($4.25) with fresh buffalo mozzarella and tomatoes. Open daily 10:30am-9pm; all orders after 8:30pm are takeout only. ❶

Cha Cha Cha, 342 Seaside Ave. (☎923-7797). Turn left down Seaside Ave. from Kalakaua Ave. and look for the tiki torches on the left. Cha Cha Cha shakes it up right with 2 Happy hours (daily 4-6pm and 9-11pm; flavored margaritas $2.50) and a fun Caribbean-Mexican menu (El Cheapo Burrito, $7; Jamaica-Me-Crazy Enchiladas, $12). You can spice things up even more with their salsa bar; try the Cholula, Jump Up and Kiss Me, or Wrong Number Chipotle Habanero Sauce. Show a copy of *Let's Go Hawaii* for a **free basket of chips and salsa.** Open daily 11:30am-11pm. MC/V. ❷

Arancino, 255 Beachwalk Ave. (☎923-5557). This small Italian restaurant has lines of people outside waiting for food bursting with big, bona-fide flavor. Candle-lit tabletops and traditional Italian music create an intimate escape from the many tourist traps of Waikiki. Spaghetti with meatballs $13. Pizzas $12-17. Homemade tiramisu $7. Half-bottle of wine $12. Open daily 11:30am-2:30pm and 5-10pm. AmEx/D/MC/V. ❸

Rainbow Drive-In, 3308 Kanaina Ave. (☎737-0177), a 15min. walk down Kapahulu Ave. until it intersects Kanaina Ave. The faded rainbow roof, burnt-out neon rainbow light, and parking lot packed with locals are testaments to Rainbow Drive-In's long-established reputation as a premium provider of plate lunches. Try the Mix Plate ($6) with steak, mahi mahi, and chicken. Open daily 7:30am-9pm. Cash only. ❶

Ono Hawaiian Foods, 726 Kapahulu Ave. (☎737-2275), about ½ mi. from Kalakaua Ave., past Rainbow Drive-In on the left. For over 40 years Ono has been serving the most traditional Hawaiian foods, from *pipikaula* (Hawaiian beef jerky) to *poi*. *Kalua* pig, *lau lau*, or chicken long rice plates come with *pipikaula*, *lomi* salmon, *haupia*, rice, and *poi* for $9.25. The combo plate includes both *kalua* pig and *lau lau* for $12. Out-the-door lunch lines are evidence that Ono lives up to its name—delicious. Open M-Sa 11am-7:45pm. Cash only. ❷

Yabusoba, 255 Beachwalk Ave. (☎926-5303), next to Arancino. Don't be alarmed when the entire staff turns and addresses you with *"irasshai"* (welcome) as you enter this authentic Japanese restaurant. Their *soba*, *somen*, and *udon* noodles are made fresh several times a day. The *Ebi Tentoji-zen* (shrimp tempura over rice in an egg-onion sauce, $10) is a favorite. Open daily 11:30am-3pm (last call 2:30pm) and 5:30-10pm (last call 9:30pm). AmEx/MC/V. ❸

Keo's, 2028 Kuhio Ave. (☎951-9355). Going west on Kuhio Ave., take a right before the Kalakaua junction with Kuamoo St. Excellent Thai and island-inspired cuisine served in a beautiful oasis of orchids. Panang curry with vegetables, chicken, shrimp, or seafood $12-15. Mango sorbet $6. Tropical drinks $6.50. Open daily 7am-2pm and 5-10:30pm, F-Sa until 11pm. Sister restaurant **Keoni's,** 2375 Kuhio Ave. (☎922-9888), serves American and Thai in a similar atmosphere. AmEx/D/MC/V. ❸

Ruffage Natural Foods, 2443 Kuhio Ave. (☎922-2042). This hole-in-the-wall sandwich shop serves fresh, local, and healthy goods at low prices. The vegan burrito ($7) and smoothies ($3.60) are favorites. Open 9am-7pm. After Ruffage closes, it becomes **I Love Sushi,** one of the best, and surprisingly unknown, sushi bars in Waikiki. There may be a wait, as rolls are painstakingly made fresh to perfection by their single sushi chef. Try the Dragon Roll or the Spider Roll for under $10. AmEx/MC/V. ❶

Top of Waikiki, 2270 Kalakaua Ave. (☎923-3877), in the revolving restaurant on the 21st floor of the Waikiki Business Plaza. To call the establishment "Waikiki's Best-Kept Secret" (as advertisements claim) is a bit much, but the revolving 360-degree view is pretty amazing. The Shrimp Carbonara with sweet potato gnocchi ($24) and the Tea Smoked Duck L'Orange ($23) are worthy splurges. Tropical drinks $7.50-8. Wine $6-8. It's best to come during the Sunset Special (5-6pm, steak kabob and lobster tail, $20), when the sun sets over the city. Reservations recommended F-Su. Open daily 5-9:30pm. Bar serves drinks and *pupus* until 10:30pm. AmEx/D/MC/V. ❺

BAKERIES

Leonard's Bakery, 933 Kapahulu Ave. (☎737-5591). Locals have been coming to Leonard's since 1952 for tasty tarts ($1-1.25), delectable danishes ($0.67), and a host of other inexpensive treats. Mouth-watering *malasadas* (Portuguese doughnuts) are worth the short trip from Waikiki ($0.66 each). Lines form in the morning, so get there early for the best selection. Open M-Th and Su 6am-9pm, F-Sa 6am-10pm. ❶

BEACHES

Waikiki Beach is the name that refers to all of the beaches on the south shore of Oahu. It begins on the Waikiki side of the Hilton Lagoon in the west and continues along the coastline of Waikiki's premier beach hotels all the way to the edge of Diamond Head Crater. Although the beach reaches moments of absolute saturation, the perpetual daytime crowds can be enlivening—the throng of people creates an audible and infectious enthusiasm. The Waikiki beaches see a variety of watersports: surfers paddle between catamarans, canoers paddle around snorkelers, and swimmers try to keep their space close to shore. If you're the type who prefers long walks on the beach, the **Waikiki Historic Trail,** which stretches two miles along the Waikiki sands and Kalakaua Ave. sidewalks, is studded with bronze statues and surfboard placards that inform the curious about such legendary figures as Duke Kahanamoku and the days when Waikiki was a marshland of taro root patches and fishponds. Quieter, romantic moments occur on the bookends of the frenetic day, at dawn and sunset, when the crowds have dispersed, and the plumeria breeze soothes sunburnt skin.

DUKE KAHANAMOKU BEACH. *(Surfing. Open daily 24hr.)* At the edge of the Hilton Lagoon, Duke Kahanamoku is the westernmost Waikiki beach. The beach is open to the public but is populated primarily by guests of the Hilton Hawaiian Village. This is where Duke Kahanamoku grew up and learned to swim and surf; some say

BEACH SERVICES. Lifeguards are asked to watch over huge numbers of beachgoers; caution and common sense go a long way to ensure safety in the water. Never swim alone, and always check with the lifeguard before entering unfamiliar water. **Landeez All-Terrain Wheelchairs** can surmount the sturdiest of dunes and are available free of charge from the beach service Prime Time Sports at Fort DeRussy Beach, off Kalia Rd. (☎949-8952).

you can still feel his *mana* (spirit) in the area. To the right of the Hilton, on the other side of the rock wall (next to the marina), is a small stretch of beach with a rocky shoreline and a few good surfing spots—**Kaiser's** and **Ala Moana Bowls,** for example—preferred by locals. There is limited free parking near the Hilton Lagoon; take Ala Moana Blvd. west to Hobron Ln. and turn left after the Renaissance Ilikai Hotel. At the stop sign, turn left and follow the road past the yacht harbor to the parking lot on the left.

FORT DERUSSY BEACH PARK. *(Open daily 9am-5pm.)* Next to Duke Kahanamoku Beach, in front of Fort DeRussy, is the aptly named Fort DeRussy Beach Park, a wide stretch of white sand before a large grassy area. The sharp shells and coral near the shore make the beach less than ideal for wading or swimming, but the park has volleyball nets, grills, and palm-shaded lawns for an afternoon picnic.

GRAY'S BEACH. *(Surfing. Open daily 24hr.)* East of the US Army Museum, stretching from the Outrigger Waikiki Shore to the jetty in front of the pink Sheraton Royal Hawaiian, is Gray's Beach, named after an inn that hosted some of Waikiki's earliest tourists. Hundreds of years ago, the area was called *Kawehewehe* (removal) because its water was believed to heal the ill. Today, Gray's Beach has a more powerful attraction for swimmers, with some of the best swimming along the Waikiki stretch due to a sand-filled channel that runs through the reef. There's also good surfing a long paddle out from the shore, and big crowds congregate there.

WAIKIKI BEACH (ROYAL MOANA BEACH). *(Surfing. Wind Sports. Open daily 24hr.)* Tourists happily cram themselves into the resort beachfront between the two Sheratons. This stretch of sand is often called **Royal Moana Beach,** or simply Waikiki Beach, and there are almost as many tourists cavorting in the water as lounging on the soft shore. Swimmers, catamarans, canoes, and all manner of pushed, pulled, and wind-propelled water toys dot the gently rolling Pacific all the way out to the surfers on the breakers.

The **Waikiki Historic Trail** continues on this section of beach, with several important sites between the seawall-enclosed swimming pools on Kalakaua Ave. The tall **Duke Kahanamoku Statue** of the Hawaiian hero, sheriff, Olympic champion, surfer, and movie star stands here, to the left of the Honolulu Police's Waikiki Substation. The frequently lei-adorned bronze Duke faces away from the Pacific, his board between him and the water.

Between the statue and the substation are four large, fenced-off stones, which are monuments to four Tahitian healers who once lived near the site and traveled the islands to dispense miraculous cures. Before leaving Hawaii, the soothsayers gave their names and *mana* (spiritual power) to the boulders—known as the **Stones of Life**—which survive as a tangible reminder of their services to many Native Hawaiians.

PARK FOR CHEAP. A great spot to park near Waikiki Beach is the Honolulu Zoo's metered lot on Kapahulu Ave., near the intersection with Kalakaua Ave. It's a 2min. walk to the beach, and parking only costs $0.25 per hr.

BABY QUEEN'S AND CANOES SURF BREAKS. Directly in front of the Duke Kahanamoku Building and police substation is a surf break favored by some locals as the safest spot to learn to surf. The area, known as **Baby Queen's,** is less dangerous and crowded than many of the sites favored by professional instructors. Just to the right of that area is another surf break called **Canoes,** which is often full of outrigger canoes and novice surfers.

KUHIO BEACH. *(Boogie boarding. Surfing. Open daily 24hr.)* Kuhio Beach extends beyond the recently improved Kapahulu Pier, or as locals call it, the "Waikiki Wall." From the overlooking pier, beachgoers watch surfers and boogie boarders catch monstrous waves in waters that often conceal shallow coral. Swimming within the calm, shallow pools formed by the seawalls is enjoyable, but inexperienced and unfamiliar boarders should not test the waves on the other side (to the right of the Kapahulu Pier). They should also avoid the strong current and the slippery rock wall. **Queen's Surf Beach,** located left of the pier, is a quiet, pleasant area popular with the gay community.

SANS SOUCI BEACH (KAIMANA BEACH). *(Open daily 9am-4pm.)* East of the Waikiki Aquarium (p. 129), on the beach, is the **Natatorium,** a WWI monument and former Olympic training pool. The Natatorium perpetually awaits further renovation before re-opening, despite a refurbishment that recently improved its appearance. Left of the Natatorium is Sans Souci Beach, commonly called Kaimana Beach by the locals who frequent the area. It's a favorite spot among families, because it's farther from the more urban, louder part of Waikiki but still close to the water and park recreation. Many people come here to swim at the flag-marked swim channel that streches 200m past the shore. It's also an especially good place to watch for the "green flash," a quick, bright flash of green light that occurs on the horizon right as the sun goes down. Beyond Sans Souci is the Outrigger Canoe Club Beach, which extends all the way to the beaches at foot of Diamond Head.

ACTIVITIES

Most rental agencies on the beach are fairly expensive and don't take credit cards. Other rental stores can be found on Kapahulu and Kuhio Ave.

Aloha Beach Services, 2335 Kalakaua Ave. (Sheraton Moana Surfrider Hotel ☎922-3111, ext. 2341 for information). In the wooden hut on the left as you walk onto the beach from Duke's Canoe Club. For $30, you can get a 1hr. lesson with a surfboard and the guarantee that you'll be able to stand up. Go early to avoid the crowds. Surfboards $15 for 1hr., each additional hour $5. Boogie boards $7 per hr., each additional hr. $3, 8am-5pm $25. Also offers outrigger canoe rides ($20 per person for 2 waves) and catamaran rides ($15 per person per hr., under 12 $5). Open daily Sept.-May 7am-4pm; June-Aug. 7am-5pm. Cash only.

Hans Hedemann Surf School, 2586 Kalakaua Ave. (☎924-7778; www.hhsurf.com), at the Park Shore Hotel. Other locations at Sheraton Waikiki (booth on beach), Outrigger Reef (sign says HH Surf School), and the Otani Kaimana Beach Hotel. The premier surf school in Waikiki, founded by famous surfer Hans Hedemann. Sign up for a 2hr. group surfing lesson ($75 per person including the board). Semi-private lesson $125, private lesson $150. Surfboard rentals are $10-15 per hr., 8am-5pm $30-45, 24hr. $45-60; $450-650 deposit required. Boogie boards $8 per hr., $15 per 4hr., 8am-5pm $20, 24hr. $30; $100 deposit. They also rent bikes for the same fees as boogie boards. Open daily 8am-5pm. D/MC/V.

Koa Board Sports, 2420 Koa Ave., 2nd fl. (☎923-0189). Rents used longboards for $25 per day and $100 per week, shortboards $20 per day and $80 per week, and boogie boards $10 per day. Open daily 10:30am-4:30pm. MC/V.

Local Motion, 1958 Kalakaua Ave. (☎979-7873). Has a large selection of surfboards and surfwear. Rents longboards and shortboards for $25 per day or $125 per week. Open daily 9am-11pm. AmEx/D/MC/V.

Outrigger Hotel Beach Services, 2335 Kalakaua Ave. (☎926-9889), on the beach in front of Duke's Canoe Club, under the blue umbrellas. Surfboards $15 for 1st hr., $7 each additional hr. 1hr. group surfing lesson $40; semi-private lesson $50 per person, private lesson $75 per person. Go before noon to avoid a long wait. Boogie boards $6 per hr. Outrigger canoe rides $15 per person for three waves. Catamaran rides $15 per person per hr. Open daily 8am-6pm. Cash only.

SIGHTS

DIAMOND HEAD. The 350-acre Diamond Head crater was created about 300,000 years ago during a single brief eruption that flung ash and fine particles into the air. These particles eventually cemented together into a rock called tuff, and geologists now consider Diamond Head one of the world's best examples of a tuff cone. Nicknamed *Leahi*, Diamond Head's 760 ft. summit resembles the *lae* (forehead) of an *ahi* (tuna) when seen from the west. The site finally earned the name "Diamond Head" when Western explorers mistook calcite crystals for diamonds in the late 1700s. In 1904, Diamond Head was purchased by the federal government for defense purposes.

At the park entrance, you'll find picnic tables, restrooms, a pay phone, and drinking water. The 30min. hike through tunnels to the 560 ft. summit is fairly easy. Flashlights are unnecessary; lights have been added to the underground walkways. If claustrophobia still holds you back, rest assured that the journey is worthwhile—the view at the top is enchanting. *(By car, take Monsarrat Ave. to Diamond Head Rd. The park comes up quickly on the right and has an easy-to-spot sign. By bus, take the #58 from Waikiki. Walk against traffic in the tunnel to the park as there is no sidewalk. Open daily 6am-6pm. Go before 8am or after noon to beat the morning rush. $1, private vehicle $5.)*

WAIKIKI AQUARIUM. Specializing in coral reef ecosystems, the aquarium keeps a wealth of tropical fish, reef sharks, and endangered Hawaiian monk seals. Although small, the aquarium reaches beyond its spatial constraints and showcases over 420 different species from the Pacific. Hordes of schoolchildren mob the place on weekdays, communicating with the animals at a high-pitched (read: grating) frequency. *(2777 Kalakaua Ave. #2 bus stops directly out front every 10min. Limited free parking on the aquarium side of Kalakaua Ave. ☎923-9741. http://waquarium.org. Open daily 9am-5pm; last admission 4:30pm. $9; locals and military $6; students and seniors over 60 $6; people with disabilities and ages 13-17 $4; children ages 5-12 $2; 5 and under free. Audio guide included with admission.)*

HONOLULU ZOO. The Honolulu Zoo has them all, and focuses particularly on animals from the African savannah. Despite prowling cheetahs and lumbering elephants, species indigenous to the Pacific Islands are curiously absent, though a *nene* goose exhibit was recently added. Rotating "Elephant Talks" discuss a different animal each day at 11am and 1:30pm. The recently expanded Children's Zoo allows kids to get close to llamas, sheep, goats, and cows, and family programs explore the zoo in depth via the Saturday "Twilight Tours" or the monthly "Snooze In The Zoo" camping program. During summer the zoo opens for free on Wednesday for an extra hour (4:30-5:30pm), followed by the popular **"Wildest Show,"** which features different live Hawaiian musical and dance performances. Bring a blanket, pack a picnic, and come early to claim dibs on lawn space. *(151 Kapahulu Ave., on the corner of Kapahulu and Kalakaua Ave. Parking lot entrance on Kapahulu Ave., $0.25 per hr. ☎926-3191; www.honzoosoc.org. Zoo open daily 9am-4:30pm; Children's Zoo open daily 9am-4pm. Twilight Tours $12, ages 4-12 $8. Snooze In The Zoo $39, ages 3-4 $15, under 2 free. Wildest*

Show: doors open 4:35pm, show 6-7pm at the stage lawn across from the Indian elephants; suggested donation $2. Zoo admission $6; ages 6-12 with adult $1, under 5 free. Family Pass $25. MC/V.)

ST. AUGUSTINE CHURCH. In 1839, St. Augustine Church was built from coconut fronds and driftwood; three renovations later the church has been transformed from the old Hawaiian chapel-hut into the grand Gothic church that stands today. St. Augustine's beautiful interior is a Waikiki rarity worth seeing. *(130 Ohua Ave., at Kalakaua and Ohua Ave. ☎923-7024. Open M-F 9am-4pm, Sa 9am-noon. Mass M-Sa 7am and 5pm, Su 6:30, 8, 10am, and 5pm.)*

ENTERTAINMENT

KUHIO BEACH TORCH LIGHTING AND HULA SHOW. In Waikiki, watching beautiful island girls shake their hips and surf-chiseled men flex in nothing but sarongs is not only socially acceptable; it's free. The Kuhio Beach Torch Lighting and Hula Show goes on at the Kuhio Beach Hula Mound, near the Duke Kahanamoku Statue across Kalakaua Ave. from Uluniu Ave. *(☎843-8002. Hula nightly 6:30-7:30pm. Waikiki style show with lesson M-Th. Hawaiian music and pageant by celebrated hula troupes F-Su. Free.)*

ROYAL HAWAIIAN SHOWS AND LESSONS. The Royal Hawaiian Shopping Center hosts free lessons and entertainment, including Hawaiian quilting, 1hr. ukulele lessons, hula lessons, and lei-making. *(☎922-2299. All classes are held in the Cultural Room in Ilima Court, 2301-C205 Kalakaua Ave., on the 2nd fl. above The Cheesecake Factory. Hawaiian quilting M, Tu and Th 9:30-11:30am; ukulele lessons M, W, F 11:30am-12:30pm; lei-making M and W 1-2pm.)*

HOTEL HULA SHOWS. Several hotels also offer free hula performances and many are open to non-guests as well. Arrive early for a better view. The Hilton Hawaiian Village's popular Friday hula show (☎949-4321, 7-8pm) is highlighted with a fireworks display. Seating is available for $12, which includes one drink. The Halekulani's House Without a Key restaurant has live Hawaiian music nightly at 5pm with a hula dancer (☎923-2311, Hula daily 5:30-8pm). The Renaissance Ilikai Waikiki's Paddles Bar (☎949-3811) is the place for a traditional sunset conch-blowing and torch-lighting ceremony daily around 6:15pm. Farther from the beach the Sheraton Princess Kaiulani Hotel hosts live Hawaiian music and hula dancing outside the Pikake Terrace Restaurant. Dinner buffet is available at the restaurant for $32.50 per person, but purchase of buffet is not necessary to watch the show (☎922-5811, daily 6-9:30pm). For more information on free events in Waikiki, check www.co.honolulu.hi.us/events.

FREE OUTDOOR FILMS. On alternate weekends, The Kuhio Beach Torch Lighting and Hula Show (see above) is followed by **Sunset on the Beach.** The Mayor's Office sets up a movie screen on the beach for a double feature of family films. Before the show, area restaurants set up portable booths on the east side of Kapahulu Pier, selling overpriced concessions to the first-come, first-seated beach blanket crowd. *(☎523-2489. Kuhio Beach Park. Most Sa-Su at sunset around 7pm. Check the Honolulu Events Calender, listed above, for film dates.)*

BLAISDELL CENTER AND WAIKIKI SHELL. The Blaisdell Center Complex, in downtown Honolulu, hosts a wide array of attractions in its arena, exhibition hall, galleria, and concert hall. The Waikiki Shell is an outdoor amphitheater near the beach with a background view of Diamond Head. Both make excellent venues for evening concerts and shows; check the website for a current schedule of events. The Royal Hawaiian Band also performs weekly (Su 1-3pm) at the Kapiolani Bandstand, near the Waikiki Shell. *(Blaisdell Center, 777 Ward Ave.,*

Win a Trip For Two to Hawaii!

Submit this sweepstakes* form at any Hilo Hattie store for your chance to win Two Roundtrip Coach Tickets on United, plus a $250 Hilo Hattie Gift Certificate.

Print Name Phone Number

Address

City State Zip

Email Address

☐ YES! Send me monthly e-mail updates from Hilo Hattie on the latest specials & products from Hawaii.

Free gift offer and "Win a Trip to Hawaii" sweepstakes are available at all of Hilo Hattie's convenient store locations:

Ala Moana Shopping Center, Oahu
Nimitz Highway, Oahu
Lahaina, Maui
Kihei, Maui
Kona, Big Island
Hilo, Big Island
Lihue, Kauai

For information, call 535-6500 (Oahu) or 1-800-233-8912. Open 365 days a year.

UNITED

*No purchase necessary. Must be at least 18 years old to participate. Give entry form to cashier and be sure to check offer on front side. Sweepstakes rules available upon request. Call 1-800-233-8912 for more information.

HILO-413

between King St. and Kapiolani Blvd. King St. gate open M-Sa 5:30am-6pm, Su and holiday hours determined by events. Box office ☎591-2211; www.blaisdellcenter.com. Open M-Sa 9am-5pm. Waikiki Shell, 2805 Monsarrat Ave., at the Diamond Head end of Waikiki.)

SHOPPING

If you're shopping in Waikiki you have two options: either the 4-for-$1 Hawaiiana and knick-knacks in the International Market and Duke's Lane, or the chic high-end (and high-priced) designer items that dominate the Royal Hawaiian Shopping Center. For everything in between, you'd be better off elsewhere.

THE INTERNATIONAL MARKETPLACE. The market is a maze of kiosk stands that hock the same wares as every kitschy tourist capital in the world. It's also the premier venue for cheap aloha wear and Hawaiian carvings, macadamia nut leis, *puka* body ornaments, jade Buddha statues, and jewelry. **Duke's Lane,** which runs along the Waikiki Beachcomber Hotel on the same block as the International Marketplace, lays things out in much the same way and sells at similar prices. *(2330 Kalakaua Ave. ☎922-2000. Open daily 8am-10pm. Most stores in Duke's Lane open 10am-10pm. Most take AmEx/D/MC/V.)*

ROYAL HAWAIIAN SHOPPING CENTER. The shopping center holds court with the nobility of the fashion world on Kalakaua Ave., including names like Bulgari, Cartier, Fendi, and Hermes. The only people you'll see wearing formal black suits in all of Waikiki are the guards in the Royal Hawaiian's Salvatore Ferragamo. The shopping center hosts a range of free entertainment and lessons (p. 130) in the Asian-inspired interior. *(On Royal Hawaiian Ave., from Lewers St. to past Duke's Lane. Info booth ☎922-2299. Open daily 9am-10pm.; shopping daily 10am-10pm.)*

DFS GALLERIA. DFS Galleria is at the crux of the lit-up, glitzy, all-for-show Kalakaua Ave., across from the Royal Hawaiian. The behemoth duty-free shopping center houses many of the same upscale stores as the Royal Hawaiian. Make sure to check out the 65,000 gallon walk-through aquarium with tropical fish, stingrays, and small sharks. There are gift shops on the first floor, American boutiques on the second, and a free hula show on some evenings. The double-decker Trolley Express runs between DFS and nearby major hotels every 30min.; schedule is posted at DFS Galleria. *(On the corner of Kalakaua and Royal Hawaiian Ave. ☎931-2655; www.dfsgalleria.com. You must show an international ticket or itinerary to gain access to the duty-free luxury brand boutiques on the 3rd fl. Free hula show W-F 5:30-7:30pm. Open daily 9am-11pm.)*

HYATT SHOPS. Two towers scrape the sky over the little Hyatt Shops. Check out everything from marine art in Wyland Galleries (☎924-3133; open daily 9am-11pm) to the plethora of gift stores and most of the usual suspects. *(Most stores open daily 10am-10pm. Call the Hyatt (☎923-1234) for more info.)*

NIGHTLIFE

CLUBS

Diamond Head Grill, 2885 Kalakaua Ave. (☎922-3734), in the **W Honolulu Hotel.** The most posh place to see and be seen, the Diamond Head Grill hosts one of the best weekend parties. DJs spin hip-hop and pack the dance floor tight. F night is most popular. Beer $5. Mixed drinks $5. Cocktails $7-8. Dress to impress; no slippers, shorts, hats, or tank tops (for men). Cover $10-20. Open F-Sa 9pm-2am. AmEx/D/MC/V.

Zanzabar, 2255 Kuhio Ave. (☎924-3939), on the 1st fl. of the Waikiki Trade Center. Despite the upscale, ostentatious exterior and hotter-than-thou vibe, clubbers get down on debaucherous theme nights. Live DJs nightly. No t-shirts, sandals, or hats for men. Exclusive VIP room for $30. 21+ Tu and F-Sa; 18+ M, W-Th and Su. Cover 21+ $10-15. Open M and W-Su 9pm-4am, Tu 8pm-4am. AmEx/D/MC/V.

Fusion Waikiki, 2260 Kuhio Ave. (☎924-2422), on the 2nd fl. across from the Waikiki Trade Plaza. Live DJs spinning house and techno keep the 2 dance floors pumping in this gay bar, starting M-Th and Su at 9pm, and F-Sa from midnight on. Red lights flash every 15min. for "Floating Red Light Specials" ($3 shots). Beer $4-5.50. 21+; 18+ the 3rd Su of each month. Cover F-Sa and event Su $5. Open M-Th and Su 10:30pm-4am, F-Sa 8pm-4am. Cash only.

Scruples, 2310 Kuhio Ave. (☎923-9530). This newly renovated nightclub provides both a chill, lounging atmosphere near the bar and a more energetic vibe on the dance floor. DJ spins by request. Strut your stuff or simply observe at the Bikini Contest (Th 12:30am). Happy hour daily 8-10pm; $2 drinks. W $1 drink night. No athletic wear. Cover M-W and Su $5, Th-Sa after 10pm $10. Open daily 8pm-4am. AmEx/MC/V.

CLUBBING FOR POCKET CHANGE. Keep an eye out for bar promoters on Kuhio Ave. during the day; they often hand out coupons for free drinks.

BARS

Duke's Canoe Club, 2335 Kalakaua Ave. (☎922-2268), inside the Outrigger Waikiki, on the beach. A Waikiki institution, Duke's is the ultimate beachside bar, mixing drinks to live contemporary Hawaiian music (daily 4-6pm and 10pm-midnight; Su local legend Henry Kapono plays) under palm-thatched umbrellas. Tropical drinks $6, beer $3.25-4.25, *pupus* $5-10. Duke's also has a busy seafood restaurant. Food served daily 7am-midnight. Lunch buffet $11. Bar open daily 4pm-1am. AmEx/D/MC/V.

Kelley O'Neil's, 311 Lewers St. (☎926-1777), across from Moose's. A laid-back Irish bar where locals and tourists enjoy pints and live music in a comfortable atmosphere. Happy hour daily 11am-8pm; domestic beer $2.25, pints $3.25, mixed drinks $2.75. Live music M-F 8:30pm-1:30am, F-Sa 5pm-3:30am, Su Irish music 4-8pm. Guinness Pie (beef marinated in Irish stout and baked into a pie) $7.50. Food served daily 11am-9pm, bar open until 4am. AmEx/D/MC/V.

Hula's Bar and Lei Stand, 134 Kapahulu Ave. (☎923-0669), on the 2nd fl. of the Waikiki Grand. In this famous Waikiki gay bar, crowds gather to watch the sunset and stay for the fun, social atmosphere. Sophisticated interior with creative black lighting, pool table, and a view of the beach. Pitchers $5.50 daily 3pm-2am, $4.50 W until 9pm. Wine and mixed drinks $2.50 daily 10am-3pm. F, Sa free *pupus* 5-9pm. Live DJ nightly, and GoGo Boyz perform Th-Sa at 10:00pm and Su at 8pm. Beach party Beerblast Su; mugs $2.50, pitchers $5. Cover Th-Sa $3, on promotional nights $5. Open daily 10am-2am. AmEx/MC/V.

Moose McGillycuddy's Pub and Cafe, 310 Lewers St. (☎923-0751; www.moosewaikiki.com). In the daytime, this laid-back sports bar is a great place to watch the game; after hours it gets a little scandalous. The bar proudly flaunts its crowd in online photo albums, check out their website for a taste. Happy hour daily 4-8pm; half-priced drinks and pupus $4-6.50, Mai Tais $1.50, mixed drinks and domestic drafts $2.50. 21+ after 8pm. Cover F-Sa after 8pm $3, Tu after 8pm $5. Food served until 10pm. Open daily 7:30am-4am. AmEx/MC/V.

Angles, 2256 Kuhio Ave. (☎926-9766), 2nd fl., above Seaside Bar and Grill. Angles is overflowing with energy on any night of the week. This lively gay bar has a swinging dance floor/stage. Hip-hop W-Su. Challenge the locals in the weekly pool tournaments M, Tu at 10pm, $5 to enter. Best Chest/Best Buns contest W at 11pm. All-Male Revue Th and Su at 11pm. Happy hour daily 10am-8pm; all drinks discounted. $2-4 drink specials M-Th and Su 10pm-2am. Free *pupus* Tu and F at 5pm, Su barbecue $3.75 cheeseburgers "with all the fixings," 3-7pm. 21+. No cover. Open daily 10pm-2am. Cash only.

FUN, AHOY! Angles hosts a gay catamaran sail every Saturday at 3pm. Go early to ensure tickets are available; $20 per person.

Nashville Waikiki, 2330 Kuhio Ave. (☎926-7911), in the basement of the Ohana West, between Walina St. and Nahua St. on Kuhio Ave. Despite being thousands of miles from the real deal, The Nashville Waikiki feels like authentic country. Line dancing and real cowboys on the scene. Line dancing lessons W 7-9pm. Happy hour daily 4-8pm; Mai Tais $2.50, domestic bottles $2.75, mixed drinks $2.70. M-Th and Su compete for gift certificates in their pool tournaments. 21+. No cover. Open daily 4pm-4am. MC/V.

Snappers, 1778 Ala Moana Blvd., Unit LL (☎947-3776). A self-professed sports pub, with a lounge, pool room, Internet jukebox, dance floor, satellite sportscast, and a TV in every corner. Drink specials change daily, but include Tequila Sunrise $4, domestic bottles $3, import drafts $4. 21+ after 10pm. No cover. Food (mainly Mexican and burgers) served until 10pm. Open M-Th 2pm-2am, F-Su 11am-2am. AmEx/DC/MC/V.

CENTRAL OAHU

PEARL HARBOR

At 7:55am on December 7, 1941, a wave of 350 Japanese fighter planes wrenched the US out of its steadfast neutrality and into the thick of WWII. Pearl Harbor, about 40min. outside of Honolulu, held the whole of the US Pacific Fleet and was the target of Japan's swift surprise attack. The assault was devastating; during the two hour onslaught, over 2400 military personnel and civilians were killed, 188 planes were demolished, and eight battleships were either damaged or destroyed. For more information, see **History,** p. 18.

ARIZONA MEMORIAL. Solemn and graceful, the *USS Arizona* Memorial is a fitting tribute to the 1177 crewmen who died aboard the ship. The 184 ft. memorial spans the partially sunken battleship's midsection, affording visitors a close, poignant view of the ship that still entombs 1100 men. Plans for the memorial began in 1943, but it wasn't until 1958 that President Eisenhower approved its creation. Alfred Preis designed the final structure that was dedicated in 1962. The memorial's unique concave shape symbolizes America's great tragedy and the country's subsequent rise above it. There are three main sections: an entry room, a central area where visitors can observe the ship, and the shrine room, which has a marble wall engraved with the names of those who died on the *Arizona*. Sixty-three years later, visitors can still see spots of oil that continue to leak from the ship. The on-shore **Visitors Center** has a museum and a somber, moving tour that includes a documentary film and boat ride to the memorial itself. The tour is free, but every visitor must pick up his or her ticket in person on a first-come, first-served basis. Come early, as wait times can reach 2hr. and on busy summer days most tickets are gone by noon. The Visitors Center offers 30 tours every day for 4500 people. The tour brochure is available in 37 different languages from the information kiosk. *(From Honolulu, take H-1 West to the Arizona Memorial/Stadium Exit 15a, which will put you on Kamehameha Hwy. Follow the signs to the Battleship Missouri Memorial and USS Bowfin Park, turning left after ½ mi. TheBus #20, 42, or CityExpress A will also get you there; the bus stop is across the street from the Battleship Missouri trolley pickup at Bowfin Park. ☎422-0561 or 422-2771. Open*

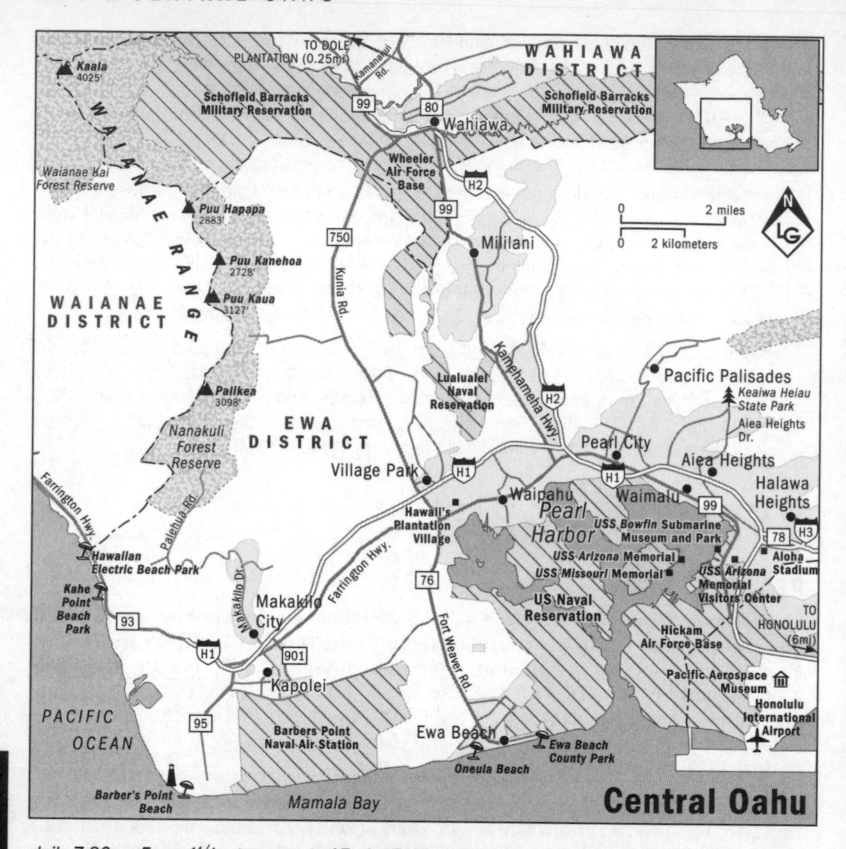

daily 7:30am-5pm. 1¼hr. tours every 15min. 7:45am-3pm. No bags, purses, backpacks, or strollers with pockets and compartments. Baggage storage available in the parking lot $2. Admission to Arizona Memorial free.)

BOWFIN PARK. One of 15 remaining WWII submarines, the *USS Bowfin* is the centerpiece of its own historical park. Called the "Pearl Harbor Avenger," the sub was set into action one year after the 1941 attack. In 1981, the *Bowfin* was pulled out of commission and given educational duty instead. Visitors can explore the insides of the submarine and several outdoor exhibits, including a waterfront memorial and various models of missiles and torpedoes (such as Kaiten, a WWII Japanese suicide torpedo). The museum exhibits submarine-related paraphernalia, paintings, photographs, battle flags, and other models. *(Adjacent to the USS Arizona Visitors Center. See directions above. ☎ 423-1341. Open daily 8am-5pm, last tour 4:30pm. Submarine and museum admission $10; military, senior citizens, Hawaii residents $7; ages 4-12 $4. Museum only $5, ages 4-12 $2. AmEx/D/MC/V.)*

BATTLESHIP MISSOURI MEMORIAL. After five decades of military service, the battleship *USS Missouri* was finally retired in 1999. "Mighty Mo" was then relaunched as a tourist attraction and has since attracted over two million visitors. The 887 ft. *Missouri* is a veteran of WWII, the Korean War, and, after an overhaul in the mid-1980s, the Persian Gulf War. Marvelously refurbished and preserved, the ship illustrates the claustrophobic monotony of sailors' daily lives. There is a strong feeling of patriotism aboard the ship—among other historic spots, guests can visit the Signature Deck, where General MacArthur accepted the Instrument of Surrender from the Japanese on September 2, 1945, ending WWII. The **Chief's Guided Tour** ($22, ages 4-12 $14) takes visitors through the restricted Combat Engagement Center. The newest attraction, the **Explorer's Tour** (1½hr.; $45, children $20), outfits visitors with hardhats and flashlights so that they can delve into the previously closed lower decks, viewing the circa-1943 analog supercomputers. Ask about combination packages for both *Bowfin* and *USS Missouri* tours. *(From Honolulu, take H-1 West to the Arizona Memorial/Stadium exit, which will deposit you on Kamehameha Hwy. Follow the signs to the Battleship Missouri Memorial and USS Bowfin Park, turning left after ½ mi. Or take TheBus #20, 42, or CityExpress A. From the USS Bowfin, take the free trolley. ☎455-1600; www.ussmissouri.com. Call for tour reservations within 24hr. of scheduled tour. Open daily 9am-5pm. Last ticket sold at the Bowfin 3:45pm. Admission $16, ages 4-12 $8, under 4 free. AmEx/D/MC/V.)*

ALOHA STADIUM

When not hosting a football game, Aloha Stadium is the site of the largest flea market on Oahu: the **Aloha Stadium Swap Meet**. Vendors sell everything from bathing suits to gadgets and ukuleles. It's the place to go for cheap jewelry, flavorful local treats, and any aloha print garb. Local edibles include homemade fruit jams, home-baked gourmet breads, and fresh-smoked marlin. Many vendors sell similar items, so shop around. Take note of your parking section, or you'll be walking in circles. *(One stop on the bus past Pearl Harbor. See directions above. Open W and Sa-Su 6am-3pm. Admission $0.50, 11 and under free.)*

WAIPAHU

Located in suburban Waipahu (pop. 33,108), **Hawaii's Plantation Village** recaptures the lifestyle, struggles, and stories of workers on Hawaii's sugar plantations back when "sugar was king." The site is composed of 30 reconstructed buildings modeled after the homes, workplaces, and social structures of the era; they are furnished with original items donated by descendants of plantation workers.

Between 1848 and 1946, plantation owners recruited over 400,000 workers from nearly a dozen different nations after diseases had ravaged the local workforce. Many Chinese, Portuguese, Japanese, Puerto Ricans, Okinawans, Koreans, Filipinos, Caucasians, and indigenous Hawaiians came to the area to work in the mills, seeking a better life. The managers segregated the workers by ethnicity in order to stymie collective wage bargaining. However, the workers began sharing food, joining in athletic competitions, and intermarrying, and they soon brought about the multi-racial International Longshore and Warehouse Union, which successfully challenged the landowners to raise the workers' wages and quality of life. A merging of these cultures became one of the roots of today's Hawaii.

A trained docent takes visitors through a range of village sites, including a 1930s barber shop, a public bathhouse, a 1940s RC Cola general store, and the last active shrine of the Inari, a minor sect of the Shinto religion often associated with the working class. Admission to the village is allowed only with one of the guided tours, which are scheduled every hour, but visitors should call ahead, as tours with insufficient demand are cancelled. A small museum shows a rotating exhibit of plantation artifacts and presents a more detailed historical background. *(94-695 Waipahu St. By car, take H-1 west to Exit 8B. Turn right onto Paiwa St. at the 2nd stoplight. Take a left on Waipahu St. The village is on the left about ½ mi. from the highway. By car, the center is 30min. from Honolulu. TheBus #43 runs from the Ala Moana Shopping Center to the gate every 30min. 7am-5pm. ☎677-0110. Open M-F 9am-3pm, Sa 10am-3pm. Tours run on the hr.; last tour at 3pm. $13, seniors $10, ages 4-11 $5, under 4 free.)*

KEAIWA HEIAU STATE RECREATION AREA

Located above Aiea Heights, a quiet residential neighborhood north of Pearl Harbor, Keaiwa Heiau State Recreation Area is a peaceful place to camp that is far from Waikiki's throngs and yet close enough for an easy daytrip. Filled with tall ironwood trees and pockets of eucalyptus, the park exudes an enveloping sense of serenity. You'll have a great view of Honolulu and Pearl Harbor while looking out over the 350-odd acres of lush vegetation.

While the natural beauty and tranquil atmosphere are the real attractions, the area's namesake *heiau* (temple) gives it cultural, spiritual, and historical significance. In the late 15th century, *kahuna lapaau* (herbal healers) practiced their craft in the *keaiwa heiau*, a squat stone structure, harnessing the natural energy of the site and medicinal properties of nearby plants. The site is considered sacred by the Hawaiian people. Today, all that remains of the *heiau* are waist-high lines of rocks where archaeologists believe walls once stood. It is disrespectful (and illegal) to move the stones or leave offerings of any kind.

The park has four **campsites,** which can accommodate 10 people each (though you'll rarely find more than five at any given site). All campsites have restrooms, shower facilities, and picnic tables. They are all recently renovated, spotless and modern. All the campsites are accessible via a 1 mi. road that circles the ridge near the entrance to the park.

Try a bit of hiking on the **Aiea Loop Trail,** an easy 4½ mi. hike through the forest, that meanders between the first and second campsites. Trailheads are behind the restrooms at each site, about a quarter mile and a half mile down the road, respectively. Superb views of the mountains and Pearl Harbor accompany the hundreds of indigenous plants along the trail. Near the end of the hike, wreckage of a 1943 C-47 cargo plane is visible through the trees. The trail takes 2-3hr. to complete; athletic shoes or lightweight hiking boots are suggested. *(By car, take Hwy. 78 west from Honolulu to the Stadium/Aiea exit and continue onto Moanalua Rd. At the 2nd light, turn right onto Aiea Heights Dr., which winds into the park, about 3 mi. up. By bus, take TheBus #11 from Alapai Transit Center. TheBus leaves daily every hr. 7am-9:30pm, last return 8:10pm. Ask the driver to let you off at Kaamilo St. The park is a strenuous 30min. walk up Aiea Heights Dr. ☎587-0300. Open daily Apr.-Sept. 7am-7:45pm; Oct.-Mar. 7am-6:45pm. See* ***Camping in Hawaii,*** *p. 75 for permit information. Camping M-W and F-Su. $5 per group.)*

WAHIAWA

Once strategically important for Hawaiian royalty, Wahiawa (pop. 16,151) is now an unremarkable town in Central Oahu. Frequent thunder claps were thought to be divine voices welcoming new royalty, though today the atmospheric booms greet the pawn shops, tattoo parlors, fast food joints, and bars that dominate the military town close to the Schofield Barracks. Wahiawa is interesting mostly for its nearby sights—an abundance of pineapples grows just a few miles north—but the town itself is best seen from the inside of a car on the way to the North Shore.

About 3 mi. north of Wahiawa, the **Dole Plantation,** 64-1550 Kamehameha Hwy. (☎621-8408; www.dole-plantation.com), fulfills any and all pineapple cravings. The new complex is becoming a major tourist attraction, with nearly one million visitors per year. Watch 20min. of staggering pineapple growth (one fruit develops in 15-18 months) on an educational train ride. (Open daily 9am-5:30pm. Trains leave every 30min. $7.50, children $5.50.) From there, you can get lost in the world's largest maze, or meander through the Dole Plantation Gardens, where you can gain an appreciation for the incredible life cycle of a pineapple plant. (Maze and gardens open daily 9am-5:30pm. Maze $5, children $3; gardens $3.75/3.) When you're done, hit up the gift shop for a well-deserved "Dole Whip," a pineapple-flavored Italian ice ($3.75).

The **Wahiawa Botanical Garden,** 1396 California Ave. (☎621-7321; www.hawaiibotanicalgardens.com), is one breath of fresh air in this decrepit town. A tropical rainforest walk passes a number of extremely rare and fascinating flora. (Open daily 9am-4pm. Free.)

Hungry travelers should stop for local fare at **Sunnyside ❶,** 1017 Kilani Ave., four blocks east of Kamehameha Hwy., in Wahiawa. Easy-to-miss, but a favorite of those in the know, Sunnyside serves cheap, super-good local food. The cheeseburger ($1.40) and the plate lunches ($5.25-6) are delicious, and people come from all over Oahu for the **cream and fruit pies** ($7), which tend to sell out by noon. Walk up to the window or sit down inside. (☎621-7188. Open M-F 6am-6pm, Sa 6am-4pm.)

To reach Wahiawa by car from Honolulu, take H-1 West, then take H-2 North to Exit 8. Follow HI-99/Kamehameha Hwy. through the middle of town. Wahiawa is also on the #52 and 62 bus lines, just over 1hr. from the Ala Moana Shopping Center hub in Honolulu.

SOUTHEAST OAHU

KOKO HEAD REGIONAL PARK AND ENVIRONS

The area east of Honolulu along **Highway 72 (Kalanianaole Highway)** from Koko Head to Sandy Beach is a county park that includes **Hanauma Bay,** the **Halona Blowhole and Cove,** and **Koko Crater.** These sites are easily accessible by car from the highway, and two major bus routes serve the area. **TheBus #22,** nicknamed the "Beach Bus," runs along the highway from Waikiki to **Sea Life Park,** and has stops at each of the destinations mentioned above, as well as Makapuu point and beach. (Departs Waikiki 8:15 and 9:15am, then every hr. at 5min. before the hr.; last departure M-F 4:25pm, Sa-Su 4:40pm; last return from Sea Life Park M-F 5:30pm, Sa-Su 5:45pm.) **TheBus #58** leaves from the Ala Moana Center and serves a similar area, but it leaves the highway to go through **Hawaii Kai,** serving the same destinations with the exception of Hanauma Bay and Sandy Beach. (Every 30min M-F 8am-6:05pm, Sa-Su 7am-6pm).

HANAUMA BAY MARINE LIFE CONSERVATION DISTRICT. *(Snorkeling. Lifeguards in summer M and W-Su 6am-7pm; in winter 6am-6pm.)* In the world of beach parks, Hanauma Bay is like Disneyland—fun, but the crowds can be maddening. Over 3000 people flock to this crater-cradled beach every day (over one million visitors annually), and while the snorkeling is among the best on the island, the legions of tourists and children detract from the experience. It's best to arrive before 10am, when throngs of tourists start to flood the water.

Hanauma means "curved bay." The wide, sandy beach is at the base of a ring of rock below **Koko Head,** and its waters bristle with hundreds of species of brightly colored fish. The concave bay is mirrored by an arcing reef about 100 yd. into the ocean; the space between the reef and the shore is shallow and encloses a beautiful latticework of coral. Once a local fishing spot, the bay has been a **Marine Life Conservation District** since 1967, protecting the area for the reproduction of aquatic life. In the past, over-fishing was the problem. These days it's overfeeding. The local fish population has become dependent on human handouts, and aggressive species foreign to the area, such as the Hawaiian Whitespotted Toby, are growing in number. Respect the bay (and the law) by not feeding the fish. Other reef etiquette is discussed in a 9min. video visitors are required to watch.

While it is a good family destination, Hanauma Bay has more serious injuries and deaths each year than any beach on the island. If you have health problems, are a weak swimmer, or are a first-time snorkeler, take precautions and heed red flags. Talk to the lifeguards to find out about surf conditions and the safe swimming areas.

The largest open area, **Keyhole,** is in the center of the bay. It is quite shallow and calm, which makes it a good spot for novice snorkelers. Snorkeling is better outside the reef, but the current is strong, and a surprise wave can throw even an experienced swimmer against the rocks. There is also a strong rip current called the **Molokai Express** (few make it to Molokai). Let's Go does not recommend swimming beyond the reef.

The two most dangerous areas of the bay are **Toilet Bowl** and **Witches Brew,** both of which are closed to public access by chain-link fences and signs threatening fines and imprisonment for trespassing. Serious injury and death occur at both sites every year, so heed the warnings. Toilet Bowl is a natural pool on the left side of the bay connected to the sea by a submerged tunnel through the rock. The water level rises with the surf and then drops 4-8 ft. almost instantly as the waves "flush" out; trespassers scurry to grab the slippery sides of the bowl, getting scraped and gashed, or worse, in the process. Witches Brew is a turbulent area on the right side of the bay near its mouth, with a notoriously strong riptide and powerful waves that have swept many unsuspecting swimmers into the sea. Do not attempt to enter the water at either location!

The park has showers, restroom facilities, changing rooms, pontoon wheelchairs for people with disabilities, a picnic area, and various cart vendors selling expensive food. Snorkeling equipment is available for rent at the park but it is cheaper in Waikiki. *(By car, take Kalanianaole Hwy. east from Honolulu. The entrance to the parking lot is on the right on top of the hill past the Foodland shopping center. Parking $1; the lot is usually full by midday. TheBus #22 runs between Waikiki and Sea Life Park and stops right in Hanauma Bay; leaves every hr. 8:15am-5:40pm. Admission $5, 12 and under free.)*

HALONA BLOWHOLE. About 1½ mi. past Hanauma Bay is the Halona Blowhole, a lava tube submerged in the ocean. Passing waves push through the tube and create a mesmerizing, geyser-like explosion of sea and sound. The quality of the spectacle depends on surf conditions. On some days the water barely bubbles out of the blowhole, while on other days it shoots high into the sky. Do not climb over the fences to get a closer look; people have been killed by the fall.

To the right of the parking lot and down a set of steep rocks is the small, sparkling Halona Cove, a quiet, sheltered lovers' beach to swim or sunbathe unmolested by crowds. Locals know the cove as **Eternity Beach,** since the Academy Award-winning flick *From Here to Eternity* was filmed here. The path was made from natural lava flow creating smooth circular boulders down to the beach. There is no easy path down, so be careful scrambling through the rocks. Look out for sea turtles at the cove. *(The parking lot is located along Kalanianaole Hwy. and the #22 bus route.)*

KOKO CRATER. Koko Crater encloses a 60-acre **Botanical Garden** and **Equestrian Center** that offers horseback-riding lessons ($50) and pony rides ($40). A pleasant 2 mi. walking trail begins in a plumeria grove and goes through the garden's far-flung plant collection, which includes species from Madagascar and other African countries. The gardens are a worthwhile stop if you're in the area for the afternoon. *(408 Kealahou St. By car, take Kalanianaole Hwy. east from Honolulu until you reach a stoplight just past Sandy Beach at Kealahou St. Turn left, and then left again after about ½ mi. onto Kokonani Blvd. TheBus #58 leaves from the Ala Moana Center and runs along Kealahou St., stopping near Kokonani. #58 runs every 30min. M-F 6:50am-6:05pm, Sa 7:10am-6:05pm, Su 8:10am-6:05pm. ☎395-2628. Stables open Tu and Th-Su 8am-7pm. Call ahead to schedule a lesson. 1hr. horseback tour through the crater $50. Gardens open daily 9am-4pm. Free.)*

SANDY BEACH PARK. *(Boogie boarding. Surfing. Open daily 24hr. Lifeguards daily.)* With the best waves on Oahu's south shore, Sandy Beach is the premier spot for experienced boogie boarders. The rocky shoreline along the east part of the beach also has two breaks—**Full Point** and **Half Point**—for advanced surfers. "Sandy's," as the beach is affectionately called, is great whether you're an advanced boarder, bodysurfer, or enthusiast. It is also among the most dangerous beaches on the island, seeing a lot of neck and back injuries. Full Point, the far left side of the beach, breaks over a deep reef bottom, while Half Point, where the wave breaks over a shallow bottom, is a bit more dangerous. The inexperienced should keep out of the water when the current is strong, and surfers and boogie boarders should be wary of a riptide when trade winds are strong. Check with the lifeguards at either station for surf information and keep an eye out for red flags, which indicate dangerous water conditions.

The beach itself is wide enough to accommodate sunbathers, and it has a reputation as a popular hangout for the island's youth come nighttime. The large grassy area to the left of the first park entrance is a popular kite-flying location and is sometimes used as a landing strip for hang-gliders. There are usually a few food stands around, and the park has restrooms and showers. *(Sandy Beach is on the #22 bus route on Kalanianaole Hwy., ½ mi. past the Halona Blowhole.)*

MAKAPUU POINT. The lighthouse marking the easternmost point of Oahu, atop the 047 ft. Makapuu Point, has been in operation for nearly 100 years. While it's fenced off, there's still an amazing view of Sandy Beach and Makapuu Beach. Farther down the road on the right is a scenic overview. Both the lookout and the lighthouse have fantastic views of **Manana** and **Kaohikaipu Islands.** Manana, the larger of the two, means "rabbit," and the island bears the name because it both resembles and is inhabited by rabbits. Kaohikaipu, the smaller island, was declared a bird sanctuary in 1972. *(The start of the 1 mi. paved hike to the lighthouse is on the right, a quarter of the way up the hill past Sandy Beach. From the opposite direction, it's ½ mi. beyond Makapuu Beach. There is no parking lot, so cars line up along the highway's shoulder.)*

SEA LIFE PARK. A standard aquatic amusement park—Oahu's largest—Sea Life Park is pricey and full of students on field trips and children dragging their parents from tank to tank. The park features a string of shows for families, including the Dolphin Cove Show and the Kolohe Kai Sea Lion Show. The park also has breeding programs for endangered animals like the giant sea turtle and Hawaiian monk seal, and capture and release programs for wounded birds and animals. The 300,000-gallon aquarium has thousands of species of fish, moray eels, stingrays, sharks, and other indigenous reef life. A spiral walkway around the tank provides views of the reef from different depths. *(41-202 Kalanianaole Hwy. By car, take Kalanianaole Hwy. east from Honolulu for approx. 35min. The park is on the left, just above Makapuu Beach. Both the #22 and 58 buses run from Waikiki to Sea Life Park; the ride is just under 1hr.; buses leave every 30min. The park also runs a shuttle service to major Waikiki hotels for those who purchase one of the extra adventures in advance. Adults $14, ages 4-12 $8. ☎259-7933; www.sealifeparkhawaii.com. Park open daily 9:30am-5pm. $30, ages 4-12 $24.)*

NEED A BREAK FROM THE SUN?

Organizations across Hawaii are always looking for volunteers. For a comprehensive list of opportunities on any island, visit www.volunteerhawaii.org. If you're reading this on the beach, here are a few examples to get you started:

For animal lovers: Wild Bird Rehab Haven (Oahu) is dedicated to the rehabilitation and eventual release of orphaned and injured wild birds. They are always looking for volunteers willing to clean cages, answer telephones, and feed baby birds. For more information, call ☎447-9274. **Eye of the Pacific Guide Dogs** (Oahu) provides guide dogs and related services to legally blind residents of Hawaii. They sometimes needs volunteers to help exercise the dogs if their owners are unable to do so. For more information, call ☎941-1088.

For tree-huggers: The Hanauma Bay Education Program (Oahu) is a non-profit organization dedicated to promoting education and awareness of Hawaii's marine wildlife. Volunteers are always welcome to staff the visitor's center, lead informational tours, and provide clerical or maintenance support. Contact ☎394-1374 for more information. **KAHEA: The Hawaiian-Environmental Alliance** (Oahu) is a community-based organization that encourages public involvement and

MAKAPUU BEACH PARK. *(Boogie boarding. Surfing. Open daily sunrise to sunset. Lifeguards 9am-5:30pm.)* Preferred hangout of hang-gliders and surfers, Makapuu Beach Park has some of Oahu's best bodysurfing and boogie boarding. The beach, located at the bottom of a steep sandhill, is rather small and surrounded by dark volcanic rocks that form a striking contrast with the white sand. Makapuu isn't only about charming vistas and scenery, however. Powerful winter waves (up to 12 ft.) retain some of their kick in the summer, too. Makapuu is almost as infamous as Sandy Beach for neck and back injuries, and has more drownings due to deeper water; be mindful of red flags, strong tides, or dangerous shore breaks. Experience is strongly recommended before boarding at Makapuu. Pack a picnic lunch and a cooler; the nearest food is overpriced at Sea Life Park. The parking lot is across the highway from Sea Life Park. Restrooms and showers are available.

WAIMANALO

Waimanalo (pop. 3,644) is the quintessential Hawaiian small town—diverse, undisturbed, and relaxed. Residents go about their lives at a slow pace, unaffected by the touristy glitz and glam of Waikiki farther south. Whether they were born and raised here or relocated from the mainland, most people here plan to stay, resulting in a largely uncommercial town. The area does have rough neighborhoods though, so don't leave your valuables unattended. Waimanalo's main attraction is its stunning **beach,** the longest (and perhaps the best) on Oahu. Backed by the Koolau Mountains, Waimanalo Beach stretches nearly five miles in an arc of white sand against the green-azure waters of the Pacific.

ORIENTATION AND PRACTICAL INFORMATION

Waimanalo is located along **Highway 72 (Kalanianaole Highway),** about 50min. by car or 1hr. on the #57 bus (every hr. starting at 7:35am) from Honolulu. **Kalanianaole Highway** is also accessible from Pali Hwy. near Kailua. The town itself is spread thinly along the highway for about 2½ mi. **Waimanalo Public and School Library,** 41-1320 Kalanianaole Hwy., has **Internet access** with a 3-month visitor's card ($10). (☎259-2610. Open M-Tu and Th-F 9am-5pm, W 1-8pm, Sa 10am-2pm.) **Waimanalo Laundry,** 41-1537 Kalanianaole Hwy., is in the Waimanalo Town Center. (☎259-5091. Wash $1.75, dry $0.25 per 5min. Drop-off service $0.80 per lb. Open daily 6am-

10pm.) **Waimanalo District Park,** 41-415 Hihimanu St., has free **Internet access.** (☎259-7436 or 259-8926. M-F 3-7pm.) **Waimanalo Post Office,** 41-859 Kalanianaole Hwy., is next to Keneke's. (☎800-275-8777. Open M-F 9am-4:30pm, Sa 9-11am. Last collection M-F 5pm, Sa 4pm.) **Postal Code:** 96795.

ACCOMMODATIONS

There aren't many budget options in Waimanalo. **Beach Houses Hawaii ❹,** at 41-866 Laumilo St., manages property and offers many beach house accommodation rentals in Waimanalo. Their studio options include the Captain and the Ohana Studio in the Ocean View Suite. Both studios include a king-size bed, kitchenette, a separate couch, private bathroom, and sliding glass doors to the backyard patio and jacuzzi. (☎224-6213; www.beachhouse-hawaii.com. Reserve well in advance. $120-145 per night.) If Beach Houses is booked, try **Paradise Found Beachside Suite ❹,** 41-928 Laumilo St., in the back of the owner's home; it has one bedroom with a queen-sized bed, a sun room with a fold-out bed, a kitchenette, and a full bath. The room sleeps up to four and has open access to the house's large and well-kept yard. (☎255-4625; www.vrbo.com/54632. 3-night min. $125 per night. $15 for each additional person. $75 additional cleaning fee. MC/V.) Several area beaches also have campsites (see **Beaches,** p. 142).

FOOD

Shima's Supermarket, 41-1606 Kalanianaole Hwy., is a one-stop market with a wide selection of *sashimi* and cheap produce. (☎259-9921. ATM inside. Open M-Sa 8am-8pm, Su 9am-6pm. D/MC/V.) **Bobby's,** 41-867 Kalanianaole Hwy., is a small local grocery with cheap beer (12-pack, $6.99) and wine (bottles under $10). It's the building three doors from Keneke's. (☎259-5044. Open M-Sa 7am-8:45pm, Su 7am-7:15pm. MC/V.) **Keneke's ❶,** 41-857 Kalanianaole Hwy., is an old-school plate lunch mecca, with mixed plates ($7) and mini plates ($4), as well as sandwiches ($3.50) and shave ice ($2) that will satisfy barefoot beachgoers (☎259-9800. Open daily 9:30am-5:20pm. MC/V.) Restaurant connoisseurs will have to be satisfied with **Ken's ❶,** 41-1537 Kalanianaole Hwy., which offers breakfast all day. Big Boy Breakfast ($4) includes two fresh eggs, rice, toast, and choice of meat. Plate lunches start at $4. (☎259-8900. Open M 6am-5pm, Tu-Sa 6am-8pm, Su 7am-5pm. AmEx/D/MC/V.)

protection of public trust resources like the Northwestern Hawaiian Islands and the summit of Mauna Kea. Volunteers are often needed in the Outreach and Education divisions to develop educational materials and plan events. For more information, call ☎524-8220.

For the *keiki* (child) in you: The Boys and Girls Club of Hawaii (Oahu) often looks for coaches, referees, and scorekeepers for seasonal sports including flag football, basketball, volleyball and soccer. Games are usually held during the afternoons and on weekends. Contact the Director of Program Operations (☎792-5111), for more information. **The Christmas Wish Program** (Big Island) provides year-round support to homeless and abused children with food, clothing, toiletries, and other necessities. They are always looking for volunteers willing to work on art projects, photograph fun events, and teach dance to children all over the state. For more information, call ☎982-8128.

For the activist: The Legal Aid Society of Hawaii (Oahu) is the largest and oldest non-profit law firm in Hawaii. Volunteer opportunities range from clerical work to website and brochure maintenance to providing legal advice. There is a 3-month minimum commitment. For more information, call ☎800-499-4392.

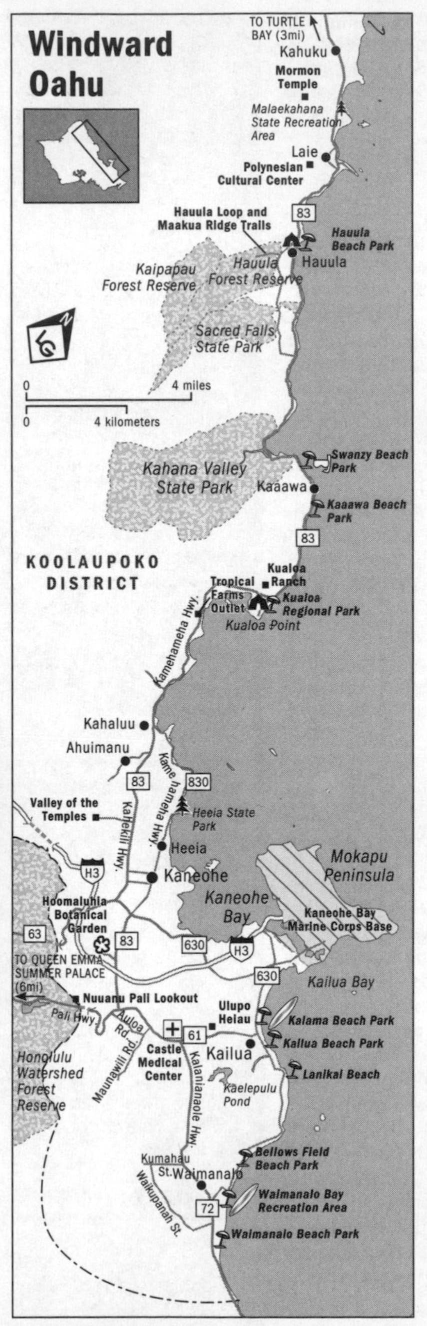

BEACHES

WAIMANALO BEACH PARK. *(Boogie boarding. Snorkeling. Open 24hr. Lifeguards 9am-5:30pm.)* Waimanalo Beach is one of the most beautiful beaches on the island, with scintillating turquoise water, a long shoreline with incredibly soft sand, and gentle surf ideal for novice ocean swimmers or beginning boogie boarders. The first beach on the right heading north from Makapuu Point to Kailua is Waimanalo Beach Park, identifiable by the city of tents along the highway. Manana ("Rabbit") Island peeks around the southern portion of the beach, and the tall ironwood trees complement the vast Koolau Mountains on the inland side of the highway. Camping (20 sites) requires a county permit available from any satellite City Hall. The permits are free, although they have to be obtained a couple weeks before camping (see **Camping in Hawaii,** p. 75, for more information). The snorkeling is decent, though the area is not quite as beautiful as other parts of the beach. There are bathrooms and outdoor shower facilities.

WAIMANALO BAY RECREATION AREA. *(Boogie boarding. Open daily 7:45am-6pm. Lifeguards 9am-5:30pm.)* One mile farther down the highway toward Waimanalo, the gorgeous Waimanalo Bay Recreation Area, locally referred to as "Sherwood Forest," has a wider beach and the most striking view amid the bay's electric-blue waters. In the summer, the water is the bunny hill of boogie boarding, but the surf picks up in winter, so be careful. Be wary of jellyfish, sharp coral, rocks, and red flags indicating dangerous surf conditions. There are bathrooms and shower facilities. Camping (10 sites) requires a county permit (p. 79). Do not leave valuables in your car.

BELLOWS FIELD BEACH PARK. *(Open F noon-M 8am. Lifeguards F-Su 9am-5:30pm.)* This beach park within the Bellows Air Force Base sits next to Waimanalo Bay Recreation Area (along the highway to Waimanalo). Enter at the first entrance to the base. Camping (50 sites) is free but requires a county permit available from any Satellite City Hall (p. 79). Picnic, restroom, and shower facilities are spartan but neat. The water is relatively calm and safe for swimming all year, making it an ideal beach for young swimmers.

WINDWARD COAST

A capricious, exuberant wind blows across the Kamehameha Highway and along the Windward Coast of Oahu. The roads that run around the misty Koolau Mountains and up the rural eastern edge of the island are chaotically unpredictable, but they promise a scenic cruise from Honolulu to the North Shore. You'll pass through a wide range of sights and scenic points, from small towns like Lanikai (of the illustrious Lanikai beach) and Laie (home to the Polynesian Cultural Center), to roadside rooster fights, hidden hiking trails, and miles of unspoiled, windswept beaches. Kailua, the major tourist destination of the Windward Coast, lures visitors with a pristine white-sand beach, brilliant turquoise bay, first-class windsurfing, and fine cuisine, all within shouting distance to Honolulu. Kaneohe, Honolulu's largest suburb on Kailua Bay, is the starting point for sightseeing tours along the Windward Coast and North Shore. The smaller settlements along Kamehameha Hwy. add distinctive beauty, and the terrain varies from rugged mountain to barren oceanscape, rainy valley to sunlit beach.

KAILUA

Kailua (pop. 36,513) is the downtown suburb of the Windward Coast, where visitors will find cozy lodgings, exceptional food, and gorgeous beaches.

ORIENTATION

Kailua, which lies south of **Kaneohe** and east of Kailua Bay, is the southernmost town on the Windward Coast. Three highways zip over the Koolau Mountain Range that separates the Windward Coast from the south shore. They are **H-3, Highway 63** (**Likelike Highway,** pronounced "lee-kay lee-kay"), and **Highway 61 (Pali Highway).** Pali Hwy. is the most direct route from Waikiki.

To reach Kailua from **Honolulu Airport,** take H-1 West to Exit 1D, H-3 East/ Kaneohe. Exit at Mokapu Blvd. and make the third right onto Oneawa St., which becomes Kailua Rd. after the Kailua town center. From **H-1 East,** take Exit 21A, Pali Hwy., and turn left. Continue straight ahead on Hwy. 61, which is called **Kailua Road** after the junction with Hwy. 72.

A complex intersection marks the center of Kailua town—if you turn left you will be on **Oneawa Street,** and if you drive straight you will be on Kuulei Rd. To stay on Kailua Rd., you must turn right at the Kailua town center intersection (following signs for Visitors Information) and then left half a mile later at the Wanaao Rd. intersection and blinking yellow traffic light. From this second left, Kailua Rd. heads straight for the western end of **Kailua Beach Park.**

TRANSPORTATION AND PRACTICAL INFORMATION

TRANSPORTATION

Bus: From Ala Moana Shopping Center in Honolulu, TheBus #56 and 57 run to Kailua. $2; seniors, disabled persons, and students $1.

Car Rental: Enterprise Kailua, 345 Hahani St. (☎261-4282; fax 261-0037). From Hwy. 61 heading toward Kailua, turn right at Hamakua Dr. and left at first stoplight onto Hahani St. Compact $25-30 per day. 21+. Collision damage waiver $17 per day, personal accident insurance $3 per day, liability $10 per day. $30 fee to return car at the airport. Open M-F 8am-6pm, Sa 9am-noon. AmEx/D/MC/V.

TOURIST AND FINANCIAL SERVICES

Tourist Information: Kailua Information Center, 600 Kailua Rd. (☎261-2727), in the Kailua Shopping Center. A friendly and reliable volunteer staff provides maps, bus schedules, phone numbers, and directions. Open M-F 10am-4pm.

City Hall: Kailua Satellite, 1090 Keolu Dr. (☎261-8575). Open M-F 8am-4pm. Camping permits available here.

Banks: First Hawaiian Bank, 705 Kailua Rd. (☎261-3372). Open M-Th 8:30am-4pm, F 8:30am-6pm, Sa 9am-1pm. Drive-up closed Sa. **Bank of Hawaii,** 636 Kailua Rd. (☎888-643-3888). Open M-Th 8:30am-4pm, F 8:30am-6pm. Drive-up hours M-F 8:30am-2:30pm. **24hr. ATMs** outside both.

LOCAL SERVICES

Kailua Public Library, 239 Kuulei Rd. (☎266-9911), 2 blocks from Kailua town center, next to the police station. Open M, W, F 10am-5pm, Tu and Th 1-8pm. **Internet access** available with a 3-month visitor's card ($10). Copies $0.15 per page.

Laundromat: U-Wash-N-Dry, on the corner of Hoolai St. and Kailua Rd. Listen to local tunes while doing your laundry in this open-air, oddly relaxing washerette. Parking available. Wash $1.75, dry $0.25 per 6min. Open 24hr.

EMERGENCY AND COMMUNICATIONS

Police: Kailua Substation, 219 Kuulei Rd. (☎262-6555).

Medical Services: Braun Urgent Care, 130 Kailua Rd., Ste. 111 (☎261-4411), in the Kailua Beach Center. Walk-in patients welcome. Open daily 8am-8pm. **Castle Medical Center,** 640 Ulukahiki St. (☎263-5500, emergency services 263-5164), at the junction of Hwy. 61 and 72, 1½ mi. south of Kailua.

Fax Office: Island Printing Centers, 25 Maluniu Ave. (☎261-8515; fax 261-9958). From Pali Hwy. continue straight through Kailua Rd. and onto Kuulei Rd. Turn left on Aulike and take the first right; continue straight to the parking lot. 1st fax page to mainland $2, subsequent pages $1.25. Copies $0.08, color $0.95 (rates decrease with more pages). Mailboxes also available ($42 for 3 months). Printing, binding, laminating also available. Open M-F 7:30am-8pm, Sa 10am-4pm, Su noon-3pm. AmEx/D/MC/V.

Internet Access: Kailua Recreation Center, 21 S. Kainalu Dr. (☎266-7652), around the corner from the Kailua Public Library. Free with registration. Access available when staffed by volunteers; call for open hours. **Morning Brew,** 572 Kailua Rd., Ste. 12 (☎262-7770), in Kailua Shopping Center. $3 per 30min. Wireless available. Open daily 6am-8pm. **Island Printing Center** also has Internet access: $2 per 15min. (see above).

Post Office: Kailua Main Office, 335 Hahani St. (☎266-3996). Last collection M-F 5pm, Sa 4pm. Open M-F 8am-4:30pm, Sa 8am-noon.

Postal Code: 96734.

ACCOMMODATIONS

The beautiful white-sand beaches and crystalline water that surround Kailua and Lanikai beckon vacationers from around the world. Small and cozy B&Bs supplant

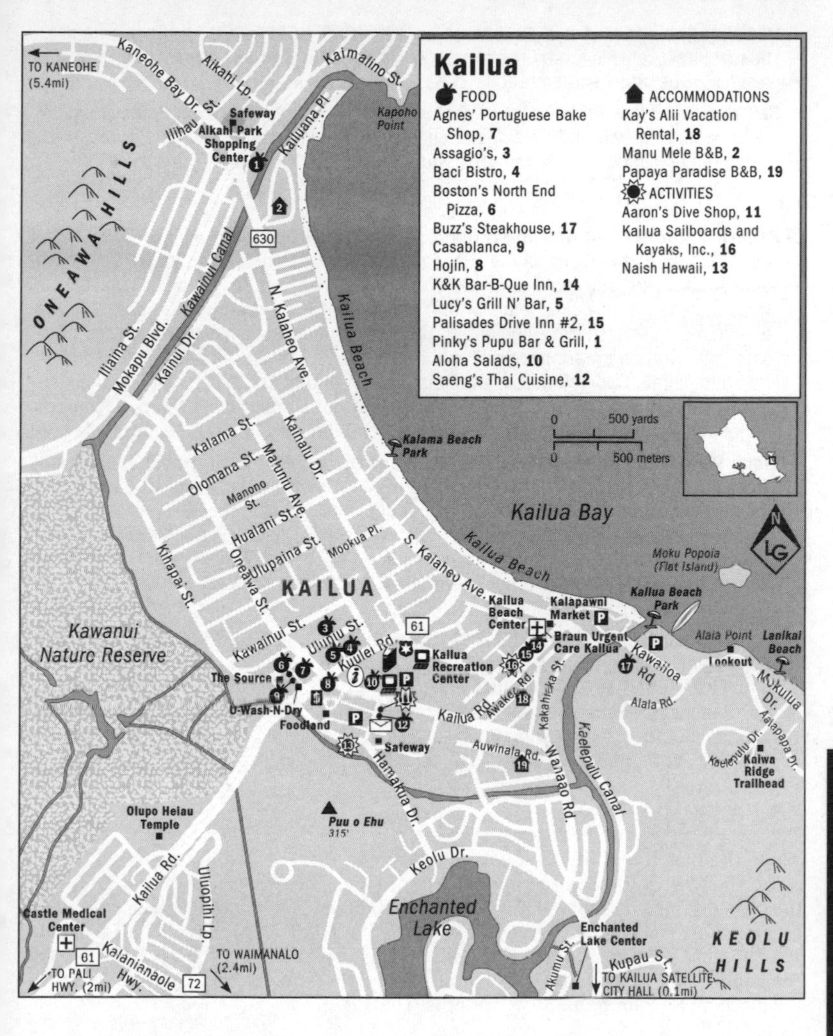

impersonal hotels, but the B&Bs tend to fill up weeks, months, and sometimes even a year in advance. It is essential to make reservations early for the best rates and availability.

BOOKING SERVICES

Many B&Bs can be found across the Windward Coast through booking agencies.

All Islands Bed and Breakfast (☎263-2342 or 800-542-0344; www.all-islands.com) matches travelers with available B&B clients based on individual preferences. Their list of clients numbers over 1000 from across the islands. Reserve 2-3 months in advance with a 20% deposit. The balance must be paid to the B&B where you're staying. Reserve online or by phone. Office hours M-F 8am-5pm. AmEx/D/MC/V.

Hawaiian Islands Bed and Breakfast (☎261-7895 or 800-258-7895; www.lanikaibeachrentals.com) is run by the owners of the **Lanikai Bed and Breakfast.** They also reserve B&Bs and vacation rentals in Kailua and Lanikai. MC/V.

Bed and Breakfast Association of Oahu, Inc., (☎262-8286; www.stayoahu.com). A network of area bed and breakfasts; send an email in with approximate dates, price range, and location. If they can offer you a place, they'll respond with availability.

BED AND BREAKFASTS

Papaya Paradise Bed and Breakfast, 395 Auwinala Rd. (☎261-0316; www.kailuaoahuhawaii.com). From Kailua Rd. continue straight onto Wanaao Rd. Turn right onto Awakea Rd. and make a quick left onto Auwinala Rd. Lovely units furnished in tropical rattan and wicker, each with a private entrance, bath, A/C, cable TV, and telephone. Guests share a kitchenette with refrigerator and microwave, and a poolside lanai with an amazing view of the mountains. Breakfast of baked goods, cereal, fruit and coffee. Boogie boards, snorkels, masks, and beach gear available to guests free of charge. 3-night min. Check-in 3pm. Check-out 11am. Doubles $95, each additional person $15. $100 refundable deposit for 3-day stay, $200 for a longer stay. ❸

Manu Mele Bed and Breakfast, 153 Kailuana Pl. (☎262-0016). Hawaiian for "birdsong," Manu Mele was named for the birds that sing by the pool. All 3 units are immaculate and self-sufficient, with mini-fridge, microwave, coffee maker, cable, and A/C. Fruits and baked goods for breakfast. This B&B's beach is popular with locals; ask to borrow beach gear from the common guest closet. 2-night min. No children. Refundable $100 deposit. Check-in afternoon. Check-out 11am. Rooms $90-100. Cash only. ❸

Kay's Alii Vacation Rental, 232 and 237 Awakea Rd. (☎262-9545; www.kaysvacations.com). Heading to town on Kailua Rd., continue onto Wanaao Rd., then turn left onto Awakea St. Kay's properties are across the street from each other, before Aumoe Rd. Rooming options vary. All rooms have cable and access to a grill and coin-op washer and dryer. 3-night min. Check-in 4pm (call ahead). Check-out 11am. Doubles $60-235; each additional adult $15, child $10. Cleaning fee $25-150. AmEx. ❸

OAHU

FOOD

While the beach is Kailua's most obvious gem, diverse and unique restaurants make the town's food scene almost as enticing. For grocery stores, Kailua has the outstanding **Kalapawai Market,** 306 S. Kalaheo Ave., that also has a deli and great coffee. (☎262-4359. Open daily 6am-9pm. MC/V.) There's also a **Foodland,** 108 Hekili St., for basic groceries, (☎261-3211; open 24hr. AmEx/D/MC/V.), and **The Source,** 32 Kainehe St., for all your natural food needs. (☎262-5604. Open M-F 9am-9pm, Sa 9am-6pm, Su 10am-5pm. D/MC/V.)

RESTAURANTS

Hojin, 609 Kalua Road, Ste. 111 (☎263-6636). This Mongolian barbecue and traditional Korean restaurant offers fresh and healthy dishes without sacrificing taste. Choose 4vegetables, any meat and any sauce for a personalized stir fry ($6.29). Daily special ($5) of Mongolian chicken, beef, pork, or vegetables from 11am-3pm. MC/V. ❶

Lucy's Grill N' Bar, 33 Aulike St. (☎230-8188), off of Kuulei Rd. Lucy's serves gourmet *pupus,* inexpensive pizzas ($9-12), and grill favorites, such as *kiawe* broiled baby back ribs ($16). Their specialty is the Ahi Tower, a stacked dish of rice, avocado and fresh ahi fish ($13). Wed. wine night: ½-priced bottles with an entree. Dinner daily 5-9pm. F-Sa bar open until 11pm. Reservations recommended. MC/V. ❸

Casablanca, 19 Hoolai St. (☎262-8196). Heading into Kailua from Pali Hwy., Hoolai St. is the last left before the town center. Well worth the splurge, Casablanca serves an exclusive 5-course *prix fixe* menu, with a choice of an entree or the house special (regular entree, $33; house special, $39). The restaurant offers a truly authentic Moroccan dining experience—patrons sit on floor cushions and eat with their hands in a luxuriously decorated interior. A shower of orange blossoms follows each meal. Belly dancers may be reserved. BYOB. Open Tu-Sa 6-8:30pm. Reservations recommended. MC/V. ❺

Baci Bistro, 30 Aulike St. (☎262-7555). Emphasizing old world know-how, Baci Bistro has earned a reputation as Kailua's best Italian restaurant. The restaurant serves a range of hot and cold antipasti (bruschetta, $6), salads ($4-8), and entrees (*Gnocchi con gorgonzola*, $14). Lunch sandwiches $5.50+. Lunch M-F 11:30am-2pm. Dinner daily 5:30-10pm. Weekend reservations recommended. AmEx/MC/V. ❸

Buzz's Steakhouse, 413 Kawailoa Rd. (☎261-4661). Take Kailua Rd. all the way to Kailua Beach Park and turn right onto S. Kalaheo; Buzz's parking lot is on the right after the bridge. This steakhouse has been a Kailua staple for 44 years. Locals flock to the all-you-can-eat salad bar ($9). Lunch serves a simpler menu of salads ($8-13) and burgers ($8-9). Lunch daily 11am-2pm. Dinner 5-10pm. Drinks and *pupus* 11am-10pm. Reservations recommended. Cash only. ❸

Pinky's Pupu Bar & Grill, 970 N. Kalaheo Ave. (☎254-6255, take-out 254-1112). Head north of town on Kalaheo Ave. Access to Pinky's driveway is past the restaurant on the right-hand side. Quantity is the name of the game at Pinky's, from the huge menu of *pupus* ($2-10) to the big entrees of Hawaiian and mainland origin ($7.50-19). 18 oz. beers $3, pitchers $5; 18 oz. Mai Tais $6. Open daily 4-10pm. AmEx/D/MC/V. ❸

Assaggio's, 354 Uluniu St. (☎261-2772), maintains a full menu of Italian dishes and an eager staff to serve them. The restaurant is well-known for its Caesar salad ($6, min. 2 orders) and colossal martinis ($5). Specialties include the *Chicken Alla Saltimboca Romana* ($12) and the Seafood Combination ($15). Bottomless baskets of homemade bread. Lunch M-F 11:30am-2:30pm. Dinner M-Th and Su 5-9:30pm, F-Sa 5-10pm. Reservations recommended. AmEx/D/MC/V. ❸

Aloha Salads, 600 Kailua Rd., Ste. 103 (☎262-2016), near the Kailua Visitor's Information Center. This leafy joint usually has a line out the door. Design your own salad from a cornucopia of toppings, or choose one of their pre-made salads. Limited seating; plan on taking it to go. Open daily 10:30am-8pm. MC/V. ❷

K & K Bar-B-Que Inn, 130 Kailua Rd., #102A (☎262-2272), in the Kailua Beach Center. Fast, local grinds a barefoot walk from the beach. Breakfast ($4-5), affordable sandwiches (hamburger $1.65), mini plate lunch ($5) or regular ($6-7), and Chinese specialties. Open M-Sa 9am-8pm, Su 9am-5pm. Cash only. ❶

Boston's North End Pizza, 29 Hoolai St. (☎263-7757). Hoolai St. is the last left on Kailua-bound Kailua Rd. before Oneawa St. A 19 in. cheese pizza pie ($14) weighs in at 3 lb. Enormous slices start at $4.25. Calzones $5. Open M-Th and Su 11am-8pm, F-Sa 11am-9pm. AmEx/D/MC/V. ❶

Saeng's Thai Cuisine, 315 Hahani St. (☎263-9727 or 263-9728). Head toward the beach on Kailua Rd. from the center of town and turn right onto Hahani St. Curry favor by leaving money on the Buddha statues that habitate this inexpensive Thai food restaurant (entrees, $7-15). The Thai curry ($8) and Panang mixed vegetables ($8) are especially popular. Open daily 11am-2pm and 5-9:30pm. AmEx/MC/V. ❷

Palisades Drive Inn #2, 130 Kailua Rd, Ste. 112 (☎261-8828), is perfect for a quick, cheap bite. They offer a variety of burgers and sandwiches ($1.35-3), Asian-influenced dishes, such as Garlic and Orange Chicken ($6.25), and breakfast until 11am. Canopied outdoor seating. Open M-Sa 9am-8pm, Su 9:30am-7:30pm. Cash only. ❶

BAKERIES

Agnes' Portuguese Bake Shop, 46 Hoolai St. (☎262-5367), across the street from Boston's North End Pizza. Agnes' is popular for its soups (cup $4.15), coffee (small $1.10), and above all, for the specialty baked goods and desserts. Call 15min. ahead for hot, fresh *malasadas*—divine, Portuguese-style doughnuts ($0.65, $6.45 per dozen). Customers can eat in an elegant cafe or take their treats to go. Internet access $2.50 per 15min. Open Tu-Sa 6am-6pm, Su 6am-2pm. D/MC/V. ❶

BEACHES

KAILUA BEACH. *(Boogie boarding. Wind sports. Open daily 24hr.)* Though proclaiming the nation's most beautiful beach is difficult, the delicately curving neck of white sand around Kailua Bay's splendid turquoise waters pleads a strong case. The fickle wind, which blows from nearly every direction, makes the bay the best windsport area on Oahu. Particularly during the winter, spectators gather to gape at the expert windsurfers and kiteboarders who careen over the whipped-up waves. In addition, kayakers frequently cross to the Bird Sanctuaries on the **Flat** and **Mokulua Islands.** The usually gentle surf makes the beach popular for swimmers and families. There are parking lots (which fill up early on weekends), bathrooms, showers, a small craft storage building, and a boat ramp in Kailua Beach Park. The secluded northern half of Kailua Beach is the grassy **Kalama Beach Park.** The virgin sand here has fewer visitors than Kailua Beach Park, and the choppier waves are free from the congestion of watersport traffic farther south. Kalama is a good learning spot for novice boogie boarders and bodysurfers. Beach facilities include a restroom, showers, and picnic tables. *(Take the Lanikai-bound bus #70 from Kailua town center. By car, turn right off Kailua Rd. onto S. Kalaheo Ave. The 1st parking lot is on the left as S. Kalaheo Ave. becomes Kawailoa Rd. before crossing the drainage canal. To reach Kalama Beach Park, turn left on N. Kalaheo Ave. from Kuulei Rd.; the parking lot is on the right at the intersection with Hauoli St.)*

LANIKAI BEACH. *(Snorkeling. Open daily 24hr.)* Fine-grained, sugar-like sand is Lanikai's calling card; even the most flattering postcards don't do justice to this utterly romantic destination. Tradewinds from the Windward Coast glide over the Koolau Mountains and lap up on Lanikai, creating an unusually soft and smooth shoreline. The offshore coral reef provides a light surf, and the tide's gentle waves are inviting to sunbathers, newlyweds, and artists alike. Lanikai is an essential destination for swimming and snorkeling. *(Public beach access to these secluded sands is on Mokulua Dr. Driving east on Kawailoa Rd. past Kailua Beach Park, make a left at the stop sign onto Alala Rd. Follow Aalapapa Dr. as it loops around Lanikai and becomes Mokulua Dr. TheBus #70 also makes a loop around Lanikai.)*

ACTIVITIES

Kailua Sailboards and Kayaks Inc., 130 Kailua Rd. (☎262-2555), in Kailua Beach Center. In Kailua, the best tours start in the water. Paddle out to Popoia and Mokulua islands, sail with sea turtles, or see the Mokulua Island Bird Sanctuary up close in one of Kailua Sailboards's tours. Guided kayak tour $119; self-guided tour $79 (lunch and transportation included). Windsurfing lessons (3hr. group lesson $89), surfing lessons (private lesson $60), and kiteboarding lessons (introductory class $119) also available. Rent kayaks (from $49 per day), surfboards ($25 per day), sailboards ($49+ per day), kiteboards ($25 per day), and bicycles ($15 per day). Weekly and half-day rates available. A Funpak allows you to use any of Kailua Sailboards's water toys for 7 days ($299 per person). Open daily 9am-5pm. AmEx/D/MC/V.

Naish Hawaii, 155 Hamakua Dr. (☎262-6068). Rick Naish, father of 1976 world champion windsurfer Robby Naish, no longer sells custom-built boards from his garage, but his family still runs this premier windsurfing rental and instruction center. Beginner boards $25+ for 2hr.; intermediate to advanced boards $40+ for ½ day, $55 for full day. Beginner group lessons $45, private lesson $75; intermediate and advanced private lessons $75. Kiteboarding beginner lesson $125. Special rates available with your own gear. Call one week in advance. Open daily 9am-5:30pm. AmEx/D/MC/V.

Aaron's Dive Shop, 307 Hahani St. (☎262-2333; www.hawaii-scuba.com). From Kailua Rd., turn right at the town center and then right onto Hahani St. Rent scuba gear for around $50 per day, or join the ranks of Tom Selleck, Jerry Garcia, and David Hasselhoff, and go on one of the daily dive trips (4-5hr.; 2-tank dive includes equipment rental, lunch, and transportation; $125). Aaron's also offers dolphin excursions starting at $90. Dive spots fill up fast—reserve 3-4 months in advance. Open M-F 7am-7pm, Sa 7am-6pm, Su 7am-5pm. AmEx/D/MC/V.

SIGHTS

ULUPO HEIAU. This sacred *heiau* (temple) is set on a peaceful plateau of lava rocks beside a shady grove with benches and a few placards. *Heiaus* were traditionally built at the orders of *kahunas* (priests) to ensure success in war and agricultural fertility. Following the abolition of the native religion in 1819 at this site, the surrounding areas became a taro root patch. Chinese buyers converted the same land into a rice paddy in the late 1800s, but it was abandoned as marshland by 1920. Thick growth conceals the bottom of the morass, home to endangered native waterfowl. For non-history buffs, the state monument still provides a nice walk through well-kept flower gardens. *(Near Kailua. Heading to Kailua from Pali Hwy., turn left onto Uluoa St., at the corner of First Baptist Church Windward, and take the 1st right onto Manu Aloha. Go to the end of the block and take a right towards the YMCA. Park behind the Windward YMCA's lot and walk around it to the heiau.)*

HIKING

KAIWA RIDGE TRAIL. *(2 mi. round-trip. ¾-1¼hr. Moderate.)* This hike climbs up the ridge behind Lanikai beach to WWII army bunkers, or "pillboxes," overlooking the beach. From the top, 600 ft. up, you can see Molokai, Lanai, and, on a superbly clear day, Maui. Despite its popularity, the trail receives minimal maintenance, and hikers are advised to use caution and not to climb the bunkers. Kaiwa Ridge is dusty, lacking moisture and vegetation common to most of Oahu's other trails. You may either return the way you came up, or continue along the trail to loop back around to Mokolea Dr. *(Take Aalapapa Dr. into Lanikai and then turn right on Kaelepulu Dr. At the Mid-Pacific Country Club, park in the turnout on the right side of the street. The dirt trailhead is unmarked, across the street on the right side at the bend in the private uphill road.)*

MAUNAWILI DITCH TRAIL. *(2¾ mi. 1¼-1¾hr. Easy.)* This equestrian, bike, and hiking red-dirt trail rises an easy 200 ft. and ends at the Waimanalo side of the **Maunawili Trail.** *(Drive 3 mi. toward Waimanalo from Castle Junction on Kalanianaloe Hwy., and turn right on Kumuhau St. At the end of Kumuhau St., turn right onto Waikupanaha St. and drive less than ¼ mi. down the street, past Mahiku Pl. Park in the pullout at the right side of the road. The narrow, unfenced trailhead is in front of this pullout.)*

MAUNAWILI TRAIL. *(10 mi. round-trip. 4-6hr. Elevation gain: 500 ft. Moderate.)* The terrain of the Maunawili ("twisted mountain") Trail varies from wet, overgrown gulches to open forest canopies as it traverses the Windward base of the Koolau Mountain Range. The voyage among *koa*, *lobelia*, *ohia*, and other vegetation ends with transcendent views of Olomana, the Koolaupoko watershed, and Waimanalo. Bikers are also allowed on this trail, but must yield to pedestrians. The freshwater streams and mud may contain *leptospirosis*. *(On Pali Hwy. from Honolulu to Kailua, drive out of the tunnels for approx. 1 mi. before turning right into the parking area marked "Scenic Point," along the turn to the left. There are yellow blinking lights and arrows pointing left. The trailhead is located at the entrance to this parking area.)*

MAUNAWILI FALLS TRAIL. *(1¼ mi. 30min. Moderate.)* The wet and muddy Maunawili Falls Trail crosses the Maunawili Stream frequently without the aid of bridges, often requiring agile rock hopping skills. The trail passes through apple and coffee trees and is universally popular with people young and old. There is a stair climb down at the last stream crossing to reach the payoff: a cool, deep pool and a short cascading waterfall. Local teenagers who visit the spot sometimes jump off of the waterfall into the pool, but it is not recommended; *leptospirosis* may be in the water and even in the mud. *(Driving toward Kailua on the Pali Hwy., turn right onto Auloa Rd. before reaching Castle Junction (Rt. 72 and Pali Hwy.). Auloa Rd. splits almost immediately; take the left fork, Maunawili Rd. Follow this road through a residential neighborhood, and look for the trailhead signs. After the signs, continue straight over the narrow bridge. Be sure to park on the right along the residential roads. Do not leave valuables in your car.)*

INSIDE THE OUTDOORS. For an insider's look at Oahu's natural side, check out www.backyardoahu.com. The site offers trail listings, descriptions, and discussion forums for backpackers and hikers and FAQs for newbies.

KANEOHE AND THE WINDWARD COAST

At the base of northbound Kamehameha Hwy., Kaneohe (pop. 34,970) is where the Windward road trip starts. Stock up here before hitting the road; farther up the coast, B&Bs are replaced by campsites, and restaurants become sparse.

ORIENTATION AND PRACTICAL INFORMATION

To get to Kaneohe from Honolulu, take **H-1** to **Route 63 (Likelike Highway)** or **Route 61 (Pali Highway)** and head northeast. Turn left onto **Route 83 (Kamehameha Highway),** which intersects both after the mountains and continues northwest to Kaneohe. From the northern part of Kailua, take North Kalaheo Ave. farther northwest and out of town as it becomes **Route 630 (Kaneohe Bay Drive),** which travels through the southern part of Kaneohe and later takes the name Rte. 63/Likelike Hwy. as it heads toward Honolulu. Kaneohe's main artery, Rte. 83/Kamehameha Hwy., runs north-south through the heart of Kaneohe and up the Windward Coast.

Bus: TheBus #55 Circle Island and #65 Kahaluu go to **Kaneohe.** The Circle Island route runs up the Windward Coast's Kamehameha Hwy. and returns to Ala Moana as the #52 via Wahiawa and central Oahu. The #65 goes through Temple Valley and stops at Windward Mall. $2; seniors, disabled persons, and students $1.

Car Rental: Enterprise, 46-003 Alaloa St. (☎247-2909). Take Rte. 83 northbound and turn left on Kahuhipa St., then onto Alaloa St. Compact $28-33 per day. 21+. Collision damage waiver $17 per day; liability $10. Major credit card required. Refundable deposit at least $100. Free pick-up and drop-off service within Kaneohe. Open M-F 8am-6pm, Sa 9am-noon. AmEx/D/MC/V.

City Hall: Kaneohe Satellite (☎235-4571), in the Windward Mall, 2nd fl. next to Sears. Camping permits available here. Open M-F 9am-5pm, Sa 8am-4pm.

Bank: Bank of Hawaii, 45-1001 Kamehameha Hwy. (☎233-4670). Turn right on William Henry Rd. to access parking lot. Open M-Th 8:30am-4pm, F 8:30am-6pm.

Library: Kaneohe Public Library, 45-829 Kamehameha Hwy. (☎233-5676). Turn right on Waikalua Rd. and make another quick right into the library's driveway, which runs alongside the police station. Open Tu, Th, Su 10am-5pm; M and W 10am-8pm; F 1-5pm. **Internet access** with a 3-month visitor's card ($10). Copies $0.15 per page.

Laundromat: Kaneohe Washerette (☎235-1238), next to the post office on Kamehameha Hwy., before the Windward Mall. Wash $1.75, dry $0.25 per 6min. Soap $0.75. Open 24hr.

Police: Kaneohe Substation, 45-270 Waikalua Rd. (☎247-2166). **Kahuku Substation,** 56-470 Kamehameha Hwy. (☎293-8565).

Pharmacy: Long's Drugs, 46-047 Kamehameha Hwy. (☎235-4511). All-purpose drug store with pharmacy and one-hour photo lab. Open daily 7am-midnight.

Medical Services: Straub Kaneohe Family Health Center, 46-056 Kamehameha Hwy. (☎233-6200), 2nd fl. inside the Windward Mall. Appointment only. M-Sa 8am-7:30pm, Su 10am-5:30pm.

Fax Office: Kinko's (with FedEx), 46-047 Kamehameha Hwy. (☎234-5500). Open M-Th 7am-10pm, F 7am-9pm, Sa 9am-9pm, Su 9am-5pm.

Internet Access: Kaneohe District Park, 45-660 Keaahala Rd. (☎233-7309). Free Internet access on 6 terminals M, W, and F 5-7pm. Also see **Kaneohe Public Library,** (p. 151).

Post Offices: Kaneohe Main Office, 46-036 Kamehameha Hwy. (☎235-1055). Open M-F 8am-6pm, Sa 9am-4pm. Last collection M-F 5pm, Sa 4:30pm. **Kaaawa Main Office,** 51-480 Kamehameha Hwy. (☎237-8372). Open M-F 8am-noon and 1-3:45pm, Sa 9:30-11:30am. **Laie Main Office,** 55-510 Kamehameha Hwy., Ste. 20 (☎293-0337). Open M-F 9am-3:30pm, Sa 9:30-11:30am.

Postal Codes: 96744 (Kaneohe); 96730 (Kaaawa); 96762 (Laie).

ACCOMMODATIONS AND CAMPING

BED AND BREAKFASTS

Alii Bluffs Windward Bed and Breakfast, 46-251 Ikiiki St. (☎235-1124 or 800-235-1151; www.hawaiiscene.com/aliibluffs). Take Kamehameha Hwy. north through Kaneohe, turn right onto Ipuka St. after S.W. King School, then take an immediate left onto Ikiiki St. This charming, antique-inspired home has 2 themed rooms (Victorian and circus). No children. Continental breakfast includes fresh fruit, cereal, juice, tea, and coffee. Laundry and parking available. Victorian room $80, circus room $70. MC/V. ❸

CAMPING

Permits for the state parks along the Windward Coast are free and available at the Divison of State Parks, 1151 Punchbowl St. Rm. 310, Honolulu (☎587-0300; www.hawaii.gov/dlnr/dsp/). The Department of Parks and Recreation in the Honolulu Municipal Bulding, 650 South King St. (☎523-4525) and any City Hall satellite in the area can issue permits for City and County Parks. See **Camping in Hawaii,** p. 75, for more information. All state, city, and county parks are open M-Tu and F-Su. Sites abound on Kamehameha Hwy:

Malaekahana Campgrounds, 1 mi. north Laie on Kamehamena Hwy. These grounds are privately owned by the Friends of Malaekahana (☎293-1736; www.malaekahana.net) and are available 7 days a week. Popular and somewhat secluded camping area has campsites, yurts, cabins and old beach cottages. Outdoor shower facilities, 24hr. security, and a swimming beach on Laie Bay. Gates locked 7pm-7am. Quiet hours after 9pm. Alcohol free premises. Check-in 3pm, check-out noon. $5.25 per person; 6-person yurt with private bathroom $130; beach cabins without bathroom $66-80. Large but aging cottage sleeps 20 for $250. MC/V. ❶

Kualoa Regional Park, 49-479 Kamehameha Hwy., on Kaneohe Bay, about 1 mi. past Tropical Farms and before the entrance to Kualoa Ranch. Families frequent this campsite for its scenic surroundings and safe swimming near the shore. Lifeguard on duty daily in summer, weekends only in winter. To reserve a space, go to a satellite City Hall 2 Fridays before you intend to camp. Get there soon after it opens, as permits are usually gone by 9am. 30 sites. Restrooms, showers, and parking on the premises. Camping M-Tu and F-Su. Park closed to public daily 8pm-7am. Free. ❶

Swanzy Beach Park, 51-369 Kamehameha Hwy., about 3 mi. north of Kualoa Regional Park, beyond Kaaawa Point. Swanzy Beach, while rocky and not great for swimming, is suitable for fishing and snorkeling. The park, also popular with families, is protected by a concrete wall with stairs leading down to the water. Basketball court, restrooms, and showers on premises. Not gated. 9 sites. Make reservations 2 Fridays in advance at the satellite City Hall (Kanohe) or the Department of Parks and Recreation in Honolulu. Camping M-Tu and F-Su. Free. ❶

Hauula Beach Park, 54-135 Kamehameha Hwy., north of Kaneohe, beyond Kahana Bay on Kamehameha Hwy. The beach is a bit littered and rocky, but Hauula's calm waves allow good swimming. The park has restrooms, picnic tables, and volleyball nets. Not gated. 15 undesignated sites. Camping M-Tu and F-Su. Free. ❶

FOOD

Travelers should check out Kaneohe's restaurants, especially before heading up the Windward Coast. Farther north, dining options are sparse. To stock up on groceries, there's a **Foodland,** 45-480 Kamehameha Hwy., in the Windward City Shopping Center in Kaneohe. (☎247-3357. Open daily 6am-midnight. AmEx/D/MC/V.) **Room Service in Paradise,** 670 Auahi St., Ste. A9, is also worth a try; they deliver from many restaurants in the area. Allow 1hr. to receive your food. Check website for participating businesses. (☎9413463; www.941dine.com. Open daily 11am-9pm. AmEx/D/MC/V.)

RESTAURANTS

Pah Ke's, 46-018 Kamehameha Hwy. (☎235-4505). Pah Ke's spacious, stylish interior is the perfect setting for their superb Chinese food. The extensive menu has something to suit every palate and price range. The fresh food is cooked in a health-conscious manner, with mostly local ingredients and no MSG. The lunch plate ($5.50) includes sweet and sour pork, *kau yuk,* pork chop suey, steamed rice, and 2 crispy won-tons. Creative seasonal salads are a house specialty ($6-18). Entrees include black pepper steak sizzling platter ($9), braised black mushrooms with vegetables ($7), and Hong Kong-style fried chicken ($6). Open daily 10:30am-9pm. AmEx/MC/V. ❷

Zia's Caffe, 45-620 Kamehameha Hwy. (☎235-9427). Zia's greets locals as well as weary Windward travelers with hearty, traditional Italian fare and an inviting atmosphere for any occasion. The lunch menu offers a selection of pasta or sandwich combos (includes soup and salad, $8-9). The real specialties, such as the Tuscan chicken penne ($15.95), emerge at dinner time. Entrees $10-23. Eat inside, out on the patio, or take it to go. Open daily 11am-10pm. MC/V. ❸

Masa and Joyce, 45-582 Kamehameha Hwy. (☎235-6129), in Kaneohe. Locals consistently crowd this bastion of Hawaiian and Japanese dishes. Choose from a selection of breakfasts (special includes 2 eggs, choice of meat, 2 scoops rice, and toast; $5), plate lunches (*kalua* pig and cabbage, $6), sushi *bentos* ($6.25), *pupus*, and *poke*. Allow 15min. prep time or call ahead for breakfast (served all day) and plate lunches. Open W-F 9am-6pm, Sa 9am-4pm, Su 9am-2pm. MC/V. ❶

Crouching Lion Inn, 51-666 Kamehameha Hwy. (☎237-8511). This roadside diner overlooks a beautiful strip of the Kahana Bay, and the extensive menu will quell any appetite. After feeding famished road trippers with a gourmet bacon cheeseburger or mahi mahi melt (both $8.50) for lunch, dinner brings out the superior house specialty: *kalua* pork with sweet steamed cabbage and *poi* bread pudding ($15). Try Crouching on the Beach, the house cocktail ($5.50). Open daily 11am-9pm. AmEx/D/MC/V. ❹

BAKERIES

Kaneohe Bakery, 45-1026 Kamehameha Hwy. (☎247-0474). The doughnuts ($1; $9 per dozen), danishes ($1.20), cakes ($9.50-12), and cream pies ($8.79-8.99) are only matched in sweetness by the service. Open daily 4am-midnight. AmEx/MC/V. ❶

SIGHTS

VALLEY OF THE TEMPLES. A Christian chapel and Buddhist temple honor the followers of all religions, races, and creeds who are buried in this beautiful and unique cemetery. According to the current temple bishop Fukuhara, "Prayers illuminate the mundane world with a bright light." Byodo-In, the Buddhist temple of equality, is a perfect replica of the 900-year-old temple in Uji, Japan, built around an enormous statue of Buddha. The ring of the temple's three-ton brass bell (said to bring good fortune to the ringers) echoes over the *koi*-filled pools and tranquil groves, which are inhabited by wild black swans and peacocks. *(47-200 Kahekili Hwy. Driving north on Kamehameha Hwy. toward Kaneohe, turn left onto Likelike Hwy. and then right onto Kahekili Hwy. To enter The Valley of the Temples, turn left onto Hui Iwa St. Open daily 8am-5:30pm. Entrance to Byodo-in Temple $2, children and seniors $1.)*

HOOMALUHIA BOTANICAL GARDEN. *Hoomaluhia* can be translated as "a place of peace and serenity," and this beautiful, 400-acre botanical garden is steeped in tranquility. The site is home to plants, trees, and flowers from major tropical climates around the world. Native Hawaiian birds nest along the smooth and well-groomed lawns surrounding the garden's lake. Driving and biking are permitted along designated paths. Visitors can participate in a free "catch and release" fishing program Saturday and Sunday 10am-2pm; equipment is available to borrow. Full moon walks are given on certain Saturdays, call ahead for the schedule. **Camping,** with a permit available from the Vistors Center, is allowed from 9am Friday to 4pm Monday. Restrooms, showers, fire pits, picnic tables, and parking lots are spread throughout the park. Campers should expect wet conditions in the rainforest-like setting—don't forget the bug repellent. *(45-680 Luluku Rd. ☎233-7323. Driving north on Kamehameha Hwy., turn left onto*

Luluku Rd. at the Aloha Gas Station. Alternatively, take TheBus #55 to this junction. The garden is 1 mi. from Kamehameha Hwy. The Visitors center is 1 mi. beyond the entrance. Open daily 9am-4pm. Guided tours Sa 10am and Su 1pm. After 4pm all cars staying in the park must be registered. Free.)

ART SMART. Call the botanical garden ahead of time to see when they will be hosting a new art exhibit in their popular gallery. Opening nights, featuring the works of local artists, offer drinks and *pupus* at a public reception.

QUEEN EMMA'S SUMMER PALACE. This small palace, also known as ***Hanaiakamalama*** (foster child of the moon), was once the retreat of Kamehameha IV's cosmopolitan queen in the mid-1800s. After the Daughters of Hawaii averted plans to turn it into a baseball park, the palace became a museum of furniture and memorabilia that once belonged to Queen Emma, including a bracelet with a lock of Queen Victoria's hair. Ask the guides to point out the furniture woodwork made of native *koa, kou, milo*, and *kamani*. *(2913 Pali Hwy. ☎595-3167. Going north from Honolulu, 2 mi. down H-1. Open daily 9am-4pm. $6, seniors $4, children $1.)*

NUUANU PALI LOOKOUT. This is the site of the Battle of the Nuuanu Pali's dramatic finish, where Oahu warriors were driven up and over the 980 ft. *palis* (cliffs) by King Kamehameha who was fighting to unite the Hawaiian Islands. Legend claims the wind is strong enough to knock a man from the cliffs and then blow him right back up. Two million years ago a catastrophic landslide sank half of the Koolau volcano into the Pacific; the Pali lookout is the edge of what remains. When standing at this point, visitors are surrounded by miles of 2000 ft. cliffs and an amazing panoramic view of the Hoomaluhia Botanical Garden, Kaneohe, Mokolii Island, Mokapu Peninsula, and the infinite horizon.

The tunnels exit immediately below the Pali Lookout, affording drivers the same sweeping bay view. If you're heading back to Honolulu from the Windward side, there is a roadside scenic point on the right as the highway begins to curve to enter the tunnels. From Honolulu to Kailua, there is a marked overlook at the left hairpin turn, 1 mi. after exiting the tunnels. There is also parking here for the **Maunawili Trail** (see p. 149). Call the Office of Forestry and Wildlife (☎587-0166) for more information. The Pali Lookout has informative placards and plenty of parking. *(North of Honolulu on the Pali Hwy. Open daily 9am-4pm. Don't leave valuables in your car.)*

THE POLYNESIAN CULTURAL CENTER. Equal parts cultural exhibit and amusement park, this 40-year-old, 42-acre mammoth tourist attraction employs an army of native and Polynesian performers, artisans, cooks, and cultural conservators to display the rich traditions of Polynesian cultures. The islands all have villages with surprisingly authentic and intriguing performances—see real Tahitian hula, or learn how Samoans start a fire with sticks, open coconuts with their bare hands, and climb palm trees to dizzying heights. The spectacular canoe pageant at 2:30pm gives a sampling of the music and dance from all of the islands. There's an IMAX screen, canoe rides, free tram tours of Laie, a spectacular night-time luau buffet and show, and much more, depending on the variety of ticket purchased. Plan to spend a few hours at the park. *(55-370 Kamehameha Hwy. ☎293-3333 or 800-367-7060; www.polynesia.com. In Laie; you can't miss the 10 ft. wooden Tiki statues that frown over the roadside and in front of the parking lot. Call for transportation reservations; a bus leaves Waikiki at 10am. Round trip $16; curbside or hotel pick-up $24. Open M-Sa noon-9pm. $50-200, children ages 5-11 $35-136. No alcohol. AmEx/D/MC/V.)*

THE MORMON TEMPLE. A sight to behold, the temple was built of crushed volcanic rock and coral, and it sits on a 6000-acre plantation purchased in 1865 by The Church of Jesus Christ of Latter-Day Saints. The temple itself is reserved for members of the Church; visitors are not allowed inside. Beyond the temple, well-manicured formal gardens drape the 11-acre site and Visitors Center. The Center's guided tours explain the church's beliefs with obvious but unobtrusive missionary overtones. The Visitors Center houses a 16 ft. commanding and majestic replica of the 1834 sculpture Christus, along with a spiritual message translated in 28 languages. *(55-645 Naniloa Loop. ☎293-9297. A free tram line runs here from The Polynesian Cultural Center through Laie every 20min. from 1-6:40pm. By car, turn left onto Hale Laa Blvd., the first street after the Laie Shopping Center. Open daily 9am-8pm. Free.)*

KUALOA RANCH AND REGIONAL PARK. The Kualoa Ranch, a privately owned 4000-acre cattle ranch-turned-tourist attraction, stretches up Kualoa, Hakipuu, and Kaaawa Valleys. Visitors can go horseback riding or off-roading on an ATV (both $45 per hr.). Other activities include a Ranch and Movie Set Tour ($15), with sites from Jurassic Park and TV series Lost, a Jeep Jungle Expedition in a six-wheel Swiss Army off-road Jeep ($15) and target shooting ($30). Ask about the self-guided tour of Secret Isle which includes kayaks, snorkel gear, volleyball nets and hammocks on the Ranch's private beach ($20 per 2hr., $30 per 4hr.). Visitors can dine inside at **Aunty Pat's Paniolo Cafe,** which offers Hawaiian specials, including a wide selection of burgers and plate lunches (all under $8). Nearby **Kualoa Regional Park,** on the coastal side of the highway south of the ranch entrance, is the closest point to Mokolii Island, commonly referred to as Chinaman's Hat, a Windward landmark nicknamed for its tapering, peaked shape. Kualoa Point, at the extreme end of the park, marks the northern edge of Kaneohe Bay. *(49-479 Kamehameha Hwy. The main entrance to the ranch is on the mauka, or mountain, side of Kamehameha Hwy., north of Kualoa Regional Park. ☎237-8515, reservations 237-7321; www.kualoa.com. Open daily 8am-5pm. Sa-Su ATV and horseback riding only. For information on Kualoa Regional Park, see Camping, p. 152. MC/V.)*

TROPICAL FARMS OUTLET. Set in the midst of Kualoa Ranch, about 1½ mi. south of Kualoa Park, Tropical Farms Outlet sells nuts from the only working macadamia nut farm on Oahu. The extensive gift shop offers free samples of freshly harvested nuts, Kona-macadamia coffee, and exotic locally produced items such as macadamia nut brittle, cooking oil, and sea salt. Visitors can explore the surrounding **Kualoa Tropical Gardens** by bus and the 800-year-old "Secret Island" fish pond by canoe on the **Alii Tour,** which also includes a presentation combining education on native culture with stand-up comedy. *(49-227A Kamehameha Hwy. ☎237-1960 or 877-505-6887. For information about the Alii Tour call ☎781-2474 or visit www.chiefsielu.com. Adults $15, children under 10 free.)*

HIKING

HAUULA LOOP AND MAAKUA RIDGE TRAILS. *(2½ mi. each. 1-1½hr. Easy.)* The trailhead for both trails is Hauula Homestead Rd., across from Hauula Beach Park (p. 152). The initial paved trail comes to a fork close to the start; to hike the **Hauula Loop Trail** take the right fork, which climbs up the ridge to cross Waipilopilo Gulch. The path then turns back toward the ocean, overlooks Kipapau Valley, and passes several waterfalls before it loops back to the beginning of the trail. Although uphill on the way out, the initial trail is fairly easy and well-suited for families. The **Maakua Ridge Trail** begins in a *hau* forest on the left side of the access road, beyond the Hauula Loop Trailhead. After a stream

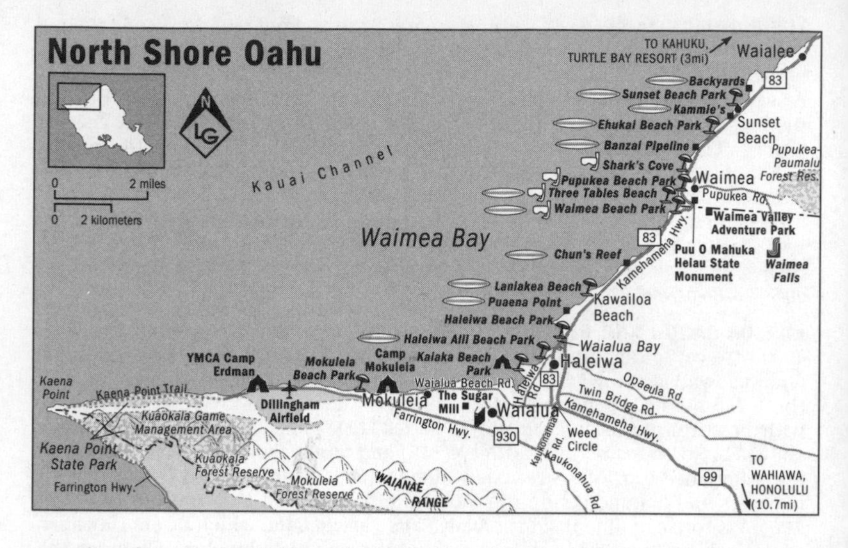

crossing, there is a switchback to a ridge-top shelter with benches overlooking seaside Hauula. The loop begins here and you may proceed in either direction up 800 ft. in moderate to difficult terrain. Both trails are accessible to mountain bikers, so use caution when heading out on foot. Watch out for Dick Cheney, this area is also a hunting ground. The water may contain *leptospirosis;* be careful and don't hike with open cuts. *(By car from Kamehameha Hwy. northbound, turn left at the 2nd entrance to Hauula Homestead Rd., at the corner with a 7-11. Where the road curves sharply to the left, continue straight onto Maakua Rd. Park roadside before the cable gate. Hauula Loop Trail begins on the right, beyond the hunter/hiker check-in station.)*

NORTH SHORE

There are only a few words to describe the break on Oahu's North Shore: gnarly, mean, and real. Surf is not a sub-culture here; it's the consciousness of an entire tight-knit community. For Oahu, this stretch of coastline is a place to kick back and relax. It's tranquil, low-key, and downright empty in certain parts. In the winter, however, the North Shore nearly explodes, as monstrous waves bring the world's best surfers in search of the perfect ride. From the rural surroundings of Turtle Bay to Sunset Beach and Waimea, one spectacular beach follows another, and some are, astonishingly, empty. Past Waimea, Haleiwa (p. 161) is the center of life on the North Shore, with first-rate restaurants, shops, galleries, and plenty of places to stock up on surf gear or Brazilian bikinis. West of Haleiwa, Wailua, once the North Shore's sugarcane powerhouse, is a rebounding town on the rise; the old sugar mill has been revamped and houses a handful of attractive local businesses. Even farther west, the small town of Mokuleia beckons thrill-seekers with myriad skydiving and mountain-biking adventures.

To reach the North Shore by car, take H-1 from Honolulu to the end of H-2, then follow Rte. 803 or Hwy. 99. Hwy. 83 (Kamehameha Hwy.) is the main road that runs along the coast through each town from Haleiwa to Kahuku, and down the Windward Coast. The North Shore is also served by TheBus #52, which runs from Honolulu via Wahiawa to Haleiwa, and then up the coast on Kamehameha Hwy. to Turtle Bay. TheBus #76 runs between Haleiwa and Waialua along Farrington Hwy.

WAIMEA AND SUNSET BEACH

Kamehameha Hwy. continues past Haleiwa along the northeastern coast of Oahu and through Waimea and Sunset Beach. Though there are no real town centers, both have clusters of roadside food stands, surf shacks, hostels, and miles of beach. This is *the* place to stay if you're serious about winter surfing, but it's also worthwhile during the calmer summer months, when in addition to the surfable "bumps," there is great snorkeling, swimming, and hiking up Pupukea (p. 160). Rollerbladers, bikers, joggers, and strollers enjoy the bike path that stretches for several miles between Sunset Beach and Waimea. Separated by thick trees and shrubbery from Kamehameha Hwy. and the houses that line it, the path provides a scenic, secluded view of the North Shore. TheBus #52 shuttles back and forth from Turtle Bay Resort in Kahuku through Sunset Beach and Waimea to Haleiwa.

ORIENTATION AND PRACTICAL INFORMATION

Kamehameha Highway is the main road from Haleiwa through Waimea and Sunset Beach. There is an **ATM** and Starbucks inside **Foodland,** at the intersection of Kamehameha Hwy. and Pupukea Rd. (Open daily 6am-11pm.) The nearest post offices are the **Haleiwa Post Office** (p. 162). and, on the Windward Coast, the **Kahuku Post Office,** 56-565 Kamehameha Hwy., past Sunset Beach. (☎293-0485. Open M-F 8:30am-4:30pm, Sa 8:30am-11:30am.) **Postal Code:** 96712 (Haleiwa), 96731 (Kahuku).

ACCOMMODATIONS

There are many vacation rentals available along the beaches near Waimea; call the real estate agents listed in Haleiwa (p. 163) for more information. Try **www.hawaiibeachfronts.com** for larger groups; they've got good prices and amazing views.

Shark's Cove Rentals, 59-672 Kamehameha Hwy. (☎638-7980; www.sharkscoverentals.com), across the Shark's Cove and Log Cabins breaks, look for 2 American flags just east of the old gas station next to Foodland. There are 3 houses, each with its own living room with cable TV, kitchen, and full bath. All rooms have bunk beds, and some also have a full-size bottom bunk. Grill, pay phone, soda machine, and coin-op laundry in the central courtyard. Free snorkel equipment for guests. Refundable security deposit $20. 3-day min. Room $75-185. MC/V. ❸

Backpackers, 59-788 Kamehameha Hwy. (☎638-7838; http://backpackers-hawaii.com), low-key and relaxed, across from Three Tables beach, has 50 beds for surfers, backpackers, and anyone else looking for the cheapest digs in town. A variety of accommodations, from 2- to 6-bed dorms to private beachfront cabins. Dorms and some private rooms share kitchen and bath; cabins have their own. Perks include free daily airport shuttle (with reservations), inexpensive nightly meals, free snorkel equipment and boogie boards, discounts on activities, Internet access ($7 per hr.), and equipment storage. Ask about **short-term work** in exchange for room and board. Linens provided. Reception 8am-7pm. Check-in after 10am. Check-out 10am. Reservations recommended. Dorms $15-18; private doubles $45-60; cottages $80-200. MC/V. ❶

AÇAÍ BOWLS

Every winter the huge North Shore waves attract a host of hopeful surfers from nearly every corner of the world. More than any other nation, the smiling Brazilian nationals have left their mark, as well as some of their countrymen. The tastiest vestige of this Brazilian influence has recently become a North Shore staple at breakfast, lunch, snack, or even dinner: açaí.

This frozen concoction is unparalleled in scrumptious goodness, and it also happens to be one of the healthiest drinks around. For $5-7, it'll keep your wallet in good shape as well.

Açaí is a dark purple berry that grows atop Amazonian palm trees. The caffeinated berry contains 10-30 times the antioxidants of red wine and over two times that of blueberries. Once the pulp is harvested, it must be processed and frozen within 24hr., in order to preserve its nutritional benefits.

The pulp is then thrown into a blender along with other berries and guarana juice. For the authentic experience, order an açaí bowl. More of a meal than a snack, the bowl is filled with sliced bananas, granola, and honey.

While there are a number of açaí sources along the North Shore, the best is at Kavaroots (☎638-5282), inside Devocean, a boutique across the street from Foodland.

Ke Iki Beach Bungalows, 59-579 Kamehameha Hwy. (☎638-8829; www.keikibeach.com), between Shark's Cove and Ehukai Beach Park. The beach bungalows have an unbeatable location directly on a long, sandy, and almost always empty beach. The view is spectacular year-round. The studio and 1- and 2-bedroom bungalows are newly renovated and landscaped, with patios and hammocks lining the beach. Surfboards are usually available to borrow. Reservations recommended. Cleaning $45-100. Streetside bungalows during low season $120-175; high season $135-190. Beachside $180-210/195-230. Discounts for stays 1 week or more. MC/V. ❸

FOOD

Foodland, 59-720 Kamehameha Hwy., by the traffic light at the intersection of Kamehameha Hwy. and Pupukea Rd., in Waimea, has the largest selection of groceries on the North Shore as well as a sushi bar, bakery, and deli. (☎638-8081. Open daily 6am-11pm.) Within Waimea and Sunset Beach, there are quite a few roadside food stands and take-out establishments that have earned solid reputations. Be sure to stop by the **North Shore County Market,** 59-530 Kamehameha Hwy., across from Ehukai Beach Park, at Sunset Beach Elementary School. Local farmers gather at this community event to sell fresh organic produce. The market is a great opportunity for travelers to catch a glimpse of the local North Shore community. (☎638-7172. Open Sa 8am-2pm.)

Island Shack, 59-254 Kamehameha Hwy. (☎638-9500), near Sunset Beach, behind a large wooden Maui Pohaku Loa statue. They say the kitchen resembles a *favela,* but you wouldn't know it after savoring the rich Brazilian grinds in Shack's breezy, chic atmosphere. Lunch plates $8.95-10.95. Dinner options include grilled chicken, fish, steak, garlic shrimp, and stir-fry vegetables. Try the *acai* berry, either in juice ($4) or bowl ($5) form. Open daily 11am-10pm. Live music F at 7pm. Cash only. ❷

Ted's Bakery, 59-024 Kamehameha Hwy. (☎638-8207), has been a North Shore favorite for 15 years. The malasadas and doughnut variations here would tempt a vegan. Some people show up later for plate lunches ($5.75-7.75), but the wise prey on the butter, egg, and cream-infused chocolate-haupia cream pie. Open daily 7am-6pm. ❶

Shark's Cove Grill, 59-712 Kamehameha Hwy. (☎638-8300). A roadside shack with a shaded patio, the grill is popular for breakfast and mid-afternoon shakes.

"Dawn patrol" breakfast of oatmeal, raisins, cinnamon, and milk ($3.50) is a popular post-surf meal. For lunch, try the fresh ahi sandwich ($6.50) and the popular banana-protein shake ($4). Open daily 8:30am-7:30pm. Cash only. ❶

BEACHES

Welcome to surfing heaven. Between Sunset Beach Park and Ekuhai Beach Park there are 12 named breaks, and from there to Waimea Bay, there are another 10. However, if riding isn't your thing, the endless stretch of sand is equally pleasant for sun-bathing and water-splashing.

WAIMEA BAY BEACH PARK. *(Snorkeling. Surfing. Open daily sunrise to sunset. Lifeguards 9am-5pm.)* Heading north after Kawailoa Beach you'll come to a bend in the road, overlooking an amazing, deep crescent of sea that is Waimea Bay. Summer mornings bring some of the clearest and calmest waters on the island, perfect for swimming and snorkeling, and in the golden afternoon sunlight, leaping visitors test their cliff jumping luck, scurrying up and off a giant rock into the bay. In the winter, sailboats and sunbathers make way as this bay comes alive, releasing an awe-inspiring energy in **big waves** that reach as high as 30 ft. The entrance to the beach is across the street from the Waimea Valley Audubon Center. Get there early, as the parking lot fills up quickly and you may be ticketed if you park on the road above. The beach has restrooms, showers, picnic tables, and lifeguards.

SHARK'S COVE. *(Snorkeling. Surfing. Open daily 24hr.)* Between the Foodland in Waimea and Kalalua Point, Shark's Cove, part of a Marine Life Conservation District, offers some of the best summer snorkeling and scuba diving on Oahu. It has caves, coral, and colorful reef fish, as well as sea turtles and an occasional white-tipped reef shark. The cove also has tide pools that are well-suited for children who wish to snorkel. A bit south of Shark's Cove, across from Foodland is **Pupukea Beach Park** (not to be confused with Pupukea, a surf spot north of Ehukai Beach Park), another good place to snorkel. The northern part of the beach park is **Three Tables Beach,** named for the plateaus of reef that emerge at low tide and make for great snorkeling in summer. In winter the waves overtake these calm waters. Snorkeling equipment can be rented at several kiosks across the street. Shark's Cove has restrooms and showers.

EHUKAI BEACH PARK. *(Surfing. Open daily sunrise to sunset. Lifeguards 9am-5pm.)* Ehukai Beach Park is renowned for its pounding waves and expert-only surf spots. Between Kalalua Point and the beach park is a long stretch of sandy beach that is practically always empty. Caution: even in the inviting summer waters, these waves break dangerously close to the shore and are challenging to negotiate. In December, surfers and fans from all over the world flock to this beach to watch the Pipeline Masters (one of the three triple crown surfing events) as they barrel down big and screaming fast waves over the most famous shallow reef break on the North Shore, the **Banzai Pipeline. Log Cabins** is farther south, and equally gnarly. Swimming is safe over the sandbar in summer months, though the rip current can still be strong. Shoreline access is marked along the path between Kamehameha Hwy. and the private beachfront homes; park at Ehukai Beach Park or wherever there is a pullout in the path and join the crowds scoping the surfers in peak season. Ehukai Beach Park is off Kamehameha Hwy., just across the highway from Sunset Beach Elementary School. Restrooms and showers are on the premises.

SUNSET BEACH PARK. *(Surfing. Open daily sunrise to sunset. Lifeguards 9am-5pm.)* The next beach north of Ekuhai, Sunset Beach entices visitors year-round. In the summer, sunbathers flock to its 2 mi. of extra-wide, white sandy beach and calm, crystal clear water. Summer swells are not unheard of here, and they often attract a flock of longboard surfers to the point break. In the winter, powerful waves bring professional surfers and enthusiastic spectators to the site of several international surfing competitions. In winter, this beach is strictly for experts; waves reach 25 ft. and there is a notorious riptide—lifeguards have saved many overly-ambitious surfers here from certain death. The park has restrooms and parking.

HIKING AND SIGHTS

WAIMEA VALLEY AUDUBON CENTER. Formerly known as Waimea Falls Park, the biggest tourist attraction in the area emphasizes the natural and cultural preservation of the valley over entertainment and features a pleasant ¾ mi. (one-way) paved "nature walk" that passes beautiful botanical gardens, cultural and historical sites, and a variety of endangered indigenous species while heading to the final waterfall. For the slightly more adventurous, the old waterfall trail to the left offers more of an unpaved, hiking experience. Swimming in the waterfall at the end of the walk is a nice cool break. Although the pool is probably more heavily infested with tourists than any deadly parasites, be sure to check in with the lifeguards lest you be scolded about the dangers of *leptospirosis*. **North Shore Yoga,** a nomadic crew of yogis led by Paul, can be reached at Cholo's in Haleiwa (☎637-3059) and makes weekly stops at the Waimea Valley Audobon Center on Tuesday and Thursday mornings for a 7:30-8:45am class. Suggested donation of $2 is well worth the price of this energizing gathering. *(59-864 Kamehameha Hwy., across the street from the Waimea Bay Beach Park. ☎638-9199; www.audubon.org. Open daily 9:30am-5pm. $8, ages 4-12 $5. Parking $2.)*

PUPUKEA. Hiking the trails at Pupukea affords a more direct communion with nature. Trails begin at the end of Pupukea Rd. next to Foodland; follow the steep and winding Pupukea Rd. about 3 mi. up the hill until you see Camp Pupukea, the Aloha Council Boy Scout's of America camp, on your left. Though you can't park in the camp, you'll have no problem leaving your vehicle on the roadside right before it. From the Boy Scout Camp, you can take the **Kaunala Loop** (5 mi.). When it rains, negotiating the muddy conditions can prove quite difficult; so rain gear, sturdy hiking boots, and mosquito repellent are strongly recommended.

KAUNALA LOOP TRAIL. *(5 mi. 2½hr. round-trip. Moderate.)* The loop trail winds through several gulches full of *ti* plants, sandalwood, and *koa* trees, as well as the occasional wild orchid. To reach the trailhead, follow the dirt road past the camp and around the locked gate; sign in at the hunters/hikers mailbox and take a peek at the trail map next to the mailbox to get an idea of where you're going. Continue down the road, keeping to the left; there's a marked trailhead on the left side when you reach the first major fork, about ½ mi. down the road. Follow the yellow hiker's arrows on the signs whenever there's an intersection or ambiguous fork. The trail connects with a dirt road; turn right onto it and follow the ridge along several ups and downs. On clear days, there are views of the shore along this leg. The road eventually loops back to the original dirt road you started on (turn right at the intersection and continue down the hill about 1 mi. to return to the parking area). On the weekends, public hunting presents another dangerous risk—wear bright clothing and a bright hat to distinguish yourself from the wild prey.

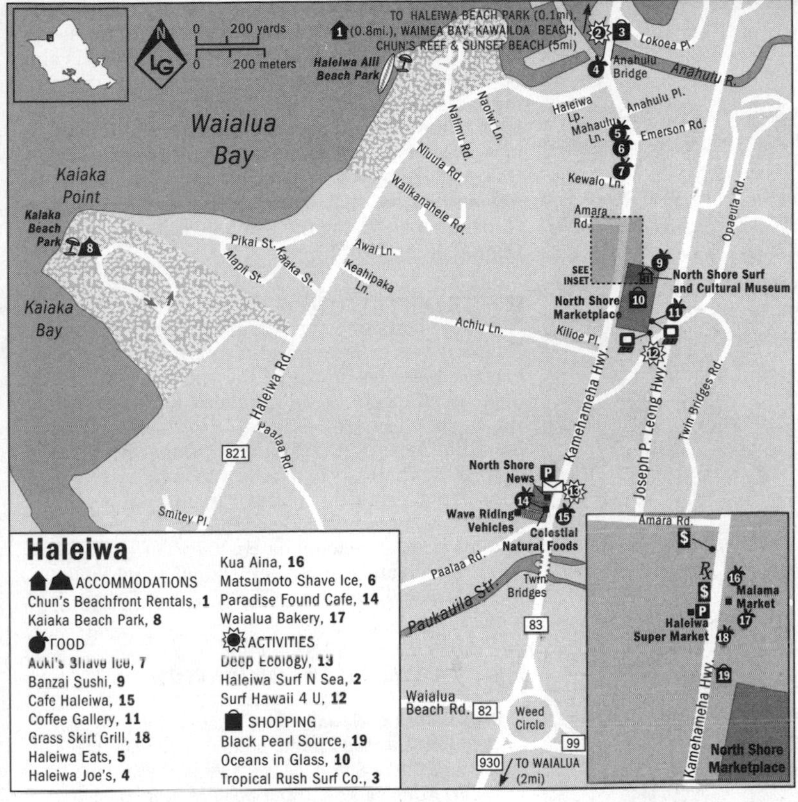

PUU O MAHUKA HEIAU STATE MONUMENT. Stop by the Puu o Mahuka Heiau for a historical and cultural reality check amongst the largely *haole* (Caucasian) surf culture below. Off Pupukea Rd., about ½ mi. from Kamehameha Hwy. and Foodland, look for a sign on your right. Follow the winding, speed bump-covered road to the remains of an ancient Hawaiian *luakini heiau,* a temple honoring the god of war, whose construction involved human sacrifice. Today, only the rock walls and stone paved floor are left at the national historic landmark, but 250 years ago a major temple stood on the site that was dedicated to success in war. High priest Kaopulupulu presided over the temple in the 1770s, and Kamehameha I's *kahuna* (priest) Hewahawa oversaw it until 1819, when the ancient Hawaiian religion was abolished. On a bluff above Waimea Valley, the monument offers a commanding view of the shoreline and the channel between Oahu and Kauai, where signal fires used to provide visual communication between the islands. The site is considered very sacred to the Hawaiian people, and a visit here can be a spiritual retreat from the frenzy of North Shore surfing.

HALEIWA

Haleiwa (pop. 2,225) is the undisputed center of life on the North Shore. Characterized by a distinctive surfer culture and renowned for its beaches, Haleiwa the

WHEN THE SHARKS BITE

I'd just flown in from the Big Island to Oahu, where I would be conducting the remainder of my research on the beaches of the famed North Shore. I was pumped. I had just spent the last five and a half weeks on an island where the sight of a group of people larger than two is an event. Oahu is a surfer's Mecca, and I was about to commence my pilgrimage.

Though in the summer, the North Shore is pretty flat, in the winter, waves come barreling over the deadly reefs at 30 ft., vestiges of turbulent storms off the coast of Alaska and other northern Pacific locales. But the surf on Oahu's South Shore is always up, and as a California boy, I felt compelled to take advantage of it.

It was a Friday, usually a crowded day in the lineup, so I was a little worried I might be told to "go home, *haole*," as some of my Big Island comrades had warned. But to my pleasant surprise, when I reached the break, there was almost no one in the water. I thought it a little peculiar, but my main concern was learning the new break and studying the reef below. I was a little nervous, looking off Diamond Head Road to the break down below—it would be a super long paddle, and at 8:45am, the wind was already picking up.

refuge of choice for Oahu's residents and a necessary stop for visitors. For surfers and locals, the town is a place to refuel on appetizing grinds and energizing rays. An entire day could be spent perusing the local craft galleries or slurping down shave ice, but be aware that store hours are often indefinite and depend on customer interest or the size of the surf. Haleiwa is the gateway to the world-famous beaches that are strung like pearls along the North Shore, earning the town its title, the "Surfing Capital of the World."

ORIENTATION

Haleiwa center is located along **Route 83 (Kamehameha Highway),** north of the traffic circle where **Highway 99** meets Rte. 83. **Haleiwa Road** runs along the harbor toward Waialua, intersecting Kamehameha Hwy. by the **Anahulu Bridge.** Haleiwa is served by TheBus #52 Wahiawa/Circle Isle, which runs from Honolulu (board at bus stop on the *mauka*, or mountain, side of Ala Moana Center) via Wahiawa up Kamehameha Hwy. to Turtle Bay, and #76, which shuttles between Haleiwa and Waialua. The trip from Honolulu to Haleiwa is about one and a half hours.

PRACTICAL INFORMATION

Banks: Bank of Hawaii, in the Haleiwa Shopping Center, and **First Hawaiian Bank,** between Haleiwa Super Market and Aoki's Shave Ice, on Kamehameha Hwy., have **24hr. ATMs** outside. (Both open M-Th 8:30am-4pm, F 8:30am-6pm.)

Pharmacy: Haleiwa Pharmacy, 66-145 Kamehameha Hwy. (☎637-9393). Enter from the back next to Flavormania Ice Cream. Open M-F 9am-1pm and 1:30-5:30pm, Sa 9am-1pm and 1:30-3:30pm.

Copy and Fax Services: North Shore News, 66-437 Kamehameha Hwy., Ste. 210 (☎637-3138, fax 637-8862), on the 2nd fl., behind the post office. Copies $0.10 per pg. Fax $3 per pg. Open M-F 9am-5pm. AmEx/MC/V.

Internet Access: Coffee Gallery (☎637-5355), in the North Shore Marketplace, has 3 terminals. $1 per 10min. Free Wi-Fi with your own laptop. Open daily 7am-8pm. **Surf Hawaii Surf School** (☎637-2622), 2nd fl., in the back right corner of the North Shore Marketplace has 3 relatively new computers. $3 per 20min.

Post Office: Haleiwa Post Office, 66-437 Kamehameha Hwy. (☎637-1711), in the building complex next to Celestial Foods on the southeast edge of town. Open M-F 8am-4pm, Sa 9am-noon. AmEx/D/MC/V.

Postal Code: 96712.

ACCOMMODATIONS

Numerous properties ranging from surfer shacks to luxurious homes line the beaches of Haleiwa. Vacation rentals are a more economical option for those traveling in groups; rates for multi-bedroom homes work out to be quite reasonable (houses that sleep 4-5 start around $100 per night). **Sterman Realty** (☎637-6200 or 800-637-6200; www.sterman.com; open M-F 9am-5pm) and **Team Real Estate, Inc.** (☎637-3507 or 800-982-6802; www.teamrealestate.com; open M-F 8:30am-5pm), both with offices in the building in the back right corner of North Shore Marketplace, handle vacation rentals on Oahu's northern coast. Both companies require a refundable security deposit (usually $300-500) and charge a one-time cleaning fee (around $60-150). Reserve at least three months in advance in high season (Nov. 15-Feb. 15), though be on the lookout for last minute discounts.

Chun's Reef Beachfront Rentals, 61-529 Kamehameha Hwy. (☎637-6417; www.hawaiibeachfronts.com). Part of a larger group of beachfront rentals, this one is in the middle of all the action. Ranging $100-475 (prices are higher Dec.-Mar.), Chun's offers 3 set-ups; the smaller studio with private bath and queen-size bed in the back ($125) is the best deal. The beachfront rooms are more "deluxe," but so are their prices. AmEx/D/MC/V. ❹

Kaiaka Beach Park, 1 mi. west of town past the fire department on Haleiwa Rd. The beach park allows free camping with a county permit M-Tu and F-Su. The scenery is unbeatable–the park sits directly on the beach. Kaiaka has 7 sites, with restrooms, showers, and picnic tables. Swimming is not safe; signs warn of a dangerous shorebreak and strong current. Camping prohibited W 8am-F 8am. Gates lock daily 6:45pm-7am. See **Camping in Hawaii,** p. 75, for more info. ❶

FOOD

From a variety of ethnic tastes to plenty of fresh fish, Kamehameha Hwy. is littered with seemingly endless dining opportunities. Shave ice is not in want, either. Vegetarians will have no problem finding their fare here—natural, organic, and meatless options abound (read: brown rice, tofu, and burritos).

When I made it out to the break, I stopped next to the surfer ahead of me and said, "Hey!" Better be friendly, I thought. Contentedly dangling my feet off my board, focused on the waves, I was glad I had done my part in breaking the often-thick surfer ice. He responded, "Yeah, hey man, it's nice when there's a shark in the water, huh?!" "Yeah," I said, "right on." Then I thought, *Wait, did he say shark!?* "Hey, did you say shark!?" "Yeah," he responded again. "It's nice, huh? No one else gets in the water!" At this point, a panic had set in, and just as I turned to my new best friend, on whom my life now seemed to depend, he vanished on a wave. "Later dude! I'm going in!" I was alone...with sharky.

As the panic began to induce paralysis, a wave miraculously swept me up, and I rode in to shore. I paddled vigorously for land and landed safe and alive on firm ground, just 15min. after I'd so courageously jumped in. I looked back and saw a surfer catch a wave, jump off, and turn back to his friends, laughing about his ride. I looked around and saw many others still enjoying the surf. And then I realized that sharks are always in the water! They live there! Someone just happened to see one that day. It was ridiculous to scurry away in fright, I later reasoned. After that, I drove as fast as I could to the North Shore, and got to work. And then I rented a longboard and surfed all day.

-Jake Levine

There are also a number of markets in and around Haleiwa. **Malama Market,** 66-190 Kamehameha Hwy., in the center of town, sells basic staples and produce. There's a deli, bakery, and ATM inside. (☎637-4520. Open daily 7am-9pm. AmEx/D/MC/V.) Across the street, **Haleiwa Super Market,** 66-197 Kamehameha Hwy., has similar offerings and an ATM as well. (☎637-5004. Open M-Sa 8am-8pm, Su 8:30am-5:30pm. AmEx/D/MC/V.) **Celestial Natural Foods,** 66-445 Kamehameha Hwy., next to the post office and across from Cafe Haleiwa, has a selection of organic produce, packaged foods, vitamins, and health care products. (☎637-6729. Open M-Sa 9am-6pm, Su 9am-5pm. MC/V.) Many opt to do their shopping at the **Foodland** in Waimea (p. 158), which has a bigger selection.

RESTAURANTS

Haleiwa Joe's, 66-011 Kamehameha Hwy. (☎637-8005). Though you could probably dine undisturbed in boardshorts and flip-flops, this is Haleiwa's most upscale dining option. *Pupus* (ahi spring rolls, $10; Tahi fried calamari, $7.75) are a popular barstool stop, and the fresh fish entrees are well-prepared, with plenty of rice and veggies on the side. Wine selection is excellent and reasonably priced (glasses $5-7). Aloha hour M-F 4:30-6:30pm; discount fish, drinks, and *pupus*. Lunch daily 11:30am-4:15pm. Dinner M-Th 5:30-9:30pm, F-Sa 5:30-10:30pm, Su 5-9:30pm. Bar features live music every other F night (21+; $10 cover). AmEx/MC/V. ❹

Banzai Sushi, 66-250 Kamehameha Hwy. (☎637-4404), in the North Shore Marketplace. This evening-only sushi bar is the local favorite for wrapping up a hard day's work. Most of the seating is on the breezy deck, where an international-surfer-bohemian crowd kicks back on the padded floor seating. Sushi and sashimi dinners $7-14. Open Tu-Su 4pm-10pm; W and Su nights go much later when the venue vibrates with local live music and $3 Red Stripe (hooray, beer!) specials. MC/V. ❷

Grass Skirt Grill, 66-214 Kamehameha Hwy. (☎637-4852). Right next to Strong Current Surf Shop, this may be the best place in town to taste the day's fresh catch. Usually ahi, mahi, or ono; have it grilled or seared with a large salad and rice on the side ($9). Open daily 11am-6pm. Cash only. ❷

Kua Aina, 67-160 Kamehameha Hwy. (☎637-6067). Seats are hard to come by at this jam-packed sandwich and burger joint. The "world's best hamburgers" are quite possibly just that; try yours with avocado or pineapple. Crispy fries ($2.60) perfectly complement the sandwiches. Burgers $6.50. Open daily 11am-8pm. Cash only. ❶

Cholo's Homestyle Mexican, 66-250 Kamehameha Hwy. (☎637-3059), in the North Shore Marketplace is fun, festive, and always packed. Try the tamales ($6.50) which contend with the ever-popular grilled ahi fish tacos ($8) as the local favorite. Head to the bar for one of Cholo's Mexican specialty drinks ($4.50-5). Open M-Th and Su 10am-9:30pm, F-Sa 9am-10pm. Bar open F-Sa until 10:30pm. AmEx/MC/V. ❷

Haleiwa Eats, 66-079 Kamehameha Hwy. (☎637-4247). A couple stops past Matsumoto, funky, flavorful Haleiwa Eats has appetizing and inexpensive grinds. A range of savory entrees ($7-15) from pad thai to shrimp *panang* are served in style. Sit in the indoor or outdoor seating area, take yours to go, or simply grab a sweet Thai iced tea ($2.25). Open Tu-Su noon-8pm. ❷

BAKERIES AND CAFES

Coffee Gallery, 66-250 Kamehameha Hwy. (☎637-5355), in the North Shore Marketplace. Everyone in Haleiwa might well come here for their daily caffeine fix. Though the menu offers specialty wraps like the smoked ahi ($4.50-5.50), patrons are drawn to the good conversation, great atmosphere, and top-quality beans. Small cups of 100% Hawaiian java will only set you back $1.30. Free Internet access with your own laptop (or on one of their two terminals for $1 per 10min.) and ATM. Open daily 7am-8pm. AmEx/D/MC/V. ❶

Paradise Found Cafe, 66-443 Kamehameha Hwy. (☎637-4540). Walk through Celestial Natural Foods to the back right corner. The wisdom of the hippie poetry on the walls is dubious, but there's no question about the quality of the made-to-order smoothies ($4-6) and vegetarian food ($7-8). Salads ($5-8) are layered with creamy avocado, heirloom tomatoes, and tangy feta. The Big Ass Burrito is a vegetarian's food fantasy ($8.25). Open M-Sa 9am-5pm, Su 10am-4pm. MC/V. ❶

Waialua Bakery, 66-200 Kamehameha Hwy. (☎637-9079), next to Malama Market, is one of Haleiwa's local highlights, known for its excellent fresh baked goods (cookies, $1-1.50) and juice bar (refreshing smoothies, $3.50-7). The fresh loaves of baked bread (honey white, $2.75; wheat, $3; cheese and herb, $4) are soft and make great sandwiches ($4-6.50); try the Hungry Hawaiian (ham, turkey, bacon, and cheese) and look for daily special breads like pineapple banana. Open M-Sa 9am-4pm. ❶

Cafe Haleiwa, 66-460 Kamehameha Hwy. (☎637-5516). Surf paintings, posters, and pictures line the walls of this diner where you can try their popular fruit bowl with yogurt and granola ($4.50) or their daily specials like banana-nut bread ($2.50). For your caffeine fix, there is hot java from the espresso bar in back. Lunch around $8. Open daily 7am-2pm. AmEx/MC/V. ❶

SHAVE ICE

Shave ice is to Haleiwa what gelato is to Venice—you're doing yourself a disservice if you pass up these cheap, colorful, and tasty treats.

Matsumoto Shave Ice, 66-087 Kamehameha Hwy. (☎637-4827). By far the most famous shave ice place—tour buses stop right outside, and the long line is a constant fixture. There is strict protocol for ordering: state how many small or large cones you want, whether you want ice cream and/or sweet *azuki* beans, and only when asked do you state your flavors (including *li hing mui, lilikioi,* and pineapple, to name a few). Small $1.30, with ice cream and beans $2.20. Open daily 8:30am-6pm. Cash only. ❶

Aoki's Shave Ice, 66-117 Kamehameha Hwy. (☎637-7017), next to Matsumoto and just as good. Aoki's has fewer flavors and a shorter line. The same ordering rules as above apply. Small $1.50, with ice cream and beans $2.25. Open daily "Hawaiian Time," usually noon-6:30pm. ❶

BEACHES

Although the beaches in town do not compare with the picture-perfect Waimea and Sunset Beaches (p. 159), Haleiwa has a few popular breaks. The beaches east of Haleiwa off Waialua Beach Rd. are frequented by sharks, but there is excellent kiteboarding farther west in Mokuleia.

HALEIWA ALII BEACH PARK. *(Surfing. Open daily 6am-10pm. Lifeguards 9am-5:30pm.)* Though placid during the summer, the winter brings three good surf breaks offshore to the left. The one farthest left is known as **Walls,** to the right of Walls is **Avalanche,** and **Haleiwa** is directly out from the beach park. The last break is a good place for beginners when the waves are small. The beach, at 66-167 Haleiwa Rd., has restrooms, showers, and picnic tables.

HALEIWA BEACH PARK. *(Surfing. Open daily sunrise to sunset.)* In winter, there are two surf breaks off the point on the right side Haleiwa Beach Park: **Puaena** and expert-only **Puaena Point** on the outside. Neither surfing nor swimming is at its best here, and Haleiwa Beach Park is less popular than other North Shore beaches. This beach does host a number of summer activities, however. For at least one Sunday during the summer canoe regatta season, the area becomes the site of an island tradition where locals compete in outrigger canoe races. In late July, this park is also host to the Haleiwa Arts Festival, a gathering of local artists that takes over the North Shore for a weekend. The beach, past Anahulu Bridge on the left when heading to Waimea Bay, has restrooms, showers, basketball courts, and picnic tables.

KAIAKA BEACH PARK. *(Open daily 7am-6:45pm.)* The 53-acre park is more appealing than the beach itself, as other beaches around are less muddy and better for swimming in the summer. But the pleasant picnic grove, seven free campsites, and clean showers make the park a great afternoon family destination. One mile west of town on Haleiwa Rd., past the fire station.

KAWAILOA BEACH. *(Surfing. Open daily sunrise to sunset.)* Kawailoa Beach is the catch-all name for the stretch of sandy and rocky coastline between Puaena Point and Waimea. Surfers head to several generally unmarked spots along this stretch to try to catch a wave. Perhaps the most "local" of these breaks is **Lani's,** local nickname of **Laniakea Beach.** Large sea turtles are commonly spotted basking close to shore; look, but don't touch, lest you incur a $1000 fine. The beach is about 1½ mi. northeast of Haleiwa Beach Park. After passing a large horse pasture on the right and driving over a short bridge, park your car on the dry side of the road before the intersection of Pohaku Lao Way and Kamehameha Hwy. Cross the street to the surf break.

On the right side of the reef when looking out to Laniakea's waters, less than ½ mi. farther up Kamehameha Hwy., is the most popular place to surf on Kawailoa Beach, **Chun's Reef.** The reef offers beachfront parking opposite a moss-covered rock formation known as **Alligator Rock.** If you park at Alligator Rock there is a surf break directly out front and two more left and over the rock (**Left Overs** and **Right Overs**). The swimming here is decent in the summer, though the crowds can be aggravating, and there's a bit of a riptide between the two surf breaks.

ACTIVITIES

If it happens in the water, you can do it in Haleiwa, which is home to a good number of outfits that provide equipment rental, surf lessons, dive trips, and whale-watching tours.

Surf Hawaii 4 U (☎637-2622; www.surfhawaii4u.com), in the North Shore Marketplace, above Team Real Estate. Edison and Bettina's hands-on and personal approach make this the best surf school around—with a stellar safety and success rate to boot. Provides surfboard rentals and lessons (3hr. group lesson $100-130, equipment included; call ☎295-1241 for reservations). Also offers Internet access (p. 162). Open daily 10am-6pm. AmEx/D/MC/V.

Deep Ecology, 66-456 Kamehameha Hwy. (☎637-7946; www.deepecologyhawaii.com), next to Cafe Haleiwa, offers snorkel tours, scuba certification, year-round diving, and coordinates 3hr. whale, turtle, and dolphin tours starting at $69. Open daily 9am-5pm. AmEx/D/MC/V.

Haleiwa Surf N Sea, 62-595 Kamehameha Hwy. (☎637-7873; www.surfnsea.com). Amid the clutter of over 1000 surfboards, this place has it all: scuba dives, scuba lessons (non-certified start at $95, equipment included), surf lessons (2hr. beginner lesson $75, equipment included), shark tours, snorkel tours (2hr. tour $45, equipment included), windsurfing lessons (2hr. beginner lesson, $75), whale watching tours (Dec.-May; $58, ages 2-12 $40), fishing charters ($300-500), and gear rental. Open daily 9am-7pm. AmEx/D/MC/V.

SIGHTS

While Haleiwa's major draw is its unique businesses and world famous surf breaks, the town also has a few cultural sights worth a quick visit.

NORTH SHORE SURF AND CULTURAL MUSEUM. "No shirt? No shoes? No problem!" If you couldn't tell from this sign hanging on the front door, we'll let you know: North Shore Surf is quite possibly the world's most laid-back museum. Curator Stephen Gould's collection of surf memorabilia includes posters, album covers, monochrome photos by legendary surf photographer LeRoy Grannis, vintage surfboards, and a very cool 1950 Ford Woody. Browse the museum's selection of jewelry and bottles collected from the ocean floor; all watches are "guaranteed *not* to work." Chat it up with "Hurricane" Bob at the front counter or catch a surfing film in the backroom theater. Most items are for sale. *(66-250 Kamehameha Hwy., behind Patagonia in the North Shore Marketplace. ☎637-8888. Usually open M, W, F 10am-6pm; Th and Sa-Su 11am-6pm. Donations appreciated.)*

LILIUOKALANI PROTESTANT CHURCH. Founded by Protestant missionaries in 1832, the church takes its name from Queen Liliuokalani, who spent her summers in Haleiwa and attended services here. Services were conducted entirely in Hawaiian until the early 1940s. The numerals on the face of the seven-dial clock are replaced with the letters of the queen's 12-letter name. *(66-090 Kamehameha Hwy., across from Matsumoto Shave Ice. ☎637-9364. Daily service at 10am.)*

SHOPPING

In addition to surf boutiques, indistinguishable tourist haunts, and Quiksilver stores, Haleiwa has a great number of unique shops and galleries worth perusing.

Haleiwa Surf N Sea, 62-595 Kamehameha Hwy. (☎637-7873), just past the Anahulu Bridge on the left. Of the town's several surf shops, Haleiwa Surf N Sea is the best-known and has the best selection of merchandise. Since 1965, they've supplied the North Shore surf community with affordable boards, accessories, and clothing. Open daily 9am-7pm. AmEx/D/MC/V.

Tropical Rush Surf Company, 62-620A Kamehameha Hwy. (☎637-8886; www.tropicalrushhawaii.com). When Haleiwa Surf N Sea is too busy, head across the street to this pristinely maintained surf shop. With the best customer service around, the shop offers a variety of gear, from clothing to surf and skim boards. They also rent equipment; inquire inside (surfboards $20 per day, $100 per wk.). Open daily 9am-7pm. MC/V.

Oceans in Glass, 66-250 Kamehameha Hwy., Ste. E-100, (☎637-3366), in the North Shore Marketplace behind Patagonia. Get a first-hand look as Krista Woodward or one of her esteemed apprentices hand-crafts intricate glass sculptures of dolphins, sea turtles, humpback whales, and colorful reef fish. The unique pieces, created with a 2000-year-old technique called lampworking, are all inspired by Krista's diving and snorkeling excursions in local coral reefs. The pieces, which start at $15 (and go way up from there), can all be packaged and shipped. Open daily 10am-6pm. D/MC/V.

Black Pearl Source, 66-220 Kamehameha Hwy. (☎637-7776). The store and its contents were designed and built by architect and jeweler Ben Thompson. Thompson's rings, pendants, and earrings are designed to cradle the high quality, natural-color Tahitian black pearls (which are often green, blue, golden, apricot, and purple) without drilling them, retaining the integrity of the pearl. These pearls are rarer and more expensive than white *akoya* pearls, but the store carries pieces to fit any budget. Open M-Sa 10am-6pm, Su 11am-6pm. AmEx/D/MC/V.

WAIALUA AND MOKULEIA

At the base of the Waianae Range on the western stretch of the North Shore, Waialua (pop. 3,761) was originally a port for the sandalwood trade and, until recently, a prime producer of sugarcane. But the town has lacked stable agricultural production since its sugar mill closed in 1996 and the "Home of the World's Best Sugar" is now in the grips of a serious insulin low. Much of the old mill has been converted into a handful of local small businesses, peddling everything from soap to surfboards. The rest of this town is rather unremarkable and predominantly residential. The respectable waves and unpopulated beaches of Mokuleia (pop. 1,839) to the west, however, draw adventurous travelers and are ideal for camping and water sports.

ORIENTATION AND PRACTICAL INFORMATION

The small commercial center of Waialua sits where Goodale Ave. meets Kealohanui St. To reach Mokuleia from Waialua, drive *mauka* (toward the mountains) on Goodale Ave. and turn right on Farrington Hwy., which cuts through the center of town and ends 2½ mi. before Kaena Point, the northwest corner of Oahu. TheBus #76 connects Haleiwa and Waialua.

The **Waialua Public Library,** 67-068 Kealohanui St., has schedules for TheBus and self-serve photocopying ($0.15 per pg.). A three-month visitor's card ($10) grants use of four relatively new computers with quick **Internet access.** (☎637-8286. 15min. max. when busy. Open Tu-Th 9am-6pm, F 9am-5pm, Sa 9am-2pm.) Wash your duds at **M and C Washerette.** (Wash $1.25, dry $1.25. Open daily 4:30am-9:45pm.) **ATMs** are located at the Waialua Federal Credit Union and The Brown Bottle convenience store (see below), both inside the plaza. If you've slept through the North Shore Yoga's 7:30am Waimea Valley class (p. 160), there's still time to make the 8:30am class at **Bikram's Yoga College of India,** 67-208 Goodale Ave. (☎637-5700), in the Waialua Shopping Center behind the library, which offers daily drop-in classes (1½hr., $14). The **Waialua Post Office,** 67-079 Nauahi St. (☎800-275-8777; open M-F 8:30am-4pm), is conveniently located. **Postal Code:** 96791.

FOOD

Between the library and the Aloha Gas Station is the **Waialua Shopping Center,** 67-208 Goodale Ave., which offers several dining options. For basic needs, visit the **Waialua General Store,** 67-272 Goodale Ave. (☎637-3131. Open daily 9am-7pm.) **The Brown Bottle** sells groceries, beer, wine, and liquor. (Open daily 7am-10:30pm.) Be sure to stock up if you plan on heading west for the night, as there are no convenience stores in Mokuleia. The holy grail of Mokuleia dining is **Lulu's Mexican Cuisine,** on the corner of Goodale Ave. and Kealohanui St. The monstrous burritos ($7) are stuffed with savory delights such as ahi, *pollo azteca*, and *carne asada*. (☎225-9055. Open M-Sa 9am until the meat runs out, usually around 3pm. Cash only.) The **Sugar Mill Cafe ❶,** 67-292 Goodale Ave., serves generous portions of local food. Plate lunches run $5-6.50. (☎637-4509. Open daily 10am-8pm.) **Waialua**

Chop Suey, 67-292 Goodale Ave., in the Waialua Shopping Center serves local favorites to go. Get the sweet and sour spare ribs ($5.25) for a quick lunch. (☎637-1688. Open M-Tu and Th-Sa 10am-8pm, Su 11am-8pm.)

ACCOMMODATIONS AND CAMPING

There are no hotels in Waialua, so travelers must move on to Mokuleia where there are places (though limited) to camp or lodge.

Camp Mokuleia, 68-729 Farrington Hwy. (☎637-6241; www.campmokuleia.org*)*, is a serene, palm-tree lined "quiet interval from the world" often booked by conference groups. Its small, windswept beach is frequented by brave swimmers and thrill-seeking kiteboarders. The tent area, in a wooded grove near the beach, has hot water showers and toilets. There are two cabins with 14-22 beds and 2 shared bathrooms in each. The camp lodge has 10 double rooms with private bath and 8 double rooms with shared bath. Facilities include a ropes course, basketball court, volleyball court, climbing tower, swimming pool, and archery targets. There's no need to go into town for a good meal; Camp Mokuleia's dining hall offers a substantial lunch ($7.50) and a hefty dinner ($9). Kayaks ($15 per hr.) are available to rent. Reception M-F 8am-5pm, Sa-Su 11am-5pm. Check-in 4pm. Check-out 1pm. Reservations required. Tents $10 per person (no alcohol and no camping W); lodge rooms $65-75; 14-person cabin $170; 22-person cabin $250. AmEx/D/MC/V. ❶

YMCA Camp Erdman, 69-385 Farrington Hwy. (☎637-4615; www.camperdman.net), about 2 mi. before Camp Mokuleia, on another beautiful, secluded beach. The friendly staff and quiet hours will make you feel like you're back at summer camp. 8-person cabins with kitchens, or 16-person cabins. Facilities include a ropes course, swimming pool, climbing wall, and tennis courts. Meal plans for individuals staying in cabins for an additional price. Also frequently rented to large groups, especially during the summer and weekends; call for availability. Reservation required. Cabins $170. Inquire about possible **work exchanges** for room and board. AmEx/D/MC/V. ❶

BEACHES AND HIKING

The beaches and hiking around Mokuleia extend from the touristy Haleiwa coast to the rugged and local Kaena Point. Visitors should use caution here; rented vehicles are easy targets for thieves. The saf-

SURFING 101

When the words "surf" and "North Shore" fall serendipitously into the same sentence, one hardly expects to find the word "school" tagging alongside. Surf Hawaii 4 U, a locally-based surf school with a lot of personality, looks to change this conception.

In the summer months, when the water is clear and the waves calm, the North Shore actually lends itself to the adventurous beginner. Edison de Paula, a world-class big wave rider, heads up the school. When he's not recklessly flying down the face of a 60 ft. wall of rushing water, Edison's focus is teaching novices to surf. Edison is an expert instructor, certified in basically every type of water rescue that exists. His enthusiasm lends itself generously to the business of beginners, and the only screams coming from the water are "yahoos!" What's more, he has an astronomical success rate; even the clumsiest tourists end up standing on a wave.

Surfing is one of the fastest growing sports on the planet, and it's no wonder—the exhiliration of taking off on a thrusting North Shore wave is tough to beat. Edison's surf school opens the door into this world, and his lesson is a foothold you should not miss. His most popular, and most useful 3hr. introductory course is $130. *Surf Hawaii 4 U, ☎295-1241; www.surfhawaii4u.com. MC/V. 66-250 Kamehameha Hwy. Ste. D204.*

est parking is in the Dillingham Airfield lot, accessible through the northwest entrance to the field.

MOKULEIA BEACH PARK. *(Wind sports. Open daily sunrise to sunset.)* The perfect winds sweep gracefully over a shallow clear blue ocean—this is a kiteboarder's paradise. The sharp reef, visible from shore and not too far beneath the surface of the water, and the strong current are hazards for both kitesurfers and swimmers. More sandy sections of the beach are on either side of the park, which is opposite the Dillingham Airfield. The park has restrooms and showers. Camping is allowed in the park by permit only between 8am on Friday and 8am on Wednesday. See **Camping in Hawaii**, p. 75, for more information.

KAENA POINT. *(2½ mi., 1-3hr. one way. Easy.)* Hike or mountain bike from the end of Farrington Hwy. along the path of the former sugarcane railroad leading to Kaena Point (p. 176), a *wahi pana* (celebrated place) for the Hawaiian people. Legend says that Kaena Point, the northwestern tip of Oahu, is a "leaping place of souls," where the spirits of the recently dead can reunite with their ancestors. The area is a precious part of Hawaiian heritage as one of the last intact dune ecosystems on the islands. Many plant and animal species are not found anywhere else in the world. If you opt to take the trek, park your car in the lot overlooking Molukeia's beaches 1 mi. past Camp Erdman. Lock your car and take valuables with you. For mountain bike rentals, check out **North Shore Raging Isle,** 66-250 Kamehameha Hwy., in North Shore Marketplace. (☎637-7707; www.ragingisle.com. Road bike rentals $70 per day; mountain bikes $40-60. Open daily 10am-6:30pm.)

KEALIA. *(2½ mi. 1½-2½hr. one-way. Elevation gain: 1600 ft. Moderate.)* Traveling west toward Kaena Point, take the 3rd and final entrance to Dillingham Airfield—this entrance is marked by an access gate with a warning sign for low-flying aircraft. Go around the end of the runway, pass a low concrete building on the left, and park in the paved lot in front of the air control tower. Travelers seeking a more ambitious hike should head to the graded ridge of Kealia. The hike is long, hot, steep, and rocks from the mountainside have been known to fall. The Kealia trail ascends a steep *pali* (cliff) en route to the summit of the Waianae Range. At the peak, hikers enjoy a scenic overlook of an undeveloped leeward valley. As always, use caution when hiking; bring water, and travel with others.

ACTIVITIES

Thrilling aerial experiences are available at **Dillingham Airfield,** on the *mauka* (mountain) side of Farrington Hwy., where several adventure sports companies operate. Go to Glider Port, the 2nd entrance to Dillingham Airfield, for plane and glider flights. Skydivers should turn in the first entrance while driving west. While two companies offer essentially the same package on paper (safe, tandem diving with licensed instructors), locals agree that Pacific, with a perfect safety record, higher dives, and bigger planes, is the superior company. Allot 2hr. to complete the skydive, allowing time to sign a safety waiver and watch an instructional video. Dives cost around $245; ask about group rates and look for substantial discount flyers and coupons in *Outrigger's Best of Oahu.*

Soar Hawaii Sailplanes, Inc. (☎637-3147; www.soarhawaii.com) offers flying lessons and scenic and aerobatic flights. Call for free hotel pickup. Rides start at $49 for 10min. and go up from there, though significant discounts are available if you buy your tickets through their website.

The Original Glider Rides (☎677-3404; www.honolulusoaring.com). 10min.-1hr. glider and sailplane rides. Also sky-surfing and aerobatic flying. Open daily 10am-5:30pm.

Pacific International Skydiving Center, 68-760 Farrington Hwy. (☎637-7472; www.pacific-skydiving.com). Groups of 4 or more qualify for a group discount. Open M-F 8am-2pm, Sa-Su 8am-sunset.

Skydive Hawaii, 68-760 Farrington Hwy. (☎637-9700). 18+. Free Waikiki hotel pickup available. Reservations recommended. Open daily 8:30am-3pm. AmEx/MC/V.

LEEWARD COAST

The Leeward Coast has been called the Wild West of Oahu. Driving from Honolulu to the Leeward side of the island is like entering New Mexico—arid brown mountains replace lush green ones, and thick tangles of dry undergrowth supplant the canopy of tall trees. The Leeward landscape has a striking, stark beauty, complemented by some of the least spoiled and beautiful beaches on the island. On calm days, the Pacific resembles a rippling mirror, and in winter, the surf can surge up to 20 ft. in height. Depending on the waves, the Leeward Coast has great conditions for snorkeling, scuba diving, swimming, canoeing, boogie boarding, and surfing. Anyone is bound to get a rush while admiring some of the most liberating swaths of land and sea Oahu has to offer.

The Leeward Coast is home to a large population of Native Hawaiians; despite foreign development in the area, many locals are very possessive of their land and way of life. The area is blessed with some of Oahu's best-preserved and least touristy natural and cultural sites, and visitors should practice common courtesy and sensitivity to the attitude of locals. While there are plentiful campgrounds, some locals joke that if you plan to camp, you'd better bring at least three friends along. Don't get caught in the Leeward area alone late at night; it's among the more dangerous areas of the island. If it's impossible to avoid confrontations, the best advice is to be as respectful as possible, and if that fails, leave the area.

TRANSPORTATION

By Bus: TheBus Country Express C, #93 Waianae Coast Express, and Rte. #40 all run up the Leeward Coast as far as Makaha. The Country Express C starts at the Ala Moana Shopping Center (1½hr.; every 30min. 5:09am-8:35pm; last bus leaves Makaha Beach Park 8:22pm) and runs frequently with the fewest stops; the #93 brings commuters from downtown in the evenings, and runs from the Leeward side to downtown in the morning. $2; seniors, ages 17 and under, and disabled $1.

By Car: Driving is by far the easiest way to get around the Leeward Coast. Car rentals are available at the airport (p. 92) and Waikiki (p. 120). Waianae is 40min. from Waikiki. Parking is plentiful on the Leeward Coast, but do not leave valuables in your car, as there is a high incidence of theft in the area.

ORIENTATION

The Leeward Coast encompasses the land west of the Waianae Mountains. To get there, take H-1 West from Honolulu for 40min.; H-1 will end at **Highway 93 (Farrington Highway).** From here, the two-lane highway goes directly up the sun-baked coast, past the rural communities of **Nanakuli, Maili, Waianae,** and **Makaha,** and peters out before the wilderness of the westernmost tip of Oahu, **Kaena**

Leeward Coast

ACCOMMODATIONS
- Makaha Resort and Golf Club, **1**
- Makaha Surfside Condos, **2**

FOOD
- Barbecue Kai, **5**
- L & L Drive-Inn, **4**
- The Red Baron, **3**
- Sun Sushi, **6**

Haleiwa Alii Beach Park
Kalaka Beach Park
Haleiwa
YMCA Camp Erdman
Mokuleia Beach Park
Waialua Beach Rd.
Haleiwa Rd.
83
Twin Bridge Rd.
Kamehameha Hwy.
99
Kaena Point
Kaena Point Trail
Dillingham Airfield
Mokuleia
930
Waialua
Farrington Hwy.
Kuaokala Game Management Area
Waialua Public Library
Kaena Point State Park
Kuaokala Forest Reserve
WAIALUA DISTRICT
Poamoho Str.
Kaukonahua Rd.
Mokuleia Forest Reserve
Farrington Hwy.
Keawaula Bay
Pahole Natural Area Reserve
Kaukonahua Str.
Puu Iki 1146'
Makua Valley Military Reservation
WAIANAE RANGE
Mokuleia Forest Reserve
Mount Kaala Natural Area Reserve
Maili 1510'
PACIFIC OCEAN
Kaneana Cave
93
Makua Keaau Forest Reserve
Kaala 4025'
Schofield Barracks Military Reservation
Keaau Beach Park
Puu Kawiwi 2975'
Waianae Kai Forest Reserve
Puu Keaau 2650'
Kaneaki Heiau
Koleaiiliili 1254'
Mauna Olu St.
Makaha Beach Park
Makaha Valley Rd.
Puu Kailio 1965'
Makaha
Puu Hapapa 2883'
Puu Kanehoa 2728'
Lahilahi Point
Waianae Valley Rd.
SEE INSET
Kaupuni Str.
Lualualei Naval Reservation
Puu Kaua 3127'
Pokai Bay
Waianae
Kaneilio Point
Waianae Mall Shopping Center
Maiiliili Rd.
WAIANAE DISTRICT
93
Palikea 3098'
Maili
Maili Beach Park
Lualualei Naval Rd.
Nanakuli Forest Reserve
Maili Point
Nanakuli
Sack 'n Save
Nanakuli Ave.
Nanakuli Beach Park
EWA DISTRICT
Hawaiian Electric Beach Park
Farrington Hwy.
Kahe Point Beach Park
TO HONOLULU (20 mi.)
93
Paradise Cove Luau Park
H1
Barber's Point Harbor
95
Barber's Point Beach
Barber's Point
0 2 miles
0 2 kilometers

Waianae

Kauiokalani Pl.
City Hall
Farrington Hwy.
Ala Hema
Lihue St.
Old Government Rd.
Waianae Park
Kaupuni Channel
Army St.
Guard St.
McArthur St.
Niihau St.
Waianae Valley Rd.
Mill St.
Waianae Store
Bayview
Lualualei Homestead
Pokai Bay Beach Park
Pokai Bay
Pokai Bay
0 250 yards
0 250 meters

Point. The paved road ends before Kaena Point, and it is effectively impossible to drive around the western tip of the island.

PRACTICAL INFORMATION

City Hall: Waianae Satellite, 85-670 Farrington Hwy. (☎696-6371), at the Neighborhood Community Center, north of where the Kaupuni Channel meets Pokai Bay. Bus schedules, bus passes, and camping permits available. Open M-F 8am-4pm.

Banks: Bank of Hawaii (☎696-4227; open M-Th 8:30am-4pm, F 8:30am-6pm), in the **Waianae Mall Shopping Center,** 86-120 Farrington Hwy. There is a **First Hawaiian Bank,** 86-020 Farrington Hwy. (☎696-7042), next to the post office. Open M-Th 8:30am-4pm, F 8:30am-6pm, Sa 9am-1pm. Each bank has an ATM.

Library: Waianae Public Library, 85-625 Farrington Hwy. (☎697-7868), offers **Internet access** with a 3-month visitor's card ($10). Open M-Tu, and Th-Sa 9am-5pm, W 1-8pm, F 1-5pm.

Equipment Rental: Hale Nalu Surf and Bike, 85-876 Farrington Hwy. (☎696-5897; www.halenalu.com), across from the Waianae Store on the right side of the highway heading north. Snorkeling gear ($8 per 24hr., $24 per week), body boards ($11/36), short boards ($18/66), long boards ($21/70), fins ($4/12), and bicycles ($21/70). Open daily 10am-7pm. AmEx/D/MC/V.

Police: Waianae Station, 85-939 Farrington Hwy. (☎696-4221). **Kapolei Station,** 1100 Kamokila Blvd. (☎692-4260).

Medical Services: Waianae Coast Comprehensive Health Center, 86-260 Farrington Hwy. (☎696-7081), heading north, turn right onto Mailiilii Rd. and head up the driveway. 24hr. Emergency Care.

Post Offices: Nanakuli Post Office, 87-2070 Farrington Hwy., next to Sack 'n' Save. Open M-F noon-4pm. **Waianae Main Office,** 86-014 Farrington Hwy. (☎696-0161). Open M-F 8am-4:15pm, Sa 9am-noon.

Postal Code: 96792 (Wainae).

ACCOMMODATIONS

There are very few accommodations on the Leeward side of Oahu. Camping at a county beach park is allowed with a permit, but it may be unsafe. Let's Go does not recommend camping at Leeward beaches.

Makaha Resort and Golf Club, 84-626 Makaha Valley Rd. (☎695-9544; www.makaharesort.net). From Farrington Hwy., turn right on Makaha Valley Rd. and follow the signs. All of the spacious and comfortable rooms have 2 doubles or 1 king-size bed, with full bath, cable TV, A/C, and mini-fridge. Amenities include a restaurant and bar, large pool, and golf course set in the striking Makaha Valley. Reception 24hr. Check-in 3pm. Check-out noon. Rooms $205-500. Call to ask about special rates. AmEx/D/MC/V. ❺

Makaha Surfside Condos, 85-175 Farrington Hwy. (☎696-6991), 1 mi. south of Makaha Beach Park. This 4-story cinder-block condominium sits on the beach and owners rent 1-bedroom, 1-bath units independently to visitors; conditions and rates vary. 2 pools, coin-op laundry. A bulletin board inside the complex lists owners who rent out rooms. Office open M-F 8-5pm. ❷

FOOD

Most of the dining options on the Leeward side are in Waianae, and many are fast-food joints; business does not support many restaurants on this sparsely populated side of Oahu. The **Waianae Store,** 85-863 Farrington Hwy., in the center of Waianae, sells inexpensive groceries. (☎696-3131. Open M-F 7am-9pm, Sa-Su 7am-8pm. D/MC/V.) A wider selection of goods can be found in **Sack 'n' Save,** 87-2070 Farrington Hwy., in Nanakuli. (☎668-1277. Open daily 5am-11pm. AmEx/D/MC/V.)

ROADFOOD. If you get hungry driving up Farrington Hwy., stop at one of the unnamed local plate lunch stands on the side of the road. They grill up fresh steak and chicken, served Hawaiian-style with rice and macaroni salad ($6-8).

The Red Baron, 85-915 Farrington Hwy. (☎697-1383), is a cozy restaurant that mixes local flavor and Italian fare, with dishes like the spaghetti plate lunch (served until 5pm; $7.50). The personal pizza ($4-7) is popular, as are house specials, including lasagna ($7.75). Beer $2.50. Open M-Th 11am-9pm, F-Sa 11am-10pm. AmEx/MC/V. ❷

Sun Sushi, 85-979A Farrington Hwy. (☎696-5518), next to Red Baron. Sun Sushi serves fresh sushi rolls and large *bentos* at low prices (6-pc. *maki,* $1-1.50; 15-pc. lunch *bento,* $4.60). Open daily 10am-9pm. Cash only. ❶

Barbecue Kai, 85-973 Farrington Hwy. (☎696-7122), at Waianae Valley Rd. Their Barbecue Mix Plate comes with chicken, teriyaki steak, and barbecue short ribs ($5.50). Open M-Tu and Th-Su 8am-11pm, W 8am-10pm. Cash only. ❶

L & L Drive-Inn, 85-080 Waianae Valley Rd. (☎696-7989), across from Barbecue Kai. Locals flock to cheeseburgers ($1.50) and chicken *katsu* plates ($5.25). Open daily 6:30am-11pm. D/MC/V. ❶

BEACHES

Beautiful beaches with uncrowded sand, clear water, and excellent conditions are the biggest draw of the Leeward Coast. Always check with lifeguards for current surf conditions, and never leave valuables in your car; beaches are some of the highest theft areas. The following beaches are off Farrington Hwy., listed from south to north.

KAHE POINT BEACH PARK. *(Snorkeling. Open daily 9am-5pm. Lifeguards daily.)* More a stretch of rocky ground than an actual beach, Kahe Point is a few hundred yards up the highway, before the rusting Hawaiian Electric Kahe Power Plant. The beach is more popular with scuba divers, snorkelers, and fishermen than swimmers or sunbathers. It also has a pavilion, restroom, shower facilities, picnic tables, and one outstanding feature: the view. Standing at the edge of the rocky shoreline, you can see straight up the Leeward Coast, and you may even spot a dolphin in the distance. Don't forget to tear your eyes away from the horizon to make sure your car is still there. Kahe Point is the first beach north of Ko Olina on Farrington Hwy..

WALKING ON BROKEN GLASS. Near Leeward beaches, parking lots which commonly have car break-ins are often littered with shards of glass. This is a good indication to park elsewhere.

HAWAIIAN ELECTRIC BEACH PARK (TRACKS). *(Snorkeling. Surfing. Open daily 9am-5pm. Lifeguards daily.)* Named for the power plant across the street, Hawaiian Electric Beach is home to a local surf spot called "Tracks," after the old railroad tracks through the sand. Although the bottom is rocky, swimming is usually safe in summer and the waves can be perfect for beginning bodysurfing. It's also popular for canoeing, fishing, and snorkeling. The power plant's warm discharge feeds coral patches and a host of marine life.

NANAKULI BEACH PARK. *(Boogie boarding. Open daily 9am-5pm. Lifeguards daily.)* This popular local beach is in the Native Hawaiian stronghold of Nanakuli. A lifeguard mans the south end of this steep, rolling, gold-sand shoreline whose calmer waters are usually gentle enough for swimming, while the north part of the beach tends to be more rough. The beach, referred to locally as "Subland," also sees traffic from canoers, fishermen, and locals who go boogie boarding. In the middle of the beach is a camping area referred to as "The Flats," with 14 sites that are primarily populated by locals. Nanakuli is north of Hawaiian Electric Beach Park. Turn left into the parking lot at Nanakuli Ave., before the school. The park has restroom and shower facilities, basketball courts, a baseball diamond, and a playground.

MAILI BEACH PARK. *(Boogie boarding. Surfing. Open daily 9am-5pm. Lifeguards daily.)* Maili's long, wide stretch of sand is especially popular among Leeward locals. There are two well-known surf spots: "Tumble Land," at the center of the beach, and "Green Lanterns," at the northernmost edge of the beach. The strong current and rocky wall mean that it's for experienced surfers only. Surfing is also popular around Maili Point, south of the beach park. The best spot to swim in the calmer summer months is near the lifeguard stands. The beach is at the south end of the town of Maili. There are picnic tables, restrooms, and showers

POKAI BAY BEACH PARK. *(Open daily 9am-5pm. Lifeguards daily.)* Thanks to the long, protective coral reef, this beach has some of the safest swimming on the Leeward Coast, though locals warn that the boat traffic can leave the water oily and unpleasant. The south end of the bay, which has picnic tables, restrooms, and lifeguard stands, also has the remains of **Kuilioloa Heiau.** The sacred temple was damaged by army training during WWII and has since been eroded by the sea. Pokai Bay is at the end of Waianae Valley Rd., off Farrington Hwy. in Waianae.

MAKAHA BEACH PARK. *(Snorkeling. Surfing. Open daily 9am-5pm. Lifeguards daily.)* Makaha is famous for its ferocious winter surf (averaging 5-8 ft., with the occasional 15-footer), several surfing competitions, and amazing sunsets. The beach is even popular on waveless days, when the calm water makes swimming safe and superior scuba diving possible in "Makaha Caverns," the coral and lava caves 500 yd. offshore, where dolphins, eels, manta rays, turtles, and white-tipped reef sharks frequently roam.

SHARK-MAN ATTACKS

A number of captivating legends revolve around the Leeward Coast and its graphic mythology. The Kaneana Cave, legendary for its ritualism and magic, is steeped with stories about its history. Most well-known is the story of Kamahoalii, the shark god and notorious shape-shifter known today as "Makua Charley," who sired a son with a Hawaiian woman. His son, a half-man, half-shark, was called Nanaue and lived in what is now Kaneana Cave. The shark-man was a bloodthirsty creature and would lure unsuspecting victims to his cave so that he could devour them. Some legends elaborate on this tale, saying that Nanaue was the lover of a beautiful girl whose parents turned her into a *moo* (lizard) to keep her away from him. Despite their efforts, the girl-lizard traveled down Kalena Stream, through Koiahi Gulch, and she lived with her shark-man lover near his cave.

Kaena Point is another area that features prominently in Hawaiian mythology. As the westernmost point on the island, and the closest to the setting sun, it was thought to be the jumping point, or *leina,* into Po, the Hawaiian spiritual underworld, or "sea of eternity." The souls of the dead were tested before they could jump off; those who had led an honest life could continue to Po, but those who did not were doomed to wander the island.

Makaha also has some of the best snorkeling on the Leeward Coast along the reef in front of the lifeguard stand by the north end of the beach. Makaha Beach Park is north of Makaha Valley Rd., off Farrington Hwy. Park on the ocean side of the road. The beach has picnic tables, restrooms, showers, and lifeguard towers.

KEAAU BEACH PARK. *(Snorkeling. Open daily 9am-5pm.)* Though Keaau isn't particularly good for swimming, the beach is a choice fishing, snorkeling, and offshore diving spot. The park's small amount of sand is bordered by rocks that make getting in the water difficult. Keaau Beach Park is north of Makaha Beach Park around Kepuhi Point. There are restrooms and shower facilities.

KEAWAULA BAY (YOKOHAMA BAY). *(Boogie boarding. Snorkeling. Surfing. Open daily 9am-5pm. Lifeguards daily.)* On the tip of the island, Keawaula Bay is the gem of the Leeward Coast. Nicknamed "Yokohama Bay," and affectionately called "Yoko's," the wide stretch of secluded white sand curves along a vast expanse of crystal-clear water. Watching the powerful waves break is a liberating experience, but only expert surfers, boogie boarders, and bodysurfers should try to tackle them. The beach catches the north, south, and west swells year-round, creating waves as large as 8 ft. in summer and 20 ft. in winter. Waves break over a sharp and shallow reef, though there is a small area close to the lifeguard stand that is safe for swimming during calm summer months. Snorkeling and scuba diving are popular in gentle water, and local fishermen crowd the point at the end of the beach, where Rte. 93 turns into an unpaved road. Keawaula Bay is at the end of Farrington Hwy., in Kaena State Park (p. 176). There are restrooms and showers.

SIGHTS AND HIKES

KAENA POINT STATE PARK. The northwesternmost point on Oahu, Kaena Point lies within the 853-acre Kaena Point State Park. *Kaena* translates to "the heat," which is appropriate as the point is one of the hottest and driest spots on Oahu. The park is almost completely undeveloped, and home to beautiful **Keawaula Bay** (see above). In 1983, **Kaena Point Natural Area Reserve,** which encompasses Kaena Point and its surroundings, was created to protect the region's rare coastal lowland dune ecosystem. Laysan albatross, Hawaiian monk seals, green sea turtles, dolphins, and various seabirds are among the animals that frequent Kaena Point. Excellent conditions for surfing, snorkeling, and scuba diving make the park any nature-lover's paradise. *(At the end of Farrington Hwy.)*

KAENA POINT TRAIL. *(2½ mi. 1-1½hr. one-way. Easy.)* Meandering through the Kaena Point State Park, Kaena Point Trail makes a great family hike. The trail was built for the Oahu Railroad and Land, and runs between the Waianae Mountains and the ocean (on the Leeward side) to Mokuleia (on the North Shore), with the awe-inspiring waves at Kaena Point halfway between. Tiptoeing along the water's edge, the trail affords hikers intimate views of the ocean, tide pools, natural stone formations, and numerous secluded coves. While the footing can be unsteady, the path is generally undemanding. You'll probably want to spend more time here than it would take to complete the hike to enjoy the tremendous scenery. *(For directions, see above.)*

KANEAKI HEIAU. This 17th-century site is Oahu's most authentically restored *heiau*. Visitors observe ancient Hawaii reincarnated with traditional prayer towers and altars. Plentiful taro root patches have led archaeologists to believe the *heiau* was originally dedicated to Kane, the god of agriculture, but it was subsequently converted to a temple for Ku, the god of war, during King Kamehameha I's conquest. The temple was restored to the sacrificial arrangement it was left in; it is very likely that it was a site of human sacrifice in the past. Today, it is a site of spiritual ceremonies for Native Hawaiians. *(Take Farrington Hwy. to Makaha Valley Rd. and turn right. Pass the Makaha Golf Resort and make a right onto Mauna Olu St. Follow the signs to the heiau. Open Tu-Su 10am-2pm. Visitors can only enter by car. Free.)*

KANEANA CAVE. This 100 yd. deep grotto, also known as Makua Cave, was carved many years ago when the seas were higher. The cave was sacred and *kahunas* (priests) performed religious ceremonies there. Today, slightly less historic broken glass and cigarette butts litter the cave floor. *(Off Farrington Hwy., about 2 mi. south of Kaena State Park. The cave is marked by several yellow concrete barriers in front and a stone marker on the opposite side of the road, where visitors can park.)*

MAKUA COVE. A blue warning sign marks this sandy beach. Dolphins frequently swim near shore each morning, and while visitors can look, remember that it is illegal to get within 50 ft. of them. *(1¼ mi. north of Kaneana Cave. An unpaved parking lot is next to a gate that is closed during the week, but visitors can still reach the beach.)*

MAKUA VALLEY. Though it looks beautiful from the highway, Makua Valley has seen much violence in its life span. As one of three valleys that compose the **Makua Military Reservation,** Makua was the site of tactical maneuvers and ammunitions practice during WWII. Undetonated training munitions remain in the valley and the area is currently closed to the public. A contract (set to expire in 2029) between the US Army and the State of Hawaii gives the Army complete control of 4190 acres of land in the area. *(Off Farrington Hwy., south of Kaena Point State Park.)*

SURFING IN HAWAII

Known as the "sport of kings," surfing was born and bred in Hawaii. *Alii*, or Hawaiian royalty, perfected the sport in the 1700s, and King Kamehameha could often be seen riding waves alongside his favorite wife, Queen Kaahumanu. In the early 1900s, Duke Kahanamoku reigned the surf scene. He and his group of Waikiki Beachboys helped turn the sport into a national trend with their surfing skill and striking looks.

As surfing's popularity swelled, so did its associated adrenaline levels. The popular slogan "Eddie Would Go," often seen on t-shirts and bumper stickers, refers to the legendary moves of Eddie Aikau on Oahu's North Shore in the early 1970s. Eddie would go where no other big-wave rider dared, swimming out in 60-foot surf, risking life and limb for the thrill of the tube. The extreme sport of tow-in surfing, though no less dangerous, has since replaced the perils of paddling through pounding waves. Jet skis tow surfers from calm, onshore harbors to beyond the break, just in time for the intrepid individual to drop in for a monster set. Maui's world-renowned Peahi Bay—also nicknamed "Jaws" for its all-consuming waves—was home to the first annual Tow-In World Championship, held in January 2002. It was also the site of the unforgettable sequence in the latest Bond movie, *Die Another Day*, in which three camouflaged stunt men (all from Hawaii) are dropped from a helicopter into the surf below.

Today, surfing is one of the world's most popular sports and has developed into a thriving industry. Movies, fashion, and music have cemented surfing's place in pop culture. New technology now allows designers to tailor boards to unique surf conditions, and surfers often own entire fleets of different models as a result. Shapers such as Dick Brewer of Kauai and Maui's Rod Ole and Jeff Timpone are the elite artists of the surfing design world.

Surfing is also the second-fastest growing sport among women. While Queen Kaahumanu may have paved the way for her gender, the past 50 years have witnessed the most rapid rise in the number of surfing kahunesses. In 1959, the first Gidget movie was released, promoting the image of female surfers. Changes in board construction have reflected this growth in interest and have made surfboards easier for women to carry and maneuver. Women finally made their way into the professional circuit with the founding of the Women's Pro Surfing Association in 1979 (though their winnings are still less than half that of professional male surfers). The best evidence for the growing popularity among women comes from *Surfer Magazine*; world pro Lisa Andersen was featured on its cover in 1995 with the line, "Lisa Andersen surfs better than you." Now, surf schools such as Surf Diva in California and Maui Surfer Girls in Maui cater primarily to women, while retailers like Girl in the Curl and Chicks with Sticks have also gained popularity. Movies have become the latest focal point for the rapidly spreading craze among *wahine* of all ages. The movie *Blue Crush*, shot on location in Oahu and released in 2002, re-introduced surfer girls to the big screen for the first time in a half-century. On any given day, women make up a solid percentage of those catching waves, dropping in, carving out their own place in this colorful pastime. *Imua!*

__Maren Lau__ was a Researcher-Writer in Hawaii for Let's Go: California & Hawaii 1997. She now lives in Maui and attends business school.

THE BIG ISLAND

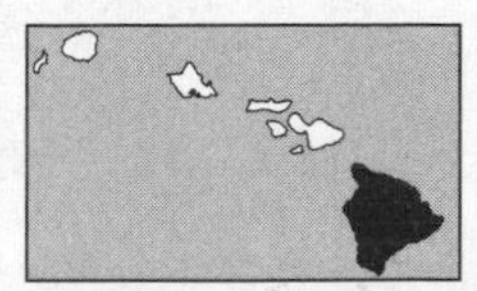

Let's come clean about the Big Island: it's not exactly the destination of choice for resort-hopping high rollers. While most Hawaiian tourists are looking for no more than a crowded Waikiki sunset, Big Island visitors watch the sun go down from empty cliffs, overlooking the Kohala Mountain range; or at the end of an unmarked trail, near a 1200 ft. waterfall; or at the summit of Mauna Kea, huddled around a warm Jeep, 1000 ft. above the clouds. Vacationers do not come here for the nightlife; they're here to explore a vastly untouched natural enigma. In this island alone, 11 out of the world's 13 climate regions are represented. From the subarctic tundra conditions of the Mauna Kea and Mauna Loa summits to the lush rainforests of the Hamakua coast to the dry and barren lava-covered Kau desert, a day of hiking can take visitors through a natural display more diverse than a roadtrip across the continental US. Yet a vacationer's paradise can still be found here; when you're done flirting with the rawest forces of nature, some of the state's most beautiful beaches are waiting, with Mai Tais practically on tap.

Spiritually, the Big Island has an unmistakable force. A legacy of the historical *mana* (spiritual power) remains on this most sacred of all the islands, which is the birthplace of Hawaii's most powerful king, Kamehameha I. In addition to the almost tangible energy that still emanates fom the ancient *heiaus* (temples) and historic villages dotted about the island, the volcanic rumble from below creates a uniquely exciting atmosphere. While development rapidly encroaches on the Kohala Coast and Kailua-Kona, the quintessence of the island is still preserved in the raw and unadulterated landscape of the rest of the island. By foot, bike, horse, surfboard, or kayak, the island is an adventure-seeker's paradise. Venturing off paved highways guarantees an encounter with a pristine nature unmatched anywhere else in the world.

HIGHLIGHTS OF THE BIG ISLAND

SNORKEL among a rainbow of fish in Kealakekua Bay (p. 196).

CLIMB DOWN to the floor of Waipio Valley (p. 239) to a secluded, mile-long beach.

TRAVERSE the Kilauea Iki Crater, a lake of lava only 40 years ago, in Hawaii Volcanoes National Park (p. 209).

EXPERIENCE PARADISE at the stunning 400 ft. Akaka Falls (p. 236).

STARGAZE from the summit of Mauna Kea (p. 203).

INTERISLAND TRANSPORTATION

The Big Island has two major airports. **Keahole-Kona International Airport,** Keahole Airport Rd. (☎329-3423), 8 mi. north of downtown Kailua-Kona off Rte. 19, is closest to South Kohala's crescent of resorts and sees the majority of international traffic. It is also served by interisland carriers. Flights from the Big Island to neighboring islands start at around $90 each way. **Aloha Airlines** (☎800-367-5250; www.alohaair.com) flies to: Honolulu, Oahu; Kahului, Maui; and Lihue, Kauai. **Hawaiian Airlines** (☎800-367-5320; www.hawaiianair.com) flies

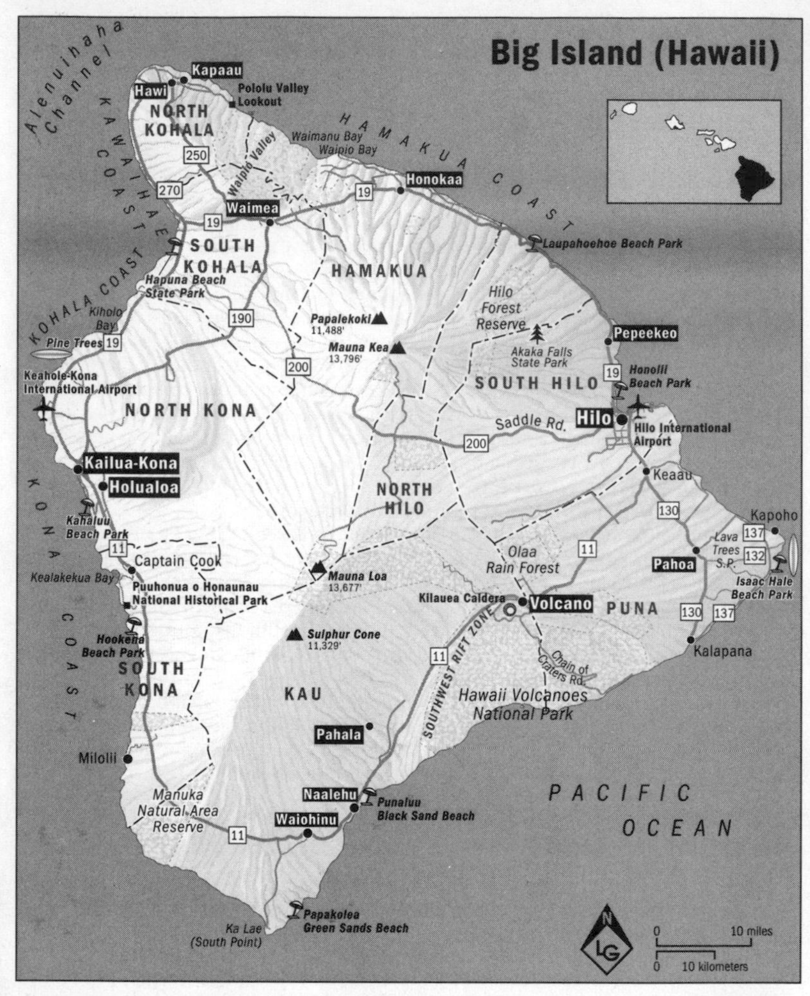

to: Honolulu, Oahu; Kahului, Maui; Lanai City, Lanai; and Lihue, Kauai (via Honolulu). The relatively new **go! airlines** (☎888-435-9462; www.iflygo.com) offers some of the cheapest rates between Honolulu and the neighboring islands. Surfers beware: Aloha and Hawaiian charge a fee for surfboards, and go! will not transport them.

A half mile south of the intersection of Rte. 11 and Rte. 19, **Hilo International Airport,** Airport Access Rd. (☎934-5840), sees mostly interisland flights, but it is also served by **United Airlines** (☎800-241-6522). **Aloha Airlines** flies to: Honolulu, Oahu; Kahului, Maui (via Honolulu); and Lihue, Kauai (direct and via Honolulu). **Hawaiian Airlines** flies to: Honolulu, Oahu; Kahului, Maui; Lanai City, Lanai (via Honolulu); and Lihue, Kauai. The visitors booth by the baggage claim provides helpful maps and brochures (open daily 6am-8pm). An $8-10 taxi ride is the only available transportation from the airport to downtown Hilo.

TRANSPORTATION

Based in Hilo, the **Hele-On Bus** (☎961-8521; www.co.hawaii.hi.us) is the Big Island's only island-wide system of public transport. Buses are clean, modern, comfortable, and free! Luggage, backpacks, and bicycles are $1 per piece. Unfortunately, catching a bus from anywhere *other* than downtown Hilo can be a challenge. This can be problematic because most inexpensive flights (especially those via Honolulu) now arrive in Kona, where the only bus out of town departs daily at 6:45am.

Renting a car is the best and most convenient way to see the Big Island. Many beaches, volcanoes, and waterfalls are otherwise inaccessible. Although 4WD is not necessary, it does make getting to more remote locations easier. Strangely enough, such vehicles are hard to come by because most rental companies only allow their cars on paved roads and reason that visitors who abide by contract shouldn't *need* 4WD. Only a handful—including Alamo, Dollar, and Harpers—guarantee 4WD upon reservation. **AAA** (☎800-736-2886) provides roadside assistance to cardholders throughout the Big Island, but excludes coverage of the Kona half of Saddle Rd. Call ahead for complete coverage information. For intercity and local transportation, consult the **Transportation** section for each town.

ACCOMMODATIONS

Budget travelers do best on the Hilo side, where a handful of hostels offer beds for $20 per night and public transportation to Volcanoes National Park and the Waipio Valley area is feasible. B&Bs have been popping up all over the Big Island (especially in South Kona and along the Hamakua Coast), offering the best mid-range accommodations. The **Hawaii Island B&B Association, Inc.** is a collection of over 50 B&B owners. Their website (www.stayhawaii.com) lists accommodations by region. **B&Bs Online** (www.bbonline.com/hi/region4.html) is another good resource, with links to B&B websites throughout the Big Island. For a longer stay, vacation rentals are another affordable alternative. In addition to the booking agencies listed in the accommodations section for Kailua-Kona (p. 185), **West Hawaii Property Services,** 78-6831 Alii Dr., Ste. 234A (☎322-6696; www.konarentals.com), is another excellent option. Hotels ($50-200) are ubiquitous in downtown Hilo and Kona, and mega-resorts ($250-the moon) line the beaches of South Kohala. Low season (Apr. 15-Dec. 15) can offer deep discounts of up to 40% at even the swankiest establishments. If you plan to stay for more than a week, **www.craigslist.org** makes finding a room to rent quite easy, especially in Kona, Pahoa, and Hilo.

KAILUA-KONA

Kailua-Kona (pop. 9,870), or Kona, as it is popularly known, is the first place many travelers to the Big Island encounter. After experiencing Kona, smart travelers will venture beyond the city for the beauty of the rest of this island shortly thereafter. Kona proper has little more to offer than a plethora of chintzy oceanfront shops and overpriced places to stay—the real beauty of Hawaii lies in the beaches of the Kohala coast to the north and Kealakekua Bay to the south.

TRANSPORTATION

Flights: Keahole-Kona International Airport, Keahole Airport Rd. (☎329-2484), is 7 mi. north of downtown Kona, off Rte. 19. Keahole is laid-back and served by international and interisland carriers: **Aloha Airlines** (☎800-367-5250; www.alohaairlines.com); **Hawaiian Airlines** (☎800-882-8811; www.hawaiianair.com); **Island Air** (☎800-323-3345; www.islandair.com); and **go!** (☎888-435-9462; www.iflygo.com).

Buses: Public transportation is minimal. The **Hele-On Bus** (☎961-8744; www.co.hawaii.hi.us), the only public transportation on the Big Island, is based in Hilo. Catching a bus anywhere else can be quite a feat. Check the website for schedules. A free bus departs M-Sa at 6:45am from the Lanihau Center on Palani Rd. and passes through **Waimea** (1hr.) on its way to **Hilo** (3hr.).

Taxis: Aloha Taxi (☎329-7779 or 325-5448). Call 24hr. in advance for their 6-person van. Other options include **C&C Taxi** (☎329-6388), **D&E Taxi** (☎329-4279), and **Mel's Taxi** (☎329-1977), which have island-wide service. Taxis usually run 6am-9pm. Taxis charge $3 initially and $2.40 per additional mi. Airport to town $25.

Car Rentals:

In the airport: Alamo (☎329-8896 or 800-462-5266). 21+. Under-25 surcharge $25 per day. Open daily 5:30am-9pm. **Avis** (☎327-3000 or 800-331-1212). 25+. Open daily 5am-9pm. **Budget** (☎329-8511 or 800-527-7000). 25+. Open 5am-9:30pm. **Dollar** (☎800-342-7398). 21+. Under-25 surcharge $20 per day. Open daily 5am-9pm. **Thrifty** (☎800-367-2277). 21+. Under-25 surcharge $20 per day. Open daily 5:30am-10pm.

Beyond the airport: **Enterprise,** 74-5583 Luhia St. (☎331-2509). Operates out of a hard-to-find office in the industrial center on Luhia St., off Kaiwi St., 8 mi. from the airport. Although it'll cost you a taxi ride to get to the office from the airport, the excellent service and basement prices make this one of the best car rental companies on the island. Get a ride from the airport with **Mel's Taxi** (see above) for a special Enterprise discounted rate ($20).

ORIENTATION

Kailua-Kona lies on the western, leeward coast of the Big Island, sheltered by cloud-covered Halualai (still considered active by volcanologists). From Keahole-Kona Airport, **Route 19** runs south toward Kona, becoming **Route 11** after crossing **Palani Road.** Take note that Rte. 11 is also referred to as **Hawaii Belt Road** or **Mamalahoa Highway,** and Rte. 19 is also called **Queen Kaahumanu Highway.** North of Palani Rd., Rte. 19 cuts through the lava fields of **South Kohala,** whose banks hide excellent beaches and a resort-lined coast. Heading south, Rte. 11 leads to the slow-paced coffee towns **Holualoa** and **Captain Cook,** and the dramatic **Kealakekua Bay.** Climbing uphill from Rte. 11, Palani Rd. ascends inland to become **Route 190** the way to **Waimea** and **Saddle Road.** Descending into town, it crosses **Kuakini Highway** and becomes **Alii Drive,** Kona's seawall-hugging main street.

PRACTICAL INFORMATION

There are two **Visitor Information Centers** (☎329-1190) at the Kona Airport, but because of staffing shortages, it is often difficult to catch an employee. Free **maps** and pamphlets are available even if no one's there to answer questions. Costco members with a car save almost $0.30 per gallon by using the **Costco gas station.** Take Hwy. 11 north past Palani Rd.; after three lights, turn right on Hina Lani Rd.

TOURIST AND FINANCIAL SERVICES

Bank: Bank of Hawaii, 75-5595 Palani Rd. (☎326-3900), next to the Lanihau Center, exchanges currency and has a **24hr. ATM.** Open M-Th 8:30am-4pm, F 8:30am-6pm.

Equipment Rental: If you're planning to snorkel for more than a week, consider purchasing your own flippers at **Wal-Mart,** on Henry St., above Hwy. 11. Full snorkel set: adult $35, junior $15. Otherwise, check out the listings below.

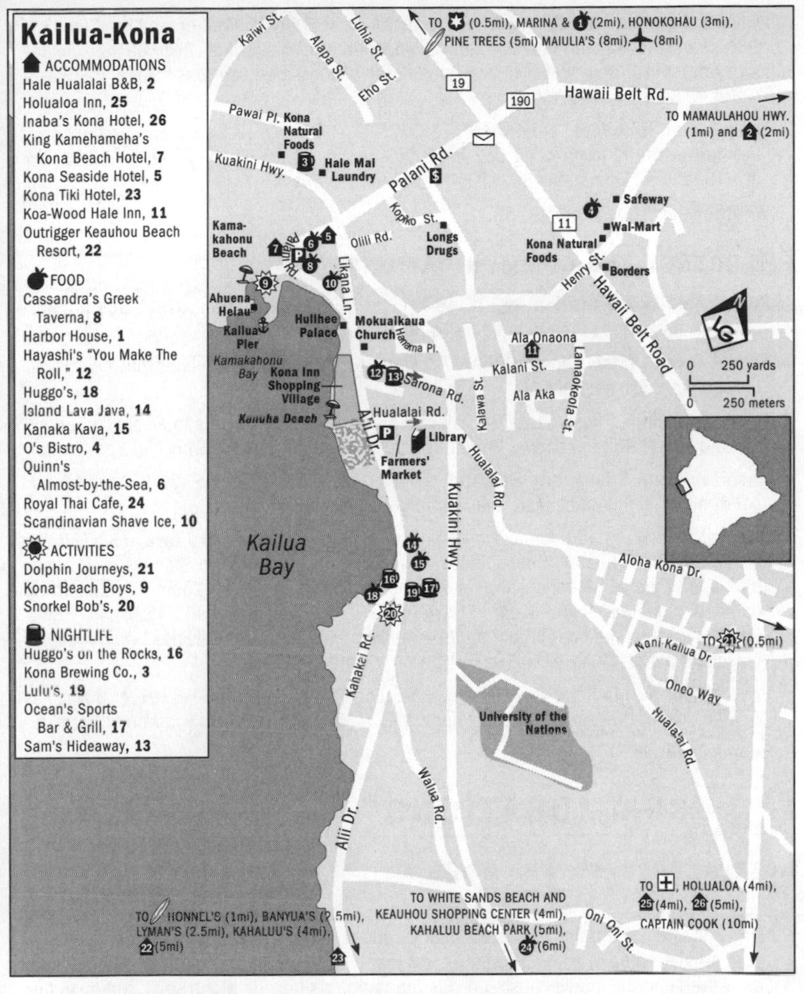

Honu Sports, 75-5744 Alii Dr., #108 (☎327-3483; www.honusports.com), in the Kona Inn Shopping Center. This place is put-together and professional. Guests meet dive crews in the Honokohau Marina for an array of dives. The Manta Ray Night Dive ($89) is the most popular. Gear available at the shop. Open daily 9am-9pm. AmEx/MC/V.

Snorkel Bob's, 75-5831 Kahakai Rd. (☎329-0770). Offers a broad selection at a range of prices. $2.50-8 per day, $9-32 per week. Package with Rx masks ($11 per day, $44 per week). Open daily 8am-5pm. AmEx/D/MC/V.

LOCAL SERVICES

Library: Kailua-Kona Public Library, 75-138 Hualalai Rd. (☎327-4327), on Hualalai Rd., connecting Kuakini Hwy. to coastal Alii Dr. **Internet access** with a 3-month visitor's card ($10). Appointment needed for one of the 3 1hr. terminals, limit 1hr. per week. 15min. walk-in terminal available. Open Tu 11am-7pm, W-Th and Sa 9am-5pm, F 11am-5pm.

Outdoor Supplies: Hawaii Forest and Trail, 74-5035B Queen Kaahumanu Hwy. (☎331-8505), next to GasPro, between downtown Kona and the airport. Sells USGS topography and trail maps, water filters, and solar shower contraptions. Open M-F 7am-5:30pm, Sa-Su 7am-4:30pm.

Laundromat: Hele Mai Laundromat, 75-5629 Kuakini Hwy. (☎329-3494), in the building next to the Kona Brewing Co. Wash $1.25, dry $1.25. Drop-off service $0.75 per lb., 10 lb. min. Open daily 6am-10pm. Last load 8:45pm.

Weather Conditions: ☎961-5582.

EMERGENCY AND COMMUNICATIONS

Police: Kealakehe Station (☎326-4646), on Queen Kaahumanu Hwy., about 1 mi. north of town, next to the Kealakehe Transfer Station.

Sexual Assault Crisis Line: ☎935-0677. Operators advise that the lines may be busy; if no one picks up, keep trying.

Pharmacy: Longs Drugs, 75-5595 Palani Rd. (☎329-1632), by the intersection of Hwy. 11 and Palani Rd., in Lanihau Shopping Center. Open M-Sa 8am-9pm, Su 8am-6pm.

Hospital: Kona Community Hospital, 79-1019 Haukapila St. (☎322-9311), 15 mi. south of Kona, in Kealakekua. 24hr. emergency room.

Internet Access: In addition to the Kona Public Library, **Island Lava Java,** 75-5799 Alii Dr. (☎327-2161), in Alii Sunset Plaza, offers Internet access for customers on 2 terminals and wireless. $3 per 15min., or $10 per hr. Open daily 6am-10pm. For something cooler than coffee, **Scandinavian Shave Ice,** 75-5699 Alii Dr. (☎331-1626), in a blue-front building by the boat harbor on the northern end of Alii Dr., provides 6 terminals for users. $8 per hr. Open M-Sa 10am-9:30pm, Su noon-9pm.

Post Office: Kailua-Kona Post Office, 74-5577 Palani Rd. (☎331-8307 or 800-275-8777), next to the Lanihau Center. Open M-F 8:30am-4:30pm, Sa 9:30am-1:30pm.

Postal Code: 96740.

ACCOMMODATIONS

HOTELS, RESORTS, AND B&BS

Kona Tiki Hotel, 75-5968 Alii Dr. (☎329-1425), just over a mile south on coastal Alii Dr., Kona Tiki maintains a 50s tropical paradise feel, and guests gather around the pool each evening to chat and watch the sunset. The hotel is built on a seawall right on the water, and the low-key husband-wife managing pair exude aloha spirit. Although the ground floor can be humid, the 2nd and 3rd floors are breezy and sunlit. Breakfast included. Reception 7am-7pm. Check-in 3pm. Check-out 11am. Reservations essential. Doubles with queen bed $65; queen and twin $79, with kitchenette $84; each additional guest $9, ages 2-12 $6. Cash only. ❸

Holualoa Inn, Mamalahoa Hwy. (☎324-1121; www.holualoainn.com), 5 mi. from downtown Kona in Holualoa Village. Turn *mauka* (toward the mountains), from Palani Rd. or Kuakini Hwy. onto Halualai Rd. Follow this road as it winds into coffee country then turn left onto Mamalahoa and look for the inn's sign on the left. Set back from the road and on a coffee estate at 1400 ft., the grounds are a vantage point for an excellent ocean view. Surrounded by Holualoa's quaint art galleries, the secluded 6 rooms in the eucalyptus-floored cedar house are an exceptional retreat. Homemade Kona coffee served at breakfast (daily 7:30-9am). Pool-side day rooms equipped with bath, shower, and luggage storage for guests with late flights. Ages 13+. Doubles $245-290; $30 per additional person. 10% off for 7 or more nights. MC/V. ❺

Hale Hualalai Bed & Breakfast, 74-4968 Mamalahoa Hwy. (☎326-2909; www.halehualalai.com). take Palani Rd. toward the mountain and turn right onto Mamalahoa Hwy. (Hwy. 180). After 1 mi., turn right at the sign. Hale Hualalai is a small, quiet retreat with splendid ocean views. The suites are large, with individual balconies, kitchens, and king-size beds. The owner (and professional chef) lives right on the premises, and cooks up a mean breakfast. Call to reserve. Suites $135 per night; weekly rates negotiable. ❹

Inaba's Kona Hotel, 76-5908 Mamalahoa Hwy. (☎324-1155), in Holualoa Village, 5 mi. from Kona. Turn left on Mamalahoa Hwy. from Halualai Rd.; the hotel is 1 mi. into town. You can't miss the building–it's all pink! Arrive with respect: the Inaba's old-fashioned residence has been a local fixture since 1926, and the owners dislike tomfoolery. **Back rooms #10** (double and twin) and **#11** (double) are steals. High ceilings, wood floors, and sweeping ocean views. Check-in 3pm. Check-out 11am. Reservations essential. 2-night min. Owners will rent any room as a single ($30), double ($35), or triple ($40). Cash only. ❷

Koa-Wood Hale Inn, 75-184 Ala Ona Ona St. (☎326-7018 or 329-9663). Heading downhill on Palani Rd., turn left onto Kalani St., then left again onto Alahou St., and right onto Ala Ona Ona St. Essentially a small apartment complex converted into hostel-like accommodations, Koa-Wood nurtures a social, relaxed environment. Dorms are single-sex, with 4 beds in a room. Private rooms on the 2nd floor share a balcony and common room. Kitchen, TV room, coin-op washing machines ($1 per load). Bedding included. Reception daily 8am-noon and 4:30-10pm. Check-in 4:30pm. Check-out 10am. Dorms $25; private rooms $55; one side of the apartment (4 people comfortably) $125. MC/V. ❶

King Kamehameha's Kona Beach Hotel, 75-5660 Palani Rd (☎922-8061 or 800-367-6060; www.konabeachhotel.com), behind Kamakahonu Beach, where Palani Rd. meets Alii Dr. Tucked away in a top-notch location, this spot is away from it all and at the same time right in the mix. Doubles $105-130, check online for deals. Check-in 3pm. Check-out 11am. AmEx/MC/V. ❹

Kona Seaside Hotel, 75-5646 Palani Rd. (☎329-2455; www.konaseasidehotel.com), on the busy corner of Alii Dr. and Palani Rd. This Triple-A hotel is practical with no frills. A/C, cable, and mini-fridge included. Special rental car deals available with Internet reservation. Reception 24hr. Check-in 3pm. Check-out noon. Doubles $98; deluxe $108. AmEx/D/MC/V. ❷

Outrigger Keauhou Beach Resort, 78-6740 Alii Dr. (☎322-3441; www.outrigger.com), 5 mi. south of Kona, in Keauhou. Keauhou offers typical resort rooms, with atypically large price reductions. Prices change daily, so bargain-hunters can enjoy ocean-view rooms with proper planning. Amenities include pool, tennis courts, spa, and access to prime snorkeling waters. All rooms have A/C and mini-fridge. Doubles $209-449. AmEx/D/MC/V. ❺

CONDOS

Visitors who plan to stay for more than a few days can often find better deals with condos than with the line of beach hotels marching down Alii Dr.

Hawaii Resort Management, 75-5776 Kuakini Hwy. (☎329-3333 or 800-244-4752; www.konahawaii.com), has some amazing deals ranging from $67-113 per day (or around $700 per week) during the low season (Apr. 15-Dec. 14). Magic Sands, Banyan Tree, Billfisher, and many other condo-complexes along Alii Dr. are advertised. ❸

Knutson and Associates, 75-6082 Alii Dr. (☎329-6311 or 800-800-6202; www.konahawaiirentals.com), in the Casa de Emdeko mall. Offers upscale options, including the Kona Riviera and Casa de Emdeko. 4-night min. Winter $90-210; summer $70-180. ❸

FOOD

Groceries are extremely expensive in Kona. Sushi is often more cost-effective than a supermarket run. Do-it-yourselfers can still try **Kona Natural Foods,** 75-1027 Henry St. (☎329-2296; open M-Sa 9am-9pm, Su 9am-7pm), in Crossroads Shopping Center, or the 24hr. **Safeway** (☎329-2207) next door. For a camping trip stock-up, consider a trip to **Costco Wholesalers.** (☎334-0770. Membership card required.) Home to charter boats that venture off the coast for deep sea fishing, **Honokohau Marina,** 3 mi. north of town off Queen Kaahumanu Hwy., is the best spot to buy fresh ahi steak, charbroiled right at the dock. At the end of each day (3:30-5pm), fishermen display their catches on Kailua Pier. For fresh fruit and vegetables, try the **farmers' market,** on Hualalai Rd. next to the library. (☎895-7970. Open Th-Su 7am-5pm.)

RESTAURANTS

Habaneros Mexican Cuisine, (☎324-4688), in the Keauhou Shopping Center on Kamehameha III Rd. right next door to Royal Thai Cafe. Habeneros is recommended, rightly so, as the best Mexican food in town. Basic burritos, quesadillas, and enchiladas $7. Breakfast ($5) until 11:30am. Open M-Sa 9am-9pm. Cash Only. ❶

Cassandra's Greek Taverna, 75-669 Alii Dr. (☎334-1066), under the striped awnings, across from the north harbor. This Greek restaurant combines open-air seating and excellent dishes with its harbor view. Dinner can be pricey ($16-20), but the lunch is more reasonable (gyros, $9). Skewered chicken *souvlaki,* marinated in wine and charbroiled, with sides of salad and garlic-heavy *tzatziki,* $18. Greek salad with tomatoes, olives, cucumbers, and feta, $8. W and F karaoke; Sa live music. Open daily 11am-10pm; bar until 2am. MC/V. ❷

Quinn's Almost-by-the-Sea, 75-5655A Palani Rd. (☎329-3822), next to the Kona Seaside Hotel, just before Palani Rd. becomes Alii Dr. This local favorite earns its keep with a friendly fisherman vibe and exceedingly fresh fare. Sit at the bar for fish and chips ($10) or have a pint. Dinner entrees $18-25. Open daily 11am-10:30pm. MC/V. ❹

O's Bistro, 75-1027 Henry St., Store 102 (☎327-6565; www.osbistro.com), this upscale spot is located in Crossroads Shopping Center, but sacrificing one night of an ocean view for this exceptional food is well worth the loss. Kona raves about the noodle bowls ($10-18), and the Grilled Eggplant Stack ($12) is out of this world. Breakfast $8-12. Dinner $24-32. Open daily 10am-9pm. MC/V. ❹

Royal Thai Cafe (☎322-8424), in the Keauhou Shopping Center on Kamehameha III Rd. Follow Alii Dr. until it becomes Alii Hwy.; the shopping center is at the corner of Alii and Kamehameha. All the Buddhas are smiling in this refined restaurant for good reason: Royal Thai keeps prices low and food quality high. Curries $9-14. Veggie dishes $8-10. Open M-F 11am-2:30pm and 4:30-9:30pm, Sa 2:30-9:30pm. AmEx/D/MC/V. ❷

Harbor House (☎326-4166), in the marina off Hwy. 19, between mi. markers 97 and 98. The house is packed during Happy hour, when an older, local crowd comes to unwind with a notorious ice-cold 18 oz. schooner ($2.75-4.25). The food, primarily seafood and chips ($8-9), is decent. Bartender Jill calls the place a Kona "Cheers," where everyone's family. Happy hour M-Sa 4-6pm, Su 4-5:30pm. Open M-Sa 11am-7pm, Su 11am-5:30pm. AmEx/MC/V. ❷

Huggo's, 75-5828 Kahakai Rd. (☎329-1493), at the south end of Alii Dr., across from the seawall. Excellent food but high prices, due in part to the restaurant's stellar location. A salty breeze and a beautiful hardwood floor beckon an eclectic set of diners. Live music nightly. Lunch-time sandwiches $12. For dinner, try Huggo's popular *lilikoi miso* ahi ($35). Vegetarian wild mushroom pasta with ginger $21. Lunch M-F 11:30am-4:30pm, dinner daily 5:30-10pm; bar open until 12:30am. AmEx/D/MC/V. ❺

CAFES AND TAKEOUT

Kanaka Kava, 75-5803 Alii Dr. (☎327-1660), down the alley in the building next to the Sunset Plaza. The first thing you'll notice about this *kava* hut is a large bowl filled with what appears to be mud water. That's *kava,* an ancient Pacific herbal beverage nicknamed "the peace drink" for its mellowing (read: numbing) effect. After a shell of *kava* ($4), try the Hawaiian food–the best in Kona. For tender-palate first-timers, a mix of *kava,* coconut milk, and pineapple juice is only $4. Plates $8-14. Open M-W and Su 10am-10pm, Th-Sa 11am-11pm. Cash only. ❶

Island Lava Java, 75-5799 Alii Dr. (☎327-2161), diagonally across from Waterfront Row. Look for the white umbrellas. Genial surfer-types serve Kona coffee and fresh-baked goods to an easy-going morning crowd. People have been known to drive for hours just to get their hands on a huge cinnamon bun ($3), but arrive before 9am, when they tend to run out. Oat-berry muffins ($3), brewed iced mochas ($4.25), and hearty sandwiches ($6-8). Dinner specials $16-18. Internet available to customers only. Open daily 6am-10pm. MC/V. ❷

Hayashi's 'You Make the Roll,' (☎326-1322), behind the Sarona Dr. Kona Marketplace Plaza. Mr. Hayashi dishes out sizable sushi rolls to go for unbelievable prices. Fill out a notecard to concoct a personal roll. There's no space inside, but ample outdoor seating includes umbrella-shaded patio furniture. Rolls $2-4. 50-pc. platters available with 2hr. advance notice ($23-25). Open M-F 11am-7pm, Sa 11am-4pm. MC/V. ❶

Scandinavian Shave Ice, 75-5699 Alii Dr. (☎331-1626). Shave ice is packed into neon blossom cups, then doused with Crayola-colored syrups. The whirring cast-iron ice shavers, swirling colors, and blaring rock music create an entertaining cacophony. Internet access available (p. 184). Small shave ice $2.50. Open M-Sa 10am-9pm, Su noon-9pm. MC/V. ❶

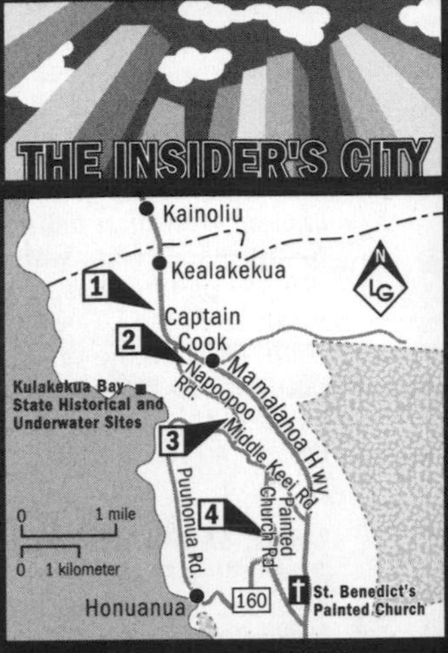

ESPRESSO WAY

South Kona is home to the farms that grow the most elite coffee in the world. Most of the 40+ farms offer free tastings, if not tours, and all are guaranteed to brew an unforgettable cup. The following are the best of the bunch.

1. **Greenwell Coffee Farms,** 81-6581 Rte. 11 (☎323-2275). Free tasting. Free tours run as people arrive. Open M-F 8am-5pm, Sa 8am-4pm.
2. **Kona Historical Society's Kona Coffee Living History** (☎323-2006). Gives a 1hr. tour of the coffee industry circa 1925-1945. $15, under 12 $10. Every hr. M-F 9am-1pm.
3. **Kona Pacific Farmers Cooperative,** 82-5810 Napoopoo Rd. (☎328-2411). This cooperative represents over 300 coffee farmers. Tours M-F 7am-4pm.
4. **Bay View Farms,** 83-5249 Painted Church Rd. (☎328-9658). Free tastings and 30-45min. tours at one of the first farms to welcome visitors. Gazebo open daily 9am-5pm.

BEACHES

The most pristine beaches in Kona are usually accessible only on foot or via unmarked roads left in disrepair to deter an avalanche of visitors. The following beaches are listed in south-to-north order along Hwy. 19.

KAHALUU BEACH PARK. *(Snorkeling. Surfing. Open daily 24hr. Lifeguards 9am-5pm.)* An ancient Hawaiian fishing harbor, Kahaluu is protected by a crumbling seawall that provides calm waters for sea turtles to hang out. The giant sea turtles are *the* compelling reason to visit this beach (it's certainly not the crude sand or lackluster view). Snorkeling is the preferred beach activity because it affords a chance to see the turtles up close. Laws require that all swimmers keep a distance of 10 ft. Surfers, there's a right/left break beyond the sea wall, but beware; the bay creates strong rip currents. *(The beach is 5 mi. south of downtown Kona on Alii Dr., near the Keauhou Beach Resort. The park is clearly marked and has plenty of parking.)*

WHITE SANDS BEACH. *(Boogie boarding. Open daily 7am-8pm. Lifeguards 9am-5pm.)* Also called Magic Sands, this beach is the area's most accessible. The promise of white, magic sand draws a large crowd, and the beach is full of boogie boarders and swimmers. *(4 mi. south of downtown Kona on Alii Dr., just past Jameson's.)*

KAMAKAHONU BEACH. *(Open daily until 7pm.)* A calm inlet amid the busy Alii Dr., this beach is for those traveling with children. The water is gentle, predictable, and usually swarming with kids in a wide variety of flotation devices. A closer view of Ahuena Heiau (p. 190) is attainable by swimming a few yards out. *(The beach is in downtown Kona near the intersection of Alii Dr. and Palani Rd.)*

OLD KONA AIRPORT PARK BEACH. *(Open daily 7am-8pm.)* When Kona's first airport closed in 1970, the runway was converted into parking for this state park. The tranquil mile of beach is close to town, but relatively unused. However, Old Kona's rocky, dangerous shoreline means swimming is only passable, and better watersports can be found elsewhere. *(To reach the beach follow Kuakini Hwy. north until it ends at a parking lot.)*

WAWALOLI BEACH. *(Surfing. Open daily until 8pm.)* Wawaloli is well known for its warm, protected tide pools, which are great for exploring and deep enough for splashing about. Explosions of surf against the protective lava bench put on quite a show for sunning spectators. Bathrooms and showers available. A mile to the right, if you face the ocean, is **Pine Trees,** the most talked about surf spot near Kona, with three breaks and a range of surfing levels. Those with 4WD should be able to access it. *(The beach is 5 mi. north of Kona on Rte. 19, between mi. markers 95 and 94, accessible via the paved entrance to the Natural Energy Lab.)*

KEKAHA KAI BEACH. *(Surfing. Open M-Tu and Th-Su 9am-7pm.)* The bumpy and twisted drive down to the beach entrance is well worth the trouble: a peaceful swath of white sand awaits the adventurous. Save the distant surf break, **Mahaiula's,** this beach is calm and quiet. Neither drinking water nor facilities exist here, and it's a long walk to the beach from the highway if you don't have 4WD. Don't forget a water bottle with your towel and sunscreen. *(10 mi. north of Kona on Rte. 19, down a bumpy, rugged road between mi. markers 90 and 91.)*

MAKALAWENA BEACH. *(Open daily 24hr.)* Isolated and unknown, Makalawena is a 20-30min. walk or a bumpy 4WD ride across baking lava fields. For those seeking exquisite sand and pure blue water and sky, look no further—just don't forget something to put on your feet; the lava rock is incredibly sharp. This beach is the best Kona has to offer. Fine sand cradles sunbathers, and tide pools provide makeshift bathtubs. No drinking water or facilities. *(The beach is north of Kona on Rte. 19, between mi. markers 89 and 90. Following the dirt path, head left whenever it forks, and then follow the shoreline until you reach white sands.)*

KUA BAY (MANINIOWALI). *(Open daily 24hr.)* Also called Maniniowali, Kua Bay is a 15-20min. walk beyond the highway pull-off. Once you reach the small beach, kick off your shoes and enjoy the fine white sand. The bay has excellent swimming when waters are calm, though when the surf's up, it's best to stay on the land. No shade, drinking water, or facilities. The beach is north of mi. marker 88, off Rte. 19.

SEVENTH HEAVEN. Our seven favorite island sunsets.

1) **Mauna Kea Summit:** The air at the summit is so clear that the astronomical viewing conditions are world-class and so are the sunsets. Besides clear air, the summit has the added benefit of being above the clouds, which makes for a unique perspective. Stay after sunset for some stargazing. For more on summit activities, see p. 231.
2) **Makalawena Beach:** From the island's highest point back down to sea level, Makalawena Beach has all the elements for a picture-perfect beach sunset. The seemingly endless horizon that may be your best chance to see the elusive "green flash." Be sure to pack a flashlight so you can find your way back from the beach.
3) **Pololu Lookout:** A few hundred feet up from an ocean crashing below, this jagged stretch of coastline bursts with sunset pastels in the evening. Highlighting the panorama, Maui looms just to the left if you're facing the ocean. For more on Pololu, including hikes, see p. 250.
4) **Waipio Lookout:** Waipio is picturesque anytime of day, but when the setting sun strikes the valley, the viewing conditions are golden in more ways than one. The lush green valley takes on an evening light that will have you frantically snapping pictures while the curving coastal waters mirror the slanting rays.
5) **Hawaii Volcano National Park, End of Chain of Craters Road:** This spot of the park is best known for the after-dark views of lava hitting the ocean, but come an hour earlier to watch day fade to night, as the lava's glow competes with the last bit of daylight.
6) **South Point:** As far south as you can go in the US, this exposed bit of land sees massive waves crashing into each other from every direction. The roar of the ocean provides the perfect sound track for the dropping sun.
7) **Huggo's on the Rocks, Kailua-Kona:** Not all the best sunsets are remote. Huggo's sets the stage for tropical paradise photo-ops with a hula dancer, Hawaiian music, frozen Mai Tais, and, oh yeah, we almost forgot—a sunset.

ACTIVITIES

SNORKELING. Although the island's best snorkeling is south of Kona in Captain Cook (p. 197), a number of companies sail snorkel cruises from the bay. Some trips provide lunch, others only snacks. Be sure to bring extra water, sunglasses, and plenty of sunscreen. For a do-it-yourself snorkel experience, head to **Snorkel Bob's** (p. 183) or Wal-Mart.

SCUBA DIVING. Even those who aren't certified can have an underwater adventure on an introductory dive for around $125. Open-water certification courses run between 3-4 days ($425). Almost every rental place, including Kona

Beach Boys (see below), books scuba dives as well. An appealing excursion for experienced divers is **Manta Ray's Night Dive.** Lights attract plankton, which in turn attract manta rays to the dive site; as you sit underwater, the mammoth manta rays will zoom around you in an underwater acrobatic act. Those hesitant to dive deep can try snuba, a shallower version of scuba diving, also available through **Kona Beach Boys** (see below).

BOOGIE BOARDING. Boogie board and surfboard rentals are not the easiest finds in town, although certain shops on Alii Dr. carry them. Try **Kahaluu Surf Rentals** at Kahaluu beach.

CANOEING. Leave the surfboard at home and come down to Kamakahonu Beach where the **Kona Beach Boys** (☎326-7686; www.konabeachboys.com) are just hangin' loose in their humble hut. More than just a paddle around the bay, their outrigger trips are adventures into Hawaii's past. The guides explain the significance of the area, focusing on Ahuena Heiau and clarifying the past importance of the outrigger canoe as a mode of transportation. *(On the shore at Kamakahonu. Canoe trips $38. 2hr. surf lesson $119 (includes rental). $10 for fins and goggles. Open daily 8am- 5pm.)*

DOLPHIN DIVING. For the intrepid traveler looking for a break from the busy Kona tourist industry, the personal, friendly dolphin tours at **Dolphin Journeys** are unforgettable. In addition to dolphin diving, Dolphin Journeys offers whale-watching and volcano tours. *(☎329-3030; www.dolphinjourneys.com. Meals included. Half-day tours $100-175.)*

SIGHTS

HULIHEE PALACE. The Daughters of Hawaii, with their impressive collection of Hawaiian artifacts, maintain this historical Kona site: a modest, but exciting piece of Hawaiian history. Hula dances and musical performances liven up the palace, built by one-time governor of Hawaii, John Adams Kuakini, in 1838. A favorite royal retreat, the grounds and oceanfront location eclipse the actual building, which only has six rooms. King Kalakua, the "Merry Monarch," was famous for being quite the socialite, and he graced the abode with countless parties. The palace lay abandoned in the early 20th century, serving as a playground for neighborhood children and an impromptu parlor for an enthusiastic group of card players. It has since been restored and contains numerous Hawaiian artifacts, including the javelins and spears of Kamehameha the Great. *(75-5718 Alii Dr. ☎329-1877; www.huliheepalace.org. Open M-F 9am-4pm, Sa-Su 10am-4pm. Guided tour available. $6, seniors $4, ages 18 and under $1.)*

MOKUAIKAUA CHURCH. Built in 1837 out of lava rock and coral lime mortar, this is the oldest church in the state. It's also the tallest structure in town; for years fishermen used the 112 ft. steeple for navigation. There is a small exhibit explaining the building's history at the entrance and beautiful stained glass over the altar. A model of the *Brig Thaddeus*, the boat that carried missionaries of the Pioneer Company to the Big Island during a 164-day voyage, sits in the back of the church. *(At the northern end of Alii Dr. ☎329-1589. Open daily sunrise to sunset. Free.)*

AHUENA HEIAU. Ahuena *Heiau* (temple) was the centerpiece of Kamehameha the Great's government from 1813-1819. Kamehameha, the only man to unite the Hawaiian islands under one ruler, was born on the Kohala coast in the 16th century. After consolidating his power over the other islands, he returned to Kona to rule (see **History,** p. 14). He built Ahuena Heiau and dedicated it to Lono, the god of agriculture and prosperity. At the top of the hut is a golden plover, a slight bird thought to have led the first Polynesian settlers from the South Pacific to the Hawaiian islands 5000 mi. away. *(At the northern end of Kailua Bay, adjacent to King Kamehameha's Kona Beach Hotel. The heiau sits on hotel property, but can be seen from the pier or water of Kamakahonu Beach.)*

NIGHTLIFE

A normal night out in Kona ends at 11pm, after the ephemeral "green flash" of the sunset, and a few Mai Tais. Those who want more do have a few options, but as Alii Dr. fills with a diverse crowd, the savvy traveler may want to turn in for the night. The scene has been known to get a little dangerous after dark, and fights are not uncommon at area bars.

BARS

Kona Brewing Co., 75-5629 Kuakini Hwy. (☎334-2739), in the North Kona Shopping Center. A happening restaurant and microbrewery with a patio perfect for enjoying one of their award-winning beers: Lavaman Red Ale or Lilikoi Passion Fruit Ale (pints $4). Or order the sampler (four 6 oz. beers for $6.50). Pizzas $8-23. Happy hour M-F 3-5pm. Free brewery tours with tasting M-F 10:30am and 3pm. Open M-Th 11am-10pm, F-Sa 11am-11pm. AmEx/D/MC/V.

Lulu's, 75-819 Alii Dr. (☎331-2633), next to the Coconut Grove Marketplace. Lulu's is the best place to party in Kona; pool tables, TVs, chili lights, and a vast upstairs lanai make it the closest thing to a nightclub you'll find on the Big Island. M open-mic night, Tu salsa night, W college night (18+), live music on most weekends. Cover F-Sa $5. Open daily 11am-2am. AmEx/D/MC/V.

Ocean's Sports Bar and Grill, 75-5819 Alii Dr. (☎327-9494), just behind Lulu's and Jake's along the small pathway. If you're looking to dance, this bar has music (live or by DJ) almost every night. Dozens of beers on draft and another dozen available by the bottle ($4-6). During the day, Ocean's also serves lunch and dinner. Open daily 11am-2am, dinner until 10pm, pupus until midnight. MC/V.

Durty Jake's, 75-5819 Alii Dr. (☎329-7366), downstairs from Lulu's. More relaxed than Lulu's and younger than Huggo's, Jake's draws young locals who enjoy drinking and watching the sun set. Beer $3-4, tropical drinks $5-6, coffee with spirits $5-6. Karaoke Th and Su. Local bands perform F-Sa. Open nightly until 2am. AmEx/D/MC/V.

Sam's Hideaway (☎326-7267), behind the Kona Marketplace, on Kakina Rd. This hole-in-the-wall is as local a place as you're likely to find. Drinks are cheap, the lighting is dim, and come midnight, everyone's drunk and singing karaoke. 21+. Beer $2-3.50; mixed drinks $2.50. Open daily 10am-2pm. AmEx/MC/V.

NIX THE 86. The 86 List in Kona is a register of all the local bad boys (and girls). Every bouncer at the Kona night spots is given a list of about 50 forbidden guests. If you're on it, you can't enter the clubs, a fate known around town as being "on the bitch list."

Huggo's on the Rocks, 75-5828 Kahakai Rd. (☎329-1493), at the southern end of Kailua Bay, next to the Royal Kona Resort. With Hawaiian music, a Hawaiian hula dancer, and a Hawaiian sunset backdrop, Huggo's embodies the *sine qua non* of a Hawaiian tropical paradise. It's a tourist spot, but one of the more fun places to go out. The only downside is the steep prices (beer, $4-7; frozen mixed drinks, $6-8), but you're paying to have the ocean's sonorous waves crash just a few yards away. Open M-Th and Su 11am-11pm, F-Sa 11am-midnight. AmEx/D/MC/V.

LUAUS

Island Breeze Luau, (☎326-4969 or 329-8111), at King Kamehameha's Kona Beach Hotel, on the beach adjacent to Kamalahonu and Ahuena. Shows Tu-F and Su nights. Reservations advised. $65, children 5-12 $29, under 5 free.

Luau at Kona Village Resort, (p. 185), 14 mi. north of Kona, takes the experience to another level. The W and F night luaus have been a tradition for over 30 years. It's the oldest continuously running luau on the Big Island, featuring traditional Hawaiian food and Polynesian dancing. Reservations are essential. Luau starts at 5:30pm. $89, ages 6-12 $54, 2-5 $30, under 2 free.

HOLUALOA

Holualoa (pop. 6,170) is a century away from nearby Kailua-Kona. One of Kona's coffee-growing centers, an influx of artists and craftspeople has remade the face of the main street, converting old pool halls and saloons into art galleries, yoga centers, and eclectic shops. One exemplary gallery, the **Ipu Hale Gallery,** 75-5893 Mamalahoa Hwy. (☎322-9069), features fantastically old French engravings of the Sandwich Isles. The store also specializes in ancient Hawaiian gourd decoration, a unique artistic technique from Niihau, rediscovered in the late 20th century.

Visitors who ascend to the hillside greenery of Holualoa tend to return often. Stay awhile at **The Holualoa Inn ❺**, or at hyacinth-pink **Inaba's Kona Hotel ❷** just up the street. For more information on either lodging, see **Accommodations,** p. 184. To reach Hulualoa, head *mauka* (toward the mountains) on Palani Rd. for a couple miles until the highway on the right, then head down Mamalahoa for about 5 mi. until Holualoa; or continue south on Rte. 11 for 2 mi. until Hualalai Rd. Turn *mauka* (toward the mountains) and drive for about 4 mi. through the windy coffee country until Mamalahoa. Turn left into town.

SOUTH KONA

On the Big Island, a few miles can make a world of difference. Kealakekua, Captain Cook, and Honaunau blithely maintain their sleepy coffee-town existence, unconcerned by and unaware of the hustle and bustle of nearby Kailua-Kona. Precariously straddling the Mamalahoa Hwy. (Rte. 11) on the slopes of Mauna Loa, this series of towns has a funky vibe all its own, along one of the most culturally and ecologically rich stretches of coastline on the island. Puuhonua o Honaunau preserves artifacts of Hawaiian history, while Kealakekua Bay's piercing blue water provides snorkelers with a fantastic glimpse of underwater life. The towns keep to an organic farming lifestyle, next to the coffee farms and organic cafes that line the highway. A few turn-offs lead to pristine, untouched beaches.

TRANSPORTATION

Driving is the easiest way to get around South Kona. Some travelers hitchhike, but it can be dangerous, and Let's Go does not recommend it. **Taxis** service the area, though they're generally expensive. **D&E Taxi** (☎329-4279; from 6am-10pm) **Paradise Taxi and Tours** (☎329-1234; 24hr.) and are two options. All taxis charge $2 initially and then $2 per mile.

The free **Hele-On Bus** (☎961-8744) runs from Honaunau north to Kailua-Kona and west to Hilo. Buses run from Honaunau Elementary School to: **Kailua-Kona** (50min.; M-Sa 5:55am) via Yano Hall in **Captain Cook,** Konawaena Schools in **Kealakekua,** and Ben Franklin in **Kainaliu;** and from Captain Cook to **Kailua-Kona** (M-Sa 10:45am, 2:15pm). See www.hawaii-county.com for the most up-to-date fares and schedules.

ORIENTATION

Route 11 (also known as the **Hawaii Belt Road** or **Mamalahoa Highway**) runs through South Kona, and most places of interest can be found along this road. A number of smaller roads branch off Rte. 11 and wind down to the coast and west up the mountain. The more significant ones are **Napoopoo Road,** which runs into **Middle Keei Road** and drops to the southern end of Kealakekua Bay, and **Route 160,** which accesses Puuhonua o Honaunau and also eventually leads to the Bay.

PRACTICAL INFORMATION

Banks: Bank of Hawaii (☎322-9377), on Mamalahoa Hwy. in downtown Kealakekua, is open M-Th 8:30am-4pm, F 8:30am-6pm. **24hr. ATM.**

Bookstore: Island Books, 79-7430 Mamalahoa Hwy. (☎322-2006), next to Sandy's Drive-in, in the Kainaliu Center, shelves an impressive collection of used and new titles, as well as used CDs and DVDs. Open daily 10am-8pm. AmEx/D/MC/V.

Library: Kealakekua Public Library (☎323-7585), on Mamalahoa Hwy. in downtown Kealakekua, offers **Internet access** with a 3-month visitor's card ($10). Appointments are recommended. Open M-Tu noon-6pm, W 1-7pm, F 11am-5pm, Sa 10am-4pm.

Laundromat: Hale Holoi Laundromat, ¼ mi. past Napoopoo Rd., next to Cap's Drive-In, north of downtown Captain Cook. Wash $1.25-1.75, dry $1.75. Open daily 6am-9pm.

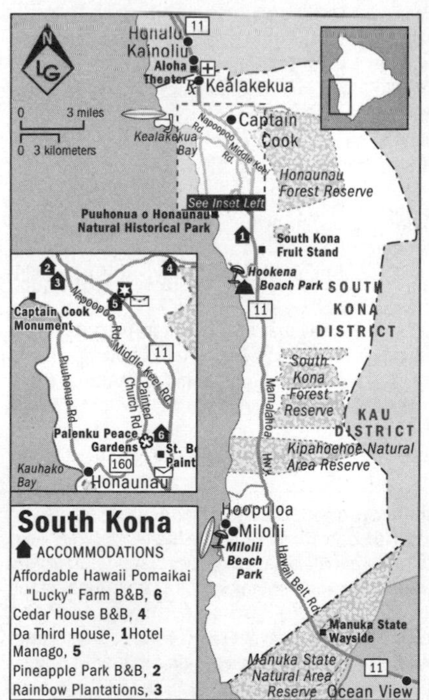

Weather Conditions: ☎961-5582.

Police: A **substation** on Mamalahoa Hwy. in the center of Captain Cook is sporadically manned. The nearest district station (☎935-3311), north of downtown Kona on Rte. 19, fields calls.

Pharmacy: Oshima Drugs, 79-7400 Mamalahoa Hwy. (☎322-3313), south of mi. marker 113. Open M-F 9am-6pm, Sa 9am-5pm.

Hospital: Kona Community Hospital (☎322-9311), on Haukapila St. in Kealakekua. Follow the signs from Rte. 11 around mi. marker 112. 24hr. emergency room.

Internet access: At the Kealakekua Public Library and **The Funkyard,** 81-6394 Mamalahoa Hwy. (☎345-7421), in downtown Kealakekua near mi. marker 111. In addition to hip t-shirts and psychedelic art, they have high-speed Internet on 4 terminals. $2 per 15min., $6 per hr. Open Tu-Sa 9am-5pm and occasionally M and Su.

Post Office: Kealakekua Post Office, Mamalahoa Hwy. (☎800-275-8777), in the Central Kona Center. Open M-F 9am-4:30pm, Sa 9:30am-12:30pm. **Captain Cook Post Office,** Mamalahoa Hwy., just past mi. marker 110. Open M-F 8am-4pm, Sa 9am-noon.

Postal Code: 96750 (Kealakekua); 96704 (Captain Cook).

ACCOMMODATIONS AND CAMPING

Cedar House B&B and Coffee Farm, 82-6119 Bamboo Rd. (☎328-8829). From downtown Captain Cook, turn uphill onto Kiloa Rd. at mi. marker 110. Kiloa becomes a single lane; turn right at the T-junction onto Kinue Rd. Take the next left onto Greenwell Mountain Rd., then left again onto Bamboo Rd. In the midst of a coffee farm high above Kealakekua Bay, rooms have a good view of the South Kona Coast. The new Hibiscus Suite is quite large, and with a private kitchenette, perfect for families. Full breakfast included. Private rooms from $110. Cottage (sleeps up to 3) $125. Hibiscus Suite $135, $810 per week. Each additional person $15. MC/V. ❸

Affordable Hawaii at Pomaikai "Lucky" Farm B&B, 83-5465 Mamalahoa Hwy. (☎328-2112; www.luckyfarm.com), south of Captain Cook between mi. markers 107 and 106, down a steep driveway. The innkeeper Nita also works a macadamia nut and coffee farm, providing a 100% pure Kona taste of Big Island eco-tourism. With a green tin roof, bare plank construction, and high ceilings, the converted Coffee Barn recalls an era before jumbo jets and vacation packages. 2 spacious "greenhouse" rooms (sleep up to 4) and 1-bed "farmhouse" double off the living room. The cook prepares killer breakfasts in the morning, fresh off the farm downstairs. Rooms $75-85; $5 off a night for 4+ nights in a row. Additional guests ages 5 and up $10 per night. MC/V. ❷

Rainbow Plantation, Rte. 11 (☎323-2393 or 800-494-2829; www.rainbowplantation.com), between Pineapple Park and the Chevron Station, just north of the turn-off for Kealakekua Bay. The "Crow's Nest" is set in a former coffee shack, and the "Jungle Queen" refers to a suite within a restored fishing boat moored permanently in the backyard. Outdoor kitchen pavilion has midnight snacks. Continental breakfast included. 2-night min. Doubles $89; each additional person $15. MC/V. ❸

Da Third House, 85-4585 Mamalahoa Hwy. (☎328-8410), is just another quaint B&B along the Mamalahoa Hwy. through South Kona. The owner, Abby, provides a continental breakfast every morning with a beaming smile. The room is merely standard, but the view is great. Check-in 3pm. Check-out noon. Reserve early. $85 per night. MC/V. ❸

Hotel Manago, Mamalahoa Hwy. (☎323-2642; www.managohotel.com). Look for the highly visible neon sign between mi. markers 109 and 110 in Captain Cook. It's one of the cheapest places to stay in South Kona. Attached to the hotel is the **Manago Hotel Restaurant ❷.** The rich and famous have been known to fly in for the pork chops ($8.75); don't forget to ask for gravy and onions. Check-in noon. Check-out 11am. Singles with shared bath $30, private bath $51-56; doubles $33/54-59. Restaurant hours 7am-7:30pm. MC/V. ❷

Pineapple Park B&B, 81-6363 Mamalahoa Hwy. (☎877-806-3800 or 877-865-2266; www.pineapple-park.com), north of downtown Captain Cook between mi. markers 110 and 111. More of a hostel than a B&B. The 4 private rooms upstairs are spacious, and there are also 2 street-side bunk rooms. Full kitchen, grill, high-speed Internet ($10 per hr.), and kayaks for rent ($40-60). If you need some cash, the landlady can often arrange some form of **short-term work.** Check-in afternoon. Check-out 10am. Dorm bunks $20; private rooms with shared bath $65, with private bath $85. MC/V. ❶

Hookena Beach County Park (☎808-961-8311; www.hawaii-county.com) is at a well-marked turn off Mamalahoa Hwy., about 2½ mi. south of its intersection with Rte. 160. Offers the only legal camping in the area and is quite crowded. Pitch your tent under palms right on the beach—just watch for falling coconuts. Showers, bathrooms, firepits, and picnic tables. Permits required, see **Camping in Hawaii,** p. 75. June-Aug. 7-day max; Sept.-May 14-day max. Adults $5, teens $2, children 12 and under $1. ❶

FOOD

Most restaurants in South Kona serve organic, homegrown food, and while the dishes have a refreshing earthy quality, expect a large bill to support the farmers who supplied the ingredients. In any case, the food is nothing to write home about; the coffee, on the other hand, is something to ship home by the pound. Kona coffee, grown in this humble part of the Big Island, is famous around the world. **Kona Pacific Farmers Cooperative,** 82-5810 Napoopoo Rd. (☎328-2411; www.kpfc.com), hosts a **farmers' market** every Friday from 8am to 4pm behind the old cooperative mill on Napoopoo Rd. and Middle Keei Rd., uphill from Kealakekua Bay. From Captain Cook, continue south on Rte. 11 to mi. marker 111. Turn right down Napoopoo Rd., and follow the signs for Kealakekua Bay. Keep right on Napoopoo Rd. at the intersection with Middle Keei Rd.; the cooperative will be half a mile down on the right. Follow the pink donkeys to the market out back.

The Coffee Shack, 83-5799 Mamalahoa Hwy. (☎328-9555), south of Captain Cook, before mi. marker 108. Perched over the coastline that's hundreds of feet below, the Coffee Shack makes breakfast (eggs benedict, $11), deli sandwiches and pizzas ($9-12), desserts ($2.50-5), and freshly-brewed coffee ($3-4.50) that are as amazing as the view. Open daily 8am-3pm. D/MC/V. ❷

Keei Cafe (☎322-9992), south of mi. marker 113 on Mamalahoa Hwy. Large portions of fresh fish draw a steady stream of customers to the lanai for fish tacos and other specialties ($13-20). Lunch M-F 10:30am-2pm; dinner Tu-Sa 5-9pm. Cash only. ❷

South Kona Fruit Stand, 84-4770 Mamalahoa Hwy. (☎328-8547), in Captain Cook between mi. markers 103 and 104 on the *mauka* (mountain) side. This fruit and vegetable farm and store is exotic, and it's definitely worth the stop. Try a spiky chayote, a gnarly-looking dragon fruit, or a guanabana. Open M-Sa 9am-6pm. AmEx/MC/V. ❶

Evie's Natural Food, 79-7460 Mamalahoa Hwy. (☎322-0739), next to Subway in Mango Court, south of Kainaliu. One of the few restaurants in the area that is 100% organic, Evie's has all-fruit smoothies ($4), creative sandwiches (Maui Taro Burger, $7), dinner combos ($8-15), and vegan options. Evie's also posts a list of **short-term work** opportunities, including farm jobs that trade room and board for labor. Open M-F 9am-7pm, Sa-Su 9am-5pm. AmEx/D/MC/V. ❶

Aloha Angel Cafe, 79-7384 Mamalahoa Hwy. (☎322-3383; www.alohatheater.com), in downtown Kainaliu, between mi. markers 113 and 114. This hip cafe warmly envelops the artsy Aloha Theater (p. 197). Its outside seating lines a long descending lanai which gives refreshing views of the wild coast below. The menu offers mango bread ($2), healthy sandwiches, and breakfast until 1:30pm. Lunch $9-12; dinner $12-24. Open daily 8am-2:30pm and 5pm-9pm. MC/V. ❹

Nasturtium Cafe, 79-7491 Mamalahoa Hwy. (☎322-5083 take-out or 322-2193 reservations), south of mi. marker 113. Offering abundant fresh foods from ahi to zucchini, this cafe wraps up healthy combos, such as chevre and artichoke. Salads ($10-13) and enticing sandwiches ($11-13). Open Tu-F 11am-5pm. MC/V. ❷

SAVE A TEAR, JUICE A NONI

The noni tree, an extremely ugly plant, grows prolifically all over the Big Island. Thriving in acidic, volcanic soil, these trees are identifiable by their enormous, shiny leaves. The fruit of the noni is the real kicker though; the juice has vast medicinal uses. Noni fruit claims to fame are: digestive, immunological, cardiac, and respiratory system benefits, as well as maintaining joint health and blood sugar levels.

How do you get the juice, you ask? In order to extract this supposedly magical sap, it takes a lot of noni. First, gather around a dozen noni fruits and stuff them into a jar. Pick them when they're white, but don't get impatient; the noni has to be translucent before it's ready to be sealed. Leave the jar out in the sunlight for a while (about a day) until the fruits begin to "weep." When a bunch of noni condensation builds up in the jar, pour it out into another container. Some advocate noni juice fermentation, another step in this mythical procedure; but most take the noni juice from the jar before this last step.

Most islanders believe in the power of the noni, and many participate in this legendary transfer of tears. As the old folk saying goes, "if a noni weeps, then we don't have to."

Teshima (☎322-9140), across from Aloha Kayaks, almost immediately after Rte. 11 and 180 merge. This place is always bustling with people seeking its unique fusion of Japanese and Hawaiian food. $10 lunch special 11am-1:45pm. Chicken Teriyaki $9. Kona Fried Rice Platter $9. Dinner meat and seafood combos $15-18. Open daily 6:30am-1:45pm and 5-9pm. Cash only. ❸

Adriana's Mexican-Salvadoran Food, 82-6066 Mamalahoa Hwy. (217-7405 or 936-8553), just below Ace Hardware building across the highway from the old Kona Theater. This place is raved about in town, and it'll only cost you between $2-9. The menu is small but tasty. Open M-F 10am-5pm. Cash only. ❶

Guy's Grinds, 79-7395 Mamalahoa Hwy. (☎322-2672), right in Kainaliu Village, diagonally across the highway from Kimura's fabrics. Grind's is a cheap local greasy spoon. Breakfasts like the egg, cheese, and ham sandwich run between $4-6, and plate lunches are all $6.75. Open daily 9am-5pm. MC/V. ❶

BEACHES

KEALAKEKUA BAY. *(Snorkeling. Surfing. Open daily 24hr.)* The steep-cliff crescent of **Kealakekua Bay** was formed when many acres of land plunged into the sea, and the bay and its spectacular coral reef haven't changed much since. What visitors see today is much like what Captain Cook saw upon his arrival over 200 years ago. The area is a **Marine Life Conservation District,** which makes this a truly fantastic place to snorkel. In addition to a launching site, the park has restrooms, picnic tables, some big surf, and **Hikiau Heiau State Monument,** a significant Hawaiian temple. To reach the park from Rte. 11, take Napoopoo Rd. between mi. markers 110 and 111. The road winds down the mountainside for a few miles before joining Middle Keei Rd. and continuing on to the bay. The only part of the bay accessible to automobiles is the southeastern end of the bay at the end of Napoopoo Rd.Hookena beach park *(Open daily 24hr.)* Another of the island's black sand beaches, Hookena doesn't stand out, but it's worth a visit, especially for those traveling with children; the beach is protected by a natural barrier which means calm waters. The waves are tame, and the full facilities make it easy to spend a day here without too many worries. For directions, see **Accommodations,** p. 195.

MILOLII BEACH PARK. *(Surfing. Open daily 24hr.)* In the no-man's-land of lava fields and dense forest between the Kona coast and the rolling pastures of

Kau is Milolii, one of the Big Island's last true fishing villages and a vestige from another era. The tortuous drive down to the town provides panoramic views of the titanic lava flow that devastated the area in 1926, and there is still so little vegetation in the black fields that the lava seems freshly cooled. At the end of the road is Milolii Beach Park, a popular local surf spot. The park offers restrooms, a sheltered picnic area, and camping. The beach is 5 mi. below Rte. 11, just after mi. marker 89. The road down to the beach twists and turns, so be alert.

SPIN THE BOTTLE-NOSE. Kealakekua Bay is one of the best spots in Hawaii to see spinner dolphins, who make this crescent of water their personal playground. They are slender dolphins, generally 7 ft. long or less, that have dark gray backs and white stomachs. Spinner dolphins travel in groups, and while they feed in the deep channels offshore, they spend much of their time resting and playing in shallow water. Seemingly natural performers, they leap out of the water to incredible heights before spinning and splashing down. While there's no schedule for this show, your best bet of catching a glimpse is in the early morning.

ACTIVITIES

Almost all of the activities in South Kona focus on the natural beauty of Kealakekua Bay and the awesomeness and diversity of its underwater inhabitants.

SNORKELING. Kealakekua Bay boasts the best snorkeling on the Big Island. The ideal location is the bay's far side, where a white obelisk marks the British monument to Captain Cook. Dolphins and sea turtles often frolic nearby, but state and federal laws mandate that snorkelers keep 50 ft. and 10 ft. away from these animals, respectively. Turtles, dolphins, and countless fish dart in and out of a coral reef that drops off suddenly 40 ft. from shore, creating a dynamic underwater landscape. Almost all of the kayak places rent snorkels as well, usually for $6-10.

KAYAKING. Kealakekua Bay offers some of the best kayaking in the Kona area, perhaps in all of Hawaii. Kayak-rental companies line Mamalahoa Hwy., but for superior service and the best orientation, try **Kona Boys,** 79-7539 Mamalahoa Hwy., north of downtown Kealakekua. Their guides are excellent, and their private guided tour consistently ranks among the best in the state. *(☎328-1234. Tours 9:30am-2pm. Lunch, paddles, backrests, life vests, dry bag, cooler, and car rack included. Private tour $225 per person; group rate $159. Kayaks $47-67 per day, $27-37 per half day. Open daily 7:30am-5pm.)*

BAY TOURS. Many companies in the area offer snorkel or kayak excursions to the Kealakekua reef. Of all the adventure companies, **Fair Wind,** 78-7130 Kaleiopapa St. (☎322-2788), is the only one with a permit to moor its catamaran in Kealakekua Bay. They have a range of tours, including the AM Deluxe Tour (daily 9am-1:30pm; $105, ages 4-12 $65, 3 and under $29) and the PM Snack Cruise (Tu, Th, Sa 2-5:30pm; $69, 4-12 $43, 3 and under free). Fair Wind sells out up to three days in advance; reservations should be made early.

SIGHTS AND ENTERTAINMENT

ALOHA THEATRE. The theater, next to Aloha Angel Cafe (p. 195), hosts screenings of mostly foreign or independent films in its single auditorium. *(79-*

7384 Mamalahoa Hwy. ☎322-2323; www.alohatheatre.com. Showings W-Su 6:30pm. $7, students and seniors $6, half-price with dinner at Aloha Angel Cafe. Tickets for live shows around $15.)

CAPTAIN COOK TRAIL AND MONUMENT. The Captain Cook Monument looms at the northwestern end of Kealakekua Bay, a 27 ft. pillar erected in Cook's honor by fellow Brits in 1878. The monument stands near the site where Cook was killed and has sparked much debate, because it is seen by some Hawaiians as a tribute to cultural domination. (See **History**, p. 15, for more on Cook's landing.) A number of ships recreating Cook's voyage have since anchored in the bay and left plaques commemorating his "discovery." A good deal more interesting to explore are the ruins of the village, Kaawaloa, which was founded when Britain was still an uncivilized hinterland of the Roman Empire.

To reach the monument, head to the **Captain Cook Monument Trail** *(4 mi., 2½hr. round-trip, moderate)*. The trail is on the downhill side of Napoopoo Rd., the first unmarked dirt road 200 yd. from the intersection with Rte. 11. The hike descends the slope to Kaawaloa Cove, passing overgrown sugarcane, exposed lava fields, and dense foliage along the shoreline. The trail follows a road for the first 100 yd. before branching off through fields of tall grass and wild brush. Farther down, the terrain opens up to *aa* (lava) fields, approaching the coast with sweeping views of the surrounding countryside. On its final descent, the path drops into shaded coastal forest. Bring plenty of water, appropriate footwear and clothing, and of course, snorkeling gear.

If you'd rather ride on horseback down the trail, **King's Trail Rides,** on Mamalahoa Hwy. between Kealakekua and Captain Cook, runs 4hr. excursions that include lunch, snorkeling gear, and 2hr. of riding. *(81-6420 Mamalahoa Hwy. ☎323-2388; www.konacowboy.com. Ages 7+. M-F $135, Sa-Su $150. $75 advance deposit required by credit card or money order to King's Trail Rides.)*

AMY GREENWELL ETHNOBOTANICAL GARDEN. The Amy Greenwell Ethnobotanical Garden gives a sense of the close relationship the Hawaiians had with the land before Cook's arrival. Home to native Hawaiian species and those brought by Polynesian settlers, this 15-acre garden provides a representative look at the plants and cultivation techniques perfected by the islanders before the arrival of Europeans. *(On Mamalahoa Hwy., north of downtown Captain Cook. ☎323-3318. Open M-F 8:30am-5pm. Tours W and F 1pm; $5. Suggested donation $4.)*

SAINT BENEDICT'S PAINTED CHURCH. John Berchman Velge, a Belgian Catholic priest, built **Saint Benedict's** between 1899 and 1904. With ordinary house paints and divine inspiration, he created the closest thing to a Gothic cathedral on the Big Island. The vibrant colors of the interior blend the islands with the Old World, from the faux marble columns blossoming into palm trees to the vaulted ceiling masquerading as a tropical sky. Be sure to look back through the doors from the aisle—the church opens to an astounding view of the ocean hundreds of feet below. *(84-5140 Painted Church Rd. Just up the hill from Puuhonua o Honaunau. Take Rte. 160 north onto Painted Church Rd., just west of mi. marker 1; or take Napoopoo Rd. and turn onto Middle Keei Rd., then right onto Painted Church Rd. ☎328-2227.)*

PUUHONUA O HONAUNAU NATIONAL HISTORICAL PARK. Once the home of Kona's royal chiefs, the reconstructed thatched buildings and lava rock walls of Puuhonua o Honaunau National Historic Park still evoke the spirit of ancient Hawaii. The area, along with the canoe landing, was historically open only to *alii* (royalty) and their attendants. All others were prohibited by *kapu* (sacred laws) from entering the grounds or marring the *mana* (spiritual power) held by the *alii*.

There are actually two parts to Puuhonua o Honaunau, the **Royal Grounds** and the *puuhonua*, or **Place of Refuge.** They are separated by a massive stone wall, built in 1550, still standing today. The walking tour of the Royal Grounds and Place of Refuge covers the points of interest highlighted in the park brochure. **Kiilae Village,** ¾ mi. from the Visitors Center along the 1871 trail, explores the daily life of early Hawaiians. You can pick up a guide booklet for the village at the Visitors Center.

A highlight of the walk, the **Waiu-O-Hina Lava Tube** opens out in the middle of a cliff overlooking the ocean, and though the park rangers say cliff-jumping is forbidden, people jump routinely anyway. **Keokea Holua,** a slide constructed out of lava rock, was used by the Hawaiians for *holua*, or sledding. The coast on either side of the park is home to numerous fish as well as rare spinner dolphins. The snorkeling beneath the cliffs and in protective coves is exceptionally good, as well as north of the park in Honaunau Cove. *(Left off Rte. 160, 4 mi. downhill from where Rte. 160 leaves Rte. 11, between mi. markers 103 and 104. The park can also be reached via Puuhonua Rd., a 4 mi., one-way road that runs from Napoopoo Beach. ☎328-2288 or 328-2326; www.nps.gov/puho. Visitors Center open daily 7:30am-5:30pm. Park open M-Th 8am-8pm, F-Su 8-11am. $5 per car.)*

KAU AND KA LAE

Tucked away in the southwest corner of the island, the Kau district (pop. 5,827) is a striking blend of landscapes, people, and ideas. The history of the region is bleak yet fascinating. In the northwest corner of Kau lies Hawaiian Ocean View Estates, a real estate development that was laid out but never finished. Another of Hawaii's old former sugar plantations lies to the south; when the sugar industry dried up, the region had to fend off the government's attempts to use the area as a rocket launch site. Today, sugar plantations have been replaced by coffee and macadamia nut farms, and the rocket debate left a land heated by divergent political ideologies. Kau has a fiery spirit that few locations in the world can match, and nowhere is this spirit better seen than in the colorful green- and black-sand beaches.

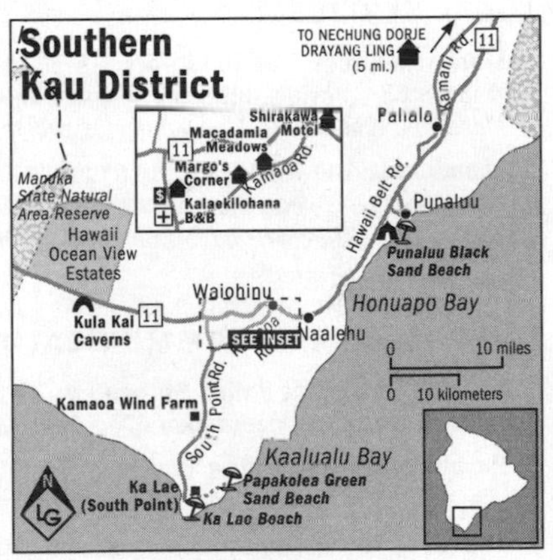

TRANSPORTATION

The only transportation to and from Kau is the free **Hele-On Bus** (☎961-8744; www.hawaii-county.com), which runs from **Ocean View Center** to Hilo (2¾hr.; M-F 6:40am) via the **Waiohinu/Naalehu** gas station (7am) and **Pahala Shopping Center,** adjacent to the bank (7:30am). Farthest from Hilo, the stop at Ocean View Center is serviced by request only. Travelers are required to phone in their request by 3pm of the afternoon prior to travel.

ORIENTATION

Route 11, also known as the **Hawaii Belt Road** or **Mamalahoa Highway,** is Kau's main thoroughfare. Ocean View, Waiohinu, Naalehu, and Pahala are all close to the route, the district's only link to the outside world. The only other major roads in the area are **South Point Road,** which runs 11 mi. between Rte. 11 and Ka Lae, and **Kamani Street,** which forks off from Rte. 11 and runs through downtown Pahala.

PRACTICAL INFORMATION

TOURIST AND FINANCIAL SERVICES

Tourist Information: Punaluu Bake Shop (☎929-7343), Hawaii Belt Rd., in downtown Naalehu, is the closest thing to a tourist office in Kau. The good-natured staff offers more sweet-bread samples than ready answers, but they will provide a few useful brochures with directions to the green- and black-sand beaches. Open daily 9am-5pm.

Banks: Kau Federal Credit Union (☎929-7334), across from the Naalehu Theatre on Rte. 11, has an ATM and is open M-Sa 9am-4pm. **Bank of Hawaii** (☎928-8356), in the Pahala Shopping Center at the corner of Kamani and Pikake St. in Pahala, has a **24hr. ATM.** Lobby open M-F 8:30am-noon and 1-3pm.

LOCAL SERVICES

Library: Naalehu Public Library, 95-5669 Hawaii Belt Rd. (☎939-2442). near mi. marker 63., provides **Internet access** with a 3-month visitor's card ($10). Call early to reserve a time on the 2 computers. Open M, W, F noon-5pm, Tu and Th 1-6pm.

Laundromat: The Wash (☎929-7072) sits adjacent to Desert Rose Cafe (p. 201), making laundry in Ocean View a potentially delicious experience. Wash $2, dry $0.25 per 6min. Drop-off service $1.50 per lb. Open M-Sa 6am-8pm, Su 7am-8pm.

Weather: ☎961-5582.

EMERGENCY AND COMMUNICATIONS

Police: Kau District Police Station (☎939-2520, non-emergency 935-3311) is southeast of Naalehu at mi. marker 62½. Open M-F 7:45am-4:30pm.

Hospital: Kau Hospital, 1 Kamani St. (☎928-8331), on Rte. 11 in Pahala, provides basic medical services and a 24hr. emergency room. Clinic open M-F 8am-4:30pm.

Pharmacy: The on-site community health clinic at Kau Hospital in Pahala doubles as the region's only pharmacy, Kau Community Pharmacy (☎928-6252). Open M, W, F 8am-5pm, Tu 8am-3pm, closed noon-1pm.

Internet: Internet Cafe (☎929-8332), on Naalehu Shopping Center's Main St. $3 per hr. Hours vary: call ahead. There's also wireless ($4 per hr.) and a computer ($6 per hr.) at the Naalehu Theatre's cafe, **Simple Good Food** (☎929-9133). Open M-Sa, 8am-4pm and during evening showtimes.

Post Office: Naalehu Post Office, 95-5663 Mamalahoa Hwy. (☎800-275-8777). Open M-F 7:45am-1pm and 2-4:15pm, Sa 10:15-11:15am. **Pahala Post Office,** next to the Bank of Hawaii in the Pahala Shopping Center, is open M-F 8am-12:15pm and 12:45-4pm, Sa 8:30-11am.

Postal Code: 96772 (Naalehu/Waiohinu); 96737 (Ocean View); 96777 (Pahala).

ACCOMMODATIONS AND CAMPING

There aren't many places to stay in Kau, so be sure to make reservations early. Good directions are also essential; the highway and backstreets are not lit at night. Comfortable accommodations can be had at the **Nechung Dorje Drayang Ling** ❷, a non-sectarian Buddhist temple, which lets rooms at prices that will calm the weariest traveler (p. 203). For campers, **Punaluu Black Sand Beach** ❶ (p. 202) allows camping by permit and has full facilities.

Kalaekilohana Bed and Breakfast, 94-2152 South Point Rd. (☎939-8052; www.kau-hawaii.com). The goal in building this B&B was to cultivate a "better-educated visitor," but between lei-making classes and traditional hat-weaving workshops, the hosts certainly did not skimp on the luxuries of a fine vacation retreat. Breakfast, often a delicious sausage, egg, rice, and mango plate, is a splendid start to a Kau day. 4 spacious rooms with rain showers and private lanais are available. Doubles $109-159; each additional guest $25. Daily workshops start at $45. Group rates available. AmEx/D/MC/V. ❸

Macadamia Meadows, 94-6263 Kamaoa Rd. (☎929-8097; www.macadamiameadows.com). Turn onto Kamaoa Rd. next to Wong Yuen Store and head up the hill. While the 8-acre working macadamia nut farm may be its biggest draw, there are plenty of amenities for guests at this lovely cedar home. Rooms are spacious yet cozy; amenities include a tennis court, swimming pool, and grill. Ask about potential work-exchange. 4 of the 5 rooms include refrigerators and microwaves. All have cable TV. Breakfast included. Check-in 3pm. Check-out 11:30am. Rooms $89-129. AmEx/MC/V. ❸

Margo's Corner (☎929-9614; www.margoscorner.com), Wakea Ave. From Kona, turn down South Point Rd. (mi. markers 69-70), and after a couple miles turn left on Kamaoa Rd. Turn right on Wakea, and look for the rainbow flag and the star window. 2 beautifully crafted suites pamper guests with luxuries like a sauna and home-cooked breakfast. Guests on a budget may also set up a tent in the front garden. Work-exchange possible after staying as a paying guest. 2-night min. Reservations appreciated. Camping $30 per person; suites $90-130; each additional person $30. Cash only. Camping ❶/Rooms ❸

Shirakawa Motel (☎929-7462; www.shirakawamotel.com), Mamalahoa Hwy., across from Wong Yuen Store in Waiohinu. The basic yet surprisingly spacious rooms are not a bad place to stay for a night. Singles and doubles $45; with kitchenette $55; with full kitchen $65; roll-away beds $10. Cash only. ❷

FOOD

Hana Hou, 95-1148 Naalehu Spur Rd. (☎929-9717), off Mamalahoa Hwy., across from Naalehu Town Center. One of Naalehu's new restaurants, Hana Hou strives to use only local ingredients in their American/Hawaiian-style dishes. Try the roast pork ($7) or the fresh fish burgers ($12). Pastries $1.50-3. Open M-Th 7am-3pm, F 7am-8pm, Sa 8:30am-8pm, Su 8:30am-3pm. MC/V. ❶

Simple Good Food (☎929-9133), in the old concession stand of the **Naalehu Theatre and Museum.** Simple Good Food is just that: no pretensions here. Serving breakfast (eggs and coffee, $5) and lunch (wraps and sandwiches, $7.50), Eric and Shannon stay open during evening screenings and events at the theater to serve a no-frills dinner. Open daily 8am-4pm, or until the last show is over. MC/V. ❷

Keoki's Cafe, 95-5587 Mamalahoa Hwy. (☎929-9437), adjacent to the 76 Gas Station in Naalehu. A popular local cafe that serves up town-famous smoothies ($3.75), burgers ($5), and fresh ahi sandwiches ($7.50). Open daily 6:30am-6:30pm. AmEx/D/MC/V. ❶

The Desert Rose Cafe (☎939-7673), on Hawaii Belt Rd., in Pohue Plaza in Ocean View. This roadside cafe charms the weary driver with its toothsome treats. Famous for their greasy burgers ($7-9), fish burgers ($12), and different vegetarian options. Desserts ($1.50-3), including Hawaiian sweet yam bites and fresh banana walnut bread, are heavenly. Open daily 7am-8pm. MC/V. ❷

Shaka Restaurant, 95-5763 Mamalahoa Hwy. (☎929-7404), in Naalehu, near the post office. Shaka is about to transform into a pizzeria with the same name and will serve hearty pizza dinners ($7-10). Baby-back ribs ($18) will still be available, but the equally good steaks will bite the dust when the wood-fire ovens come in. Open daily 10am-9pm; bar open until 10pm. MC/V. ❷

Punaluu Bake Shop (☎929-7343), on Mamalahoa Hwy., in Naalehu Town Center. Their famous sweetbreads are Hawaiian modifications of the traditional Portuguese treat. Everything is baked on-site and is shipped around the island. They also serve plate lunches ($8) and offer an array of dry goods in their small general store. Open daily 9am-5pm. AmEx/D/MC/V. ❶

BEACHES

The 12 mi. road that goes from the Hawaii Belt Rd. (between mi. markers 69 and 70) to South Point is like a runway to another world. Lush green valleys give way to the **Kamaoa Wind Farm** and to brown pastures full of cattle. Most rental companies don't permit their cars on this road, but 2WD cars can make it to the entrances of all areas of interest without any problems. Near the coast, the road enters the 710-acre **Ka Lae District** and eventually forks. The right fork heads to a parking lot and the 30 ft. cliffs of South Point. The left fork leads to a set of abandoned buildings and a parking lot convenient to **Green Sand Beach.** A little north of South Point, **Punaluu** is the most famous black-sand beach on the island and a natural wonder that simply can't be missed.

PAPAKOLEA GREEN SAND BEACH. *(Open daily 24hr.)* From the parking lot (see above), Green Sand Beach, or Papakolea, is a 3 mi. trek along the coast, often over craggy lava rocks and torn-up, off-road paths. This beach is for the adventurer, not the sun-bather. The unusually beautiful sand is caused by a geological phenomenon; the olavine from aged lava is eventually eroded by the sea, forming a green-ish slope that falls into a turbulent sea. The vista from up top is unique, but the climb down and dip in the ocean can be dangerous because of steep sharp pathways and rough windy seas. Don't forget sturdy shoes, plenty of water, and perhaps a sweater; the winds are ripping here. Also, be mindful of the surroundings— many locals do not appreciate guests.

KA LAE BEACH/SOUTH POINT. *(Open daily 24hr.)* A 5min. walk from the end of the right hand fork after the Ka Lae Historic Landmark District sign, Ka Lae is a spectacular spot—the convergence of currents from the windward and leeward sides of the beach creates intense surf. Although swimmers may leap into the rip current below, the ladders that used to support these thrill seekers are no longer there. Try not to get tangled in the dozens of fishing lines stretching out to sea. "The Point" itself is beyond the parking lot at the extremity of the island. It is thought to be the spot of the Polynesians' first landing in the Hawaiian Islands and has been important throughout Hawaiian history because of the Kalalea Heiau, a temple which still stands today.

PUNALUU BLACK SAND BEACH. *(Open daily 24hr.)* Eight miles northeast of Naalehu and 5 mi. south of Pahala along Rte. 11 between mi. markers 56 and 57, is Punaluu Beach, the island's largest black-sand beach. The dazzling volcanic sand is home to a large population of hawks bill turtles and an even larger contingent of tourists. Punaluu has some wicked surf that makes for messy boarding at best. For the more cautious beachgoer, swimming usually affords a close look at turtles, whose primary feeding ground is around the lava rocks near the shore. You can also sometimes spot them from shore or from underneath the coconut palms that shade the sparkling sand. Just south of the beach are county park facilities, including protected picnic areas, restrooms, showers, and campsites. A permit is required to camp; see **Camping in Hawaii,** (p. 75) for more information.

SIGHTS AND ACTIVITIES

KULA KAI CAVERNS. Over 1000 years old, the Kula Kai Caverns are some of the island's most spectacular lava tubes. Trips range from an easy walking tour to an all-out spelunking extravaganza in Maelstrom Cave. *(In the town of Ocean View, on Hwy. 11, 40min. south of Kona. ☎929-9725; www.kulakaicaverns.com. Tours daily by appointment only. 30min. walking tour $12. 3-4hr. Maelstrom Cave tour $65. Call for details.)*

MANUKA STATE NATURAL AREA RESERVE. Cast off the chains of resort packages in favor of the natural calm of **Manuka State Natural Area Reserve.** The 2 mi. **Manuka Loop Trail** runs through eight acres of land that were set aside in the 1930s for 48 species of native Hawaiian flora and 150 other species from around the Pacific. The trail is rocky in some places and buggy in all places, so wear proper hiking shoes and bring insect repellent. The park, which has bathrooms and shaded picnic tables, is a quiet locale for a lunch or rest stop. *(Between mi. markers 81 and 82 on the Hawaii Belt Rd.)*

NECHUNG DORJE DRAYANG LING. Once a Japanese mission, this Buddhist temple was established by Nechung Rinpoche in 1973 as a non-sectarian center for Buddhist teachings and is worth even a short visit. The entire complex is colored in the traditional Tibetan style and beautifully maintained. The Dalai Lama visited the temple in 1980 and again in 1994, giving a talk to several thousand people. The immaculate grounds, home to a number of peacocks and shaded by bamboo and palm trees, add to the tranquility. Accommodations are available for those wishing to prolong their stay. *(From Rte. 11 take Kamani Rd. when it forks off the highway to Pahala. Take the 3rd right onto Pikake St. and follow the paved road 5 mi. The temple will be on the right. ☎928-8539; www.nechung.org. 2-night min. Dorms $35; singles $50; doubles $70. Suggested donation for viewing the temple $5.)*

HAWAII VOLCANOES NATIONAL PARK

Home to the world's most active oceanic hot spot and the only two active volcanoes on the Hawaiian Islands (Mauna Loa and Kilauea), Hawaii Volcanoes National Park is constantly changing. Along the park's southeastern coast, 2000°F lava flows enter the Pacific Ocean, constantly redefining the island's coastline. Between 1983 and 2005 the current eruption from Kilauea's Puu Oo vent added 525 acres of new land to the state. Perhaps the most remarkable part of the process is its proximity to any adventurous visitor. Both Mauna Loa and Kilauea are shield volcanoes with gentle slopes that rise gradually over many miles. Although they aren't characterized by the dramatic steep-angle peaks formed by more violent volcanoes, their slow, continuous activity makes them much more accessible for scientific study and general viewing. The Kilauea Caldera is often jokingly referred to by rangers as "the drive-in volcano." On any given day, visitors can witness lava flows oozing and dripping from the East Rift Zone near the end of Chain of Craters Road. One of the most unforgettable experiences in the park is the hike (see **Going with the Flow,** p. 212) that many visitors take after sunset to watch lava flows light the night sky.

WHAT THE HELL IS A CALDERA? A "caldera" and a "crater" look very similar, but the terms are not interchangeable. A caldera (from the Portuguese *caldeira*) is a volcanic crater with a large diameter that is formed by collapse of the central part of a volcano or by explosions of extraordinary violence.

The National Park, near Volcano Village, a small town a mile north of the park entrance, is a melange of some of the most advanced geologic research and technology. Day-hiking through desolate lava fields, visitors witness first-hand the slow rebirth of life. Once the sun sets, a trek across the most recent lava flows to watch the lava river meet the ocean is a once-in-a-lifetime chance to view an indescribable battle between natural elements.

AT A GLANCE: HAWAII VOLCANOES NATIONAL PARK

AREA: 333,000 acres.

FEATURES: Kilauea, Mauna Loa, Kau Desert, Puna Coast, Puu Loa Petroglyphs.

HIGHLIGHTS: Hiking over *aa* and *pahoehoe* lava rocks, steam vents, cinder cones, pit craters, ancient petroglyphs, and active lava flows along the East Rift Zone of the Kilauea Caldera.

QUICK FACT: NASA astronauts have trained for lunar landings in the Kau Desert and Kilauea Iki Crater, because of their similarity to the moon's surface.

GATEWAY TOWNS: Volcano, 1 mi. (p. 203). Hilo, 30 mi. (p. 221).

CAMPING: Camping is free and reservations are unnecessary at designated campsites (p. 206). Stays limited to 7 days per month and no more than 30 days per year. Registration required for backcountry camping.

FEES: $10 per vehicle; $5 per pedestrian, bicyclist, or motorcyclist.

FOR MORE INFO: ☎985-6000.

ORIENTATION

The only entrance to the park is from **Route 11 (Hawaii Belt Road),** 30 mi. southwest of Hilo and 96 mi. southeast of Kona. There used to be another entrance from Hwy. 130 (Kalapana Rd.) in the southeast, but this route has been closed since 1989, when lava took out more than 8 mi. of highway. Within the park there are two main roads: the 11 mi. **Crater Rim Drive,** which circles Kilauea Caldera, and the 20 mi. **Chain of Craters Road,** which descends along the east side of Kilauea toward the coast and ends abruptly where it meets an active flow. This area serves as the trailhead for the night hike to see the lava flow. **Hilina Pali Road** accesses the remote western portion of the park, and **Mauna Loa Road** ascends Mauna Loa and ends at the trailhead to the summit.

TRANSPORTATION

Volcano (p. 214) is the nearest gateway town and can satisfy all visitors' basic needs. A car is indispensable (unless participating on a guided tour); however, if renting a car is impossible, the Kau/Hilo **Hele-On Bus** runs between the park's Visitors Center and the Mooheau Bus Terminal in Hilo. (☎961-8744; www.co.hawaii.hi.us. Leaves Volcanoes National Park M-F 8:10am, arrives in Hilo 9:20am; leaves Hilo 2:40pm, arrives in Volcanoes National Park 3:45pm. Free.)

PRACTICAL INFORMATION

Much of the park is **wheelchair accessible,** including the Kilauea Visitors Center, Jaggar Museum, Volcano House Hotel, Volcano Art Center, Devastation Trail, and the pathways to the Steam Vents, Keanakakoi, Pauahi Crater, and Muliwai a Pele.

CLIMATE HOPPING. In his *Letters from Hawaii,* Mark Twain remarks in awe of the diverse volcano landscape; one "could see all the climes of the world at a single glance of the eye, and that glance would only pass over a distance of 4 or 5 miles as the bird flies." Twain wasn't too far off; visitors should come prepared for extremes of hot and cold, as well as wet and dry, often within the same day. Covering elevations from sea level to 13,677 ft., the range of ecosystems in such a small space is nothing short of extraordinary.

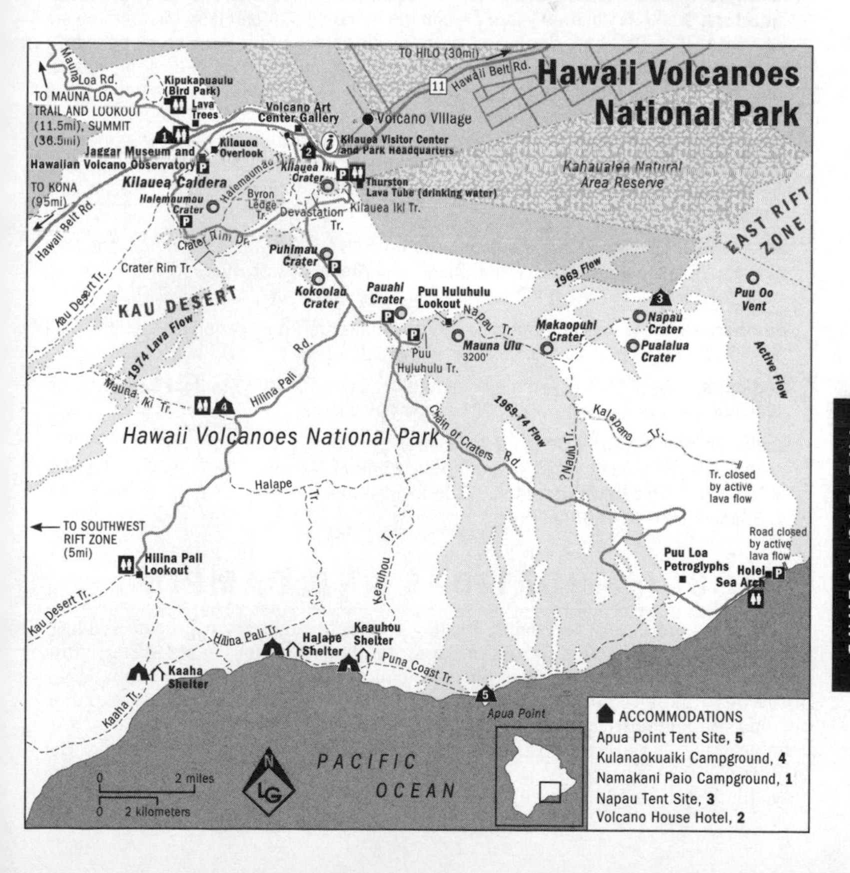

Information: Hawaii Volcanoes National Park, P.O. Box 52, Hawaii National Park, 96718-0052 (☎985-6000; www.nps.gov/havo).

Hours: Open 24hr. Ranger hours vary by location: at the Visitors Center 7:45am-5pm; at the end of Chain of Craters Road 7:45am-midnight. Hours subject to change; be sure to check in at the Visitors Center for the most accurate information.

Fees, Permits, and Regulations: $10 per car or $5 per pedestrian, bicyclist, or motorcyclist; good for 7 days. Year-long Hawaii Volcanoes Pass $20.

Guided Hikes and Events: The Visitors Center shows a 25min. introductory film about the park daily 9am-4pm on the hr. Ranger-led lectures and walks also offer a good introduction to the natural history and geology of the region. Daily schedule for lectures and walks varies; consult the Ranger Activity bulletin board at the Visitors Center. Check the National Park Website, www.nps.gov/havo, for a schedule of events and a list of hikes.

Camping Equipment: Hilo Surplus Store, 148 Mamo St. (☎935-6398), in Hilo, sells tents, backpacks, stoves, sleeping bags, and rainwear at discount prices. **True Value Hardware,** in Volcano Village, also sells basic supplies, including iodine tablets for water purification (p. 215).

Facilities: Kilauea Visitors Center (☎985-6000; www.nps.gov/havo) and **Park Headquarters,** a couple hundred yards beyond the entrance station along the northern arc of Crater Rim Dr., has maps and eruption updates. Visitors Center open daily 7:45am-5pm. **Showers** are available at Namakani Paio Campground, 3 mi. west of the park entrance along Rte. 11. Shower keys ($3) are available from Volcano House (p. 207). **Drinking water** is available at the Visitors Center, Jaggar Museum, Thurston Lava Tube, and Namakani Paio Campground. However, drinking water is scarce, so it's a good idea to store up. Catchment water that must be treated is available at 6 backcountry shelters: 2 on Mauna Loa and 1 each at Halape, Keauhou, Kaaha, and Pepeiau.

Gas: The archaic pumps of the **Volcano Store** (☎967-7210), next to the Volcano Post Office, still function daily 5am-7pm. There is an **Aloha Gas Station,** 19-3972 Old Volcano Rd. (☎967-7555), at Kilauea General Store. Open daily 6:30am-7:15pm.

Weather: For weather conditions, eruption information, and general questions, call ☎985-6000. The park also broadcasts on AM 530.

Medical Services: The nearest major medical facility is the **Hilo Medical Center,** 1190 Waianuenue Ave. (☎974-4700). 24hr. emergency room.

Banks: There is a **24hr. ATM** in the Volcano House Hotel, across the street from the Visitors Center. The nearest banks are in Hilo: **Bank of Hawaii,** 120 Pauahi St. (☎935-9701), and **First Hawaiian Bank,** 1205 Kilauea Ave. (☎969-2211). Both open M-Th 8:30am-4:30pm, F 8:30am-6pm.

ACCOMMODATIONS AND CAMPING

The park is completely accessible for day and night hikes from Volcano Village, where comfortable accommodations are readily available. On the other hand, anyone with the urge to really explore Volcano Park should plan to camp. Many of the best hikes require a solid day of walking, and camping greatly expands options. **Backcountry camping** is allowed at designated cabins, shelters, and campgrounds by permit only. Permits are free and can be easily obtained at the Visitors Center on a first-come, first-served basis no earlier than one day before. Stays limited to seven days per month and no more than 30 days per year. Tent sites, a small shelter, pit toilets, and water catchments are available on the coast at **Kaaha, Halape,** and **Keauhou Shelters. Apua Point** has tent sites but no shelter or water. The **Pepeiao Cabin,** in the Kau desert, has three bunks and water catchment. **Napau Crater** has only tent sites and pit toilets. There are two cabins en route to the summit of Mauna Loa, one at Red Hill (7½ mi. from the trailhead) and the second at the summit caldera (11½ mi. from Red Hill). Both have bunks and mattresses. Stays are limited to three nights per site and to groups of no more than 12. Be aware that the water catchments at all of these sites must be treated before drinking. Backcountry campers are encouraged to follow "leave no trace" ethics. No fires are allowed; ask the ranger about camp stoves when you pick up your permit. Camping is strictly prohibited anywhere other than the sites listed above.

Volcano House Hotel (☎967-7321; www.volcanohousehotel.com), along Crater Rim Dr., across from the Visitors Center. Perched on a ledge overlooking the Kilauea Caldera, Volcano House was built in 1877 to lodge everyone who flocked to the great lava lake that filled the Halemaumau Crater. Unfortunately, the boiling fire drained away along with much of the charm. Simple rooms are comfortable, but with crater views starting at $200, you might expect more. Restaurant serves buffet-style breakfast ($11.50, ages 2-12 $7.25) and lunch ($14/$9), and sit-down dinners ($18-25). Reception 24hr. Check-in 3pm. Check-out noon. Reservations required. Singles and doubles $95-225; each additional person (up to 2) $15. AmEx/D/MC/V. ❸

Namakani Paio Cabins (☎967-7321), in the Namakani Paio Campground. All cabins have 1 full bed and 1 bunk bed, linens, a sheltered picnic bench, and fire pit. There are lights in the cabins, but no electrical outlets. Check-in 3pm. Check-out noon. Reservations required well in advance through the Volcano House reception desk. Singles and doubles $50 (linen included, extra blankets are suggested); each additional person (up to 2) $8. ❷

Namakani Paio Campground (☎985-6000), 3 mi. west of the park entrance on Rte. 11. Sheltered in a grove of giant eucalyptus and *koa* trees, Namakani provides a tranquil escape from a day of volcano exploring. Campsites are free and available on a first-come, first-served basis. The 2 large fields and pavilion are often crowded, but campers usually find enough room to set up a tent. Restrooms and fire pits. Shower keys ($3 per 24hr.) can be obtained from the Volcano House reception desk. 7-night max. A ½ mi. path directly across from the entrance on Hwy 11. leads to the Jaggar Museum, useful for people without cars. Free. ❶

Kulanaokuaiki Campground (☎985-6000), off Hilina Pali Rd., 4 mi. southwest of Chain of Craters Rd. In the midst of the Kau Desert, the seclusion gives a sense of the backcountry without the trek. There's no shade or water, and you'll be sleeping on lava, but there's probably not another person for miles. 8 sites with more on the way. Pit toilets and fireplaces but no drinking water. Free. ❶

SIGHTS

Almost all of the major attractions are accessible by car along **Crater Rim Drive, Chain of Craters Road,** and **Mauna Loa Road.** Below, the sights are divided up by the roads they're on (the first three are by the park entrance). Crater Rim Dr., which circles Kilauea Caldera and Halemaumau and Kilauea Iki, is the busiest. In the evening, Chain of Craters Rd. sees a decent amount of traffic as park visitors head to the end of the road for the night hike. Mauna Loa Rd., off Hwy. 11, is part of the park, though it is not past the park's entrance (meaning you don't have to pay to see the sights off Mauna Loa Rd.).

GALLERIES AND EVENTS

VOLCANO ART CENTER GALLERY. Adjacent to the Kilauea Visitors Center, the Volcano Art Center Gallery holds a large collection of visual and literary works by over 200 local artists, all inspired by the volcanoes. The woodwork (handmade *koa*, *ohia*, and *milo* crafts) and drawing are exceptional, and the photography (by G. Brad Lewis, apparently the only photographer to witness the last major eruption) is worth a glance. *(☎967-7565. Open daily 9am-5pm. AmEx/D/MC/V.)*

AFTER DARK IN THE PARK. On most Tuesday evenings, guest speakers give lectures and slide presentations on topics ranging from water catchment to vent creation. *(In the Kilauea Visitors Center Auditorium. Tu 7pm. Free.)*

KILAUEA CULTURAL FESTIVAL AND OTHER EVENTS. In mid-July, the park hosts Hawaiian artists and musicians from across the islands during the Kilauea Cultural Festival. Hawaiian music and hula, instruction in Native Hawaiian crafts and games, and demonstrations of island traditions are all part of the festivities. A hula performance is in late May or early June, and a procession to Halemaumau Crater is at the end of August. The (free) food is delectable. *(On the grounds of the Kilauea Military Camp, 1 mi. west of the Visitors Center on Crater Rim Dr. Admission included in the park entrance fee. Check at the park information desk or at www.nps.gov/havo for updated information.)*

CRATER RIM DRIVE

Beginning at the Visitors Center, Crater Rim Dr. is an 11 mi. loop that circles the Kilauea Caldera and passes through a cross section of recent and past lava landscapes. There is a lot that you can miss from the car, so if you have time, consider walking at least part of the 11 mi. Crater Rim Trail. The sights from the Jaggar Museum to the Kilauea Iki Overlook are especially groovy on foot. Overlooks and points of interest are marked by road signs and clearly labeled on the Visitors Center maps. Traveling counterclockwise from the Visitors Center, you will pass sulfur banks, steam vents (or Pele's Saunas), crater pits, cinder cones, lava tubes, and deep fissures along the southwest rift zone. Placards explain the geology, history, and legends of each sight. The following are a few highlights of Crater Rim Drive.

KILAUEA CALDERA. Don't be fooled—the barren summit crater that you will be circling for the next 11 mi. is one of the most active volcanoes in the world. From the 1800s until 1954, the caldera was the site of Kilauea's most dramatic eruptions, including fountains of lava up to 2000 ft. and a boiling lava lake. However, after 1955, most of the action has shifted to Kilauea's Southwest and East Rift Zones. Nonetheless, evidence of volcanic activity, past and present, is still visible around the caldera.

Halemaumau emits strong sulfur fumes—children, pregnant women, and people with heart and/or respiratory problems should avoid the crater.

JAGGAR MUSEUM AND HAWAIIAN VOLCANO OBSERVATORY. This museum, while a bit dated, is a fascinating introduction to the science behind the park. Stop in pre- or post-hike for a better understanding of both the current geological research at the park and the ancient Hawaiian legends that surround the volcanoes. Pele's hairs and tears, for example, are explained in scientific detail, as well as in the context of their mythical conceptions. The observatory, right next door, is closed to the public, but the Jaggar Museum sometimes shares a part of their current research. *(On Crater Rim Dr. ☎985-6049. Open daily 8:30am-5pm. Admission included in park entrance fee.)*Halemaumau Crater

Until 1924, Halemaumau was the site of a dramatic lake of lava which captivated the world. The crater visible today was formed in 1924 when the lava suddenly drained and the ground dropped several hundred feet. According to legend, the fire goddess Pele settled in Halemaumau after fleeing her sister, Namakaokahai, the goddess of the sea. The legend insists that she still resides there today. Although Pele's home is visible from all of Crater Rim Dr., it is seen best from the Jaggar Museum (p. 208) or the Steaming Bluff Lookout. Kilauea Iki Crater and PuU PuaI Cinder Cone

In November 1959, the cliff walls of Kilauea Iki ("Kilauea the Little") burst open, flooding the crater with liquid fire 400 ft. deep. Lava soon started blasting vertically in fountains nearly 2000 ft. high—the highest ever recorded on Kilauea. When it was over, a massive crater remained; it measures 1 mi. long, 3000 ft. across, and 380 ft. deep.

During the eruption, lava splatter from the fountain oxidized, forming the red-brown Puu Puai cinder cone. The cinder cone formed on the southwest side of the crater, because the splatter and ash were carried by the prevailing trade winds. For a closer look at Kilauea Iki, hike the Kilauea Iki Trail (p. 211).

DEVASTATION TRAIL. *(1 mi. round-trip. Easy.)* This self-guided plank trail stretches through a portion of rainforest buried in pumice cinders during the 1959 eruption of Kilauea Iki. The rain of volcanic debris left only a skeleton of what was once a densely forested area—hence the name.

THURSTON LAVA TUBE. Lava tubes are formed when a river of hot lava cools enough so that the outer edges of the flow crust over while the molten interior continues to move, leaving a tunnel behind. In 1913, Lorrin Thurston, a local newspaperman, was the first non-Native to discover the tube, and it has been a popular attraction ever since. The first portion of the Thurston Lava Tube is lit up, and you can walk down and investigate. Although stairs lead back to the surface after a couple hundred yards, the tube extends another 300 ft. Damp and dark, this extra stretch is far more exciting than the short, guided part. You will, of course, need a flashlight. Much of the tube is overrun with a living canopy of roots that have penetrated the rock, revealing the density of *ohia* and fern rainforest above.

JIM VERSUS THE VOLCANO

While buzzing around Volcanoes National Park, I swung an interview with Jim Kauahikaua, Scientist-in-Charge at the Volcano Observatory.

LG: Why in the hell should anyone feel safe here?

A: (chuckle) Well, obviously, many people live here without dying from an eruption. That being said, this volcano is responsible for the most deaths now [of volcanoes] in the U.S.

LG: One question: Pele or Science?

A: That's two questions! A lot of information is conveyed in the Pele stories, as with any Native Hawaiian literature. Clearly, the Hawaiians were very aware of their surroundings, and the Pele stories represent native science intelligence. There are many accounts of eruptions. And just the idea of Pele is astounding. Her characteristics mirror the science. She is often recounted in legend as having a dual personality: she could be a young beautiful woman, or an old, violent hag. For the Hawaiians to ascribe these characteristics to a volcano that is often calm with frequent spurts of violent outbursts was very precocious.

LG: One visitor while I was out there said, "I feel so unsafe here." Others were perched over the cliffs. Reaction?

A: Cliffs collapse. And if you're standing on the part that's still there and thinking that it's not going to collapse, you're a fool.

CHAIN OF CRATERS ROAD

The drive along Chain of Craters Rd. is about 40 mi. round-trip, and there is neither gas nor water available below the Visitors Center, so make the necessary preparations before leaving. Chain of Craters is also the road most likely to be closed due to lava flow or fires; check with the Visitors Center about current conditions.

HILINA PALI ROAD. This road intersects with Chain of Craters Rd. after about 2¼ mi. Heading into the heart of the Kau Desert, the 9 mi. Halina Pali Rd. is an escape into barren solitude, one missed by most visitors. It ends at the Hilina Pali Overlook, where a vast horizon of ocean and sky meets the edge of the 2280 ft. Halina Cliff. Notwithstanding numerous scenic overlooks, perhaps the coolest part is where the road ends, cut short by the massive lava flow from the Puu Oo vent.

PUU LOA PETROGLYPHS. One of the most striking features of Volcanoes National Park is its juxtaposition of old and new. The petroglyphs lining the slopes of Puu Loa, the largest collection in Hawaii (over 15,000 carvings), are the perfect place to find such a contrast. From the parking lot along Chain of Craters Road, a 2 mi. round-trip trail leads to a boardwalk that allows a close look at the symbols and figures tattooing the rock.

HOLEI SEA ARCH. Although sea arches are common on the coasts of Hawaii, where large waves provide the raw power for erosion, the Holei Arch is exceptional. Standing more than 90 ft. tall, this is the site where Hawaiian legend says a great battle took place between Pele and her sister Namakaokahai, goddess of the sea. It is also an unusual example of a sea arch formed by the creation of new land (by oozing lava), not by the usual erosion.

END OF CHAIN OF CRATERS ROAD. Since Puu Oo first blew her top on January 3, 1983, the Puu Oo-Kupaianaha rift zone has been erupting continuously, though things have calmed down since the dynamic early years, when lava fountains blasted 1500 ft. high. Today, the eruption is characterized by gentler *pahoehoe* flows and lava tubes. With tubes insulating the lava from heat loss, these flows are able to travel across the long *palis* (cliffs) all the way to the ocean, where they continue to add substantial landmass to Hawaii's youngest island in a display almost as spectacular as the fountains two decades ago. In total, more than 8 mi. of highway have been swallowed, and between 1989 and 1991 the entire town of Kalapana was destroyed. Since 2003, the park ranger satellite building at the end of the road has had to move considerably south to flee the encroaching flows—the shack and facilities are all on wheels down here. The volcano's power is viscerally apparent; if you hike northeast along the coastal lava rocks from the end of the road, you'll come upon a series of road signs ("reduce speed ahead," "stop") buried by lava that make for ironic pictures.

MAUNA LOA ROAD

This scenic drive starts 2 mi. west of the park entrance off Rte. 11. The road climbs 3000 ft. through rainforest to the **Mauna Loa Lookout** (13½ mi. from Rte. 11), a secluded spot perfect for a quiet moment of reflection. This trailhead also happens to be one of the best bird-watching spots on the island, with a diverse range of native and non-native species cruising overhead.

Mauna Loa is the world's tallest mountain if measured from the ocean floor. Climbing 18,000 ft. to the surface of the Pacific and then another 13,677 ft. above

CellularAbroad

With Cellular Abroad,
talk is not only cheap,
it's free.
Unlimited FREE
ncoming calls
nd no bills
r contracts
or overseas use!
1-800-287-5072
ww.cellularabroad.com

Otel.com

DO NOT
DISTURB
US & CANADA
1-800-820-4171 OR 1-212-594-8045
EUROPE
00-800-468-35482 OR 44-207-099-2035

sea level, Mauna Loa dwarfs even Mt. Everest. In sheer bulk, it's 100 times the size of Mt. Rainier. If the enormity of what rests beneath your feet doesn't overwhelm you, watching the sun set might.

Near the beginning of the road there is a turn-off to see the **lava trees.** These phantoms of the old forest were formed when *pahoehoe* lava flows engulfed a tree that carried a lot of water (usually *ohia*) and hardened around it before the tree burned away. Just over 1 mi. on Mauna Loa Rd. after the turn-off from Hwy. 11 is **Kipuka Puaulu,** an enclave of native forest that has managed to avoid the torrents of lava. This oasis of upland forest is full of *koa* and *ohia* trees, as well as many other native plants, insects, and birds that have been partially sheltered from invasive foreign species by the surrounding fields of lava. An easy 1¼ mi. trail offers a good view of this treasure.

HIKING

The hiking in Hawaii Volcanoes National Park is some of the best on the island, and with over 150 mi. of well-maintained trails, there's certainly a lot of it. A list of suggested hikes at the Visitors Center includes routes for all abilities and endurance. Whatever the adventure, sunscreen, a hat, lots of water, sturdy close-toed shoes, rain gear, a flashlight, long pants, and all-purpose gloves are highly suggested. Most of the hikes offer little shade and cover hot black lava rock fields; drinking water and replenishing electrolytes (found in sports drinks) is a must if you plan on avoiding heat stroke and dehydration. Trails over lava flows are loosely marked by piles of neatly arranged rocks known as *ahu* (rock piles) or lighted beacons. Strong winds can knock down even the best *ahu*, though most trails are fairly well trafficked, making it possible to guess the direction of the next *ahu* while keeping the last *ahu* in sight. Don't spend all your time at the Visitors Center (which features an informational film given "two thumbs up" by park rangers) or the Jaggar Museum—many of the park's highlights are accessible only by hiking.

KILAUEA IKI TRAIL. *(4 mi., 2-3hr. round-trip. Moderate.)* The trail starts from the lava tube parking lot along Crater Rim Dr. If you only have time for one hike in the park, this may be it. Just over 40 years ago, the surface of Kilauea Iki Crater was a boiling lake of molten lava. Today, hikers revel in the experience of walking on what might be called hell frozen over. The hike itself is not very long, but give yourself plenty of time to enjoy the view from the crater floor. The first part of the hike descends 400 ft. through *ohia* and *hamuu* (tree fern) rainforest. Once in the crater, the desolate moon-like landscape provides a rare opportunity to witness the first stages of ecological development following an eruption. Just 40 years after the lava drained from Kilauea Iki, signs of life are everywhere: fern fiddles have broken through and *ohia* trees have planted their first roots.

HALEMAUMAU TRAIL. *(3 mi. one way, but many trail combinations possible. Moderate.)* This trail leaves from the Volcano House Hotel and traverses the smooth *pahoehoe* lava on the Kilauea Caldera floor to the Halemaumau Crater. The trail is perhaps the best way to experience the massive scale of the caldera, because it takes you directly through the center. The ground is often so hot that thermal updrafts create their own system of wind currents—if you're lucky, you may spot the *io*, a small red-brown hawk native to Hawaii, on a late afternoon glide. The Halemaumau trail connects to many other trails, and the best connections are with the Kilauea Iki Trail and the Byron Ledge. Consult a map before heading

GOING WITH THE FLOW. Exploring lava flows past the end of Chain of Craters Rd. requires vigilance and care; the newly formed land is unstable and lava flows are unpredictable, not to mention scorching hot. However, when proper precautions are taken, the experience is unparalleled. The hike, which changes every day with the movement of the flow, is easier in the daytime but much more rewarding around sunset. As the sky darkens, "skylights" through the upper crust of a lava tube often appear. Before you set out, be aware of the dangers of lava. Whether the flow is 3hr. or 30min. from the end of the road, it pays to heed warnings. Consult the ranger station or national park service for eruption updates and safety information, watch the safety video at the Visitors Center (every hr. on the hr. daily 9am-4pm), and be prepared by bringing the necessary gear (sunscreen, hat, sturdy boots or shoes, plenty of water, a flashlight, long pants, and all-purpose gloves.) Perhaps most importantly, stay on Pele's good side; what you actually see at the end of the road will depend wholly on her temperament at the time of your visit. There is always the possibility that conditions may be too dangerous to allow hikers onto the flow or that there might not be any visible lava. Here are a few precautions to keep in mind:

Stay off "benches" created by lava flowing into the sea, and don't go near the water! Benches are extremely unstable and inevitably crash into the ocean below. The water itself is independently dangerous, because splashing waves can carry molten lava into curious crowds.

Watch for fires! Lava can easily set grasslands on fire. With a bit of wind, this can be very dangerous. Also, burning organic material causes the buildup of methane gas underground, which can ignite in powerful methane explosions.

out. This trail traverses **heavy sulfur emissions** from the caldera; persons with respiratory problems or heart difficulties, pregnant women, infants, and young children should avoid this area.

PUU HULUHULU TRAIL. *(3 mi. round-trip. Moderate.)* This short hike leaves from the Mauna Ulu Overlook and takes you to the summit of Puu Huluhulu ("shaggy hill"), a 150 ft. cinder cone formed by buildup from the eruption of Mauna Ulu in 1974. From here, you can see just about everything on a clear day: Mauna Loa, Mauna Ulu, Puu Oo's steaming vent and Kilauea's east rift zone, the beach, and the dramatic course of the 1969 and 1974 lava flows as they seared across the forest, leaving *kipukas* (islands of untouched forest) in their wake. Hiking beyond this point requires pre-registration and a permit from the Visitors Center, so most visitors turn back. To go farther into the heart of the current eruption, see the next hike.

NAPAU TRAIL. *(14 mi., 6-9hr. round-trip. Challenging.)* Taking up where the Puu Huluhulu trail leaves off, the Napau trail, due to Puu Oo's unpredictability, remote location, and risk, is the only dayhike that requires hikers to register at the Visitors Center. Napau is also the only trail that brings you as close as legally possible with the heart of the current eruption at the Puu Oo vent. If you were able to walk to the rim of Puu Oo and peer in, you'd see a giant, bubbling lava lake. Unfortunately, the land around Puu Oo is too unstable, so you can only go as far as Napau Crater to watch the billowing clouds of volcanic gas. On a clear day, the sight humbles even the bravest hikers. Be prepared to hike over long stretches of *aa* and *pahoehoe* flows, and bring a lot of water; the trail is hot and there are no facilities.

KEAUHOU AND PUNA COAST TRAILS. *(16½ mi. through Keauhou or 19 mi. through Halape. Challenging.)* The hike leaves from Mau Loa o Mauna Ulu on Chain of Craters Rd., and descends the Hilina and Puueu cliffs through an ever-changing landscape of black lava, *ohia* forest, and grasslands. Interspersed throughout the hike are thin slivers of golden lava rock, known as Pele's hair, and small drops of shiny black lava rock, Pele's tears. At the end of Keauhou trail (5 mi.) you can head straight to the rocky tide pools of Keauhou Shelter (2 mi.) or continue to **Halape Shelter** (3 mi.).

If you have time, don't skip Halape. After hours of hiking, it appears on the horizon—a palm tree oasis in the desert. The white-sand beaches here are a popular nesting site for endangered hawks bill and green sea turtles. Halape is only accessible by hiking 19 mi., and many travelers opt to camp at the backcountry campsite. For those interested in exploring, there are two spots at Halape not to miss. The first is **Kumu Niu,** popularly called Halape Iki ("Halape the little"), a cove of white sand and palm trees that's great for snorkeling. To reach it, hike southwest along the coast for about 20min.; you can't miss it. The second spot is a freshwater swimming hole. To get there, stand with your back to the ocean, facing the pit toilet at Halape. You will notice a cliff that drops off into a ravine. Head toward the cliff and follow the ravine to your left until you see the pool. Swim all you want, but don't drink this water without purification.

Although not quite as magical as Halape, Keauhou is also a great place to camp in the area. Beware of high surf and dangerous rip currents at all sites, and check weather forecasts before leaving. As for the facilities, expect pit toilets, and bring water-purification tablets as all three sites offer only non-potable water.

KAU DESERT AND HILINA PALI TRAIL. *(1-21 mi. Easy to challenging.)* The adventure starts at the Kau Desert Trailhead, along Rte. 11, 10 mi. west of the main park entrance, and can last as long as you want it to. In total, there are more than 21 mi. of trail between Crater Rim Drive and Hilina Pali Overlook, but hiking any portion gives a taste of the desert and the intense heat and solitude that characterize this region of rock and sun. From the trailhead, it's an easy 1 mi. walk to the Footprints Trail, left in the desert rock after the 1790 eruption of Kilauea. A band of warriors was traveling across the desert back to Kau when the volcano spewed clouds of gas and ash that suffocated the men and immortalized their path.

DESERT RAINS. A quick trip around Kilauea Caldera reveals a strange anomaly: within minutes the barren landscape of the Kau Desert in the southwest suddenly becomes a region of lush rainforest. The transition is so abrupt it seems impossible. The fact is, the Kau Desert is not technically a desert—it receives about as much rainfall as a tropical rainforest. The catch is, this rain, contaminated by volcanic sulfer dioxide gas, is almost as acidic as vinegar; it has a pH level of about 3.4 during eruptions. Pacific trade currents guide the acid rain over the Kau Desert, creating a stark contrast with the lush rainforest to the northeast. For more information, contact the US Geological Survey, Hawaii Volcano Observatory (☎967-7328; http://volcanoes.usgs.gov).

MAUNA LOA TRAIL. *(36½ mi., 3-4 days round-trip. Challenging.)* The trailhead is the Mauna Loa Strip Rd. This steep 7000 ft. route climbs at an average of 388 ft. per mi. The ascent to the summit of Mauna Loa passes through a moon-like expanse of barren *aa* and *pahoehoe*. Most hikers spend a night in the cabin at Red Hill (7½ mi. from the lookout) in order to pace themselves and acclimatize before trekking to Mauna Loa Cabin, at 13,250 ft. (For an intense day hike, just hike to Red Hill and back.) The immensity of the Mokuaweoweo Caldera may blow you away—that or the year-round flash-snow storms, which occur at such a high altitude. The ascent is recommended only for experienced and well-equipped backpackers. Altitude sickness is a frequent problem even among the extremely fit, causing dizziness, headaches, nausea, and fatigue. Prospective hikers should consult the rangers at the Visitors Center. Mauna Loa can also be reached by a less rigorous trail starting at the Mauna Loa Weather Observatory, accessible via Saddle Rd. (p. 230).

PUNA

Cloaked in a high canopy of lush green leaves and veiled with an edgy, alternative aura, Puna is perhaps the Big Island's best-hidden secret. Perched along the northern slopes of Hawaii's only two active volcanoes, Kilauea and Mauna Loa, Puna's risky nature evades the tourist and development craze that has destroyed much of the island's natural beauty. Although almost 80% of the rainforest here has been hacked away in recent decades, Puna is still a fertile haven for yogi, hippie, and generally open-minded travelers. The spectacular black-sand beaches, natural lava pools, and convenient volcano access welcome an amazing array of adventurers.

VOLCANO

Nestled in the thick of a pleasantly cool ancient *hamuu* (tree fern) and *ohia* rainforest, Volcano Village (pop. 2,231) sits at an elevation of nearly 4000 ft. During the 19th century, the fertile volcanic soil of the village attracted workers from around the world to labor in local sugarcane plantations. Drawn from across continents, these immigrants brought fragments of life from their native homes. Today, the native rainforest is interlaced with bamboo, wild orchid, ginger, Portuguese fire trees, and the purple lasiandra—a visual display of the cultural patchwork in Volcano's history. Just over one mile northeast of Volcanoes National Park, Volcano Village has two historic general stores and beautiful B&Bs that accommodate the heavy traffic without losing the distinctive sense of community established long ago. Unless you plan on camping, stay here for the best volcano experience.

ORIENTATION

Life in Volcano centers on **Old Volcano Highway (Old Volcano Road),** which forks off **Route 11** and runs parallel to it for slightly over 1 mi. before stopping in a dead end at the northeast end of the village. **Haunani Road** and **Wright Road,** perpendicular to Volcano Rd., connect the village to Rte. 11. A car is the best option for getting to and from Volcano. Alternatively, the **Hele-On Bus** runs from the Mooheau Station in Hilo to the Visitors Center in Volcanoes National Park (p. 203), 1½ mi. away, and might detour upon request.

PRACTICAL INFORMATION

Tourist Information: Volcano Visitor Center, 19-4084 Volcano Rd. (☎967-8662), in Volcano Village. Usually unmanned but full of brochures. Open daily 9am-5pm.

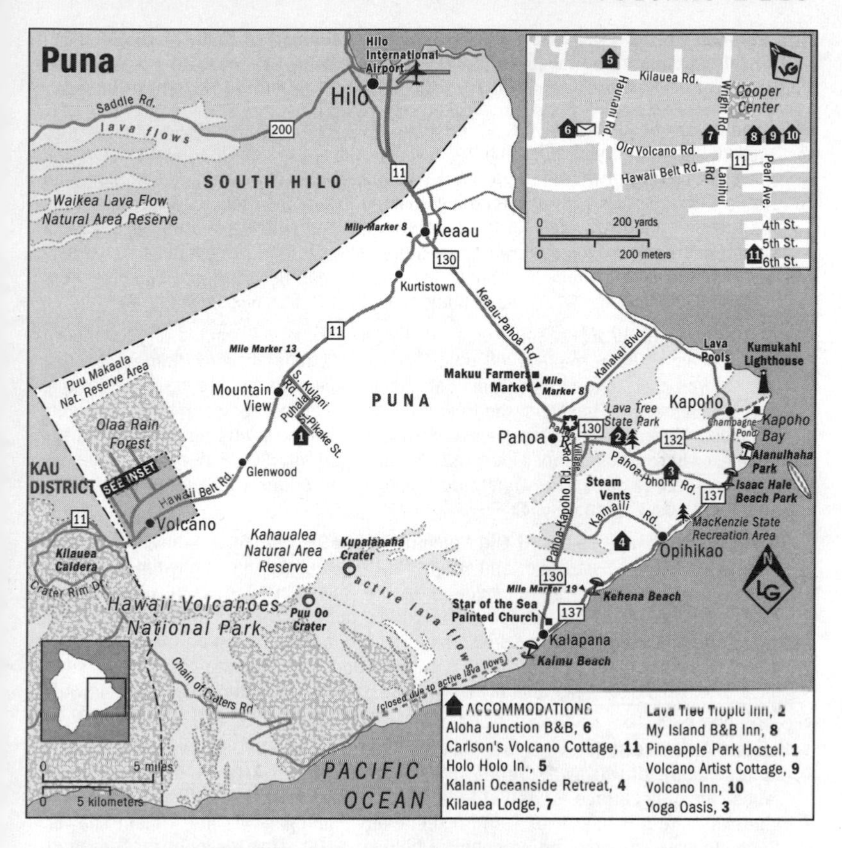

Laundromat: Volcano Wash and Dry, in Volcano Village, behind Volcano True Value. Wash $2.50, dry $1.50. Open daily 8am-7pm. Last wash 7pm.

Supplies: Volcano True Value (☎967-7969), in Volcano Village, carries batteries, flashlights, and water-purifying iodine tablets. Open daily 7:30am-5pm. AmEx/D/MC/V.

Police Station: The nearest police station (☎966-5835) is on Old Volcano Rd. in Keaau, just outside of Hilo.

Internet Access: Lava Rock Cafe (☎967-8526), on Old Volcano Rd. $4 per 20min, $10 per 24hr. Open M 7:30am-5pm, Tu-Sa 7:30am-9pm, Su 7:30am-4pm. Talk to **Steve Young** (☎985-9977) for digital camera and photo services. MC/V.

Post Office: Volcano Post Office, 19-4030 Old Volcano Hwy. (☎800-275-8777), next to the Volcano Store. Open M-F 7:30am-3:30pm, Sa 11am-noon.

Postal Code: 96785.

ACCOMMODATIONS

Since many visitors to Volcano decide to spend the night last minute, a lot of places have surcharges for one-night stays, and it's a good idea to book reservations before taking a trip to Volcano. **Volcano Lodging** (☎967-8617 or 800-908-9764), the **Volcano Village website** (www.volcanovillage.com), and the Volcano Visitor Center (see above) are good resources for finding local accommodations.

Carson's Volcano Cottages, 6th St. (☎967-7683; www.carsonsvolcanocottage.com). Detached from the main strip, Old Volcano Rd., Carson's is off Pearl Ave., before mi. marker 26 heading toward Hilo on Rte. 11. Take a right on Pearl and another right onto 6th St. If you're aching for a pampering, look no further than this B&B located in the heart of the rainforest. Most of the ornate rooms and cottages feature luxuries like wood-burning stoves, goose-down comforters, cable TV, and private hot tubs. Breakfast buffet included. Check-in 3-5pm. Check-out 11am. Reservations recommended. Doubles $115; cottage $170; each additional guest $15. AmEx/D/MC/V. ❸

Holo Holo In, 19-4036 Kalani Honua Rd. (☎967-7950; www.enable.org/holoholo). From Volcanoes Park, make a left onto Volcano Rd.; turn left onto Haunani Rd. just past the Volcano Store and left again onto Kalani Honua Rd. Built to create an inviting spot for international travelers, the Holo Holo In is a backpacker's dream, with laundry facilities, showers, a spacious kitchen, free Internet access, and an eclectic (mostly Japanese) library collection. Linens $1. Wash $1.50, dry $0.25 per 7min. Check-in 4:30-9pm. Check-out 11am. Quiet hours 10pm-6am. Dorms $18; doubles $45, with private bath $60. Cash only. ❶

My Island B&B Inn, 19-3896 Old Volcano Rd. (☎967-7216; www.myislandinnhawaii.com), between Pearl Ave. and Wright Rd. The owner of this family-run B&B, Gordon Morse, has written several guides to the Hawaiian Islands, all of which are available to guests. The house was originally built by the Lyman family (the Big Island's first missionaries) in 1886, and all of the rooms–though on the small side–are quaint and charming. Breakfast is creative and delicious; the crowning achievement is the signature "My Island Papaya." Reservations recommended. Rooms $55-105. MC/V. ❷

Volcano Artist Cottage, 19-3436 Old Volcano Rd. (☎985-8979; www.volcanoartistcottage.com), drawn away behind the **Volcano Garden Arts** gallery and natural foods cafe, this cottage is a quiet little getaway for two. The room is simple but elegant with one queen-size bed and a remarkably indulgent granite walk-in shower. Contemplative gardens and greenhouse behind. $109, 10% discount for 3 or more nights. MC/V. ❸

Aloha Junction B&B, 19-4037 Post Office Ln. (☎967-7289; www.bnbvolcano.com), off Old Volcano Hwy., behind a gate, next to the post office. Clean, extremely well-maintained, and equipped with a state-of-the-art entertainment room, Aloha Junction is furnished with big comfy beds, high-speed Internet, equipment closet for guest use, and a hot tub to recuperate after a long day of *pahoehoe* hikes. Full kitchen. Breakfast included. Check-in 3-6pm. Check-out 10am. Rooms with shared bath $75, with private bath $100-125; each additional guest $15. MC/V. ❷

Kilauea Lodge, Old Volcano Rd. (☎967-7366; www.kilauealodge.com), between Haunani and Wright Rd. The community spirit is still evident around the 1938 "Fireplace of Friendship" at this old YMCA summer camp, but with a ski chalet vibe and plenty of inviting reading nooks, the rooms are nothing like the average camp. Hot tub available. Check-in 3pm. Check-out noon. Reservations recommended. Rooms $150-190; each additional person $15. AAA discount 10%. AmEx/MC/V. ❹

Volcano Inn, 19-3820 Old Volcano Rd. (☎896-6851; www.volcanoinn.com). Surrounded by a nice lanai, this custom-designed house is full of niches to cozy up in as well as modern amenities, such as wireless Internet. Units include a private bath, phone, refrigerator, cable TV/VCR, and, in some suites, stained-glass windows. Continental breakfast included. Check-in 2pm. Check-out 10am. Reservations recommended. Rooms $110-135. AAA discount 10%. D/MC/V. ❸

FOOD

Volcano has two general stores at which daytrippers to the park can stock up on food and supplies. **The Volcano Store,** 19-4005 Haunani Rd., at the corner of Old Volcano Hwy. and Haunani Rd., has groceries and general supplies. (☎967-7210. Open daily 5am-7pm. AmEx/D/MC/V.) **Kilauea General Store,** 19-3972 Old Volcano Hwy., between Haunani and Wright Rd., serves a soup of the day ($3.75) and pizza by the slice ($2.25), and stocks general supplies. (☎967-7555. Open M-Sa 7am-7:30pm, Su 7am-7pm. AmEx/D/MC/V.) The **Volcano farmers' market** sets up shop on Sundays (7am until the merchandise runs out—usually before 8am) at the Cooper Center, near the corner of Old Volcano Rd. and Wright Rd.

Volcano's Lava Rock Cafe, Old Volcano Rd. (☎967-8526), behind Kilauea General Store. A little obsessed with the volcano theme, this cafe offers "seismic sandwiches," "lava tube plates," and "tsunami salads," and at around $8 for every item on the menu, this place is a steal. Favorites include sweetbread french toast with 2 eggs ($7) and grilled mahi mahi ($8). Internet access available (p. 215). Open M 7:30am-5pm, Tu-Sa 7:30am-9pm, Su 7:30am-4pm. MC/V. ❷

Thai Thai Restaurant, 19-4084 Old Volcano Rd. (☎967-7969), in Volcano Village, next to True Value. Classic Thai cuisine adds another dimension to Volcano's fiery mix. Massaman curry $11, with shrimp $16. Thai basil stir-fry $10. Dinner $10-16. Open daily 5-9pm. AmEx/D/MC/V. ❸

Kiawe Kitchen (☎967-7711), next to the Old Volcano Store, off Old Volcano Rd. After a day of hiking in the park, Kiawe's 10 in. pizzas ($11 and up) hit the spot. Sandwiches, like the wood-fired roasted chicken ($10), are tasty, but a little pricey. Specials change daily. Open M-Tu and Th-Su noon-2:30pm and 5:30-9:30pm. MC/V. ❷

PAHOA

The hippie center in Puna, Pahoa (pop. 962) is perhaps best known for its beach gatherings and cultural and health retreat facilities, where visitors come to rejuvenate their spirits with yoga, dance, and meditation in one of Hawaii's unspoiled regions.

LEGALIZING MARIJUANA?

In 2000, Hawaii became the eighth state to pass a law allowing the possession and use of marijuana for medicinal purposes. Although legislation allowing for medicinal marijuana is becoming more prevalent, the campaign to legalize recreational marijuana still has many hurdles to overcome.

For Brian Murphy, head of the political group Maui County Citizens for Democracy in Action, these obstacles include bureaucratic hang-ups with the initiative process. This group is gathering signatures to put an initiative on the ballot that would tax and regulate medicinal marijuana as well as allow anyone over the age of 21 to posses one ounce of the substance. Because a certain number of registered voters must sign the petitions, the group has attempted to obtain signatures as well as register new voters. Murphy has been frustrated by the fact that the County only allows him 300 voter registration forms a month. County officials have also made it clear that the five voters who started the initiative must oversee the collection of all signatures, limiting the efficiency of the group and narrowing the window of opportunity to get the initiatives passed and on the November ballot. For now, it seems that only qualified patients can possess marijuana, while the rest of Hawaii must wait to see how the initiatives play out.

Set on striking lava flows, the area around Pahoa offers a diverse natural environment that is best captured as a roadtrip from Rte. 130, to Rte. 132, to the historic coastal Rte. 137, and back to Rte. 130. On weekends, pass through one of Pahoa's popular farmers' markets and assemble a fresh picnic lunch before hitting the long stretch of black-sand and lava-cliff beaches on Rte. 137.

ORIENTATION

From Volcano, **Route 11** heads northeast where it intersects **Route 130 (Pahoa-Kapoho Road).** Pahoa is located to the south, off Rte. 130 near its intersection with **Route 132**, slightly under 20 mi. south of Hilo. Heading *makai* (toward the ocean), take a right at the sign for Pahoa Village onto **Pahoa Village Road** (also called **Old Pahoa Road** or **Government Main Road**); most of Pahoa's attractions can be found along this 1 mi. stretch through town, although accommodations and activities are down the hill. Most of the whole area's sights are in the triangle formed by Routes 130, 132, and 137 (a scenic ocean highway that is cut off by an old lava flow). These highways are often labeled by the towns they connect; for instance, part of Rte. 130 is known as **Pahoa-Kapoho Rd.,** and Rte. 137 is often referred to as the **Red Rd.,** because it used to be a red clay road.

PRACTICAL INFORMATION

Banks: First Hawaiian Bank (☎965-8621), on Government Main Rd., has a **24hr. ATM.** Open M-Th 8:30am-4pm, F 8:30am-6pm.

Libraries: Pahoa Public Library, 15-3070 Pahoa-Kalapana Rd. (☎965-2171), adjacent to the school at the intersection of Hwy. 132 and Hwy. 130. Coming from town, turn right just before the stoplight. **Internet access** is available with a 3-month visitor's card ($10). 3 terminals available on the hr. Open M 1-8pm, Tu-F 9am-5pm.

Laundromat: Suds 'N Duds (☎965-2621), off Old Pahoa Rd. in Pahoa Village Center. Wash $1.50-2.50, dry $0.25 per 5min. Open daily 7:30am-7:30pm.

Swimming Pool: There is a free public swimming pool behind Pahoa Cash & Carry. Open M-F 9am-6pm, Sa-Su 9am-5pm.

Internet access: Enjoy a cup of joe or a fresh smoothie while surfing the web at **Aloha Outpost Cafe** (☎965-8333), in the Pahoa Village Marketplace just off Rte. 130. $4-6 per hr., rates are cheaper during the middle of the day; F $4 per hr. all day. Open M-F 8am-6pm, Sa-Su 8am-5pm. AmEx/D/MC/V.

Police: Police Satellite (☎935-3311), on Government Main Rd., across from Pahoa Hardware. Phone outside the station connects to dispatcher.

Pharmacy: Pahoa Rx Pharmacy (☎965-7535), in the Pahoa Village Center. Open M-F 9am-5pm, Sa 9am-noon; closed 12:30-1:30pm for lunch.

Post Office: Pahoa Post Office, 15-2859 Puna Rd. (☎800-275-8777). Open M-F 8:30am-4pm, Sa 11am-2pm.

Postal Code: 96778.

ACCOMMODATIONS

In addition to the places below, it is possible to camp in Mackenzie State Recreation Area (p. 221), which offers some of the best camping along the coast. There is also roadside camping in Isaac Hale Beach Park (p. 220).

Yoga Oasis, 13-678 Pohoiki Rd. (☎965-8460; www.yogaoasis.org), about 2 mi. from Rte. 137. The colorfully-flagged driveway marks a rollicking route towards relaxation and rejuvenation. Most guests stay in cabins painted with invigorating colors and luxuriously adorned with soft linens and inviting tubs. Others stay in the main house, while bargain hunters camp on the lawn. All stays include morning yoga class and a lavish breakfast spread. Classes ($10) open to non-guests each day at 8am. Call for reservations. Camping singles $35; doubles $60. Cabins $75-125/ $100-145. MC/V. ❶/❸

Kalani Oceanside Retreat, RR2 Box 4500, on Rte. 137 (☎965-7828; www.kalani.com), between mi. markers 17 and 18. This New Age oasis of creativity is a unique experience. Spectacular oceanfront setting, sumptuous vegetarian and vegan options ($11-22), a tight-knit community of volunteers, and a variety of classes including yoga, ecstatic dance, waterdance, salsa, and hip-hop during the week (prices vary from donations to $12). Free Internet access in the cafe 7pm-10pm. The 1 or 3 mo. volunteer program provides a unique **short-term work** alternative. Quiet hours after 10pm. Check-out 11am. Reservations recommended. Campsites $30; dorms $60; rooms with shared bath $105-110, with private bath $125-260. AmEx/D/MC/V. ❷/❸

Lava Tree Tropic Inn, 14-3555 Puna Rd. (☎965-7441; www.lavatreetropicinn.com), next to Lava Tree State Park; follow the sign about 500 yd. past the park entrance and turn right up the driveway. This house upon a hill sits in a patch of sunlight among the dark green forest beyond. The heavy iron gate at the bottom of the driveway is unlocked—just slide it across yourself and drive in. The rooms are neat and spacious. Breakfast included. Check-in 3pm, check-out 11am. Rooms $95-100, $10 extra for one-night stays. MC/V. ❸

Pineapple Park Hostel, 7927 Pikake St. (☎323-2224; www.pineapple-park.com). In Mountain View, heading west on Rte. 11, turn left onto South Kalani Rd. after mi. marker 13. At the T-junction, turn right onto Pohala St., follow it to the end of the pavement, and turn left onto Pikake St. Although a bit out of the way, Pineapple Park sees a lot of student traffic and has a large kitchen with complimentary snacks, grill, laundry facilities, Internet access, and bunks. Wash $1, dry $2. Ask about trading a bed for a few hours of housekeeping per week. Quiet hours after 10pm. Bunks $25; private rooms $75; VIP suite $95. MC/V. ❶/❸

FOOD

Weekends in Pahoa offer endless options to explore local farmers' markets and craft villages. The largest two are the **Makuu Farmers Association Cultural and Craft Village** on Sundays from 8am to mid-afternoon (located on Hwy. 130 just over 2 mi. north of Pahoa near mi. marker 8; look for the "slow down" signs), known for its signature **Cane Juice Stand** offering juices, sorbet, and hemp seed and cane ice cream ($2-3); and the **Pahoa farmers' market** (☎965-9990), weekends from 6am to 3pm, on Pahoa Village Rd. at the intersection with Kauhale St., which has great fresh fruit and produce. **Raisin' Cane,** 15-2958 Pahoa Village Rd. (☎965-5486), hidden in a clothing store just in front of Yoga Shala, has some of the best homemade sorbet on the island. The free "Discovery Tour of the Dipper Freezer" is well worth the hunt. One scoop $2; smoothies $6.

Ning's Thai Cuisine, 15-2955 Pahoa Village Rd. (☎965-7611), is a popular Pahoa dinner destination known for its reasonable prices and luscious spices. The coconut soup ($5) has almost reached celebrity status around town. Try the yellow curry with brown rice (with chicken, beef, pork, fish, or tofu, $8-12). Vegetarian-friendly. Entrees $8-12. Open M-Sa noon-3pm and 5-9pm, Su 5-9pm. AmEx/D/MC/V. ❷

Island Natural Groceries, 15-1403 Pahoa Village Rd. (☎965-6263), next to the Pahoa Natural Emporium. If it isn't organic or all-natural, you won't find it here. Products are a tad pricey but have attracted a cult following. Hot vegetarian plate of the day is $6 per lb. Sandwiches $3.30-4. A "waterman" in the parking lot allows you to fill up for $0.50 per gallon. Open M-Sa 7:30am-7:30pm, Su 7:30am-6pm. AmEx/D/MC/V. ❶

Ludi's (☎965-5599), next to Paolo's on Pahoa Village Rd. Quality Filipino cuisine at low prices. Unassuming setting, usually inhabited by fiercely loyal customers. Lunch plates $7. Open M-Sa 9am-6pm. Cash only. ❶

Paolo's Bistro, 333 Pahoa Village Rd. (☎965-7033). This quaint and cozy restaurant feels like home–if home had an award-winning Italian chef in the kitchen, that is. Follow your nose past the kitchen and onto the flowery garden gazebo seating area for a breath of fresh air over dinner. Entrees like the pasta primavera ($15) run between $11-17. Open Tu-Su 5:30-9pm. MC/V. ❸

Baraka Foods Cafe, 15-2945 Pahoa Village Rd. (☎965-0305). Organic food, teas, juices, and smoothies are the name of the game. Sandwiches, like the Mediterranean avocado pesto sandwich, go for around $7. Smoothies $6.75. Open daily 5-9pm and W-Sa 11am-2pm. MC/V. ❶

Pahoa Fresh Fish, (☎965-8248), in the Pahoa Village Marketplace. This is the ideal stop before a barbecue or fishing outing; besides fresh fish, they sell tackle and other supplies. Whole ahi $2.50 per lb.; mahi mahi $11.99 per lb.; fish and chips $7.75. Open daily 8am-6pm. MC/V. ❷

BEACHES

KEHENA BEACH. *(Open daily 24hr.)* One of the few undiscovered places left on the island, this secluded black-sand beach is private and quiet during the week. Weekends are busy, especially on Sunday afternoons, when the Kalani ecstatic dance crowd meanders down for a drum circle that lasts until sunset. **Nudity** may be illegal on Hawaiian beaches, but bikinis and boardshorts are used here as makeshift pillows, more often than not. Roadside parking is somewhat questionable, so be sure to lock up before trekking down. The beach is located at mi. marker 19 on Hwy. 137. The path is marked by the "Government Property" sign to the left of the parking area when you're facing the ocean.

ALANUIHAHA PARK. *(Open daily 7am-7pm. Lifeguards 9:30am-4:45pm.)* A quarter mile past mi. marker 10 on Hwy. 137, Alanuihaha Park is an ocean- and spring-fed pool protected from strong tides by a man-made wall. The site is one of the few places on the southeast coast where swimming is safe, making it a popular weekend attraction for local families. Toilets and shelters are available.

ISAAC HALE BEACH PARK. *(Surfing. Open daily 24hr.)* One of the few surfing spots on the Big Island, Isaac Hale is fun for both surfers and spectators, as the bay allows those on the beach to get close to the action. It's also a popular launching spot for local fishermen and a favorite place for roadside camping, with toilets and picnic shelters. For the surfers, this beach goes by the moniker **Pohoiki,** after the street that hits Rte. 137 at the Beach, Pohoiki Rd. There are four breaks here, from south to north, **1st Bay, 2nd Bay, Shacks,** and **Bowls.** From Pohoiki Bay take Hwy. 137; the beach is near mi. marker 11, less than 1 mi. south of Alanuihaha.

SIGHTS

The triangle defined by Routes 130, 132, and 137 makes an exceptional daytrip, and the drive itself, especially along the coastal highway (Hwy. 137), is as enjoyable as any of the sights. The scenery alternates between old forests and lava fields, and the ocean views are captivating. But be careful: the surf can be dangerous. The calmest water is at Champagne Pond and Alanuihaha.

LAVA TREE STATE PARK. As you head east toward Lava Tree State Park on Hwy. 132, giant albizia trees arch over the road where an eruption from Kilauea's East Rift Zone in 1790 drowned the surrounding rainforest in *pahoehoe* lava. Originally formed as lava cooled around water-holding *ohia*, the trees eventually burned away, leaving a hardened forest of shells behind. The park allows visitors a closer look as well as restrooms and picnic shelters.

KUMUKAHI LIGHTHOUSE. Continuing east on Hwy. 132, the road ends just shy of the ocean on flows that lead to the old Kumukahi Lighthouse. Rather than turning onto Hwy. 137, continue straight on the dirt road toward the ocean. The old lighthouse has been replaced by a new and unremarkable steel structure that is useful mostly as a landmark for the popular **Champagne Pond** and the great-for-snorkeling tide pools of **Kapoho Bay.** Champagne Pond (often bubbling, hence the name) is one of the island's most talked about swimming havens, protected from the turbulent surrounding surf by the bay and heated by volcanic activity below. *(From the lighthouse, the road to the ponds is only accessible with 4WD, but the walk (1.5 mi.) isn't too bad. The tide pools of Kapoho Bay are more easily reached by Kapoho-Kai Rd. off Hwy. 137.)*

LAVA POOLS. Wade through this natural pool as the waves crashes continuously against a craggy wall of *aa* lava. The pools are somewhat difficult to find, but well worth the chase. *(3 mi. north on Rte. 137 after the intersection with Rte. 132, turn down a well-covered dirt driveway beneath a low ceiling of trees. Continue for about 1500 yd. until you reach the ocean, then turn left and walk for another 100 yd. Those without 4WD should walk.)*

MACKENZIE STATE RECREATION AREA. Set on elegant cliffs overlooking the Pacific under the shade of an old Ironwood grove, this area is quiet, secluded, and probably the best place to camp along the coast. Permits are required for camping, but not for lava-tubing! To get to the entrance, face the ocean and walk left for approximately 100 yd. See **Camping in Hawaii**, p. 75, for permit information. *(Off Hwy. 137 between mi. markers 13 and 14. Note: The stretch of road between Isaac Hale and Mackenzie often floods during high tide.)*

KALAPANA. Although Kalapana was once home to a thriving Hawaiian fishing village and world-renowned black-sand beaches, Pele's merciless lava flows covered this town between 1989-1991, and barely anything was spared. **Verna's,** (☎965-8234), however, survived. This fast-food drive-in now has an excuse to be as pricey as it wants, but when that *pahoehoe* starts heating up, the $4.55 milkshakes are worth every penny.

STAR OF THE SEA PAINTED CHURCH. Spared by the flow that wiped out Kalapana, the church was hauled from Kalapana in 1996 to its current resting place along Rte. 130. In the middle of the 20th century, Father Evarist taught himself to paint to communicate the gospel to his congregation. The result is a gorgeous set of biblical frescoes that adorn the interior if this lime green church. The church, constantly battling financial hardship, no longer conducts services, but it occasionally hosts weddings and other ceremonies on the grounds. *(On Hwy. 130 just north of its intersection with Hwy. 137, near mi. marker 20. Open daily 9am-4pm.)*

HILO

Kona and Hilo (pop. 40,759) may be the only two cities on the Big Island, but they are worlds apart. Kona is a tourist magnet, and Hilo is the opposite pole: a

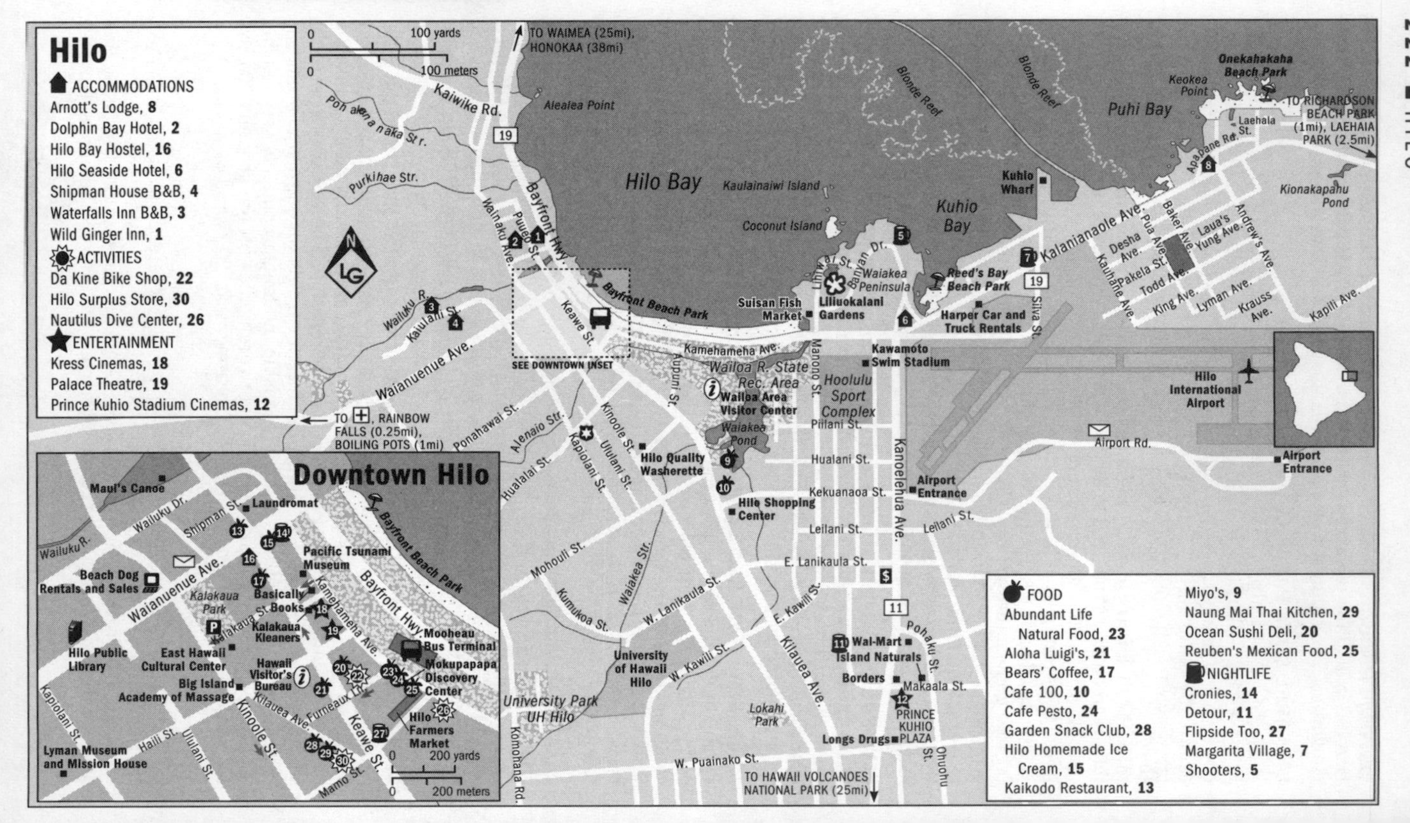
Hilo
ACCOMMODATIONS
Arnott's Lodge, 8
Dolphin Bay Hotel, 2
Hilo Bay Hostel, 16
Hilo Seaside Hotel, 6
Shipman House B&B, 4
Waterfalls Inn B&B, 3
Wild Ginger Inn, 1
ACTIVITIES
Da Kine Bike Shop, 22
Hilo Surplus Store, 30
Nautilus Dive Center, 26
ENTERTAINMENT
Kress Cinemas, 18
Palace Theatre, 19
Prince Kuhio Stadium Cinemas, 12
FOOD
Abundant Life Natural Food, 23
Aloha Luigi's, 21
Bears' Coffee, 17
Cafe 100, 10
Cafe Pesto, 24
Garden Snack Club, 28
Hilo Homemade Ice Cream, 15
Kaikodo Restaurant, 13
Miyo's, 9
Naung Mai Thai Kitchen, 29
Ocean Sushi Deli, 20
Reuben's Mexican Food, 25
NIGHTLIFE
Cronies, 14
Detour, 11
Flipside Too, 27
Margarita Village, 7
Shooters, 5
TO WAIMEA (25mi), HONOKAA (38mi)
TO RICHARDSON BEACH PARK (1mi), LAEHAIA PARK (2.5mi)
TO RAINBOW FALLS (0.25mi), BOILING POTS (1mi)
TO HAWAII VOLCANOES NATIONAL PARK (25mi)
SEE DOWNTOWN INSET
Hilo Bay
Kuhio Bay
Puhi Bay
Hilo International Airport
Downtown Hilo
Bayfront Beach Park

laid-back town that sees comparatively little outside traffic. Due to driving ocean winds, Hilo's beaches pale in comparison with those on the leeward coast. However, the area makes up for its dearth of sand and swimming with a sprawling rainforest and opportunities for adventure. Hilo offers endless road and mountain biking trails, good summer surfing, easy access to Saddle Road, and captivating natural sights. The charming streets of Hilo's old-fashioned downtown also offer a glimpse into the city's turbulent past. Devastated by tsunamis in 1946 and 1960, the city remembers the natural disasters through park memorials and the Pacific Tsunami Museum. This city is a breath of fresh air, clear from the tourism that clogs up the Kona side of the island. Whether leisurely strolling through downtown or boldly leaping into the lush green outskirts, a trip to Hilo will undoubtedly prove a lesson in the aloha spirit of Hawaiian life.

TRANSPORTATION

INTERCITY TRANSPORTATION

Bus: Hilo is the hub of the **Hele-On Bus** (☎961-8744; www.co.hawaii.hi.us for schedules); it is easier to get around the island from here than from anywhere else. Buses depart from the green-roofed **Mooheau Bus Terminal,** at the corner of Mamo St. and Kamehameha Ave. Open M-F 8:30am-4:30pm. The office, which employs a very helpful staff, is a light in the dark of an utterly confusing bus system. Every Hele-On bus is free, but the schedules are hard to follow. Still, going from Hilo to the major sights is entirely feasible and economical with the Hele-On. Hele-On runs to: **Kailua-Kona** (3¼hr., M-Sa 1:10pm) via **Honokaa** (1½hr.); **Waimea** (2¼hr.); **Kau** (2¼hr.) via **Hawaii Volcanoes National Park** (1hr., 2:40pm); **Pahala** (1¾hr.); **Naalehu/Waiohinu** (2¼hr.); **Ocean View** (2½hr.); **Pahoa** (1hr., M-F 5 times a day). See **Interisland Transportation,** p. 179, for more information on transportation and the Hilo International Airport.

LOCAL TRANSPORTATION

Bus: Hele-On (☎961-8744) also runs an intra-Hilo bus system that makes stops throughout town, including Banyan Dr., Prince Kuhio Plaza, Hilo Library, and Hilo Medical Center via Mooheau Bus Terminal (M-F 7:05am-4:30pm).

Taxis: A-1 Bob's Taxi (☎959-4800 or 963-5470) serves Hilo, Puna, Volcano, and Hamakua. **Hilo Harry's** (☎935-7091), based in Hilo, covers most of the island. Both operate approximately 5am-10pm. **Shaka Taxi** (☎987-1111) has 24hr. service and 6-person vans. All taxis charge $3 initially, then $2.40 per additional mi.

Car Rental: All national chains have offices at the airport (☎934-5840), on Airport Access Rd., off Rte. 11 about ½ mi. south of the intersection of Rte. 11 and Rte. 19. **Alamo** (☎961-3343). 21+. Under-25 surcharge $25 per day. **Budget** (☎935-6878, ext. 25 or 26). 21+. Under-25 surcharge $25 per day. Both open daily 6am-8:30pm. **Harper Car and Truck Rentals of Hawaii,** 456 Kalanianaole Ave. (☎969-1478), rents 4WD vehicles and economy cars. Unlike other companies, it has few travel restrictions. 25+. Open M-Th 6:30am-5pm, F-Su 6:30am-6pm. The **Enterprise** (☎331-2509) in Kona (p. 182) has very low rates; call before reserving elsewhere.

Bike Rental: Da Kine Bike Shop, 12 Furneaux Ln. (☎934-9861), off Kamehameha Ave. Run by a group of cycling enthusiasts, Da Kine is at the center of the Big Island's cycling scene. The community of riders is very welcoming; newcomers may find themselves invited on biking excursions around the island. Although they don't technically rent their bikes, their "sell and buy back" program ends up around $10-20 per day. Open M-Sa noon-6pm. D/MC/V.

ORIENTATION

Hilo lies on the Big Island's east coast, at the intersection of **Route 19 (Bayfront Highway),** from the Hamakua Coast and Waimea, and **Route 11,** from Hawaii Volcanoes National Park. Kailua-Kona is 87 mi. away, across Saddle Rd. Rte. 19 and **Kamehameha Avenue** run parallel to each other next to Hilo Bay, and Kamehameha serves as downtown's de facto Main St. Farther back from the water, **Kilauea Avenue** (which turns into downtown's Keawe St.) and **Kinoole Avenue** are the main arteries that run roughly parallel to the bay. **Waianuenue Avenue** is the major cross street and becomes Kaumana Dr., and then Saddle Rd. Rte. 11 **(Kanoelehua Avenue),** southeast of downtown, goes from the oceanfront to the airport.

PRACTICAL INFORMATION

TOURIST AND FINANCIAL SERVICES

Tourist Information: The Hawaii Visitor's Bureau, 250 Keawe St. (☎961-5797 or 800-648-2441; www.bigisland.org), at the corner of Keawe and Haili St., is primarily a marketing agency for the island but provides a decent map and helpful directions. Open M-F 8am-4:30pm. The **Mooheau Bus Terminal** (p. 223) also doubles as a Visitors Center.

Banks: Visitors should have no problem finding a bank in Hilo. **Bank of Hawaii** and **First Hawaiian Bank** have multiple locations, most with **24hr. ATMs.**

LOCAL SERVICES

Bookstores: Otherwise known as "The Map Shop," **Basically Books,** 160 Kamehameha Ave. (☎961-0144), on the waterfront, stocks the reliable Nell's Maps and shelves of Hawaiiana. Open M-Sa 9am-5pm, Su 10am-4pm.

Library: Hilo Public Library, 300 Waianuenue Ave. (☎933-8888), is blessed with a dynamic and welcoming staff. Centered around a grassy courtyard, a good half of this library is open-air. High-speed **Internet access** on 6 computers is available with a 3-month visitor's card ($10). Open Tu-W 11am-7pm, Th and Sa 9am-5pm, F 10am-5pm.

Laundromats: Hole-in-the-wall and unnamed, Hilo's cheapest laundromat is around the corner from Hilo Bay Hostel, at the intersection of Keawe and Shipman St. Wash $1, magma-temperature dry $0.25 per 5min. Open daily 4am-11pm. Last wash 10pm. Hilo Quality Washerette, 210 Hoku St. (☎961-6490), near the corner of Kinoole, behind 7-Eleven. Wash $1.50-4, dry $0.25 per 5min. Open daily 6am-10pm. Last wash 8:45pm.

Swimming Pool: 799 Piilani St. (☎961-8698), in Hoolulu Sports Complex. Facing the waterfront in downtown Hilo, take Kamehameha Ave. south toward Volcano-bound Rte. 11 and turn right on the street before Kanoelehua St. Olympic-size pool open to public daily, but hours are subject to lifeguard availability. Three designated public swim sessions daily, 9-10:45am, 1:30-3:45pm, and 6-7:10pm.

Equipment Rental: Hilo Surplus Store, 148 Mamo St. (☎935-6398). Much of the equipment here is military surplus, and another large portion is second-hand. Open M-Sa 8am-5pm. AmEx/D/MC/V. Scuba divers should drop by **Nautilus Dive Center,** 382 Kamehameha Ave. (☎966-8773), across from the bus terminal, next to the farmers' market. Instruction, certification, and rentals. Open M-Sa 9am-4pm.

Weather Conditions: ☎935-8555. The Internet-connected touch screen outside of Mokupapapa Discovery Center, on Kamehameha Ave. near the farmers' market, next to Cafe Pesto, also provides detailed weather and surf conditions. 24hr.

EMERGENCY AND COMMUNICATIONS

Police: Hilo Police Station, 349 Kapiolani St. (☎935-3311), at the corner of Kapiolani Ave. and Hualalai St.

Rape Crisis Hotline: ☎935-0677. 24hr.

Pharmacy: 111 E. Puainako St. (☎959-5881), in Prince Kuhio Plaza, next to Safeway. Open M-F 8am-10pm, Sa-Su 8am-9pm.

Medical Services: Hilo Medical Center, 1190 Waianuenue Ave. (☎974-4700). 24hr. emergency room.

Internet Access: When the library is closed, try **Beach Dog Computer Services,** 62 Kinoole St. (☎961-5207), at the corner of Kinoole and Waianuenue. $2.50 for first 20 min, $0.13 per min. thereafter; $8 per hr. **Hilo Bay Hostel** (☎933-2771) also has 4 Internet terminals for $5 per hr.

Post Offices: Hilo Main Post Office, 1299 Kekuanaoa St. (☎800-275-8777), on the road to the airport. Open M-F 8am-4:30pm, Sa 8:30am-12:30pm. **Downtown Hilo,** 154 Waianuenue Ave. Open M-F 8am-4pm, Sa 12:30-2pm.

Postal Code: 96720 (Main Post Office); 96721 (Downtown Hilo).

ACCOMMODATIONS

Hilo Bay Hostel, 101 Waianuenue Ave. (☎933-2771; www.hawaiihostel.net), on the corner by Keawe St. This is a clean, airy, well-run hostel in a perfect downtown location. Crisp cotton linens provided. Well-kept kitchen available until 9:45pm. High-speed Internet access $3 per 30min., $5 per hr. Refundable $10 key deposit. Check-out 11am. Quiet hours after 10pm. Dorms $20; single with shared bath $42; double with shared bath $54; 2 double beds (up to 4) with private bath $65. MC/V. ❶

Dolphin Bay Hotel, 333 Iliahi St. (☎935-1466; www.dolphinbayhotel.com). Take Keawe St. over the Wailuku River north of town and make the 2nd left onto Iliahi. A short walk from downtown, this meticulously maintained hotel is one of the best values in Hilo. All 18 large rooms have a full kitchen and cable TV; some have their own lanai. Local coffee, fresh papaya, and bananas are available in the lobby, along with warm cinnamon rolls shipped from a local bakery. Check-out 11am. Reservations recommended. Doubles for 4 $79-89; suites for 6 $109-129; each additional guest $10. MC/V. ❸

Arnott's Lodge, 98 Apapane Rd. (☎969-7097; www.arnottslodge.com). From the end of Rte. 11 by the Hilo waterfront, turn right onto Kalanianaole St. and continue for over 1 mi. until the left on Apapane Rd. This well-run hostel has plenty of camping space, dorm beds, and private rooms. Internet access and full laundry and kitchen facilities. Also rents bicycles, snorkeling equipment, and runs tours to Volcanoes National Park, Mauna Kea, and Hamakua Coast (guests $50-60, non-guests $75-90). A lot of info on **short-term work** available in the area. Check-out 10am. Camping $10 per person; bunks $20; singles with shared bath $47; doubles $57, with bath $70; 2-bedroom suite with kitchen for 6 $130. AmEx/D/MC/V. ❶

Waterfalls Inn, 240 Kaiulani St., (☎969-3407; www.waterfallsinn.com). In the same spirit of the Shipman House down the road, this wonderful old house, built at the end of the Victorian period, is aware of its tropical surroundings, with windows that reach from the floor to the roof, and a breakfast nook with a 270° view of the lush outdoors. Two-person whirlpool tub. Rooms $140-210. AmEx/D/MC/V. ❹

Hilo Seaside Hotel, 126 Banyan Dr. (☎935-0821; www.hiloseasidehotel.com), near the intersection with Kalanianaole Ave. Overlooking a quiet sliver of Hilo Bay, this low-key hotel is a no-frills place for a night. Clean and simple rooms with A/C, ceiling fans,

IN THE MARKET FOR A GOOD TIME?

For a small city that often seems to have its eyelids half-closed and a similarly sleepy cloud cover, a lively farmers' market is an invigorating alarm clock. On Wednesday and Saturday mornings (technically the market is open daily, but the people-watching is best on W and Sa), the town jumps into a hidden fifth gear.

The farmers' market was traditionally a showcase venue for all of the sugar plantations that dotted the eastern coast of the Big Island. Today, over 100 local farmers and crafters have set up shop to cater cheap fruits, produce, clothing, and B movies to locals and tourists alike. Baked goods have taken over the western end, while to the south, clothing and crafts have sunk their roots. Fruits, vegetables, and summer wraps (spring rolls, not fried) are ubiquitous throughout. To the far southern end, alternative and somewhat unusual shops stake claims.

Most of all, however, the farmers' market has become a social epicenter—it's the Hilo scene. Some residents have begun shopping there on the off-days, just to save a half-hour of gab. The "stop and chat" is the foundation of the Hilo farmers' market, and what results is a fast-paced marketplace that hardly resembles the slow creep of normal Hilo life. The Hilo farmers' market is a double shot of espresso for this drowsy town—it's a real trip.

refrigerators, lanais, and cable TV. Swimming pool. An attached (but unaffiliated) restaurant, **Coconut Grill,** serves up seafood and steak dinners just beyond the hotel lobby. Check-in 3pm. Check-out noon. Rooms $78-98. AmEx/D/MC/V. ❸

Wild Ginger Inn, 100 Puueo St. (☎935-5556; www.wildgingerinn.com). From downtown Hilo, take Keawe St. over the river; the street becomes Puueo St. It's a large beige building with sea green trim. "Bamboo" doubles have hardwood floors and private bath. Quaint tropical garden and outdoor barbecue facility. 2 hammocks hang in the lobby. Fruit and bread breakfast included (8-10am). All rooms have a fridge and TV. Self-service laundry: wash $1.25, dry $1. No children under 9 or visitors at night allowed. Check-in 3pm. Check-out 11am. Rooms $59-105. Monthly rates including utilities available: $630 single, $700 double. MC/V. ❷

Shipman House Bed and Breakfast, 131 Kaiulani St. (☎934-8002; www.hilo-hawaii.com). From Rte. 19, take Waianuenue Ave. 5 blocks, turn right on Kaiulani St., and cross over the rumbling bridge. Victorian-style house with spacious rooms, porches, lofty ceilings, and classy ambience. All with private bath: 1 with claw-foot tub and 1 with magnificent ocean view. Robes and kimonos provided. Continental breakfast included. Check-in 3-6pm. Check-out 10am. Reservations recommended. Doubles $205-225; each additional guest $25. AmEx/MC/V. ❺

FOOD

The colorful **Hilo farmers' market,** on Mamo St. between Kamehameha and Kilauea, runs all day, every day. **Island Naturals,** 303 Makaala St., in the Waiakea Center, is Hilo's best natural food store. Their gourmet takeout buffet has a **vegetarian lasagna** that rivals any Italian grandmother's. (☎935-5533. Hot dish and salad buffet with vegan options. $7 per lb. Open M-Sa 8am-8pm, Su 9am-7pm. AmEx/D/MC/V.) **Suisan Retail Market,** 85 Lihiwai St., near the intersection of Lihiwai and Banyan Dr., has fresh fish at market prices. (☎935-9349. Bidding starts M-F 7:30am. Store open M-F 8am-5pm, Sa 8am-4pm. D/MC/V.)

Miyo's, 400 Hualani St. (☎935-2273), #19A2, in Waiakea Village. A peaceful view over the Waiakea Pond gives this homestyle Japanese restaurant an unparalleled natural ambiance. The food is equally exquisite, plentiful, and surprisingly affordable. Sesame chicken and sashimi served over a bed of rice and garden greens, with a bowl of miso on the side, $9.50. Donburi and noodles range $5-9. Live music W nights. Open M-Sa 11am-2pm and 5:30-8:30pm. MC/V. ❶

Kaikodo Restaurant, 60 Keawe St. (☎961-2558), across from the Hilo Bay Hostel at the corner of Keawe and Wainuenue Ave. NYC-born owners have imported a cosmopolitan flair to downtown Hilo. Live jazz frequently Sa-Su nights. Affordable appetizers: seared tofu with ginger and seaweed salad $5. Miso-glazed seared salmon $21. Open daily 5:30-9pm; W and F nights bar open late with live DJ. AmEx/MC/V. ❹

Bears' Coffee, 106 Keawe St. (☎935-0708), between Waianuenue and Kalakaua, just around the corner from Hilo Bay Hostel. Despite the flurry of changing owners, locals convene daily for early morning conversation over Big Island coffee ($1.50-3) and sizeable breakfasts at low prices. Waffles $3.50; eggs $3-4; and granola, fruit, and yogurt $5. Sandwiches $4.25-5. Open M-Sa 7am-5pm, Su 8am-noon. Cash only. ❶

Aloha Luigi, 264 Keawe St. (☎934-9112), a two story pastel-painted joint, bright and unmistakable. Luigi insists it's an Italian specialty restaurant, but the Mexican fare is the star of the menu. The famous huevos rancheros—featuring Luigi's hand-made corn tortillas—are only $6.95. Slice of pizza $2.50. Open Tu 9am-3pm, W-Th and Sa 9am-7pm, F 9am-7:30pm. MC/V. ❶

Naung Mai Thai Kitchen, 86 Kilauea Ave. (☎934-7540), near the corner of Kilauea and Mamo St., behind Garden Exchange. Everything at this authentic Thai restaurant is done with unassuming grace, from the exquisite food to the table arrangement. Spring rolls $7-8. Curries $10-12. BYOB; corking fee $1 per glass. Lunch M-F 11am-2pm. Dinner M-Th 5-8:30pm, F-Sa 5-9pm. MC/V. ❸

Garden Snack Club, 80 Kilauea Ave. (☎933-9664), right next door to Nuang Mai Thai Kitchen. A very friendly staff and hip local crowd gather for a healthy dinner. Chef and owner Tina cooks up fresh and tasty Thai-Hawaiian fusion; try the black bean fish ($15), or the ahi salad ($9). Sandwiches $5-7. Open Tu-Sa 11am-9:30pm. MC/V. ❷

Abundant Life Natural Foods and Cafe, 292 Kamehameha Ave. (☎935-7411). This bayfront market and cafe makes both a great morning coffee spot and a late lunch sandwich stop. Mixed plate combos $6-8, salads and sandwiches $4-7, bagels $3, smoothies $4. Check out the adjacent market for some alternative foods shopping. Open M-Tu and Th 8:30am-7pm, W and Sa 7am-7pm, Su 10am-5pm; cafe closes at 5:30pm. MC/V. ❶

Island Bake Shop, (☎934-8227) Mamo St., beyond the farmers' market. Get coffee ($1) and delicious baked goods, like their famous bran muffins ($1). Open M-Sa 5am-7pm. Cash only. ❶

Ocean Sushi Deli, 239 Keawe St. (☎961-6625), near the corner of Haili St. A bustling business that rolls up lunch for most of downtown Hilo. The staff is happy to assist novices navigate the giant selection. *Nigiri* $2.50-4. *Hosomaki* and *temaki* $1.40-4.50. Specialty rolls $5-7. BYOB. Open M-Sa 10am-2pm and 5-9pm. AmEx/MC/V. ❶

Cafe Pesto, 308 Kamehameha Ave. (☎969-6640), near the corner of Kamehameha Ave. and Mamo St. Enormous bayfront windows, checkerboard floor, high ceilings, and candlelight create a unique ambience. The designer thin-crust pizzas ($9-18) are top-notch. Lunch sandwiches $9-11. Organic salads $5-11. Dinner pasta $11-12. Open M-Th and Su 11am-9pm, F-Sa 11am-10pm. AmEx/D/MC/V. ❸

Reuben's Mexican Food, 336 Kamehameha Ave. (☎961-2552). Reuben's Mexican flavor is spot on, and the food is delicious. Combo plates with beans and rice go for $9.50-15; two chile rellenos $10.50. Perhaps the best plate is a simple fish taco ($5). Open M-F 11am-9pm, Sa noon-9pm. AmEx/D/MC/V. ❶

Cafe 100, 969 Kilauea Ave. (☎935-8683), near the corner of Kekuanaoa St. and Kilauea. Birthplace of the *loco moco,* this is fast food, Hawaiian-style. Most meals, like the Kilauea Loco (homestyle chili, sausage, Spam, 2 eggs, rice, potato salad) are right around $5; all items under $7. Open M-Th and Sa 6:45am-8:30pm, F 6:45am-9pm; phone order 10:30am-2pm. Cash only. ❶

Hilo Homemade Ice Cream, 41 Wainuenue St. (☎933-1520), at Keawe St., in a nook downhill from the Hilo Bay Hostel. In addition to traditional flavors, they scoop ginger, banana macadamia nut fudge, and *poi* and cream. Kona mocha-almond hot fudge sundae $4. Single scoop $2; double $3.25. Open M-F 10:30am-7:30pm, Sa noon-6pm, Su noon-4pm. Cash only. ❶

BEACHES

Hilo is not known for its beaches, in part because it's dominated by rocky coastline. The best places to go are east of downtown Hilo along Kalanianaole Ave. **Onekahakaha Beach Park,** a little less than 2 mi. northeast of the intersection of Rte. 11 and Kalanianaole Ave., has a sandy-floored swimming pool and a lawn for the perfect picnic, with basic facilities. A bit of black sand masquerading as beach, **Richardson Ocean Park,** at the end of Kalanianaole Ave., about 4 mi. east of Hilo, has picnic tables, rest rooms, showers, and lifeguards on duty 8am-4:30pm. The protected cove's calm water sees plenty of snorkelers, and the dozens of natural pools make for a scenic sunset. To hit what little surf there is, head to **Honolii Beach,** north of Hilo, just before the Honolii Bridge. Surfers pack in here before and after work, but the water is somewhat cold and murky. Families sometimes head to **Reed's Bay,** where the water is calm and perfect for small swimmers.

SIGHTS

MERRIE MONARCH FESTIVAL. When **King David Kalakaua** ascended the throne in 1883 following half a century of missionary influence, he took great measures to reassert Hawaiian culture. Kalakaua (also known as the **Merrie Monarch** for his support of dance and music) brought hula back into the public sphere by including it in his coronation ceremony. Hilo celebrates the reign of this last Hawaiian king 160 years later, the week after Easter. The celebration, which includes a giant parade and other festivities, culminates in a hula competition among dancers from all the islands of the Pacific. Take a look at any of the photo books by Kim Taylor Reece; nearly half of his shots are from Hilo's Merrie Monarch Festival. Tickets go on sale on New Year's Day and sell out quickly. *(For tickets, call the Hawaii Naniloa Resort at ☎935-9168.)*

IMILOA ASTRONOMY CENTER OF HAWAII. This recent addition to Hilo museum community prides itself on bridging the gap between Hawaiian history and state-of-the-art astronomical technology. The mind-blowing planetarium shows screen three times a day (11am, 1, and 2:30pm), while the rest of the building is a comprehensive tour through the origins, navigation, and celestial underpinnings of ancient Hawaiian culture. This veritable journey through time is child-friendly and bilingual (Hawaiian and English). Don't miss the "Sky Tonight" show ($5) on the last Saturday of every month. *(600 Imiloa Pl. at the UH Hilo Science and Technology Park. On the corner of Komohana and Puainako St., at the back of the UH Campus. ☎969-9700; www.imiloahawaii.org. $14.50, children ages 4-12 $7.50.)*

LYMAN MUSEUM AND MISSION HOUSE. The Lyman Mission House, built in 1839, is the oldest frame building on the Big Island and has been restored to represent the lifestyle of missionaries to Hawaii during the mid 19th century. A guided tour takes you through the home, which includes many original furnishings, tools, and household items. Next door is the Lyman Museum, itself a fascinating inquiry into Hawaiian history. Galleries explore topics like the formation of the islands, Hawaiian culture from the arrival of the first Polynesian settlers through the waves of international immigrants, and the astronomical observations on the summit of Mauna Kea. It also features rotating exhibits of modern Hawaiian art. *(276 Haili St. ☎935-5021; www.lymanhouse.org. 30min. guided tours of Mission House 10am-3pm on the hr. Open M-Sa 9:30am-4:30pm. $10, seniors $8, students $3, family rate $21.)*

PACIFIC TSUNAMI MUSEUM. The museum's diagrams that explain tsunamis become all the more profound alongside detailed chronicles of Hilo's history, a city ravaged twice by tsunamis, once in 1946 and again in 1960. Knowledgeable tour guides provide insightful introductions, and exhibits shed light on tsunamis recorded around the world. One of the most compelling sections of the museum is a video entitled "Raging Sea." *(130 Kamehameha Ave., at the corner of Kalakaua St. ☎935-0926; www.tsunami.org. Open M-Sa 9am-4pm. $7.)*

PANAEWA RAINFOREST ZOO. Panaewa is the only tropical rainforest zoo in the US. Over 75 animal species are kept here, including a white Bengal tiger, water buffalo, Aldabra tortoise, and pygmy hippo. Families can find plenty of shade (and nice picnic spots) under the many different palm trees, and the petting zoo (Sa 1:30-2:30pm) will certainly delight young children. *(A few mi. south of Hilo on Mamaki St., off Rte. 11. From Hilo, turn right onto Mamaki St., between mi. markers 4 and 5. The zoo is about ¾ mi. down. ☎959-9233; www.hilozoo.com. Open daily 9am-4pm. Free.)*

KALAKAUA PARK. A statue of Hawaii's Merrie Monarch, David Kalakaua, sits beneath the park's immense Banyan tree with a hula drum and taro root leaf in hand. The park, a splendid bit of green in the midst of sidewalks and streets, makes a good resting place on a tour of Hilo. In the summer, the Hilo Community Players produce their annual Shakespeare in the Park rendition here. *(In downtown Hilo at the corner of Kinoole St. and Waianuenue Ave.)*

EAST HAWAII CULTURAL CENTER. Bordering one edge of Kalakaua Park is the East Hawaii Cultural Center, which promotes visual and performance art on the Big Island through different forums. While they produce festivals in the arts year-round, their biggest production is the **Big Island Hawaiian Music Festival,** which happens in late July (tickets, $15). The building, the old Hilo police station and courthouse, is one of the city's most elegant, and it houses an art gallery where many local artists display their work. *(141 Kalakaua St, across from the park. ☎961-5711; www.ehcc.org. Open M-Sa 10am-4pm. Donations are appreciated.)*

RAINBOW FALLS. This powerful waterfall drops over a rock ledge to the river below. A swimming hole behind the falls contrasts starkly with the thunderous crashing water. To reach the hole, take the left-hand trail through the trees, passing to the right of the enormous Banyan tree. Restrooms available. *(From downtown, follow Waianuenue Ave. 2 mi. uphill; turn right onto Rainbow Dr. Look for the green sign.)*

BOILING POTS. Broken waterfalls cascade down a rocky ledge surrounded by a jungle at Boiling Pots, a scene so tropical you should stop just for the photo-op. Near Rainbow Falls, this is a lesser-known but equally worthwhile sight. Restrooms are available. *(From downtown, follow Waianuenue Ave. past the turnoff for Rainbow Falls; turn right onto Peepee Falls Dr. Look for the green sign. Park open daily 7am-6:30pm.)*

KAUMANA CAVES. Right off Saddle Rd., Kaumana Caves County Park is a quick subterranean diversion. The park contains a series of caves with fascinating rock formations and hanging tree roots. Restrooms and pavilions at the rest stop. Appropriate footwear and a flashlight needed for exploration. *(When coming from Hilo, between mi. markers 4 and 5 on the right-hand side of Saddle Rd.)*

NIGHTLIFE AND ENTERTAINMENT

Despite being the largest city on the island *and* a college town, Hilo's nightlife is fairly unremarkable. There are, however, plenty of movie showings, from artsy and foreign shows at **Palace Theatre** to $1 Hollywood flicks at **Kress Cinemas.** If you're up for more adventure, take Saddle Rd. (p. 230) up to Mauna Kea for a free nightly stargazing session.

BARS

Club Kaikodo, 60 Keawe St. (☎961-2558). This hip Manhattan-style restaurant opens up as a club on W and F nights. A live DJ spins eclectic tunes in the back while the bar serves pricey ($10) cocktails. Open W and F 9pm-2am. MC/V.

Detour, 124 Makaala St. (☎920-8687). This warehouse-turned-sports-bar is brand new, equipped with lush leather couches and multiple plasma-screen TVs. Weekend nights fill up fast. Heavy appetizers are often free with drinks, and *pupus* are served until around 10pm. Open M-F 2pm-2am, Sa-Su noon-2am. MC/V.

Margarita Village, 11 Silva St. (☎961-3290), just east of downtown Hilo, near the Port of Hilo. Drafts $2.50-3.50, and dozens of creative margaritas for $5.95. Open Tu-W and Su 11am-1:30am, M and Th-Sa 3pm-1:30am. MC/V.

Cronies, 11 Waianuenue Ave. (☎935-5158), on the corner of Kamehameha St. and Waianuenue Ave. 2 fluorescent-lit pool tables attract the most attention in this large bar, which also has electronic dart boards and a big-screen TV. Cronies is known for the best crab cakes ($8) and *sashimi* ($9) in town. Karaoke M-W and F-Sa 10:30pm-1:30am. Food served M-Sa 11am-11pm; bar open until 2am. AmEx/MC/V.

Shooters, 121 Banyan Dr. (☎969-7069). A boisterous crowd of all ages packs the tiny dance floor while a DJ spins (W-Sa after 10pm). Happy hour daily 3-7pm; domestic drafts $2.25, imports $3.25. W and Sa nights $1 beers. Variety of drink specials, themes vary by weeknight. 21+; Th 18+. Open M-W 3pm-2am, Th-Sa 3pm-3am.

Flipside Too, 94 Mamo St. (☎961-0057), just beyond the Hilo farmers' market, this is an authentic local watering hole at any time of day. Beers are cheap ($3), and there's plenty of pool or foosball to be played. Open M-F 10am-2am, Sa noon-2am. MC/V.

MOVIES

Kress Cinemas, 174 Kamehameha Ave. (☎935-6777), on the corner of Kamehameha and Kalakaua St. New Hollywood films for back-in-the-day prices. Reels arrive a few weeks after mainland release. Shows $1. Matinees before 6pm $0.50. Tu all day $0.50.

Palace Theatre, 38 Haili St. (☎934-7010, box office 934-7777), between Kamehameha Ave. and Keawe St. A relic from Hilo's glory days, the theater plays a single art-house (often foreign) film each week, hosts local and visiting musicians, and puts on live theater performances. Most film showings M-Tu and F-Sa 7:30pm, Su 2:30pm; sometimes Th 7:30pm. $6; children, students, and seniors $5. Palace also shows children's films F-Sa mornings 9-11am, $2.

Prince Kuhio Stadium Cinemas, 111 E. Puainako St. (☎959-4595; www.wallacetheaters.com), in Prince Kuhio Plaza. 1st-run Hollywood films. $8.25, seniors and ages 3-11 $5.25. Matinees M-F before 6pm, Sa-Su before 3:30pm $5.50.

SADDLE ROAD

Saddle Rd. (Rte. 200) climbs up and down a topographic cross-section of Hawaii. The only major route through the middle of the Big Island, Saddle Rd. starts on the Kona coast and rolls across the grasslands of Parker Ranch before cutting between the two highest points on the Big Island—Mauna Kea to the north and Mauna Loa to the south. As the road comes down from the mountains and into Hilo, the foliage becomes more dense and luxuriantly green from the moisture in the air on the windward side.

POTHOLES AND PITFALLS. From Kona to Hilo, saddle up and keep your eyes open, because Saddle Rd. is as wild as it is captivating. On the Kona side, the road is decrepit and crumbling; not only does it see heavy action from military vehicles making the trip between Pohakuloa Military Training Area and Kawaihae Harbor, but the Kona side also has much less funding to spend on maintaining its roads. It's no surprise then, that as you head toward Hilo, the road improves drastically. Almost all rental car companies, except for local Harper Car and Truck Rentals (p. 223), forbid you from driving on it. In reality, the road is absolutely fine between Hilo and the Mauna Kea Access Rd., around mi. marker 28. After this point, only the center lane is well-maintained and, as a result, cars tend to drive (sometimes speeding) down the middle. Stay alert over blind hills and sightless turns on the Kona side of the road–it's seen its fair share of head-on collisions. Don't forget to fill up your tank, your water bottles, and throw on a sweater; except for the Mauna Kea Observatory Visitors Center, there are no places to stop for food, gas, or warmth along this road.

ORIENTATION

On the Kona side, **Saddle Road** leaves Rte. 190 about 6 mi. south of Waimea and 33 mi. northeast of Kailua-Kona. On the Hilo side, **Waianuenue Avenue** splits just above downtown Hilo, and one fork, **Kaumana Drive,** becomes Saddle Rd. in the foothills outside of town. Saddle Rd. runs 54 mi. from end to end.

From Hilo, the road climbs between Mauna Loa and Mauna Kea in a series of twists and turns that is made more difficult to navigate by the fog; it can get so thick that it's hard to see the road in front of you. Mi. marker 28 indicates an unmarked turnoff to the road up Mauna Loa, where you will find a weather observatory and sparse parking. Another unmarked road, the Mauna Kea Access Rd. (John A. Burns Way), near mi. marker 28, leads up Mauna Kea to the **Onizuka Center for International Astronomy.** A graded track continues from there onto the mountain's summit. Seven miles farther down Saddle Rd. is the **Mauna Kea State Recreation Area,** about 19 mi. from the intersection of Rte. 190 and Saddle Rd. From here the road descends into the Kona Coast.

MAUNA KEA

Towering 13,796 ft. above sea level, Mauna Kea, or "White Mountain," is notable less for its size than its world-class astronomical viewing conditions. The summit's dry, stable air and extremely dark sky have led 11 countries to set up telescopes on the mountain and drawn innumerable travelers to gaze and gape at the night sky.

The Onizuka Center for International Astronomy, 6 mi. up Mauna Kea Access Rd., from mi. marker 28 of Saddle Rd., teaches visitors about the advanced telescopes on the summit. The access road's nearly 3000 ft. ascent up Mauna Kea leads to more than just stargazing; it also has vistas of the saddle between Mauna Loa and Mauna Kea's cinder cones

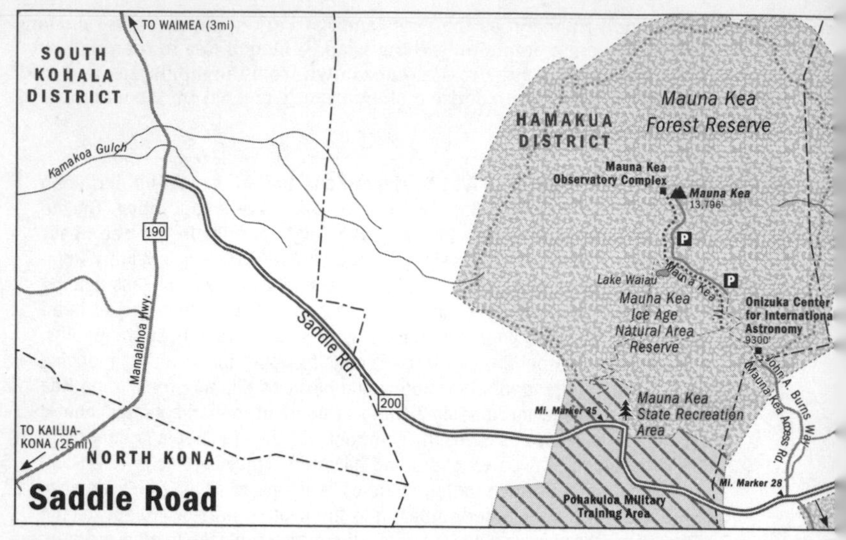

Saddle Road

SIGHTS

MAUNA KEA STATE RECREATION AREA. Near mi. marker 35, 7 mi. west of the Mauna Kea summit road and 25 mi. southeast of Waimea, this simple park is a good base for an exploration of Saddle Rd. The park has restrooms, picnic tables, a pay phone, and a short hike with good views of Mauna Kea, Hulalai, and Mauna Loa. There are also four **cabins** for rent with kitchens and non-drinking water but no bathrooms or showers. *(To reserve a cabin, call the Department of Land and Natural Resources, State Parks Division, 75 Apuni St. ☎974-6200. $35 per night.).*

WATCH FOR INVISIBLE COWS. Free roaming cattle are a hazard that is taken quite seriously on Mauna Kea Access Rd. Dark cattle hide so well under the cover of the nightfall that they're almost impossible to see. Signs warn drivers to "Watch For The Invisible Cows." Be careful. Those cows are out there.

ONIZUKA CENTER FOR INTERNATIONAL ASTRONOMY. Perched on the slope of Mauna Kea at 9200 ft., the center for the summit telescopes is an invaluable resource. Named after Ellison Onizuka, an astronaut from the Big Island who died in the 1986 *Challenger* explosion, the center's exhibits detail the form and function of the 13 summit telescopes, used by 11 countries. The powerful Keck and Subaru Telescopes on the summit boast enormous dual 10m and 8m (the world's largest single piece optical telescope) mirror diameters, respectively, and the Onizuka Center offers a 4 in. refractor and a pair of 14 in. and 16 in. reflective amateur telescopes for free public viewing.

The center also observes the night sky in nightly **stargazing** sessions. The program begins with an orientation video, followed by a discussion of Mauna Kea and astronomy in general. Visitors are able to see a variety of stellar phenomena, including stars in their many stages of life (from red giants to white dwarfs), globular clusters, binary stars, planets, constellations, and perhaps most fascinating, entire distant galaxies. It is essential to dress warmly; temperatures drop to 40-50°F during the summer and 25-50°F during the winter.

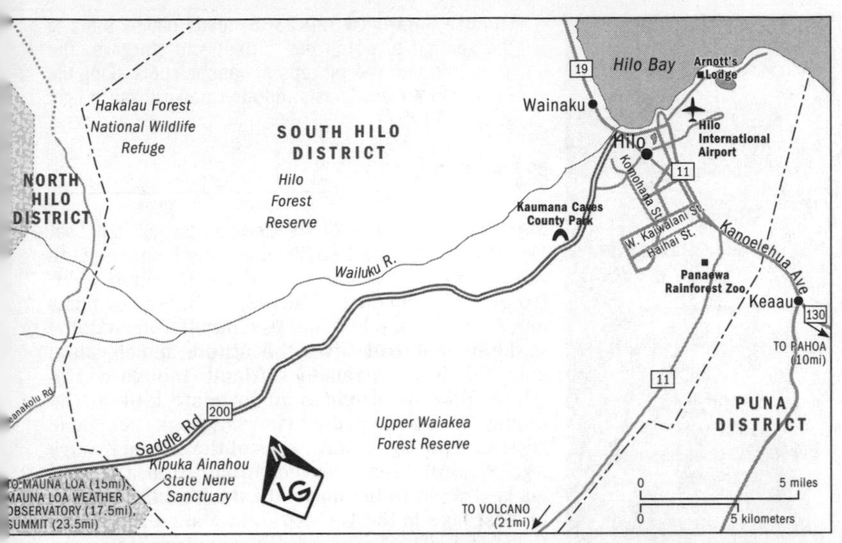

If you have your own 4WD vehicle, consider going on one of the center's weekend **summit tours.** The 4hr. tour includes an orientation video, acclimatization period, caravan to the summit, overview of all the telescopes, and a guided visit to one or two of them. *(From Saddle Rd., turn onto the Mauna Kea Access Rd. at mi. marker 28. The center is 6 mi. up the road. ☎961-2180; www.ifa.hawaii.edu. Open daily 9am-10pm. Coffee, hot chocolate, tea, and snacks available; $1 donation requested for beverages. Stargazing daily 6-10pm. Free. Summit tours Sa-Su 1-5pm. Free. Children under 16 and pregnant women not allowed on tours due to high-altitude health hazards. Scuba divers should be careful: going to the summit can produce the same effects as flying immediately after diving. Free.)*

The air on the summit has 60% of the oxygen available at sea level, causing many people to suffer altitude sickness. Symptoms include shortness of breath, dizziness, confusion, and fatigue. Pregnant women, children, individuals who are overweight or in poor health, and people with a history of heart or respiratory problems are advised not to make the trip.

DRIVING TO THE SUMMIT. If you have 4WD, you could also drive to the top yourself. Visitors are allowed on the summit only from sunrise to 30min. after sunset, as car headlights interfere with observations after dark. The road to the observatories is well maintained but unpaved until the last few miles, and its extremely steep grade makes 4WD a necessity. The drive from the Onizuka Center to the summit is 8½ mi. and should take about 30min. Once there, both the University of Hawaii telescope and the WM Keck Observatory have **Visitors Centers.** While the telescope's technological sophistication makes for an unrivaled view of space, the crystal clear night sky is spellbinding even to the naked eye.

ACTIVITIES

Arnott's Lodge, 98 Apapane Rd. (☎969-7097; www.arnottslodge.com), in Hilo. Trips from Hilo to Mauna Kea for sunsets and stargazing several times a week. Parkas and a stop at a grocery store provided. M, W, F departure time seasonally adjusted; trips usually last from 3 to 9 or 10pm. $60, nonguests $90.

Paradise Safaris (☎322-2366) leads nightly tours to the summit to watch the sunset and stargaze. The 7½hr. trip includes pickups at various spots along the Kona and Kohala Coasts, hooded parkas, and a light supper, $185.

HIKING

MAUNA KEA TRAIL. *(6½ mi. Elevation gain: 2250 ft. Challenging.)* The Mauna Kea Trail climbs from the Onizuka Center to the summit and takes around 4-5hr. to complete round-trip. The path is marked by posts and *ahus* (rock piles) and essentially runs parallel to the summit road. Given the altitude and elevation gain, this is an extremely difficult (though worthwhile) hike. It provides an intimate look at the mountain and compelling views. Among the unique sights are the eerie landscapes of the Mauna Kea Ice Age Natural Area Reserve. In addition, the trail leads straight to the magical **Lake Walau,** the third-highest lake in the US, set amid Mauna Kea's lava fields at 13,020 ft. The lake is considered to be the physical manifestation of the goddess Waiau and is therefore extremely sacred.

MAUNA LOA

East of the Mauna Kea turnoff, a serpentine road climbs the Mauna Loa volcano for 7 mi. to the **Mauna Loa Weather Observatory,** 11,000 ft. above sea level. The drive takes about 45min. and though the road is slowly crumbling, it is passable in any car. The observatory is purely scientific and there is no Visitors Center.

HIKING

OBSERVATORY TRAIL. *(6 mi. one way. Elevation gain: 1250 ft. Challenging.)* The paved road ends at the Mauna Loa Weather Observatory, which is the trailhead for a hike to the summit of Mauna Loa or the cabin on the opposite rim of Mokuaweoweo Caldera. There is nothing easy about this hike; a good portion of your time will surely be spent scrambling across the precariously loose rubble of *aa* (lava) fields in temperatures that consistently drop below freezing on the summit. Inclement weather is common here. While it is easy enough to follow the *ahu* (rock piles) up the mountain, this hike should not be done without a partner. Proper hiking gear and plenty of water are also essential; dehydration is a deadly process at high altitudes. However, for all the obstacles of the trail, the gap-

W. M. KECK TELESCOPES

Ever succesfully bend and distort a perfectly polished and extremely precise circle of glass with a diameter of 10 meters? It's nearly impossible, and hardly practical. But for the W.M. Keck Telescopes, a two-telescope array atop Mauna Kea, creativity trumped the physical limitations of the world in which we live.

University of California astronomer Dr. Jerry Nelson was the innovative scientist who dreamed up this seemingly ludicrous idea. Instead of using one single piece of reflective glass, Nelson used 36 different mirrors to act as one giant one. Amazingly, these 36 hexagonal shaped mirrors are deployed in a perfect hyperbolic shape adjusted in one-millionth-of-an-inch increments, twice a second, to counteract the movement of the telescope and the wind. If this technological marvel weren't enough, in recent years, adaptive optics adjustment mirrors have been installed on both Keck telescopes, that have the ability to change the mirrors' shape 670 times per second, adjusting for atmospheric distortions of incoming starlight and sharpening resolution of a factor of 10 to 20 times. Additionally, instead of crafting just one of these technological wonders, the W.M. Keck Foundation funded the construction of an array, two 10m telescopes spaced 85m apart, effectively creating a reflective telescope with a primary mirror diameter of 85m.

ing expanse of the Mauna Loa summit is a reward well worth the hardship suffered on the way up. For more information about hiking Mauna Loa, see **Hawaii Volcanoes National Park,** p. 203.

HAMAKUA COAST

The drive along Rte. 19 (Hawaii Belt Rd.) between Hilo and Waimea features some of the most spectacular scenery on the island. Waterfalls peek around each bend and brilliant blossoms dot the mountainside. Although Hamakua was once the sugarcane gold mine of the Big Island, not a single plantation remains today. Attempting to fill the void left by sugar's decline, the area has become actively engaged in historical preservation—the coast's official name is the Hilo-Hamakua Heritage Coast. From Hilo's historic downtown to the Hawaii Tropical Botanical Garden and Honokaa's early-1900s facades, a drive down the coast is a journey into the Hawaii of yesteryear. While much of what is preserved belongs to a past that cannot be reclaimed, the grandeur of the waterfalls and flora is timeless.

PEPEEKEO SCENIC DRIVE

The well-marked **Pepeekeo Scenic Drive** (also known as **Papaiko Rd.**) starts about 5 mi. north of Hilo. Watch for the blue scenic route sign leading right off Rte. 19. Before connecting up again with Rte. 19, the 4 mi. winding road stretches across narrow one-lane bridges, curls through lush rainforest, and negotiates steep twists over the crashing surf below.

About 1½ mi. in, the road leads to the **Hawaii Tropical Botanical Garden,** 27-717 Old Mamalahoa Hwy., overlooking Onomea Bay. Home to over 2500 species of tropical plant life from around the globe, the botanical gardens started as one couple's desire to cull the world's rarest plant species, often endangered, and allow them a space to grow in Hawaii. The garden slopes downhill from the old highway to the sea; a 1 mi. trail meanders through scenery rich with bromeliads, flowering orchids, and different types of ginger under Banyan and palm trees. The solar-powered aviary, new in 2006, is an impressive addition. The only drawbacks to this mesmerizing locale are the price and the mosquitoes; bring plenty of bug spray. (☎964-5233; www.hawaiigarden.com. Open daily 9am-4pm. $15, ages 6-16 $5, under 5 free. 1 yr. family pass $35.)

Even more riveting than watching the dome open and shift along its altitude-azimuth track as the sun sets over Mauna Kea, are the intensely precise measurements behind such movement. Although the weight of each piece of glass is 14.4 tons, it requires just 10 lb. of pressure to rotate the mirror; each one sits on a bed of oil lubricant a mere 50 nanometers thick. As for the entire structure, each telescope weighs in at a low 270 tons, frozen during the daytime with high-powered air conditioners to reduce the stress of gravity over time and increase the life-span of these super seeing structures.

Ultimately, these elaborate sets of measurements, precise ion polishing processes, and long trails of fiber optics cables combine to answer fundamental questions for all of humanity: who are we? Where did we come from? And, perhaps the most pressing: how much does the expansion rate of the universe vary over history, and where is its missing mass?

For more information about how you can get involved with this exciting research, contact the Institute for Astronomy. ☎956-8312; www.ifa.hawaii.edu. Additionally, the University of Hawaii at Manoa has one of the country's top-ranked graduate programs in astronomy. See their website, www.uhm.hawaii.edu, for information on applying to the program.

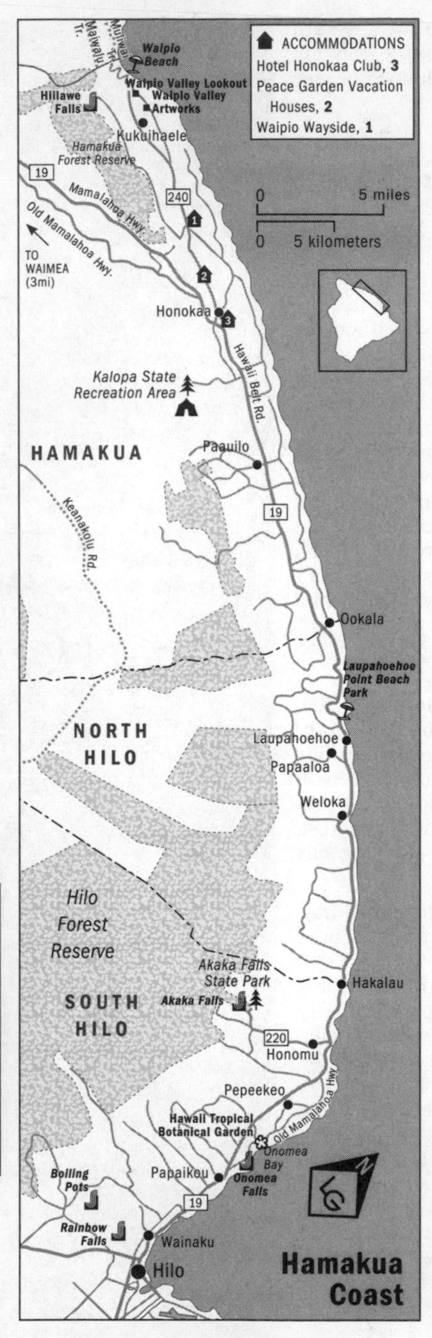

Before returning to the highway, the drive passes **What's Shakin' ❶**, 27-999 Mamalahoa Hwy., a stand that blends superior smoothies ($5.75). Their concoctions—with names like Papaya Paradise and Peanut Bruddah—use no added sugar or ice, only fresh fruit and juice, milk, and peanut butter. (☎964-3080. Open daily 10am-5pm. MC/V. Credit card min. $15.)

AKAKA FALLS STATE PARK

The lofty and delicate **Kahuna Falls** (400 ft.) and **Akaka Falls** (442 ft.) make Akaka Falls State Park a highlight of the Hamakua Coast. The tiny park is packed with delights, including the awe-inspiring falls and a well-kept walking path. The half-mile paved loop begins at the parking lot and travels between the two falls, and then turns back for a short trek through a vibrant rainforest filled with orchids, redhead ginger, mossy Banyan trees, gigantic ferns, and bamboo groves. While the trail never gets close enough to Kahuna for more than a glimpse of the long free-falling water, at Akaka Falls visitors can look down a couple hundred feet to where the water splashes into a calm pool. The park is 15 mi. north of Hilo, about 4 mi. up the side of Mauna Kea. From Rte. 19, a marked turnoff between mi. markers 13 and 14 leads to Rte. 220; the falls are about 3¾ mi. up the road. Restrooms and picnic tables are next to the parking lot.

HONOKAA

For much of the 19th and 20th centuries, Honokaa (pop. 2,233) occupied a lofty position in the Big Island's sugarcane production until the industry waned, and Honokaa's last mill closed in the 1990s. However, Honokaa has rallied, forging a future on its own terms. The 1920s-era storefronts of the town's main street still house a hardware store and a five-and-dime, but recently, funky art galleries, antique shops, and restaurants have filled the spaces around them. The range of establishments mirrors the diversity of Honokaa's residents, a tightly-knit group, passionate about pretty much everything that's going on in this small town, from family to the feisty local concerts at the Honokaa Club. This town is a great jumping-off point for much of the Hamakua Coast.

ORIENTATION AND PRACTICAL INFORMATION

Honokaa sits along **Route 240,** off Rte. 19, about 40 mi. northwest of Hilo and 15 mi. east of Waimea. **Waipio Valley** is 9 mi. northwest of town, at the end of Rte. 240. Life in Honokaa centers on **Mamane Street** (Rte. 240), which is home to almost all of the town's businesses; a handful more lie along Rte. 19 up the hill. From Waimea, **Plumeria Street** leaves Rte. 19 and drops down through Honokaa, meeting Mamane St. in the center of town.

Honokaa is on the main route between Hilo and Kona and receives more **Hele-on Bus** traffic than any other small town. Buses run from the high school to Hilo (1¼hr.; M-Sa 5:50, 8:30am, 3:15, 5:10, 5:25pm) and Kona (1¾hr.; daily 2:40pm) via Waimea (40min.) from the Dairy Queen on Rte. 19.

Tourist Information: Honokaa Visitor Center (☎775-0598 or 966-5416; www.hawaii-culture.com), is actually the gift shop of Tex Drive-in along Rte. 19. It offers a few brochures and some basic maps, as well as public restrooms. Open daily 9am-5pm.

Banks: Bank of Hawaii, 45-574 Mamane St. (☎775-7218) has a **24hr. ATM.** Open M-Th 8:30am-4pm, F 8:30am-6pm.

Library: Honokaa Public Library, 45-3380 Mamane St. (☎775-8881), offers **Internet access** on 1 of 3 terminals with a 3-month visitor's card ($10). Open M and Th 11am-7pm, Tu-W 9am-5pm, F 9am-3pm.

Laundromat: PJ Sudo Washerette, 45-493 Kika St. (☎987-7731), on Kika St., near the corner of Kika and Mamane St., turnoff next to First Hawaiian Bank. Wash $2.50, dry $0.25 per 4min. Open daily 6am-9pm. Last wash 8:30pm.

Swimming Pool: Honokaa Swimming Pool (☎775-0650), on Mamane St., next to the high school; turn away from the ocean onto Pakalana St. Open weekday mornings 10-11:30am for adult lap swim; 12:45pm free swim. Hours vary during school year.

Weather: ☎961-5582.

Police and Fire Department: Honokaa Station (☎775-7533), on Mamane St., near mi. marker 1.

Pharmacy: Hamakua Family Pharmacy, 45-3551A Mamane St., #4, (☎775-0496), located across from the Bank of Hawaii. Open M-F 8:30am-6pm, Sa 9am-1:30pm.

Post Office: Honokaa Post Office, 45-490 Lehua St. (☎800-275-8777), on the corner of Lehua and Mamane St. Open M-F 9am-4pm, Sa 8:15-9:45am.

Postal Code: 96727.

ACCOMMODATIONS AND CAMPING

Waipio Wayside (☎775-0275; www.waipiowayside.com), on the way toward Waipio Valley, a few miles west of downtown Honokaa near mi. marker 4, recognizable by a small white sign in the front lawn. Formerly a plantation house, this secluded inn offers an incredible view of the Pacific. Each bedroom is comfortable, but the gazebo and decks are the best places to enjoy the soothing tropical atmosphere. Pastry and organic fruit breakfast included. Rooms $99-180; $10 surcharge for 1-night stays. MC/V. ❸

Peace Garden Vacation Houses, 45-4623 Waipio Rd. (☎775-1505; www.hawaiipeacegardenvacationhouses.com.) This is the perfect spot for relaxation, rejuvenation, and self-reflection. This luxurious facility has it all: a spa with sauna, hot tub, cold tub, and showers, hammocks with a view, yoga spaces, and a focus on privacy and indulgence. Fresh fruit in the morning. Two different houses offer accommodations to either groups, couples, or individuals. 3-night min. $75-150, $20 extra for 3rd-6th person. MC/V. ❸

Hotel Honokaa Club, Mamane St. (☎775-0678; www.hotelhono.com), just past Maile St. across from the sign for Honokaa Park. You can't miss this rambling establishment, built in 1908 as a club for plantation managers. When the sugar industry died, it was remade into a hotel; the eccentrically decorated rooms are reminiscent of an earlier era. Basic continental breakfast included. Linens not included in dorms. Reception 8am-1pm and 4-8pm. Check-in 4pm. Check-out noon. Dorms $20. Doubles with shared bath $30-40, with private bath $60-80; 2-bedroom suites for 4 $85. MC/V. ❶

Kalopa State Recreation Area, off Rte. 19, 5 mi. south of Honokaa and 1 mi. south of the intersection of Rte. 19 and Rte. 240. Excellent grassy tent sites under an *ohia* and eucalyptus canopy at a cool 2500 ft. Tent sites available on a first come, first served basis. It rains here quite often, so look to the adjacent cabins for a drier stay. Reserve cabins by calling ☎974-6200, or speak to the caretaker at the park entrance for a free permit (before 4pm). Cabins include access to the recreation hall and kitchen. Bedding provided. Check-in 2pm. Check-out 10am. 5-day max. stay. Camping $5; cabins $55-175; rates rise as the number of guests increases. ❶

FOOD

Cafe Il Mondo, 45-3626A Mamane St. (☎775-7711). The folks behind the counter love what they're doing, and the fresh aroma of baking dough and homemade sauce makes us love them. Slices $2.75-3.25. Pizza $10-19. Open Tu-Sa 11am-8pm. Cash only. ❶

Simply Natural (☎775-0119), on Mamane St. Aloha with an edge served here. Breakfast is the highlight with taro-banana pancakes ($5.95), but a variety of deli and veggie sandwiches (like the spicy tuna melt, $7.95) can satisfy any hunger. The decor is cute, with rainbow ceiling fans and a colorful menu. Open M-Sa 9am-3:30pm. Cash only. ❶

Cafe Rendezvous, 45-3490B Mamane St. (☎775-9230), next door to Hotel Honokaa. This is your morning cafe and baked goods stop ($3-5). For more hearty portions, the friendly waiters at this French-style, open-air eatery serve both salty and sweet crepes ($7.95-9.95). Specials include chef's salad and barbecue chicken ($8-10). Open M and Th-Su 10am-4pm; F-Sa 10am-9pm. Cash only. ❷

Jolene's Kau Kau Korner Restaurant (☎775-9498), on the corner of Mamane and Plumeria St., across from True Value. A friendly local joint serves Hawaiian favorites, including mahi mahi and teriyaki anything. Plate lunches $6.50-8. Dinners $8-17. Open M, W, F 10am-8pm, Tu and Th 10am-3pm. Cash only. ❶

Tex Drive-In, 45-690 Pakalana St. (☎775-0598), off Rte. 19 above downtown Honokaa. Owner Ada makes *malasadas* (Portuguese doughnuts) famous throughout the Big Island ($0.95). The beef for her excellent burgers ($3-6) comes from right up the street. Heaping fish salad $9. Open daily 6am-9pm. MC/V. ❶

SIGHTS AND ENTERTAINMENT

WHile much of the surrounding land has been destroyed by sugarcane production, the 615-acre **Kalopa State Recreation Area** has been protected since 1903. This reserve encompasses 100 acres of virgin Hawaiian rainforest at 2000 to 2500 ft. above sea level and receives approx. 100 in. of precipitation a year. An easy ¾ mi. loop, the **Native Forest Nature Trail** passes through the heart of the *ohia* forest. In addition, the **Gulch Rim Trail,** which skirts Kalopa Gulch and Hanaipoe Gulch, is in the greater forest reserve area. Group cabins, a campground, and a picnic area (see **Camping in Hawaii,** p. 75) are available to the public. The park is off Rte. 19, about 1 mi. south of the intersection of Rte. 19 and Rte. 240. Watch for the green sign marking the turnoff south of Honokaa. The park is 3½ mi. up a series of narrow winding roads; signs clearly mark the way.

Back in town, **Honokaa People's Theater,** on Mamane St. (☎775-0000), has been meticulously restored and shows a wide range of movies, from art-house films (Tu-W) to Hollywood blockbusters (F-Su). Adjacent **People's Cafe** functions as the concessions stand. (Shows 7pm. $6, seniors $4, under 12 $3.)

LAUPAHOEHOE

Laupahoehoe ("leaf of smooth lava") was once a bustling and active sea village. Much like Kalapana, which was rubbed off the map by merciless lava flows in 1989, Laupahoehoe also fell victim to the violent whim of Mother Nature. The deadly 1946 tsunami devastated the entire developed town and surrounding neigborhood, and it swept over 20 unfortunate students and four teachers into the sea. Most of the victims had gone to investigate the unusually low tide that day, hunting for fish and previously underwater sights. When the wave hit, they were too far out to make an escape, and they perished at sea. Today, the point is home to the well-maintained **Laupahoehoe Point Beach Park** with a monument dedicated to those lost in the tragedy. Facilities include volleyball courts, restrooms, showers, picnic tables, and campsites. The park is halfway between Hilo and Honokaa, 1 mi. off Hwy. 19 near mi. marker 27.

In the town of Laupahoehoe, the **Laupahoehoe Train Museum,** right on Hwy. 19, is housed in a railroad worker's old abode. An introductory video informs visitors of Laupahoehoe's storied past; artifacts and photos supplement the video as reminders of the long-gone era of trains and sugarcane. The staff is gracious, knowledgeable, and eager to share what they know. (☎962-6300. Open M-F 9am-4:30pm, Sa-Su 10am-2pm. Adults $3, students and seniors $2.)

WAIPIO VALLEY

Walled in by 2000 ft. *palis* (cliffs), the mile-wide Waipio Valley is a world unto itself. The wide, twisting **Waipio Stream** channels fresh water from the Kohala Mountains to the sea. This natural irrigation nourishes a wealth of fruit trees ripe for the picking. Lush taro root patches dot the landscape and trees bend under the weight of avocados, coconuts, mango, guava, and passion fruit. With a stunning gray-sand beach, striking waterfalls, myriad vistas, and canopied rainforest, the valley is, in a word, paradise.

Before the arrival of Captain Cook in 1778, between 4000 and 10,000 Native Hawaiians had established a private Eden in the crevices of Waipio Valley, which once served as the cultural center of the Big Island. Until the 1946 tsunami, a diverse people and developed land characterized this valley, established solely on the economic prosperity of 16th-century taro root fields. Today, no more than 100 residents call the valley home, and much of the cultivated land has been reclaimed by the rainforest. The valley's days as the center of Big Island agriculture are over, but the beauty of this fertile land remains.

ORIENTATION

Route 240 ends here; it dead ends at the parking lot for the Waipio Valley Lookout. From here, an extraordinarily steep paved road winds down 900 ft. to the valley floor. With grades of 20-35% and sharp hairpin turns, it is passable only with a hearty 4WD in first gear. Descending vehicles must yield to ascending traffic. An eerie graveyard of rusting truck spines at the bottom of the ravine stands testament to this road's treacherous conditions. Visitors with a 2WD can park at the lookout and hike ½ mi. to the valley floor.

ACTIVITIES

If you've been down to the valley floor already and want to see things from a new perspective, there are several companies that run tours along the Waipio rim.

ON HORSEBACK

Waipio Naalapa Stables (☎775-0419; www.naalapastables.com) offers 2½hr. adventures in the valley. Trips begin at Waipio Valley Artworks in Kukuihaele. M-Sa 9:30am and 1pm. Reservations required. Ages 8 and up. $85. MC/V.

Waipio on Horseback and ATV (☎775-7291). Leisurely excursions highlight the waterfalls and one of the largest taro root farms. Meet at the Last Chance Store in Kukuihaele for a drive to the valley. M-Sa 9:30am and 1:30pm. Reserve 24hr. in advance. $85. The same outfit offers guided tours on ATV through the valley. Sa-Su 9:30am and 1:30pm. 2½hr. tour with snack $100; 4hr. tour with picnic $150. Ages 16 and up. MC/V.

BY WHEEL OR SPOKE

Waipio Valley Shuttle (☎775-7121) leaves from Waipio Valley Artworks. The 2½hr. tour features views of Hiilawe Falls and taro root patches, and it is led by knowledgeable guides who narrate Hawaiian history and legends. M-Sa 9, 11am, 1, 3pm. Reservations recommended. $45, ages 11-17 $35, 10 and under $20.

Waipio Valley Wagon Tours (☎775-9518) departs from the Last Chance Store in Kukuihaele. Explore the taro root fields, tropical vegetation, and waterfalls of the valley in a 1½hr. tour from the seat of a mule-drawn covered wagon. M-Sa 9:30, 11:30am, 1:30, 3:30pm. Reservations required. $55, children $27.50, under 3 free.

HIKING

While you can get a decent look from the **Waipio Valley Lookout** at the top of the eastern cliff, it is far more rewarding to hike through the valley. Below are some of the available hikes; stay on the trails and avoid trespassing. For a guided adventure, **Hawaiian Walkways** (☎775-0372 or 800-457-7759; www.hawaiianwalkways.com), on Mamane St. in downtown Honokaa, leads 5hr., fully equipped hikes into the valley. Other trips hike in Volcanoes Park or along Saddle Rd. (Open M-F 8am-5pm. $95-135 per person.)

WAIPIO VALLEY BEACH TRAIL. *(40min. one-way. Challenging.)* From the lookout, a steep (but relatively short) paved road plunges to the valley's floor. Hikers and motorists share the road, so be alert. All rented vehicles are prohibited below the valley rim, so strap on a pair of sturdy shoes and start trekking.

Turning right at the fork takes you on a muddy 10min. walk to the peerless **Waipio Beach,** known for its dynamic currents and gnarly shore break. Spectacular cliffs and tumbling cascades border the sandy expanse, which is splashed with a shallow shore break. A tight-knit group of surfers call this beach home; these guys start up early and are *pau* (finished) when the trade winds perk up at around 8:30am. Surfers brave the mighty riptides, but be aware of a deceptively powerful current. Waipio Stream splits the beach in two on its way to the ocean; if you plan to visit the western end (which offers an expansive beach and hiking access), the easiest avenue is a quick wade through the stream.

KALAUAHINE FALLS. *(45min. one-way. Moderate.)* From Waipio Beach, you can see Kalauahine Falls sparkling in the east. There's a rough trail along fairly loose lava rock that runs from the intersection of the cliffs and the ocean to the falls.

MAIWALU TRAIL. *(7½ mi. one-way. Challenging.)* At the western end of Waipio Beach, opposite the stream from the lookout, a switchback trail leads up the cliffs and over to **Waimanu Valley.** The switchback panoramas surpass even the astounding views from the lookout. This trail reveals unique and unparalleled waterfall and valley views. However, during rainfall, this trail can be quite treacherous, with narrow and slippery cliff-side passes and unclear paths. Most hikers plan on spending 3 days on the excursion; don't forget to pack enough water, food, rain gear, and insect repellent. While you can't camp in Waipio, it is possible to get a free backcountry camping permit from the Division of Forestry and Wildlife, 19 E. Kawili (☎974-4221), in Hilo, to camp in Waimanu Valley.

HIILAWE FALLS. *(2-2½hr. one-way. Challenging.)* At the end of the descent into the valley where the beach trail forks right, take the left path back into the interior of the valley, revealing views of the shimmering Hiilawe Falls (1200 ft.), Hawaii's highest single-drop waterfall. From here, it's about a 2hr. bushwhacking and stream-crossing session until reaching the falls. Continue on the road and turn left just before the river into the dense forest. The faint path to the falls zig-zags under at least two barbed-wire fences and across the river numerous times. The rocks are slippery, and getting soaked is unavoidable; come prepared with appropriate footwear, water, and insect repellent. Hikers with open cuts may want to avoid this trek; stream-walking exposes swimmers to *leptospirosis.*

WAIMEA

A history of Waimea (pop. 7,028) is a history of Parker Ranch. This is cattle country, a cross between the American Rockies and Scotland. Though only 10 mi. from balmy Kohala beaches, the air is crisp and cool. The Parker story began in 1793, when George Vancouver gave a herd of cattle to King Kamehameha. He then bade them go forth and multiply and declared hunting them to be *kapu* (forbidden). This lasted for 10 years, during which the cattle became a ferocious lot, notorious for rampaging and even chasing Hawaiians from their homes. By the early 19th century, King Kamehameha had hired Massachusetts-born marksman John Palmer Parker to round up the cows, shoot the wild ones, and tame the rest. Parker did as ordered and garnered royal favor, so much, in fact, that he was granted a small plot of land on the slopes of Mauna Kea, beginning a collection of land that would reach 225,000 acres and become the vast Parker Ranch.

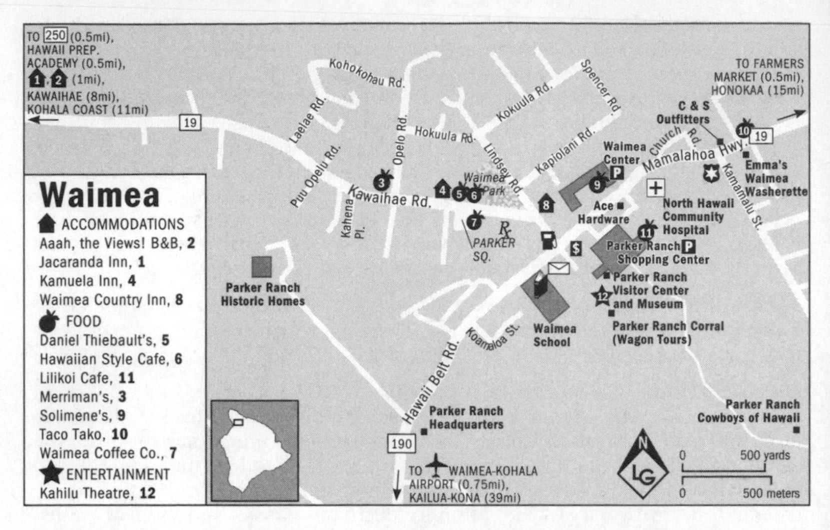

More than a decade after the death of Samuel Smart, the ranch's last heir, the board of the multi-million dollar Parker Corporation still runs this town, and 44% of the Big Island's real estate. In addition to financing several public service trusts and many of Waimea's town festivals, Waimea's private prep school and public hospital are both funded solely by the copious Parker cash flow. The presence of the Parker millions has distorted Waimea's trajectory as a small Hawaiian town; it has provided the community with economic resources and opportunities while transforming the downtown area into a suburb of the South Kohala resorts.

TRANSPORTATION

Flights: Waimea-Kohala Airport is 1½ mi. south of Waimea Center, off Rte. 190, heading toward Kona. The primary carrier, **Pacific Wings Airlines** (☎887-2104; www.pacificwings.com) runs flights to **Honolulu** and **Kahului** daily. All express service flights are $81, while flights operating out of the bigger airports are subject to much higher fares. Open F-Su 8am-noon and 5-6pm.

Bus: The free **Hele-On Bus** (☎961-8744) passes through Waimea with some consistency. Trips to Hilo from Ace Hardware (1¼hr.; daily 2:55, 4:55pm), the Parker Ranch Center (1¾hr., M-Sa 8:05am), and to Kailua-Kona from the Parker Ranch Center (1¾hr., M-Sa 3:20pm).

Taxis: Alpha Star Taxi (☎885-4771), based 10 mi. out of town, is the only taxi company in the Waimea area. Drivers will not pick up or drop off at the airport. $3 initial charge; $2.40 per additional mi.

ORIENTATION

Forty miles northeast of Kona and 54 mi. northwest of Hilo, Waimea is set in the Kohala hills in the northern part of the Big Island, at the intersection of **Route 190 (Mamalahoa Highway)** and **Route 19 (Hawaii Belt Road).** From the Parker Ranch Plaza, the eastern half of Rte. 19 runs 15 mi. to Honokaa and the Hamakua coast. The other half of Rte. 19 heads toward Kawaihae, while **Route 250 (Kohala Mountain Road)** splits off toward Hawi.

PRACTICAL INFORMATION

Banks: Bank of Hawaii, 67-1191 Mamalahoa Hwy. (☎885-7995). Open M-Th 8:30am-4pm, F 8:30am-6pm. **First Hawaiian Bank** (☎885-7991), in front of the Parker Ranch Center at Mamalahoa Hwy. and Kawaihae Rd. Open M-Th 8:30am-4pm, F 8:30am-6pm, Sa 9am-1pm. Both have **24hr. ATMs.**

Library: Thelma Parker Memorial Library, 67-1209 Mamalahoa Hwy. (☎887-6067), behind the Waimea middle school gym, offers **Internet access** with a 3-month visitor's card ($10). Open M-Tu and Th 9am-4:30pm, W 12:30-7pm, F-Sa 9:30am-1:30pm.

Laundromat: Emma's Waimea Washerette is the yellow building on Mamalahoa Hwy., north of the intersection with Hwy. 19. Wash $2.25, dry $1.75. Open M-Th and Su 5:45am-9pm, F-Sa 5:45am-11pm.

Swimming Pool: Hawaii Preparatory Academy, 65-1692 Kohala Mt. Rd. (☎881-4028), off Rte. 250 just past the split with Rte. 19. Open M-F noon-1pm, Su 1-4pm. $3.

Police: Waimea Police Station (☎935-3311), at the top of the hill in the Waimea Civic Center, at the corner of Kamamalu St. and Mamalahoa Hwy. Open daily 24hr. Emergency phone outside.

Pharmacy: Village Pharmacy, 65-1267 Kawaihae Rd. (☎885-4824), in the Hale Ola Pono Health Center. Open M-F 8:30am-5:30pm, Sa 8:30am-2pm.

Hospital: North Hawaii Community Hospital, 67-1125 Mamalahoa Hwy. (☎885-4444), next to Ace Hardware.

Post Office: Kamuela Post Office, 67-1197 Mamalahoa Hwy. (☎800-275-8777), off Hwy. 190, across from the Parker Ranch Shopping Center. As there are 2 other Waimeas on Kauai and Oahu, be sure to address mail to Kamuela, not Waimea. Open M-F 8am-4:30pm, Sa 9am-noon.

Postal Code: 96743.

ACCOMMODATIONS

Jacaranda Inn, 65-1444 Kawaihae Rd. (☎885-8813; www.jacarandainn.com). From the intersection of Rte. 19 and Rte. 190 in Waimea Center, continue west down Rte. 19 (Kawaihae Rd.) toward Kawaihae; Jacaranda is just past mi. marker 85. With rich interiors and quaintly decadent architecture, Jacaranda offers luxury at a fraction of the resort price. The understated plantation feel is complemented by four-poster beds, hot tubs, hardwood floors, chandeliers, and a wood-paneled library. Each room is unique. Breakfast included. Check-in 3-6pm. Check-out 11am. Reservations recommended. Rooms $159-225; 3-bedroom cottage $450. MC/V. ❺

"Aaah, The Views!" Bed and Breakfast, 66-1773 Alaneo St. (☎885-3455; www.aaahtheviews.com). Take Kawaihae Rd. about ½ mi. past the Rte. 250 turnoff from Waimea, take a left on Akulani St., then a right on Alaneo. Aaah is a comfortable, friendly, and low-key B&B—with some pretty decent stream and mountain scenery. With a few lofted rooms and a famous "chocolate breakfast," this place is great for the whole family. Rooms from $65. MC/V. ❸

Kamuela Inn, 65-1300 Kawaihae Rd. (☎885-4243; www.hawaii-bnb.com/kamuela.html), west of Waimea Center along Rte. 19 (Kawaihae Rd.) and past the ball field. More of a stylish motel than an inn, Kamuela is Waimea's best mid-range value.

Spacious, clean rooms exhibit an Upcountry motif. Breakfast included. Check-in 3pm. Check-out noon. Doubles $59-72. AmEx/D/MC/V. ❷

Waimea Country Lodge, 65-1210 Lindsey Rd. (☎885-4100; www.castleresorts.com/wcl), off Kawaihae Rd. west of Waimea Center, before the Parker school. The motel's central location, optional kitchenettes, and smiling staff make this a great value for longer stays. Reception 7am-11pm. Check-in 3-11pm. Check-out noon. Reservations recommended. Rooms $105; with kitchenette $125. AmEx/D/MC/V. ❸

FOOD

Some of the best gourmet restaurants on the island are in Waimea. You can also pick up fresh produce and bouquets at the **Homestead farmers' market** (Sa 7am-noon), in the parking lot of the State of Hawaii Department of Home Lands, 2 mi. east of Waimea center at mi. marker 55 on Rte. 19.

Merriman's (☎885-6822), on Kawaihae Rd. at Opelo Rd. Specializing in cutting-edge Hawaiian cuisine, Merriman's is consistently ranked the best restaurant on the Big Island. Fresh Big Island products and inventive, delectable dishes, like the wok-charred ahi and sesame-crusted fresh catch, will undoubtedly measure up to the high praise. Lunch $10-14. For dinner, the ponzu-marinated mahi ($35) or prime cuts ($40), are worth the astronomical prices. Lunch M-F 11:30am-1:30pm. Dinner nightly 5:30-9pm. Reservations recommended. AmEx/MC/V. ❺

Lilikoi Cafe, 67-1185 Mamalahoa Hwy, Ste. 143 (☎887-1400), in the Parker Ranch Shopping Center. This cafe is a winner; their creative dishes are succulent and healthy, made with fresh fruit and a smile. Rotating salads like chicken papaya and avocado mango $5. Sandwiches and hot entrees ($5.50-11) are equally delicious. Open M-Sa 7:30am-4pm. MC/V. ❶

Waimea Coffee Co, 65-1280 Kawaihae Rd. (☎885-4472), in the Parker Ranch Square. This is a local stop with great coffee, tasty sandwiches, wraps, sweet pastries, a friendly staff, and free wireless Internet. Turkey and avocado wrap $7.95. Open M-F 7am-5pm, Sa 8am-5pm, Su 9am-3pm. MC/V. ❶

Solimene's, 65-1158 Mamalahoa Hwy. (☎887-1313), in the Waimea Shopping Center. This pizza, pasta, and panini place is a quick dinner spot. The father-son staff is friendly, possessing an uncanny knack for remembering your favorite dish. Try the Napa pizza with artichoke hearts, olives, roasted peppers, red onion, mozzarella, and fresh herbs. Pizza $17-24. Pastas $9-13. Open Tu-Su 11am-3pm and 5-9pm. MC/V. ❷

Hawaiian Style Cafe (☎885-4295), on the right side of Kawaihae Rd. coming from town, ¼ mi. from the intersection of Hwy. 19 and Hwy. 190. Steak and chicken $7-9. Specials, like their famous smoked pork omelet, go for $7.25. Open M-F 7:30am-12:30pm, Su 7:30-10:30am. Cash only. ❷

Tako Taco, 64-1066 Mamalahoa Hwy. (☎887-1717), across from the Parker Ranch Center. Straight out of Baja beach, this cheerful tin-roof taqueria is the place to pick up cheap Mexican food. Indoor counter, stools, and umbrella-shaded outdoor seating. Burritos $6.25-8.50. Tacos $3.50-8.50. Salads $6.50-8.50. Open daily 11am-8pm. AmEx/MC/V. ❶

Daniel Thiebaut's, 65-1259 Kawaihae Rd. (☎887-2200). From the center of town it's a yellow house on the left-hand side of the road. Housed in what was a general store in 1900, Daniel Thiebaut's gourmet restaurant caters unabashedly to the Kohala resorts down the hill. The crab-crusted mahi mahi receives high accolades ($37). Lunch $7.50-11.50. Dinner $20-35. Rack of lamb $35. Nice attire encouraged, especially for dinner. Excellent selection of wines. Lunch M-F 11:30am-2pm. Dinner daily 5:30-9pm. Reservations recommended. AmEx/D/MC/V. ❺

ACTIVITIES

Welcome to *paniolo* (cowboy) country: tighten your spurs, dig out your jeans, and jump on a horse. The misty rolling chartreuse of the Kohala Mountains are a landscape best explored in the saddle. A number of quality outfits operate horseback tours both in Waimea and a few miles north toward North Kohala. Reservations should be made in advance. Bring a raincoat for the strong winds, rain, and fog.

Dahana Ranch (☎885-0057; www.dahanaranch.com), take Rte. 19 5 mi. toward Hilo, then bear right onto Mamalahoa Hwy. Continue 2½ mi, and turn right at Dahana Rough Riders sign. Dahana's open range rides are outside Parker estate, and even farther outside the conventions of guided horseback tours. At Dahana, you're encouraged to lead the horse off the trail. Guides still navigate the rolling pasture, and invite tourists to help on **weekly cattle drives**–an unparalleled experience ($130). Reservation required. 1½hr. rides at 9, 11am, 1, 3pm; $60. 2hr. advanced ride; $100. MC/V.

Paniolo Riding Adventures (☎889-5354; www.panioloadventures.com), 14 mi. north of Waimea Ct. on Rte. 250, just past mi. marker 13 in Kohala. Guides lead riders across the open expanses of a working ranch, all the more exciting during calving season. 1½hr. sunset ride $79, 2½hr. *paniolo* ride $96, 3hr. picnic ride $124, 4hr. wrangler ride $149.

Parker Ranch Wagon Tours (☎885-7655; www.parkerranch.com/wagonrides.php). In Parker Ranch Corral, next to the Parker Ranch Visitor Center. A tame 45min. spin around a small section of Parker Ranch in a covered *paniolo* wagon. Every hr. Tu-Sa 10am-2pm. $15, seniors and ages 12 and under $12.

SIGHTS AND ENTERTAINMENT

PARKER RANCH HISTORIC HOMES. These exquisitely maintained homes illustrate two different eras in the history of Parker Ranch. Mana Hale is the New England-style wooden saltbox that served as John Palmer Parker's home during his first years as a rancher. Palmer actually hauled the lumber from Mauna Kea to the house's site, 12 mi. away. Puuopelu, or "meeting place," was built in 1862 and was home to Richard Smart, a 6th-generation Parker, until his death in 1992. The home is an excellent showcase for his French Impressionist and Chinese art collection. *(Off Rte. 190, 1 mi. south of town; the turnoff is on the right heading from Waimea to Kona. ☎885-5433. Open M-Sa 10am-5pm, last admission 4pm. $8.50, seniors $8, children $6.50. Joint admission to museum and historic homes $14/13.50/11.50.)*

PARKER RANCH VISITOR CENTER AND MUSEUM. A small exhibit explores a bit of early Hawaiian history before focusing on the ranch's owners—from John Palmer Parker in the early 1800s to the 6th-generation Parker who died in 1992. A 25min. video details the ranch's history. *(67-1185 Mamalahoa Hwy., in the Parker Ranch Center. ☎885-7655; www.parkerranch.com. Open M-Sa 9am-5pm. Last admission 4pm. $6.50, seniors $5.50, children $5.)*

KAHILU THEATRE. This is where the Big Island comes for big-name performances. 2005 brought the Kronos String Quartet and the Spanish Harlem Orchestra, among many other internationally-acclaimed acts. The theater starts its season in September and continues until May. It also hosts local performers and screens independent and blockbuster films throughout the year. *(67-1186*

Lindsey Rd., behind the Parker Ranch Center. ☎885-6868; www.kahilutheatre.org. Box office open M-F 9am-noon and 1-4pm. Tickets for major events $28-45. Movies $6, children 12 and under $4.)

HULA HAPPENS. Waimea Town is home to some of the best hula *halaus* (schools) in the state. Many of the local churches open their doors on weekend mornings and allow the public in to see an authentic *halau* practicing for a tournament. If you hear music, poke your head in—you may have just stumbled across the most authentic part of your Hawaiian vacation.

NORTH KOHALA INCLUDING HAWI AND KAPAAU

North Kohala is living history. On this northern perch, the unforgiving winds and racing ocean currents have sculpted the island's oldest volcanic mountain range into one of the state's most striking vistas. Hawi (pop. 938) and Kapaau (pop. 1,159) used to be powerful fixtures in Hawaii's sugarcane industry and royal history; King Kamehameha rose to power and united the entire island chain from this windy range. Today, a row of stores (and empty storefronts) lines the sides of Akoni Pule Hwy. in a jungle of wild sugarcane. These once-booming towns and the surrounding hills are the perfect place to get a glimpse into Hawaii's past; the slopes of the Kohala Mountains are lined with ancient *heiaus* (temples) and reminders of the not-too-distant caning industry. Hike up, kayak down, or just tear right on through--the alluring charm of North Kohala is ubiquitous.

ORIENTATION

Hawi is at the intersection of **Route 250 (Hawi Road)** and **Route 270,** 19 mi. north of Kawaihae and 20 mi. northwest of Waimea. This stretch of Rte. 270, also known as **Akoni Pule Highway,** is the town's main road. It continues east from Hawi, through **Kapaau,** and ends 7 mi. later at the Pololu Valley Lookout (p. 250).

North Kohala is the one district not linked via the Hawaii Belt Rd. The free **Hele-On Bus** (☎961-8744) leaves daily from downtown Kapaau (6:20am) to **Hawi** and the six resorts in **South Kohala;** it returns from the last of those resorts, the Hilton Waikoloa, at 4:15pm (1¼hr.).

PRACTICAL INFORMATION

Bank: Bank of Hawaii, 54-388 Akoni Pule Hwy. (☎889-1073), in downtown Kapaau. **24hr. ATM.** Open M-Th 8:30am-4pm, F 8:30am-6pm. Another ATM can be found in Hawi at **Kohala Mailbox,** 55-3419 Akoni Pule Hwy., #28 (☎889-0498). Open M-F 8:30am-4pm, Sa 9am-2pm.

Gas: Hawi Shell Station, 55-503 Hawi Rd. (☎889-5211), on the corner of Hawi Rd. and Akoni Pule Hwy. Open M-F 5:30am-6:30pm, Sa 6am-6:30pm, Su 8am-4pm.

Bookstore: Kohala Book Shop, 54-3885 Akoni Pule Hwy. (☎889-6400), in downtown Kapaau. The largest used bookstore on the island has an extensive collection of Hawaiiana. Open M-Sa 11am-5pm. Closed in Sept. MC/V.

Library: Bond Memorial Public Library, 54-3903 Akoni Pule Hwy. (☎889-6655), on Akoni Pule Hwy. in downtown Kapaau, offers **Internet access** with a 3-month visitor's card ($10). Open M noon-8pm, Tu-Th 9am-5pm, F 9am-1pm.

Police: North Kohala District Police Station, 54-3900 Akoni Pule Hwy. (☎889-6540; Hilo dispatch 935-3311), in Kapaau, behind the Kamehameha statue and North Kohala Civic Center. Office open daily 8am-4pm.

Pharmacy: Kamehameha Pharmacy, 54-3877 Akoni Pule Hwy. (☎889-6161), in downtown Kapaau. Open M-Tu and Th-F 9am-12:30pm and 1:30-5pm, W 9am-1pm.

Hospital: Kohala Hospital, 54-383 Hospital Rd. (☎889-6211), on the ocean side of downtown Kapaau, off Hwy. 270.

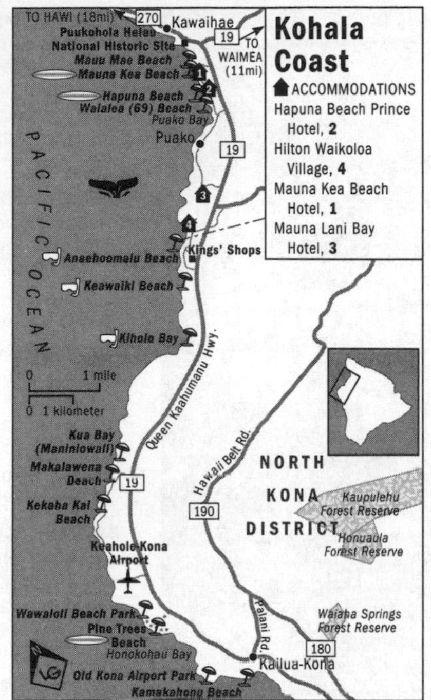

Internet Access: In addition to the library (see above), **Kohala Computer Center,** 55-3407 Akoni Pule Hwy. (☎889-1002), in downtown Hawi, provides superior tech support and Internet access. $3 per 15min., $10 per hr. Open M-F 8am-4:30pm. **Kohala Mailbox,** 54-3419 Akoni Pule Hwy. (☎889-0498) charges $3.50 per 15min. Fax $5.25 per page; copies for $0.16 per page.

Post Offices: Hawi Post Office, 55-515 Hawi Rd. (☎800-275-8777), near the corner of Rte. 250 and 270. Open M-F 8:30am-noon and 12:30-4pm, Sa 9-10am. **Kapaau Post Office,** 54-396 Union Mill Rd. (☎889-6766). Open M-F 7:30am-4pm, Sa 9-10:30am.

Postal Code: 96719 (Hawi); 96755 (Kapaau).

ACCOMMODATIONS AND CAMPING

Kohala's Guest House, 52-277 Keokea Park Rd. (☎889-5606; www.kohalaguesthouse.com), about 3 mi. east of Kapaau. Turn *makai* (toward the ocean) from Hwy. 270 onto the road that leads to Keokea Beach. The white Guest House is less than ¼ mi. in on your right; look for a labeled mailbox. Check-in 2pm. Check-out 11am. Single room $49. 1-bedroom with use of kitchen and common area $79. Either side of a fully furnished duplex house equipped with full kitchen, 3 bedrooms, TV, and washer/dryer $125; $600 per wk. ❷

Kohala Country Adventures Guest House (☎889-5663; www.kcadventures.com), ¼ mi. above Kapaau. Turn away off Hwy. 270 onto the road between the Bank of Hawaii and the statue of Kamehameha; the guest house is on the right at the end of the road. "Cozy" is an understatement; here, you're at home. Rooms vary in size, though all have refrigerator and kitchen access. Check-in 3pm. Reservations recommended. Doubles $85-160; each additional guest $15. AmEx/D/MC/V. ❸

Kohola Village Inn, 55-514 Hawi Rd. (☎889-0404), in Hawi, at the corner of Rte. 250 and 270. The rooms here are convenient, and nicer and cheaper than in most places. TV and continental breakfast. Check-in 3-9pm. Check-out 11am. Quiet hours after 9pm. Doubles $65; triples $75; 2-room suites $100-120. MC/V. ❷

Mahukona Beach Park, less than 1 mi. north of Lapakahi Historical Park on Hwy. 270, before mi. marker 15. Although the campsites have little shade relief, many locals come to snorkel in this unique "industrial underwater." The snorkeling reveals an underwater treasure trove with all kinds of fish and sights, including yellow tang and underwater debris. The ambitious diver can follow an anchor chain from the port to the remains of a sunken steamboat that rests largely intact under 20 ft. of water. The campground has showers, a pavilion with electricity, and toilets, but bring your own water. Permits required; see **Camping in Hawaii,** p. 75, for information. ❶

Kapaa Beach Park, turn toward the ocean from Hwy. 270 between mi. markers 15 and 16. This small rocky beach has water calm enough for swimming. Restrooms and picnic tables surround a covered structure that is often converted into a makeshift camper's luau. Permits required; see **Camping in Hawaii,** p. 75, for information. ❶

FOOD

Despite being in the Big Island's backcountry, North Kohala has some surprisingly good places to eat. From Mexican to sushi, the hungry hiker will find plenty of satiating options. Plan on eating in Hawi—the food options in Kapaau are quite limited. **Nakahara Grocery Store** (☎889-6359), on Hawi Rd., is Hawi's local grocer, with the added bonus of an informal farmers market that congregates on the grass outside. (Open M-Sa 8am-7pm, Su 8am-3pm.)

Sushi Rock, 55-3435 Akoni Pule Hwy. (☎889-5900), in Hawi, just east of the intersection with Hwy. 250. This upscale sushi studio rolls creative lunches and dinner ($3-7). Also try their irresistible salads, like the baked macadamia nut chevre with caramelized onions ($7). Fish and chicken dishes $11-15. Open M-Tu, Th, Su noon-3pm and 5:30-8pm; F-Sa noon-3pm and 5:30pm-9pm. AmEx/D/MC/V. ❷

Kohala Coffee Mill (☎889-5577), across from Bamboo, on Akoni Pule Hwy. in Hawi. Heaping scoops of Tropical Dreams Hawaiian Ice Cream ($2-4), fruit smoothies ($4), and a wide selection of tea and coffee

PURPLE PASTE HAS NEVER TASTED SO GOOD

A short introduction to the fine art of Hawaiian food.

Plate Lunch: One entree (such as chicken teriyaki, deep-fried mahi mahi, beef stew, or kalua pig) with 2 scoops of rice and 1 scoop of macaroni salad.

Loco Moco: 2 eggs on 2 hamburger patties on 2 scoops of rice, slathered with gravy.

Shave Ice: not ice cream or a snow cone, neither smooth nor crunchy; boasts the taste of an ICEE without the artificiality.

Kalbi Beef: short beef ribs, a staple of Korean barbecue.

Spam Musubi: a fried slab of the locals' favorite spiced ham in a can, set on a hunk of sushi rice and wrapped in nori (seaweed).

Kalua Pig: succulent pork roasted in an imu (an underground pit oven) and shredded.

Lau Lau: pork, beef, fish, or taro root leaves wrapped in *ti* leaves and steamed or roasted in an imu.

Lilikoi: Passionfruit.

Malasada: a Portuguese doughnut, fried and sugared.

Poi: a thick purplish paste made from pounded taro root. Often eaten with kalua pig or lomi salmon, but it can be eaten alone and sweetened as well.

Poke: sliced raw fish, seaweed, Hawaiian salt, and chile peppers served together as an appetizer.

Haupia: coconut-milk custard; a popular dessert, especially scrumptious in pie.

($1.75-4). Burgers $4.50. Ice cream flavors rotate daily and include white chocolate ginger, banana-mango, jamocha-macadamia nut, and white pineapple sorbet. Lunch specials, like the angel hair pasta with mahi, around $7. Open M-F 6:30am-6pm, Sa-Su 7am-5:30pm. MC/V. ❶

Bamboo, 55-3415 Akoni Pule Hwy. (☎889-5555), in downtown Hawi. Quality Hawaiian-style local plates have become *the* reason many people come to Hawi. Favorites include *kalua* pork and cabbage ($13.95), *Puaa A Opai* (pork tenderloin and black tiger shrimp on papaya salad), and their original passion fruit margarita. Try a bit of everything Hawaiian on the sampler plate ($13). Dinner around $30. Live Hawaiian music F-Sa. Open Tu-Sa 11:30am-2:30pm and 6-9pm, Su 11am-2pm. MC/V. ❸

Short N Sweet Bakery and Cafe, 55-3419 Akoni Pule Hwy. (☎889-1444), in Hawi. This baker turns dessert into fine art; they've also got delicious panini sandwiches served on home-made focaccia (mozzarella and Italian ham, $8.95). Salads $3.95-7.95. Scrumptuous treats $2-5. MC/V. ❷

Hula La's Mexican Kitchen, 54-3419 Akoni Pule Hwy. (☎889-5668), in the Kohala Trade Center in Hawi. A basic *taqueria* with satisfying burritos ($6-7.50). 4 varieties of salsa are so popular they sell by the pound ($10) or the more reasonably sized bowl ($1.50). Open daily M-F 11am-8pm, Sa-Su 11am-4pm. MC/V. ❶

Kava Kafe, 54-3419 Akoni Pule Hwy. (☎896-6073), in the Kohala Trade Center just behind Hula La's. It's the local kava hole, and a great place to unwind after a long day's hike. Open **M-F 4:21pm-8:59pm,** call for Sa-Su hours. Cash only. ❶

Rainbow Cafe, 54-3897 Akoni Pule Hwy. (☎889-0099), in Kapaau. One of the few eating options in Kapaau, people come here for the friendly ambience. Try their most popular sandwich, the Hawaiian Bleu (grilled chicken, ham, and pineapple topped with a lilikoi dressing, $8.95). Salads and wraps $7.50. Sandwiches $8. Burgers $10. Open M-F 10am-5pm, Sa-Su 10am-3:30pm. MC/V. ❷

SIGHTS AND ACTIVITIES

LAPAKAHI STATE HISTORICAL PARK. When Polynesian sailors arrived at the sheltered coves of Lapakahi nearly 600 years ago, they agreed upon its security and built a village. Soon thereafter, many of the villagers hiked into the wetter Kohala Mountains, where extensive farming was more feasible. For nearly 500 years, a trade arrangement between the upland farmers and their coastal counterparts called *ahupuaa* united these Kohala natives. Their exchanges included fresh fish from the coast and coconut, *kamani* nuts, taro root, and *ulu* (breadfruit) crops. In 1918, when struggling sugar plantation owners diverted the seven streams that fed Lapakahi, lush fields quickly dried to a red-sand desert and the fate of Lapakahi became a common tragedy for Native Hawaiians. Today, Lapakahi is the only Native village that has been at least partially restored.

The Visitors Center at Lapakahi has maps of a 1 mi. trail, indicating canoe landings, houses, salt pans, fish shrines, burial grounds, and the fragments of the taro-for-fish trade road that once connected the mountains and the coast. The trail is faint, but ambling around the grounds is as rewarding as the self-guided tour.

In its time, Lapakahi was considered a sacred healing ground because of the high number of medicinal roots and plants that grew on its coast. Many traditional healers still frequent the site for ceremonies and ask that visitors respect the sacredness of their historic home. Signs request that visitors not bring their picnics to the beach. The **snorkeling** is exceptional but is only permitted in the cove accessible by a path directly *makai* (toward the ocean) from the visitors center. Ask before leaving to be sure you are swimming in the right spot. The water is so clear that you can see a rainbow of fish from the rocks without any snorkel equipment. *(The park is off Hwy. 270; turn toward the ocean near mi. marker 14. ☎889-5566. Bring your own water and sunscreen. Open daily 8am-4pm, gate closes 3:30pm. Free.)*

MOOKINI LUAKINI HEIAU AND KAMEHAMEHA'S BIRTHPLACE. Hawaiian chants and oral histories stress that the most important factor in building a sacred *heiau* (temple) is not the building's design, but the choice of the site. On a windy green cliff overlooking the Pacific and Haleakala Mountain on Maui, the Mookini Heiau is undoubtedly a site of great *mana*, or spiritual power. Although most *heiaus* tend to be dedicated to Lono, the god of harvest, the *heiau* at Mookini is dedicated to Ku, the god of war. Known as *luakini heiaus*, temples dedicated to Ku were the only spiritual sites to offer human sacrifices. Built in 480 BC, the Mookini Heiau has 30 ft. walls, which according to legend were transported by a 9 mi. long human chain that extracted volcanic stones from the Pololu Valley. Traditionally restricted to *alii* (royalty) and *kahunas* (priests), in 1963, Mookini Luakini Heiau was designated the first National Historic Landmark in Hawaii and opened to the public.

A few hundred yards down the coast from the *heiau* there is a large enclosure reputed to be the site of Kamehameha's birth. The exact date is disputed, but according to oral tradition, Kamehameha was born on a stormy night following an unusual celestial light that was seen rising in the east. Maude Makemson, an astronomer at Vassar College, determined that it must have been the 1758 appearance of Halley's Comet that signaled the great king's birth. Towering at a peak of 5480 ft., the North Kohala mountains would provide Kamehameha with a commanding view of Maui, allowing him strategic vision in his advance to unify the islands. *(Both of these sacred sites are almost unmarked. To reach the heiau, turn toward the ocean at the sign for Upolu Airport at mi. marker 20 on Rte. 270. Follow the road for 2 mi. At the airport, turn left on the rutted dirt road that runs parallel to the coast. This road is often swamped with large mud pools, making it impassable for cars with low clearance or 2WD. Most people choose to walk at this point. After about 1½ mi. you will see a signpost indicating the direction of each historic site; the heiau is on the hill to the left. Kamehameha's birthplace is another ¼ mi. down the right-hand fork, just up from the coast. For more information about the heiau call ☎591-1170 or 591-1142.)*

KAMEHAMEHA STATUE. On the *mauka* (mountain) side of the highway through Kapaau, this "true-to-scale" 8 ft. tall statue of King Kamehameha asserts the legendary status of Hawaii's uniting king. It's a popular sight, but heavily touristed and really not worth the stop.

POLOLU VALLEY LOOKOUT. This is a fantastic place for a stop; the view is spectacular and would probably halt traffic even if the road continued forward. The parking lot at the end of the highway looks out over rocky cliffs and waves crashing against a black-sand beach. Behind this, the start of the seven valleys (from Pololu to Waipio) stretch out in sharp green arcs. Thousands of years of Pacific erosion carved these lush valleys from the Kohala Mountains: a miracle of time, water, and circumstance found nowhere else on the island. Waipio is the only other valley accessible by car from the east. If the view ensnares you, several trails into the valley start from the parking lot. For more information, see **Hiking,** p. 251. *(7 mi. past Kapaau on Rte. 270 at the end of the road.)*

FLUMIN' DA DITCH. A unique option for seeing the North Kohala countryside, Flumin' Da Ditch coordinates wet and bizarre group kayak adventures that explore the area's undeveloped rainforests and remnants of the long-gone era of sugar plantations. Kids who grew up on these plantations were known to grab anything that floated and go flumin' in the ditches, tunnels, and flumes of

Kohala's irrigation system. After the sugar industry died, a group of locals decided to revive the tradition on a larger scale with kayak rides through 3½ mi. of the Kohala Ditch. Over the course of the trip, guides explain the design, construction, and history of the Kohala Ditch Project and the 600 Japanese laborers who made it possible. The guides all grew up flumin' da ditches as children and have stories about life in North Kohala. The ride is very cool: little paddling is involved, and the guides are as entertaining as the scenery. Flumin' also runs 3hr. **HMV Tours,** a drier venture into the same rainforests and past the same waterfalls. *(55-519 Hawi Rd. Above the intersection of Hwy. 250 and 270 in Hawi. ☎889-6922; www.flumindaditch.com or www.hmvtours.com. Both trips daily 8:15am and 12:15pm. $89, children 5-18 $68. AmEx/D/MC/V.)*

ATV OUTFITTERS. This is a rumbling, bumpy, muddy, and spectacular way to see the North Kohala mountains and waterfalls. These guides, all of whom are 4th, 5th, and 6th generation Kohala natives, lead groups along the King Kamehameha and Kohala sugar plantation trails. They offer ATV trips on the Historical Ocean Cliff Trail (1½hr., $114), 15 mi. Waterfall Adventure (2hr., $176), and 22 mi. Deluxe Adventure (3hr., $249). Reservations required. *(Just off Rte. 270 in Kapaau; turn toward the ocean at the sign. ☎889-6000; www.outfittershawaii.com. Open M-Sa 7am-4pm. Ages 16 and up to drive, 7 and up to ride with a guide. AmEx/D/MC/V.)*

HIKING

The landscape of the northwest corner of the Big Island is often overlooked. However, the valleys, beaches, and rainforest yield some of the most adventurous and scenic hikes on the island. Bring water, sturdy shoes, and, for stream hikes, be prepared for extensive wading and aggressive mosquitoes. Rock-hopping is much easier in a pair of water-proof shoes, such as tevas, chacos, crocs, or tabis.

KAPU. Signs that read "*kapu*" (forbidden) are common throughout the Kohala range. This sign is not just a decoration–it marks private property. Always be respectful when hiking, and consult tourist offices for the most up-to-date information on the following trails. Let's Go recommends asking landowners for permission before venturing into *kapu* territory.

POLOLU VALLEY TRAIL. *(15-20min. one-way. Easy.)* The Pololu Valley Trail leaves the Pololu Valley Overlook at the end of Rte. 270 and quickly drops down the slope to the valley's gray-sand beach. This short and easy (though steep) jaunt wraps around the cliff, bringing the tip of at least four valleys, the thick vegetation of Maui, and the boundless Pacific into view.

HONOKANENUI VALLEY TRAIL. *(3-4hr. round-trip. Moderate to challenging.)* Honokanenui trail is a long and energizing hike from Pololu Valley Beach to the next valley: bring water, good hiking shoes, bug spray, and sunblock. The trail is well maintained but not always well marked, and at least once, the trail crosses into private property. The Honokanenui Trail begins on the other side of the stream from the end of the Pololu Valley Trail (see above). Following the beach initially, the trail eventually climbs to a ridge with an arresting view. It then twists back down through bamboo, pineapple trees, and a host of other plants before ending at a stream, just before the point of absolute sensory overload. From here, it is possible to continue hiking through the seven valleys; however, the trail becomes more challenging and only experienced hikers should attempt to go farther. The trip to Waipio takes at least 9 days and involves serious backcountry camping and extreme hiking conditions. Returning from Honokanenui, a trail (trail markers are any three or more stacked stones) just before the stream leads to a boulder beach. With wonderful cliff views and crashing waves, this is the place to break for lunch before making the return hike.

WAIKAMA FALLS HIKE. *(¼ mi., 20min. one-way. Challenging.)* The trailhead is on the mountain side of Rte. 270 about ½ mi. from the Pololu Valley Overlook (p. 251). Look for a plain white post; the trailhead is otherwise unmarked, just follow the stream. Strap on a pair of waterproof shoes and prepare for a slippery, muddy, and buggy adventure. Note that stream hiking with open cuts can result in *leptospirosis* infections; think twice before walking into the water with exposed wounds. Hopping from one rock to the next, few hikers manage this without slipping at least once. At the end of the "trail," you'll stand sweaty and wet in a murky pool in the middle of a rainforest as a waterfall tumbles over large boulders.

KAUHOLA POINT LIGHTHOUSE. *(15-20min. one-way. Easy.)* The trail starts in Kapaau off Hwy. 270. Turn toward the ocean at the ATV Outfitters sign. A dirt road takes you to a gate; park on the right and head through the gate, making sure to close it behind you. The dirt path to the lighthouse is nothing more than a straight shot to the ocean. Although the trail lacks scenery, it leads to an austere white lighthouse that towers over a jagged coastline with water spraying against brown cliffs.

SOUTH KOHALA

The most luxurious resorts of South Kohala are islands within an island; there are no true towns, only resort endeavors backed by multi-million dollar budgets. The South Kohala coast enjoys a near-perfect 363 days of sun annually. The resorts take meticulous care of the beaches, combing the sand smooth and providing beach chairs, cool showers, and hammocks along some stretches. Because the entire Hawaiian shoreline is public access by law, even travelers on a shoestring can live it up on the beaches of the most exclusive resorts—just don't forget your bag lunch. Hwy. 19 carves through these desolate lava flows on its way toward the Kohala mountain range; it is along this formidable route that men and women run the grueling marathon leg of the annual Ironman Triathlon.

ACCOMMODATIONS

In South Kohala, the overwhelming majority of the accommodations are pricey resorts. Vacation rentals in nearby Waikaloa and Puako are sometimes available online. Try **www.sunquest-hawaii.com** for condo rentals in Waikaloa. **Vacation Rentals** (☎882-7000; www.vacationbigisland.com) offers more reasonably priced condos and cottages in Puako. For those interested in the full South Kohala experience, resort and all, a good deal can be saved by giving up the ocean view.

Mauna Kea Beach Hotel, 62-100 Mauna Kea Beach Dr. (☎882-7222; www.maunakeabeachhotel.com), 32 mi. north of Kona on Hwy. 19, between mi. markers 68 and 69. Far and away the best of South Kohala, the opulence of the Mauna Kea is intoxicating. Breeze-swept buildings overlook a stunning crescent of sand—one that Laurence Rockefeller first visited in 1960, just 5 years before beginning construction on the hotel. 40 years later, the entire complex is as swank—and ridiculously expensive—as ever. 6 restaurants, 2 golf courses, and 13 tennis courts. Tu night luau starts at sunset ($82, ages 5-12 $40). Reservations recommended. Check website for special rates. Check-in 3pm. Check-out noon. Rooms $390-660; suites $975-1650. AmEx/D/MC/V. ❺

Mauna Lani Bay Hotel, 68-1400 Mauna Lani Dr. (☎855-6622; www.maunalani.com), north of the Kona airport on Hwy. 19, between mi. markers 73 and 74; continue around the 2nd right at the rotary. In one of the most intimate of the South Kohala resorts, guests in search of tranquility are rewarded. Rooms are thoughtfully designed, with a marble-floored baths and sizable balconies. Ask about the ancient fishponds, settlement remains, and the extensive petroglyph collection. Standard room $430, with ocean view $670; bungalow $5200-5900. Cash only... just kidding. AmEx/D/MC/V. ❺

Hapuna Prince Hotel, 62-100 Kaunaoa Dr. (☎880-1111; www.hapunabeachprinceho-tel.com), on the mountain side of Rte. 19, south of the Mauna Kea entrance. Although you head *mauka* (toward the mountains) to get to this resort, the Hapuna boasts at least a partial ocean view for every one of its rooms. The resort is perched at the north end of Hapuna Beach and offers myriad amenities, golf and fitness in particular. More price flexibility than at other resorts. Check online for discounts. Check-in 3pm. Check-out noon. Rooms $370-650; suites $1250-7000. AmEx/D/MC/V. ❺

Hilton Waikoloa Village, 425 Waikoloa Beach Dr. (☎886-1234; www.hiltonwaikaloavil-lage.com). Turn onto Waikoloa Beach Dr. from Rte. 19 between mi. markers 76 and 77 and go past the Waikoloa Beach Marriot and Kings' Shops. Extravagance and indulgence hardly seem to be sufficient words to describe this playground for the privileged. Recreation options include: 7 restaurants, 2 golf courses, 8 tennis courts, a multi-million dollar art collection, 4-acre lagoon, monorail, slow-cruising boat-shuttle, and a full lineup of entertainment options for young and old. Legends of the Pacific Luau F $78, under 12 $39. Check-in 3pm. Check-out noon. Room rates are subject to change, call ahead. $199-549; suites $995-5800. AmEx/D/MC/V. ❺

BEACHES

Kohala's got sunshine on a rainy day; when it's gray to the north or south, the sky is usually blue over the Kohala coast. Some of the island's best white-sand beaches, listed here from south to north, are only a paved resort driveway away. Just don't forget the sunblock.

KIHOLO BAY. *(Snorkeling. Open daily 24hr.)* Although this bay lacks sand and the narrow beach is all but invisible when the tide is up, the water is more than able to entertain visitors. Green sea turtles make their home here; remember that these creatures are protected by state and federal laws, and touching them is illegal and harmful to the turtles. To reach the beach, turn toward the ocean onto the gravel road between mi. markers 82 and 83. As the road forks, stay right; once the road nears the shoreline, there is a parking area. From there, walk to the shore and, facing the ocean, turn right. The beach is about a 20min. walk.

ANAEHOOMALU BEACH. *(Snorkeling. Wind sports. Open daily 6am-8pm.)* Waikoloa Beach Resort sits on a white-sand beach that stretches south toward Kona along a picturesque bay. Known to locals as "A-Beach," or "A-Bay," its consistently calm waters and sandy bottom make it one of the most popular swimming, snorkeling, and windsurfing spots around. Part of a state park, the beach has showers, toilets, and drinking water at its southern end.

At the northern end of A-Beach, **Ocean Sports,** the beach hut on the sand, arranges all sorts of aquatic activities in the area—from snorkeling ($6 per hr., $50 per wk.) to sunset cruises to scuba diving and windsurfing. (☎886-6666. Open daily 8am-5pm. Cruises M, W, F-Sa 4:30pm. $73, ages 3-12 $53; windsurfing lessons $60 per hr.; rental $30 per hr.; snacks and drinks $1-3.) Past Ocean Sports to the north, at the Marriot, nonguests are free to enjoy a volleyball net, a running/circuit training loop, and rows of beach chairs. To reach the beach, make the turn for the Waikoloa Beach Resort between mi. markers 76 and 77, 8 mi. south of Kawaihae and 25 mi. north of Kailua-Kona. The beach parking lot is the first left turn on the road across from the Kings' Shops.

WAIALEA BEACH (69 BEACH). *(Open daily 24hr.)* This little-known stretch of white sand was given its scandalous moniker because of the privacy and seclusion it once offered. It's much busier these days, but it's still a good find. A white tree twists out over the beach, providing visitors with shade and a place to spend a day without worrying about sunburn. Full facilities, but no lifeguard. Turn toward the ocean onto Puako Rd. from Hwy. 19 between mi. markers 70 and 71. Take your first right at the dump gate onto a single-lane road and drive until telephone pole #71, indicated by small gold numbers about 10 ft. up. A dirt path leads to a parking lot and the beach.

HAPUNA BEACH. *(Boogie boarding. Open daily 7am-8pm. Lifeguards 9am-4pm.)* One of America's best beaches, this ½ mi. stretch of sand is exactly what you'd picture when you think of Hawaii. It's not a secret either: expect crowds, as tourists and locals plant themselves firmly on the sand from the early morning until the fabled green flash of the sunset. Swimming is excellent in the calm seas, and when the surf kicks up, the beach becomes a boogie boarder's heaven. Public entrance is off Rte. 19 between mi. markers 69 and 70. **Paradise Grill,** on the northern end of the grassy walk down to the sand, offers a full menu of beach food (fish tacos, $8) and a healthy inventory of beach rentals ($10 each; open daily 9am-4pm).

MAUNA KEA BEACH. *(Surfing. Open daily sunrise to sunset. Lifeguards 8am-sunset.)* At the end of the luxury resort, yet another flawless crescent of sand awaits. Check with the hotel lifeguards on the surf conditions—in the winter this beach sees some impressive swells. Mauna Kea has full facilities. Thirty-two miles north of downtown Kona on Rte. 19 between mi. markers 68 and 69, there is access the beach through the road to Mauna Kea Hotel. Those not staying at the hotel have to stop at the gate and get a beach parking pass, valid from sunrise to sunset. Parking is limited, so come early.

MAUU MAE BEACH. *(Open daily 8am-5pm.)* Although at the same resort as Mauna Kea, Mauu Mae couldn't be more different. Smaller, shady, and murky, Mauu Mae rarely hosts any resort guests, though it does offer a great spot to park it beneath a tree and get out of the sun. Like Mauna Kea, this beach is accessed through the Mauna Kea Beach Hotel Rd. (see directions above). The hotel provides free parking passes and directions. The beach is the third right inside the resort; follow the road as it crosses two bridges and park just before the road turns to dirt. Follow the trail and go left at the sign post.

SIGHTS

PUUKOHOLA HEIAU NATIONAL HISTORICAL SITE. According to legend, Puukohola played a key role in Kamehameha's unification of the islands. Today, though, stripped of some of its natural splendor by nearby development, it nevertheless retains its historic and cultural significance and commanding position on the coastline. The park's Visitors Center gives out pamphlets for a self-guided tour of three *heiaus* (temples). Don't miss the 3min. video—it's surprisingly worthwhile. The first site along the walking path is the sprawling **Puukohola**

Heiau, built by Kamehameha in the late 18th century. Farther down the hillside is **Mailekini Heiau,** an older structure thought to have been built for war or agricultural purposes. The final *heiau,* **Hale o Kapuni Heiau,** submerged offshore, was dedicated to the shark gods. Although initially built above the high-water mark, it has been underwater since the 1950s. Like the Mookini Luakini Heiau to the north, this temple is believed to have been built with volcanic rock extracted from the Pololu Valley and carried along a chain of human laborers to the final sacred site. King Kamehameha is believed to have labored on this *heiau* alongside his men. Across Rte. 270 and off the self-guided walking trail in the corner of the park is **John Young's homestead.** Young, a stranded British sailor, became a trusted military adviser to Kamehameha. *(10 mi. west of Waimea and 34 mi. north of Kona along Rte. 270, near the intersection of Hwy. 19 and 270. ☎882-7218; www.nps.gov/puhe. Open daily 7:30am-4pm. Free.)*

MAUI

The second-oldest, second-largest, and second most-developed island in the Hawaiian chain, Maui is far from second-best. Not as developed as Oahu, but with more attractions than Kauai and much of the same natural beauty, Maui stakes a solid claim that *Maui no ka oi!* (Maui is the best!) Families delight in the beach activities of Kaanapali and Kihei, and honeymooning couples romance on secluded coasts and waterfall hikes.

Most visitors first become familiar with the dry leeward side, where the resorts have turned *kiawe* tree deserts into golf courses. The less developed, dense rainforest of the windward side of the West Maui mountains grows acres of ripe fruit trees and ferns. At the high altitudes of Haleakala Crater, rainforest gives way to forests of towering pines, redwoods, and eucalyptus. The central valley, located in the narrow isthmus between Haleakala and the West Maui mountains, is carpeted from end to end with sugarcane: the heart of agriculture on Maui. Maui is the only island that retains a significant sugarcane crop (43,000 acres), staving off residential and commercial development in the valley.

Maui's water bristles with marine life, including hundreds of species found only in the island's reef. Winter (December through April) is high season, when the largest group of humpback whales (about 3000 of them) gather off the south coast. Big-wave surfing on the North Shore coincides with whale-watching and attracts its own onlookers. Surfing, boogie boarding, windsurfing, and kiteboarding are popular year-round and form the center of both tourism and island life. Countless young people move to Maui to work and surf.

As commercial as Maui has become, the identity of the Hawaiian community remains strong and is constantly evolving. Grassroots movements have sprung up to reclaim sacred lands, educate visitors about Hawaiian history and culture, and deal with internal community issues. The lively debates in the editorial pages of *Maui News* provide a glimpse into the most current concerns, and there is a growing number of opportunities for visitors to learn actively from locals about native traditions. Maui's rich local culture is the essence of what makes the island so special—a fusion of ethnic groups whose love of the island is contagious.

HIGHLIGHTS OF MAUI

BE THE FIRST TO SEE DAY BREAK from the summit of Haleakala (p. 311) as the sun lights up the horizon.

DRIVE THERE AND BACK AGAIN along the Hana Highway (p. 294), stopping to enjoy the waterfalls along the road and the Pools of Oheo past Hana.

SHED YOUR INHIBITIONS at Little Beach (p. 292) in Makena.

ADMIRE the majestic grace of hundreds of humpback whales (p. 289) as they frolic off the coast of Maui from December to April.

SNORKEL IN THE FISHBOWL, a secret cove in the Ahihi-Kinau Natural Area Reserve (p. 292).

INTERISLAND TRANSPORTATION

Flights from the neighboring islands start around $120 round-trip, although some cost as much as $200, and prices vary depending on the season. Maui's

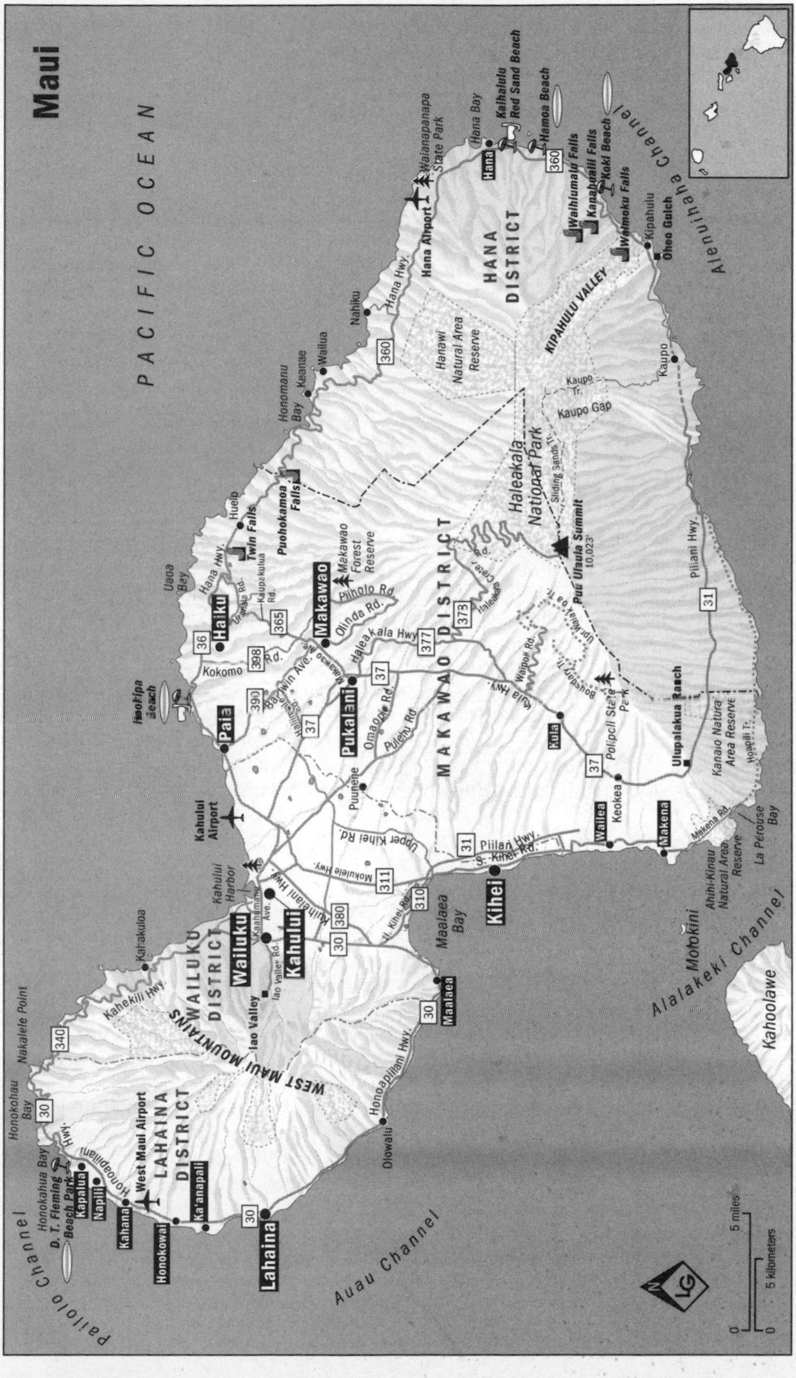
Maui
PACIFIC OCEAN
Pailolo Channel
Auau Channel
Alalakeki Channel
Alenuihaha Channel
Kahoolawe
Molokini
LAHAINA DISTRICT
WAILUKU DISTRICT
MAKAWAO DISTRICT
HANA DISTRICT
WEST MAUI MOUNTAINS
Lahaina
Honokowai
Kahana
Napili
Kapalua
Ka'anapali
West Maui Airport
D. T. Fleming Beach Park
Honokahua Bay
Honokohau Bay
Nakalele Point
Kahakuloa
Kahekili Hwy.
Honoapiilani Hwy.
Olowalu
Maalaea
Maalaea Bay
Iao Valley
Wailuku
Kahului
Kahului Harbor
Kahului Airport
Kihei
Wailea
Makena
Keokea
Kula
Pukalani
Makawao
Haiku
Paia
Ho'okipa Beach
Kokomo
Puunene
Uaoa Bay
Huelo
Twin Falls
Puohokamoa Falls
Makawao Forest Reserve
Honomanu Bay
Keanae
Wailua
Nahiku
Hana Hwy.
Hana Airport
Waianapanapa State Park
Hana Bay
Hana
Kaihalulu Red Sand Beach
Hamoa Beach
Koki Beach
Wailua Falls
Kanahuali Falls
Waimoku Falls
Kipahulu
Oheo Gulch
KIPAHULU VALLEY
Hanawi Natural Area Reserve
Haleakala National Park
Kaupo Gap
Kaupo Tr.
Kaupo
Sliding Sands Tr.
Puu Ulaula Summit 10,023'
Polipoli State Park
Ulupalakua Ranch
Kanaio Natural Area Reserve
Hoapili Tr.
Piilani Hwy.
Ahihi-Kinau Natural Area Reserve
La Pérouse Bay
Makena Rd.
S. Kihei Rd.
Piilani Hwy.
Upper Kihei Rd.
Mokulele Hwy.
Kuihelani Hwy.
Haleakala Hwy.
Kula Hwy.
Omaopio Rd.
Pulehu Rd.
Olinda Rd.
Piiholo Rd.
Baldwin Ave.
Makawao Ave.
Waipoli Rd.
Haleakala Crater Rd.
Kaupakulua Rd.
Ulumalu Rd.
Iao Valley Rd.
Kaahumanu Ave.
N. Kihei Rd.
30
31
36
37
311
310
340
360
365
373
377
380
390
398
0
5 miles
5 kilometers
LG

major airport is **Kahului International Airport (OGG),** in Kahului in Central Maui. International and interisland carriers fly to Kahului, and their flight schedules change constantly. **Aloha Air** (☎800-367-5250; www.alohaair.com) and **Hawaiian Airlines** (☎800-367-5320; www.hawaiianair.com) fly to Hilo, the Big Island; Honolulu, Oahu; Hoolehua, Molokai; Kona, the Big Island; and Lihue, Kauai. **Pacific Wings** (☎873-0877 or 888-575-4546; www.pacificwings.com) offers daily service to Hana, Maui; Hilo, the Big Island; Honolulu, Oahu; Kona, the Big Island; the Kalaupapa Peninsula, Molokai; and Waimea, the Big Island. There are two other airports on Maui: **Hana Airport (HNM),** on Maui's east coast, which sees a lot of commuter flights and unscheduled air traffic; and **Kapalua Airport (JHM),** which handles only prop planes and commuter flights.

The **Molokai Princess** (☎667-6165 or 800-275-6969; www.molokaiferry.com) makes daily trips between Maui and Molokai. It leaves from Lahaina Harbor (1½hr.; daily 6pm, M-Sa 7:15am; one-way $40, children $20). **Expeditions** (☎661-3756 or 800-695-2624) runs ferries from Lahaina Harbor to Lanai (45min.; 5 per day 6:45am-5:45pm; one-way $25, children $20). The easiest and most convenient way to get around Maui is to rent a car. For intercity and local transportation, consult the **Transportation** section for each town.

ACCOMMODATIONS

In Maui, travelers can stay in budget hostels in Wailuku, Paia, or Lahaina for about $20 per night, in condominiums in Kihei from $70 per night, in B&Bs anywhere from $75 per night, in vacation rentals from $45 per night (check www.vrbo.com for an extensive listing), or in hotels from $125 per night. For long-term accommodations, check the *Maui News*, in print or online at www.mauinews.com. Studios start around $500 per month.

Whatever you decide, make reservations as soon as you know the dates of your trip. High season runs between December 15 and April 15, and rates are highest during December and January. During high season, accommodations are booked three to four months in advance (even longer for popular B&Bs). Summer is a second peak season; fall and spring are the least popular times to visit.

WEST MAUI

West Maui's mountains are older than Haleakala and have been scarred over the years with deep rifts from stream erosion. Their hulking mass rises out of the cane fields in velvety folds before disappearing into the cloud cover. Unlike the valleys northwest of Wailuku, which get almost 400 in. of rainfall per year, the *pali* (cliffs) on the leeward side are extremely arid. Despite the lack of rainfall, West Maui has continued to grow, and resorts now stretch 10 mi. north of Lahaina from Kaanapali to Kapalua. The popularity of real estate in the area is certainly understandable: the western coast is lined with gorgeous beaches, and few sunbathers would trade the dry heat for the windward side's rain showers.

There is only one road in and out of West Maui: Hwy. 30, or Honoapiilani Hwy., which becomes Rte. 340 (Kahekili Hwy.) past Honokohau. Hwy. 30 is a two-lane road that hugs the scenic coastline from Maalaea north. Near Maalaea, Hwy. 30 intersects with Rte. 380 (Dairy Rd.), which goes northeast to Kahului, and Rte. 310/31, which heads southeast to Kihei. Although the northern route (Rte. 340) may be the quickest between Kapalua and Wailuku, it can be dangerous. The road narrows down to one lane, which in many places is scarcely the width of a car, and hugs the cliffs with no guardrail protection from the water

below. This route can be done as a scenic drive at a leisurely pace, but for everyday travel, stick to Hwy. 30. When accidents close Hwy. 30, Rte. 340 might also get shut down so that people won't be tempted to take the hazardous back route. If this happens, be prepared to wait for a few hours, or just turn around and go to the beach!

LAHAINA

Lahaina means "merciless sun," and visitors will quickly find that the city is aptly named—in any season, Lahaina (pop. 9,118) is *hot.* Although it may be difficult to visualize, Lahaina was once prized by the Hawaiian royalty for its abundance of fresh water, and its natural harbor and convenient location halfway up the west coast made it a bustling port. From the 1820s to the 1840s, King Kamehameha III made Lahaina his home, turning it into the capital and center of the emerging Hawaiian democracy. Remnants of Lahaina's history are still visible in the restored buildings and sites of the downtown historic district, though they are overwhelmed in many places by t-shirt shops, activity booths, and theme restaurants. Lahaina has become a tourist trap, but that doesn't keep people from enjoying it. Sitting on the seawall on Front St. provides endless entertainment people-watching as well as front row seats to a dazzling sunset.

TRANSPORTATION

Bus: Service available between Central, South, and West Maui. On West Maui, buses make the following stops: Maalaea Harbor, Lahaina Center, Whalers Village in Kaanapali, Kahana, Napili, and Kapalua. In Lahaina take **route D** from Lahaina Cannery Mall to Whalers Village where you can then pick up **route E** to go all the way north to Kahana, Napili, and Kapalua. All routes are $1 one-way and times are staggered throughout the day. Call the **Maui Transit Office** (☎270-7511) or check www.mauicounty.gov/bus for the most up-to-date information. The bus system is operated by **Roberts Hawaii** (☎871-4838), and they can often tell you the easiest way to get where you need to go.

Ferry: An easy and inexpensive way to reach Maui's neighboring islands is by ferry out of Lahaina Harbor. The **Molokai Princess** (☎667-6165 or 800-275-6969) makes daily trips to **Molokai.** For more information, see p. 256. The **Expeditions Ferry** (☎661-3756 or 800-695-2624) sails to Manele Harbor on **Lanai** (45min.; 5 per day 6:45am-5:45pm; one-way $25, children $20) and back (5 per day 8am-6:45pm).

Taxis: Although the town of Lahaina is pedestrian-friendly, cabs might come in handy for travelers staying slightly north or south of town. You'll have to call in advance to get a cab; they rarely search for passengers. Several taxi companies operate out of Lahaina, including **Island Taxi** (☎667-5656) until 11pm, **Paradise Taxi** (☎661-4455) until 2am, **La-Taxi** (☎661-4545) 24hr., and **AB Taxi** (☎667-7575) 24hr.

Car Rental: Most national chains operate out of Kahului, near the airport (see p. 276), but some, like **Enterprise,** have branches near Lahaina or the Kapalua Airport.

Mopeds: Cruising around Lahaina on a moped is an efficient and fun way to reach some of the best beaches in West Maui. **Island Riders,** 126 Hinau St. (☎661-9966), rents mopeds in addition to exciting sports cars. $45 for use 8am-5pm, $54 for 24hr.

Bikes: Lahaina is more than manageable on 2 wheels. **West Maui Cycles** (☎661-9005) rents regular beach riders for $15 per day and $60 per week as well as road bikes for $50 per day or $200 per week.

ORIENTATION

Lahaina sits on the ocean, halfway up Maui's western coast. **Highway 30 (Honoapiilani Highway)** runs through the city and all the way north past Kaanapali and Napili. In light traffic, it takes about 25min. to drive the 10 mi. from Lahaina north to Kapalua. Lahaina's main road, **Front St.,** parallels the highway along the waterfront and is connected to it by six cross streets (from south to north: Shaw St., Prison St., Dickenson St., Lahainaluna Rd., Papalaua St., and Kenui St.). Drivers cannot make left turns onto the highway from Prison and Kenui. **Wainee St.** runs the length of Lahaina, between the highway and Front St.

PRACTICAL INFORMATION

TOURIST AND FINANCIAL SERVICES

Tourist Office: Lahaina Visitor Center, 648 Wharf St. (☎667-9193; www.visitlahaina.com), in the Old Lahaina Courthouse, in Banyan Tree Sq., directly across from the harbor and the lighthouse. Maps and brochures are available. Gift shop, museum, and restrooms. Arranges 10 annual events and festivals. Open daily 9am-5pm.

Banks: American Savings Bank, 154 Papalaua St. (☎667-9561; open M-F 9am-6pm, Sa 9am-1pm) and **Bank of Hawaii,** 32 Papalaua St. (☎661-8781; open M-Th 8:30am-4pm, F 8:30am-6pm) are located near the Old Lahaina Center and have **24hr. ATMs.**

LOCAL SERVICES

Library: Lahaina Public Library, 680 Wharf St. (☎662-3950). Copies $0.20. **Internet access** with a 3-month visitor's card ($10), limited to 1hr. session each day. Open Tu noon-8pm, W-Th 9am-5pm, F-Sa 10:30am-4:30pm.

Laundromats: One Hour Martinizing Dry Cleaning, 3350 Lower Honoapiilani Hwy. (☎661-6768). Coin-op laundry M only; quick dry-cleaning daily. Open daily 8am-5pm.

EMERGENCY AND COMMUNICATIONS

Police: Lahaina Police (☎661-4441), located north of Lahaina on Honoapiilani Hwy. above Wahikuli Wayside Park; follow the road that curves behind the post office.

Pharmacies: Longs Drugs (☎667-4384), in the Lahaina Cannery Mall, sells everything from film to fine wine. Open M-F 8am-6pm, Sa-Su 8am-5pm. **Lahaina Pharmacy** (☎661-3119), in the Old Lahaina Center, is open M-F 9am-5:30pm, Sa 9am-2pm.

Medical Services: Kaiser Permanente Clinic, 910 Wainee St. (☎662-6900, after hours 243-6000), and **Maui Medical Group,** 130 Prison St. (☎661-0051), are both open M-F 8am-5pm, Sa 8am-noon.

Internet Access: Travelers can go online at the **Lahaina Public Library** and the following locations:

Breakwall Cafe, 505 Front St., Ste. 142 (☎661-7220), has 2 DSL terminals and serves coffee, sandwiches, salads, and smoothies. $0.10 per min., $6 per hr. Free wireless connection for laptop users. Open M-Sa 7am-2pm. Cash only.

Buns of Maui, 878 Front St. (☎661-5407), in the Old Lahaina Shopping Center, next to the Maui Theater. With 6 stations and A/C, this is the cheapest place to check your email. **$0.08 per min.** with no minimum. Printing $0.25 per page ($0.50 for color). Sweet, gooey cinnamon rolls ($2) are available. Open daily 7:30am-8:30pm, including holidays. AmEx/D/MC/V.

Post Offices: The downtown **Lahaina Post Office,** 132 Papalaua St. (☎661-0904), in the Old Lahaina Center, tends to have long lines and is open M-F 8:15am-4:15pm. The **main branch,** at 1760 Honoapiilani Hwy. (☎800-275-8777), 1 mi. north of town at the intersection of Leialii Parkway, offers more flexible hours and general delivery pick-up. Open M-F 8:30am-5pm, Sa 9am-1pm.

Postal Code: 96761.

ACCOMMODATIONS AND CAMPING

Staying in Lahaina is possible on any budget, and the affordable accommodations in the old town have more character than the chain hotels and condos in the resorts farther north. If you plan to partake in Lahaina's nightlife, it's a good idea to stay in town to avoid a drive home.

Patey's Place, 761 Wainee St. (☎667-0999). There's no sign on the door of this hostel; just look for the street number and wooden fence with surfboards. Patey's offers the cheapest beds in West Maui and a strong sense of community. Many young people stay, as well as several long-term guests. Shared kitchen, laundry, TV room, coin laundry, and back porch. 2 of the private rooms have their own bathrooms; other guests share. The hostel has quiet hours 10pm-8:30am; common areas are off-limits and guests either sleep or head to the beach or bars. Reception 8:30am-noon and 5-10pm. Check-in and check-out 10am. 4-bed dorms $22; singles $50; doubles $60. MC/V. ❶

Old Lahaina House, 407 Ilikahi St. (☎667-4663 or 800-847-0761; www.accommodationsmaui.com), 1 block south of Shaw St. on the corner of Ilikahi and Kauaula Rd. Nestled in the residential end of Lahaina, this pink house is only a minute from a pretty beach. Gracious owner sees that rooms are equipped with beach towels and picnic cooler. Rooms have A/C, TV, phone, microwave, fridge, coffee maker, and private bath. Guests can enjoy the pool in the house's tropical courtyard. Owner also manages a gorgeous 1-bedroom cottage across the street, furnished with A/C, laundry, and full bath. Activities booked for no extra fee. 3-night min. Reserve with 50% deposit. Rooms Dec.-Apr. $89-129; May-Nov. $69-119; cottage $130-150. AmEx/MC/V. ❸

Lahaina Inn, 127 Lahainaluna Rd. (☎661-0577 or 800-669-3444; www.lahaininn.com). Perfect for a romantic stay in old Lahaina, the Inn offers 10 rooms and 2 suites uniquely decorated with turn-of-the-century furnishings and stocked with yukata robes for guests. Modern comforts include in-room classical music, A/C, and a phone. Guests can enjoy watching passers-by from the rocking chairs on lanais. Parking $7 per day. Check-in 1pm. Check-out 11am. Reserve with 50% deposit. Rooms $130-180. AmEx/MC/V. ❹

Lahaina Budget Accommodations, 252 Lahainaluna Rd. (☎661-6655), at the corner with Honoapiilani Hwy, across from the 76 gas station. Run by the same owner as Old Lahaina House; rooms come with A/C, fridge, and microwave. 4 single rooms share a bath. Private double has its own bath. Ask Adam at the front desk anything about the city, and he'll point you in the right direction. Rooms $59; $10 nightly cleaning fee for stays less than 3 nights. AmEx/MC/V. ❸

Makai Inn, 1415 Front St. (☎662-3200), on the quieter northern end of Front St. All suites have a bedroom, small sitting area, full kitchen, and modern bathroom, though no TV, phone, or maid service. Rooms are cooled by the ocean breeze. All suites face the inner courtyard garden, and the pricier rooms have ocean views. On-site parking and coin-op laundry. Check-out 11am. Reserve with credit card; no deposit required. Discounts for stays of 1 week or longer. Rooms $95-156. AmEx/MC/V. ❸

Camp Pecusa, 800 Olawalu Village Rd. (☎661-4303), 6 mi. from Lahaina, between mi. markers 14 and 15, off Honoapiilani Hwy. down a small gravel road which is easy to miss; look for a small white sign about ½ mi. south of the Olawalu General Store. The camp's secluded sites are right on the water and offer a nice, quiet place to spend the night. Shower, sink, portable bathroom, clothesline, tables, and simple cooking sites available. No reservations. Camping $10 per person. ❶

Papalaua Beach Park, between mi. markers 11 and 12, just north of the tunnel on Honoapiilani Hwy. This beachfront county-maintained campsite can be noisy, and even dangerous, since it's close to the road and frequently crowded. Every Thursday all campers must leave for cleaning. Permits required. See **Camping in Hawaii,** p. 75, for more information. Permits $5 per night, $0.50 per child. ❶

FOOD

Nearly every restaurant in Lahaina caters exclusively to tourists; however, inflated prices do purchase a larger selection of options. With a few exceptions, Lahaina restaurants stop serving by 9pm, so plan accordingly. For groceries, there is a 24hr. **Safeway,** 1221 Honoapiilani Hwy. (☎667-4392), in the Lahaina Cannery Mall, and a **Foodland** in the Old Lahaina Center. (☎661-0975. Open daily 6am-midnight.) **Down to Earth Natural Foods Store,** 193 Lahainaluna Rd., on the corner of Wainee St., has organic produce, packaged food, smoothies, and a salad bar. (☎667-2855. Open M-Sa 8am-8pm, Su 9am-8pm.)

RESTAURANTS

Blu Maui, 839 Front St. (☎661-9591). This restaurant sits right on the water and proudly boasts of providing the best sunset for its patrons. Along with several classic Greek and Mediterranean dishes, Blu Maui's tandoori oven produces tantalizing daily specials. Try the *souvlaki* ($13). Lunch menu 11am-3:30pm; dinner Su-Th 5-10pm and F-Sa 5-11pm, burgers and appetizers can be ordered in between. Happy hour 3-6pm and 9-11pm. Drafts $2; mixed drinks $3.50. AmEx/D/MC/V. ❸

Kimos, 845 Front St. (☎661-4811), offers seafood, steak, and burgers with a fun and vibrant atmosphere. Dinner entrees are filling but pricey ($20-28), and the wait can sometimes be very long. Lunch is your best bet ($8-13): the grilled teriyaki chicken sandwich with pineapple is heavenly. Ask to be seated near the water if possible, because the sea breeze is wonderful and the sunset is always spectacular. Lunch daily 11am-3:30pm; dinner 5-10pm. AmEx/D/MC/V. ❹

Lahaina Coolers, 180 Dickenson St. (☎661-7082), a block from Front St., serves decent food in a relaxed, open-air atmosphere with good classic rock music. Hearty menu includes the MocoLoco: an egg on top of a hamburger patty, placed on a layer of rice and covered in gravy ($9.50). Egg and griddle breakfasts $6-11. Lunch $13. Dinner entrees $9-25. Happy hour daily 3-6pm; mixed drinks and microbrews $3.25. Open daily 8am-2am; full menu until midnight. AmEx/D/MC/V. ❸

Thai Chef, Old Lahaina Shopping Center (☎667-2814). This cozy Thai restaurant has an extensive menu of curries, seafood dishes, and vegetarian and vegan options ($9-13). BYOB. Lunch M-F 11am-2pm; dinner nightly 5-9pm. D/MC/V. ❸

CAFES AND TAKE-OUT

Penne Pasta Cafe, 180 Dickenson St. (☎661-6633). Sizeable portions of pasta with homemade sauce (*bolognese fettuccine,* $8.25) are served in an understated, classy atmosphere slightly removed from bustling Front St. Pizzas, flatbreads ($2-8), and sandwiches ($6-8) also on the menu, but save room for dessert (tiramisu, $6). Open M-F 11am-9:30pm, Sa-Su 5-9:30pm. Delivery available. MC/V. ❷

Aloha Mixed Plate, 1285 Front St. (☎661-3322; www.alohamixedplate.com), right on the harbor next to the Old Lahaina Luau. A great place to sample Hawaiian food: *kalua* pig and other meat are served plate lunch style. The ocean view is first-class, and drumbeats emanating from the luau next door accompany dinner. Plate lunches $5-10, mini-plates $3-4.50. Sandwiches $4.50-8. Cocktails $4. Outdoor seating only. Happy hour 2-6pm; Mai Tais $2.50, beer $1.75. Open daily 10:30am-10pm. MC/V. ❶

Maui Tacos, 840 Wainee St. (☎661-8883), in Lahaina Sq. Sells cheap, filling, Hawaiian-named tacos and burritos with 5 kinds of homemade salsa. Open for breakfast (egg burrito, $3.50; *huevos rancheros,* $5.50). Additional locations in Napili Plaza and Kihei (p. 283). Takeout or eat at one of the small tables outside. Open M-Sa 9am-9pm, Su 9am-8pm. Delivery available 11am-2pm. AmEx/D/MC/V. ❶

House of Saimin, 845 Wainee St. (☎667-7572), in the Old Lahaina Center next to the Lahaina Pharmacy. Steaming bowls of *saimin* ($3.30-6.55), a ramen-like noodle soup, are served on a red U-shaped counter, beneath photos of the local Little League teams. Open Tu-Th 5pm-2am, F-Sa 5pm-3am. Cash only. ❶

Vinny's Pizza, 840 Wainee St. (☎661-6773), in Lahaina Sq. toward the back row of shops. The only place to grab a quick slice of pizza, Vinny's offers slices for $2.50 and a special lunch deal (2 slices and a soft drink, $5). Specialty pies include the three meat combo, all veggies, or Da Kine (pineapple, ham, and onions). Delivery available. Open 11am-10pm. AmEx/D/MC/V. ❶

BEACHES

Lahaina itself is not the place for sunbathing and swimming. The few sandy beaches have somewhat murky water and are only good for watching the sunset. There is a sandy beach behind the Lahaina Shores Resort (with public access a few blocks south of the resort on Front St.) and a good surf break a block south of the hotel. Generally, though, the beaches north and south of town are much better. **Puamana Beach Park,** the first beach south of Lahaina, is nice for a beachside picnic. **Launiupoko Wayside Park,** a mile farther south at mi. marker 18, has restrooms, showers, and a surf break popular with beginners. No camping is allowed at Launiupoko. **Ukumehame Beach Park,** ½ mi after mi. marker 13, also has picnic tables and is usually a little less crowded. All three parks have small surf and are often filled with families and a mix of locals and young visitors. **Baby Beach,** north of town, is another popular beach; the shallow water is good for children and beginning snorkelers. However, these beaches are unimpressive compared to the beaches north of Lahaina in **Kaanapali** and **Napili** (p. 270), and **Kapalua** (p. 272). Note that no Lahaina beaches have lifeguards. For lifeguards, head to **D. T. Fleming Beach Park** or **Kapalua Beach** in the Kapalua area, or to **Kaanapali Beach** or **Hanakaoo Beach** in the Kaanapali area.

ACTIVITIES

The activity booths that line Front St. offer an exciting number of choices, and it's easy for the budget traveler to become overwhelmed by glossy flyers and smooth-talking agents. This is a big business; companies market thrills by air, land, and sea, from helicopter rides to biking and parasailing. Watch out for false advertising; many of the super-low rates on activity boards are only for visitors with timeshares. There are also activities (boogie boarding, snorkeling, or hiking) that cost little or nothing and don't require a middleman. If you do opt to go with an activity booker, *Let's Go Hawaii* recommends **Best Hawaii Activities,** 252 Lahainaluna Rd., (☎661-6655), a pink house at the corner of Honoapiilani Hwy. across from the 76 gas station. Ask Adam for the cheapest way to get your favorite activity booked. **Tom Barefoot's Cashback Tours,** 834 Front St. (☎888-222-3601; www.tombarefoot.com), doesn't require a timeshare, but offers a wide selection of well-organized activities at a discount. **Boss Frogs,** 150 Lahainaluna Rd. (☎661-3333) is a cheap place to rent snorkel gear ($1.50-8 per day; $9-30 per week), boogie boards ($5 per day; $15 per week), or surfboards ($20 per day; $75 per week). Customers can return equipment at any of six shops. Open daily 8am-5pm. AmEx/D/MC/V.

SNORKELING. Before you splurge on a boat excursion, keep in mind that there is excellent snorkeling at beaches all along the West Maui coast. A self-guided adventure will cost you only a few bucks for the mask and fins. Many companies in Lahaina rent snorkel equipment for $2-10 per day. **Maui Dive Shop** (☎661-6166) is courteous and professional, with several locations, including one at the Lahaina Cannery Mall. The best West Maui snorkel spots are north of Lahaina in **Honolua Bay** (p. 273), **Kapalua Beach** (p. 272), **Kahekili Beach Park** (p. 270), and **Black Rock** or **Kaanapali Beach** (p. 270). Other good snorkel spots can be found near mi. marker 14 by the small town of Olowalu, and at **Slaughterhouse Beach.** Kahekili has free parking, and if you walk 15min. down to the end of the beach toward the Sheraton, **Black Rock** offers some of the best snorkeling around. If you want to take a boat excursion, head to the submerged crater of **Molokini.** On a good day, visibility at Molokini is over 150 ft. Plan on spending anywhere from $60 to $95; excursions typically take a few hours, and include equipment, drinks, and lunch. Conditions vary, and many snorkelers set on Molokini have ended up at "Turtle Town" or "Coral Gardens," less glamorous spots that have decent snorkeling, but are not appreciably better than what you can see from beaches for free.

SWIMMING WITH THE FISHES. Snorkeling is a great way to explore the deep blue waters of the Pacific, and an upgrade in snorkeling gear is definitely worth the money. Deluxe masks and snorkels with one-way valves run only about $8, and the splurge is well worth it. Better equipment will keep contact lenses dry and lungs salt water-free.

SCUBA DIVING. The most popular places for offshore dives near Lahaina are the neighboring island of **Lanai** and the back wall of **Molokini.** There are multiple companies competing for boat dive business in Lahaina. **Extended Horizons** (☎667-0611 or 888-DIVE-MAUI; www.extendedhorizons.com) is known for good service on boat dives, and beginner dives are offered on Tu and Th for $99. **Maui Dive Shop** (☎661-6166; www.mauidiveshop.com) is larger and less personal, though still reliable. For shore dives, **Kahekili Beach Park** is a good place for beginners (most certification classes start here). **Black Rock,** below the Kaanapali Sheraton, and the right side of **Honolua Bay** in summer are also popular West Maui dive spots. For shore dives, **Pacific Dive** (☎667-5331) is reputable and reasonably priced with intro dives for $69. Numerous companies give introductory classes, starting around $70; 2-day full certification classes run $290 and higher.

SURFING. Driving into Lahaina from the south, you'll see surfers from the road. **Olowalu** and **Launiupoko** (p. 263) usually have reliable breaks, though conditions change daily. There is a surf spot about a block south of the Lahaina Shores Beach Resort that is usually uncrowded and good for beginners, but watch out for waves breaking in the shallow water over the coral. **Honolua Bay** is famous for its winter surf, but beginners should stick to watching from the sand. Board rentals start at about $20 per day with discounts for weekly rentals. Expect to pay about $55 for a 2hr. group lesson and twice that for a private lesson. For mid-priced, reliable surf lessons, contact **Goofy Foot Surf School,** in the 505 Front St. Shopping Center. Teaching surfers of all ages, from the young to the young at heart, beginners are guaranteed to stand and ride at least one wave in their first lesson, or it's free. Intermediate lessons also available (☎244-9283; www.goofyfootsurfschool.com). Beginner lessons daily 8, 11am, and 2pm. Shop hours M-Sa 7:30am-9pm. Reservations by phone Su 9am-7pm. Group lesson $55, private $125. Intermediate level lesson $200 for 2 people, $275 for 3 people. 6hr. surf camp $250.

BOOGIE BOARDING. Catching waves on a boogie board is a lot easier than surfing. Driving toward Lahaina from the south, just look for places with good conditions and other boarders, pull over, and jump in. **Puamana Beach** (p. 263), just south of Lahaina, is usually good, but slightly rocky. Some of the beaches in Kaanapali are also excellent for boogie boarding, especially the blissfully deserted **Oneloa Beach** (p. 273) and the south end of **Kaanapali Beach**—though the waves may break too quickly there. Many recommend **D. T. Fleming Beach** (see p. 273), which is sandy and lifeguarded. All the surf shops in Lahaina also rent boogie boards ($5-8 per day; $20 per week). For a great deal on rentals, hit up **West Maui Sports,** 1287 Front St., which offers boards for $2.50 per day or $15 per week. (☎661-6252. Open M-Sa 8am-8pm, Su 8am-6pm. AmEx/D/MC/V.)

SAILING. Lahaina looks even better from offshore than on land. Although legal issues have made it harder for companies to rent sailboats, many companies have sunset and daytime sailing trips (some include dinner, others just snacks and drinks) on schooners or catamarans. **Trilogy,** 180 Lahainaluna Rd., is by far the biggest operator. In addition to its beautiful boats, another boon is Trilogy's excursion to Lanai; it is the only company that owns property on the island, enabling it to land and fix a nice barbecue lunch or dinner. (☎874-5649 or 888-225-MAUI; www.sailtrilogy.com. Trips $59-229.)

PARASAILING. Parasailing looks scarier than it is; the ride is a gentle glide that lasts about 10min. Companies only operate from May to December, to avoid whale breeding season. **Parasail Kaanapali** has a good deal for singles ($40) or tandems ($35 per person; weight min. 320 lb.) and leaves from Mala Wharf on the north end of town. (☎669-6555. Prices depend on the season and time of day—early runs are $10 cheaper.) Another option is **UFO Parasail,** whose rates are a bit higher, but they offer a simulated free fall at no extra charge if you buy the 800 ft. ride. (☎661-7836; www.ufoparasail.com. $47-62, depending on length of ride and time of day.) **West Maui Parasail** also offers singles, tandems, and early bird specials. (☎661-4060. $50-70.)

TRAIN. The **Lahaina Kaanapali Railroad** runs up and down Maui's northwest coast and is an entertaining way to get from Lahaina to the Puukolii Station in Kaanapali. The historic steam engine replicates the way islanders traveled during Maui's booming sugarcane era. Panoramic views of the island make a ride on the train a fun afternoon diversion. On Thursday nights, view the gorgeous Maui sunset aboard the train while enjoying a delicious barbecue dinner; the train leaves Puukoli Station at 5pm. $78; children $46. *(975 Limahana Pl. Turn right on Hinau St. off Honopiilani Hwy. and take another right on Limahana Pl. ☎667-6851 or 800-499-2307. Daily departures from Lahaina 11:05am, and 1, 2:30, and 4pm. $20, ages 3-12 $14. Free parking available.)*

HELICOPTERS. Beautiful from the ground, West Maui and Molokai are spectacular from the air. Most companies tour both locations during a 1hr. trip, peeking at the waterfalls hidden in the West Maui mountains, zipping across to circle the sea cliffs of Molokai, and returning to Iao Valley on Maui. This ride generally runs around $250 per person, but **Tom's** (p. 264) sells trips at about $125 per person for 30min.; the trip is almost guaranteed to be cheaper if booked through an activity vendor. Almost all trips leave from Kahului. Of all the companies that offer trips, **Alexair** (☎877-4354) is the only one that has two-way headsets so you can talk to the pilots. **Blue Hawaiian** (☎871-8844) also has an excellent reputation.

WHALE-WATCHING. From mid-December to mid-April (peaking in February and March), hundreds of humpback whales come to Maui to breed before continuing to Alaska. All along the southern and western coast, the whales put on quite a show, and you don't need to leave shore to see them breaching and spouting. If you do want a closer look, contact the Pacific Whale Foundation, 612 Front St., a nonprofit organization that contributes to whale research and conservation. (☎249-8811; www.pacificwhale.org. 2hr. whale-watch is $38, starting Dec. 15.)

SIGHTS

The **Lahaina Restoration Foundation,** a non-profit agency, maintains many of Lahaina's historic sites and publishes a brochure entitled *Lahaina: A Walking Tour of Historic and Cultural Sites,* available for free at **The Village Gift and Fine Arts,** 120 Dickenson, on the corner by Front. St., and the **Old Lahaina Courthouse Museum** and the public library, on Dickenson and Luakini St. The walking tour describes many sites in Lahaina's historic district, recounting the town's history through its whaling and missionary days and detailing the churches and cultural centers of Lahaina's various immigrant groups who were brought to the island to work the sugar plantations. For those interested in Hawaiian history but lack the budget or inclination to take the guided tour (see below), this is a better option.

That said, the most fulfilling way to explore Lahaina is to spend the $40 it costs to take a guided tour with **Maui Nei,** an award-winning grassroots organization devoted to relating the history of Lahaina from a Native Hawaiian's point of view. Local guides, working from oral histories, traditional chants, and archival research, lead small groups along a 2hr. walking tour of Lahaina's harbor and backstreets. In addition to breathing life into the historical sites, Maui Nei offers insight into what visitors can't see. The tour ends on what was once the sacred island of **Mokuula,** the home and burial site of Hawaiian royalty. (☎661-9494; www.mauinei.com. Tours are conducted only a few times each month, depending on interest. Call for more information.)

HIKING

LAHAINA PALI TRAIL. *(5½ mi. 2½-3hr. Elevation gain: 800 ft. Challenging.)* This trail is most rewarding during whale season (Dec.-Apr.), when the view from the top of the ridge can include hundreds of whales cavorting in the channel—bring binoculars. This hike works best if you have two cars, or can be dropped off at mi. marker 5 and picked up at mi. marker 11. Starting from the eastern trailhead allows you to get the tough part over with before finishing at the beach. The path begins with a steep climb up to Kealaloloa Ridge; once there, hikers are treated to a view of the central valley and Haleakala, and Kahoolawe, Molokini, and Lanai offshore. The trail will meet up with a service road; at this junction stay left and don't go up the hill towards the windmills. Stay on the road for a short stretch until the trail picks back up. The trail will then cross over a gravel construction road and descend gradually from the ridge. *Kiawe* trees provide modest shade along the way. The hike ends across the highway from the beach. This hike gets incredibly hot; hikers should be equipped with sturdy hiking boots, plenty of water, and sunscreen. *(The eastern trailhead is on the mountain side of Hwy. 30 at mi. marker 5, just south of the jct. with Rte. 380. Parking is available for a 2nd car at mi. marker 11 on the mountain side of Hwy. 30, just north of the tunnel.)*

ENTERTAINMENT

HULA. To get a free dose of hula, head to the **Center Stage** at the Lahaina Cannery Mall; see **Polynesian Hula** Tuesdays and Thursdays at 7pm, and come back on Saturdays and Sundays at 1pm for your weekend fix of **Keiki** (children's) **Hula.**

LUAU. If your visit to Maui won't be complete without a luau, Lahaina is definitely the best place to attend one. Many of the hotels offer their own versions of this traditional Hawaiian feast, but the most authentic is the **Old Lahaina Luau,** 1251 Front St., held nightly on the waterfront near Mala Wharf, across from the Cannery Mall. Guests are greeted with fresh orchid leis and a Mai Tai from the open bar. Along the water, craftspeople demonstrate lei-making and display their wares. Just before sunset, the *kalua* pig is unearthed from the *imu* (underground oven) in an intimate ceremony, and the feast begins. An exciting hula performance narrates the Polynesians' arrival in Hawaii and continues through the missionary and plantation periods to modern times. There are also two morning shows on Wednesdays and Fridays, which feature breakfast, a history of the islands, and a short hula show. Although not as authentic as the nightly luau, the morning shows are cheaper, and a fun cultural excursion. (☎667-1998 or 800-248-5828; www.oldlahainaluau.com. Reserve 2-4 weeks in advance, but last-minute cancellations may accommodate those without reservations. $89; 12 and under $52.)

SHOWS. Ulalena, 878 Front St., in the Old Lahaina Center, offers a modern interpretation of ancient Hawaiian myths and recent Hawaiian history, communicated through dance, song, chant, text, images, and remarkable aerial acrobatics. A live percussion group provides the performance with a pounding rhythm. (☎877-688-4800 or 661-9913; www.ulalena.com. Limited parking. Tu-Sa 7:30pm. $48-58; 1 child under 12 for free; additional children ages 3-10 $28-38. AmEx/D/MC/V.) Another fantastic, though not *quite* Hawaiian, show is **Warren & Annabelle's Magic Nightclub,** 900 Front St. Annabelle, an invisible ghost, opens the show by playing piano, then Warren amazes guests with up-close magic. (☎667-6244; www.warrenandannabelles.com. 21+. Daily 5pm. Show $49.50; drinks, appetizers, and dessert extra.) There is also a family show, performed by guest magicians, which runs seasonally. (Daily 4pm. Ages 6-12 $20, 13-17 $26, 18+ $36.)

NIGHTLIFE

When the young families and newlyweds turn in early after eating ice cream and checking out the shops, a younger late-night crowd emerges to hit up the various bars. Special $1 draft nights and different happy hours make for some good bar hopping with live music on certain nights. Pick up a copy of **Maui Time Weekly,** a publication free at many restaurants and stores, to learn more.

Moose McGillycuddy's, 844 Front St. (☎667-7758), is lively, especially on Tu, when drinks are $1, and tourists and locals dance to live music. If dancing is not your thing, you can always hit up the Ms. Pac-Man machine. $3 Mai Tais. $5 cover. Happy hour 3-6pm. Food served until 10pm. Open daily 7:30am-2am.

Gaby's Pizzeria & Deli, 505 Front St. (☎661-8112). Some locals head to Gaby's for the award-winning food and nightly Happy hour specials. From 3-6pm and 9-11pm domestic drafts $2; pizza slices $3. Open daily 11am-midnight.

Bamboo's, 505 Front St. (☎667-4051). Good for a drink after work and reasonably priced sushi. Happy hour 1-4pm and 8-10pm. Food until 9:30pm; sushi until closing except M. Open daily 11am-1:30am.

Spat's, (☎661-1234) in the basement of the Hyatt at Kaanapali, fills with people on Sa when the lounge transforms into a nightclub for the evening. Valet parking available; regular parking is difficult to find. Dress code for men: collared shirt, no jeans, no flip-flops. 21+. Cover $15. DJ and dancing 10pm-3am.

Longhi's, 888 Front St. (☎667-2288; www.longhis.com), is a classier venue for cocktails and dancing with live music every F. Complimentary valet parking nightly 5-11pm. F night 21+. Happy hour 4-6pm. Open daily 7:30am-10pm. AmEx/D/MC/V.

Waveriders Bar and Grill, (☎661-1200), in the Lahaina Center behind the Hard Rock Cafe. Empty on most nights, this large place fills up fast on W nights when $1 drafts draw a mix of both locals and tourists. Billiards and dance music add to the entertainment. $5 cover. Open W-Sa 6pm to close. AmEx/D/MC.

SHOPPING

Lahaina is a shopper's delight; countless small stores and boutiques line **Front St.** There are a number of large shopping centers in town. At the north edge of town is the **Lahaina Cannery Mall.** For light beach reading, head to the **Old Lahaina Book Emporium,** at 834 Front St., on the right side of a small alley. Selling new and used books, the Emporium has an extensive Hawaiian section, fiction, mysteries, poetry, and more. (☎661-1399. Open M-Sa 10am-9pm, Su 10am-6pm.) Less than a block off Front St. is **Take Home Maui, Inc.,** 121 Dickenson St., where you can break out the markers, decorate a coconut husk, and mail it home for $23. They also ship pineapples, papayas, and macadamia nuts, which make great, though expensive, gifts. Their small deli is known for its smoothies. (☎800-545-6284 or 661-8067. Open daily 7:30am-6:30pm, deli closes at 4:30pm.) **Maui Maui,** 156 Lahainaluna Rd., is the cheapest place to buy board shorts ($10), and if you're really on a budget and need to get some gifts, six t-shirts for $20 is the way to go. To get some relief from the hot sun, check out the straw hats at **Lahaina Hat Co.,** 705 Front St. (☎661-8230. Open daily 9am-10pm. AmEx/D/MC/V.)

KAANAPALI

Kaanapali (pop. 1,375) has long been a resort community. Hawaiian chiefs once prized its beaches for surfing; now tourists use them for every beach activity imaginable. All the major hotel chains own property on Kaanapali Beach, a 3 mi. stretch of golden sand punctuated by the volcanic Black Rock, which makes for spectacular snorkeling, scuba diving, and cliff jumping. This is one of the most prized (and beautiful) places to stay in all of Maui; hotels run at least $200 per night. Travelers on a budget may have more luck staying in Lahaina or renting a condo in Napili or Honokowai (p. 271).

ORIENTATION. Kaanapali is located on **Highway 30 (Honoapiilani Highway),** just north of Lahaina. Pristine beaches can all be accessed from this road, which is punctuated by expensive, elaborate resorts.

ACCOMMODATIONS. The best deal on the beach is the **Kaanapali Beach Hotel ❺,** 2525 Kaanapali Pkwy., more subdued and relatively

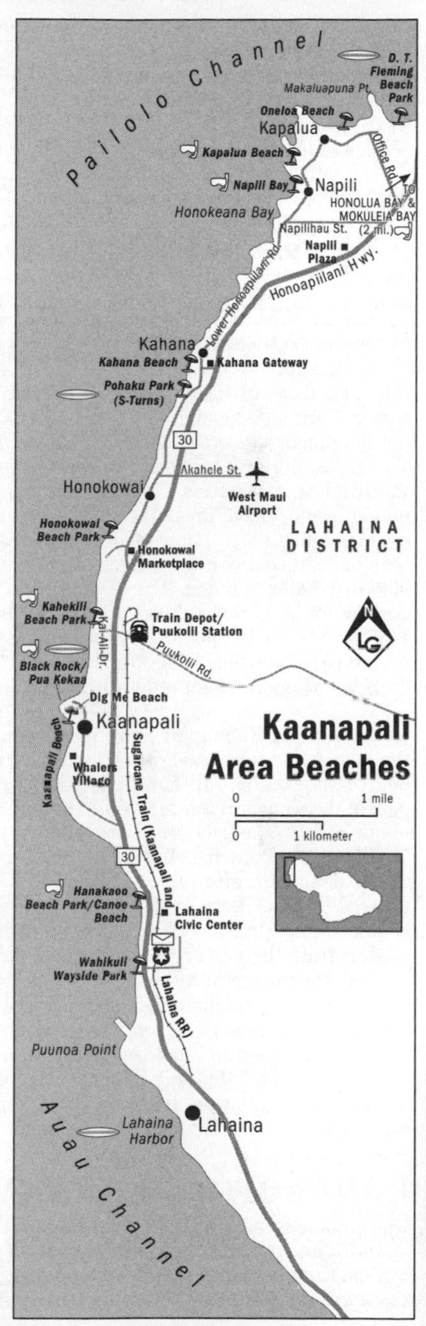

cheaper than its posh neighbors. (☎800-262-8450; www.kbhmaui.com. Rooms $210-310 depending on view; suites $275-630.) Of the major hotels on Kaanapali Beach, the **Hyatt Regency Maui ❺**, 200 Nohea Kai Dr., is the biggest and most luxurious, with an incredible tropical lobby, lush garden with swans and flamingos, and set of ornate swimming pools. (☎661-1234 or 800-233-1234; www.maui.hyatt.com. Rooms $364-700; suites $850-3000.) The **Sheraton Maui ❺**, 2605 Kaanapali Pkwy., has a great location on the cliff at Black Rock. (☎661-0031; www.sheraton-maui.com. Rooms $450-650; suites from $830.) A paved path runs between the Hyatt and the Sheraton; even if you're not staying at one of the resorts, a stroll along this path can be nice, especially at sunset and during hotel luaus and live music concerts.

FOOD. Most of the restaurants in Kaanapali are located in the hotels and are expensive (entrees $25-40), but locals eat at **Jonny's Burger Joint ❶**, 2291 Kaanapali Pkwy. Jonny's is a hole-in-the-wall that serves the best burgers on the coast ($6-11) and cheap drafts ($2.50). A full bar, pool table, and jukebox can be found inside. Parking is available. (☎661-4500. Open daily 11:30am-2am; food served until midnight.) **Hula Grill ❺**, 2435 Kaanapali Pkwy., on the waterfront in Whalers Village, is one of Kaanapali's more reasonable dining options, serving salads, sandwiches, and pizzas ($8-16) for lunch, and seafood specialties ($20-29) for dinner. (☎667-6636. Live Hawaiian music daily 3-5pm and 7-9:30pm. Hula show 8:30pm. Open daily 11am-11pm; dinner 5-9:30pm.) For family-style dining and really cheap Happy hour drinks, stop by **Rusty Harpoon Restaurant and Tavern ❶**, also in Whalers Village. The "Daiquiri Capital of the World" serves the frozen concoction in about a dozen flavors for $3.50 (daily 2-6pm and 10pm-1:30am). Watch a variety of sporting events on the big screen TVs. Early bird special for dinner ($17) at 5:30pm. (☎661-3123. Early-bird dinner special 5:30pm $17. Open daily 8am-2am; food served until 10pm.)

BEACHES. Kaanapali's southernmost beach, **Hanakeoo,** or **Canoe Beach,** is the launch site for canoe races, jet skiing, and other activities. Canoe Beach has decent snorkeling, full facilities, and lifeguards on duty daily. It is technically part of the same stretch of sand as **Kaanapali Beach,** a popular beach lined by the major hotels. The section of shoreline between the Kaanapali Beach Hotel and The Whaler is known as **Dig Me Beach.** The sunsets (if not the people) are particularly beautiful, although parking ($3 per hr.) is pricey. Kaanapali Beach is marked by **Black Rock** or **Puu Kekaa,** an ideal place for snorkeling and beginning scuba lessons, but beware of strong currents. King Kahekili's warriors used to demonstrate their bravery by jumping off the rock; those with a penchant for danger still attempt it today.

For cheaper parking and a lovely beach, drive to **Kahekili Beach Park,** on Kai Ala Pl. off Honoapiilani Hwy., on the north end of Kaanapali. Although close to a few hotels, this long, narrow beach is surprisingly quiet and uncrowded; its grassy park, shaded picnic tables, grills, restrooms, and showers make Kahekili a desirable destination. Its clear, calm waters have won favor with families and are frequently used for introductory scuba classes.

HONOKOWAI, KAHANA, AND NAPILI

One condominium development after another lines Lower Honoapiilani Rd., and it's difficult to distinguish where each of the three "towns" ends and the next begins. Honokowai, the first development north of Kaanapali, offers a few good restaurants. Kahana, the next town, has 1970s-style condos along its rocky beaches. Finally, wedged between Kahana and Kapalua, Napili has condos surrounding the sandy crescent of Napili Bay, a popular family beach.

ACCOMMODATIONS

The condos in this area are generally more moderately priced than the hotels in Kaanapali and the resorts in Kapalua. It's a good vacation home base, with easy access to West Maui beaches and activities. Staying in a condo is also convenient for families who want more than just a place to sleep. *Let's Go Hawaii* recommends **Accommodations Hawaii ❸❹❺**, a vacation rental company based in Lahaina that handles 30 properties and over 200 units in Kaanapali, Honokowai, Kahana, and Napili. All units are privately owned and the prices are reasonable. Pictures, rates, and details of the properties are on the website. (☎661-6655 or 877-661-6655; www.accommodationsmaui.com. Rentals around $75-350 per night. Weekly and monthly rates available.)

FOOD

The **Honokowai Marketplace,** off Lower Honoapiilani Rd. immediately after the turnoff to the highway, hosts several takeout places and a **Star Market** grocery store. (☎442-4700. Open daily 5am-2am.) The **Napili Market** grocery store, 5095 Napilihau Rd., in Napili Plaza, has an **ATM** inside and a copy machine. (☎669-1600. Copies $0.20 per page. Open daily 6:30am-11pm.) **Farmers' Market of Maui,** 3636 Lower Honoapiilani Hwy., directly across from Honokawai Beach Park, has several fresh produce stands offering local produce along with a full salad and soup bar. Some organic foods available. (Open M, W, F 7-11am.)

Soup Nutz & Java Jazz (☎667-0787), in the Honokowai Marketplace. This funky sandwich shop by day and classy bistro by night is a pleasant reprieve from the standard strip-mall ambience. Its subtle lighting and background jazz makes it a great place to relax from the heat and enjoy some great food. Sandwiches $8-10. Entrees $18-26. Open M-Sa 6am-9pm, Su 6am-5pm. MC/V. Lunch ❷/Dinner ❺

Honokowai Okazuya and Deli, 3600D Lower Honoapiilani Rd. (☎665-0512), in the shopping center with AAAAA Rent-A-Space. The quality takeout makes Okazuya a West Maui staple. There is something for everyone, from deli sandwiches and pasta to spicy Szechuan eggplant and mahi mahi. Little seating so

IN RECENT NEWS

THE LOWDOWN ON B&BS

Bed and breakfasts are becoming more and more popular across Maui as travelers look for cheap, comfortable places to stay and homeowners renovate and rent out spare studios and cottages. For many residents, running a B&B can be a full time job and provides a nice income, yet many places throughout the island are not registered. Roughly 90% of the B&Bs operate without a county permit and the number is likely to increase if the present registration system is not changed.

To register, a homeowner must go through the burdensome process of notifying all residents within a 500 ft. area, as well as making a trip to the county seat in Wailuku to fill out paperwork. The county is in the process of rewriting the regulations to make it easier to register. Under the new system, it will be easier to get a license, but rules will be strictly enforced. Since parking and noise complaints are the two main issues with B&B licensing, owners will be required to provide parking and will be held to strict standards on noise complaints. The new system seems to be a win-win situation, since owners will be able to register easily and operate legally, and the county will be able to collect more taxes from newly registered accommodations.

everything is made to order and taken to go. Plates $7-10. Open M-Sa 10am-2:30pm and 4:30-9pm. Cash only. ❶

Maui Tacos (☎665-0222), in Napili Plaza. Serves a filling meal for under $6 with 5 kinds of salsa to choose from. Open M-Sa 9am-9pm, Su 9am-8pm. AmEx/D/MC/V. ❶

The Coffee Store (☎669-4170), next to Maui Tacos and the grocery store. Blissfully air-conditioned with soothing music, delicious roasts (try the Vanilla Macadamia Nut), and **Internet access** ($0.20 per min., $2 minimum with cash and $5 with credit card). A great place to pick up some coffee as a gift. Open daily 6:30am-6pm. D/MC/V. ❶

BEACHES

NAPILI BAY. *(Boogie boarding. Snorkeling. Open daily 24hr.)* The best beach in this area is a crowded crescent of sand—many families and small children come here to swim and snorkel. You can also expect seasonal high surf good for boogie boarding. Because the condos along the beach do not allow beach visitors in their parking lots, parking is difficult. Access to the shore is on Hui Dr. and Napili Pl., both off Lower Honoapiilani Rd., where a few cars manage to park.

LOOK LOCAL. Theft from parked cars at beaches is not uncommon. To protect your valuables, always lock your car, and try putting a Hawaiian flag on your dashboard to look more like a local (and less like a target).

KAHANA BEACH. *(Open daily 24hr.)* A pleasant little cove in front of Kahana Beach Resort Condos, this beach has a sandy bottom and a lot of nasty seaweed. Access to the beach is a bit difficult since the condos are private, and the public access puts you at a rocky cove a bit south of the actual beach. The nearest parking lot is for Puhaku Beach or S-Turns Park, which has a small strip of sand and a few picnic tables but no facilities.

HONOKOWAI BEACH PARK. *(Open daily 24hr.)* With grills, tables, restrooms, and a playground, Honokowai Beach Park is a good place to picnic. Don't bother swimming or sunbathing: the view is not great and the water has large rocks and concrete blocks. There is easy parking access right off Lower Honoapiilani Rd.

KAPALUA AND BEYOND

Tall Cook pines line the carefully planned roads of Kapalua (pop. 467), the most exclusive resort area in Maui. The elegance of the **Ritz Carlton Kapalua** ❺ (☎669-6200 or 800-241-3333.) is a departure from all the glitz of Wailea. The impressive and world-famous golf course dominates the grounds. Aside from the gloriously free beaches, there is little in Kapalua for a budget traveler.

BEACHES

KAPALUA BEACH. *(Snorkeling. Open daily 24hr.)* A lovely white-sand spot with clear, calm waters, Kapalua Beach is great for swimming, lounging, diving, or snorkeling. Rare Hawaiian monk seals also enjoy sunning here. Kapalua is very popular with families and condominium renters in the area. The beach can get crowded, and the small parking lot does fill up. To reach the beach from Lower Honoapiilani Rd., look for a blue shoreline access sign immediately north of Napili Kai Beach Club as you go uphill and around a bend in the road.

ONELOA BEACH. *(Boogie boarding. Open daily 24hr.)* Farther up the coast, Oneloa is usually nearly empty and perfect for secluded sunbathing. It's better suited for boogie boarding than swimming, though, as the sand gives way to reef and the waves are rather large. To reach public parking and beach access, take Office Rd. (the main road leading from the highway into Kapalua), turn left at the end, and then right on Ironwood Ln. Parking is before the gate, and the small blue sign points to an access path opposite the parking lot.

D. T. FLEMING BEACH PARK. *(Boogie boarding. Surfing. Open daily sunrise to sunset. Lifeguards 8am-4:30pm.)* Ranked America's best beach in 2006, Fleming Beach Park has full facilities, lifeguards on duty, a large parking area (although it's often full), shade, and a mighty riptide. In winter the waves can be great for boogie boarding and surfing. Turn left off the highway after mi. marker 31; the beach is at the end of the road.

MOKULEIA BAY AND HONOLUA BAY. *(Snorkeling. Surfing. Open daily 24hr.)* Between mi. markers 32 and 33, these bays offer some of the best snorkeling on the island when the water is calm. Mokuleia Bay, also known as Slaughterhouse Beach, has a sandy entrance to the water; just follow the concrete steps down through the cove. A small parking area is at the top of the steps. Visitors to Honolua park on the side of the road a quarter mile past this parking area and walk down a dirt path and past a gate. Farther down the dirt path, and through a gorgeous jungled forest, the rocky Honolua Bay emerges. Snorkelers enter the water via an old boat ramp in the center of the bay. Be careful though: huge swells roll into Honolua in winter, and only experienced surfers should take them on.

SIGHTS

One of the most beautiful and heart-pounding drives on Maui, **Route 340 (Kahekili Highway)** winds along the coast for 20 mi. between Kapalua and Wailuku. In some places, the one-lane road narrows to the width of a car, with a cliff on one side, no guardrail, and the ocean 100 ft. below. The road is paved, so 4WD is not necessary, just alertness and resignation to the 10 mph speed limit. You'll be glad for the slow speed if you encounter a car coming from the other direction and have to back up around hairpin turns. If you drive from Lahaina, you're less likely to encounter people coming the other way. Allow at least 90min. for the drive.

CLICK IT OR TICKET. As with driving anywhere, in Hawaii it's best to adhere to the speed limit. On coastal highways, the limit changes frequently, and cops love to pull over motorists who aren't paying attention to signs. Be sure to buckle up, since fines for driving without a seat belt run around $100.

PUNALAU BEACH. *(Open daily 24hr.)* Traveling from Kapalua to Wailuku, the road continues as part of Hwy. 30 in two lanes past **Honolua Bay** (see above). About three-quarters of a mile past mi. marker 34, you'll have to get out of your car and walk down a trail to find Punalau Beach. The beach is surrounded by cliffs and lava arches, making it great for walking or picnicking, but it's too rough for swimming or snorkeling. Because it is the farthest north, this beach is usually deserted, providing a good place to lounge around and sunbathe.

NAKALELE BLOWHOLE. The blowhole is at the second major turnout, about half a mile past mi. marker 38. The water comes crashing up into the rocky cliffs, creating a misty mix of blue, white, and black. At high tide, the blowhole is visible just paces from the pullout, but there is also a dirt trail (30min. one-way.) leading down that allows for a closer look. There are two long ladders extending down a steep cliff toward the water. Do *not* use these ladders; they are old and unsafe. Use extreme caution: visitors have been killed when they venture too close and the spray catches them with surprising force.

OLIVINE POOLS. Past the end of the state highway, near mi. marker 16, is a site some call the Olivine Pools. These blue-green pools are lovely places to swim and relax. The road narrows to one lane between mi. markers 15 and 26.

KAHAKULOA. This remote village of less than 100 people is tucked into a small valley as Kahekili Hwy. dips between the two ridges. There are a few stands selling shave ice and banana bread to refresh hot drivers. After the short detour of Kahakuloa, a rock formation known as **Kahakuloa Head** towers 636 ft. above the water and together with **Kahulianapa** behind it, the two hills form a distinctive silhouette identifiable from beaches on the North Shore. There's not much between Kahakuloa and Wailuku besides some gift shops, sculpture gardens, and galleries.

LANGUAGE LESSONS. To learn more about local values and beliefs, note words that are never translated into English. *Ohana* can loosely be translated as "family," but is usually kept in Hawaiian because it denotes something deeper and stronger than blood relation. Similarly, *kapu*, which means something like "forbidden," is often in Hawaiian on rural signs because the word carries the connotation of being cursed. It implies a respect for the power of the land that "forbidden" does not.

WAIHEE VALLEY. As you near Wailuku, you enter the lush Waihee Valley, which receives almost 400 in. of rain per year. To access this drive coming from the other direction, take Market St. straight out of Wailuku, or go along the coast from Kahului Beach Rd. to Waiehu Beach Rd. and turn right at the end onto Rte. 330.

CENTRAL MAUI

Central Maui refers to the valley that stretches between the West Maui Mountains on one side and the Haleakala Volcano on the other. The valley receives a fair amount of rain, and the clouds and strong winds make it cooler than the west side. Aside from the county seat of Wailuku and the commercial center of Kahului, there isn't much in the valley but vast fields of sugarcane. Kaahumanu Ave. and Rte. 32 (Main St.) run along the northern part of the valley all the way to the spectacular Iao Valley (p. 280) in the West Maui Mountains. Rte. 36 and 37 connect the valley with the North Shore (p. 293) and upcountry towns in the east (p. 307), Rte. 350/311 (Puunene Ave./Mokulele Hwy.) leads toward the towns and beaches of South Maui (p. 282), and Rte. 30 (Honoapiilani Hwy.) goes from Wailuku to Lahaina.

KAHULUI AND WAILUKU

On the northern coast of the Central Maui Valley, these two uncharming towns offer several options for budget travelers, including two inexpensive hostels. Kahului (pop. 20,146), the site of Maui's main airport, is largely a sprawl of shopping centers. Wailuku (pop. 12,296), west of Kahului, is more cohesive. Clusters of mom-and-pop stores and restaurants give Wailuku more character than its larger neighbor, though there's still not much draw other than its location and

Kahului and Wailuku

ACCOMMODATIONS
Banana Bungalow, **7**
Maui Beach Hotel, **2**
Maui Seaside Hotel, **1**
Northshore Hostel, **9**
Old Wailuku Inn, **17**

FOOD
Alive & Well, **14**
Café Marc Aurel, **12**
Da Kitchen Cafe, **6**
Mair St. Bistro, **16**
Mañana Garage, **3**
Pizza in Paradise, **5**
Saigon Cafe, **15**
Saeng's, **10**
Tasty Crust Restaurant, **8**

SHOPPING
Beads of Paradise, **11**
Maui Swap Meet, **4**
Requests, **13**

0 — 1000 yards
0 — 1000 meters

Kahului Bay
Kahului Harbor
Hobron Point
Kahului Harbor County Park
Kanaha Beach Park
Kanaha Pond Wildlife Sanctuary
Kanaha Pond
KAHULUI
WAILUKU
PUUNENE
Keopuolani County Park
Maui Arts and Cultural Center
Maui Memorial Park
Maui Memorial Medical Center
Kaahumanu Shopping Center
Kahului Shopping Center
Maui Mall
Longs Drugs
Maui Go Karts
W & F Washerette
Dairy Center
FedEd Kinko's
Maui Marketplace
Down to Earth Natural Foods
Kahului Beach Rd.
Kaahumanu Ave.
Puunene Ave.
Hana Hwy.
Dairy Rd.
Haleakala Hwy.
Pulehu Rd.
Honoapiilani Hwy.
Kahekili Hwy.
Waiale Rd.
E. Main St.
N. Market St.
W. Main St.
Mill St.
Waihee Ditch
Mill Reservoir
Hopoi Reservoir
TO PAIA (5mi), HANA (49mi)
TO DAIRY ROAD (Rt. 380), SUGAR MILL & MUSEUM (1mi), KIHEI (7mi)
TO LAHAINA (22mi)
TO MAALAEA (7mi), LAHAINA (20mi)
TO TROPICAL GARDENS OF MAUI (2mi), KEPANIWAI PARK/HAWAII NATURE CENTER (2.5mi), IAO VALLEY (3mi)
SEE DOWNTOWN INSET

Downtown Wailuku

Bailey House Museum
Maui Bowling Center
Iao Theater
Open Market
Copy Services
Honolii Park
Vineyard St.
Church St.
Main St.
Central Ave.
Kaniela St.
Wells St.
High St.
Kaohu St.

friendly accommodations. There are no attractions of note in Wailuku itself, but it is the gateway to the Iao Valley.

TRANSPORTATION

Flights: Kahului International Airport (OGG), on the northern coast of Central Maui, in Kahului. Kahului is the main airport for Maui, served by international carriers as well as **Hawaiian Airlines** (☎800-367-5320; www.hawaiianair.com), **Aloha Air** (☎800-367-5250; www.alohaair.com), **Pacific Wings** (☎888-575-4546; www.pacificwings.com), and **go!** (☎888-495-3468; www.iflygo.com).

Bus and Van Services: Executive Shuttle (☎669-2300) charges $20-30 to go to the bigger cities. The **MEO (Maui Economic Opportunity) Public Shuttle** (☎877-7651; www.meoinc.org) is free and runs between Kahului and Wailuku. Routes #1 and 2 operate M-Sa approx. every 2hr. with multiple stops between the center of Wailuku and the Kahului shopping plazas. **Robert's** (☎871-4838) runs buses for $2 from Maalaea to Wailea via Kihei (M-Sa every hr. 6:55am-6:55pm), Kahului to Lahaina via Maalaea (M-Sa every 2hr. 7:33am-5:33pm), and Kahului to Wailea via Kihei (M-Sa every 2hr. 7:20am-3:20pm). Check www.co.maui.hi.us/bus for schedules.

Car Rental: National car rental chains operate out of Kahului airport; see **Essentials,** p. 36. Local car rental companies may have a more limited selection of vehicles, but they often offer better rates and less conspicuous cars, though none sell full liability insurance.

Maui Cruisers Car Rental (☎249-2319 or 877-749-7889; www.mauicruisers.net) rents cars $29 per day and $147 per week in the summer; winter prices are higher. 21+.

Aloha Rent-a-Car (☎877-4477 or 877-452-5642; www.aloharentacar.com) offers reasonably priced rentals. Compact cars for $25 per day and around $150 per week; Jeeps $40 per day.

ORIENTATION

Most of the stores in Kahului sprawl along the main road, **Kaahumanu Avenue,** and along **Dairy Road,** on the east side of town. Wailuku is centered around **West Main Street,** the continuation of Kaahumanu Ave.

PRACTICAL INFORMATION

Tourist Information: Maui Visitors Bureau, 1727 Wili Pa Loop (☎244-3530; www.visitmaui.com), off Imi Kala St., across from the Wailuku post office. Maps and brochures available to those who make the trek. Open M-F 8am-4:30pm.

Banks: Major banks line Kahului's highways. **24hr. ATMs** are located at all of the banks and in most shopping centers and malls. In Wailuku, there's a **Bank of Hawaii** at 2105 W. Main St. (☎871-8200) and a **First Hawaiian Bank** at 27 N. Market St. (☎877-2377). Both are open M-Th 8:30am-4pm, F 8:30am-6pm.

Libraries: Kahului Public Library, 90 School St. (☎873-3097), off Kamehameha Ave. Open Tu 1-8pm, W-Sa 10am-5pm. **Wailuku Public Library,** 251 High St. (☎243-5766). Open M-W and F 9am-5pm, Th 1-8pm. **Internet access** at both is unlimited with a 3-month visitor's card ($10). Both offer copies at $0.20 per page.

Laundromats: There are several laundry centers scattered throughout Kahului, including **W & F Washerette,** 125 S. Wakea Ave. (☎877-0353). Wash $1.75, dry $0.25 per 5min. Snack bar and video arcade. Open daily 6am-9:45pm. In Wailuku, **Happy Valley Laundry,** 340 N. Market St. (☎244-4677), is a few doors down from the Banana Bungalow. Wash $1.75 (double load $2), dry $0.25 per 5min. Open daily 6am-9pm. Both have coin machines.

Pharmacies: In Kahului, head to **Longs Drugs** (☎877-0041), in the Maui Mall. Open daily 8am-midnight; pharmacy open M-Sa 8am-9pm, Su 8am-7pm. In Wailuku, **Wailuku Professional Pharmacy,** 1900 Main St. (☎244-9099), is open M-F 9am-5:30pm, Sa 9am-1pm.

Medical Services: Maui Memorial Medical Center, 221 Mahalani St. (☎244-9056), serves both areas and has 24hr. emergency service. In Wailuku, **Maui Medical Group,** 2180 Main St. (☎242-6464), has a night clinic. Open M-F 8am-9pm, Sa-Su 8am-noon.

Copy and Fax Services: In Kahului, go to **Kinko's,** 395 Dairy Rd. (☎871-2000), in the Dairy Center in Kahului. Open M-F 7am-11pm, Sa-Su 9am-9pm. In Wailuku, **Copy Services,** 1975 Vineyard St. (☎242-7651), is just south of Market St. $0.10 per page, color $1. Open M-F 9am-5pm.

Internet Access: Kinko's (see above), $0.20 per min.

Post Offices: Kahului Post Office, 138 S. Puunene Ave., next to the Shell station. Open M-F 8am-4:30pm, Sa 9am-noon. **Wailuku Post Office,** 250 Imi Kala St., off Mill St. Open M-F 8am-4:30pm, Sa 9am-noon.

Postal Code: 96732 (Kahului); 96793 (Wailuku).

ACCOMMODATIONS AND CAMPING

Accommodations in Kahului and Wailuku are relatively budget. Wailuku's hostels attract backpackers, windsurfers, and hangabouts, while Kahului's functional hotels draw business travelers looking for a bed near the airport. Lodgings in these towns provide a convenient base for exploring the natural beauty of the Iao Valley, and many visitors stay here and take daytrips to see the rest of the island.

Banana Bungalow, 310 N. Market St. (☎244-5090; www.mauihostel.com), a few blocks from central Wailuku. The free tours to Haleakala, Hana, and other popular destinations are the reason to stay at this humble hostel. A lively, mostly international crowd congregates in the large kitchen, TV lounge with foosball table and billards, and other common areas. Numerous bathrooms and showers are a plus. Luggage storage and safe available. Linens included. Coin-op laundry. Free Internet. Reception 8am-11pm. Check-out 10am. Quiet hours after 10pm. Reservations strongly recommended. 4- and 6-bed dorms $25; singles $38; doubles $52; triples $64. Call about short-term work. MC/V. ❶

Northshore Hostel, 2080 W. Vineyard St. (☎986-8095; www.northshorehostel.com). The entrance is down an alley between Market and Church St. in downtown Wailuku. This spacious hostel full of easygoing surfers will make you feel right at home. A comfortable common area merges with a shared kitchen and often sees amiable guests watching surfing movies or TV. Renovations are improving all rooms, especially the bathrooms. Usually free airport pickup depending on driver availability. Breakfast included. Luggage storage available. Laundry $1.75. Free Internet and local phone calls. Reception 8am-10pm. Check-out 10am. Dorms $25; singles $50; doubles $65. Inquire about short-term work. MC/V. ❶

Old Wailuku Inn at Ulupono, 2199 Kahookele St. (☎244-5897; www.mauiinn.com). Follow Main St. (Rte. 32W) through central Wailuku and turn left on High St. (Rte. 30); the 3rd left is Kahookele. Rooms decorated with native wood carvings and handmade quilts. Gourmet breakfast each morning. All rooms with private bathrooms. 2-night min.

Reception 9am-5pm. Check-in 2pm. Check-out 11:30am. Reserve 60 days in advance with $50 deposit. Doubles $140-190; each additional person $20. AAA and seniors 10% discount. D/MC/V. ❹

Maui Beach Hotel, 170 Kaahumanu Ave. (☎877-0051), between Lono Ave. and S. Kane St., near the Kahului airport. There's no beach, though some rooms do overlook Kahului Bay. Convenience and price attract travelers to these rooms, which have a TV, refrigerator, and A/C. The restaurant on the 2nd fl. offers a breakfast buffet ($7-9), lunch buffet ($13), and dinner menu (all-you-can-eat sushi buffet Tu-W 5:30-8pm). Free shuttle to and from airport runs hourly 6am-9pm. Internet available in the lobby ($3 for 10min.). Reception 24hr. Check-in 3pm. Check-out noon. Credit card required for reservations; 72hr. notice required for cancellation. Standard room $105; superior $125; ocean view $155; oceanfront $225. Group rates available. MC/V. ❸

Maui Seaside Hotel, 100 Kaahumanu Ave. (☎877-3311; www.mauiseasidehotel.com), next to Maui Beach Hotel, near the Kahului airport. This family-owned hotel is well kept and has an outdoor pool and ocean view. You can walk right into Kahului harbor from the nice inner courtyard. All 200 rooms have A/C, cable TV, and fridge; about half have private lanais. Car rental $29-54 per day. Reception 24hr. Check-in 3pm. Check-out noon. Reservations recommended. Standard ground-floor $118, with pool view and breakfast $126, with bay view and breakfast $140. AAA discount 10%. AmEx/MC/V. ❹

Kanaha Beach Park, off Amala Pl. From central Kahului, take Hobron Ave. off Kaahumanu Ave. The 1st right is Amala Pl.; follow this coastal road past the factories and look for the park entrance on your left. Centrally located with the convenience of outdoor showers, restrooms, and picnic tables. Pitch your tent in the shaded park grounds or right on the beach. Campground closed Tu-W for maintenance. See **Camping in Hawaii,** p. 75, for permit information. ❶

FOOD

In Kahului, restaurants and supermarkets are located in the shopping centers along Kaahumanu Ave. **Down to Earth Natural Foods,** 305 Dairy Rd., in Kahului, has an impressive (and expensive) variety of organic produce, packaged foods, and a popular salad- and hot-bar buffet. (☎877-2661. Open M-Sa 7am-9pm, Su 8am-8pm.) There's an also an **outdoor market** that sells fresh local produce and homemade baked goods right on Market St. (☎276-4966. Open M and Th 7am-6pm.) For a small town, Wailuku offers an impressive selection of international cuisine along Vineyard St., W. Main St., and N. Market St.

Tasty Crust Restaurant, 1770 Mill St. (☎244-0845), off N. Market St. in Wailuku. Tasty Crust is as local and cheap as they come; if you eat here twice in the same week, the gracious staff will remember your order. Locals crowd the 50-year-old Wailuku staple in the early morning for big, fluffy pancakes ($1.60 each) and cups of freshly brewed joe ($1). Lunch and dinner are good but less popular (sesame chicken with steamed rice and macaroni salad, $6.50). Open daily 6am-10pm. Cash only. ❶

Mañana Garage, 33 Lono Ave. (☎873-0220), off Kaahumanu Ave. in Kahului. Stuck between car dealerships and gas stations, Mañana Garage is a pleasant surprise. Bright purple walls create an inviting atmosphere that complements the creative Latin American cuisine. The dinner entrees are a bit pricey (citrus-jalapeño glazed salmon, $22; fajitas, $22), but they're all **half-price** M and Su. Tempting desserts (chocolate mousse cake, $7), martinis, and margaritas ($22 per pitcher) round out the menu Cocktails $5-7. Live Latin music W-Sa. Happy hour M-F 3-6pm. Open M-Tu 11am-9pm, W-Sa 11am-10:30pm, Su 5-9pm. AmEx/D/MC/V. ❺

Saigon Cafe, 1792 Main St. (☎243-9560). In Wailuku, take Central Ave. to Nani St. and then turn right onto Kaniela St. The restaurant is on your left, though there's no sign. This unassuming Vietnamese restaurant is constantly filled with locals and hungry tourists. The service is quick and friendly, and the portions are heaping. The house specialty *banh hoi* (vegetables, meat, and noodles that you roll in rice paper; $11-13) is especially popular. Crispy noodles ($10) are also an excellent choice, served hot with shrimp, calamari, and vegetables in a garlic sauce. Open M-Sa 10am-9:30pm, Su 10am-8:30pm. MC/V. ❸

Cafe Marc Aurel, 28 N. Market St. (☎244-0852), in Wailuku center. Rich roasts, gypsy teas, light fare (quiches, muffins, and scones), and Häagen-Dazs go down well with the soothing background music. If you brought an appetite, try one of the sophisticated salads or sandwiches ($7-10). Happy hour 4-6pm. Coffee $1.25-4. Single espresso drinks $2-3. Open M-F 7am-6pm, Sa 7am-1pm. MC/V. ❶

Main Street Bistro, 2051 Main St. (☎244-6816), in Wailuku. This breezy and comfortable bistro serves hearty, unique meals. The lunch menu offers a variety of interesting salads and sandwiches, while the dinner menu boasts ambitious dishes, such as duck with grilled polenta ($13). Open M-F 11am-2:30pm and 3-7pm. D/MC/V. ❸

Da Kitchen Cafe, 425 Koloa St. (☎871-7782), in Triangle Sq. off Hana Hwy. in Kahului before the turnoff for the airport. Da Kitchen's spacious booths and indoor umbrella tables offer plenty of seats from which to enjoy this classic local spot. This fun cafe serves heaping plates of *loco moco, kalua* pork, and teriyaki chicken ($7.50-9), and even hearty eaters may find themselves taking home leftovers. Takeout available. Open M-F 11am-8pm, Sa 11am-3pm. AmEx/D/MC/V. ❷

Pizza in Paradise, 60 E. Wakea Ave. (☎871-8188), in Kahului. If paradise can't be complete without pizza, then swing by and enjoy a quick slice or grab some friends and split a huge pie. Diners chow on incredible "upper crust" pizzas ($16.50-24), oven-baked subs ($6.50), and filling pasta dishes ($6.50). Pizza by the slice $1.50. Free delivery in the Kahului/Wailuku area. Open M-Th and Su 11am-9pm, F-Sa 11am-10pm. MC/V. ❷

Saeng's, 2119 Vineyard St. (☎244-1567), at N. Church St. in downtown Wailuku. Saeng's stands out for its elegant, dimly-lit dining room and handsome open-air garden lanai. The extensive Thai menu features 3 colors of curry (Pineapple Red Shrimp Curry, $10) and highlights local seafood (mahi mahi ginger, $12). Saeng's also offers a large selection of creative vegetarian options (Evil Prince Tofu, $7.50). Lunch served M-F 11am-2:30pm, dinner 5-9:30pm. MC/V. ❸

Alive and Well, 2010 Main St. (☎244-5950), on the corner of Market St. Wraps, salads, and sandwiches made with healthy and organic ingredients at this NYC-style cafe. Don't let the emphasis on vegetables scare you; the Philly cheesesteak ($7) ranks with the best of them. Open daily 10am-3pm. AmEx/MC/V. ❶

BEACHES

KANAHA BEACH. *(Wind sports. Open daily 11am-sunset.)* In Kahului, Kanaha Beach is the place windsurfers and kiteboarders go to play. Some say the swimming isn't too bad as long as you turn off the road before the beach park, but the murky water and choppy waves may make you think otherwise. After 11am, when windsurfers and kiteboarders are allowed in the water, it's a great place to watch colored sails jump through sea and sky as adventurous boarders catch air. **Action Sports** offers kiteboarding lessons and will deliver the equipment to the beach. (☎871-5857. 3hr. private lesson $240.) **Kanaha Beach Park** has large grassy areas, grills, picnic tables, and a few volleyball courts, making it nice for a barbecue. Parking spaces are abundant; remember to take your valuables with you. The beach is located off Amala Pl., behind the airport.

SIGHTS

SUGAR MILL AND MUSEUM. Across the street from the functional sugar mill in Puunene (just south of Kahului), the Alexander & Baldwin Sugar Museum offers a sample of the sights, sounds, and tastes of Maui sugar. Photographs, models, and artifacts document the history of the industry—focusing on the white plantation owners and the immigrant field and mill workers. A 10min. video guides guests through the process of creating sugar, from planting to harvesting and filtering.-*(3957 Hansen Rd., at Puunene Ave. From Kahului, take Puunene Ave. south. There are signs for the sugar museum before Hansen meets Puunene. ☎871-8058; www.sugarmuseum.com. Open M-Sa 9:30am-4:30pm. $5, ages 6-17 $2.)*

BAILEY HOUSE MUSEUM. This 1833 mission house, run by the Maui Historical Society, contains a small museum with early Hawaiian artifacts. The front room showcases portraits of the Baileys, the sugar moguls who operated a girls' school here. The Hawaiian Room on the left displays the tools and ornaments of early Hawaiians, and the room to the right houses paintings of Maui's landmarks created by the Renaissance man and self-taught artist Edward Bailey, a former headmaster. Scattered throughout these rooms are utensils and other artifacts that illustrate the style arising from the fusion of European and Hawaiian culture. The upstairs bedrooms hold period furniture and handmade quilts. *(2375 Main St., outside Wailuku center on the road to Iao Valley. ☎244-3326; www.mauimuseum.org. Open M-Sa 10am-4pm. $5, seniors $4, ages 7-12 $1.)*

TROPICAL GARDENS OF MAUI. This magnificent three-acre garden showcases tropical trees and flowers from all over the world, including many rare native Hawaiian plants. If you're on the way to Iao Valley, you might consider stopping for a picnic and a leisurely stroll (20-30min.). Orchids, hibiscus, and the rare *nanu* (Hawaiian gardenia) are just some of the blossoms that grow along the garden paths that wind across a small bridge, around a small pond, and past a lovely gazebo. In the adjacent greenhouse, plants are for sale. *(200 Iao Valley Rd. ☎244-3085; www.tropicalgardensofmaui.com. Open M-Sa 9am-5pm; last entrance 3:15pm. Ages 8 and up $5, under 8 free.)*

KEPANIWAI PARK AND HAWAII NATURE CENTER. Farther up the road, **Kepaniwai Park** and the Heritage Gardens commemorate Hawaii's immigrant groups with sculptures and pavilions. Numerous covered tables and restrooms make the park a decent stop for a picnic lunch. Farther along the road, the **Hawaii Nature Center,** just up the hill from the gardens, houses a great interactive nature museum for all ages and offers pricey guided tours of the valley. *(Iao Valley Rd. Park open daily until 7pm. Free. Museum open daily 10am-4pm. $6, ages 4-12 $4, under 4 free. Rainforest Valley Tour $30, ages 5-12 $20, under 5 not allowed. 2hr. tours M-F 11:30am and 1:30pm, Sa-Su and holidays 11am and 2pm; call ☎244-6500 ext. 15 for reservations, or check out www.hawaiinaturecenter.org.)*

KAHUNA PROFILE. Half a mile past Kepaniwai Park and the Hawaii Nature Center, a sign on the right side of the road indicates the viewing point for a profile of the rock formations of Pali Eleele gorge. Local Hawaiians claim the profile is of a powerful ancient *kahuna* (priest), but many visitors see the face of President John F. Kennedy. Then again, there are also those who see, well, rock.

IAO VALLEY STATE PARK AND THE IAO NEEDLE. The result of thousands of years of water pressure eroding volcanic rock, the Iao Needle rises 2250 ft. above Iao Valley. The beauty of the mountains and needle is inspiring. Hawaiians affectionately call the structure *Kukaemoku*, after the phallus of the sea god Kanaloa. The valley was considered a sacred space—*alii* (royalty) were buried here—and it's also the site of many important battles. In 1790, Kamehameha I won a bloody victory here over the rival chief of Oahu, which ultimately led to his coronation as the first Hawaiian king. Exactly 133 steps lead to the top of the path for a more intimate view. The paved path meanders down to the fast-moving Iao Stream, where local kids are unconcerned by the "no swimming" signs and frolic in the water that once irrigated taro crops on the lush valley floor. The valley can be windy and chilly even when it's sunny in downtown Wailuku, so bring along a light jacket just in case. *(Take Main St. through Wailuku and continue for 3 mi. The road ends at Iao Valley Park. Although it seems like a hike through the valley would be gorgeous, there is no off-trail hiking in Iao Valley. Allow 35min. to see the entire park via the paved paths and steps. Open daily 7am-7pm. Free.)*

ENTERTAINMENT

For evening entertainment, **Mañana Garage** (p. 278) occasionally has live music. In Wailuku, the **Iao Theater,** 68 N. Market St. (☎242-6969; www.mauionstage.com), and the **Maui Arts and Cultural Center (MACC),** 1 Cameron Way (☎242-2787; www.mauiarts.org), off Kahului Beach Rd., both hold live performances. The latter attracts international stars as well as local artists. The two movie theaters in Kahului are both off Kaahumanu Ave.: the **Maui Mall Megaplex Cinemas** (☎871-6684; $8.50, seniors and children $5.75, matinee $6.25), in the Maui Mall and the **Kaahumanu 6 Theaters** (☎873-3137; $8.50, seniors and children $5.25, matinee $6.25), in the Queen Kaahumanu Center. The **Maui Film Festival** screens art films at the Castle Theater at the MACC, with live music and food before and after the first screening, and also at the McCoy Theater. Showtimes vary; call for an updated schedule. (☎572-3456; www.mauifilmfestival.com. Screenings 5 and 7:30pm. $10.) Sometimes there is free entertainment at the **Queen Kaahumanu Center;** call ☎877-4325 for details.

Wailuku is home to the **Maui Bowling Center,** 1976 Vineyard St., just south of Market St. Get your roll on for $2.25 a game. (☎244-4596.-Open Tu 9am-10pm and W-Su 10am-10pm.) For fast-track action, **Maui Go Karts,** 191 Vevau St., across the street from the Kahului Foodland, can speed up a lazy Hawaiian afternoon or evening. A minigolf course and a few carnival games can keep the younger children busy while the big kids race. (☎871-7619. Open M-Th and Su 10am-8pm, F-Sa 10am-11pm. 5min. ride $6; 5 rides $25. MC/V.)

SHOPPING

Almost every major shopping chain has a store in Kahului. The town's highways are more like strip malls, and within a few miles' radius, shoppers can locate practically anything they forgot to bring from home. The **Maui Swap Meet,** on Puunene Ave. next to the Kahului post office, is *the* place to buy amazing local produce and Hawaiian clothing and jewelry or to simply peruse the giant junk sale. (☎877-3100. Open Sa 7am-noon. Admission $0.50.)

North Main Street and **Market Street** in Wailuku are lined with antique stores, galleries, hair salons, pawn shops, and bookstores. For music lovers, **Requests,** 10 N. Market St., can easily fill a rainy afternoon. This secondhand music store has an impressive selection of new and used CDs ($8 and up), from hard-to-find indie labels to rows of reggae, and tons of vinyl in the basement. (☎244-9315. Open daily 10am-6pm.) If you need a book for your travels, check out **Maui Book Sellers,** 105 Market St., on the corner with Vineyard. This small bookstore offers new and used books and serves coffee and cookies inside. The small stage hosts an occasional poetry slam which can draw quite a crowd. (☎244-9091. Open M-F 10am-7pm, Sa 10am-5pm.) **Beads of Paradise,** 1930 Vineyard St., offers beads of every color, size, and shape. (☎242-8317. Open M-F 10am-5pm, Sa 10am-4pm.)

SOUTH MAUI

Stretching from Maalaea to Kihei, Wailea, and Makena on the southwest slope of Haleakala Volcano, South Maui encompasses a vast and varied region. Kihei has expanded rapidly into a 6 mi. strip of condos and touristy restaurants. Past Kihei, the swank resorts of Wailea occupy the best beachfront property. Farther down, you'll find the most impressive beaches in Makena, with dramatic cliffs, sandy shores, and views of Kahoolawe and Molokini across the water. Beyond Makena, the paved road becomes an ancient path, winding past lava fields and coves that are swimming with fish. South Maui is hotter and drier than the rest of the island—December through April is the best time to visit. In addition to the more pleasant weather, it's also whale-watching season, when hundreds of humpback whales migrate to Hawaii's coastal waters each year to breed.

MAALAEA

There isn't much to see in Maalaea (pop. 454), but what's there is concentrated in Maalaea Harbor Village, 300 Maalaea Rd., a complex off Rte. 30 between Lahaina and Kihei. Tour companies depart from the harbor on boating and fishing trips.

FOOD. There is a **restaurant** and **snack bar** in the Ocean Center, as well as several dining options in Maalaea Harbor Village. The **Maalaea Grill ❹,** part of the Cafe O'Lei chain, combines upscale seafood cuisine (sauteed mahi mahi in ginger butter with papaya salsa, $17), with an equally posh location overlooking the ocean. Lunch sandwiches ($7-11) are more affordable. (☎243-2206. Open M 10:30am-3pm, Tu-Su 10:30am-5pm and 5:30-9pm. AmEx/D/MC/V.) Satisfy your sweet tooth with a snack from **Hula Homemade Cookies and Ice Cream ❶.** (Cookies around $1.50, shave ice $4. Open M-Sa 10am-6pm, Su 10am-5pm.)

BEACHES. A narrow strip of sandy beach lines Rte. 30, but the current here is quite rough, and better swimming can be found farther south beyond Kihei. When the surf is up, experienced surfers and boogie boarders rip the swells that roll unobstructed into **Maalaea Harbor;** you can watch them from the seawall behind the Harbor Village. Restrooms are located to the right of the restaurant.

ACTIVITIES. In the port behind the Harbor Village, there are a number of boats that run **snorkel** trips to Molokini, as well as **sunset cruises, fishing expeditions,** and seasonal **dolphin- and whale-watching trips.** Several different companies run boats, all of which are represented in the activity kiosk in Maalaea Harbor Village. Prices vary based on the length of the trip, number of passengers aboard, and the food and drink served. The boats with an open bar tend to adopt a frat-party feel; if you don't intend to drink, your money is better spent elsewhere. Known for their eco-friendly and educational tours, the **Pacific Whale Foundation** (☎249-8811; www.pacificwhale.org), a non-profit organization dedicated to marine research and conservation, runs several trips led by certified naturalists, including the toothed whale and dolphin tour held year-round. (Call ahead, trips and sightings vary by season.) In addition to the location in the Maalaea Harbor

Village, the foundation has several other branches throughout Maui. Pacific Whale also offers volunteer programs; for more information, see **Beyond Tourism,** p. 66.

SIGHTS. The other main attraction in Maalaea is the **Maui Ocean Center,** an indoor and outdoor aquarium that showcases the mind-boggling diversity of Hawaii's marine life. The admission price is a bit steep, but the fish don't disappoint—many of the beautiful and bizarre species displayed can only be found in local waters, and even experienced snorkelers and scuba divers will be impressed by the range of creatures here. The Shark Dive is a new program which allows certified scuba divers to actually dive in the 750,000-gallon tank and enjoy the fish, sharks, and stingrays first hand. Tactile displays, like the Touch Pool, entertain small children, while the placards beside the visual displays aim to educate visitors of all ages. *(192 Maalaea Rd., off Hwy. 30 in Maalaea Harbor Village. ☎270-7000; www.mauioceancenter.com. Open daily 9am-5pm; July-Aug. daily until 6pm. $22, seniors $19, ages 3-12 $15.)*

KIHEI

Cruising the busy Kihei strip, it's hard to believe that 50 years ago Kihei (pop. 16,749) was just a small town on an unpaved road. In the last few decades, development has exploded; for several years, Kihei ranked among the fastest-growing towns in America. While some consider Kihei, with its traffic and noise, the least attractive of Maui's cities, others enjoy a vacation made affordable by the town's condos, takeout tacos, and cheap drink deals at local Happy hours. If you do choose to stay in Kihei, reserve a place far in advance. Make sure you find time to leave too—the best South Maui beaches lie beyond Kihei in Wailea and Makena.

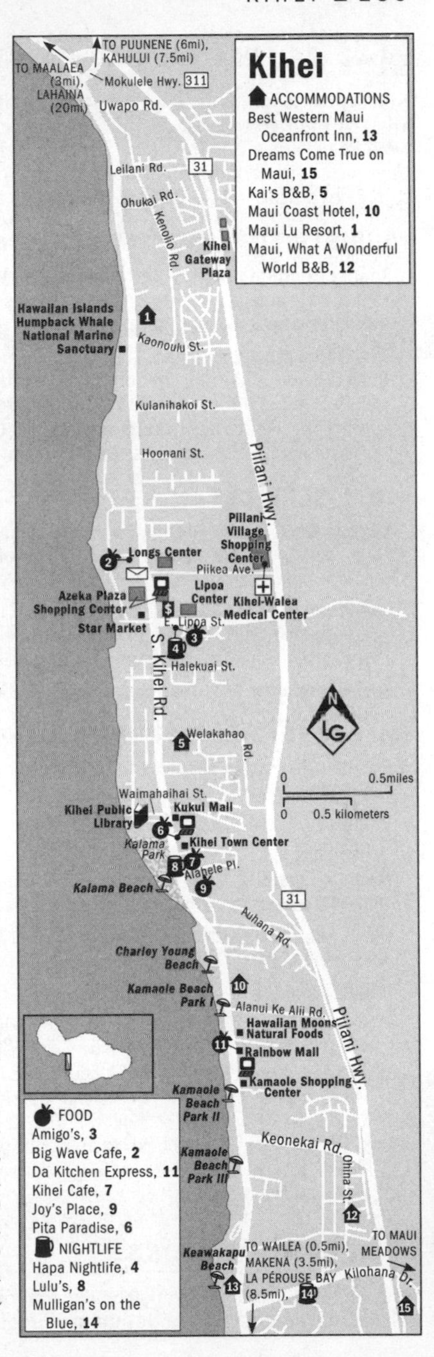

ORIENTATION AND PRACTICAL INFORMATION

Kihei sprawls along the southwest shore of the Haleakala volcano, which gradually rises above the condos and hotels on the *mauka* (mountain) side. **South Kihei Road** runs along the coast, studded with traffic lights and shopping centers. Cars move slowly here any time of day; the inland **Route 31 (Piilani Highway)** that runs above Kihei all the way to Makena is a good alternate route.

TOURIST AND FINANCIAL SERVICES

Tourist Information: Maui Information and Visitors Center (☎874-4919) offers a personal concierge service, making reservations for car rental, accommodations, activities, etc. free of charge. Call with questions. **Expedia!Fun,** Kihei-Kalama Village (☎879-8676), books snorkel trips, helicopter rides, and other activities at low prices.

Banks: Banks and ATMs dot both S. Kihei Rd. and Piilani Hwy. **American Savings Bank,** 1215 S. Kihei Rd. (☎879-1977), in Longs Shopping Center. Open M-F 9am-6pm, Sa 9am-1pm. **First Hawaiian Bank** (☎875-0055), in the Lipoa Center. Open M-Th 8:30am-4pm, F 8:30am-6pm, Sa 9am-1pm.

LOCAL SERVICES

Library: Kihei Public Library, 35 Waimahaihai St. (☎875-6833), across from the Kukui Mall, behind the fire station. Unlimited **Internet access** with the purchase of a 3-month visitor's card ($10). Open Tu noon-8pm, W-Sa 10am-5pm. Copies $0.20 per page.

Laundromat: Lipoa Laundry Center, 41 E. Lipoa St. (☎875-9266), near Hapa's Night Club in Lipoa Center. Wash $2, dry $0.25 per 5min. Change machine. Open M-Sa 8am-9pm (last wash 8pm), Su 8am-5pm (last wash 4pm).

Surf Conditions: High Tech Surf Report (☎877-3611).

EMERGENCY AND COMMUNICATIONS

Police: (Non-emergency ☎244-6400.) Next to Foodland in the Kihei Town Center. Office open M-F 7:45am-4:30pm.

Pharmacy: Longs Drugs, 1215 S. Kihei Rd. (☎879-2259), in Longs Shopping Center. Open daily 8am-midnight, pharmacy open M-Sa until 9pm, Su until 7pm.

Medical Services: Kihei-Wailea Medical Center, 221 Piikea Ave. (☎874-8100), in the Piilani Village Shopping Center. Open M-F 8am-8pm, Sa-Su 8am-5pm.

Copy and Fax Services: Mail Boxes Etc., 1215 S. Kihei Rd. (☎874-5556), in Longs Shopping Center. M-F 8:30am-5:30pm, Sa 9am-4pm. AmEx/D/MC/V.

Internet Access:

The Coffee Store, 1729 S. Kihei Rd. (☎875-4244), in Azeka Mauka. $0.20 per min. $2 (cash) or $5 (credit card) minimum. Open M-Sa 6:30am-8pm, Su 6:30am-7pm. AmEx/MC/V.

Cyberbean Internet Cafe, 1881 S. Kihei Rd. (☎879-4799), near Foodland in the Kihei Town Center. $0.20 per min. with 12min. minimum. Membership ($13 per yr.) entitles the whole family to a $0.10 per min. rate. Open M-Sa 7am-9pm, Su 8am-8pm. AmEx/MC/V.

Post Office: 1254 S. Kihei Rd. (☎879-1987), next to Azeka Plaza. Open M-F 8:30am-4:30pm, Sa 9am-1pm.

Postal Code: 96753.

ACCOMMODATIONS

Without any hostels or campsites, accommodations in Kihei are in the higher price ranges; unremarkable condominiums abound. However, many places do have price breaks for stays of more than seven days. A stay at a B&B is a good alternative to the condo scene, although reservations in advance are essential.

NO PLACE LIKE HOME. Many Maui homeowners will rent rooms; check local newspapers for listings. These unofficial B&Bs are a good last resort if everything else is booked. Despite the popularity of these unregistered B&Bs, travelers should always exercise caution in such establishments.

BED AND BREAKFASTS

B&Bs are generally located in residential neighborhoods close to the Kihei restaurants and beaches, but a world away from the noise. **Linda Little** (☎879-7865 or 888-333-9747) books cottages, B&Bs, condos, and vacation homes for no fee. She also rents a room in her home for $80 with breakfast.

Kai's Bed & Breakfast, 80 E. Welakahao Rd. (☎874-6431; www.mauibb.com), off the *mauka* (mountain) side of S. Kihei Rd. Each of the 3 rooms has cable TV, microwave, and refrigerator. Breakfast included. Beach towels, boogie boards, snorkel gear, bicycles, garden hot tub, and washer/dryer are available for guest use. Check-in 2pm. Check-out 10am. 3- to 5-night min. Reserve with 50% deposit at least 2 mo. ahead in low season, earlier for high season; balance due 30 days prior to arrival. Rooms $70-100; $450-600 per week; slightly less in low season. AmEx/MC/V. ❸

Aloha Journeys (☎875-4840), in Maui Meadows. Includes 2 cottages, 2 larger houses overlooking a pool, and a garden path that wanders by tropical fruit trees. Cottages are pleasant, and houses are great for families or groups. All have TV, bathroom, and kitchen. Guests have access to hot tubs and can borrow snorkel or beach gear. $50 cleaning fee. Check-in 3pm. Check-out 10am. Cottages 5-night min.; houses 7-night min. 50% deposit, balance due on arrival. Cottages and houses $80-265. MC/V. ❸

Dreams Come True on Maui, 3259 Akala Dr. (☎879-7099), from Piilani Hwy., turn left on Mapu Pl. and then right on Akala Dr. 2 small suites with kitchenettes, breakfast included. Wireless Internet access and free laundry in "Rainforest" suite. Cottage has full kitchen, computer with Internet, TV/VCR, and washer/dryer. A huge movie screen dominates the common room available to all guests. Beach and snorkel gear for loan. Suites 4-night min.; cottages 6-night min. Check-in 3pm. Check-out 11am. $200 deposit, balance due 40 days before arrival. Suites $82; cottage $125 in low season, $92-139 in high season. MC/V. ❸

Maui, What a Wonderful World Bed and Breakfast, 2828 Umalu Pl. (☎879-9103). The 4 suites in this friendly B&B all have their own entrance, bathroom, TV, and A/C; 2 have a kitchenette and 1 has a full kitchen. Extended continental breakfast served in the spacious, nicely furnished common area or breezy lanai. Free laundry. Check-in 4pm. Check-out noon. Reserve 2-3 mo. ahead with 50% deposit. 1-bedroom $89-99; ocean suite $110-120; garden and patio suites $120-135. MC/V. ❸

Eva Villa, 815 Kumulani Dr. (☎874-6407), in Maui Meadows. From Piilani Hwy., turn left on Mikioi Pl. and take the 1st right on Akala Dr. Turn left onto Hoala Dr. and then left on Kumulani Dr. Accommodations include a pool-side studio, 2-bedroom suite, and a cottage with full kitchen, laundry facilities, and grill. Kitchens stocked with continental breakfast food. Shared pool, hot tub, and cable TV. Snorkeling and beach gear for loan ($5). No children. 4-night min. Check-in 3pm. Check-out 10am. $200 deposit; balance due on arrival. Suite $145, studio $155, cottage $175. Cash or checks only. ❹

CONDO RESERVATION SERVICES

If staying in Kihei for more than a few days, condos are your best bet. In addition to the price of a room, be prepared to pay the 11.42% tax on accommodations

FIRST-RATE SUSHI AT HALF-PRICE

Much to the delight of South Shore seafood lovers, the success of Sansei, a sushi restaurant in Kapalua, led to the opening of a second Sansei in Kihei. Sansei's popularity is well deserved–the ambience is swanky, and (more importantly) the sushi is exceptionally good. The nigiri is made with fresh, sweet fish and the perfect amount of seasoned rice. Yet the real highlights of the menu are the maki rolls, creatively assembled into caterpillars and pink Cadillacs. The menu also includes cooked entrees and noodle dishes ($16-24), which infuse local produce with Japanese flavor, and an informative sake and wine list that will help you pair your meal with the perfect cool or dry beverage. The elegant setting and *ono* (delicious) food doesn't come cheap (nigiri, $4.25-9.50; maki, $4-16), but early-bird and late-night specials make things far more affordable. You won't be the only one taking advantage of the early-bird specials–the line starts forming well before 5pm, and by 5:29 it's wrapped all the way around the plaza.

1881 S. Kihei Rd. (☎879-0004), in the Kihei Town Center. Open M-W and Su 5:30-10pm, Th-Sa 5:30pm-2am. 25% off all food Tu-Sa 5:30-6pm; 50% off late-night food (pupus and sushi), $1 off draft beverages Th-Sa 10pm-1:30am. Free 21+ karaoke until closing. AmEx/MC/V.

and the fee or commission charged by the booking service. Some condos also charge a cleaning fee when you check out (around $50).

AA Oceanfront Condo Rentals, 1279 S. Kihei Rd. Ste. 107 (☎800-488-6004; www.aaoceanfront.com). From $90 per night. Reservation fee $25.

Affordable Accommodations Maui, 2825 Kauhale St. (☎888-333-9747; www.affordablemaui.com). From $90 per night. No fee.

Kihei Maui Vacations, 2395 S. Kihei Rd., Ste. 206 (☎879-7581; www.kmvmaui.com). From $77 per night. 10% commission charge.

HOTELS

There are only three hotels in Kihei, all of which offer an alternative to the minimum stay and cleaning fees that condominiums require.

Best Western Maui Oceanfront Inn, 2980 S. Kihei Rd. (☎879-7744; www.mauioceanfrontinn.com), on Keawakapu Beach. With the best beach location in Kihei and reasonable prices, the Maui Oceanfront is a great value. Each unit of this Best Western has a queen-size bed, A/C, TV, coffee maker, and fridge. Check-in 3pm. Check-out 11am. Reserve with credit card; 3-day cancellation policy. Standard rates start at $169, but specials can bring prices down to $119, and rooms start at $139 when they're under 75% full. Suites $239-339. AmEx/D/MC/V. ❺

Maui Coast Hotel, 2259 S. Kihei Rd. (☎874-6284), across the street from Kamaole Park I. Fitness center, pool, tennis courts, 2 outdoor hot tubs, and activity desk. The 265 rooms all have A/C, lanai, cable TV, mini-fridge, and coffee maker. Live pool-side entertainment nightly and free shuttle for guests. Check-in 3pm. Check-out noon. From Dec. 21-Mar. 31 reserve with 2-night deposit; 7-day cancellation policy. From Apr. 1-Dec. 20, reserve with 1-night deposit; 3-day cancellation policy. Standard double $215; suites $245-275. Credit card required. AmEx/D/MC/V. ❺

Maui Lu Resort, 575 S. Kihei Rd. (☎879-5881). Maui Lu sits on 28 acres on the northern Kihei coast, a trek from Kihei's best beaches. In lieu of the ocean, swimmers can enjoy the resort's Maui-shaped pool. All rooms have fridge, A/C, and cable TV. Check-in 3pm. Check-out noon. Reserve with 1-night deposit. Rooms $119-232. MC/V. ❹

FOOD

Kihei restaurants run the gamut from fast food to fine cuisine, though it can be hard to find a good value. There are several supermarkets in the shopping centers on S. Kihei Rd., including a 24hr. **Foodland,** (☎879-9350) in the Kihei Town Center, and a 24hr. **Safeway,** (☎891-9120) in the Piilani Village Center. The hot bar at **Hawaiian Moons Natural Foods,** 2411 S. Kihei Rd., has healthy takeout meals and organic salads that you can enjoy at the beach across the street. (☎875-4356. Open M-Sa 8am-9pm, Su 8am-7pm. AmEx/D/MC/V.) **Aloha Discount Liquors,** 2439 S. Kihei Rd., in the Rainbow Mall, is the best bet for cheap beer, wine, and liquor. (☎874-8882. Open daily 9am-11pm. AmEx/D/MC/V.)

Kihei Cafe, 1945 S. Kihei Rd. (☎879-2230), across from Kalama Park. Serving breakfast classics for $6 or less, including French toast, 2 eggs with bacon, home fries and biscuit, and the Papaya Delight (papaya filled with yogurt, granola, and raisins). Quick service and fresh Kona coffee make this the busiest breakfast place in Kihei. Lunch salads, sandwiches, and burgers around $7. Open daily 5am-3pm. Cash only. ❶

Joy's Place, 1993 S. Kihei Rd. (☎879-9258), in the Island Surf Building at Auhana Rd. Tan, fit women in bikinis flock to Joy's, where organic, wholesome eating is a way of life. Plenty of vegan and vegetarian options include organic sandwiches, salads, and wraps ($4-8.50). Mostly takeout, but a few pleasant tables are available. If you like what you taste, cooking classes are also offered. Open M-Sa 10am-5pm. ❶

Pita Paradise, 1913 S. Kihei Rd. (☎875-7679), in the Kihei Kalama Village across from Kalama Park. Gyros, kabobs, wraps, salads, and pitas ($8-15) are staples at this relaxing cafe. Greek salad ($6.25) and delectable baklava ice cream cake ($6) are also on the menu. Takeout available. Open M-Sa 11am-9:30pm, Su 5-9:30pm. MC/V. ❷

Da Kitchen Express, 2439 S. Kihei Rd. (☎875-7782), in the Rainbow Mall. This no-frills restaurant sells cheap, freshly prepared food. Try the Hawaiian Plate smorgasbord (pork *lau lau, kalua* pork, chicken long rice, and *lomi* salmon; $10), or the classic Hawaiian Loco Moco (grilled hamburger patty, topped with 2 eggs, onions, mushrooms, and gravy; $8.25), both served with rice and macaroni salad. Breakfast features hearty omelets ($8) and sweetbread french toast ($6). Open daily 9am-9pm. AmEx/D/MC/V. ❶

Royal Thai Cuisine, 1280 S. Kihei Rd. (☎874-0813), in Azeka Makai. Plain decor and savory, cheap food. The "Royal Favorite" comes with chicken, beef, shrimp, or tofu ($8-10). Lunch M-Sa 11am-3pm. Dinner daily 5-9:30pm. AmEx/MC/V. ❷

Vietnamese Cuisine, Azeka Place 1 (☎875-2088), in Azeka Makai. Serves decent food, including rice, noodle, and vegetable dishes. The Vietnamese burritos, or *banh hoi*, are also good ($11). Plenty of vegetarian options ($8-10). Open M-Sa 10:30am-9:30pm, Su 10:30am-9pm. AmEx/D/MC/V. ❸

Amigos, 41 E. Lipoa St., (☎879-9952), in Lipoa Center next to Gold's Gym. This taco shack serves some of the quickest and most filling Mexican food in Kihei. Individual tacos are only $2-3, and larger combo meals with rice and beans are $6-8. Mostly takeout with delivery available from 5-8:30pm. Open daily 9am-9pm. MC/V. ❶

Big Wave Cafe, 1215 S. Kihei Rd. (☎891-8688), in Longs Shopping Ctr. Create your own omelet ($8), or choose from standards like eggs benedict or eggs florentine ($9). Open daily 7:30am-9pm with breakfast until 2pm. MC/V. ❷

BEACHES

The sandy expanse between Maalaea and Makena is one long beach broken up by lava formations. The North Kihei beaches are popular for windsurfing and sailing; beaches farther south are better suited for swimming. **Kalama Beach Park** is popular with skaters and has tennis courts and sports fields. Volleyball courts, picnic tables, and restrooms are scattered throughout the long park, while the southern edge is the best place to swim. South of Kalama, **Charley Young Beach** is a large stretch of sand around volcanic rock that is usually filled with sunbathers. All the **Kamaole Beach Parks (I, II, and III)** have showers, lifeguards, and beautiful golden sand; Kam. II and III are set farther from the road than Kam. I and have some shaded areas. All have small parking lots and some parking on the streets. **Keawakapu Beach,** past Kam. III, is usually uncrowded and may be worth the walk although there are no facilities (parking is past the Maui Oceanfront Inn, in a lot on the left). More beaches are farther south, in **Wailea** (p. 290) and **Makena** (p. 291).

ACTIVITIES

SNORKELING. With over 450 different fish, 25% of which are found only in Hawaii (and 20% of those only in Molokini!), Maui is a can't-miss snorkeling experience. Nearly every beach has lava rocks that jut into the sea where fish gather. **Kamaole I, II, and III** are great for novices. In Wailea, **Ulua Beach** (p. 290), just past the Renaissance Wailea Hotel, has a rocky point and a reef that extends farther out. **Ahihi Bay** (p. 292), 2 mi. past the Maui Prince Hotel in Makena, is a marine life preserve where fishing is prohibited, making it spectacular for snorkeling. Two miles past Ahihi Bay, the fish preserve at **La Pérouse Bay** is suited for advanced snorkelers who can handle the difficult entrances along the rocky coast and battle with sometimes rough water caused by the strong winds. If you get there early (5:30am) you may see a pod of dolphins, though by law you must keep 50 ft. away. Several companies run snorkel trips to **Molokini** and **Turtle Arches,** including the eco-friendly **Pacific Whale Foundation** (p. 282) and the **Maui Dive Shop** (below), both of which include gear in the cost of excursions. Kihei has plenty of purveyors of snorkel gear that rent daily or weekly; one of the most visible is **Boss Frog's,** 2395 S. Kihei Rd. (☎875-4477. $1.50-8 per day. Rx mask $10. $20-30 per week.)

SCUBA DIVING. Sea conditions change daily and, as a result, so do the best diving spots. Several dive shops on Kihei Rd. are more than willing to give advice; most shops that offer excursions plan their itineraries on a daily basis. Many companies also rent gear and offer certification classes, in addition to leading guided trips. **Dive and Sea Maui** (☎874-1952) runs a boat with a two-tank dive every day (including equipment, lunch, and drinks; trips leave around 7:30am and return around 12:30pm. $120 if certified; $130 with gear; AmEx/MC/V) and charter tours. **Maui Dive Shop** (☎879-3388), has four locations in Kihei and offers basic certification ($350), 2-tank dives ($120, with gear $130), advanced classes, combination packages for gear and charters, and other discounted activities (helicopter trips, Haleakala bike rides, etc.). **Scuba Shack** (☎879-3483) rents equipment ($22.50 per day) and offers a 3-day certification class including a boat dive ($350 per person), and advanced classes and boat dives ($125 per person for a 2-tank dive).

SURFING AND BOOGIE BOARDING. Summer is the season for South Shore surfing, but even then the big waves don't come every day—ask a local surfer or call the **High Tech Surf Report** (☎877-3611). Many places along Kihei rent surfboards (approx. $20 per day) and boogie boards (approx. $15 per wk.). Most surf schools operate out of Lahaina (p. 265).

KAYAKING. Kayaks are an increasingly popular way to see some of Maui's more secluded coves. The **Ahihi Bay** fish preserve, between Makena and La Pérouse

Bay, is a popular kayak and snorkel destination. Many companies also head to Makena Landing, but locations change depending on wind conditions. **Maui Eco-Adventures** (☎891-2223) gives 3 and 4hr. guided tours starting at $60. **South Pacific Kayaks and Outfitters** (☎875-4848) leads 2½ and 4½ mi. tours starting at $65 per person and rents single kayaks for $40 per day and doubles for $50 per day. Reserve rental kayaks a day in advance. Pick-up is at 7am, and the rental is good until noon.

HORSEBACK RIDING. Move beyond the crowded beaches and tourist traps and enjoy the beauty of South Maui on horseback. **Makena Stables** (☎879-0244), located past Makena at the end of the road near La Pérouse Bay, offers both an early morning ride and a sunset ride. Experienced local guides take you up the mountain side, offering incredible views of La Pérouse Bay and the expansive lava flows. Rides are around 3hr., and groups are limited to six. Ages 13+. Morning rides leave around 8am, and sunset rides start around 3:45pm. Morning rides are $145, and sunset rides are $170. The stables are located at the end of Makena Alanui Rd., which goes through Makena State Park and the Ahihi-Kinau Reserve. Parking is at La Pérouse Bay and the stables are 100 yd. up the road. MC/V.

WHALE-WATCHING. In South Maui, from December to April, you can see whales wherever you can see the ocean, and you can hear them anywhere you stick your head underwater. This unparalleled natural spectacle is truly marvelous. The **Ocean Center** (p. 283) in Maalaea, the **Whale Observatory** near Kaleolepo Park off S. Kihei Rd. (south of Ohukai), and any of the hotels in Wailea make especially good whale-watching sites. To get close, whale-watching cruises can be fun and educational (**Pacific Whale Foundation,** p. 282, our eco-friendly favorite).

To learn more about these creatures, stop by the **Hawaiian Islands Humpback Whale National Marine Sanctuary,** 726 S. Kihei Rd. (☎879-2818; www.hihwnms.nos.noaa.gov), just south of Kaonoulu St. on the *makai* (ocean) side of the road. This free educational center is managed through a partnership between the State of Hawaii and the National Oceanic Atmospheric Administration (NOAA) to conduct research and educate the public about humpback whales and their habitat within the islands. At the sanctuary, you'll find friendly volunteers, colorful displays about whales from scientific and cultural perspectives, and free brochures. Open M-F 10am-3pm. Free.

MOLOKINI CALLING

When traveling on a limited budget, it's difficult to convince yourself to shell out the extra cash for a nice dinner or a tropical frozen drink, and as much as you may want those aloha print car seat covers, you just can't have 'em. However, there's one splurge in Maui that's definitely worth the expense.

As soon as you set foot on Maui, activity centers barrage you with glossy brochures advertising fun-filled snorkeling excursions to the small crater-shaped island of Molokini, situated midway between Maui and Kahoolawe. No matter how much snorkeling you've done at various beaches and coves around the island, Molokini still calls.

With snorkel gear and mask de-fogger in hand, board the boat and enjoy the leisurely ride to "Molo," as locals call it. When you get in the water, you'll understand what all the fuss is about. Molokini and Makena (on Maui's southern coast) bring you face-to-face with turtles, gorgeous humpback whales spouting and breaching, and more vibrant fish and coral than you could ever imagine.

Several activity centers book snorkel trips to Molokini: Maui Dive Shop runs trips from Kihei Boat Harbor (☎879-3388; $50), Pacific Whale Foundation runs out of Maalaea Harbor (☎249-8811; $88, reserve 4-5 days in advance), and Boss Frog's runs out of Kihei (☎875-4477; $60).

NIGHTLIFE

Kihei is generally known as the nightlife hot spot in Maui. Kihei Kalama Village is a small but happening area with several bars. Pick up a free copy of Thursday's *Maui Time Weekly*; its nightly entertainment listings will point fun-seekers in the right direction.

Lulu's, 1945 S. Kihei Rd. (☎879-9944), at Alahele Pl. in Kihei Kalama Village. Lulu's is Kihei's newest up-and-coming nightlife venue: the decor is fun, bartenders are outgoing, and drinks flow readily. An open patio fronts the large 2nd-story room, with couches and a pool table in back. Several large TVs show various sports. Priding itself on "red carpet service at shag rug prices," Lulu's offers food and live music. Happy hour M-F 2-6pm, Sa-Su 4-6pm; domestic drafts, Mai Tais, and mixed drinks $3. Food served until 11pm. Open daily 11am-2am. MC/V.

Hapa's Nightclub, 41 E. Lipoa St. (☎879-9001), in the Lipoa Center. The best known club in Kihei, Hapa's draws a sizable crowd every night. Uncle Willie K., a Hawaiian entertainer and local favorite, plays on M; W Dolla Balla with $1 beers until midnight; Th Retro Nite; F Wild Party; and Sa Flirt with 808 Boogie. M-Sa 21+. In summer, Su doors open 6:30pm for an all-age–but mostly under-18–dance party. Cover $5-10. Open nightly 9pm-1:30am.

Life's A Beach, 1913 S. Kihei Rd. (☎891-8010), in Kihei Kalama Village. Home of the $1 Mai Tai, this drinking den fills up with an eclectic mix of bikers and surfers over the night. Features karaoke and the occasional live band. Happy hour 4-7pm. 21+ after 10pm. Open daily 11am-2am.

Mulligan's on the Blue, 100 Kaukahi St. (☎874-1131), at the Wailea Blue Golf Club. Take S. Kihei Rd. toward Wailea, veer left on Okolani Dr., turn right on Wailea Alanui Dr., then left after the Fairmont Kea Lani Hotel. Mulligan's is the only Irish pub in Maui: the perfect place to savor a Guinness or a gorgeous view of the ocean. $6 drafts. Su night brings the Celtic Tigers, a toe-tapping Irish fiddle band. Happy hour 4-6pm and 10pm-midnight; $1 off drinks, *pupus* $2-3. Open daily 8am-1:30am. AmEx/D/MC/V.

WAILEA

"Affordable paradise" is not the first thing that comes to mind driving along the impeccably landscaped Wailea Alanui Dr. World-class golf courses line one side of the road and five-star resorts the other. But everyone can take advantage of Wailea's beautiful beaches, even if they can't afford the $200+ price tag. All Hawaiian beaches are public, and even the exclusive resorts with beachfront property are required to provide public access to the shore.

FOOD. If you want to splurge on a gourmet beach picnic, head to **Caffe Ciao ❷**, behind the pool in the Fairmont Kea Lani hotel. This boutique grocer sells sandwiches ($9.50), high-end wine, cheese, pastries, and delicious desserts. They also make custom picnic baskets great for roadtrips to other parts of the island. (☎875-4100. Open daily 6:30am-10pm. AmEx/MC/V.) There are also a number of fine dining options within the **Shops at Wailea,** 3750 Wailea Alanui Dr. (☎891-6770; www.shopsatwailea.com), a collection of expensive specialty shops and restaurants in the middle of Wailea's resorts.

BEACHES. There are five main beaches in Wailea, each occupying a crescent of soft sand bordered by outcroppings of volcanic rock. The first beach,

Keawakapu, stretches ½ mi. along the border between Kihei and Wailea. Less of a scene than Kihei beach parks, Keawakapu offers great swimming and snorkeling on an artificial reef 400 yd. offshore. Parking is available in the lot at the entrance to Wailea, on the *mauka* (mountain) side of S. Kihei Rd. To enter the parking lot, make a left shortly before the sign for Wailea; it's on the right. **Mokapu** and **Ulua** are both pleasant but generally crowded with resort guests from the Renaissance Wailea Hotel. The rocky point between the beaches also provides excellent snorkeling. The entrance to both is south of the entrance to the Renaissance Hotel; parking is down the hill. Showers and restrooms available. Sandwiched between the Grand Wailea Resort and the Four Seasons, **Wailea Beach** is the widest beach in Wailea. An access road between the hotels ends in a parking lot. Music from the resort luaus can be heard, and the beach has great swimming and snorkeling along the left side. Public restrooms and showers are available. A walkway leads from Wailea to **Polo Beach,** a narrower beach on the fringe of an immaculate park with picnic tables, grills, showers, and restrooms. While the north part of Polo Beach can be packed with Fairmont Kea Lani vacationers, the southern cove is generally less crowded. Parking for Polo Beach is down a marked road just past the entrance of the Fairmont Kea Lani, 1 mi. south of the Shops at Wailea.

MAKENA AND BEYOND

Until very recently, Makena (pop. 5,671), south of Wailea, was entirely undeveloped. There is still only one hotel in Makena, the Maui Prince Resort, but the golf courses and tennis clubs on the *mauka* (mountain) side of Makena Alanui (the main and only road) stretch ever farther south. After the Maui Prince and the last golf course, the *kiawe* tree desert resumes, and dirt roads on the *makai* (ocean) side lead to the best beaches in Maui. Past the last sandy beach, a number of mansions have sprung up, but even big houses don't detract from the area's rugged beauty.

 BEACHES

POOLENALENA BEACH. *(Open daily 24hr.)* After the Fairmont Kea Lani, but before the Maui Prince, 1¾ mi. south of the Shops at Wailea, there is a small sign for Poolenalena Beach. Also known as Chang's or Paipu Beach, this is the least crowded of Makena's beaches, has ample parking space, and is a find at any time of day. Even with the windswept reddish sand and frequently strong current of this isolated coastline, the beach is still a favorite among locals. You can see the Maui Prince down at the far southern end, but otherwise, the view touches on completely undeveloped land. Camping is not legal.

MAKENA LANDING. *(Snorkeling. Open daily 24hr.)* Heading south, the next cove is Makena Landing. Once Maui's busiest port, it is now an unimpressive, if placid, beach. Kayaking companies often take advantage of the sheltered waters. The Beach Park at Makena Landing has showers, restrooms, a boat-launching ramp, and good snorkeling on the south side of the landing. To get there, head south on Makena Alanui Rd., turn right on Honoiki St., and then right again on Makena Rd. for the beach, which is identified by a wooden sign. Turn left to reach the quaint and beautiful **Keawalai Church** (built in 1832 from offshore reef coral), which still holds Hawaiian-Anglo church services on Sundays at 7:30 and 10am; all are welcome. After Keawalai Church, Makena Rd. comes to an end at a cul-de-sac by the edge of the Maui Prince Hotel.

MALUAKA BEACH. *(Open daily 24hr.)* Continuing south on Makena Alahui Rd., take the first right after the Maui Prince Hotel to the public parking for the golden Maluaka Beach, the best swimming beach in Makena and a family favorite. The paved path leads to the hotel but also provides public access from the parking lot. Public restrooms, showers, and picnic tables are available. Due to erosion and steep slopes, hiking is discouraged.

BIG BEACH (ONELOA BEACH). *(Open daily 24hr.)* Big Beach is part of **Makena State Park.** There are toilets and picnic tables by the northernmost entrance. Camping is not legal, and the area may be dangerous after dark. The last sandy beach for miles, Big Beach may look tempting, but its clear waters are deceptive. Powerful waves break right on the shore, sweeping swimmers and boogie boarders off their feet and onto the sand at forces strong enough to break necks and backs. **Swimming and bodysurfing is not recommended.**

LITTLE BEACH. *(Open daily 24hr.)* At the north end of Big Beach, beneath Puu Olai, volcanic rocks hide a short, steep trail that leads to Little Beach. A lingering hippie hangout, Little Beach is unofficially "clothing optional," though nudity is illegal on Hawaii's beaches. Sunday afternoons, the hippie contingent holds a drum and dance circle that can be quite a spectacle for the uninitiated observer. The surf at Little Beach may look choppier than at Big Beach, but it's generally safer since the waves break farther out. Still, the riptide and currents are incredibly strong—make sure someone is watching you, and signal if you feel yourself being pulled out.

ACTIVITIES

AHIHI-KINAU NATURAL AREA RESERVE Past the last entrance to Big Beach, the road narrows to one lane and winds through the 2000-acre Ahihi-Kinau Natural Area Reserve. Since fishing is prohibited in the reserve, any calm spot along the coast makes for excellent snorkeling. As you enter the reserve, several protected coves of Ahihi Bay are visible from the road, including Ahihi Cove, which has good snorkeling but is often crowded with families. Past Ahihi Cove, the road winds inland through a lava field—the path of the flow during the last eruption of Haleakala around 1790. The area formed by the lava path is Cape Kinau, and the water around it is part of a protected reserve.

No longer a secret but still an adventure, a 35min. hike through the lava field ends in a sheltered and less crowded spot for snorkeling—the **Fishbowl.** If you plan to hike, bring your snorkel gear and wear sturdy shoes. To find the trailhead, look at the numbers posted on the telephone poles. Around pole #14 (6 mi. from the intersection of Wailea Ike Dr. and Wailea Alanui Dr.), there is a large dirt lot where you can park, but don't leave valuables in your car. Walk 10min. up the road to pole #18. When you reach this pole, face the ocean and climb about 20 ft. over the lava rocks until you see a brown sign marking the trail. With a view of the ocean ahead and the rolling pastures of Haleakala behind, the walk is worthwhile for the surroundings alone. The path ends in a protected cove, and the narrow black-sand and pebble beach on the left is the easiest entrance for snorkeling. Underwater plants have grown on the volcanic rock, and the area is populated by colorful fish. Only venture beyond the cove if you are an experienced snorkeler and the water is calm, because currents are strong.

About seven miles from the Wailea Ike/Wailea Alanui intersection and a few hundred yards before the end of the road, a sign on the *makai* (ocean) side of the road begins the trail to the **Aquarium.** The trail is marked by two yellow reflectors, and it goes through a cove of trees along a barbed wire fence until it comes out onto the lava formations. Park at La Pérouse Bay and walk about 200 yd. up the road to the trail. Many beautiful fish swim in this large, protected cove. It's easy to lose the rugged trail. Make sure to turn left when the trail splits about 5min. in, and wear sturdy shoes. As you approach the Aquarium, you'll see a lot of white spray paint leading down to the water. Since there's no sand, just rough, volcanic rock, bring water shoes or the equivalent to make entrances less painful. Many of the inlets on the way to the Aquarium also offer good snorkeling. At the end of the road is **La Pérouse Bay,** or Keoneoio, a spot that European explorer La Pérouse "discovered" in 1786. Visitors will find porta-potties and a splendid ocean view.

NORTH SHORE

Hana Hwy. begins right outside Kahului, but most travelers feel the road to Hana really begins in Paia, a town that epitomizes the laid-back surfing lifestyle on Maui. Past Paia lies Haiku, which goes unnoticed a few miles inland of the highway. Twin Falls, on the east end of Haiku near Huelo, are only a few of the innumerable waterfalls along Hana Hwy. Unfortunately, a lot of these falls are

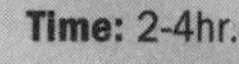

Time: 2-4hr.

Distance: 45 mi.

Season: Any

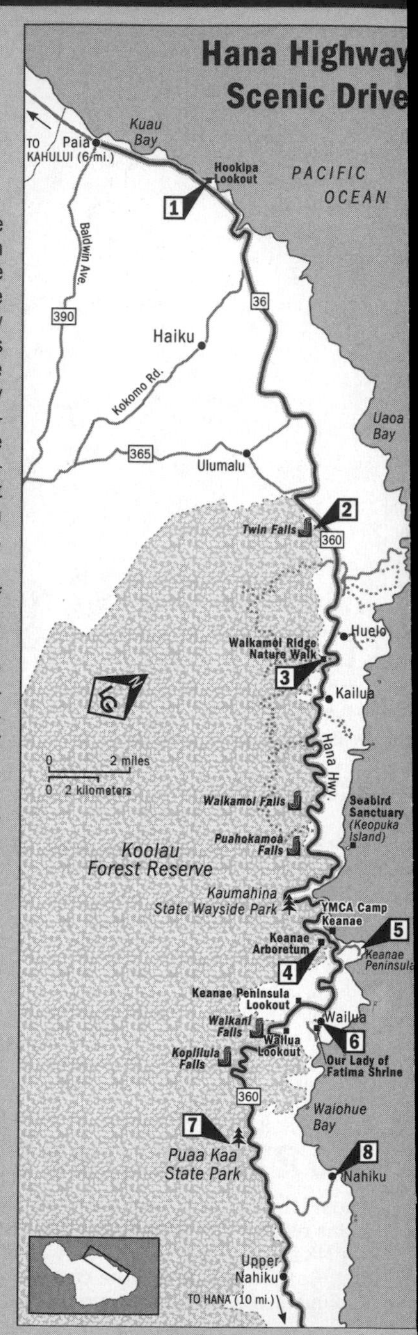

The 45 mi. trip from Paia to Hana is one of the world's most impressive coastal drives. With more than 600 turns and over 50 single-lane bridges, the "Road to Heaven" offers incredible views of Maui's rainforests and waterfalls, many of which are visible from the road. While it takes about 2hr. to drive, the experience is much more rewarding if you stop along the way. If you only have a day for the road to Hana and back, consider skipping some of these sites to leave time for the Pools of Oheo and the nearby hikes. Highlights of the journey are outlined below, but there's always more to explore. Fill up on gas in Paia (there are no gas stations along the way), pack a cooler with snacks and water, and go!

1 HOOKIPA LOOKOUT. About 2 mi. east of Paia on the *makai* (ocean) side of Hana Hwy., Hookipa Lookout offers a killer view of Hookipa Beach. In summer, windsurfers fly over the choppy waves at lightning speed while longboard surfers wait patiently for a wave. In winter, the surf changes entirely, and swells over 10 ft. high (some over 25 ft.) fill the bay.

2 TWIN FALLS. If you want to make this a worthwhile excursion, go at 7am or take your chances, because by 8:15am the parking lot is typically full and the narrow trail to the falls is packed with Hana-bound tourists. As with most waterfall hikes, don't stop at the first fall—keep going! Usually where you see one fall, there is a bigger one above, and another above that—Twin Falls is no exception. If you beat the crowds, you may enjoy a lovely secluded swim beneath the falls—just you and the mosquitoes (don't forget your bug spray). To get to the falls, pull over when you see the fruit stand past mi. marker 2, after Hana Hwy. turns into Rte. 360. Pass through the gate onto the dirt road; after 2min., a few small trails branch off to the left to a rope swing and small pool. While many stop here for a quick dive, this is not the main attraction. After 10min., the trail forks at a small, hand-painted rock. The path to the left leads to the most popular waterfall and a lovely pool beneath it. The path to the right includes a akeshift bridge over an irrigation canal and continues to a concrete step where the path splits. oing uphill to the left leads you through a forest where you can find the top of the falls on the ft. Stay right at the concrete block to continue through a jungle-like cove to a less populated, but onetheless breathtaking, waterfall and pool.

WAIKAMOI RIDGE NATURE WALK. On the *mauka* (mountain) side, between mi. markers and 10, there is an excellent short hike among native ferns, bamboo, eucalyptus, mango, and trawberry guava. Picnic tables are at the start of the trail above the parking area, and a more cenic and less crowded picnic area is at the top of the trail. Just above the parking area, the ail forks into 2 nested loop trails. To take the longer one (about 1 mi. total), bear left, then left gain past the second bench. The trail climbs a bit past strawberry guava and *hala* trees before eveling out and making a switchback to another bench. To the right, the trail continues through stand of bamboo. It ends under mango trees in a quiet, grassy clearing, with a picnic shelter verlooking the ocean. To loop back down to the parking lot, either backtrack down the trail or alk down the old road (bearing right when it splits). The ride from here to the next stop offers ome of the most gorgeous views of the coast as the road winds in and out in large curves.

KEANAE ARBORETUM. Right after the YMCA Camp Keanae, before mi. marker 17, the eanae Arboretum offers another chance to stretch your legs. A corridor of impatiens and trees eads to the main park, a garden of labeled trees and flowers that includes taro, breadfruit, and ugar cane. The 6-acre park is pleasant, but extremely damp, and the mosquitoes can be worse ere than in other areas, which may discourage you from staying long. However, in the dry season, it may not be bad at all.

KEANAE PENINSULA. The taro farming village of **Keanae** lies on a wave-thrashed coast, a eft turn off Hana Hwy. shortly after the arboretum. Here you'll find a peaceful Hawaiian town, entered on the **Keanae Congregational Church,** built in 1860 at the tip of the peninsula. Before you reach the church, you'll see a snack shop on the right, which sells delicious banana read, as well as fruit and smoothies. At the end of the road is a park with public restrooms. Picnic tables overlook the rocky beach, where waves crash against the coast. Please respect the ocals who live here by coming and going quietly.

6 WAILUA. Just past mi. marker 19, the **Wailua Lookout** offers views of the tiny village of Wailua. The pride of the town is the **Our Lady of Fatima Shrine,** built in 1860, and the bougainvillea gardens maintained by many of Wailua's residents. The view is pretty, but you won't egret skipping it if you're in a hurry.

7 PUAA KAA. Between mi. markers 22 and 23 are the freshwater pools of **Puaa Kaa State Park.** The 2 swimmable pools connected by a small waterfall make for a refreshing dip, but because they are less than a 2min. walk from the car, they are frequently crowded. The park also has shaded picnic tables, restrooms, and a pay phone. Parking is available on the *makai* (ocean) side of the highway.

8 NAHIKU. Between mi. markers 25 and 26, a road leads seaward to **Nahiku,** a small fishing village that is home to an historic Christian church, built in 1867. Nahiku is East Maui's wettest town, getting more than 300 in. of rain per year. The real draw here is the road–about 2½ mi. one way, it winds through lush rainforest growth and is particularly beautiful in the wet season. At the end of the road is a nice ocean view. From Nahiku, it's another 10 mi. to Hana town.

! **HANA HIGHWAY DRIVING TIPS.** Please keep in mind that many residents commute several times a day on this road. Use your **rearview mirror,** and use the pull-outs along the road to let cars pass you. **Do not stop on the road** to look at scenery or take pictures; this is dangerous and inconsiderate. On **one-lane bridges,** obey the yield signs but do not stop if you can see that the road ahead of you is clear. On steep downhill passages, **switch to a lower gear** rather than riding your breaks.

on private property, and hiking to them is technically trespassing. Beyond Huelo, the road winds around 617 hairpin turns, hugging the resplendent coastline all 53 mi. to Hana. A few small towns lie between Huelo and Hana, including the taro root farming town of Keanae, but for the most part the road is surrounded only by unspoiled tropical forest. Hana, a peaceful town with beautiful beaches and parks, warrants more than a glance from the car, though it might be worth hurrying a bit to make time for Oheo Gulch, where you can swim in freshwater pools and hike to waterfalls. Those who haven't promised their rental company otherwise can continue around the southern coast of Haleakala on Hwy. 31, returning to Kahului via Kula and the arid Kaupo Valley.

PAIA

Surfing and healthy living go hand in hand in Paia (pop. 2,499): organic food stores and yoga studios abound near the North Shore's biggest waves. Its beaches are renowned for windsurfing in summer; winter brings staggering waves and the most daring surfers. At any time of year, Paia attracts surfer dudes, bikini-clad Maui chicks, and aging hippies. With a mix of restaurants and beach bars, Paia is arguably the best town on Maui for good, cheap food. It's also a wonderful place to experience the laid-back attitude characteristic of Maui without the lofty price tag.

ORIENTATION AND PRACTICAL INFORMATION

Paia is at the intersection of **Highway 36 (Hana Highway)** and **Baldwin Avenue,** which runs from Paia to **Makawao** (p. 317). This is the commercial center of the town, called Lower Paia. Actual Paia is farther inland on Baldwin Ave.

The **Nagata General Store,** 96 Hana Hwy., sells basic necessities along with limited fish, meats, and produce. (Open M-F 6am-6:30pm, Sa 6am-6pm, Su 6am-noon.) There are three gas stations in Paia along Hana Hwy. It's a good idea to fill up on the way to Hana; the only gas station after Paia is in Hana itself, and gas there is usually $0.30 per gallon more. Other services include: **Bank of Hawaii,** 35 Baldwin Ave., with a **24hr. ATM.** (☎579-9511; open M-Th 8:30am-4pm, F 8:30am-6pm), and a **laundromat,** 129 Baldwin Ave. (wash $1.75, dry $0.25 per 5min.; open daily 6am-9pm). Head to **LiveWire C@fe,** 137 Hana Hwy., for **Internet access,** coffee, homemade cheesecake or lava cake ($3.50), or the frequent live music on the outdoor patio. (☎579-6009; www.livewirecafe.com. Internet $3 per 20min. AmEx/D/MC/V.) The **Paia Post Office** is on Baldwin Ave., just south of town. (Open M-F 8:30am-4:30pm, Sa 10:30am-12:30pm.) **Postal Code:** 96779.

ACCOMMODATIONS

Paia is one of the few places on Maui where good beaches, restaurants, and bars converge. It's easy to find a cheap place to stay and many places offer long-term rates. Travelers interested in private vacation rentals can look for postings on bulletin boards in town or contact **Hookipa Haven,** 62 Baldwin Ave., for a range of studios, apartments, and cottages in Paia and Upcountry Maui. (☎579-8282; www.hookipahaven.com. Open M-F 9am-4pm. Rentals $85-350 per night, often with cleaning fees for stays shorter than a week. MC/V.) For a great, inexpensive room, see **Peace of Maui** (p. 318), in Haliimaile, a 10min. drive from Paia.

Rainbow's End Surf Hostel, 221 Baldwin Ave. (☎579-9057). Well-maintained and friendly, this hostel, usually filled with windsurfers and young backpackers, is only a short walk from the beach. Parking available. Linens included. 4 dorms and 3 private doubles share a living room with TV/VCR, 2 kitchens, and 3 bathrooms. Quiet hours after 10pm. Reserve far in advance with $50 deposit. Dorms $25 per night, $135 per week, $375 per month; doubles $55/300/750. Rates higher Oct.-Apr. Cash only. ❷

YMCA Camp Keanae, 13375 Hana Hwy. (☎248-8355), about halfway between Paia and Hana, before mi. marker 17. Pitch a tent on the gorgeous property, or stay in one of the co-ed dorms or cabins. Dorm guests and campers share toilets and single-sex shower rooms, grill pit, charcoal grill, and gym. Two 4-person cottages, each with full bathroom, kitchenette, lanai, and grill. Linen not included in dorms. Coin-op laundry. The entire camp is frequently rented to large groups in the summer; call for availability. Check-in 3pm. Check-out noon. Camping and dorms $17; cottages $125. MC/V. ❶

The Inn at Mama's Fish House, 799 Poho Pl. (☎579-9764), 1½ mi. east of Paia on Hana Hwy., turn left on Kaiholo Pl., which dead ends into Poho Pl. at the end of the shady parking lot across from Mama's Fish House restaurant. Cottages have A/C, full kitchen, TV/VCR, DVD, stereo, grill, and beach access. Single rooms with bath also available occasionally, call to inquire. 3-night min. Check-in 3pm. Check-out 11am. Reserve in advance with credit card deposit. Singles from $60. Cottages $175-475. AmEx/D/MC/V. Singles ❷/Cottages ❺

Aloha Maui Bed and Breakfast, 101 Loomis Rd. (☎572-0298; www.alohamauicottages.com). Turn off Hana Hwy. right before mi. marker 2 onto Ulalena Ln. Follow the gravel road over a small bridge, and at the fork stay left onto Loomis Rd. Veer right at the next fork at the sign "Private Rd., Invited Guests Only." Follow this turn-off to the driveway at the end. Set in a beautiful rainforest, Aloha Maui provides a relaxing and removed getaway. Tropical flowers surround 3 cottages which use solar energy and run filtered rainwater through their pipes. Continental breakfast included. All cottages have full kitchens or kitchenettes. 3-night min. Reserve with 50% deposit, balance due on arrival. Cottages $65-135. Weekly rates available. D/MC/V. ❸

FOOD AND NIGHTLIFE

There are plenty of excellent places to dine out in Paia. In addition, **Mana Foods,** 49 Baldwin Ave., a health-food haven, sells bulk food, organic produce, and packaged groceries. (☎579-8078. Open daily 8:30am-8:30pm. AmEx/MC/V.)

RESTAURANTS

Paia Fishmarket, 100 Hana Hwy. (☎579-8030), at the corner of Baldwin Ave. A Paia stand-by, filled with familiar people at long wooden tables eating good food and sipping their favorite beers (Hefeweizen, $4; domestics, $3.50). The mahi mahi burgers ($8) are the best on the island. Sashimi appetizer $13. Fries, fish tacos, salads, seafood entrees $12-16. Open daily 11am-9:30pm. D/MC/V. ❷

Jacques Northshore, 120 Hana Hwy. (☎579-8844). A windsurfer hangout with surf paraphernalia and live local music M, Jacques offers creative appetizers (spicy ahi roll, $9.50). While many entrees are on the steep side (up to $27 for fish and meat), curries and pastas are easier on the wallet ($11-18). In fact, most locals skip the food altogether and head straight for the beer and music. F nights are especially happening (bar open until 1am). Dinner daily 5-10pm. Sushi bar open Tu-Sa 5:30-10pm. MC/V. ❹

Charley's Restaurant and Saloon, 142 Hana Hwy. (☎579-9453). With swinging wooden doors and lazy ceiling fans, this old-time saloon serves 3 meals a day, including hearty breakfasts with massive pancakes ($4-7.25) and *ono* (delicious) eggs benedict ($11.75). Dinner ($14-22) features standard pub food, including burgers, ribs, pastas, and pizza. Charley's is one of the few places in town that stays open past dinner for hit-or-miss nightlife: M and Sa live music, W DJ 10:30pm-1am. Open daily 7am-1am; food served until midnight. AmEx/D/MC/V. ❸

CAFES AND BAKERIES

Cafe des Amis, 42 Baldwin Ave. (☎579-6323). The scrumptious crepes at this intimate and funky cafe are equally popular with the morning latte crowd and Merlot-toting diners. Savory crepes ($7-9) are substantial enough for a full meal, while sweet crepes ($2.50-4.75) finish things off nicely (try the sugar and lime juice). Curries pack a tasty punch. BYOB. Open daily 8:30am-8:30pm. MC/V. ❷

Moana Bakery and Cafe, 71 Baldwin Ave. (☎579-9999). Breakfast is a treat—homemade pastries, Belgian waffles, and hearty omelets—while dinner is a decadent tour of the best cuisine (island pesto pasta with macadamia nuts and ginger, $13; chili-seared ahi with mango salsa, $24). Lunch includes some of the same dishes at a better value (pasta, $9-10; lamb and hummus wrap, $11). On weekends, brunch (8am-3pm) is a Moana specialty, with crab cake eggs benedict ($12). Relax and enjoy some of the live music starting at 6:30pm. Hula Honeys play on W, Haiku Hillbilly's Th, and jazz F. Open M and Su 8am-3pm, Tu-Sa 8am-9pm. MC/V. ❹

Cafe Mambo, 30 Baldwin Ave. (☎579-8021). Contemporary art hangs on brightly painted walls in this funky, fun Spanish cafe. The menu includes omelets ($7 and up), sandwiches ($6-9), fajitas (lunch, $8-13; dinner, $11-16), and a variety of tapas. Dessert ($5) includes the lime cheesecake or crème brûlée. Happy hour 4-6pm. Open daily 8am-9pm. MC/V. ❸

Cakewalk Paia Bakery (☎579-8770), next to Paia Fishmarket, sells baked goods ($1.35-4) and appetizing sandwiches ($6.50). You can also special order custom-made cakes. Open M-Sa 7am-5pm, Su 8am-2pm. AmEx/MC/V. ❶

Anthony's Coffee Co., 90 Hana Hwy. (☎579-8340). A good place for an ice cream snack. Sells sandwiches and coffee as well. Open daily 5:30am-6pm. AmEx/MC/V. ❶

Aloha Island Shaved Ice, 77 Hana Hwy. (☎579-8747), across from Shell gas station. Regular ($3.50), large ($4.50), or jumbo ($5.50) shaved ice in a variety of tropical flavors makes this small store a great place to stop by on a hot afternoon. Also offers a few plate lunches. Open daily 11am-5pm. MC/V. ❶

BEACHES

PAIA BAY. *(Boogie boarding. Open daily 24hr.)* A few minutes west of town, Paia Bay is a first-rate beach for summer swimming, and it is usually uncrowded, particularly late in the day. The surf picks up in winter, and the beach becomes popular with boogie boarders. Parking is available at the Youth and Cultural Center and the Paia Town Public Parking Lot. Left of Paia Bay, a trail leads to a small, generally unpopulated, unofficial nude beach (although public nudity is illegal in Hawaii).

H. A. BALDWIN BEACH PARK. *(Open daily sunrise to sunset. Lifeguards 8am-4:30pm.)* Half a mile west of town, H.A. Baldwin Beach Park is a long, wide beach with playful surf and an occasionally dangerous shorebreak. The small cove on the right side of the beach is a great place to swim. There are changing rooms, showers, picnic tables, and a big picnic shelter. A large recreational field separates the beach from Hana Hwy. Coming out of Paia, look for the sign and field on your right.

SPRECKLESVILLE TOWN BEACH (BABY BEACH). *(Open daily 24hr.)* Under a mile west of H.A. Baldwin Beach Park, the beach turns into Sprecklesville Town Beach, which is also accessible by veering right onto Nonohe Pl. off Hana Hwy. and then turning left onto Kealakai Pl. Parking is in the red sand lot at the end of Kealakai Pl.; do not leave valuables in your car. The beach is also known as Baby Beach for the protected swimming area to the right of the parking perfect for *keiki* (children). Both Baby Beach and Baldwin Beach Park are subject to strong winds that can kick up brutal sandstorms or make the water too rough to swim.

KUAU BAY. *(Open daily 24hr.)* A small stretch of sand, Kuau Bay Beach has some rocks and coral in the water, making it tough to swim but great for laying in the sun. Look for the blue shoreline access sign half a mile east of the intersection of Hana Hwy. with Baldwin Ave.

HOOKIPA BEACH. *(Snorkeling. Surfing. Wind sports. Open daily sunrise to sunset. Lifeguards 8am-4:30pm.)* Hookipa Beach is famous for the windsurfers who race along the west end of the water in the summer; relatively small waves attract longboarders and beginning surfers to the east end. The east end also has some coral that is great for snorkeling if the wind isn't too strong. The entrance is rocky, making it less ideal for swimming; the best place to swim is the far west end in front of the lifeguard stand. In winter, the bay is rocked by giant waves, and only experienced surfers should paddle out. To get there, drive 2 mi. east of Paia on Hana Hwy.; look for the sign for Hookipa Lookout. Porta-potties and picnic tables are available.

SHOPPING

Aloha Bead Company, 43 Hana Hwy. (☎579-9709), behind the Maui Crafts Guild. The Bead Company sells a wider variety of beads in 2 rooms than you'll find in most craft warehouses. Limited selection of expensive pre-made jewelry (around $60) and some cheaper bracelets and necklaces ($4-12). Open daily 11am-6pm. AmEx/D/MC/V.

Da Kine Hawaii (☎575-2495), in Haiku. This famous surfboard manufacturer, next door to Pauwela Cafe (p. 302), sells surf and windsurf accessories. Open M-F 9am-1pm.

Maui Girl, 12 Baldwin Ave. (☎579-9266). Burn up the beach in one of Maui Girl's original bikinis that will seduce you and everyone else on the beach (around $100). The tops and bottoms on the sides are cheaper. Open daily 9am-6pm. AmEx/D/MC/V.

Northshore Tropix, 90 Hana Hwy. (☎579-9816). For over 25 years, Tropix has provided Maui with quality surf gear and the exclusive Maui Built brand (whose logo graces local truck bumpers). Surfboards, stickers ($1-20), t-shirts ($19), and sunglasses ($25 and up). Also in Kahului and Lahaina. Open M-Sa 9am-6pm, Su 10am-6pm. AmEx/MC/V.

HAIKU

Sleepy Haiku (pop. 6,758) is as poetic as its name. While its downtown is little more than a cluster of stores, small restaurants, and a post office, the sprawling outskirts occupy a chunk of Upcountry Maui and spill down North Shore along Hana Hwy. Frequent rain showers keep the land lush and the air cool and humid. Ginger speckles the verdant landscape with brilliant color, while plumeria and soft orange *puakenikeni* flowers infuse the air with heavy floral perfume.

ORIENTATION

Hana Highway defines the northern edge of Haiku, Paia is to the west, and Huelo is to the east. **Haiku Road** loops inland from Hana Hwy., intersecting Kokomo Rd.,

Time: 1-2hr.

Distance: 30 mi.

Season: Any

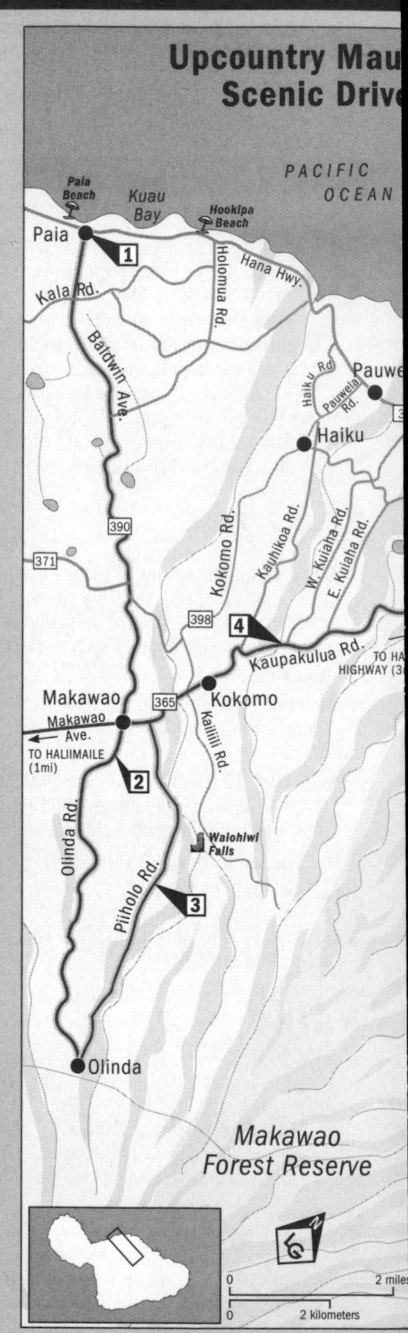

1 PAIA. Begin in this former plantation town, now the haven of health-conscious New Agers and devoted surfers. Take Baldwin Avenue southeast, past the old sugar mill, and through the rustling cane fields.

2 OLINDA RD. After 7 mi., Baldwin Ave. ends in the town of Makawao. At the end, cross Makawao Ave. (between Polli's and Casanova's restaurants) to Olinda Rd. The farther you go on Olinda, the prettier it gets—ranches and country pastures give way to fragrant eucalyptus groves, which can be better appreciated with the windows rolled down. The rodeo grounds are on your left. As the road climbs to 4000 ft. in elevation, the switchbacks get steeper, the shoulder narrows, and the corners become more difficult to see around—take your time and drive carefully.

3 PIIHOLO RD. Just before mi. marker 12, turn left on Piiholo Rd. to loop back down. The turns here are tighter still; switch to a lower gear to save your brakes. Eucalyptus trees line the way and the rural homesteads grow more eccentric. In the last mile or so before town, the landscape opens up to fields of pineapples. A left takes you back to Makawao, where you can easily backtrack to Paia.

4 KAUPAKULUA RD. You can also continue the scenic drive by turning right at the end of Piiholo onto Makawao Avenue. This becomes **Kaupakulua Road,** which ends 6 mi. later when it meets Hana Hwy. See Hana Highway scenic drive, p. 294.

This drive can also be reversed, starting from Hana Hwy. in Haiku, taking Kaupakalua to the Piiholo-Olinda loop, and going back through Makawao on Baldwin Ave. to Paia. The advantage of this direction is that you have an ocean view along Baldwin heading toward Paia; the disadvantage is that it's a bit harder to find the streets. If you have a good map and are attentive, you should have no problem.

W. Kuiaha Rd., and E. Kuiaha Rd., before reconnecting with Hana Hwy. All three intersected roads run southeast to **Kaupakulua Road,** which connects Haiku to **Makawao.** Kaupakulua ends at Hana Hwy. just before Twin Falls. The center of Haiku is at the intersection of Haiku Rd. and Kokomo Rd., where Haiku Rd. makes a turn to the left and Kokomo Rd. continues inland.

TOW-IN SURFING AT JAWS. Every year in December and January, there is a grand *Pohai na keiki nalu* ("gathering of the surf kids") to witness one of the biggest spectacles in the islands: tow-in big-wave surfing at Jaws. When the waves break just right off the coast below a pineapple field in Haiku, surfers have jet skis tow them into waves that reach heights of 100 ft. from crest to trough (though the average height is 25-40 ft.). Surfers are strapped into their boards, allowing them to rip nasty tricks on their way down the wave—it's like skiing down an avalanche. After the ride, surfers hold their breath and wait for the jet ski to tow them back to safety before the next wave. Surfers train for years, holding onto heavy rocks below the surface to increase their lung capacity, which they'll need to survive the powerful wave breaking above them. Lifeguards wait outside the impact zone should they be needed. The event also has a hefty price tag, as the cost for the tow-in is a few thousand dollars, unless the surfer is backed by a sponsor or a movie company trying to make a film. News of surfing at Jaws spreads by word of mouth—keep your ears open for a chance to see this crazy event.

PRACTICAL INFORMATION

Almost everything you'll need in Haiku is in the Haiku Marketplace, 810 Haiku Rd., in the old cannery building, including an **ATM** in both supermarkets, the **medical clinic** (☎575-7531; open M-F 8am-noon and 2-6pm; MC/V), **pharmacy** (☎575-7522; open M-F 9am-6:30pm, Sa 9am-noon; AmEx/D/MC/V), and **laundromat** (☎575-9274; open daily 6:30am-9pm; wash $1.75, dry $0.25 per 7min.). **Internet access** is available at **1 Stop Postal Shop,** 810 Haiku Rd., in the Haiku Marketplace, which has four computers and copiers. (☎575-2049. Internet $0.15 per min., $2 min. Copies $0.10 per pg. Open M-F 8am-6pm, Sa 9:30am-3:30pm.) The **Haiku Post Office** is on Haiku Rd. in the town center. (Open M-F 8:30am-4:30pm, Sa 9-11am.) **Postal Code:** 96708.

ACCOMMODATIONS

Many privately rented cottages are listed at www.vrbo.com. Price and quality vary. **Hookipa Hale ❹,** 1350 Kauhikoa Rd., is located three quarters of a mile from the intersection of Kauhikou Rd. and Haiku Rd. Guests have everything they need in a remote location at the right price. A bright pink country home has basic accommodations including a two-bed/two-bath apartment, and a two-bed/two-bath cottage. The gracious hosts provide beach chairs, boogie boards, and snorkel gear. (☎575-9357; www.hulahuts.com. 7-night min. 50% deposit due a month before arrival. Apartment $120; cottage $225. MC/V.)

FOOD

For groceries, visit the **Haiku Grocery Store,** in the Haiku Cannery Marketplace (☎575-9291; open daily 7am-9pm; MC/V), or **Fukushima General Store** across the street (☎575-2762; open M-Sa 6:30am-8pm, Su 7am-4pm. AmEx/D/MC/V).

Colleen's at the Cannery, 810 Haiku Rd. (☎575-9211), in the Haiku Marketplace, offers flaky pastries, hearty sandwiches (with a fresh cookie, $7), salads, and fish and burgers ($6-10). Breakfast also includes the Hangover Cure: sauteed potatoes, cheddar cheese, ham, onions, and mild green chiles, along with sides of salsa and sour cream ($6.75; with 2 eggs, $2). Young locals flock here for the food and casual atmosphere. Happy hour daily 3:30-5:30pm. Open daily 6am-9pm. D/MC/V. ❷

Lyn's Cafe, 810 Kokomo Rd. (☎575-9363), in the Haiku Town Center. A simple cafe, but a great place to grab some breakfast. 2 eggs and choice of breakfast meat comes with choice of rice, toast, or hash browns ($6). Also serves sandwiches and plate lunches. Open M-Sa 6:30am-7pm, Su 7am-2pm. ❶

Veg Out (☎575-5320), also in the Haiku Town Center. A casual, fun place that caters to vegetarians and vegans with healthy, wholesome, and palatable sandwiches (around $5), tacos ($5), smoothies ($3), juice ($2.50-4), and entrees ($8-9). Open M-F 10:30am-7:30pm, Sa-Su 11:30am-7:30pm. MC/V. ❶

Pauwela Cafe, 375 W. Kuiaha Rd. (☎575-9242), take Haiku Rd. out of Haiku and turn left on W. Kuiaha Rd.; Pauwela Cannery will be on your right. Another local cafe, loved for its fresh-brewed coffee, quick and filling breakfasts ($4.50-6.50), and delicious sandwiches and salads ($4-7). Open M-Sa 7am-2:30pm, Su 7am-1pm. MC/V. ❶

Hana Hou Cafe (☎575-2661), at the Haiku Marketplace in a separate building from the main cannery. Chow down on a burger or plate lunch ($7-10) in a pleasant courtyard with screened-in patio seating that hides the fact that you're in the middle of a parking lot. Open M-Sa 11am-9pm, Su 7am-10pm. AmEx/MC/V. ❶

Island Tacos, a makeshift stand at the edge of the Haiku Marketplace parking lot with 2 picnic tables. Good for a fish or chicken taco on the go ($3). Open daily 11am-4pm, or until tacos run out. Cash only. ❶

HANA

Since Hana Highway's 617 hairpin turns and 53 bridges were paved in 1984, the town has undergone a considerable tourist boom. Yet Hana (pop. 709) remains relaxed and visitors still stop to smell the plumeria and take a vacation from their vacation, exploring caves, watching the sun rise, strolling along secluded red- and black-sand beaches, or joining the entire town to cheer on the local ball team.

TRANSPORTATION

Hana Airport is on Alalele Rd., off of Hana Hwy. 4 mi. north of Hana. **Pacific Wings** (☎873-0877) offers regular nonstop service to Honolulu and Kahului; other airlines fly less frequently. The only rental car company in Hana is **Dollar,** at the airport. (☎800-800-4000. Open M-F 9am-noon and 2-4:30pm, Sa 3:30-4:30pm, Su 10am-noon and 2-4:30pm.)

A **gas station** at 5170 Hana Hwy., in the south end of town, charges about $0.30 more per gallon than elsewhere on Maui. (Open daily 7:30am-7:30pm.) For 24hr. emergency road service and repair between Keanae and Kaupo, call **East Maui Towing and Mechanics** (☎248-8085).

ORIENTATION AND PRACTICAL INFORMATION

Approaching Hana from the north, **Hana Highway** splits at the **Hana Police Station** (☎248-8311). Hana Hwy. continues down the right fork, past the Hotel Hana-

Maui. Left of the police station, **Ua Kea Road** leads to Hana Beach Park and accommodations on Hana Bay. The **fire station** (☎248-7525) is also at the intersection, along with the **Hana Community Health Center.** (☎248-8294. Open M-Tu and F-Sa 8am-5pm, W-Th 8am-8pm.) Ua Kea Rd. ends after the community center and the Hana Ball Park; turn right on **Hauoli Street** to return to Hana Hwy. Hauoli St. crosses Hana Hwy. by the Wananalua Congregational Church, north of Hana's business district. A **Bank of Hawaii** is in the Hana Ranch Center, at the center of town. (☎248-8015. Open M-Th 3-4:30pm, F 3-6pm.) **ATMs** are located in both the **Hasagawa General Store,** 5165 Hana Hwy. and the **Hana Ranch Store,** up the hill from the Hana Ranch Center. The **post office,** 1 Mill St., is by the Bank of Hawaii. (Open M-F 8am-4:30pm.) **Postal Code:** 96713.

ACCOMMODATIONS AND CAMPING

Vacation rentals in **Hamoa Bay,** 2 mi. south of Hana, have a prime location on Hana's best beaches. For an extensive list of accommodations in Hana, look under lodging on the local website (www.hanamaui.com).

Joe's Place, 4870 Ua Kea Rd. (☎248-7033; www.joesrentals.com), offers the cheapest private rooms in town. The spartan, economical rooms are kept very neat. Guests share a common kitchen, living room with cable TV, and recreation room. Check-in 3pm. Check-out 10am. Quiet hours after 10pm. Reserve in advance. 7 rooms with shared bath $45; 1 with private bath $55. MC/V. ❷

Aloha Cottages, 73-79 Keawa Pl. (☎248-8420). Each cottage comes with a full kitchen and sleeps 6 comfortably. A walk from Hana Beach Park, these no-frills units are a great value. 2-person studio $65; 2-bedroom cottages $115-125; 3-bedroom cottage $170; each additional guest $10. Cash only. ❸

Napualani O'Hana, 95 Kalo Rd. (☎248-8935), off of Hana Hwy., about 5 mi. north of Hana between mi. markers 30 and 31. A bit out of the way, these cheap rooms are a good value, with their own bathrooms and kitchens. Check-out 11am. Studios $50; 2-bedroom units $75; each additional guest $10. Cash only. ❷

Hana Kai-Maui Resort, 1533 Ua Kea Rd. (☎248-8426; www.hanakaimaui.com), across from Joe's Place. Hana Kai's standard condo-style units are comfortable. The 16 studio and 1-bedroom units are on the black-sand beach next to Hana Beach Park. Full kitchens and private lanais in each unit; ocean views in some. Check-in 2-5pm. Check-out 11am. Quiet hours

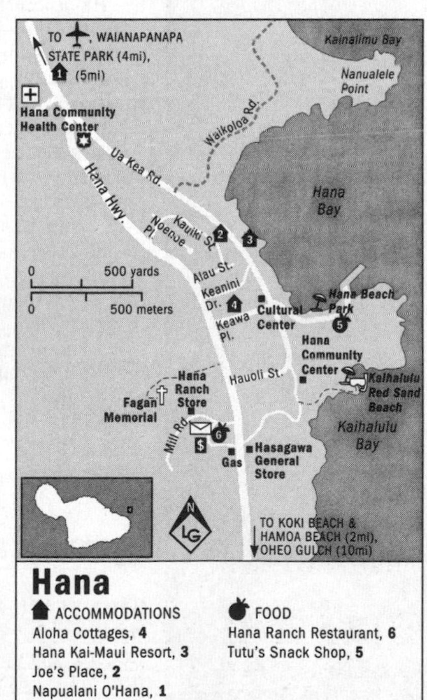

CYCLING MAUI

Many of Maui's highways not only offer travelers beautiful scenic drives, but also varied, spectacular training courses for cyclists. With several miles of windy coastal highways, steep uphill climbs, and long flat roads in the central valley, a cyclist can find any kind of ride. Several athletes train in Maui as they prepare for the legendary Ironman Triathlon.

Crater Rd. slowly winds its way up to the top of Haleakala volcano and is a tough climb for any rider. While many companies offer bike trips down the volcano, the steep climb and high altitude make it a very challenging ride uphill—the perfect training for the hardcore cyclist.

There are several good routes throughout the island and the various combinations are endless. Starting in Maalaea and traveling north on Rte. 30, you'll have a few climbs as you pass through the tunnel, then the route descends through Lahaina and gradually begins to climb through Kaanapali. Continuing north on Rte. 340 takes you on the windy coastal route with several climbs and descents as you make your way to Wailuku. The whole route is roughly 60 mi. Another good route is along Kula Hwy., down through Ulupalakua.

To rent a good road bike, try Go Cycling Maui in Haiku (575-7464). $60 per day; $45 each additional day; $300 per wk. Open daily 8am-6pm.

after 10pm. Reserve in advance. Studios $145; 1-bedroom units $155-190. Weekly rates available. AmEx/MC/V. ❹

Waianapanapa State Park (☎248-4843), 4 mi. north of Hana, on Honokalani Rd. off of Hana Hwy. Waianapanapa's campsites are steps from the park's lava tube caves and coastal hiking trails. Facilities include restrooms, picnic tables, outdoor showers, and grills. Campsites and a limited number of 6-person cabins available. Cabins come with bedding, towels, electricity, hot water, bathroom, kitchen, and miscellaneous cooking utensils. Reserve cabins far in advance. Campsites $5; 4-person cabins $45; each additional guest $5. See **Camping in Hawaii,** p. 75, for permit information. ❶

FOOD

Bring groceries with you if you are staying for more than a day or two. The two general stores in the center of town have a limited selection of produce, meat, and fish, and other items are expensive. Services include: the **Hasagawa General Store,** 5165 Hana Hwy., (☎248-8231; open M-Sa 7am-7pm, Su 8am-6pm) and the **Hana Ranch Store** (☎248-8261; open daily 7am-7:30pm). There are numerous fruit stands on the road north and south of Hana. If you want fresh fish, try fishing off the pier in Hana Bay, or if you see a boat trailer parked at the pier, wait until the fishermen return and ask if they will sell to you.

Tutu's Snack Shop ❶, at Hana Beach Park, sells burgers ($4), ice cream, cold drinks, and a handy map of Hana. (☎248-8224. Open daily 8am-3:45pm.) The **Hana Ranch Restaurant ❷,** left of the Hana Ranch Store, is open for lunch and dinner, but it's a bit overpriced (ranch bacon cheeseburger, $15)—like everything else in Hana. (☎248-8255. Lunch daily 11:30am-3pm. Dinner W-Sa 6-8:30pm; reservations required. AmEx/D/MC/V.) For a better deal, try the **take-out window ❶,** also at Hana Ranch, for plate lunches, burgers, and saimin, all under $7. (Open M-F 9am-4pm, Sa 9am-3:30pm, Su 10am-3pm. AmEx/D/MC/V.) The only other place to eat is the astronomically expensive restaurant at the Hana-Maui Hotel.

BEACHES

HANA BEACH PARK. *(Open daily 6am-10pm. Lifeguards in summer 8am-4:30pm.)* Hana Beach Park, off of Ua Kea Rd., occupies a stretch of dark sand along Hana Bay. The bay is protected, and the calm water makes it popular for families with small children. Facilities include picnic tables, restrooms, and Tutu's Snack Shop (p. 304). The beach is set against the red cliffs of Kauiki Head. Because of the steep grade and exotic plant life, hiking on Kauiki Head is discouraged.

KAIHALULU RED SAND BEACH. *(Snorkeling. Open daily 24hr.)* On the south side of Kauiki Head, a crescent red-sand beach has been carved from the cliffs above. The deep turquoise water that abuts the beach is incredibly clear and ideal for snorkeling. Although an outcropping of rock keeps larger waves out, there is still a surprisingly swift current. To get to the beach, follow Ua Kea Rd. to the end and park on the left side before the lot for Hotel Hana-Maui guests. Parking in the private lot or on the opposite side of the street may get you ticketed or towed.

KOKI BEACH. *(Boogie boarding. Surfing. Open daily 24hr.)* Koki Beach is one of Hana's two best swimming and surfing beaches; Hamoa is the other (see below). Red cliffs rise above the rocky sand on the left, while **A-lau Island,** a seabird sanctuary, lies to the right. Koki can be busy at the height of the day, so go in the morning or evening, when it's calmer. Ask locals about hazards, be wary of a potentially dangerous shorebreak, and never swim alone. The beach is 2 mi. south of Hana toward Kipahulu; turn left off Hana Hwy. onto Haneoo Rd., where there is a sign to Koki Beach, the first beach on the left.

HAMOA BEACH. *(Boogie boarding. Surfing. Open daily 24hr.)* Hamoa Beach is a beautiful stretch of soft sand open to the public and maintained by Hotel Hana-Maui. Surfing and boogie boarding are popular here, and although the strong currents make the water rough at times, swimming is generally safe. Hamoa Beach gets crowded in the afternoons but is virtually empty in the mornings and evenings. Follow the directions to Koki and continue down the road. Public restrooms and outdoor showers are available.

ACTIVITIES AND SIGHTS

WAIANAPANAPA STATE PARK. Four miles north of Hana, Honokalani Rd. turns off Hana Hwy. on the *makai* (ocean) side to Waianapanapa State Park. In addition to the campsite and cabins (p. 304), the park encompasses several miles of shoreline along the rocky lava coast. The King's Highway Coastal Trail is a well-defined path that parallels the coast all the way to Hana town, past ancient Hawaiian burial sites and *heiaus* (temples). The captivating view and lava rock formations make any part of the trail a joy to hike. The 1½ mi. of the trail from the park headquarters to the Ohala Heiau and back is surrounded by *hala* tree groves on one side and the turbulent sea crashing through arches and blowholes on the other. Left of the campsite, a short loop leads through the lava tube caves. Though the caves are steeped in poetic myth about a murdered princess, the mosquitoes and stagnant water may be a disappointment. Below and to the right of the caves is a black-sand beach. The shore area is small, and the surf can be strong; watch out for rip currents. **Popolana Beach,** a more substantial black-sand beach, is closer to town in the cove north of Hana Beach Park. *(☎248-4843. Pick up park maps and camping information at the park office, located in the caretaker's cottage. Office open M-F 7am-6pm, Sa-Su 8am-4pm.*

KAYAK AND SNORKEL TRIPS. Hana-Maui Sea Sports leads kayak and snorkel trips that benefit from guides' knowledge and experience. People paddle in tandem out into Hana Bay and slide into the water to see fish, coral, other marine life, and sometimes even a sea turtle. *(☎248-7711; www.hana-maui-seasports.com. 2-2½hr. trips daily 9:30am and 2pm; $79. 6 person limit. Private charters available. Call for reservations.)*

DENGUE FEVER. The last outbreak dengue fever in Hawaii occurred in 2001; however, mosquitoes along all of the hikes are still plentiful, so wear plenty of insect repellent. Dengue fever can only be contracted from a day-biting mosquito. Symptoms appear in 3-14 days, and include headache, fever, and nausea. If you feel sick, seek medical attention immediately. See **The Great Outdoors,** p. 75, for more information on dengue fever.

HANA CULTURAL CENTER. On a small hill overlooking Hana Bay, the Hana Cultural Center runs a small museum with *kapa* (barkcloth) tapestries, woodcarvings, artifacts, thatched *hales* (huts), and native Hawaiian plants and trees. Preservation of Hawaiian culture and teaching visitors the history of this tradition-steeped town are a top priority. *(4974 Ua Kea Rd. ☎248-8622; www.planet-hawaii.com/hana. Open daily 10am-4pm. Free tours available by request. Donations accepted.)*

FAGAN MEMORIAL. Hana's landmark cross stands prominently atop the large hill overlooking Hotel Hana-Maui and Hana Bay. The memorial was built in 1960 to honor Paul Fagan, the founder of Hana's first hotel. A good view of the coastline, Kauiki Head, and the town of Hana rewards those who make the trek up the steep hill. *(Take the trail that begins in the guest parking lot across from Hotel Hana-Maui. 20min.)*

KIPAHULU AND OHEO GULCH (HALEAKALA NATIONAL PARK)

This portion of Haleakala National Park is unlike the lonely, barren summit of Haleakala Volcano that rises above the clouds (p. 311). Here, dense foliage, freshwater swimming pools, and a multitude of waterfalls welcome visitors.

ORIENTATION

Ten miles south of Hana on Hana Hwy., a swath of **Haleakala National Park** stretches down to the coast through **Kipahulu Valley** and **Oheo Gulch,** home to the famous and delightful **Pools of Oheo.** Consider staying in Hana overnight to get an early start and have more time for the plethora of outdoor activities. It is important to note that this part of the park is not connected to the rest of Haleakala (p. 311).

PRACTICAL INFORMATION

The road to Kipahulu is narrow but easily negotiable in any vehicle. Maps and information about the park can be obtained at the **Kipahulu Rangers' Station,** located in the main parking lot. The rangers' station offers free 15min. natural and cultural history talks and guided hikes. (☎248-7375 for schedule and to confirm pools are open. Open daily 9am-5pm. $10 per vehicle, good for 7 days.) **Camping** (3-night max.) in the park does not require a permit. Campground facilities include porta-potties, picnic tables, and grills, but no drinking water, so visitors must bring their own. Don't forget plenty of insect repellent to fend off the legions of mosquitoes. Sturdy shoes are recommended for the waterfall hikes.

HIKING

POOLS OF OHEO. *(½ mi. 10-15min. Easy.)* The trail starts next to the parking lot and leads to the Pools of Oheo, the Hawaiian name for the freshwater pools, also called the **Seven Sacred Pools.** From the bluff above the pools, you can usually see clear across the channel to the Big Island. The water is nice for a quick swim before or after a hike, but it is often crowded. Under no circumstances should you swim in the ocean beyond the pools; sharks gather around the mouth of the Oheo Stream. The path continues up on the left where it connects with the road. The one-lane bridge offers a great view of the pools, though traffic can be hazardous.

PIPIWAI TRAIL. *(3¾ mi. 1¾-2¼hr. Moderate.)* The first half-mile of this trail, which starts next to the parking lot, follows the path of the Pipiwai Stream. At the Makahiku Overlook, you can sometimes see a 185 ft. waterfall. The upper part of the trail is more rewarding; it crosses over many pools, passes waterfalls, and ambles through a serene bamboo forest, past a banyan tree, and around a guava grove. The trail ends at the base of a 400 ft. awe-inspiring waterfall; it is best to heed warnings about the danger of falling debris. Return the same way you came.

THE ROAD FROM HANA

The road from Hana along Highway 31 (Piilani Highway) from Kipahulu to Kula couldn't be more different from Hana Hwy. Gone are the lush rainforests and roadside waterfalls. In their place, arid plains and stark, desolate valleys give a sense of the vastness of Haleakala Volcano. In some ways, this drive is even more spectacular than the fabled Hana Hwy., and it's certainly the road less traveled.

ORIENTATION. Because it is often narrow and paved in patches or not at all, the road takes about 30min. longer than Hana Hwy. Most rental companies do not permit their cars here, though 4WD is not essential. Falling rocks and unseen hazards make the road particularly dangerous after dark.

SIGHTS. A mile south of Oheo Gulch, a dirt road to the *makai* (ocean) side just past mi. marker 41, leads to Palapala Hoomau Church, the site of **Charles Lindbergh's grave.** Eight bumpy miles past Kipahulu, you'll encounter the quiet town of Kaupo at the base of the Kaupo Valley. The **Kaupo Store** merits a stop merely to peruse its antique cameras, pocket watches, and miscellaneous relics that have been sitting on the shelves since the early 20th century. The store also sells cold drinks and snacks. (☎248-8054. Open M-Sa 9am-5pm.) The three-day hike from the Haleakala crater (p. 316) ends in Kaupo; the store is a good place to have a car meet you if you plan on attempting the hike. Past Kaupo, there's nothing but ranch land for 20 mi. The road heads north above Makena to **Ulupalakua Ranch and Tedeschi Vineyards.** If you arrive during business hours, stop in for wine tasting and refreshment (p. 310). Past Ulupalakua, the road meets **Highway 37 (Kula Highway),** which leads through the upcountry to Kahului.

UPCOUNTRY MAUI

Upcountry Maui loosely encompasses the rural townships built on the slopes of the ancient Haleakala Volcano. Although the region is only minutes from the busy commercial center of Kahului, you'll feel a world away in Upcountry's quaint villages, rolling landscapes, and cool temperatures. In the heart of Upcountry's pastoral hills, Kula grows much of the island's produce, including sweet corn, greens, tomatoes, avocados, and papayas. Kula is home to magnificent floral gardens, many of which include the unique protea flower. South of Kula along Rte. 37 (Kula Hwy.), the tiny hamlet of Keokea has a coffee shop, art gallery, general store, gas station, and thousands of acres of ranch land. *Paniolo* cowboys ride and hog-tie every year at the Fourth of July rodeo in Makawao, the only town in Upcountry with a sizeable main street. The old cowboy town is also home to a string of charming shops and galleries. North of Makawao, serene Haiku connects Upcountry to the North Shore.

KULA

Driving through Kula (pop. 7,060) is a treat—every side road you venture down reveals something unexpected. The countryside is patched with green rural hillside, eucalyptus patches, and fields of exotic flowers. Each turn reveals spectacular views of the Central Maui Valley spreading 4000 ft. below. Feathery clouds that hug the rolling slope of the volcano cast shadows on roaming cattle herds. And of course, there is Haleakala itself (p. 311), rising majestically to 10,023 ft. and occupying a full range of climate zones, from cloud forest to craterous desert.

ORIENTATION AND PRACTICAL INFORMATION

To reach Kula from Kahului, take **Route 36** east to **Route 37 (Haleakala Highway),** which becomes **Kula Highway,** the main north-south road through Kula. Kula Hwy. runs south through Kula and Keokea all the way to the Ulupalakua Ranch, where it becomes **Highway 31** and runs along the southern coast all the way to Hana (p. 307). **Route 377 (Haleaka Highway** or **Kekaulike Avenue)** strays from Rte. 37 and makes for a very scenic drive past flowering jacaranda trees. **Route 378 (Haleakala Crater Road)** heads up the side of Haleakala from Rte. 377. The **Kula Post Office** (open M-F 8am-4pm, Sa 9-11:30am) is located on Rte. 37 after the sign for the Holy Ghost Church. **Postal Code:** 96790.

ACCOMMODATIONS

Several cottages and B&Bs in Kula provide Upcountry peace and solitude. Nights are cool at these high altitudes, so pack a few sweaters and a pair of long pants. The beach is at least 30min. from here, but Haleakala's right in your backyard.

Star Lookout, 622 Thompson Rd. (☎907-346-8028; www.starlookout.com). Drive up Rte. 37 past mi. marker 16 in Keokea, turn left at the fork across from Grandma's Coffee House, and make an immediate right onto Thompson Rd. The perfect setting for a peaceful retreat, the front of Star Lookout's cottage looks down onto the Central Maui Valley. 6-person cottage with full kitchen. Landscaped gardens, bonfire pit, gas grill, hot tub, and telescope. Cable TV/VCR, wireless Internet, fresh fruits and vegetables from the garden (when in season), and a wood-burning stove. Washer/dryer available. 2-night min. Reserve well in advance. $200 per night. AmEx/D/MC/V. ❺

Kula Lodge and Restaurant (☎878-1535), on Rte. 377, ½ mi. north of the intersection with Haleakala Crater Rd. This lodge is as close to Haleakala National Park as you can get without camping. Popular with older guests, rooms have a loft, fireplace, and private lanai. On-site restaurant with great views (lunch, $14-18; dinner, $16-28). Check-in 3pm. Check-out 11am. Reserve with full payment; cancel 30 days in advance with a $25 fee. 2-person chalets $115-175; each additional person $20. AmEx/D/MC/V. ❹

FOOD

Curiously, given how much the area has grown, Kula has few restaurants. **Morihara Store,** across from Cafe 808 on Lower Kula Rd., is the closest thing to a grocery store in Kula; it also sells beer, wine, and liquor. (☎878-2578. Open M-Sa 7am-8pm, Su 8am-8pm. MC/V.) **Fong's Store,** 9228 Kula Hwy., next to the Keokea Gallery and Grandma's Coffee House in Keokea, has basics and is a good place to stop for snacks and drinks. (☎878-1525. Open daily around 7:30am to 5:30pm. Cash only.)

Grandma's Coffee House, 9232 Kula Hwy. (☎878-2140), in Keokea, is an Upcountry institution that serves excellent coffee, a hearty breakfast (eggs, sausage, toast; $6.50), sandwiches ($6-8), a daily hot special, and decadent cakes and pastries. Open daily 7am-5pm. AmEx/MC/V. ❶

Cafe 808 (☎878-6874), on Lower Kula Rd., up from the Holy Ghost Church, is a local joint that serves hearty breakfast ($5-7), deli sandwiches ($6-8), and plate lunches (teriyaki chicken or chicken katsu, $7) in a plain, cafeteria-like space. Open daily 6am-8pm. Cash only. ❶

Kula Sandalwoods Cafe (☎878-3523), on the *mauka* (mountain) side of Rte. 377, between the Kula Lodge and the intersection with Rte. 378. With a view to match the restaurant's at Kula Lodge, Sandalwoods serves fancy sandwiches and salads ($6-9) and espresso drinks. Breakfast also available. Omelets $9. Eggs benedict $10. Open M-Sa 6:30am-3pm, Su 6:30am-noon; hours vary. MC/V. ❷

ACTIVITIES

Explore the Kula countryside on horseback just like the *paniolos* (cowboys) with **Thompson Ranch and Riding Stables,** on Polipoli Rd. From Rte. 37 in Keokea, turn left onto Polipoli Rd. before Grandma's Coffee. (☎283-6209. 1½-1¾hr. ride $75. 200 lb. weight limit. 8-person max. Reserve in advance.) For a high-powered look at Maui's countryside, **Maui ATV Tours,** on the left just before the Ulupalakua Store & Deli coming from Kula, offers tours of Upcountry Ranchland on one- and three-passenger ATVs. (☎878-2889; www.mauiatvtours.com. 2hr. tour 2-4pm $90, 4hr. tour 8am-noon $125.)

SIGHTS

ENCHANTING FLORAL GARDENS. Visitors to Enchanting Floral Gardens will find a milieu of other tourists and beautiful, carefully labeled plants. *(2505 Kula Hwy. ☎878-2531. Open daily 9am-5pm. $7.50, seniors $5, children 6-11 $1.)*

KULA BOTANICAL GARDEN. Kula Botanical Garden, established in 1969, is a family-run operation showcasing native Hawaiian plants, as well as unique specimens from around the world. Laminated maps direct you along several paths as you wind your way past the koi pond, the bird cages, and the newly-carved tiki exhibit. *(638 Kekaulike Ave., about ½ mi. from the intersection of Kula Hwy. and Rte. 377. ☎878-1715. Open daily 9am-4pm. $7.50, children 6-12 $2.)*

MAUI AGRICULTURAL RESEARCH CENTER. The University of Hawaii operates this 35-acre center in Kula for proteas and other flora of the southern hemisphere. Visitors are invited to stroll around the grounds for free, which support a colorful spectrum of unique protea hybrids and an impressive rose garden. Visitors must check in at the main office before entering. *(424 Mauna Pl. To reach the Research Center from Rte. 37, take a left onto Copp Rd. between mi. markers 12 and 13. After ½ mi. on Copp, turn left onto Mauna Pl. ☎878-1213. Open M-Th 7am-3:30pm. Free.)*

ART GALLERIES. The **Keokea Gallery** is an intimate space featuring contemporary art. Inside the Kula Lodge, on Rte. 377, the **Curtis Wilson Cost Gallery** showcases the works a realist painter who finds inspiration in the Maui landscape. *(The Keokea Gallery is located on Rte. 37 next to Grandma's Coffee House. ☎878-3555. Open daily 9am-5pm or by appointment. Curtis Wilso Cost Gallery ☎878-6544. Open daily 8:30am-5pm.)*

ULUPALAKUA RANCH AND TEDESCHI VINEYARDS. Ulupalakua is a 25,000-acre ranch on the site of a former sugar plantation and rose garden. The ranch's gem, **Tedeschi Vineyards,** is a winery that produces local vintages from grapes, pineapples, and raspberries. The road to the ranch is stunning, but the **free wine tasting** certainly doesn't detract from the journey. One room exhibits history from the *paniolo* cowboy tradition on Maui and provides interesting food for thought as you decide between the Ulupalakua red or passion fruit-sweetened Maui Blush. The cowboy-themed gift shop is across the street at the **Ulupalakua Ranch Store and Deli ❶,** where you can pick up a juicy ranch burger ($7), or splurge and buy yourself an elk steak ($18) to throw on the grill. *(Take Hwy. 37 south from Kula for 5 mi. past Grandma's Coffee in Keokea or on the way back from Hana via Hwy. 31. ☎878-6058; www.mauiwine.com. Tasting room open daily 9am-5pm. Free 30-40min. guided tours 10:30am and 1:30pm. Gift shop open daily 9:30am-5pm. Deli open daily 9:30am-1pm. Grill open daily 11am-1:30pm.)*

POLIPOLI SPRING STATE RECREATION AREA

Polipoli Spring State Recreation Area is secluded high above Kula, which lies 6200 ft. above sea level on the western slope of Haleakala. The park's damp forest of redwoods and eucalyptus is used mainly by locals for pig-hunting and camping. Views from the park look down across the rolling upcountry hills.

Polipoli's trails are excellent for hiking or mountain biking, though only some trails allow biking; check the signs at each trailhead. The trails have been reconstructed by Na Ala Hele, a group committed to preserving and maintaining Hawaii's state and county parks. Their work is evident in clean trails, well-marked with lucid signs. Since official publications are limited, head to a local bookstore for a hiking guide that includes maps of the park. *Day Hikes on Maui*, by Robert Stone, will do the trick.

ORIENTATION

Visitors access the park via **Waipoli Road,** off Rte. 377. Follow a series of switchbacks on the narrow one-lane road for 5 mi. (about 30-40min.), until you reach a hunter check-in station that also serves as a trailhead for a few Polipoli hikes. To reach the campground, continue on Waipoli Rd., which becomes unpaved and hazardous 1 mi. or so after the check-in station. Signs indicate it's passable with 4WD only. Full of rocks, mud, and potholes, the road forks a grueling 4¼ mi. from the check-in station; bear right and continue for a little over ½ mi. to the parking, picnic, and camping area. If the road is impassable, satisfy yourself with the earlier trails or bring a mountain bike to pedal to the campground.

CAMPING

Since hikes are long, and it takes a while to get to Polipoli in the first place, camping in the park makes sense. The campground is very basic, with restrooms and picnic tables but no drinking water. The temperature can drop below freezing at night, and the ground is a damp place to pitch a tent. Other than a few pig-hunters, you might be the only person at the campground; think twice before camping by yourself. Another option is to reserve a **rustic cabin** ❷ from the Division of State Parks. See **Camping in Hawaii,** p. 75, for more information on the cabins and permits. Polipoli's cabin doesn't have cooking utensils or dishes, but there is a gas stove and a wood-burning stove.

HIKES

WAIAKOA LOOP TRAIL. *(4½ mi. 1½-2hr. Elevation gain: 600 ft. Moderate.)* To reach the trailhead, walk ¾ mi. down the grassy road at the hunters' station (5 mi. down Waipoli Rd.) to the large sign marking the trail. Remember to shut the gate behind you. The loop is a 2¾ mi. trek through pine forests and open hills. The pine needles which blanket the ground can be slippery, so watch your step.

BOUNDARY-WAIOHULI LOOP. *(5¾ mi. 2-2½hr. Elevation gain: 850 ft. Moderate.)* To get to the Boundary Trailhead, head 1½ mi. up Waipoli Rd. from the hunter check-in station. About ¼ mi. after the paved road becomes a dirt road, you'll pass through a cattle gate, and the trailhead will be on your right. This hike, which passes through stands of redwood, ash, and cedar trees, is a great option for those unable to reach the top of Waipoli Rd. From the trailhead, take the Boundary Trail for 2¾ mi. until it terminates at the junction of the Waiohuli and Redwood Trails near an old cabin. For a longer hike, take the Redwood Trail to the campground at the top of Waipoli Rd., adding another 2¾ mi. round-trip. Otherwise, turn left and take the Waiohuli Trail for a 1½ mi. hike back to Waipoli Rd. When you reach the road, turn left, and from there it's another 2½ mi. down Waipoli Rd.

POLIPOLI LOOP. *(5 mi. 1¾-2¼hr. Elevation gain: 1000 ft. Moderate to challenging.)* This loop takes you along four different trails in a 5 mi. loop. The trailhead is at the Polipoli Campground, at the top of Waipoli Rd. From the campground parking lot, take Redwood Trail 1¾ mi. to Plum Trail, near an old bunkhouse. Turn left onto Plum Trail and walk for 1¾ mi. until you reach Haleakala Ridge Trail. Turn left again onto Haleakala Ridge Trail and take it for 1 mi. until it intersects Polipoli Trail. For a pleasant view and different vegetation, continue on the Haleakala Ridge Trail for ¼ mi., where it reaches the Skyline Trail (a dirt road). Otherwise, turn left onto Polipoli Trail for the final ¾ mi. back to the campground parking lot.

HALEAKALA NATIONAL PARK

The gradually sloping volcano of Haleakala ("house of the sun") dominates the island of Maui. Haleakala National Park stretches from the upper slopes of the volcano down to Kipahulu (p. 306), on the southeast coast past Hana. The extreme landscape of Haleakala is an incomparable site of striking diversity; from the Kipahulu coast to the 10,023 ft. summit, there are as many climate zones as there are between Central Mexico and Alaska. The National Park was established to preserve the fragile ecosystems of Haleakala's summit, and park rangers are still actively involved in the protection of the rare native Hawaiian species that live here. The most impressive feature of Haleakala is the "crater" at the summit; geologists have since determined that the gigantic depression was actually formed by erosion instead of a volcanic explosion. Watching the **sunrise** from above the cloud line atop the summit has become a customary pilgrimage for visitors to the island. Sunset is also beautiful and usually much less crowded. The hikes from the top can be modified to suit both the casual day-hiker and the camping trekker. The switchback road runs from the moon-like crater down through subalpine shrubland, cloud forest, rolling pastures, and intensely fragrant eucalyptus, providing a magnificent scenic drive and leaving visitors humbled by the lonely majesty of the mountain.

AT A GLANCE: HALEAKALA NATIONAL PARK

AREA: 30,183 acres.

HIGHLIGHTS: Hiking the huge crater at Haleakala's summit; observing endangered wildlife such as the silversword plant and *nene* goose; watching the sun rise from the slopes.

GATEWAY TOWNS: Kipahulu, p. 306; Kahului, p. 274; Kihei, p. 283; Kula, p. 308.

FEATURES: Haleakala Volcano, Kipahulu Valley, Oheo Gulch (p. 306).

CAMPING: Camping is free and available at 2 drive-in campgrounds, 2 wilderness campgrounds, and 3 wilderness cabins.

FEES: Entrance fee $10 per vehicle, good for 7 days. $5 for walkers, cyclists, or motorcyclists.

PRACTICAL INFORMATION

Information: Haleakala National Park, P.O. Box 369, Makawao, 96768. ☎572-4400; www.nps.gov/hale.

Hours: The park is open 24hr., though the road may be closed in extreme weather.

Fees, Permits, and Regulations: The entrance fee is $10 per vehicle, good for 7 days at both entrances to the park (the other entrance is in Kipahulu, south of Hana). There is a $5 fee for pedestrians, cyclists, or motorcyclists. Permits are required for camping at wilderness sites (not accessible by road) and can be picked up at Park Headquarters. Camping permits are free and issued on a first come, first served basis on the day of the trip (though they rarely run out). 3-night max.; 2-night per campsite. Hunting, firearms, in-line skates, and skateboards are prohibited. Pets and bikes are not allowed on trails. Do not pick flora or feed fauna in the park. Hikers must stay on the trails.

Driving: From Kahului, take Rte. 37 to Rte. 377 to Haleakala Crater Rd. Allow at least 2hr. from Kihei and 2½hr. from Kaanapali and Napili to reach the summit. It takes a good 45min. to ascend the final 22 mi. off Haleakala Crater Rd. Once you enter the park, the road is a series of steep switchbacks; take your time and watch for bikers, cattle, and other hazards. Stop at overlooks instead of trying to see everything from behind the wheel. On the way down, switch to a lower gear to prevent brake overheating and failure. Slower vehicles must use turnouts to let cars by. **Do not attempt to pass cars.**

Weather: Call ☎877-5111 for current weather conditions and time of sunrise and sunset, or check http://banana.ifa.hawaii.edu/crater/ for a webcam of the crater and current weather data. Weather conditions at the summit can change rapidly. Strong wind, intense sunlight, and variable cloud cover make forecasts impossible, and the current weather doesn't guarantee anything about the next hour. For sunrise, prepare for the

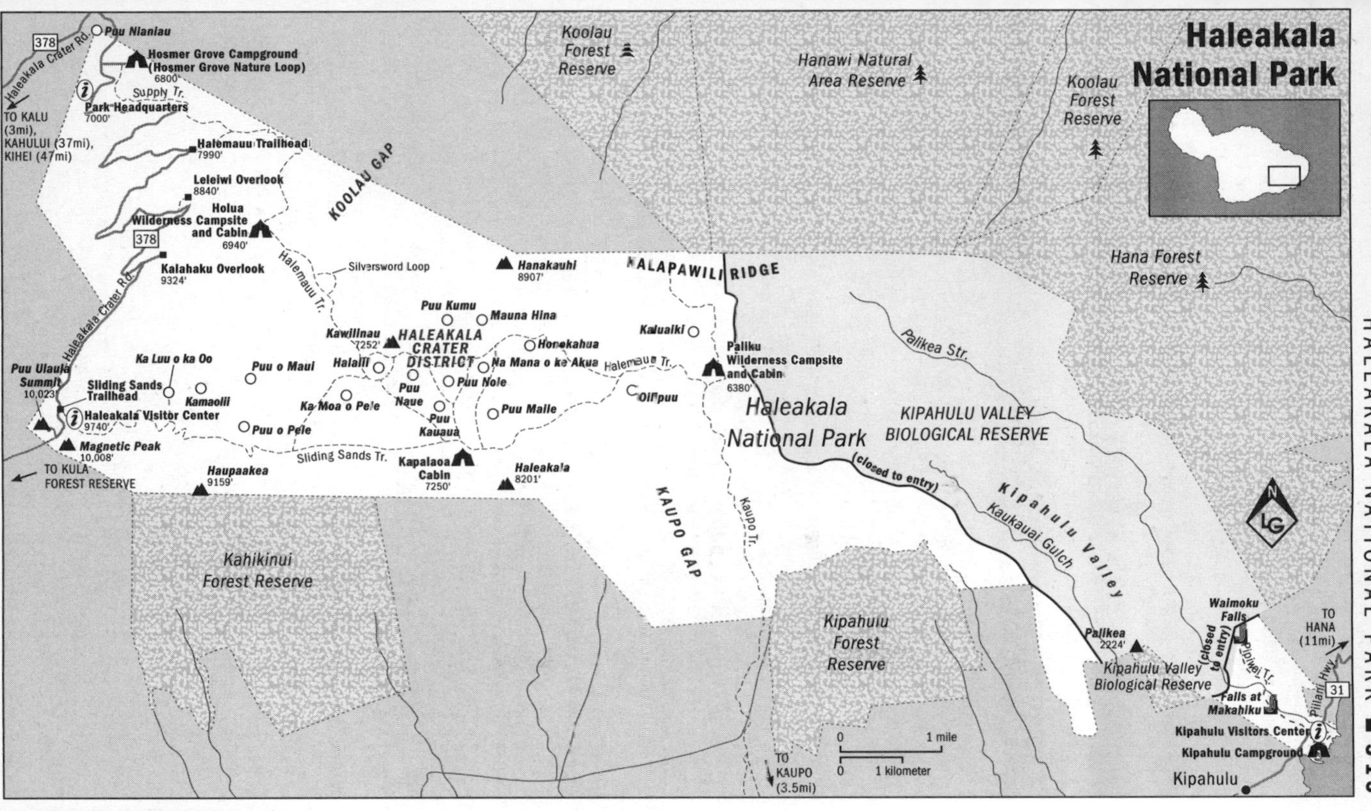

Haleakala National Park
Koolau Forest Reserve
Hanawi Natural Area Reserve
Koolau Forest Reserve
Hana Forest Reserve
378
Haleakala Crater Rd.
Puu Nianiau
Hosmer Grove Campground (Hosmer Grove Nature Loop) 6800'
Supply Tr.
Park Headquarters 7000'
TO KALU (3mi), KAHULUI (37mi), KIHEI (47mi)
Halemauu Trailhead 7990'
Leleiwi Overlook 8840'
Holua Wilderness Campsite and Cabin 6940'
KOOLAU GAP
Kalahaku Overlook 9324'
Halemauu Tr.
Silversword Loop
Hanakauhi 8907'
KALAPAWILI RIDGE
Puu Kumu
Mauna Hina
Kawilinau 7252'
HALEAKALA CRATER DISTRICT
Honokahua
Kaluaiki
Paliku Wilderness Campsite and Cabin 6380'
Ka Luu o ka Oo
Puu o Maui
Halalii
Na Mana o ke Akua
Halemauu Tr.
Puu Ulaula Summit 10,023'
Sliding Sands Trailhead
Kamaolii
Puu Naue
Puu Nole
Oilipuu
Haleakala Visitor Center 9740'
Ka Moa o Pele
Puu Kauaua
Puu Maile
Puu o Pele
Magnetic Peak 10,008'
Sliding Sands Tr.
Kapalaoa Cabin 7250'
Haleakala 8201'
TO KULA FOREST RESERVE
Haupaakea 9159'
Haleakala National Park
KIPAHULU VALLEY BIOLOGICAL RESERVE
Palikea Str.
(closed to entry)
Kipahulu Valley
Kaukauai Gulch
KAUPO GAP
Kaupo Tr.
Kahikinui Forest Reserve
Kipahulu Forest Reserve
TO KAUPO (3.5mi)
0 1 mile
0 1 kilometer
Palikea 2224'
Kipahulu Valley Biological Reserve
Waimoku Falls
(closed to entry)
Pipiwai Tr.
Falls at Makahiku
TO HANA (11mi)
Piilani Hwy
31
Kipahulu Visitors Center
Kipahulu Campground
Kipahulu

cold (30-50°F) by wearing layers and bringing blankets. If you are hiking, prepare for hot, cold, wet, and windy conditions. Sunscreen and water are essential.

Emergency: Visitors are responsible for their own safety in the park. There is a public phone in front of Park Headquarters at 7000 ft. The nearest hospital is 2hr. away, and in bad weather, helicopter rescues may be difficult or impossible.

Facilities: There are 3 Visitors Centers in the park. **Park Headquarters,** at 7000 ft., issues camping and cabin permits and has phones, restrooms, maps, books, and information on the park. Open daily 8am-4pm. The **Haleakala Visitors Center,** at 9740 ft., has bathrooms, geologic and environmental displays, an overlook of the crater, and a helpful staff that dispenses hiking maps and information. Open daily in summer 6am-3pm, in winter 6:30am-3pm. **Kipahulu** also has a **Visitors Center** and public phones. Open daily 9am-5pm. There is no food or gas in the park. There is no water in Kipahulu. Water from the sources in the wilderness area must be boiled or treated before drinking.

Guided Hikes and Events: 10-20min. talks on natural and cultural history are held at the Summit building daily; check with the Visitors Center for details. Park rangers lead guided hikes. The Waikamoi Cloud Forest Hike meets M and Th at 9am at the Hosmer Grove shelter. You must reserve in advance by calling ☎572-4400. The 3hr., 3 mi. hike is moderate, with a 500 ft. elevation change. Ask at the Visitors Center for information about other guided hikes.

Activities: Dozens of independent companies offer activities in the park, including biking down the volcano and horseback riding in the crater. Bike tours range from about $50-150 per person, depending on the company and the time of day. **Maui Sunriders** (☎579-8970) offers sunrise tours for $70 and later trips at 9am for $45. **Mountain Riders** (☎877-4944) offers 15% off their price (around $150) if you book at www.mountainriders.com. **Maui Downhill** (☎877-8787) also has a sunrise tour for $155 and an early morning tour for $115. Tours generally include hotel pick-up, breakfast, thermal suits, helmets, and equipment. Check-in for sunrise rides is usually around 3am.

ALTITUDE SICKNESS. The summit of Haleakala is over 10,000 ft. above sea level. Hiking at high altitudes can cause shortness of breath, headaches, dizziness, nausea, and dehydration. Take it slowly, drink plenty of water, and go back down if you have serious symptoms. People with respiratory and heart conditions, pregnant women, and young children should consult with a doctor first.

CAMPING AND CABINS

Overnight facilities include two drive-in campgrounds, two wilderness campgrounds, and three wilderness cabins. The two drive-in campgrounds do not require any permits. The wilderness campgrounds and cabins require free permits that are issued on the day of the hike (8am-3pm) at Park Headquarters.

Hosmer Grove Campground. Near Park Headquarters at 6800 ft. Accessible to cars. Tables, grills, drinking water, and porta-potties. Conditions are often cool, windy, and rainy. No permit required.

Kipahulu Campground. A 40min. drive south of Hana on the coast, Kipahulu is located at a 20 ft. elevation, 15 mi. beyond Waianapanapa State Park. Kipahulu is not connected to the rest of the park by trails or roads. Accessible to cars. Tables, grills, and porta-potties. No water. Conditions are often warm and wet (with lots of mosquitoes). No permit required.

Holua Wilderness Campground. A 4 mi. hike down the Halemauu Trail, Holua is the most accessible wilderness site. Pit toilets; water must be boiled or treated before drinking. No open fires. Free permit required.

Paliku Wilderness Campground. At the base of a rainforest cliff, accessible by a strenuous 10 mi. hike up either Sliding Sands or Halemauu Trail. Paliku is the last campsite before the descent into the Kaupo Gap. Pit toilets; water must be boiled or treated before drinking. No open fires. Free permit required.

Wilderness Cabins. There are rustic cabins at Holua and Paliku, and at Kapalaoa, 6 mi. down the Sliding Sands Trail in the cinder cone desert. Each cabin has a wood burning stove, propane stove, cooking utensils and dishes, 12 padded bunks, pit toilets, limited non-drinking water, and firewood. No electricity. Cabin reservations are awarded by monthly lottery. Applications must be submitted in writing at least 3 months prior to requested date. A flexible request improves your chances of getting a cabin. No phone or fax requests accepted. Calls regarding vacancies and cancellations are accepted daily 1-3pm (☎572-4459). Full payment must be received 3 weeks ahead of time, or your reservation will be cancelled. Cabins $75 per night per group (1-12 people). Mail applications to: Haleakala National Park, P.O. Box 369, Makawao 96768.

FLORA AND FAUNA. The extreme conditions on Haleakala make the diversity of life there even more incredible. The rare *ahinahina,* or silversword plant, is endemic to the volcanic uplands of Maui and the Big Island of Hawaii. Its silvery spines grow for 10 to 50 years and then blossom once with hundreds of purplish blooms, after which the plants shrivel and die. Silver geraniums are easy to identify along the Halemauu Trail, with white, five-petal flowers blossoming in summer and early fall. Not too many creatures live in the summit lava fields, so the inch-long black wolf spider is at the top of the food chain. This spider carries its young on its back and hunts for food on the ground instead of building a web. The *nene* (the Hawaiian goose, and the State Bird) is nearly extinct but frequently makes an appearance in the park. Never feed a wild *nene* or any fauna in the park. It is illegal to pick flowers or disturb plants in the park.

HIKING

The drive to the summit, scenic overlooks along the road, and the summit itself give visitors a sense of the range of landscapes the park has to offer. However, to truly experience these diverse biomes, you must hike them. The park offers hikes of all levels with trails of various lengths and elevation changes; some can be completed in an hour or two while others can take several days. There are two main trails from the summit area—**Halemauu** and **Sliding Sands**—which connect on the crater floor. Before attempting any of these hikes, be sure to bring the map provided upon entrance to the park or buy the more detailed hiking guide ($5) from the Visitors Center. The times listed below should only be used as a guideline; be sure to plan for extra time and bring plenty of food and water. The elevation changes listed are for round-trip hikes.

A CINDER WHAT? A cinder cone is a conical hill that is formed when airborne lava cools and accumulates around a volcanic vent. The tallest cinder cone is Puu o Maui, with a height of 600 ft. measured from the valley floor.

HOSMER GROVE NATURE LOOP. *(½ mi. 20min. Elevation change: 240 ft. Easy.)* To reach this trail, park at Hosmer Grove Campground, 1 mi. from Park Headquarters. The trail is clearly marked at the end of the parking lot. Brochures describing the flora and fauna on this ½ mi. nature walk are available at the trailhead and in the Visitors Center.

HALEMAUU TO VALLEY RIM. *(2¼ mi. 1-2hr. Elevation change: 800 ft. Easy.)* The first leg of the Halemauu trail, to the valley rim and back, is a short, fairly level hike. Follow the signs off Haleakala Crater Rd. for the Halemauu trailhead (8000 ft.), 3½ mi. above Park Headquarters. The trail begins with a clearly defined path and winds through an aeolian meadow before opening to the mist-filled Keanae Valley. About 1 mi. in, you reach the rim of the vast crater, with 300 ft. reddish cinder cones rising from the crater floor. You can turn back, or continue down the switchbacks to the valley floor, adding about another 3 mi. and 1200 ft. elevation change.

SLIDING SANDS TO THE FIRST CINDER CONE. *(5¼ mi. 2-4hr. Elevation change: 2800 ft. Moderate to challenging.)* Sliding Sands is a steep and windswept descent through the dramatic landscape of the crater. The trailhead is at the bulletin board in the Visitors Center parking lot (9740 ft.). After the winding descent, the trail forks; the left fork leads to **Ka Luu o ka Oo,** the first cinder cone. Because of the altitude and steep grade, hiking back up takes twice as long as it does on the way down. Even if you don't have much time or aren't in the best of shape, doing the first ½ mi. of the trail will reward you with an incredible view of the desert crater.

HALEMAUU TO SILVERSWORD LOOP. *(10 mi. 5-7hr. Elevation change: 2500 ft. Moderate to challenging.)* Follow the directions for the first leg of the Halemauu trail. After reaching the valley rim, continue down the series of switchbacks to the valley floor. The view of the crater from the trail is phenomenal. About 4½ mi. from the trailhead, past the Holua cabin, a spur trail loops around past a field of the rare *ahinahina* (silversword) plant. Again, plan on spending twice as long climbing the trail as it took to get down.

SLIDING SANDS TO HALEMAUU TRAILHEAD. *(11 mi. 6-10hr. Elevation change: 4600 ft., including a 3200 ft. drop and 1400 ft. climb. Moderate to challenging.)* If you've come to Haleakala for the hiking, then this is the trail to do. This combination allows you to experience the drastically different terrain of both trails. After the steep descent to the crater floor (a little under 4 mi. from the Sliding Sands trailhead), you'll see the intersection with the Halemauu Trail, which leads off to the left. After another 3½ mi., you'll reach Holua cabin; from the cabin, it's a challenging 3¾ mi. uphill trail along switchbacks to the Halemauu parking lot. The trailheads are 6 mi. apart on the steep Haleakala Crater Rd., so before hiking into the crater, many hikers leave cars at the Halemauu Trailhead and hitchhike to the Sliding Sands Trailhead at the summit. Let's Go does not recommend hitchhiking.

KAUPO GAP. *(17¾ mi. one way. 1-3 days. Challenging.)* This long and almost completely downhill trek starts from the Haleakala Visitor Center and traverses the crater floor descending through the rainforest in the southern valley of the park. It can be completed in one day if you're extremely fit, but it is recommended as a two- or three-day hike. To do the Kaupo hike, request a brochure at the Visitors Center or Park Headquarters; you may also want to arrange a ride back.

PUKALANI

Pukalani (pop. 7,380), is primarily a residential community and draws travelers with its grocery stores, banks, and commercial plazas. For tourists in Kula or Makawao, Pukalani is a quick drive for basic necessities.

ORIENTATION AND PRACTICAL INFORMATION. Pukalani rests along **Route 365 (Makawao Ave.),** 2 mi. south of Makawao and 6 mi. north of Kula on **Route 37.** From Kahului, take Rte. 37 (Haleakala Hwy.) for about 6 mi. If you're headed directly to Haleakala or Kula, take the **Pukalani Bypass,** which avoids the town center and is a direct route to more popular destinations. **Pukalani Square,** 81 Makawao Ave., is just northeast of the intersection of Rte. 365 and Rte. 37. In this square, **Upcountry Medical Center** offers drop-in medical care. (☎572-9888. Open M-F 8am-5pm, Sa 9am-noon.) Next door is **Paradise Pharmacy,** which also has a copier. (☎572-1266. Copies $0.15. Open M-F 9am-6pm, Sa 9am-4pm.) The square is also home to **First Hawaiian Bank** with a **24hr. ATM.** (☎572-7238. Open M-Th 8:30am-4pm, F 8:30am-6pm.) The **Pukalani Terrace Shopping Center** is located at 55 Pukalani St., off Rte. 37. (From Makawao Ave., turn right at the light onto Rte. 37; Pukalani St. will be ½ mi. down on your left.) Here you'll find an **American Savings Bank** (☎572-7263; open M-F 9am-6pm, Sa 9am-1pm) and **Bank of Hawaii** (☎572-1530; open M-Th 8:30am-4pm, F 8:30-6pm) both with **24hr. ATMs. Majestic Laundry and Dry Cleaning** will satisfy your laundry needs. (☎573-8382. Wash $2, dry $0.25 per 5min. Open M-F 8am-9pm, Sa-Su 7am-9pm. Last wash 7:30pm. Dry cleaning also available. MC/V.) The **Pukalani Post Office** is also here. (☎572-0019; open M-F 9am-4pm, Sa 10am-noon.) **Postal Code:** 96768 or 96788 (P.O. boxes only).

FOOD. There are two main grocery stores in Pukalani. The **Pukalani Superette,** on the corner of Makawoa Ave. and Haleakala Hwy., is a full grocery store with all the basic necessities. It also has several hot pre-packaged plate lunches and a decent produce and deli section (☎572-7616). There is also a 24hr. **Foodland** (☎572-0674) located in the Pukalani Terrace Shopping Center. **Serpico's Pizzeria ❶,** 7 Aewa Pl., off Old Haleakala Hwy., is a good place for mouth-watering pizza, pasta, and subs (☎572-8498. Open daily 11am-10pm. AmEx/MC/V.) For cheap, filling plate lunches ($6-8), join locals at **Mixed Plate ❶** in the Pukalani Terrace Shopping Center. (☎572-8258. Open daily 6am-1pm. Cash only.) Part of the same counter, **Maui Fresh Tamale ❶** will satisfy cravings for Mexican food for less than $10. (☎573-2998. Open daily 10am-7pm. AmEx/D/MC/V.)

MAKAWAO

Makawao (pop. 6,327) is the only Upcountry town with shops, restaurants, and a discernible main street. The western-style storefronts hint at Makawao's cowboy past, but aside from the annual Fourth of July rodeo, Makawao is a tourist town. Store after store of aloha wear lines up next to a plethora of local art and craft galleries. Nightlife isn't totally desolate either: Casanova's features live music and DJs, and, as you would expect from the heart of cow country, the steak here is prime.

ORIENTATION AND PRACTICAL INFORMATION

The central district of historic Makawao is located where **Makawao Avenue** intersects **Baldwin Avenue,** which continues seven miles northwest to **Paia. Kaupakulua Road** continues north to **Haiku** from the end of Makawao Ave. and eventually connects with Hana Hwy. There's a public parking lot on Makawao Ave. close enough to walk to all of Makawao's shops, galleries, and restaurants.

The **Makawao Public Library,** 1159 Makawao Ave., is next to Down to Earth Natural Foods. (☎573-8785. Open M and W noon-8pm, Tu, Th, and Sa 9:30am-5pm. Copies $0.20 per page.) For **Internet access** and copy services, head to **1 Stop**

Postal Shop, a little way down Makakawao Ave. past the library. (☎572-3088, fax 572-3671. Internet $0.15 per min., $2 min. Copies $0.10 per pg. Open M-F 8am-6pm, Sa 9:30am-3:30pm.) Internet is also available at the public library with a 3-month visitor's card ($10). The **Makawao Post Office** is a little farther down at 1075 Makawao Ave. (Open M-F 8:30am-4:30pm, Sa 8:30-11am.) **Postal Code:** 96768.

ACCOMMODATIONS

Makawao is a convenient base from which to explore Upcountry Maui and the North Shore; the galleries and shops downtown will only fill an afternoon. There are no hotels in Makawao, but several B&Bs are located just outside of town.

Peace of Maui, 1290 Haliimaile Rd. (☎572-5045; www.peaceofmaui.com). From Kahului, take Haleakala Hwy.; Haliimaile Rd. will be on your left. From Paia, take Baldwin Ave.; Haliimaile Rd. will be on your right. Surrounded by pineapple fields and possessing great views of Haleakala, Peace of Maui has 6 hostel-style rooms which share toilets, showers, a common living room, and a kitchen. 4 rooms have queen-size beds; 2 have 2 twin beds. All have TV, fan, and access to coin-op laundry, hot tub, and free Internet. A 2-bedroom cottage sleeps 2-4 people, with full bath, kitchen, and lanai. The owner is happy to suggest other accommodations in the area if there are no vacancies. Somewhat flexible 7-night min. for cottage. Full payment due 30 days in advance. Singles $50; doubles $55; cottage $120. AmEx/D/MC/V. ❷

Wild Ginger Falls, 355 Kaluanui Rd. (☎573-1173; www.wildgingerfalls.com). Take Baldwin Ave. out of Makawao toward Paia; turn right onto Kaluanui Rd. ¼ mi. past the Hui Noeau Visual Arts Center. Continue on Kaluanui for ¾ mi. and turn left through the iron gates just over the bridge. Descend into a tropical jungle to find this cozy studio cottage nestled among banyan trees and kahili ginger. Queen-size bed, full kitchen, TV, DVD player, gas grill, private screened porch, and a spa. 3-night min. Reserve with 50% deposit 45 days in advance. Check-in 3pm. Check-out 11am. $130. ❹

Banyan Tree Vacation Rentals, 3265 Baldwin Ave. (☎572-9021), ¾ mi. from Makawao. The grounds of Banyan Tree Rentals are lush, luxurious, and feature a large swimming pool. Guests also enjoy the hammocks and old-fashioned rope swings on the property. The bungalows offer "a taste of Old Hawaii," and a bit of peeling paint only adds to the rustic quality. 4 studio cottages $110-135; a luxurious and spacious 3-bedroom, 3-bath house with living room and full kitchen $390. AmEx/D/MC/V. ❹

FOOD

There are several good places for a light lunch on Baldwin Ave., in addition to heavier Mexican and steak house options for dinner. For more selection, **Paia** (p. 293) is only a 10-15min. drive away. Natural food store **Down to Earth,** 1169 Makawao Ave., next to the library, has healthy groceries and salad. They also sell the food left in their hot bar for half-price daily 6-7pm. (☎572-1488. Open daily 8am-8pm. MC/V.) The **Rodeo General Store,** 3661 Baldwin Ave., is an old-fashioned market stocked with basic groceries and super-cheap pre-packaged salads, sushi, and sandwiches. They also carry local meat from the Maui Cattle Co. (☎572-2404. Open daily 7am-10pm. AmEx/MC/V.)

RESTAURANTS

Casanova's Italian Deli, 1188 Makawao Ave. (☎572-0220), at the intersection of Baldwin Ave. Casanova's Deli is more reasonably priced than the upscale Italian restaurant of the same name next door, and it maintains a similarly funky atmosphere. Mirror mosaics deck the walls, and there are a few wooden tables in the back to sit with counter-service sandwiches (baked eggplant and smoked mozzarella, $6). Open M-Sa 7:30am-6pm, Su 8:30am-6pm. MC/V. ❶

Stopwatch Sports Bar & Grill, 1127 Makawao Ave. (☎572-1380). Paintings of bright Hawaiian flora decorate this sports bar. Decent for a burger ($6.50-8.50) and beer ($3.50). "Buy 1, get 1 half-off" dinner special (W-Th 5:30-8:45pm) and homemade fruit and cream pies ($5). Sample Maui-brewed beers on tap, like Kona Longboard and Firerock Pale Ale. Local bands F-Sa 9pm-1am ($3 cover). Happy hour daily 4:30-6:30pm; $1 off mixed drinks and some beers. Food served until 9pm. Open daily 11am-midnight. AmEx/D/MC/V. ❶

Polli's, 1202 Makawao Ave. (☎572-7808), at the intersection of Baldwin Ave. Polli's offers heaping Mexican dishes, many for under $12. The setting is intimate, the staff spunky, and the margaritas free-flowing. Entrees are hearty; chips and salsa come with every meal. Vegetarian-friendly. The bar is filled with locals, especially during happy hour (M-F 4-5:30pm), when domestic beers are $2.50, margaritas are $3.50, and *pupus* and nachos are $2. Open daily 7am-10pm. AmEx/D/MC/V. ❷

CAFES AND BAKERIES

Cafe del Sol, 3620 Baldwin Ave. (☎572-4877), in the plaza behind Maui Hands, next to Hot Island Glass. Serves local greens, sandwiches (roasted chicken salad on a croissant, $8), and freshly baked muffins and pastries. The atmosphere is relaxed and playful; local artwork hangs on the walls. Shady outdoor patio dining is removed from busy Baldwin Ave. Breakfast M-Sa 7:30-10:45am. Lunch M-Sa 11am-4pm. MC/V. ❶

Makawao Garden Cafe, 3679 Baldwin Ave. (☎573-9065), tucked in the Paniolo Courtyard. Formerly a Cafe O'Lei, the new owner has maintained the same creative menu and high quality using the freshest local ingredients. Focaccia sandwiches (snow crab and avocado, $8.50), salads (taro root and Molokai sweet potato on Kula greens, $8.50), and the daily specials are reliably delicious. Open daily 11am-4pm. Cash only. ❷

Kitada's Kau Kau Corner (☎572-7241), on Baldwin Ave. across from Maui Hands gallery. Squeeze in among the locals for a cheap breakfast or lunch. Breakfast M-Sa 6-11am. Lunch until 1:30pm. Sandwiches $2.50-4. Plates $5-7. Cash only. ❶

Komoda Store and Bakery, 3674 Baldwin Ave. (☎572-7261), is famous for their *malasadas* (Portuguese doughnuts), cream puffs, and freshly baked doughnuts. The bakery's large brown building is unmarked, so just follow the scent of fresh pastries. Open M-Tu and Th-F 7am-5pm, Sa 7am-2pm. Cash only. ❶

GALLERIES

Craft stores and galleries line Baldwin Ave. and sell handmade wooden bowls, jewelry, paintings, and prints. Although they aren't cheap, you may find a unique trinket that suits you.

Hui Noeau Visual Arts Center, 2841 Baldwin Ave. (☎572-6560), 1¼ mi. from Makawao Center. This beautiful estate, farther out of town than the other galleries, offers 6 exhibits per year of pieces by contemporary local artists. Hui Noeau also sponsors visiting artists, offers classes, and leads painting, photography, printmaking, jewelry, woodworking, and ceramics workshops for all ages. The house and landscaped grounds, once part of the Baldwin estate, are worth a stroll. While the art is expensive, the gift shop offers lovely handmade items starting around $10. Open M-Sa 10am-4pm. Suggested donation $2.

Hot Island Glass, 3620 Baldwin Ave. (☎572-4527), behind Maui Hands. Visitors come in droves to marvel at Maui's only hand-blown glass gallery (glassblowing most days

10:30am-4pm, call to confirm). Most budget travelers will just come to look (glass starfish $60 and up), but slightly flawed unsigned seconds and small souvenirs are more affordable ($15 and up). Open daily 9am-5pm. AmEx/MC/V.

David Warren Gallery, 3625 Baldwin Ave. (☎572-1288). This family-owned artistic showcase was Makawao's 1st gallery. It has since evolved into a family co-op that displays the work of the talented Warrens, including unusual and reasonably priced woodwork (Maui driftwood vase, $25), funky creations made from forks and spoons, and other crafts. Open daily 10am-6pm. AmEx/D/MC/V.

Maui Hands, 3620 Baldwin Ave. (☎572-5194), in the Courtyard. Handcrafted ceramics, glass, wood, and prints by over 250 local artists are on display. Open M-Sa 10am-6pm, Su 10am-4pm. AmEx/MC/V.

Randy Jay Braun Gallery, 1156 Makawao Ave. (☎573-1176; www.randyjaybraun.com). Braun's black-and-white photographs are subtly hand-colored, and his collection captures the aloha spirit of the island's faces and spaces. Gallery also includes work by other local artists in a variety of media. Open M 10am-5:30pm, Tu-F 9:30am-5:30pm, Sa 10am-6pm, Su 10am-3pm. AmEx/D/MC/V.

NIGHTLIFE

Both **Polli's** and the **Stopwatch Sports Bar and Grill** (p. 319) house bars that attract a local crowd of devotees, but upscale Italian restaurant **Casanova's,** 1188 Makawao Ave., is the real pulse of Upcountry nightlife. Wednesday's ladies' night ("Wild Wahine Wednesday"), billed as the best late-night entertainment in Maui, packs the place by 10:30pm. Thursdays occasionally feature salsa/Latin music and dancing. Fridays and Saturdays also attract a crowd for live bands or DJs at 10pm. Pizza is served until 11:30pm. Check the free publication *Maui Time Weekly* for Casanova's entertainment schedule. (☎572-0220. 21+ after 10pm. Cover $5-10.).

HULA

A Brief History

he hula dance and hula dancers are arguably some of the most recognized icons of ławaiian culture, but the images adorning ostcards and photo books represent a ıore modern form of the dance. This conemporary version grew out of an ancient ral tradition, that of a chant accompanied y pantomimed movements.

For the ancient Hawaiians, the hula dance as of secondary importance; the chant was he main part of the hula. While there are ıany different forms of hula dance which ary depending on the implements used, the hant remains constant throughout these ariations. In its most basic form, a beat is reated by thumping a hollow gourd *(ipu)* n the ground, and drumming on it with the alm of the hand. This creates the basis for he pantomimed movements, while the hanting over the sound of the beat gives he movement meaning and conveys culural stories. Many such stories celebrated he volcano goddess Pele, while others lescribed historic events as a mode of preerving Hawaiian history. Through chant ınd pantomimed movements, hula dance erved as a vehicle for oral history to be assed from generation to generation.

Chant and hula dance were not performed n their own, however, but were merely part f a more elaborate religious practice that ccurred in the *heiau*—a temple where religious rites were performed. The dance itself ook place in the *halau*, a portion of the *eiau* reserved especially for it. The *halau*, n addition to being a structure devoted to hula dance, was also a term denoting a school for hula instruction which would be associated with a *heiau*—a definition that continues to this day, although the religious significance has all but disappeared.

The arrival of Western missionaries in the late 18th and early 19th centuries marks the beginning of hula's dark ages. The missionaries viewed the hula dance as a heathen practice and sought to eliminate it from Hawaiian culture first by limiting its practice, and eventually by banning it altogether. The hula dance saw a revival under the reign of King Kalakaua—nicknamed the Merrie Monarch—and Queen Kapiolani during the late 19th century. These two monarchs legalized the dance, and in fact, held several hula festivals during their 20-year reign. Kalakaua's important role in the revitalization of the hula dance is honored every April during the Merrie Monarch Hula Festival, held on the Big Island, which showcases both ancient and modern hula styles.

It was under Kalakaua and his successor Queen Liliuokalani that the hula began to evolve and take on the more modern form that most would recognize today. The early 20th century saw the introduction of the ukulele, borrowed from Portuguese immigrants, and the use of band music and Western rhythms to accompany the hula dance. With the beginning of the tourist boom in the mid 20th century, the hula dancer was transformed into the common image that most think of today—complete with grass skirt, flower *lei*, and ukulele.

***Christine Yokoyama,** whose family hails from Oahu, was the map editor for Let's Go: Hawaii 2004, Let's Go: Australia 2004, Let's Go: Boston 2004, and Let's Go Road Trip USA: 2005. Despite having extensively researched the hula dance, she does not hula, save for one horribly awkward experience at Waiamea Falls.*

MOLOKAI

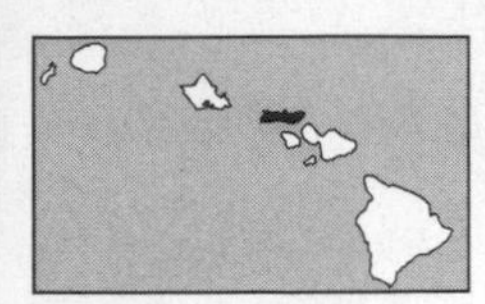

Amid Hawaii's many resorts and tourist traps, Molokai is the closest you can get to old Hawaii. Fishponds dating from the 14th century, several of which are still operational today, line the southern coast, and some residents choose to spend a portion of the year living in true Hawaiian fashion—at beach campsites. The island's population is over half Native Hawaiian, and Molokai is fighting to preserve its current traditional state. Within the island, there is a divide between members of the community over issues of development and the expansion of tourism. The most recent controversy stems from Laau Point on Molokai's eastern end, which has been zoned for 200 millionaire estates on traditional hunting and fishing grounds. While cruise ships are not allowed to stop on Molokai, an extensive ferry system has recently begun which will transport cars and passengers between all the islands, making Molokai much more accessible to tourists.

At one time, Molokai was respected and revered for its many powerful *kahunas* (priests). Visitors from all over made pilgrimages to the island to seek the priests' counsel. The island was called *Pule Oo* (Powerful Prayer), and was considered a refuge place for *kapu*-breakers (taboo-breakers). For a time, the island was free from armed conflict because it was considered sacred. Now, however, Molokai retains little of its former influence, and the island is struggling. Jobs are scarce and unemployment rivals some of the mainland's most depressed counties.

Nonetheless, Molokai's laid-back residents maintain a positive outlook on life. The birthplace of both the aloha spirit and hula, Molokai is known as "The Friendly Isle" for a reason, and drivers often smile and wave amiably at passersby. Molokai's roads are traffic light-free, although the slow pace of some of the island's 7000 inhabitants sometimes causes a bit of a back-up. Nobody seems to mind, however, since there's no reason to be in a hurry. A sign that greets visitors at the airport says it all: "Aloha! Slow down: this is Molokai." With some of the state's least-developed coastal areas, Molokai's beaches and the warm personalities of her residents are not to be missed.

HIGHLIGHTS OF MOLOKAI

STAND IN AWE at the Iliiliopae Heiau, the second-largest traditional Hawaiian temple in the islands (p. 341).

BASK IN THE SUN on a deserted beach cove at Make Horse Beach, one of Hawaii's most beautiful white sand beaches (p. 348).

GET BACK TO NATURE at the rugged Kamakou Preserve, home to 219 endemic plant and animal species (p. 334).

SOJOURN to the sobering former leper colony at Kalaupapa Peninsula (p. 331).

ROPE A STEER in *paniolo* lessons at the Molokai Ranch in Maunaloa (p. 345).

INTERISLAND TRANSPORTATION

Molokai is most easily accessible by plane, though there is also a ferry service from Maui. Flights to Molokai generally arrive at the Hoolehua Airport (6.5 mi. northwest of Kaunakakai, 10 mi. east of Maunaloa), although there is also an airport at Kalaupapa.

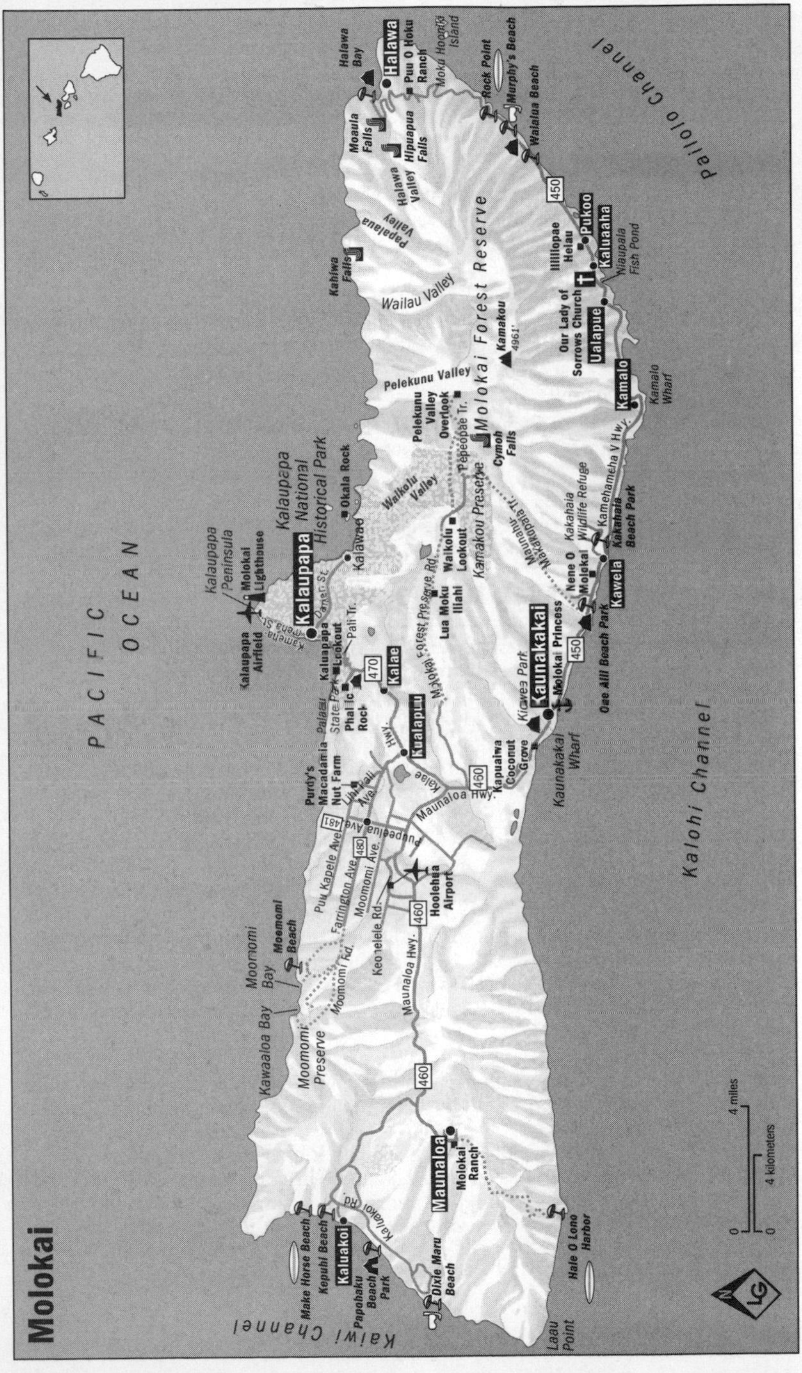
Molokai
PACIFIC OCEAN
Kaiwi Channel
Kalohi Channel
Pailolo Channel
Kaluakoi
Make Horse Beach
Kepuhi Beach
Papohaku Beach Park
Dixie Maru Beach
Kaluakoi Rd.
Maunaloa
Molokai Ranch
Hale O Lono Harbor
Laau Point
Kawaaloa Bay
Moomomi Preserve
Moomomi Bay
Moomomi Beach
Moomomi Rd.
Farrington Ave.
Puu Kapele Ave.
Keonelele Rd.
Maunaloa Hwy.
460
480
481
Hoolehua Airport
Moomomi Ave.
Puupeelua Ave.
Lihi Pali Ave.
Purdy's Macadamia Nut Farm
Kualapuu
Kalae Hwy.
Maunaloa Hwy.
450
Kapuaiwa Coconut Grove
Kaunakakai Wharf
Kiowea Park
Kaunakakai
Molokai Princess
Palaau State Park
Phallic Rock
Kalae
470
Kaluapapa Lookout
Pali Tr.
Kalaupapa Airfield
Kamehameha St.
Kalaupapa
Damien St.
Kalaupapa Peninsula
Molokai Lighthouse
Kalawao
Kalaupapa National Historical Park
Okala Rock
Molokai Forest Preserve Rd.
Lua Moku Iliahi
Waikolu Lookout
Waikolu Valley
Kamakou Preserve
Pepeopae Tr.
Mauna Mahana Tr.
Ooe Alii Beach Park
Kawela
Nene O Molokai
Kakahaia Wildlife Refuge
Kakahaia Beach Park
Kamehameha V Hwy.
Cymoh Falls
Pelekunu Valley Overlook
Pelekunu Valley
Molokai Forest Reserve
Kamakou 4961'
Kamalo
Kamalo Wharf
Our Lady of Sorrows Church
Ualapue
Niaupala Fish Pond
Kaluaaha
Iliiliopae Heiau
Pukoo
Wailau Valley
Kahiwa Falls
Papalaua Valley
Halawa Valley
Moaula Falls
Hipuapua Falls
Halawa Bay
Halawa
Puu O Hoku Ranch
Moku Hooniki Island
Rock Point
Murphy's Beach
Waialua Beach
0 4 miles
0 4 kilometers

The Molokai Princess (☎661-8397 or 667-6165; www.molokaiferry.com) at Kaunakakai Wharf. Ferry goes to and from **Lahaina, Maui** (90min.; departs Maui daily 7:15am and 6pm, departs Molokai daily 5:30am and 4pm; one-way $42.40, children ages 3-12 $21.20, under 3 free.) Two bags allowed; additional bags, surfboards, or bikes will be charged $15 each. Package deals also available from Maui to visit Kalaupapa, take an island tour, or rent a car. Opportunities for whale-watching Dec.-Apr.

George's Aviation, 10 Lagoon Dr. (☎866-834-2120 or 553-8554; www.georgesaviation.com), in Honolulu. From Honolulu, round-trip $95, one-way $65. From Maui, round-trip $110, one-way $70. This is an unscheduled flight service, but there is typically one flight a day (2 on M and F) between Honolulu or Maui and Molokai. Book in advance for weekend travel.

Molokai Air Shuttle, 99 Mokuea Pl. (☎545-4988), in Honolulu, along Lagoon Dr., just behind the airport. There is also an office at the Molokai airport (☎567-6847). From Honolulu, 6 flights per day (round-trip $100). Also flies to Kalaupapa ($25 each way to and from the Molokai Airport; one-way $70, round-trip $110 from Honolulu). Office open M-Sa 6am-6pm.

Pacific Wings (☎888-575-4546; www.pacificwings.com). Flights from Honolulu and Kahului ($95 each way). Flies to the Kalaupapa Peninsula ($96 each way). 10% discount online.

Island Air, 99 Kapalulu Pl. (☎800-323-3345; www.islandair.com), on Lagoon Dr., behind the airport in Honolulu. From Honolulu (9 flights per day) or Maui (9 flights per day); one-way from $60, round-trip from $120. 5% discount online.

LOCAL TRANSPORTATION

Once on the island, renting a car is a necessity, as there is no public transportation. A single highway stretches 50 mi. from one side of the island to the other, making Molokai Hawaii's easiest island to navigate.

Budget has an office in the Molokai Airport (☎567-6877 or 800-527-0700; www.budget.com) as does **Dollar** (☎567-6156; www.dollar.com). Both offices are open daily 6am-7pm. Check for Internet specials. **Island Kine Auto Rental,** 242 Ilio Rd. (☎553-5242 or 866-527-7368; www.molokai-car-rental.com), is just north of Ala Malama Ave. This local outfit rents cars, trucks, vans, and ATVs from their lot south of town on Ala Malama Ave. They will pick you up from the airport and orient you to the island. ($40-66 per day. Open daily 7am-7pm.) Try **Molokai Outdoors** (☎552-4477) for bargain car rentals ($25 per day, 4-day min.), as well as **shuttle** service from the airport ($13.75 per person one-way to Kaunakakai). **Taxis** are astronomically expensive, but are available early morning to 8pm from **Molokai Off-Road Tours & Taxi** (☎553-3369), which operates all over the island (airport to Kaunakakai, $26.80). **Hele Mai Taxis** (☎336-0967), who also operates islandwide, may be your cheapest bet (airport to Kaunakakai, $19; airport to Maunaloa, $22).

No rental cars, including those with 4WD, are technically permitted off paved roads by any rental car companies. Even in a 4WD vehicle, never drive off-road in the rain; you will get stuck, and getting stuck on Molokai is a major inconvenience.

Gas prices on Molokai are often substantially higher than on Oahu or Maui. Always drive with your fuel level in mind, as there are only three gas stations on the island—none are east of Kaunakakai or near the airport. If you need assistance, call one of the full-service stations in Kaunakakai. **Shirley Rawlins' Chevron,** 20 Maunaloa Hwy. (☎553-3214), is a good bet. (Open M-Th 6:30am-8:30pm, F-Sa 6:30am-9pm, Su 7am-6pm.)

ACCOMMODATIONS

Molokai isn't an easy place to find budget accommodations, especially if you're traveling solo. There are no hostels and most of the less expensive options are condos or beach houses that are better suited for two or more people. Couples can find great deals at the various **B&Bs** on the island; try them before staying at a hotel or condo. For a list of nearly all the accommodations available, including a large number of properties leased directly by their owners, pick up the **Molokai: Hawaiian by Nature** brochure at the **Molokai Visitors Association,** 28 Kamoi St., in Kaunakakai.

Molokai Vacation Rentals (☎800-553-8334 or 800-367-2984; www.molokai-vacation-rental.com), at the intersection of Hwy. 460 and 470, rents houses, condos, and cottages for a wide range of prices. Most two- or three-bedroom houses go for $100-150. (☎800-553-3648, rentals 553-8334; www.island-realestate.com. Open M-F 8am-4:30pm. AmEx/MC/V.) **Friendly Island Realty,** 75 Ala Malama Ave. (☎553-3666 or 800-600-4158; www.molokairesorts.com), leases dozens of properties all over the island, from studio apartments ($75-90) to one-bedroom condos ($85-125) to full beach houses from $125. (Open M-F 8am-5:30pm, Sa 8am-3pm. MC/V.)

KAUNAKAKAI

Located in the middle of the south shore, Kaunakakai (pop. 2,726) is a mellow, easy-going town. The leisurely amble of cars along Ala Malama Ave. might initially frustrate anxious travelers, but after adjusting to Molokai's slow pace, those same travelers will appreciate the rustic appeal of this old-fashioned town. Half-century old facades and friendly locals make Kaunakakai feel like a step back into a less stressful past. It takes less than an hour to walk all of Kaunakakai's paved roads, and after 9pm, you may have them to yourself. Kaunakakai is also home to the majority of Molokai's grocery stores, restaurants, and shops, as well as its police station, hospital, and banks. Every visitor to the island is sure to stop in Kaunakakai at least once, and there's plenty here to reward the savvy visitor.

ORIENTATION

To get to Kaunakakai from Hoolehua Airport, turn immediately right, and then left on **Route 460 (Maunaloa Highway) East.** Kaunakakai center begins at the intersection of Route 460 and **Ala Malama Avenue.** There's a Chevron gas station in the northwest corner of the intersection, and both of the town's banks are located across the street in the Molokai Center, a business complex that stretches north along the first block of Ala Malama. At the end of the block, Ala Malama turns east for another four blocks; most of the town's shops and restaurants are located here. Rte. 460 continues east, but its name changes to **Route 450 (Kamehameha V),** or "Kam 5," as it leaves town. The easiest way to navigate either route is by the highway mile markers, which begin at mi. 0 in Kaunakakai and ascend in both directions.

PRACTICAL INFORMATION

TOURIST AND FINANCIAL SERVICES

Tourist Office: Molokai Visitors Association, 2 Kamoi St., Ste. 200 (☎553-3876; www.molokai-hawaii.com), just north of the highway, offers brochures and recommen-

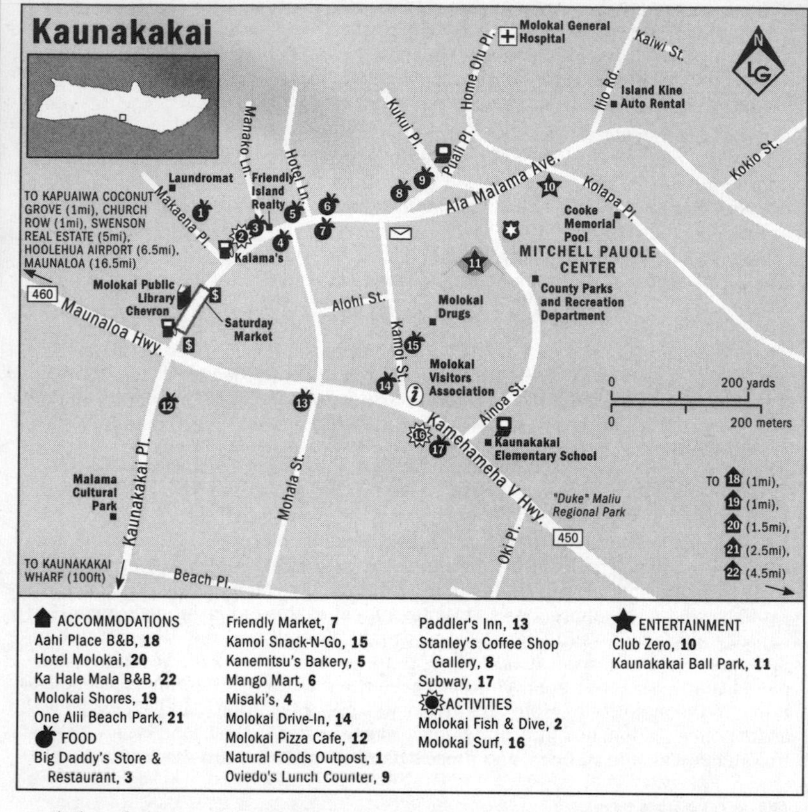

dations for many of the island's activity centers and accommodations, but has less information about non-commercial attractions. Open M-F 8am-4:30pm.

Banks: Bank of Hawaii, 20B Ala Malama Ave. (☎888-643-3888), in the Molokai Center on the right side of the street as you turn on Ala Malama from the main highway. Open M-Th 8:30am-4pm, F 8:30am-6pm. **24hr. ATM** out front.

LOCAL SERVICES

Library: The **Molokai Public Library,** 15 Ala Malama Ave. (☎553-1765), in the Civic Center across from the banks. Knowledgeable staff, well-stocked Hawaiiana book section, 6 computers with **Internet access** and printing with 3-month visitor's card ($10). Open M and W noon-8pm, Tu and Th-F 9am-5pm.

Internet Access: The fastest Internet connection is at **Stanley's,** 125 Puali Pl. (☎553-9966), the island's only Internet cafe. $1 per 10min. **Kaunakakai Elementary School,** 30 Ainoa St. (☎553-1730), has a computer lab with set hours for public use a few days a week (not during the summer), though this time is generally reserved for the local community members. Call ahead for schedule.

Laundry: A self-service laundromat is located just off Ala Malama on Makaena Pl., behind the Natural Foods Outpost. Wash $1-2, dry $0.25. Change and detergent available at Kalama's gas station 2 stores down. Open daily 7am-9pm.

Recreation: Mitchell Pauole Center, 90 Ainoa St. (☎553-3204), ½ block south of Ala Malama next to the police station. Recreation facilities open to the public free of charge. **The Cooke Memorial Pool,** 20 Kolapa Pl. (☎553-5775), is open in summer M-Tu and Th-Sa 9am-4:30pm, W 10am-4:30pm. W and F night swim 6-8:30pm. Closes daily 11:45am-1pm. Winter hours vary. The **gym** (☎553-5141) is open for basketball M-F 11am-3pm, Sa 10am-3pm and weight room open M-F 10am-9pm. Tennis courts, a skateboarding park, and baseball fields. Also sells **camping permits.**

EMERGENCY AND COMMUNICATIONS

Police: 110 Ainoa St. (☎553-5355), south of Ala Malama between the Mitchell Pauole Center and the fire department.

Pharmacy: Molokai Drugs, 28 Kamoi St., Ste. 100 (☎553-5790), in the Kamoi Professional Center, behind the post office. Wide selection of Hawaiian CDs, magazines, and souvenirs. Open M-F 8:45am-5:45pm, Sa 8:45am-2pm.

Hospital: Molokai General Hospital, 280 Home Olu Pl. (☎553-5331), 4 blocks north of Ala Malama; blue signs clearly indicate the way from Ala Malama on the eastern end of downtown. 24hr. emergency room.

Post Office: 120 Ala Malama Ave. (☎553-5845). Open M-F 9am-4:30pm, Sa 9-11am.

Postal Code: 96748.

ACCOMMODATIONS AND CAMPING

While there are no accommodations within walking distance of Kaunakakai, the first 5 mi. east of town along Hwy. 450 have a range of quality places to stay, including hotels, condos, B&Bs, and campgrounds.

Ka Hale Mala Bed & Breakfast, 7 Kamakana Pl. (☎553-9009; www.molokai-bnb.com). Before the 5 mi. marker east of town on Hwy. 450, turn left on Kamakana Pl. It's on the left near the end of the small cul-de-sac. Ka Hale is one of Molokai's nicest B&Bs and certainly one of its best values. It occupies the 1st floor of a secluded private residence, and its spacious suite has a master bedroom, dining room with a full kitchen, living room, and a private lanai surrounded by a manicured garden. Sleeps 4. Affable owners will pick you up at the airport and are happy to share their knowledge of the island over breakfast. Snorkels, beach towels, and picnic gear are free for guests to borrow. Hawaiian-style breakfast for an additional $5 per guest. Suite $70 (1-2 guests); each additional person $15. Cash only. ❸

Aahi Place Bed & Breakfast, 215 Aahi Pl. (☎553-8033; www.molokai.com/aahi), located 1½ mi. east of town, on the left side of Aahi Pl., at the top of the steep hill and right before the road swings to the east. This B&B's lofty location offers an ocean view and a variety of accommodations, including a roomy cottage, one-bedroom trailer, and a small room off the main house with its own entrance. All guests have access to the kitchenette, washing machine, grill, phone, and cable TV on the porch. Approachable and friendly owner **Steve** offers sizeable discounts for longer stays and advice about island activities. Reserve the cottage months in advance in high season. Cottage $75; trailer $35; room $35. Cash or travelers checks. ❷

Hotel Molokai, Kamehameha V Hwy. (☎553-5347, fax 553-5047; www.hotelmolokai.com), before the 2 mi. marker east of town. Set on tiny Kamiloloa Beach with a great view of Lanai, Hotel Molokai is a cluster of two-story bungalows with bamboo-accented interiors. Rooms have phone, lanai, TV, fridge, and laundry access. A pool is next to the hotel restaurant and bar, which hosts F night Hawaiian music jam sessions. **Molokai Outdoors** (p. 329), a major activity center, and the beach front **Hula**

Shores Lounge and Restaurant, are also on the premises. Guests receive a 10% discount on some Molokai Outdoors tours. Rooms $115-190. AmEx/D/MC/V. ❹

One Alii Beach Park I, just past the 3 mi. marker on the *makai* (ocean) side of Kamehameha Hwy., was once a favorite beach spot for *alii* (Hawaiian royalty). One Alii is actually 2 parks, One Alii I and One Alii II, located next to each other. One Alii I, the only park available for camping, has lights, electrical outlets, restrooms, and showers. Both parks are hot and windy during the day and are not appealing places to swim or snorkel. The parks are mostly used by locals, especially during the weekends when the pavilion is frequently used for parties. 3-night max (waived if demand is low). Camping permits required and can be obtained at the Mitchell Pauole Center. $3 per night per camper, children $0.50. See **Camping in Hawaii,** p. 75, for more info. ❶

Kiowea Park at Kapuaiwa Coconut Grove, west of Kaunakakai, past mi. marker 1 on the *makai* (ocean) side of Maunaloa Hwy. This very popular camping spot sits in the middle of King Kamehameha's historic coconut plantation, and is one of the best places to experience the magnificent Molokai sunset. Though there is not much of a beach, a protective reef makes for calm waters great for swimming and fishing. Restrooms, pavilion, electricity, grill, water, and showers are available. Be sure to book well in advance. Pavilion $50 deposit, $20 per night, see **Camping in Hawaii,** p. 75, for more info. Warning: pitch your tent well away from coconut-laden trees! ❶

FOOD

Organic, local produce abounds at **Natural Foods Outpost,** 70 Makena Pl., just ½ block off Ala Malama, where it turns east. **Internet access** is available from the back parking lot for a $1 donation. (☎553-3377. Open M-Th 9am-6pm, F 9am-4pm, Su 10am-5pm. AmEx/D/MC/V.) Locals flock to **Friendly Market,** 90 Malama Ave., the largest grocery store on the island. (☎553-5821 or 553-5595. Open M-F 8:30am-8:30pm, Sa 8:30-6:30pm. AmEx/MC/V.) On Saturday mornings, local merchants set up a **farmers' market** on the sidewalk in front of the Molokai Center on Ala Malama Ave. Vendors start setting up and selling as early as 6am. Sample tropical fruits and look for vintage aloha shirts (from $5), locally-made drums, and letter openers carved from the antlers of the local axis deer. Arrive early if you want fresh produce; it sells quickly.

Kamoi Snack-N-Go, 28 Kamoi St. (☎553-3742), in the same complex as Molokai Drugs, behind the post office. Molokai's only ice cream parlor offers 32 unique flavors from green tea to Hawaiian mud pie (single scoop, $2.25; double, $3.25). Kamoi also offers a range of snack food and quick meals (barbecue sandwich, $2; mini pizza, $3). Open M-F 10am-9pm, Sa 9am-9pm, Su noon-9pm. MC/V. ❶

Kanemitsu's Bakery, 79 Ala Malama Ave. (☎553-5855). For a unique experience, venture down Hotel Ln. (1 block east of the bakery), and then down the colorful alley on your left. Loaves of warm French bread with fruit toppings ($4.25-5.25) sold fresh Tu-Su 10:30pm-2am, from the window marked "knock here." The bread is also available for purchase during the day ($2.20), but come early, as it sells out fast. Pastries, lavosh, and saimin sold as well. Open M and W-Su 5:30am-6:30pm. MC/V. ❶

Paddler's Inn, 10 Mohala St. (☎553-5256), on the corner of Mohala and Kam 5 Hwy. This latest addition to Molokai's nightlife scene has a full bar (wine, $3.50; beer, $3; mixed drinks, $4-5) and restaurant decorated with canoe gear in honor of Molokai's paddling past. Try their Paddler's Saimin with Fantail Shrimp—fresh noodles with wonbok, spam, fishcake, green onion, egg, and golden fantail shrimp ($7) or Auntie Rosie's Island famous pies (different every day, $4). Breakfast served M-F 7-11am, Sa-Su 9am-noon; lunch and dinner served daily 11am-8:30pm. Bar open until midnight. Th-Sa draw large crowds to watch local and island bands play until 2am. AmEx/D/DC/MC/V. ❶

Stanley's Coffee Shop Gallery, 125 Puali Pl. (☎553-9966), north of Ala Malama on the eastern end of town. The best place to have a latte ($2.75) on Molokai, Stanley's supplies plush leather booths and couches for its clientele—mostly tourists and a few locals. High-speed Internet connection available ($1 per 10min.). Mango, tropical burst, and pineapple milkshakes ($3.25), a Molokai breakfast plate ($5), and the "best saimin in town" ($3.25). M-F 6:30am-4pm, Sa 6:30am-2pm. MC/V. ❶

Molokai Pizza Cafe, 15 Kaunakakai Pl. (☎553-3288), 1 block south of Rte. 460 on the wharf road. Kaunakakai's popular family restaurant serves a variety of food in its diner-style interior. Pizzas named after each Hawaiian Island (small, $10.20-$17.80; large, $15.15-24.35). Also serves subs ($8.25), burgers ($7-9), pasta ($8-11), *hulihuli* chicken ($11), fresh fish, and on W a Mexican menu with burritos and fajitas ($10). Open M-Th 10am-10pm, F-Sa 10am-11pm, Su 11am-10pm. Cash only. ❷

Molokai Drive-In, 15 Kamoi St. (☎553-5655), on the corner of Rte. 460. Fast food island-style—greasy, good, and dirt cheap. 2 eggs, meat, hash browns, and drink $5.30. Plate lunches $7.25-8.75. Hamburgers ($2.15), tacos ($2), and saimin ($3.25). Serves fish caught daily. Takeout available. Open M-Th and Su 6am-10pm, F-Sa 6:30am-10:30pm. Cash only. ❶

Big Daddy's Store and Restaurant, 67 Ala Malama Ave. (☎553-5841). Part convenience store, part Filipino plate lunch stop (2 choices, $7.65). Sells delicious shave ice ($2.75) and fresh *poke, shoyu,* and *limu ogo* sashimi salads ($9.99 per lb.). Open daily 8am-9pm; kitchen 10am-4pm. Cash only. ❶

Oviedo's Lunch Counter, 145 Puali Pl. (☎553-5014), 1 block north of Ala Malama. Serves Filipino food like crunchy roast pork and chicken papaya, or pigs' feet and tripe stew for the daring. Lunch ($9.50) comes with rice and a main dish. Takeout available. Open M-F 10am-5:30pm, Sa-Su 10am-4pm. Cash only. ❷

ACTIVITIES

Molokai offers a range of outdoor activities; some of the most popular are hiking, kayaking, and snorkeling. Surfing and golf are also possible, but the surfing spots and golf course are not on par with those found elsewhere in Hawaii. A few outfits near Kaunakakai offer rentals and guided trips of all kinds. Almost all of Molokai can be explored on your own, but you may find it more rewarding to

REEF: IT'S WHAT'S FOR DINNER

Molokai lays claim to many records: the highest sea cliffs, the tallest ocean-terminating waterfall in the world, the largest beach in Hawaii, and the coolest mule ride on earth. Perhaps a less recognized treasure is the barrier reef that sits off Molokai's South shore. The only barrier reef north of Australia, it stretches almost 28 miles and is the longest in Hawaii. Students come from all over the world to study the diversity of life that is found in these teeming waters, including several species of rare fish and coral. Honu (green sea turtles), rays, reef fish, octopi, and several species of shark all call the reef home. The critically endangered hawksbill turtle even nests on the unprotected beaches along this shore, feeding on the reef. There are a variety of snorkeling and diving services offered in Kaunakakai to explore this hidden treasure, but there is no need to fork out big bucks and hire a guide to see it—just dive in! One of the best places for snorkeling is 20 Mile (Murphy's) Beach, where the reef connects to the shore and swimming is safe. Be wary of the current that pulls to the west. Stepping on the coral often causes irreparable damage—try to have as little impact as possible on this delicate ecosystem.

go with a local guide. **Molokai Outdoors,** at Hotel Molokai, is a great source of information about everything outdoors, including trips to the Kalaupapa Peninsula (p. 331), and hiking in Halawa Valley. Most rental equipment can be taken out for same-day, 24hr., and weekly rentals. All 24hr. rentals include snorkeling gear ($6), kayaks (single $26, double $39), surfboards ($13-21), and boogie boards ($5). They also offer a few half-day and full-day guided tours of the island ($64-156) for those who want to see everything in a short period of time. Most popular is the **Alii Tour** which covers Kaunakakai, St. Joseph's Church, the fishponds, Kalaupapa Lookout, Coffees of Hawaii, and Purdy's Macadamia Nut Farm. (☎553-4477. Open M-Sa 8am-5pm, Su 8am-4pm. $96.) **Molokai Fish and Dive,** 61 Ala Malama Ave., in Kaunakakai, also offers tours and rentals. They rent kayaks ($33 per day), snorkel gear ($10 per day), boogie boards ($11 per day), and surfboards ($25-35 per day), and employ full-time guides who lead cultural hikes ($50-75), bike tours ($60), surf lessons ($150 for the first hr., $75 for each additional hr.), and horseback rides ($85). Ask also about their whale-watching, kayaking, fishing and scuba diving adventures. (☎553-5926 or 552-0184; www.molokaifishanddive.com. Open daily 7:30am-6pm.) Serious surfers should check out **Molokai Surf,** 130 Kam. V, Ste. 103, for surf clothing, equipment, and advice from the 30-year Molokai surf veteran and store owner, Jerry Leonard. (☎558-8943. Open M-F 9:30am-5pm.) Molokai is easily navigable on two wheels, so try **Molokai Bicycle,** 80 Mohala St. (☎553-3931). The owner will drop-off/pick-up a bike to any location on the island and all rentals include a helmet, lock, map, and water bottle. (☎553-3931 or 800-709-2453; www.bikehawaii.com/molokaibicycle. $15-20 per day, discounted weekly rates available.)

SIGHTS

Although the main attractions on Molokai are the beaches on the east and west ends of the island and the Kalaupapa peninsula, there are also several pleasant things to see around Kaunakakai. About a mile or two west of town lies the **Kapuaiwa Coconut Grove.** The coconut grove, an 11-acre expanse of coconut trees is on the south side of the highway. It was originally planted in the 1860s by Prince Lot, a Molokai resident who became King Kamehameha V, to provide shade for visiting royalty as they bathed in the sea. It is one of the few remaining royal coconut groves in the state and has been renovated as a campground (p. 328) by the Hawaiian Home Lands Department.

Across the highway from Ala Malama Ave., the road becomes Kaunakakai Pl. and leads out to the **Kaunakakai Wharf,** stretching a quarter mile from the highway. The longest wharf in Hawaii offers great views of the mountains, and three-quarters of the way out on the west side there is a small area with showers and restrooms where locals swim. This is also the arrival and departure point of the **Molokai Princess** (p. 324). The wharf's main activity is still fishing; the **Molokai Ice House,** a fishermen's cooperative established in 1988, makes its home at the end on the east side. The cooperative no longer acts as a restaurant and fish market, but sometimes fishermen sell their catch on the wharf early in the morning or late in the afternoon. In winter, when the barge can only make it a few times across the dangerous channel, locals gather here to greet it and help unload long-awaited necessities like **toilet paper and beer.** Many fishing, snorkeling, and whale-watching expeditions leave from the wharf. **Satan's Doll** (☎553-5852) offers snorkeling and sportfishing expeditions and **Gypsy Sailing Adventures** (☎345-4412) offers whale-watching and sailing charters.

During June and July, every other Saturday morning, from 9am to *pau* (finish), a raucous crowd gathers to watch **outrigger canoe races** and sip cold drinks from concession stands run by local canoe clubs. Anyone 12 and up can participate in one of Molokai's clubs, which start training in spring for the summer races.

Just before the wharf on the west side of Kaunakakai Pl., a stone platform is all that remains of King Kamehameha V's vacation home. Although it looks more like an overgrown parking lot than a park, the area is designated **Malama Cultural Park,** and archaeologists believe it was once a *heiau* (temple).

ENTERTAINMENT

The best of local Molokai nightlife takes place at Paddler's Inn (p. 328), which has live local bands Thursday to Saturday until 2am. The **Hula Shores Lounge** at Hotel Molokai often attracts hundreds of islanders and tourists to watch the weekly Na Kapuna jam session on Fridays from 4-6pm. Locals play ukuleles and slack key guitars, and there is informal singing and sometimes hula dancing as well. A live band usually comes on after the jam session and plays until the bar closes (around 10:30pm). During the rest of the week, the Hula Shores Lounge offers live island music; ask at the front desk for a schedule. (Breakfast $5-11; lunch $5-9; dinner $15-20. Breakfast and lunch daily 7am-2pm; dinner M-Th and Sa-Su 6-9pm, F 4-9pm. Bar open daily 10am-10:30pm.)

Across from the **Mitchell Pauole Center** at the intersection of Ala Malama Ave. and Ainoa St. is the **Kaunakakai Ball Park,** where the Molokai Farmers have a substantial home field advantage over the competition, players from Maui or Lanai. The locals take their Little League very seriously: almost the entire town comes out for the Maui County Championship game. The Little League schedule is available at the Mitchell Pauole Center. Basketball leagues also run in the nearby gym, where stands afford visitors a chance to catch a game.

For the under-21 crowd, **Club Zero,** a youth center in the Mitchell Pauole Center, has pool tables, great couches, a 64-in. cable TV, and video games. The club is part of a larger youth center that runs other programs; ask about volunteering opportunities. Super-friendly staff welcome youth of all ages. (☎553-3675. Open in summer M-F 10am-8:30pm, Sa 11am-7:30pm. Call ahead for school-year hours.)

CENTRAL MOLOKAI

KALAUPAPA PENINSULA

Kalaupapa is a flat, leaf-shaped land formation on Molokai's northern shore. It is separated from the "topside" (the rest of Molokai) by a 2000 ft. wall of mountains passable only by a steep switchback trail or plane. A volcanic eruption created the peninsula and the Kauhako Crater, which is one of the deepest lakes in the US (800 ft.). Dubbed "the grotto" by locals, the crater is marked by a cemetery and large white cross, visible from sea. Kalaupapa's history is painful. Its many stone walls attest to the area's past as a fertile farming land, until 1866, when it was converted into an infamous quarantine colony for lepers. The quarantine was lifted in 1969, although a few ex-patients continue to live here. The hundreds of graveposts that emerge from its green grasses, standing silent testament to the deep suffering of the peninsula's residents, make the beauty of the peninsula all the more evocative.

KALAUPAPA'S STORY

The first documented case of leprosy on the Hawaiian Islands was in 1835. When it developed into a serious epidemic in 1860, King Kamehameha V became afraid that leprosy would infect his people and destroy his kingdom. To prevent this catastrophe, he chose the most isolated spot in all the islands, a cove called Kalawao on the southeastern part of the Kalaupapa peninsula, and in 1866, began to exile the lepers there.

Thought to be incurable and highly contagious, patients diagnosed with leprosy were rounded up with little or no notice, separated permanently from their families, put on a ship, and dumped into the water near Kalawao, sometimes hundreds of yards offshore. Some drowned, others succumbed to hunger or exposure, but none returned. Until 1890, when the survivors moved from Kalawao to the drier and more hospitable village of Kalaupapa, death was so common that the colony was described as a living cemetery.

By 1870, a few Christian missionaries had arrived in Kalaupapa to attend to the sick, but hardly any stayed on the peninsula for more than a few months. Nevertheless, Joseph de Veuster, a Belgian Catholic priest nicknamed Father Damien, set a new precedent. Known for his exceptional carpentry skills, Damien was originally sent to Kalaupapa to repair the roof of St.

! The only way to travel through the Kalaupapa Peninsula is as part of an organized tour. It is against state law to explore the peninsula on your own, as well as disrespectful to the area's residents.

TRANSPORTATION

There are three ways to get to Kalaupapa: you can hike down the strenuous but magnificent cliff trail, fly to an airstrip on the far side of the peninsula, or ride a mule down the trail. Advance reservations are required for all three. State law requires that you be 16 years or older to enter the peninsula as part of the tour.

BY FOOT. Hiking the challenging 2.9 mi. **Pali trail** is by far the cheapest and most rewarding option. It descends over 1600 ft. along 26 numbered switchbacks until it finally reaches sea level. It then continues east for ¼ mi. to the end of the road, where tours begin. To get there from Kaunakakai, take Hwy. 460 west, then turn right at Hwy. 470. The trail entrance is 15min. down the highway, past the mule stables, on the right at a metal gate with a sign warning not to enter without a permit. Although the laws requiring permits to hike the trail have expired, you must have an advance reservation with **Damien Tours** (see below), or else you will be turned away at the bottom of the trail.

If you plan to hike, be certain to start 1hr. before the mules leave at 8:30am to avoid the worst of their droppings on the way down (it's unavoidable on the way up) and bring plenty of water. The hike can take as little as 25min. or as much as 1hr. if you allow time to appreciate the view. At the base of the trail, walk right toward the settlement. You'll pass a black-sand beach (one of the island's most dangerous due to insane currents, large waves, and submerged rocks), and as you enter an open area, you'll see the bleachers where you wait for the tour.

BY AIR. If you prefer to fly, you will need to arrange both a flight and a tour reservation with **Damien Tours,** unless your airline explicitly states that they will handle the tour reservation. The prices listed here are for the flight only and do not include the tour. Consider hiking down and flying back, or vice versa, as the hike is very enjoyable. **Molokai Air Shuttle** is the cheapest option. (☎567-6847. $25 each way to and from the Molokai Airport in Hoolehua; from Honolulu one-way $70, round-trip $110. Office open M-Sa 6am-6pm.) Other options include **Pacific**

Wings, which flies from Honolulu (☎873-0877 or 888-575-4546, $96 each way).

BY MULE. The third option, **Molokai Mule Ride,** offers rides that include both lunch and a tour ($165 per person; AmEx/D/MC/V). The trip begins at 8:30am (plan to arrive by 8) at the stables across the street from the Pali Trailhead. The trailhead is at the entrance to Palaau State Park, 5 mi. up Hwy. 470 from its intersection with Hwy. 460. Although many people enjoy the ride, it is very bumpy, and some may prefer to hike. Nevertheless, mule riders are safely above the mule doodie that hikers otherwise encounter below. Bring long pants and lots of water; in addition, riders must be in good health and weigh no more than 240 lb. Book at least two weeks in advance because space is limited and fills up quickly. Molokai Mule also offers package deals that include flights from Maui ($345) or Honolulu ($319).

You can also book package deals (flight, mule, hike/tour in any combination) through **Molokai Fish and Dive** (p. 345). A cheaper option is to book the trip and tour together through **Damien Tours.** (☎567-6171. Call between 4-8pm. Tours M-Sa 10am-1:30pm. Flight $90; hike $40. Cash only.)

ACTIVITIES

Damien Tours (☎567-6171) operates all the tours of Kalaupapa. Bring your own lunch; once you arrive at the bleachers near the mule corral, wait for the big blue bus and your tour guide (sometimes a former patient or resident) to pick you up. The tour stops at the docks, where residents gather once a year to receive supplies, at **St. Francis Church,** whose walls are fixed with images of **Father Damien,** and at the grave of **Mother Marianne.** There is also a stop at the **Visitors Center,** which is filled with books about Damien and Kalaupapa. *Yesterday at Kalaupapa* or *The Lands of Father Damien* are excellent choices for their photography; *Separating Sickness* contains some of the better narratives about residents' lives. The latter portion of the tour goes around the old Kalawao settlement. From the park, you can see dome-shaped **Okala Rock,** the only place in the world where miniature okala palms grow in the wild.

The most poignant part of the tour is the history of Father Damien's life, which is recounted at **St. Philomena Church.** Though his remains are in Belgium, his grave is located outside. In order to protect the privacy of the residents during the tour, no stops are made at residential establishments such

Philomena Church. However, when he saw the suffering and depravity of Kalaupapa's residents, he decided to stay.

Over the course of several years, Father Damien built nearly 300 box-like houses and dug new graves each day. Unfailingly compassionate and accepting, he always welcomed patients into his house, dipped his hands in the same bowls of poi as his guests, and shared his tobacco pipe with anyone who asked. Though leprosy is among the least contagious of all diseases, Damien was diagnosed with leprosy in 1884; he died in 1889. Although over 1000 volunteers have followed Damien's example and worked on the peninsula since 1870, Damien is the only documented case of infection.

In the 1940s, sulfone antibiotics were discovered as an effective treatment for leprosy, and by the 1960s, the disease was no longer considered as dangerous. Nevertheless, until the quarantine on Kalaupapa was lifted in 1969, children born to residents were taken by the state and put up for adoption. After 1969, no new residents were admitted and residents were free to leave, but many feared reintegration into society and chose to stay.

During its years of operation, over 7000 people were sent to the Kalaupapa colony. Down from a peak of 1800 residents in 1970, there are fewer than 38 today.

as the post office or hospital and residents stay indoors. Also be aware that **photography of residents is strictly prohibited.**

KAMAKOU PRESERVE

The 3000-acre preserve next to Kamakou Peak is home to more than 250 different species of plants, 219 of which can be found only in Hawaii, and it is the last patch of native rainforest on Molokai. The plants feed indigenous insects and snails, which in turn support the local bird population. Look for the happy-faced spider—distinguished by its yellow body and bright red grin. Pine, eucalyptus, and kukui trees envelope the area, and the bright red native honey creeper *(apapane)* feeds from the same-colored flowers of the *ohia lehua* tree. You will also find the *hapuu*, a tall endemic fern used in the past for mattress stuffing and roof thatch, and *pukiawe*, a short shrub with pinkish berries, used by Hawaiian chiefs before making public appearances, supposedly to reduce their godly status.

The preserve owes its existence to the generosity of the Molokai Ranch (and the proprietors of the luxurious Maunaloa Lodge), which sold the land rights to the Nature Conservancy in 1982; the rights to the Moomomi Preserve were sold six years later (p. 338). The ranch maintains control of the water rights which provide 60% of the island's water via a tunnel to the Kualapuu Reservoir. The **Nature Conservancy** (☎553-5236) encourages visitors to call before visiting the preserve. The Conservancy can provide you with valuable information about the state of the preserve's roads.

The destruction of the sandalwood forests and the subsequent overgrazing of cattle caused severe erosion in this area in the mid-19th century. In the 1930s, Molokai, like many of the Hawaiian islands, was reforested with non-native eucalyptus, ironwood, and Norfolk island pines in an effort to stabilize the soil and protect Molokai's watersheds. Today the activity of feral pigs, goats, and axis deer in the area destroys delicate native plant ecosystems and is a further source of erosion. Red soil washes down the slopes of Kamakou to the ocean where it can choke and kill the coral reef. In an effort to control this devastation, the Nature Conservancy builds and maintains fences around preservation areas. They also sponsor monthly hunting trips into Pelekunu, Kamalo, and Kawela. The hunters that live in these areas are given first priority to go on the hunts, but it is possible for anyone to reserve a spot on the trip. In general, hunting is permitted on weekends and state holidays in the reserve, so it is a good idea to wear brightly colored clothing and stay on marked trails when hiking.

GETTING THERE. If you're not on a guided tour and are trying to drive to the preserve yourself, a **4WD vehicle** is essential. In a 2WD vehicle, **turn around at the first sign of rain.** In the event that you get stuck, you'll have to hike all the way back to call your rental agency or one of the gas stations in Kaunakakai (and suffer the embarrassment and expense of car retrieval). Keep in mind that the last few miles of the road are at high elevation; they can be rainy even when it is sunny at the bottom. Use first gear and go slowly, driving around (not over) the manhole covers that appear at odd intervals along the road. Try not to drive in ruts; instead, straddle them with the wheels of your vehicle, or drive up on the shoulder to avoid them. If you lose traction and start to slide, ease up on the gas and turn into the skid. Lastly, avoid stopping if your vehicle is on an upward incline—many parts of the road are passable only with momentum.

ORIENTATION AND PRACTICAL INFORMATION. The road that leads to the preserve begins west of Kaunakakai on **Highway 460.** Turn right before mi. marker 4; there is a sign that says "Homelani Cemetery." The pavement ends and the dirt road begins just past the cemetery. The first 5 mi. of this road are fairly easy-going, until you pass the entrance sign for the **Molokai Forestry Reserve.** Although the massive trees may be beautiful, the road is not. Even 4WD may encounter traction problems while trying to climb the steep grades after this point.

This part of the island was a popular place to live back in the days of Kamehameha the Great, but the only people you'll see today are hikers, locals checking on remote *pakalolo* (marijuana) plants, and a woodcutter, who sells carvings slightly past the forest reserve entrance. Honk your horn or ring the bell by the gate if you want a tour of the woodshop. There's a restroom outside his gate, too.

After around 10 mi., you will be able to make out **Lua Moku Iliahi,** or the Sandalwood Measuring Pit, on the left. This 75 ft. long pit was used to ensure that the trees harvested would fit in the hold; the wood was then hauled on the backs of workers down to Kaunakakai wharf.

After 1 mi., you will reach the entrance to the Kamakou Preserve and the **Waikolu Lookout.** Waikolu, or "three waters," refers to the many waterfalls that run over the mountains and into the region's streams. At 3700 ft., the lookout has staggering views of the surrounding valleys. Although Waikolu's frequent afternoon rain and clouds can obstruct the view, early morning is often clear. With squat toilets and a picnic area but no drinking water, this camping site is popular with pig hunters and preserve explorers, though it can be a bit chilly and wet. Free camping permits are available through the **State Division of Forestry and Wildlife.** You must notify the state of your stay (2-night max.) and have your permit in hand when you camp. For more information, see **Camping in Hawaii,** p. 75. Camping is only permitted in the state forest reserve, not the preserve.

GUIDED TOURS. If you are concerned about getting to and hiking through the preserve yourself, or if you'd simply like to avoid the long walk from the Waikolu Lookout, consider arranging a guided hike with the **Nature Conservancy** (p. 334). Because you are driven directly to the trailheads, guided hikes are generally less time-consuming. The tour leaders often have worthwhile background knowledge about the region. The Conservancy runs an eight-person trip, usually on the first Saturday of the month. Hikers meet at the airport at 8:30am for the 3 mi. round-trip hike and return by 4pm. A $25 donation is suggested and advance reservations (with a $25 refundable deposit) are required.

HIKING. The Nature Conservancy asks that you stay on the roads and marked trails in the preserve to avoid damaging the surrounding vegetation or hurting yourself. From the Waikolu Lookout, the road is impassable in anything but 4WD, and you'll have trouble even then. Unless you have extensive off-road driving experience—or people to get out and push, the safest course of action is to park at the lookout and walk to the trailheads. Before you leave the lookout, sign in on the Nature Conservancy's log sheet, which often has information about road conditions. In addition, be sure to bring lots of water, rain gear, and sturdy shoes or hiking boots that you won't mind getting muddy.

The main trail in Kamakou Preserve is the **Pepeopae Trail.** Its trailhead is 2.2 mi. down the main road, past the Waikolu Lookout, and is clearly marked. The trail is a 6-8 in. wide boardwalk that is covered in chicken wire for better traction. It winds for slightly over a mile through one of Hawaii's wettest regions. There are no handrails, so you may want to bring a walking stick. The substantial rainfall (over 170 in. annually) and acidic soil have stunted the plant population and maintained the 10,000 year old **Pepeopae Bog.** The bog is humid and cool and the surrounding landscape is brilliantly green. Stay on the boardwalk; it gives hikers a chance to experience the remarkable vegetation without damaging the environment.

At the end of the boardwalk is a tiny patch of grass on the edge of a cliff known as the **Pelekunu Valley Overlook.** The overlook offers truly arresting views of high grassy cliffs towering over the Pelekunu River and the turquoise waters of the Pacific to the left. On a good day, wispy clouds just barely wreath the tops of the cliffs. The 5760-acre Pelekunu Valley is under the care of the Nature Conservancy and closed to the public, as it is one of the few remaining breeding grounds for several species of marine and terrestrial life.

KALAE AND KUALAPUU

Kalae, the area toward the end of Hwy. 470, 5 mi. up the road from Hwy. 460, is blessed with a lot of sun and a cooler climate due to its elevation (1500 ft.). Three miles farther the tiny agricultural town of Kualapuu (pop. 1,936), at Farrington Ave. and Hwy. 470, was the island headquarters of the Del Monte Company in the 1930s. When they closed shop in 1982 headed for more profitable pineapple lands in the Philippines and Thailand, the town's economy suffered. In recent years, the coffee bean has replaced the pineapple—the town's main attraction is now a coffee plantation.

FOOD

Next door to Kualapuu Cookhouse on Farrington Ave., the **Kualapuu Market,** a well-stocked grocery store (one of two west of Kaunakakai) carries periodicals and magazines, and rents VHS tapes and DVDs. (☎567-6243. Open M-Sa 8:30am-6pm. Video store open M-W and F-Sa 3-6pm. AmEx/MC/V.)

Coffees of Hawaii, Inc., 1630 Farrington Ave. (☎567-9490), at Hwy. 470. The Espresso Bar and Cafe serve local brew any way you like it. Cool off with the shop's signature frozen drink, the Mocha Mama (vanilla ice cream, espresso, and chocolate, $3.95). Sandwiches and other light fare ($3-6) are also available. A 45min. walking tour takes visitors through the 500-acre plantation to see the phases of coffee production. You can also hike through the plantation to the top of Kualapuu Hill for a 360-degree view of the island. Cafe open M-F 7am-4pm, Sa 8am-4pm, Su 8am-2pm. Walking tour M-F 10-11am; $25, 15 and under $10, 2 and under free. Gift shop M-F 8am-5pm, Sa 8am-4pm, Su 8am-2pm. Call ahead for tour reservations and hiking information. ❶

Kualapuu Cookhouse, P.O. Box 1715, (☎567-9655), a few doors down from Coffees. The original cookhouse for pineapple plantation workers and the only restaurant between Kaunakakai and Maunaloa, Kualapuu is considered by many locals and visitors to be the best place to eat on the island. The lemon chicken ($7.50) is superb, and the hamburgers ($3.50) are large and juicy. Double the size of any meal by ordering it "Kanaka size" ($4). Dine in the shady outdoor seating or the tropical-themed interior, or take your food to-go. Open M 7am-2pm, Tu-Sa 7am-8pm. Breakfast until 11am. Dinner specials Tu-Sa ($12-19). Cash only. ❶

ACCOMMODATIONS AND CAMPING

One of the only places to stay in central Molokai is the **Hale Malu Guesthouse ❷,** 23 Kalama Rd., after mi. marker 4 on Kalae Hwy. The guesthouse is on the left near the bottom of the hill. With an extremely convenient location, Hale Malu consists of a quirky round cottage and two separate guest rooms. All guests have access to the kitchen, living room with cable TV and VCR, washer/dryer, phone, and Internet in the main house. (☎567-9136. 2-night min. Cottage with A/C, TV, fridge, shower, and lanai; $80. Rooms with communal bathroom and shower; $50.) For camping, take Hwy. 470 north to **Palaau State Park** ❶ (☎587-0300). With picnic tables, restrooms, outdoor showers, and a surrounding forest, this peaceful state park is a great bet. Palaau suffers from frequent drizzles and a lack of drinking water, but it is one of Molokai's best camping spots. If you don't mind getting a little damp, bring your own water and pitch a tent on the soft needles on the ground—chances are you'll have the park to yourself. No need to set your alarm, wild roosters will ensure you are up at dawn. Camping permits are necessary. See **Camping in Hawaii,** p. 75, for more information.

SIGHTS

PALAAU STATE PARK. Daytime visitors will find a large pavilion and lawn near the entrance of the park before reaching the campsite road turn-off; a smaller picnic area with tables and trash cans is farther down on the right. At the end of the road, a display describes the park's two main attractions. The first, Kaule o Nanahoa (Phallic Rock), deserves a visit. By foot, the rock is 5min. from the end of the highway along a marked trail down the left fork in the path. A sign claims that the rock is a natural formation which has only been carved "to some extent" by humans. Legend has it that a woman who brings offerings to the rock and sleeps a night next to it will wake up pregnant. Two minutes down the right fork is the Kalaupapa Lookout which has an exceptional view of the peninsula of the same name. Five placards recount the history of the peninsula and the lepers exiled there. If you don't hike down to the colony (p. 332), at least check out the view—it's one of Molokai's best, especially in the morning before clouds shroud the peninsula. The lookout is perched on nearly vertical cliffs at an elevation of 1500 ft., so stay behind the rock wall and be prepared for high winds. *(At the end of Hwy. 470, about 5 mi. from Hwy. 460.)*

PURDY'S MACADAMIA NUT FARM. Purdy runs what may very well be the most hospitable macadamia nut farm in the world, and certainly one of Molokai's best-known tourist attractions. Visitors are welcomed by the man himself and given a full tour of the working farm. Because Purdy does not prune his trees or use irrigation, fertilizer, pesticides, or chemicals of any kind, visitors have the privilege of wandering freely and taste-testing throughout the property. The 50 trees on his tiny farm are 85 years old, producing nuts year-round. Purdy will insist you crack your own nut before helping yourself to samples of macadamia honey on slices of fresh coconut. A small gift shop stocks treasures like rare macadamia woodworking ($5-55), macadamia blossom honey ($6.50), and the nuts themselves. *(On the right side of Lihi Pali Ave., ½ mi. from the intersection with Farrington Ave. From Hwy. 470, turn left on Farrington Ave., then right on Lihi Pali after 1 mi. ☎567-6601. Open Tu-F 9:30am-3:30pm, Sa 10am-2pm, weather permitting. Tours on the hr. Park on the road outside. Free.)*

IRONWOOD HILLS GOLF COURSE. Ironwood Hills is a pleasant nine-hole course set in a rustic upcountry venue. While the fairways are not perfectly manicured, Ironwood Hills is a great place to enjoy a casual afternoon of golf. The unpretentious pro shop is run out of a trailer by a good-natured caretaker. *(About 3¾ mi. from the intersection of Hwy. 460 and Hwy. 470, down a long dirt road on the left, before the Molokai Museum and Cultural Center. ☎567-6000. Open daily 7:30am-6pm. $24. Club rental $12.)*

MOLOKAI MUSEUM AND CULTURAL CENTER. It took 16 years to restore the smallest sugar mill in Hawaii to full working condition, but it now sits proudly on a hill above the main museum building. The mill spewed out cane sugar over 100 years ago, though it went out of business in just a decade due the low price of sugar and cane disease. In addition to the mule-driven cane crusher and other authentic mill parts, the museum has an ever-changing display of old Molokai artifacts and photos. Be sure to stop at the information desk for advice on local activities, seminars, hiking tours, exhibits, and festivals. *(On Kalae Hwy., turn left at the sign, just past the Ironwoods Golf Course and before mi. marker 4. ☎567-6436. Open M-Sa 10am-2pm. $3.50, students and children $1. Cash only.)*

HOOLEHUA

This large, dry area west of Kalae divides eastern and western Molokai. Most of the land in the area is under the auspices of the department of Hawaiian Home Lands, which provides homesteads to Native Hawaiians.

PRACTICAL INFORMATION. The **Hoolehua post office** (☎567-6144), at Puupeelua Ave. (Hwy. 480) and Farrington Ave., is home to the **Post-A-Nut** service—you can send a Molokai coconut to your friends back home for the price of postage (US $6-9, international $11-20). The smiling postmaster provides the nuts along with a few felt pens to write on their husks. If you want to keep things cheap, ask to weigh the coconut before you decorate. (Open M-F 8:30am-noon and 12:30-4pm.) **Postal Code:** 96729.

SIGHTS. One of the only coastal sand dune ecosystems left untouched by development in Hawaii, the **Moomomi Preserve** is home to a half-dozen endangered plants that cannot be found anywhere else on the planet. Its pristine coast is a breeding ground for green sea turtles, rare on other parts of the island, and the many white-sand beaches are expansive and perpetually empty. Most beaches are rocky, however, and in many cases have nasty offshore currents, making them ill-suited for swimming or other aquatic activities.

The Moomomi Preserve is one of two Molokai preserves that are managed by the **Nature Conservancy** (p. 334) and open to the public (the other is Kamakou Preserve, p. 334). Maps and information are available at the Conservancy's office, where the staff encourages visitors to stop in to get up-to-date information before they visit the preserve. The office is in the second cul-de-sac on the right in the Molokai Industrial Park. (Turn down Oha St., which leads south from Hwy. 460. ☎553-5236; www.nature.org/hawaii. Open M-F 7:30am-3pm.)

There are three ways to access the preserve. The first is by hiking a trail (¾ mi.) to the east from the Moomomi Pavilion. To get to the trail, take Hwy. 460 from Kaunakakai, turn left onto Hwy. 480 (Farrington Ave.), and continue straight until the asphalt ends. The dirt road straight ahead is smooth most of the way, and generally passable in good weather, although a few monster ruts may tilt your vehicle at odd angles. The road runs for about 2 mi. and passes through a gate about halfway down before it reaches the Moomomi Recreation and Cultural Park on the eastern edge of Moomomi Bay. The pavilion here is owned and maintained by the Hawaiian Home Lands Department (as is all the land in the area) and has restrooms, an outdoor shower, picnic tables, and room to park. Camping is not permitted here. From the parking area, the trail leads left along the shore of Moomomi Bay and Kawaaloa Bay until it reaches the preserve. Wear athletic shoes as the terrain can be rough. Within the preserve there are a number of endangered plants, so after leaving the bay, be absolutely certain to hike only on trails or roads. The trail stays along the coast for 1 mi. and offers some of the most magnificent views of untouched beaches and sand dunes you can imagine. The trail ends at a deserted beach and sandstone cliff. Look for the endangered Hawaiian monk seal basking in the sun or a *pueo* (Hawaiian owl) surveying the dunes in search of prey. Remember that it is illegal to remove or disturb any part of the preserve, be it animal, vegetable, or mineral.

The two other ways to enter the preserve are by car or on a guided tour. The Nature Conservancy occasionally grants visitors permission to use the 4WD roads through the preserve with advance notice. Instead of turning right at the fork in the road, keep left; there are two grassy parking lots at the end and the preserve trail begins near the first. Guests must contact the Conservancy and ask for a key to the various gates along this road. Finally, the Conservancy leads guided hikes on the third or fourth Saturday of each month for a suggested donation of $25. Hikers are picked up at the Hoolehua airport at 8:30am and returned by 2:30pm. A $25 refundable deposit is required to reserve a spot on the hike; try to reserve well in advance as these trips are popular. The hike is 2 mi. round-trip.

Beyond Moomomi Bay along the same trail, **Kawaaloa Bay** is characterized by a similar (but much longer) stretch of sandy beach. Again, the surf is strong, and rocks make swimming difficult and potentially dangerous, but the beach is long, beautiful, and secluded.

EAST OF KAUNAKAKAI

The drive east from Kaunakakai becomes progressively more rural, and the road becomes narrower and less-traveled. The towns listed here are really nothing more than houses clustered along the road. Other than the **Iliiliopae Heiau,** (p. 341) most sights are visible from the road, making this a great place to sightsee with the windows down. The highway is dotted with a string of tiny beaches, often deserted. After many twists and hairpin turns, the end of the road reveals one of Molokai's most stunning and secluded scenes—the **Halawa Valley and falls** (p. 343).

A variety of private cottages, beach houses, and condos are found along Molokai's southeast shore. There are some great deals, especially if traveling in a larger group; most are easily booked via Molokai Vacation Rentals (☎553-8334) or Friendly Isle Realty (☎553-3666), (p. 325). **Kamalo Plantation Cottage ❸,** through the gate next to mailbox 300 on the *mauka* (mountain) side of the highway, is just across from St. Joseph's Church, before mi. marker 11. A stay on this lush 5-acre property is truly an island-style experience. The guest cottage is a lovely, well-furnished studio with a king-size bed, kitchen, bird-watching deck, indoor and outdoor showers, tons of privacy, and access to the nearby luau hut, which has a gas grill. (☎558-8236; www.molokai.com/kamalo/. 2-night min. Cottage $95.) The owners also rent the bright white A-frame **Moanui Beach House ❹,** at mi. marker 20, across the road from the golden sand of Murphy's Beach. Both the cottage and house come with fruit from the family's plantation and home-baked bread for breakfast. The house has two airy bedrooms with king-size beds, a kitchen, and living and dining rooms. Kayaks, snorkels, and other beach gear are available for use. (3-night min. House $150; each additional guest $30.) The **Wavecrest Resort ❸** is located at mi. 13. A laid-back condo complex, the resort sits on an attractive lagoon with a good view of Maui. There are two tennis courts, a shuffleboard, and a putting green. A swimming pool is complemented by a large pool house with bamboo fans. All rooms have a kitchen, lanai, TV, and ceiling fans. No A/C or guest telephone. (☎558-8101. 1-bedroom $70-85; 2-bedroom $85-135; cleaning fee $70 for stays under 1 wk.) Just past mi. marker 19 is the **Waialua Pavilion and Campground ❶,** a private facility run by the Waialua

Congregational Church, but available for public use most of they year. (☎558-8150. $10 per night, under 18 $8. Call ahead for permit.)

Besides Puu O Hoku Ranch, the only place to grab groceries or lunch on the east side of the island is **Manae Goods & Grindz** ❶ (☎558-8186 or 558-8498), just before mi. marker 16. In addition to the small but well-stocked market, the food counter serves up tuna melt sandwiches on whole wheat bread ($3), fresh mahi mahi burgers ($4), and other treats. Video rental is also available for $3.50. (Open M-F 10am-5pm, Sa-Su 8am-5pm.)

KAWELA

A small residential development between mi. markers 4 and 6, Kawela is notable for its views and its memorable history. Kawela is home to Pukuhiwa battleground, where Kamehameha I defeated Molokai's warriors on his way to uniting all the islands. It is said that in the hills above Kawela is a *puuhonua*, an ancient place of refuge for the defeated warriors. For a great view of Lanai, drive up any of the streets on the mountain side of the road. Especially good are the views from the top of Onioni Dr. (turn just past mi. marker 5, before the "Kawela Plantation I" sign). **Kakahai'a Beach Park,** at mi. 5½, is a narrow stretch of picnic tables with beach access. Across the street is the **Kakahai'a National Wildlife Refuge,** an ancient fishpond that is now a bird sanctuary for the endangered Hawaiian state bird, the *nene.* It is generally closed to the public, but the wetlands are visible from the highway. You can see the birds and get information about other bird-watching spots at **Nene O Molokai,** a nonprofit facility for breeding and releasing nene, at mi. marker 4, on the *makai* (ocean) side. There is usually a tour once a week; ask for details about getting permission to explore the Wildlife Refuge. (☎553-5992; http://aloha.net/~nene. Call ahead to visit.)

If you see a wild *nene,* do not approach or try to feed the bird. The state of Hawaii enforces a $50,000 fine for harassing *nene.*

KAMALO

Between mi. markers 10 and 11, Kamalo (pop. 147) was once the economic and civic center of the island. The **Kamalo Wharf** can be accessed via the dirt road on the right at the major bend in the highway about 100 yd. after mi. marker 10. Once the main port for Molokai's old pineapple industry, the wharf, now reduced to stones, is home to a few semi-permanent campers and an occasional outrigger race. Due to the large shark population, this area is not a popular destination for swimmers. However, the wharf is a great place for fishing, as many locals can attest. The wharf provides a spectacular view of the inland mountains; look for the highest point on the island, Mt. Kamakou, 4,961 ft. About ½ mi. farther down the road is **St. Joseph's Church,** built in 1876. It is one of two remaining churches that Father Damien constructed on "topside" - Molokai slang for anything outside and above the Kalaupapa peninsula. A small statue of him adorned with leis and pearls and a plaque commemorate his selfless work among the lepers of Kalaupapa, which resulted in his own death after contracting leprosy in 1889 (p. 332). The church is simple and no longer holds weekly services, but it still gets its share of visitors who often sign the logbook inside. About 1 mi. farther, an obscured wooden sign on the right denotes the **Smith-Bronte Landing Site,** where the first civilian flight from the mainland to Hawaii ended in a "safe" crash-landing in 1927. The flight took 25 hours and was originally intended to touch down in Honolulu.

UALAPUE AND KALUAAHA

The village of Ualapue (pop. 4,702) is clustered just past mi. marker 13, and about 1 mi. later, on the *mauka* (mountain) side of the highway in Kaluaaha, is the old **Kaluaaha Church,** built in 1835 by the first missionary to the island. Only the church's 3 ft. thick concrete outer wall remains, but monthly services are still held under a tarp inside the great walls of the worn church. If the gate is padlocked, park outside and walk in. Just ¼ mi. farther is the well-known **Our Lady of Sorrows Church.** A 10 ft. tall wooden cross makes the parking lot for the church unmistakable. Today's building is the 1966 reconstruction of the original, which was built by Father Damien in 1874. Services are held Sundays at 7am. A bit past and across the street from the church is the **Niaupala Fishpond,** one of the easiest ancient fishponds to see on the south shore.

PUKOO

Located within the tiny village of Pukoo, the colossal **Iliiliopae Heiau** is not to be missed. To reach the *heiau* (temple), watch for the small Mapulehu bridge, about ½ mi. past mi. 15 on Rte. 450. On the south side of the road before the bridge, check out the mango trees; this used to be an expansive working plantation with over a dozen different kinds of mango. The path to the *heiau* is the first dirt road on the left, marked by mailbox #488 and a sign that reads "No Hunting, Private Property, Keep Out, Keep Gate Closed," immediately past the bridge. Fortunately, in recent years, the site has been opened to the public, provided that visitors stay on the road and don't make their presence obtrusive. The gate is broken, so the road is easy to access, and could be driven in a 4WD but it is short enough to walk. Follow the dirt road for almost ½ mi., until you get to a clearing ideal for car parking. A narrow path leads into the forest on the left, underneath a hand-painted sign that reads "*heiau.*"

This is an awesome and holy place. Legend has it that this *heiau* was built in one marathon night by a massive human chain that snaked its way inland over the mountain to Wailau Valley. The flat stone surface of the *heiau* rivals a football field in size, over 3000 sq. ft. and almost 22 ft. tall. The surface is remarkably level, and as with many *heiaus*, it is widely believed that Iliiliopae was two or three times its present size when it was in use. Iliiliopae is the second-largest *heiau* in Hawaii and was used as a temple for human sacrifice, as well as a training ground for *kahunas* (priests) from all the islands. It is holy to the Hawaiian people and is a stunning reminder of a mighty civilization that has all but disappeared.

Heiaus are sacred spaces for Hawaiians. Some Native Hawaiians believe that *heiaus* are *kapu* (forbidden) to non-Hawaiians, so treat the temple with respect by not touching any of it. For a more stimulating visit, contact Walter Naki (☎558-8184), who offers *heiau* tours through Molokai Action Adventure, and can bring the ancient legends and uses of the place to life. Walter also does fishpond tours, hunting trips, and is most well-known for his boat trips to Molokai's rugged north shore.

EAST TO HALAWA BAY

From roughly mi. marker 20 onward, the road is basically one lane and has a fair number of cliff-edge hairpin turns. The view is justly earned after braving the ride; sea cliffs, secluded beach coves, and wide-open pastures await. The road is paved and smooth all the way to Halawa Bay, but use caution nonetheless, especially the first time you make the trip. Don't hesitate to honk your horn as a warning when you approach tight corners, and drive very slowly. Be certain that your first time driving beyond mi. marker 20 is not at night; not only is it dangerous, but you'd also miss the view. There is a string of various unnamed and unmarked tiny beaches along this road—if you see a small place to pull off the road and park, chances are there is beach access nearby.

Before reaching Waialua Beach, there are also a few hidden spots in Pukoo. Between mi. markers 15 and 16, look for the "Public Beach Access" sign and follow the road down to the water. The water here is a little murky, but it is shallow for a long time and offers good snorkeling. The adventurous can try their hand at lobster diving. On all Molokai beaches, be extra wary of heavy currents and high surf. It may be best to wait for high tide before attempting to snorkel at any of these beaches—check one of the local newspapers for a tide table.

WAIALUA BEACH. *(Snorkeling. Open daily 24hr.)* Two hundred yards before mi. marker 19, Waialua Beach is a popular place among locals who gather here to sunbathe, snorkel, and socialize. Legend has it that Kamehameha I was raised here solely on taro leaves. The narrow beach, stretching west a couple hundred yards from where Waialua Stream meets the ocean, is a good spot for swimming. In the summer, children jump from Honouli Wai Bridge into the stream to rinse off before heading home. Limited parking is available on the side of the road. To access the beach, enter near the western end of the beach, where the highway runs along the beach. Many other secluded beaches await; you should be able to find a place all to yourself on the east side.

MURPHY'S BEACH (20 MILE BEACH). *(Snorkeling. Open daily 24hr.)* Murphy's Beach is the east shore's most popular swimming and snorkeling spot. The waters are unique: Murphy's Beach is at the eastern end of the 28 mi. barrier reef that extends along the south shore of Molokai. The snorkeling off Murphy's is notable for its ease of entry and the spectacular diversity of fish and local turtle population. The shallow reef connects right to the shore, so be wary of sharp coral when wading in the surf. Plenty of parking is available in the grassy lawn on the south side of the highway beyond mi. marker 20. Like Waialua, Murphy's Beach is distinctly Molokaian: no shower or restroom facilities, but still a fabulous place to relax, enjoy the day, and let what little worries you have drift away into the sand.

POHAKULOA POINT (ROCK POINT). *(Surfing. Open daily 24hr.)* Past Murphy's Beach and around a bend before mi. marker 21 is a rocky area aptly named Rock Point. To access the break, park next to the lone 10 ft. tall boulder on the ocean side of the road. Natives call this the Whispering Rock: if you whisper the right question, the rock will whisper back your answer. The area is one of the island's most popular surf spots, especially in winter, but it can be dangerous. Beginning surfers should look elsewhere, as the steep wave faces and shallow, sharp coral bottom are particularly dangerous. Check with local surfers for the best entry points along the rocky outcropping and arrive before noon when the break frequently becomes blown out by the onshore trades. There is no sandy beach here; however, right at mi. marker 21 is a small strip of sand across from a couple of houses. This unnamed beach has a protected shoreline and makes for decent swimming. Parking is limited here. Half a mile farther down the road is an unnamed cove even better for swimming; it's also larger and sandier with more parking.

PUU O HOKU RANCH. After mi. marker 21, the road winds its way upward into the cattle pastures of the Puu O Hoku Ranch. Around mi. 24, the road levels and widens, and you should be able to see **Moku Hooniki Island.** Originally used for target practice during WWII, it is now protected as a bird sanctuary. This 14,000-

acre ranch contains a certified organic farm which grows papaya, avocado, sugarcane, corn, asparagus, and kava, a plant that has been used as a ceremonial drink in the Pacific for centuries. At mi. marker 25, the main office of the ranch doubles as the **Last Chance Store** (☎558-8109 or 336-0969; www.puuohoku.com. Open daily 9am-4pm. MC/V.), where you can pick up organic snacks and sodas ($1-3) before venturing further down to Halawa Bay.

The ranch also has two delightful vacation **cottages ❹**. The **Sunrise Cottage** is a two-bedroom, two-bath house for six with a kitchen and covered lanai. The **Grove Cottage** is a 2100 sq. ft., four-bedroom, three-bath house for nine with a fireplace, a sunny master bedroom, and spectacular views of Maui. Guests are welcome to take advantage of hiking on ranch trails. (2-night min. 1-2person cottages $140; each additional person $20. Weekly stays $840.)

The ranch also offers horseback riding. Take a 1hr. guided trail-ride ($55) or one of two specialty rides: a half-day beach ride with time to snorkel and swim ($120) and a full-day waterfall ride ($145). Make reservations 24hr. in advance; there are discounts for group rides.

HALAWA VALLEY AND BAY. *(Boogie boarding. Snorkeling. Surfing. Open daily 24hr.)* About ½ mi. past mi. marker 26, a mesmerizing lookout over Halawa Valley has views of Moaula, Hipuapua Falls, and two beach coves below. As you descend into the valley, be mindful of the stone wall on the edge of the highway and drive slowly, especially while passing oncoming traffic.

Thought to be the site of Molokai's first settlement in AD 700, Halawa Bay typifies the primal and untouched essence of Molokai. Although the area had quite a few taro-harvesting residents at one time, tsunamis in 1946 and 1957 left so much salt behind that the farmland became fruitless and all but half a dozen residents moved out. Though camping on the beach is not permitted, the rule is not strictly enforced, and some locals pitch semi-permanent tents on the far side of the beach during summer.

At the bottom of the highway is a small green church, **Jerusalem Hou,** and a little farther on the right is **Halawa Park,** which has a bathroom and an outdoor shower (though the water here is not safe to drink). When the paved road ends, follow the dirt road to a grassy area where you can park. The main beach is accessible by wading across a stream by the parking area, and it is a great place for swimming, snorkeling, boogie boarding, and surfing. Be careful, as the waves break over shallow rocks and it can be difficult to see sharks in the murky water. To the right, a smaller beach, separated from the main beach by a rocky point, is a more sheltered place to sunbathe or swim.

For a place to camp, head down an unmarked driveway on the mountain side between the ruins of a church and Halawa park to **Koko's Halawa Campground ❶.** The campground has showers and a bathroom, but no drinking water. Ask about working in the taro fields in exchange for free camping. (☎553-8033. 2-night min. $25.)

MOAULA AND HIPUAPUA FALLS. Halawa's real attraction, aside from its overall grandeur, is the hike up Halawa Stream to two magnificent waterfalls: **Moaula Falls** and **Hipuapua Falls.** The hike crosses private property and is closed to visitors except as part of a guided tour. Intermittent fighting between local landowners and the state parks department has resulted in a recent increase of local landowner vigilance. Let's Go recommends hiring a tour guide through **Molokai Outdoors** or **Molokai Fish & Dive** (p. 346) to get to these incredible falls, though deals are also available through a less-advertised local service.

Depending on the weather and recent rainfall, the hike to Moaula Falls takes at least 1hr.; you'll need another 30min. to get up to Hipuapua Falls. The total round-trip distance for the hike to both falls is 4½ mi. The hike itself is half the fun, as *heiaus* (temples) are interspersed among the thick tropical vegetation along the trail. The Moaula Falls hike is gentle the whole way, but getting to Hipuapua Falls involves scrambling over river rocks and through some muddy patches—it might be difficult for those unaccustomed to hiking through the woods. Nevertheless, the obstacles are well worth the trouble. The pool below Moaula Falls is wide, deep, and swimmable (though be careful of falling rocks) and the waterfall itself (250 ft. tall) is two-tiered and carries an impressive volume of water down the mountain. Hipuapua Falls (500 ft. tall) is narrower and single-tiered, allowing you to see the top of the falls from the pool at its base as water cascades down the cliff face. The pool below Hipuapua is shallower, but it's still a great place to enjoy the solitude.

LEGENDS OF THE HIDDEN LIZARD. Legend has it that there is a great *moo* lizard sleeping in the pool beneath the Moaula Falls in the Halawa Valley who's quite particular about who can swim in his pool. Visitors are advised to drop a *ti* leaf into the pool before entering. If the leaf floats, the *moo* is accepting. If it sinks, the lizard will not tolerate any disturbance to his lair, and those who enter will drown. Don't anger the *moo*—keep out!

NORTH SHORE SEA CLIFFS AND WAILAU VALLEY

The north shore of Molokai is home to the world's tallest sea cliffs (4000 ft.). The cliffs were formed when the Makanalua Peninsula, a large chunk of the island created by the Kauhako Volcano, sank into the sea after thousands of years of pounding surf eroded its foundation. The stunning masses of rock and earth are spotted with swaths of bright green grass and the occasional herd of mountain goats, grazing high above the ocean's surface. In wet weather, dozens of waterfalls spill over the cliffs into the ocean above a shoreline dotted with hidden coves and sea caves. The north shore sea cliffs are a remote part of an already remote island.

Four major valleys span the 12 mi. of coastline from Halawa to the Kalaupapa Peninsula: from east to west they are Papalaua, Wailau, Pelekunu, and Waikolu. **Papalaua Valley** is the smallest of the four, but home to one of the most impressive waterfalls visible from the sea, **Papalaua Falls.** The cliffs just beyond Papalaua Valley are home to **Kahiwa Falls,** the longest waterfall in the state. This thin stream of water spills down the face of the cliffs from an elevation of 1750 ft., eventually plunging into the sea. You might recognize **Wailau Valley** from Hollywood's *Jurassic Park 3.* It is about an hour boat ride from Halawa Bay and where many locals go to escape the "hustle and bustle" of Kaunakakai. The largest of the north shore valleys, Wailau was once accessible via the dangerous Wailau Trail, which started at Iliiliopae Heiau and climbed over the mountains. Today, the trail is in disrepair, and only passable for those with experience. **Pelekunu and Waikolu Valleys** cover the rest of the north shore all the way to the Kalaupapa Peninsula. They are remote, uninhabited, and completely untouched. Nestled along their coasts are decade-old fishing buoys and debris washed ashore from thousands of miles away. Both can be seen from lookouts in the Kamakou Preserve (p. 334), but they are virtually impossible to visit on foot.

The sea cliffs are only accessible by boat. The ocean below the cliffs can be quite rough, but it is a popular spot for advanced sea kayaking: the current flows swiftly away from Halawa, so kayakers must arrange a boat in advance to retrieve them before they reach the restricted area of Kalaupapa Peninsula. Boat tours of the north shore are an easier way to get a look at Molokai's sea cliffs. **Molokai Action Adventures** (☎558-8184) makes excursions from Halawa two to five times per week for sightseeing, fishing, diving, snorkeling, and whale-watching (in winter). Sightseeing trips sometimes include an hour-long stop in Wailau Valley and are sure to come with plenty of stories. Try calling early in the morning or late at night, and be flexible—the weather can make it hard to pin down an exact date for a tour. The standard north shores boat tour runs 6hr. and costs $125 per person, but prices are negotiable and family rates are offered. **Molokai Fish and Dive** (☎553-5926) also offers sea cliff tours. (Tours Sa 7am-1pm. $150.)

WESTERN MOLOKAI

The beaches on this side of Molokai are by far the best on the island and, given that western Molokai is for the most part uninhabited, you can find at least one to yourself. The Molokai Ranch, established in the 1850s by King Kamehameha V, was once roamed by Molokai's *paniolo* (cowboys) and is still operational today. It owns almost one third of the land in this region and is home to over 7000 cattle. Aside from the small town of Maunaloa and the condo developments around the now-defunct Kaluakoi Hotel, the area is mostly empty pasture land. Dry and dusty, the west gets 12 in. of rain or less each year, and water has to be piped in from the wetter eastern side to support human habitation.

MAUNALOA

To reach Maunaloa (pop. 230), take Hwy. 460 West to mi. marker 17, where it becomes the main road of the town. The **Maunaloa Post Office** is located across from the general store. (☎522-2852. Open M-F 8am-noon and 12:30-4:30pm. **Postal Code:** 96770.) Once there, the only place to stay is the **Molokai Ranch ❺**, 100 Maunaloa Hwy., a 65,000-acre ranch that moonlights as a first-class luxury resort. You can stay in either the ranch's lodge (the first turn on your right as you round the corner into Maunaloa), or the Kaupoa Beach Village (9 mi. from Maunaloa on a pleasant beach down the Hale o Lono harbor road). The lodge has 22 opulent rooms equipped with A/C and footed bathtubs; a fitness center, restaurant, bar, and spectacular pool round out the available facilities. (☎660-2824 or 888-627-8082. Rooms $288-508. AmEx/D/DC/MC/V.) The lodge's **restaurant ❹** is the only place to eat west of Kualapuu. The restaurant features all-you-can-eat Chinese buffet on Sunday nights ($22, ages 5-12 $11, under 5 free), and their own Kapuna Jam (ukulele and slack-key guitar entertainment) starting at 5pm. They have other dinner specials ($10-30) and entertainment throughout the week, including a Friday luau ($31; reservations ☎660-2824) at the Kaupoa Beach Village. (Restaurant and bar open daily 7am-9pm.) The **Kaupoa Beach Village** is an upscale campground populated by 40 "tentalows," solar-powered steel-and-canvas structures on a raised platform, each with two bedrooms, a lanai, and open-air restroom and shower. There are plenty of hammocks scattered around, and snorkel equipment and boogie boards are available to borrow. **Kaupoa Beach House,** the lone building at the campground, serves three meals a day to guests and has electrical outlets and Internet access. (Breakfast 7-8:30am, lunch 11:30am-1pm, dinner 6-8pm. $15/15/31, under 12 free. Open F-Sa nights to the public.) The ranch offers a shuttle service to beach locations; schedule available from the lodge's front desk. (100 Maunaloa Hwy. ☎552-2741 or 888-627-8082; www.molokairanch.com. 2-person rooms $238-288; 2-person tentalows $158-188; each additional person $50 in lodge, in tentalows $25. Discounts available during periods of low occupancy.)

The only reason to visit Maunaloa, a one-block town, is to buy a kite and fly it, watch a movie in the only theater on Molokai, or see the Molokai Ranch. The town's 300-odd residents are almost all employed by either the ranch or the condo developments down the road. The **Big Wind Kite Factory,** 120 Maunaloa

HULA, HULA BABY

The goddess Laka is said to have given birth to the hula in Kaana, on Western Molokai. Originally a religious practice, the dance had eight dancers accompanied by a sharkskin drum called a *pahu.* Both dancers and drummer made regular offerings to Laka. However, after Christian missionaries converted local chiefs in the early 1800s, the hula was deemed heathen and forced underground.

During the late 1800s, King Kalakaua encouraged the teaching and open practice of the hula. A new incarnation, known as hula kui, used an ipu gourd as a drum rather than the pahu, out of respect for the holiness of the older ritual. By the mid-1900s, Hollywood had sensationalized the dance. Tourists were more interested in the sexually suggestive moves of coconut bra-clad dancers than the cultural and religious significance of the hula, and the traditional chant was abandoned in favor of a more catchy accompaniment.

The birth of the hula is celebrated the 3rd weekend in May at Papohaku Beach. The festival is called Ka Hula Piko, and the dancing begins late at night. The dancers are visible at first only as shadows against the stars; as the sky brightens, a traditional chant begins, and the dancers try to match the rise and fall of the waves. Dancing continues with workshops by renowned hula teachers every evening.

Hwy., is well worth the trip to Maunaloa. Hand-painted kites ($28-200) of all colors and styles hang from the walls. Beyond kites, the store connects to the **Plantation Gallery** next door, which offers a delightful array of merchandise ranging from Indonesian jewelry, intricately-carved coconut light covers ($25), and woodworking to one of Molo's most substantial collections of Hawaiiana books, souvenirs, CDs, clothing, and knickknacks. (☎552-2364. Open M-Sa 8:30am-5pm, Su 10am-2pm. AmEx/D/MC/V.)

Molokai Fish and Dive (☎552-0184), at the lodge, runs an activity center renting every kind of equipment and offering activities to hotel guests and the general public for fairly steep prices. Options include various hikes ($50-75), sea kayaking ($90), learn-how-to-lasso-a-steer *paniolo* lessons ($85), mountain biking ($40-70), snorkel gear ($10 for 24hr.), boogie boards ($11 for 24hr.), and surfboards ($25-35 for 24hr.). They also have a location in Kaunakakai (p. 329).

For groceries, try the well-stocked **Maunaloa General Store,** 200 Maunaloa Hwy. (☎552-2346. Open M-Sa 8am-6pm, Su 8am-noon.) **Lucky's Gas and Oil,** behind the general store, is the only gas station east of Kaunakakai. (☎552-2627. Open M-F 7am-1pm, Sa 10am-2pm.) The only movie theater on Molokai, the **Maunaloa Town Cinema** has three screens and shows two main-stream movies on each screen per day. (☎552-2616 or 552-2707. ATM inside. $6.50, ages 3-11 and 62+ $4.)

KALUAKOI

Much of this area is grassland dotted with a few millionaire estates and miles of sandy and secluded beaches. So far, tourism on Molokai has not proven to make further development of Kaluakoi profitable, but developers are hopeful that the planned renovation of the deserted Kaluakoi Hotel will turn things around. In the meantime, there are several condo developments offering vacation rentals. About 1½ mi. before Maunaloa, just before mi. marker 15, a turnoff from the highway on the right leads 4 mi. down Kaluakoi Rd. to several condo developments, as well as most beaches of the west side. Turn right at Kakaako Rd. and then left at Lio Pl. to find **Paniolo Hale ❹**, a beautiful 77-unit condominium complex. Condos are available there or through Friendly Island Realty (☎800-600-4158), Molokai Vacation Rentals (☎800-367-2984), or the directory at the Molokai Visitors Association (p. 325). Most are well-furnished condos that feel like houses, all with full kitchens, living rooms, and some with screened lanais. The grounds include a swimming pool, barbecue grills, and prime beach access. (2-person studio $135; 4-person bedroom $145; 6-person suite $275.)

Across the street from the Kaluakoi Villas, on your right heading down Kepuhi Pl. from Kaluakoi Rd., is **Ke Nani Kai ❸,** another condo complex with slightly smaller rooms. Though set further away from the ocean than others, it's a perfectly nice place to stay. Friendly Island Realty or Molokai Vacation Rentals (see above) have rental information. (Condo manager ☎552-0237. Office open daily 1:30-5pm. 1-bedroom $95 and up; 2-bedroom $110 and up.)

Kaluakoi Villas ❹, on the left just down from Ke Nani Kai, has frequent Internet specials that can save you 20% or more. Try booking through Friendly Island Realty (see above) for discounted prices. (☎552-2721, reservations 545-3510. Studio $145 and up; 1-bedroom with kitchenette $175 and up.) At the end of the road is the abandoned Kalauakoi Hotel, and just past that is Molokai Ranch's 18-hole **Kaluakoi Golf Course.** A more scenic (and pricey) option than Ironwood Hills in Kalae, this course spreads itself dramatically along the Kepuhi and Make Horse beaches. (☎552-0255. Open 7:30am-3pm. 18 holes with cart $75, 18-hole club rental $15, 9-hole afternoon special $35.)

WEST END BEACHES

PAPOHAKU BEACH. *(Open daily 24hr.)* Over 2½ mi. long, Papohaku Beach is the king of West End beaches. It has the most surface area of any beach in Hawaii (up to 60 yd. in width, depending on the time of year and the tide) and has so much sand, in fact, that some of it was sent to Oahu during the mid-1950s to create Waikiki Beach. Papohaku is backed by a number of small dunes, and the wind frequently picks up sand, creating some nasty sand storms that torment unsuspecting sunbathers. The water is not good for snorkeling, but it's perfect for a dip between sunbathing sessions to take refuge from the biting sand. Although you may see the occasional bodysurfer, the water is known for a strong undertow—exercise caution. Do not enter the water near the steeper sections of the beach where gigantic barreling waves break feet from the shore, and do not swim at all in winter.

Papohaku Beach has three main access points from **Kaluakoi Road,** all with outdoor showers and signs reading "Beach Access, Public Right of Way"; however, these signs have the tendency to fall apart and, in some cases, flat-out disappear. From north to south, the first is **Papohaku Beach Park,** which is also the only **campground** on the West End. The site has showers, restrooms, picnic tables, barbecue grills, lots of parking, and is usually uninhabited and peaceful. Camping permits can be purchased at the Department of Parks and Recreation (p. 75).

The second access point, **Lauhue,** has the most pleasing setting. Located about ½ mi. from Papohaku Beach Park, it's surrounded by taller dunes and is one of the wider sections of the beach. It has more beach area than the third access point, **Papapa.** Look for the letters "Papapa Pl." written on a stop sign pole and turn right here. Papapa Beach is the site of **Ka Hula Piko,** a hula festival held the third week of May.

DIXIE MARU BEACH. *(Snorkeling. Open daily 24hr.)* At the southern end of Kaluakoi Rd., turn right when the road comes to a T; the beach is on the right off the cul-de-sac at the end of the road. Dixie Maru is a dazzlingly beautiful, protected cove that is almost circular. The surrounding rocks and vegetation give the place an aura of privacy, and the water is calm and good for swimming and snorkeling. Locals and visitors soak up sun, swim, and picnic in the pleasant setting of the beach. While the surf is inconsistent, there is a dredging left reef point break that is fun in smaller waves. The bay just before Dixie's is a better place to surf on a larger swell. As always, be careful in the Hawaiian ocean—especially in this notoriously current-ridden west end of Molokai.

KEPUHI BEACH. *(Open daily 24hr.)* At the northern end of Papohaku Beach, Kepuhi is accessible by turning off Kaluakoi Rd. on Kakaako Rd. and then left at Lio Pl. to get to Paniolo Hale. Park here and walk through the condo complex and across the golf course. The narrow Kepuhi Beach is the most crowded of all the beaches on the west side because of its proximity to the condos, but it's a fun place to bodysurf and take shelter on a windy afternoon.

MAKE HORSE BEACH. *(Surfing. Open daily 24hr.)* For far better sand and sun, walk down the dirt road. Follow the faded arrow sign that says "beach," at the parking lot just before turning into Paniolo Hale to Make Horse—one of the best beaches in Hawaii. You can also drive down; the road is bumpy but passable, and there is room to park at the bottom. Make Horse spans three crescent-shaped bays of white sand, separated by high rocks that obscure the other bays from sight. If you have too much company at the first bay, try the others to the right. The beach is a favorite local fishing spot and has good surf in the winter, but it's not the place to snorkel. Make (pronounced "mah-kay") means "dead"; the beach earned its name when locals slaughtered horses during the 19th century by running them off the high plateau to the right of the beach. Despite its grisly past, the beach is one of the world's most beautiful and sheltered.

HALE O LONO HARBOR. *(Surfing. Open daily 24hr.)* The only part of the southwest shore that is open to the public, the harbor is accessible via a dirt road beyond the Molokai Ranch Lodge in Maunaloa down Mokio St. Following signs to Kaupoa, you will eventually pass the locked gate to Molokai Ranch's Kaupoa beach on your right (access requires getting the key from the Molokai Lodge front desk). The road swings to the east as it nears the water and there are various access points, both sandy and rocky. The road ends at a quiet beach where there's a picnic table and primitive restrooms. A surf break on the left side of the beach shows its colors during summer south swells.

LANAI

Travelers in search of peaceful serenity, friendly locals, and outdoor adventure should head to Lanai. A quiet, slow-paced paradise, with just one small town and only a few paved roads, Lanai isn't known for touristy Hawaiian glitz and glamour. Though its industry now centers on two secluded luxury resorts, the island was once home to the world's largest pineapple plantation. Its 15,000 acres accounted for over 90% of total US pineapple production, and many of the island's older residents are former field laborers. The community is small and close-knit, and people are genuinely amiable and polite—it is considered common courtesy to wave at all oncoming drivers and pedestrians, especially outside of town. Prices on Lanai are a bit higher than those on other islands, but if an escape the dense tourism of Oahu and Maui is what you seek, you'll get what you pay for here.

Lanai has been under the control of nearby Maui since before recorded history. It is still part of Maui County but with just over 3000 residents, it has too few voters to hold much sway in local politics. Castle & Cooke, a private company, owns

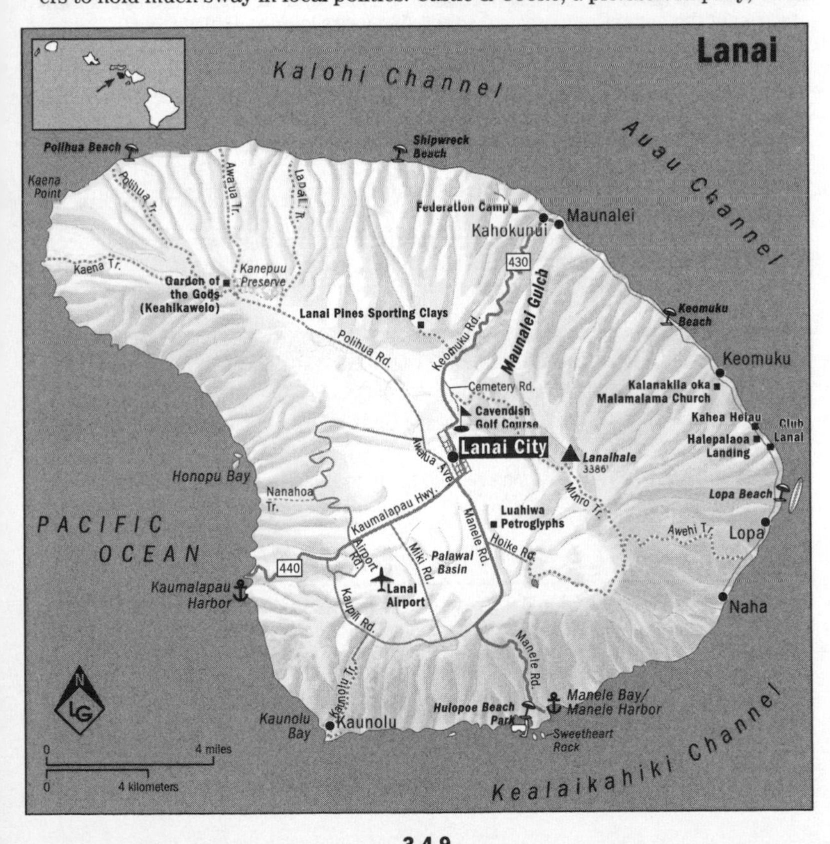

98% of the island, and Castle & Cooke resorts employ 80% of the population. Lanai, however, hasn't always enjoyed such a peaceful and simple existence. For generations, Maui chiefs believed that evil spirits inhabited the island. Prince Kaululaau, the unruly son of King Kakaalaneo, is said to have used trickery to rid Lanai of its spirits during his exile there in 1400. As a reward, Kaululaau was given control of the island and he encouraged immigration from other islands. Life on Lanai remained relatively calm until King Kamehameha came over to take control, slaughtering people on every part of the island. His wrath was so fierce that when Captain George Vancouver sailed past the island in 1792, he didn't bother to land because of Lanai's apparent lack of villages and population.

Deterred by treacherous ocean swells and the lack of natural harbors, travelers to Lanai were scarce until 1861, when a group of Mormon missionaries led by Walter Murray Gibson arrived and began to build a holy city in the Palawai Basin. In 1864, it was discovered that Gibson had been using church funds to acquire land for himself, and he was excommunicated. Unfazed, he befriended King Kalakaua, who eventually appointed him Prime Minister (apparently in order to establish links with the US). As such, Gibson effectively controlled the entire kingdom. After Gibson's death, his daughter and her husband acquired more land to form the Lanai Company, and they tried their hands at cattle ranching. New Zealander George Munro was hired as foreman, and he is credited with planting the tall pine trees that still shade the central portion of the island. In 1917, the Baldwin Brothers bought the Lanai Company and sold it five years later to James Dole.

At Harvard, Dole had studied agriculture and specialized in canning. He built Kamalapau Harbor and Lanai City, and he is also responsible for much of the island's infrastructure. Thanks to his business savvy, the exotic pineapple became a household staple for millions of Americans. By the late 1930s, the Great Depression and the availability of cheap land and labor in Southeast Asia lured Dole overseas, and the Castle & Cooke Company bought out his interest in the island. David Murdoch is the current CEO of Castle & Cooke, and the two resorts on Lanai are his brainchildren.

The hotels have experienced a steady rate of growth in recent years. Most locals doubt that Lanai's character will change and hope that the resorts will continue to provide jobs without jeopardizing the island's quaint charm and hospitality.

HIGHLIGHTS OF LANAI

OFF-ROAD on the rugged Munro Trail and experience untamed Lanai (p. 355).

TRAVEL BACK IN TIME in the Garden of the Gods, with its ancient stone formations and mythical history (p. 356).

COMMUNE WITH NATURE at Manele Bay, home to Lanai's best beach and only official campsite (p. 358).

INTERISLAND TRANSPORTATION

The easiest and least expensive way to reach Lanai is on the **Expeditions Ferry** (☎661-3756 or 800-695-2624), which runs from **Lahaina, Maui** to **Manele Harbor** (45min.; 5 per day 6:45am-5:45pm; one-way $25, children $20) and back (5 per day 8am-6:45pm).

The only other way to get to Lanai is by flying. Schedules change frequently and rates vary by availability, so check with the airline for departure cities, times, and prices. **Island Air** (from the US ☎800-323-3345, from Hawaii 800-652-6541; www.islandair.com) flies from Honolulu (30min., 7 per day, cheapest flight approx. $65 one-way). **Hawaiian Airlines** and **Aloha Airlines** also fly to Lanai City.

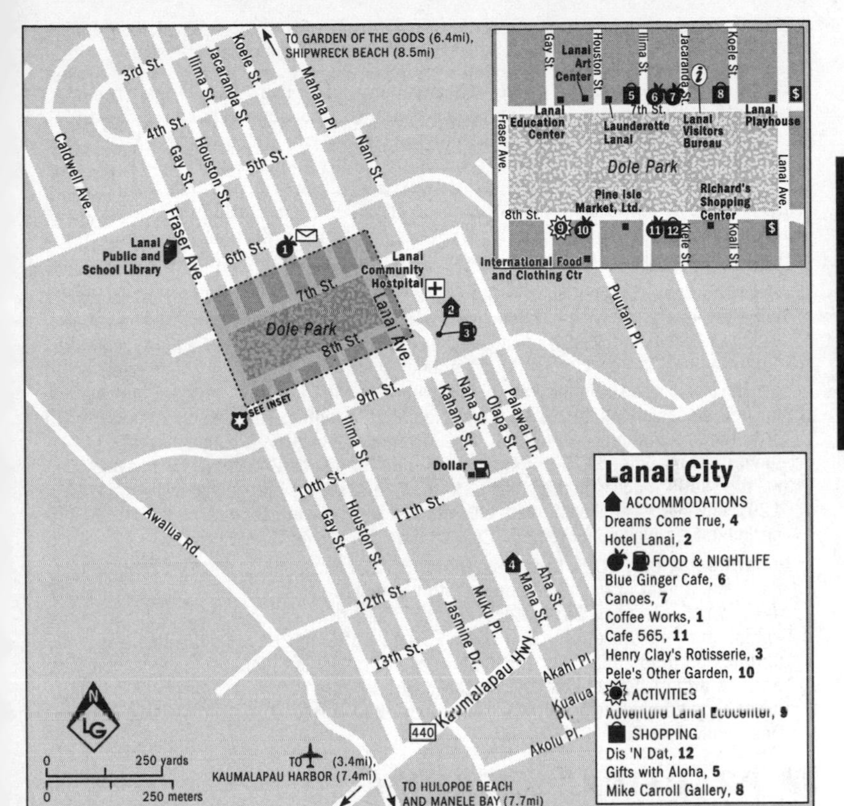

LANAI CITY

Lanai City—less a city than a quaint town—is the social and cultural center of the island, though the distinction is not hard to come by, as it is also the only town on Lanai (pop. 3,164). Built by Jim Dole in 1922 to house plantation workers and their families, Lanai City was the first planned community in Hawaii. Almost all of Lanai's inhabitants live in the brightly painted houses here. At an elevation of nearly 1700 ft., Lanai City is cooler than the beaches below. Visitors won't see a single stoplight or fast-food joint, but they will find a charming community of restaurants, shops, and art galleries.

ORIENTATION

Lanai City surrounds **Dole Park,** a large, rectangular grassy area that runs basically east-west. It is bordered by **7th Street** to the north and **8th Street** to the south. Most of the town's stores and eateries are located along these streets. The boundaries of town are marked roughly by **Fraser Avenue** to the west and **Lanai Avenue** to the east. All streets are at right angles, and those running east-west are numbered 3rd-13th, with 3rd St. the farthest north. Those running north-south start with Fraser in the west and end with Queens in the east.

LOCAL TRANSPORTATION

From the **Lanai Airport,** you'll need to rent a car since there is no local transportation other than hotel shuttles and **Rabaca's Limousine Service.** (☎565-6670. Open 24hr. $10 per person from the airport to town; $15 to Manele Bay. Two-person min. for the trip to town.) The island's dirt roads require 4WD. Lanai is covered in loose red dirt, so get a hard top and close your windows unless you want to end up coated in dust and mud. The only **gas station** on the island is Lanai City Service, on the Dollar property (see below). Gas is pricey, often almost $4 per gallon.

Adventure Lanai Ecocentre, 338 8th St. (☎565-7373; www.adventurelanai.com), is a laid-back operation run by Kayak John, a.k.a. "Mikey," a relaxed and helpful islander with an uncanny knowledge of all Lanai has to offer. The gang at Adventure Lanai rents safari-style 4WD Jeep Wranglers with snorkel gear, towels, and an ice chest for $104 per day. Unlike the competition, they let you take their vehicles anywhere and will tow for free. Reservations are highly recommended. Adventure Lanai also rents every kind of outdoor equipment you can imagine. They run several tours, including ATV adventures ($99 per 2hr., $129 per 4hr.; ask Bubba for a Let's Go discount), a kayak/snorkel trip ($99), a downhill road bike trek ($99), and surfing and scuba diving trips ($99-129). Adventure Lanai also offers bike rentals at the cheapest rates on the island ($25 per day). Free pick-up for renters. Call anytime; tours everyday.

Dollar Rent A Car, 1036 Lanai Ave. (☎565-7227 or 800-533-7808), south of Dole Park, has a fleet of brightly colored Jeep Wranglers ($139 per day) and Jeep Cherokees ($145 per day). Cars, which are restricted to paved roads by both the rental agreement and the terrain, run from $60 to $129 per day. Dollar also has daily updates on road conditions and a shuttle that runs customers to and from the ferry and the airport. Be sure to stay on the proper roads; otherwise, you could pay hundreds to get towed. Reserve well in advance. 21+. Under-25 surcharge $15 per day. Open daily 7am-7pm. AmEx/D/MC/V.

PRACTICAL INFORMATION

Tourist Information: Lanai Visitors Bureau, 431 7th St. Suite A (☎565-7600; www.visitlanai.net), near Canoes, about 20 ft. from 7th St. The staff is very helpful and knowledgeable and carries brochures for popular island activities.

Banks: Bank of Hawaii, 460 8th St. (☎565-6426), **First Hawaiian Bank,** 644 Lanai Ave. (☎565-6969). Both open M-Th 8:30am-4pm, F 8:30am-6pm (Bank of Hawaii is closed daily 1-2pm). Both have 24hr. ATMs.

Laundromat: Launderette Lanai, at 7th St. and Houston St. Wash $1.50, dry $0.25 per 5min. No change machine. Open daily 5am-8:30pm.

Police: Lanai Police Department, 855 Fraser St. (☎565-6428). Office open 7:45am-4:30pm. On duty for emergencies 24hr.

Hospital: Lanai Community Hospital, 628 7th St. (☎565-6411), east of Lanai Ave. Emergency room open 24hr., administrative office open M-F 8am-5pm.

Copy Services: At the Lanai **Education Center** of Maui Community College, at 7th St. and Gay St. Copies $0.05 per page. Open M-F 9am-5pm. Also at the **Lanai Public and School Library,** 555 Fraser Ave. (☎565-7920), for $0.20. Open M-W and F 9am-4:30pm, Th 2-8pm.

Internet Access: The **Education Center** (see above) has 12 computers that are open to the public M 1-5pm and Tu-Th 10am-12pm, 1-5pm (mornings are your best bet). Internet is also available at the **Lanai Public and School Library** (see above) with a 3-month visitor's card ($10); 1hr. time slots begin at the top of each hour.

Post Office: Lanai City Post Office, 620 Jacaranda (☎565-6517), north of Dole Park, right behind the Mike Carroll Art Gallery. Open M-F 9am-4pm, Sa 11:30am-1:30pm.

Postal Code: 96763.

ACCOMMODATIONS AND CAMPING

Lanai is famous for its five-star resorts: **Lodge At Koele** ❺ (☎565-3800 or 800-321-4666), north of town, and its sister resort, the **Four Seasons at Manele Bay** ❺ (☎565-7700). Though a room at either of these illustrious spots ($350-3500) might break the bank, a walk through their grounds is free and worth the time. The gardens at the Lodge at Koele are serene, while the view of Manele Bay from the Four Seasons is breathtaking. For a true island experience, some Lanai residents rent rooms. Gail, of **Pua's Place** (☎565-7088), will rent her two rooms ($50 for one person, slightly more for two) to anyone who gets along with her terrier, Pua.

Hulopoe Beach Park, near Manele Bay. There are 6 official campsites that can accommodate 6 people, each with a grill and access to restrooms. The showers that line the beach have sunlit pipes and warm water. There are often groups of locals in semi-permanent campsites on the beach. If all the campsites are booked (not uncommon on weekends), try to find a local sponsor, which may allow you to camp for free. For any price, Hulopoe Beach is simply gorgeous. $5 registration fee, plus an additional $6 per person per night. For reservations, contact Castle & Cooke (☎565-7700) or call the park ranger (☎565-2345; office open daily 8am-5:30pm). ❶

Dreams Come True, 1168 Lanai Ave. (☎565-6961 or 800-566-6961; www.dreamscometruelanai.com). Each room in this bright, cheery 4-bedroom B&B has a TV and VCR, private marble bath, whirlpool tub, and bathroom skylight. Rooms share access to a full kitchen, laundry room, and backyard garden deck. Singles and doubles $112. Entire house (sleeps 10) $450. AmEx/D/MC/V. ❹

Hotel Lanai, 828 Lanai Ave. (☎565-7211 or 800-795-7211; www.hotellanai.com), next to the hospital, at the top of a semicircle driveway. Fantastic value for the service: the staff is warm and friendly, and 10 welcoming rooms showcase elegant furniture and immaculate bathrooms. Complimentary continental breakfast and shuttle to the beach. Check-in 2pm. Check-out 11am. A 50% deposit is required for reservations and cancellations must be 14 days in advance in order to get a full refund. 1-3 person rooms $105-135; private cottage $175. AmEx/MC/V. ❸

FOOD

The hotel restaurants on Lanai are all exorbitantly priced with the exception of **Henry Clay's Rotisserie** ❺, at Hotel Lanai, which serves superb Cajun-fusion cuisine with prices that are within reach of a budget traveler's splurge. (Appetizers $7-15; entrees $19-33. Open daily 5:30-8:45pm.) On Saturday morning, there's a **swap meet** in Dole Park where locals serve homemade ethnic dishes and socialize.

GROCERY STORES AND MARKETS

Pine Isle Market, Ltd., 356 8th St. (☎565-6488). Equal parts grocery store, hardware store, and drug store, Pine Isle is the closest thing to a supermarket on Lanai. It has a deli counter with fresh meat and fish and also carries beer and wine. Open M-Sa 8am-noon and 1:30-7pm.

Richard's Shopping Center, 434 8th St. (☎565-6488). Another grocery/hardware store combo, with a decent selection of produce. Sells ice, coolers, and the requisite beer, wine, and liquor. Open M-Th 8:30-noon and 1:30-6:30pm, F-Sa 8:30am-6:30pm.

International Food and Clothing Center, on Ilima St behind Pine Isle Market. This small store has only five aisles, but it fills basic food and hardware needs. With a nice wine and liquor selection, it offers generally lower prices and a key duplication service. Open M-Tu 9am-7pm, W-F 9am-9pm, Su 8am-4pm.

RESTAURANTS

Canoes, 419 7th St. (☎565-6537). Open for breakfast and lunch, Canoes is a popular gathering place for locals in the morning. Burgers and sandwiches $2-6. Plate lunches $6-8.50. Open M-Tu and Th-Su 6:30am-1pm. Cash only. ❶

Coffee Works, 604 Ilima St. (☎565-6962; www.coffeeworkshawaii.com), north of Dole Park, serves the best coffee in town, according to locals. They ship coffee across the country, but you can enjoy yours on the large deck out front. The house special espresso milkshake ($4.50-6) is worth every penny. Ice cream, pizza bagels, sandwiches, cinnamon buns, and other fare $2-6. Open M-Sa 6am-4pm, Su 6am-noon. AmEx/MC/V. ❶

Cafe 565, 408 8th St. (☎565-6622). Known mainly for giant calzones ($10-12), filled with beef, chicken, or vegetables. They also sell pizza ($2 per slice; $12.95 by the pie), sandwiches ($7-10), salads ($5-9), and entrees, including a popular Korean chicken dish. Lunch M-Sa 10am-3pm, dinner M-F 5-8pm. Cash only. ❷

Pele's Other Garden, 811 Houston St. (☎565-9628), on the corner of 8th St. By day, Pele's is a New York deli-style eatery that serves decent sandwiches ($6-8). By night, the staff changes the lighting, tablecloths, music, and menu to create an Italian bistro catering mainly to the resorts. The bruschetta ($6.25) is delicious. Pasta dishes ($17-20) are satisfying but pricey. Dinner reservations recommended. Open M-F 10am-2:30pm for lunch, M-Sa 5-8pm for dinner. AmEx/D/MC/V. ❸

Blue Ginger Cafe, 409 7th St. (☎565-6363). Blue Ginger is Lanai's all-purpose eatery and a good place to grab a cheap dinner. 2 eggs, choice of meat, rice, and toast $5; bigger portions $8. Plate lunches $6-9. Dinner specials $13-15. Known for its fresh fish, usually *ono* or mahi mahi. Variety of daily specials; Mexican food on Tu. Open M-Th and Su 6am-8pm, F-Sa 6am-9pm. Cash only. ❷

ENTERTAINMENT AND ACTIVITIES

There isn't much to do on Lanai after dark other than see a first-run movie at the **Lanai Playhouse,** 465 7th Ave. (☎565-7500. $8, ages 3-12 and seniors $5, under 3 free.) This one screen theater shows one movie twice a night (except W and Th). The only bar in town is at **Henry Clay's Rotisserie** (p. 353) in Hotel Lanai (beer $2.75-4.50, mixed drinks about $6). An agreeable way to spend the evening is to wander the streets just before sunset, when locals tend their gardens and children play in the streets.

For daytime excitement, head north of town on Keomuku Rd. toward Shipwreck Beach, and turn left after 1½ mi. at the **Lanai Pine Sporting Clays** sign, where you can blast compressed fertilizer discs with a 12-gauge shotgun on a gorgeous sporting clay range. Dollar Rent A Car provides a voucher for 10 free shots, and it's worth taking advantage of the offer if you have time. (☎559-4600; www.islandoflanai.com. Reservations highly recommended. $85 for 50 clays and $145 for 100. Open daily 9am-4:30pm.) If shooting clay discs isn't your bag, try archery ($45 for a 45min. introductory session, $35 for experienced shooters). If you're a sharpshooter, or you're just feeling lucky, ask about the Pineapple Challenge.

To play the nine-hole, par-36 **Cavendish Golf Course** (on Keomuku Rd., north of town), a public course on the grounds of the Lodge at Koele, simply show up and tee off. ($5-10 donations appreciated in the box by the first tee.)

SHOPPING

The calm pace of life in Lanai City provides an inspiring and creative forum for the arts on the island. The few art galleries and shops that have recently opened around Dole Park allow visitors to peruse the work of local artists and craftsmen.

Mike Carroll Gallery, 443 7th St. (☎565-7122; www.mikecarrollgallery.com), next to the Lanai Playhouse. This cozy gallery, which also serves as the artist's studio, features island-inspired paintings, photography, prints, and cards created by local artists and complemented by the Chinese furniture on display. While original works sell for $500-2500, decent-sized prints are reasonable ($18-75). Shipping available. Open Tu-Sa 10am-5:30pm, or by appointment.

Lanai Art Center, 333 7th St. (☎565-7503), near Houston St. Artists of all ages take lessons, exhibit work, and sell art at this community art center. Postcards $1.50-5. Paintings, photos, and prints $15-35. Shipping available. Open M-Sa noon-4pm.

Dis N' Dat, 418 8th St. (☎565-9170; www.suzieo.com). A charming shop with hundreds of wind chimes ($19-250) and an eclectic mix of bric-a-brac, including "slippah" jewelry (miniature flip flops that hang from necklaces and earrings, designed by the store's owner, Suzie) and reproductions of Tiffany stained glass lamps. Features local artists' work and a variety of exotic antiques. Open M-Sa 10:15am-5:30pm.

Gifts with Aloha, 363 7th St. (☎565-6589; www.giftswithaloha.com). Local artwork, handcrafted jewelry, and aloha-inspired clothing and keepsakes. Shop owners Kim and Phoenix Dupree claim that this is the only store on the island that sells musical instruments—ask them to serenade you with one of their ukuleles! Shipping services available. Open M-Sa 9:30am-6pm.

THE MUSIC OF THE UKULELE

Along with surfing and hula, a prominent symbol of Hawaiian culture is the ukulele. This musical instrument, which is often described as a miniature guitar, was first brought to the islands by the Portuguese explorers. The name ukulele comes from *uku* (head lice) and *lele* (jumping). When the native Hawaiians saw how the fingers of the Portuguese sailors jumped rapidly all over the fretboard when they played, the only word they could use to describe the enchanting instrument was ukulele.

The ukulele has only four strings: G, C, E, and A. Unlike the guitar, the strings are strummed over a fretboard, rather than over an open soundboard. There are soprano and tenor ukuleles, as well as a larger baritone ukulele, which is the easiest for guitar players to learn. Hawaiian music is very similar to reggae, and emphasis is placed on the offbeats; "Jawaiian" is a term used to describe the blend of Jamaican and Hawaiian rhythyms and styles. To absorb as much of the Hawaiian culture during your travels as possible, try listening to the famous ukulele stylings of artists such as Troy Fernandez, Raiatea, or the famous Israel "Iz" Kamakawioole, who is known best for his haunting version of "Over the Rainbow."

SIGHTS

CENTRAL LANAI

MUNRO TRAIL. If you only have time for one off-road trek while you're on Lanai, this is the ideal island drive. The Munro Trail is named for the New Zealand naturalist who planted Lanai's magnificent pines. Much of the trail provides. excellent views of Maui, Molokai, Kahoolawe, the Big Island, and Oahu, as well as the former pineapple fields of Lanai far below.

OFF-ROADING OFF CHANCES. Many of the best sights on Lanai are accessible only by driving over rough, unpaved terrain. 4WD vehicles are best suited to this activity, and even then, getting stuck in sand or mud is possible. Cell phone coverage is spotty at best, so pack some food and water before you go, and be prepared to wait for rescue if your excursion gets mired.

Be certain to stay on the main road. Side roads are often very muddy because they only exist for water drainage purposes; it should be clear which is the most-traveled road. Two miles from the start of the trail, there's a turn-off to the left that leads visitors to a lookout over the gigantic Maunalei Gulch, the island's original source of drinking water. The main road bears right, and it takes you as close as you can get to **Lanaihale,** Lanai's highest point (3368 ft.). After another mile or two, past the communications tower on the left, the road affords a great view of Hookio Gulch, the site of the Lanaian warriors' defeat by King Kamehameha.

At the end of the trail, an exit sign points to the left. Continue down the road and then veer right at the first major fork (if you reach a large orange pipe with a small wooden shed, then you've gone too far). Follow the steep road until it ends, then turn left and proceed until reaching Manele Rd. Turn right to return to Lanai City. *(To reach the trail from town, take Lanai Ave. toward the Lodge at Koele. Past the Lodge, take Keomoku Rd. toward Shipwreck Beach, and then take a right onto Cemetery Rd. With the cemetery on your right, veer left after the pavement ends and look for a sign that marks the trailhead. The trail is about 8½ mi. long with a 1600 ft. elevation change and can take anywhere from 1¼-3hr. to complete with 4WD, depending on road conditions. Also expect to spend about 30min. making your way from the end of the trail back to the highway. The trail is also good for hiking (4-8hr.) or mountain biking.)*

Munro Trail is in generally good condition, but it can only be navigated with 4WD. Be absolutely certain not to attempt the trail if it has rained in the last 24hr., and watch out for mud puddles and boulders that have fallen onto the trail. There are several places where an inopportune skid could send your vehicle over the edge of the road and into a deep ravine. Check with a car rental agency for an update on the conditions. Drive slowly and use 1st gear.

THE NORTH SIDE

GARDEN OF THE GODS (KEAHIKAWELO). Keahikawelo, or Garden of the Gods, is a vast, desert-like expanse of red earth marked by thousands of rock towers. The winding topography of the wind-swept terrain is both surreal and awe-inspiring. The towers are concentrated at the beginning of the garden, but to fully appreciate the splendor of the place, drive all the way through. Late afternoon is the best time to visit the garden, when the towers cast long shadows and the warm tones of the setting sun complement the colors of the landscape.

Some claim that Hawaiians believed that the rock towers were created by the gods and that locals followed suit with their own man-made versions. However, the larger towers were actually created by natural forces, and it was tourists who built structures to imitate them. Hawaiian legend has it that Kawelo, a young sorcerer, challenged his master on Molokai to a contest. Each had to build a bonfire, and the person whose bonfire lasted the longest would have their island blessed with prosperity. Kawelo, it is said, burnt everything in sight, leaving the beautiful, though dry, terrain seen today in the Garden of the Gods. *(The*

Garden is approximately 25min. from town, ½ mi. beyond the Kanepuu Preserve (see directions below). The drive requires 4WD, but the road is usually in decent condition if it hasn't been raining. There are a few places where you might tip your vehicle if careless, but the drive is less challenging than most others on the island. Brave drivers can continue on to the gorgeous Polihua Beach, but road conditions are sometimes very unfavorable.)

KANEPUU PRESERVE. A road leading over three sets of cattle grates enters the silvery ironwood and pine forest at the beginning of the 460-acre preserve. After a mile on the road, you'll see a sign for a self-guided trail on the right. The walk takes about 15min., and plaques along the path provide information on the rare vegetation in the preserve. Some 48 native species can be found in the largest **native Hawaiian dry forest** on the island, including endangered Lanai sandalwood and rare Hawaiian gardenia. *(Take Lanai Ave., which turns into Keomuku Rd., north toward the Lodge at Koele. Just past the Lodge, turn left onto the dirt road between the tennis courts and the stables. Past the stables, turn right at the intersection.)*

SHIPWRECK BEACH. Enjoy the simple beauty of the drive to Shipwreck Beach—short dune grass flows along Keomuku Rd. and around hills, winding to the blue Pacific. The narrow road offers arresting views of both Molokai and Maui as well as the forsaken, rusting hulls of two large ships that give the four-mile stretch of white-sand beach its name. This part of the island gets less than a dozen inches of rain per year, and the vegetation is just sparse enough that the burnt red dirt unveils itself, creating a rough-hewn patchwork of contrasting colors.

The first sight along the dirt road is **Federation Camp,** about 1½ mi. from Keomuku Rd. The deserted fishing shacks were built as vacation homes in the early 20th century by the island's pineapple plantation workers. A few minutes beyond the houses is a turnaround area with picnic tables. Park here and continue walking along the road over bumpy rocks for about 50 yd. On the left you will see a small straw house and patio tucked into a cove of bushes. Continue towards your right where you will find the cement foundation that once supported a lighthouse. Walk down the small ramp of the lighthouse foundation and continue away from the sea and slightly to the right for about 200 yd. (toward a boulder that warns "Do Not Deface"). Climb down the rocks to the right of this boulder to reach well-preserved petroglyphs. Look carefully on the undersides of the large rocks to see these ancient drawings of warriors and animals, believed to date back to AD 500-900. To reach **Shipwreck Beach** from the petroglyphs, backtrack and walk down from the lighthouse.

Once on the beach, walk along the coast toward the shipwreck, which becomes visible almost immediately, though you'll have to walk over rocks for about 10min. to reach it. As you continue, keep your eyes peeled for dozens of piles of sand next to holes in the ground; the holes are crab homes. Sea turtles have also been known to lay eggs on this beach at night. After about 20min. of walking, you'll reach the closest point to Liberty Ship, a WWII-era frigate that became stuck on the reef due to navigational error. There are nearly a half-dozen other shipwrecks along the beach. Most wrecks are no longer visible, except the one at Awula, six miles beyond the Liberty Ship and accessible via a dirt road beyond the Garden of the Gods. *(Take Keomoku Rd., the highway north of town, until it ends. Turn left onto a dirt road at the end of the highway. Be careful not to drive into any of the large ruts in the road. The road is usually passable, but do not attempt it with 2WD or in the rain. Under no circumstances should you drive on the beach itself—doing so is illegal and you may get stuck.)*

KEOMUKU BEACH AND ENVIRONS. From the end of Keomuku Rd., the beach road heads southeast to Halepalaoa Landing. The ocean next to the road is shal-

ROMPING AROUND LANAI

All-terrain vehicles (ATVs) are four-wheeled, gas-powered bikes that can go just about anywhere. If you want to romp around the hills and across the beaches of Lanai, talk to the folks at Adventure Lanai Ecocentre. They offer two- and four-hour ATV trips and will take you anywhere you want to go. If you want to drive, they'll teach you, or you can cruise on the back of your guide's ATV.

One adventure goes through the basin and down the whole length of the Awehi Trail, a beautiful and bumpy steep downhill ride with amazing views of the Maunalei Gulch, a valley carved by lava and eroded by the ocean. A gorgeous 2hr. trek traverses the entire Munro trail, ideal for anyone who prefers cool, high elevations and the shade of trees. Another trail goes through the Garden of the Gods to the remarkable Polihua Beach, an awesome chance to see a long, wide, pure beach without sinking your car into it. Be careful not to run over any turtles lying on the beach; they can look quite log-like from a distance.

To book a tour, contact Adventure Lanai Ecocentre (☎565-7373; www.adventurelanai.com). 2hr. tours $99, 4hr. tours $129; if you're an experienced rider, ask about getting one for the whole day. Ask for "Bubba" for a Let's Go discount.

low, rocky, and rife with marine life. Until 1900, this was the most densely populated part of Lanai; now it's empty, save the occasional fisherman or campsite. After about five miles you will reach Keomuku Village, a former sugar plantation. The only noteworthy sight is **Kalanakila oka Malamalama,** an abandoned wooden church built after the collapse of the island's sugar industry. About a mile out from the village, a walking trail on the right leads inland to **Kahea Heiau,** a temple once the site of human sacrifices, which was partially dismantled by the Maunalei Company to build a railroad. The railroad moved sugar to the **Halepalaoa Landing,** south of the *heiau* (temple). A few minutes past the landing is the abandoned **Club Lanai,** whose run-down gazebos and broken fountain conceal a secluded beach with views of Molokai and Maui.

Lopa Beach, a good surfing beach, lies another five miles down the road. Naha, over 12 mi. from the end of the highway, is the site of an ancient fishpond and probably not worth the trek, though Maui residents sometimes charter boats that drop them at the beach there for the day. *(To get to Keomuku Beach from the end of the highway (Keomuku Rd.), go straight on the dirt road at first and then veer right. The village is about 5½ mi. down. The road is very bumpy and impossible to navigate in poor weather. Do not drive along the beach—you might get stuck. Check with your rental agency to see if the road has been re-graded before heading out.)*

THE SOUTH SIDE

MANELE BAY AND HULOPOE BEACH PARK. Dominated by the luxurious Manele Bay Hotel, Manele Bay is home to Lanai's most popular beach, only official campground, and a small harbor where you can catch the ferry to Maui (see **Interisland Transportation,** p. 350). From town, take Manele Rd. south. As the road straightens out, you'll be driving through the caldera of an extinct volcano. This tree-lined **Palawai Basin** was once the center of the Dole Plantation.

At the very end of the highway, after a series of sloping switchbacks down to the shore, the road forks. To the left is Manele Harbor, the ferry landing and the island's principal port until the construction of the commercial harbor at Kaumalapau. To the right is Hulopoe Beach Park, the island's best beach for swimming and snorkeling. Although the surf is nothing remarkable in the summer, the beach gets much busier in the winter (but the sandy white expanse is large enough that it won't seem crowded). Both the beach and the harbor are part of a conservation district that prohibits boat fishing and the removal of any objects, including rocks. Hulopoe also has the island's only campsite, with picnic tables, grills, showers, and restrooms (p. 353).

From the beach, you can walk uphill and to the left along the bay. At low tide, take the steps on your right down to the vibrant tide pools. Continue along the bay to reach Puu Pehe Rock, also known as **Sweetheart Rock.** According to Hawaiian legend, a local fisherman decided to build his home in a cave to prevent other men from laying eyes on his beautiful wife, Pehe. One day, a sudden storm swept his home into the sea, taking his wife with it. Her family recovered the body and brought it back to town. Late that night, the fisherman stole her body and, with the help of the gods, scaled the 150-ft. rock tower and buried her on top. Overcome with grief, he jumped off the rock to his death. The tomb structure is visible on top of the tower and is called *Kupapau Puupehe* (tomb of Puu Pehe). This southeastern lookout is a romantic spot to watch the morning sunrise or to glimpse nearby Maui.

While at Hulopoe Beach, you can stroll around the grounds of the Manele Bay Hotel. If you face the water and stand toward the back of the beach, you'll see a path a few feet wide off to the right that takes you up to the resort. At night this path is illuminated with tiki torches. You'll pass the luau grounds on your right and arrive at Manele Bay's pool area. The facilities are only for the use of registered guests, but the view of the beach from the hotel is worth the quick walk. If you prefer not to visit the resort, follow the path that starts on the resort end of the beach. The path starts out on the sand, guided by a line of rocks and supplemented by plaques with historical information. If you cross the low point of the path and climb up and slightly toward the right, you'll see a sign for the "Lanai Fisherman's Trail," which crosses in front of the resort. The views from the trail are exceptional.

LUAHIWA PETROGLYPHS. Lanai's largest collection of petroglyphs is scattered throughout a four-acre area. The ancient etchings of bird heads, dogs, circle patterns, and people on horseback are still visible centuries after their initial inscription, though some are quite weathered. Be careful as you scramble around the hill; the footing can be tricky. And refrain from taking rubbings of the petroglyphs, since doing so damages them. You don't need 4WD to get here, but you do need lots of clearance off the ground—a regular car won't cut it. At the time of publication, the access road was under construction; it is advisable to check the road's status before heading out. *(From town, take Manele Rd. toward Manele Bay. After mi. marker 7, look for a pumphouse with a red roof and 3 small trees next to it and turn left. 1 mi. down the broken asphalt road, make a sharp left at a fence post where the road rises. Continue ½ mi. along this road until you see a large pipe in the ground. Cross over the pipe and onto the high road. Follow both the road and the pipe about ¼ mi. to a turnaround. The petroglyphs are on the right.)*

KAUMALAPAU HARBOR. Though there isn't much here, you'll probably make the quick trip to Kaumalapau Harbor simply because it's connected to town by a paved road. The drive itself is worth the trip, with remarkable views of the Pacific Ocean and the western slopes of the island. At one time, over a million pineapples a day were sent to canning plants on Oahu via the harbor, but today it's the drab commercial facility of an oil company. It's also the landing site for the weekly barge that supplies Lanai with goods such as cars, furniture, industrial equipment, and wholesale products retailed at grocery and hardware stores. Since coming under the control of Homeland Security, the harbor is under renovation and soon will be able to receive two large shipments every week. The area is rarely populated after 5pm, and the stone wall next to the road is a great place to watch the sunset.

KAUAI

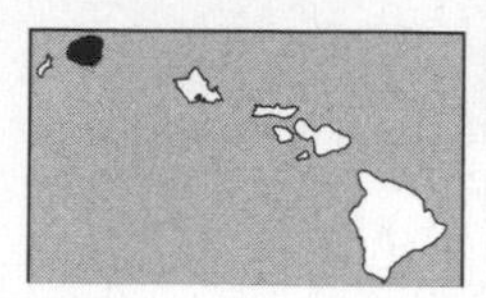

Hawaiian spirit burns brightly in the island's 65,000 residents—locals are fiercely proud of their heritage and Kauai's lack of commercial development (law prohibits any buildings taller than a palm tree). The oldest and northernmost major island, Kauai is at the lonely end of the chain, next to only Niiahu and the tiny Northwest islands. Aptly nicknamed "The Garden Isle," Kauai's plentiful rains nurse the verdant land and support local agriculture, including coffee, sugar, and taro root. Kauai's rainforest jungle is best described as primordial (*Jurassic Park* was filmed here), and markers of the island's six million years of weathering are visible in its impressive landscape. The cliffs of the Na Pali Coast and the jagged Waimea Canyon were carved by millennia of rainfall, and Waialeale Mountain is the wettest spot on earth, receiving over 450 in. of rain per year. Kauai's miles of sandy shoreline testify to the land's relative age, and the beaches are among the most beautiful and raw in the state.

Kauai's tranquil isolation, untamed landscape, and opportunities to commune with nature once lured hippies from the mainland. Today, Kauai still draws a more rugged and independent traveler than Maui or Oahu. Many visitors who come here blaze their own paths through the "real Hawaii" of the Na Pali Coast and its spectacular Kalalau Trail. Whether you want to lose yourself on the island's trails, bask on its beaches, or steep in the infectious and irresistible aloha spirit, opportunities for exploration are endless.

HIGHLIGHTS OF KAUAI

EXHALE INTO the shimmering sand of remote Polihale Beach (p. 421) as you watch the fiery sunset paint the sky with a vibrant palette.

SWIM WITH SEA TURTLES at PKs, one of many beautiful beaches by Poipu (p. 400).

SCALE DOWN into the Waimea Canyon (p. 414), the "Grand Canyon of Kauai."

TAME the Kalalau Trail, the hard-core hiker's mecca on the Na Pali Coast (p. 392).

INTERISLAND TRANSPORTATION

All commercial flights fly into **Lihue Airport (LIH).** Direct flights to Kauai from the mainland are rare—most passengers connect in Honolulu. However, **American Airlines** (☎800-433-7300; www.aa.com) has daily nonstop service to Kauai from Los Angeles, and **United Airlines** (☎800-241-6522; www.united.com) flies direct daily from Los Angeles and San Francisco. For island-hopping, **Aloha Airlines** (☎800-367-5250; www.alohaairlines.com) flies to: Honolulu, Oahu; Kahului, Maui; and Kailua-Kona, the Big Island. **Hawaiian Airlines** (☎800-367-5320; www.hawaiianair.com) flies to: Honolulu, Oahu; Hilo, the Big Island; and Kahului, Maui. Flights to Kauai begin around $180 round-trip. Schedules and prices change frequently; be sure to check online or call for the most current information.

EAST SHORE

Anchored by Lihue, the county seat, the East Shore is Kauai's center of government and commerce. Most of the island's population is concentrated up and down the East Shore, and a multitude of restaurants and shopping centers cater

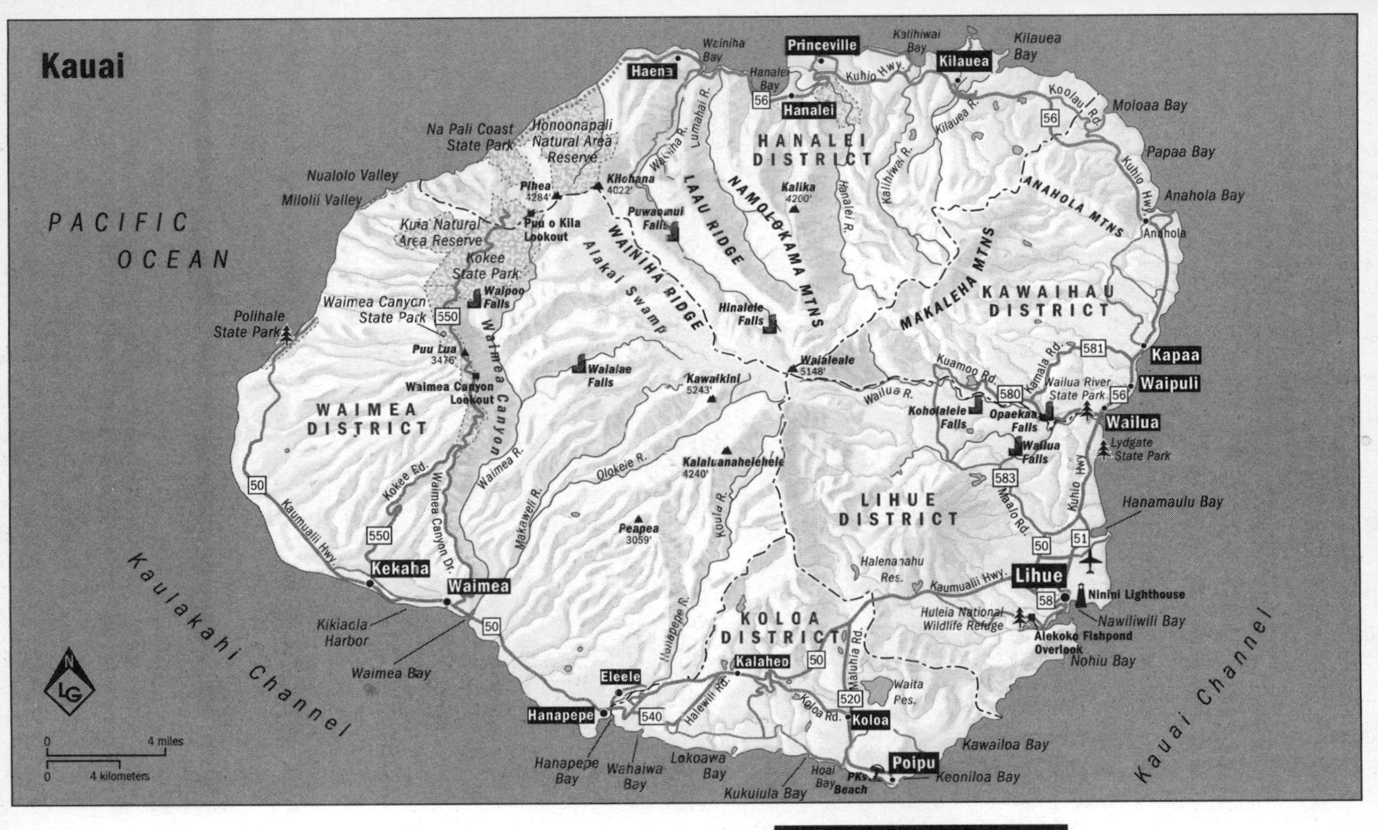
Kauai
PACIFIC OCEAN
Kaulakahi Channel
Kauai Channel
HANALEI DISTRICT
KAWAIHAU DISTRICT
LIHUE DISTRICT
KOLOA DISTRICT
WAIMEA DISTRICT
ANAHOLA MTNS
MAKALEHA MTNS
NAMOLOKAMA MTNS
LAAU RIDGE
WAINIHA RIDGE
Alakai Swamp
Waimea Canyon
Haena
Wainiha Bay
Princeville
Hanalei Bay
Hanalei
Kalihiwai Bay
Kilauea
Kilauea Bay
Moloaa Bay
Papaa Bay
Anahola Bay
Anahola
Kapaa
Waipuli
Wailua
Lydgate State Park
Wailua River State Park
Hanamaulu Bay
Lihue
Ninini Lighthouse
Nawiliwili Bay
Alekoko Fishpond Overlook
Nohiu Bay
Huleia National Wildlife Refuge
Halenanahu Res.
Waita Res.
Koloa
Poipu
Kawailoa Bay
Keoniloa Bay
PKs. Beach
Hoai Bay
Kukuiula Bay
Kalaheo
Lokoawa Bay
Wahaiwa Bay
Eleele
Hanapepe
Hanapepe Bay
Waimea
Waimea Bay
Kikiaola Harbor
Kekaha
Polihale State Park
Waimea Canyon State Park
Nualolo Valley
Milolii Valley
Na Pali Coast State Park
Honoonapali Natural Area Reserve
Kuia Natural Area Reserve
Kokee State Park
Pihea 1284'
Kilohana 4022'
Puu o Kila Lookout
Waipoo Falls
Puu Lua 3476'
Waimea Canyon Lookout
Waialae Falls
Hinalele Falls
Kalika 4200'
Waialeale 5148'
Kawaikini 5243'
Peapea 3059'
Kohalalele Falls
Opaekaa Falls
Wailua Falls
Kuhio Hwy.
Koolau Rd.
Kuamoo Rd.
Kamala Rd.
Maalo Rd.
Kaumualii Hwy.
Maluhia Rd.
Koloa Rd.
Halewili Rd.
Kokee Rd.
Waimea Canyon Dr.
Wainiha R.
Lumahai R.
Hanalei R.
Kalihiwai R.
Kilauea R.
Wailua R.
Waimea R.
Makaweli R.
Olokele R.
Koula R.
Hanapepe R.
56
581
580
583
51
50
58
520
540
550
0 4 miles
0 4 kilometers
N
LG

KAUAI

to tourists and visitors. Drop your bags and buy your groceries here, but seek beauty and adventure elsewhere. The area north of Lihue, also known as the Coconut Coast, provides an easily accessible sample of many of Kauai's attractions, from *heiaus* (temples) to boat rides on the Wailua River.

LIHUE

Welcome to the big city. Expect shopping, good food, and relatively inexpensive housing in Lihue (pop. 5,674); posh resorts and popular sights are found elsewhere on the island. Though plenty of tourists come to Lihue for its historical sights and decent beach, few stay the night. However, for travelers on a budget, Lihue's affordable hotels and central location shine up an otherwise lackluster town. Lihue restaurants usually serve local food in large portions at a low price.

TRANSPORTATION

Flights: Lihue Airport, 3901 Mokulele Loop (☎246-1400), 2 mi. east of town. See Interisland Transportation, p. 360.

Bus: The Kauai Bus (☎241-6410) runs 6 bus routes M-Sa around the island, offering affordable, but infrequent (every 30min.-4hr. depending on route and day of the week) and often inconvenient transportation. **Rte. 700** runs M-F within Lihue. **Rte. 100** has a stop at the Lihue Airport. The other main routes stop at every town as they run across the south shore to Kekaha and up and across the North Shore to Hanalei. Carry-ons are limited to 10x17x30in., and oversized backpacks, suitcases, and surfboards are prohibited—this rule is generally not enforced, especially if the item will fit on your lap. Bikes are permitted in the bike rack at front. In addition to the regularly scheduled stops, riders can request on-call pick-up at a number of locations. Schedules are available at the Kauai Visitors Bureau and most of the larger stores in town (Lihue Big Save and Wal-Mart) or at www.kauai.gov/OCA/Transportation. $1.50, seniors and ages 7-18 $0.75, 6 and under free; monthly pass $15, available for purchase from the County of Kauai Transportation Agency at 3220 Hoolako St. Bus runs M-F 5:15am-7:15pm, Sa 7:15am-3:15pm.

Taxis: Cabs charge $2 initially, and $3 for each additional mi. Most companies add $0.50 per bag and $5 per surfboard and can provide vans upon request. The following companies service the entire island: **Akiko's Taxi** (☎822-7588), **City Cab** (☎245-3227), **North Shore Cab** (☎828-6189), and **South Shore Cab** (☎742-1525).

Car Rental: Rent-a-Wreck, 3501 Rice St., Ste. 112A (☎632-0741), the turquoise building across the street from Nawiliwili Bay, in Harbor Mall, rents inexpensive used cars and a few new rentals. Rates vary with the age of the car and the length of the rental, but start around $25 per day; discounts may be negotiated with the friendly management. Must provide proof of personal car insurance. Open daily 8am-11pm. In addition, **Alamo** (☎246-0645 or 800-327-9633), **Avis** (☎245-3512 or 800-831-8000), **Budget** (☎245-9031 or 800-527-7000), **Dollar** (☎866-434-2226 or 800-800-4000), **Hertz** (☎245-3356 or 800-654-3131), **National** (☎245-5636 or 800-227-7368), and **Thrifty** (☎246-6252 or 800-847-4389), all at the airport, charge similarly higher rates. Package deals and AAA membership can usually swing a discount.

ORIENTATION

There are two main streets in Lihue: **Rice Street** runs through downtown and **Nawiliwili Road** meanders near the coast. Most of the cheaper accommodations are downtown, while luxurious hotels and Kalapaki Beach line the waterfront. From the beach, Nawiliwili Rd. heads north to Kauai's largest shopping center, **Kukui Grove,** and ends at its intersection with **Highway 50,** which leaves Lihue southwest for Koloa and Poipu. **Highway 56 (Kuhio Highway)** leaves town from the north on the way to Wailua and Kapaa.

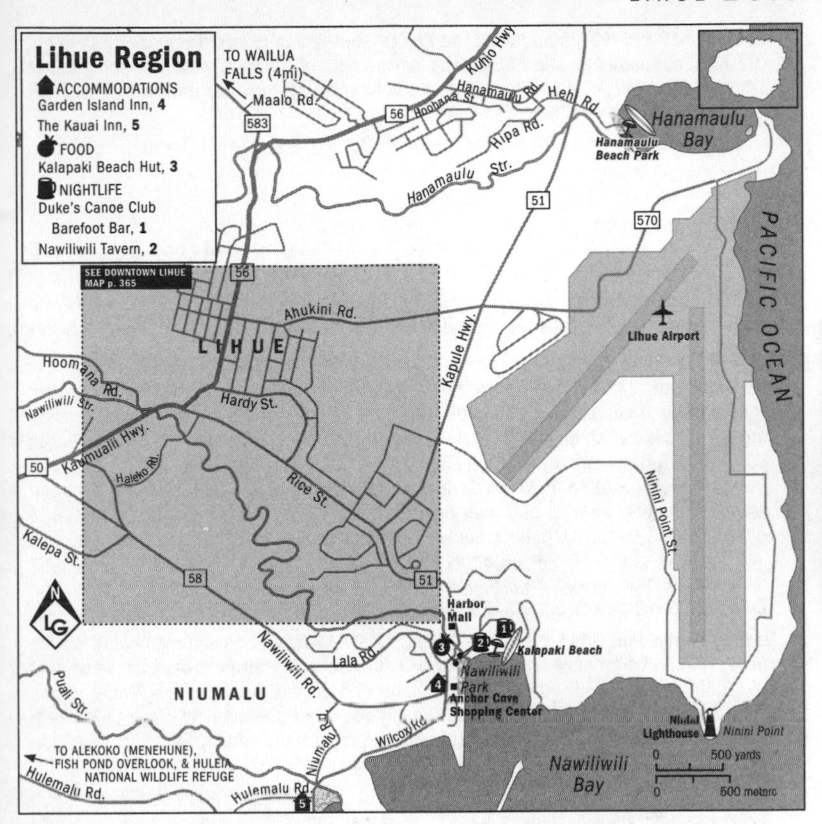

PRACTICAL INFORMATION

Tourist Information: Kauai Visitors Bureau, 4334 Rice St., Ste. 101 (☎245-3971; www.kauaivisitorsbureau.com), in the Watamull Plaza, has maps and brochures. Open M-F 8am-4:30pm.

Banks: Bank of Hawaii, 4455 Rice St. (☎245-6761), next to the post office. Open M-Th 8:30am-4pm, F 8:30am-6pm, Sa 9am-noon. **24hr. ATM.**

Library: 4344 Hardy St. (☎241-3222). **Internet access** is available with a 3-month visitor's card ($10). Use of 6 computers is limited to 1 session per day per person. Printing $0.10 per pg. Also has a wide selection of DVDs ($1 per rental). Open M and W 11am-7pm, Tu and Th-F 9am-4:30pm.

Laundromat: Lihue Laundromat, in Rice Shopping Center. 24 washers, 28 dryers. Wash $1.75, dry $0.25. Open 24hr.

Weather Forecast: ☎245-6001.

Police: Kauai Police Department, 3990 Kaana St., Ste. 200 (☎241-1711).

Hospital: Wilcox Memorial Hospital, 3420 Kuhio Hwy. (☎245-1100).

Internet Access: Harbor Mall Information Center, in Harbor Mall, Ste. 100 (☎632-0192), take Nawiliwili Rd. or Rice St. toward the harbor. $4 per 15min., $6 per

30min., $10 per hr. Alternatively, you can try your luck at **Kauai Community College,** 3-1901 Kaumualii Hwy. (☎245-8233), on the right of Kaumualii Hwy. heading out of Lihue toward Poipu, about ¼ mi. past Kilohana's. 15min. per day of free Internet access to the public, although students have priority.

Post Office: Lihue Post Office, 4441 Rice St. Open M-F 8am-4pm, Sa 9am-1pm.

Postal Code: 96766.

ACCOMMODATIONS

Anyone looking for luxury and spectacular surroundings will peel right out of Lihue for the resorts on the North Shore and southern coast. But for everyone else, the central location and affordable accommodations make Lihue a great choice.

The Kauai Inn, 2430 Hulemalu Rd. (☎245-9000; www.kauai-inn.com), near Nawiliwili Harbor on the *mauka* (mountain) side. Take Rice St. toward the harbor, turn left on Wilcox St. at Hale Kauai, follow it over the 1-lane bridge, and turn right onto Hulemalu Rd.; the inn is immediately on your left. Removed from the well-trodden path, the family-owned Kauai Inn offers great value and plenty of amenities. Beautifully landscaped grounds, tropical flowers, and lush palm trees surround a small swimming pool and pleasant courtyard. Their deluxe rooms—with private lanai, refrigerator, microwave, ceiling fan, and cable TV—are arguably the best deal in Lihue. Continental breakfast included. Coin-op laundry $1 per load. Reception 10am-5pm. Basic room $99; with A/C $109; 2- to 4-person suite $129. AmEx/D/MC/V. ❸

Garden Island Inn, 3445 Wilcox Rd. (☎245-7227; www.gardenislandinn.com), across from Nawiliwili Harbor. All 21 units have A/C, cable TV, refrigerator, microwave, wet bar, coffee maker with complimentary Kona coffee, and fresh flowers. Nicer rooms have a private lanai and ocean view. The cheerful staff provides solid advice on local restaurants and sights. Reception 8am-9pm. 4-night min. Rooms $95-150; 6-person condo from $150. AmEx/D/MC/V. ❸

Motel Lani, 4240 Rice St. (☎245-2965). Lots of plants and a friendly staff brighten up the 6 basic rooms with beds, a bath, mini-fridge, and A/C. 2 larger rooms come with TV but no A/C. Tidy and centrally located, Motel Lani is a deal, especially if you'll spend the day out and about. Reception 6:30am-9:30pm. Doubles from $34; each additional guest $14. Cash only. ❷

Tip Top Motel, 3173 Akahi St. (☎245-3333), above Tip Top Cafe. Turn onto Akahi St. from either Hardy St. or Ahukini Rd. With 34 clean, simple hotel rooms, Tip Top has provided visitors with a cheap place to stay since 1965. Key deposit $30. Reception 6:30am-11pm. Rooms $65. MC/V. ❸

FOOD

Lihue hosts a surprising assortment of restaurants. A typical restaurant features Asian, Hawaiian, or American cuisine (or a mix of all three) and focuses more on quality of ingredients and affordable prices than sophisticated decor. For something fancier, save up for a splurge in Poipu or Princeville. **Vim 'n Vigor,** 3122 Kuhio Hwy., Ste. A9, across from McDonalds, is one of Lihue's only health food stores, carrying grain, soy products, vitamins, packaged organic sandwiches on local bread ($3-5), and salads for $3-4. (☎245-9053. Open M-F 9am-7pm, Sa 9am-5pm.) For groceries, try **Star Market,** in Kukui Grove Shopping Center. (☎245-7777. Open daily 6am-11pm. MC/V). **Wal-Mart,** 33300 Kuhio Hwy., on the north side of town, has a pharmacy. (☎246-1599. Open daily 6am-11pm.

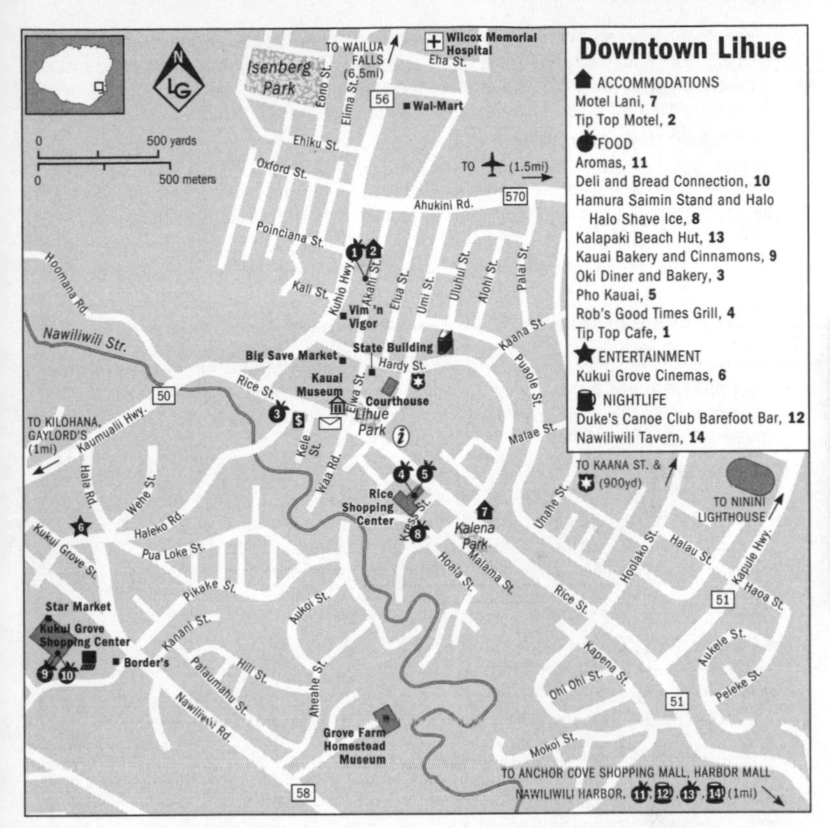

Pharmacy open M-F 9am-7pm.) Lihue holds weekly outdoor sales of Kauai-grown fruit, vegetables, and flowers, known as **Sunshine Markets,** Fridays at 3pm behind Vidinha Stadium.

Deli and Bread Connection (☎245-7115), next to Macy's in Kukui Grove Shopping Center. A deli, bakery, and kitchenware store in one, the Connection is a popular lunch stop. The sweet bread, endless variety, and reasonable prices make the wait worthwhile. A number of vegetarian selections (veggie burger, $5.50) and fresh daily soups complement the tasty sandwiches (BLT, $5; crab and shrimp "Crimp," $5). Open M-Th and Sa 9:30am-5:30pm, F 9:30am-9pm, Su 10am-4pm. MC/V. ❶

Kauai Bakery and Cinnamons (☎246-4765), in Kukui Grove's outdoor mall, between Sears and Star Market. This hole-in-the-wall has a steady flow of eager customers and a staff of friendly bakers hard at work. All the best baked goods are fresh out of the oven, including doughnuts ($0.75) and pastries ($1-3). Don't miss the divine banana bread, perfect apple turnovers ($1-3), delicious ham and cheese roll ($1.75), or the chocolate, cream, or red bean-filled *malasadas* ($1). Most of the good stuff sells out by noon. Open M-Th and Sa 7am-7pm, F 7am-9pm, Su 7am-6pm. Cash only. ❶

Kalapaki Beach Hut, 3474 Rice St. (☎246-6330), across from Harbor Mall. Juicy, flame-broiled burgers ($4-6.50), an amazing amount of toppings, and a prime location make the Beach Hut very popular for lunch. Try the Aloha Classic ($5.75) with teriyaki glaze, pineapple, and cheese. Although seating is available, most people take their burgers to Nawiliwili Beach Park for an entertaining view of beginning surfers. Breakfast includes omelets ($5-7), pancakes, french toast, or an egg sandwich ($4). Kids meals ($4) come with a burger, fries, and drink. Open M 7am-9pm, Tu-Su 7am-8pm. AmEx/D/MC/V. ❶

Aromas, 3501 Rice St. (☎245-9192), on the 2nd fl. of Harbor Mall. Aromas serves delicious Mediterranean-Pacific fusion all day in a chill atmosphere. Omelets and toast served with potatoes or rice ($7.50-10), and bajitos (Baja-style fish tacos, $13) are among the breakfast and lunch dishes. Dinner features vegetarian dishes (pasta angelo, $13) and guava mac nut ribs ($22). Open Tu-Sa 11:30am-2:30pm and 4:30-8:30pm, Su 8am-2:30pm and 4:30-8:30pm. MC/V. ❹

Hamura Saimin Stand and Halo Halo Shave Ice, 2956 Kress St. (☎245-3271), at Halenani. Lihue's unquestioned *saimin* headquarters: hordes of locals slurp island famous bowls of noodle soup. Try the barbecue chicken or beef sticks ($1.50) with a bowl of *saimin* ($4-7) for one of the cheapest meals in town. Shave ice ($2-3) available M-F 10am-4pm. Open M-Th 10am-11pm, F-Sa 10am-1am, Su 10am-9:30pm. Cash only. ❶

Oki Diner and Bakery, 4491 Rice St. (☎245-5899), on the corner of Haleko Rd. Plenty of parking in back. Oki serves award-winning hotcakes in a comfortable diner with a covered patio. The selection, service, and prices make Oki an easy and reliable place for a bite, and it's just about the only late-night option in town. Meals $10-14. For a break from sandwiches, order an Oki bento box (a midsize lunch of teriyaki chicken, corned beef hash, an omelet, and rice; $6) the day before. Open M and Th-Sa 6am-3am, Tu-W and Su 6am-midnight. Cash only. ❸

Pho Kauai, 4303 Rice St. #B-1 (☎245-9858), in Rice Shopping Center. Delicious Vietnamese soup ($7), rice with stir-fried tofu and vegetables, or chicken with lemongrass in a spicy sauce ($6.75). Bubble tea addicts will be delighted with their selection of flavors (from taro to mango, $3). Open M-Sa 10am-9pm. Cash only. ❶

Tip Top Cafe, 3173 Akahi St. (☎246-0176). Turn on Akahi St. from either Hardy St. or Ahukini Rd. The cafe attracts a mostly local crowd with cheap, good food served in its diner-style interior. The plush, gray booths are a comfortable place to try their popular oxtail soup or surfer special (grilled mahi mahi and shrimp tempura, $9.25). For breakfast they have pancakes ($5) and omelets ($7). At night the cafe converts into the **Sushi Katsu Japanese Restaurant,** serving delicious, cheap sushi. Cafe open Tu-Su 6:30am-2pm. Restaurant open 5:30-9pm. MC/V. ❷

BEACHES

KALAPAKI BEACH. *(Boogie boarding. Surfing. Open daily sunrise to sunset.)* Given the commercial development around it, Kalapaki is an unexpectedly pretty beach, drawing eager beachgoers to its quarter mile of fine white sand. The bay, one of Kauai's historic surfing sites, creates gentle waves ideal for swimming, sailing, boogie boarding, and learning to surf. You'll probably have to elbow through abandoned catamarans, volleyball nets, and the beach chairs of Marriott guests for an empty spot on the sloping beach. West of the beach, **Nawiliwili Park** provides tables, grills, bathrooms, outdoor showers, and grass perfect for picnicking aficionados. Public parking is available on the far east side of the Marriott via the main entrance to Marriott; follow the beach access signs. Parking is also available behind Anchor Cove Shopping Center in the Nawiliwili lot.

HANAMAULU BEACH PARK. *(Boogie boarding. Surfing. Open daily sunrise to sunset.)* Two miles east of Lihue, a trip to the dusty town of Hanamaulu will yield prime

JELLYFISH RISING. Box jelly fish swim to the southern Kauai shores 9-10 days after a full moon; always heed jelly fish warning signs on beaches. If you are stung, use vinegar to clean the area and prevent further stinging. Remove remaining tentacles with a stick or other object, and apply ice.

beachfront campsites. Silty water laps Hanamaulu Beach's narrow crescent of fine sand. Gentle swells, an all-sand bottom, and a few small breakers make this beach great for kids, swimming, boogie boarding, and beginning surfing. The slightly battered facilities include grills, picnic tables, trash cans, showers, and a pavilion. The campers are mostly locals; for more information, see **Camping in Hawaii,** p. 75. After driving 2 mi. east of Lihue on Hwy. 56, take a right onto Hanamaulu Rd. at the "Welcome to Hanamaulu" sign, then the third right onto Hehi Rd. for parking.

SIGHTS

Well before Wal-Mart's ascendancy, Lihue was Kauai's commercial center. The town's location next to the island's main port, Nawiliwili Harbor, supported the sugar plantations that directed the course of Kauai's history. Today, historical sights take visitors back to the island's sugar age and the time of its great kings.

ALEKOKO (MENEHUNE) FISHPOND OVERLOOK. According to legend, the *menehune* were a race of mischievous, pot-bellied elf-like creatures who lived in the forest and could complete complicated building projects overnight. Many years ago, a Hawaiian king asked the *menehune* to build a fishpond, and they happily complied. Yet despite their prodigious effort, the *menehune* were unable to finish, and as the sun began to rise, they hurriedly washed their hands (scratched and bleeding from the rough lava rock) in the pond before disappearing. *Alekoko* ("rippling blood") filled the pond with fish and provided the Hawaiian Royalty with their main source of protein from that point on. *Amaama* (striped mullet) and *awa* (milk fish) continue to thrive in the pond today, laying their eggs amid the tangled roots of mangroves that have taken hold along the walls. The overlook itself is a small structure along the edge of the river valley, hundreds of feet above the pond, with a sign describing the history and present-day fishy occupants of the pond. The view is beautiful, though it is a trifle disappointing that the walls of the pond are shielded from the overlook by plant growth. *(From Nawiliwili Rd., turn onto Wilcox Rd. at Hale Kauai or onto Niumalu Rd., farther to the northwest. Both eventually lead over a 1-lane bridge, after which you turn right onto Hulemalu Rd. Drive about 1 mi. up to a small lookout on the left.)*

GROVE FARM HOMESTEAD MUSEUM. Those who reserve one week or more in advance can enjoy an informative 2hr. walking tour of the 22,000-acre estate of **George "G. N." Wilcox,** Kauai's first and greatest sugar baron. The tour, capped at six people, begins in G. N.'s office with a brief biography of the industrious man (he funded his Yale education by gathering *guano*). The tour's next stop is Wilcox's austere cottage and the spectacular house he gave his brother and family. Gleaming *ohia* floors, a grand *koa* staircase, beautiful paintings, and a vast library are just a few luxuries inside. The tour also includes visits to the kitchen, a plantation cottage, and a guest house that puts his own humble cottage to shame. A devout Christian, Wilcox preferred to spend his hard-earned money helping others—he furnished both the land and funds for Nawiliwili Harbor. The grounds have been landscaped with tropical gardens, orchards, and acres of pastures. *(Northbound on Nawiliwili Rd., turn right at the small sign onto a private dirt*

KAUAI

road about 1¼ mi. from the harbor. ☎245-3202. 2hr. tour M and W-Th 10am and 1pm; may be cancelled on rainy days. Reservations required. Requested donation $10, ages 5-12 $5.)

KILOHANA. Built in 1935 by G.N. Wilcox's youngest nephew, Gaylord Parke Wilcox, and his wife, Ethel, Kilohana was once the most elegant and expensive house on Kauai. Wilcox and his Grove Farm Plantation were the height of the sugar era on Kauai and the lavish dinner parties thrown by Gaylord and Ethel were famous throughout Hawaii. The word *kilohana* translates as "not to be surpassed," which was Gaylord's intent when he built it. Today, the 15,000 sq. ft. Tudor-style mansion's eight bedrooms and bathrooms have been converted into shops retailing art, jewelry, and collectibles. The living room, hallways, and other rooms have been restored to their original condition with furniture and artwork dating to the 1930s. Unlike other historic homes, Kilohana encourages guests to truly experience the house—you can even sit on the furniture. Guests are also free to wander 35 acres of flowering gardens, cottages, and the working farm around the main house, which provide a spectacular view of the inland mountains. The galleries are worth browsing, if only to see the innovative ways the owners have put the space to use. A Clydesdale-drawn carriage tour is an opportunity to learn more about Kilohana's history. *(1½ mi. north of Lihue on the mauka, or mountain, side of Hwy. 50. ☎245-5608. House and galleries open M-Sa 9:30am-9:30pm, Su 9:30am-4:30pm. 20min. carriage rides daily 11am-6pm; $12, ages 12 and under $6. 1hr. sugarcane wagon rides M-Tu and Th 11am and 2pm; reservations required, call ☎246-9529; $29, ages 12 and under $15. Luau Kilohana Tu and Th 5pm; ☎245-9593; $68, seniors and ages 13-18 $64, ages 4-12 $36, under 4 free.)*

KAUAI MUSEUM. Small but informative, the Kauai Museum introduces you to everything you could possibly want to know about the island. A self-guided tour begins in the Wilcox building (one of two that comprise the museum) with a sweeping aerial video of the island. Comprehensive displays illustrate Kauai and Niihau's indigenous and immigrant histories and the geologic origins and ecology of the Hawaiian islands. *(4428 Rice St., at Eiwa. ☎245-6931; www.kauaimuseum.org. Guided 1½hr. tours M-F 10:30am; free with price of admission. Open M-F 9am-4pm, Sa 10am-4pm. $57, seniors over 65 $45, ages 13-17 $3, ages 6-12 $1, under 6 free. 1st Saturday of every month free.)*

WAILUA FALLS. Hawaiian *alii* (royalty) would dive from the cliffs overlooking the pool at Wailua Falls to prove their courage; many did not survive. Today, classic television fans may recognize the falls from the opening scenes of *Fantasy Island*. The south fork of the Wailua River flows to the falls where the magnitude varies with rain and the river's flow. Come early to avoid the crowds and watch the morning sun sparkle against the falls. Afternoon visitors will likely share the view with at least a dozen others, but not grudgingly—there is plenty of room. The easy convenience of the lookout doesn't detract from the powerful sight—a must-see if you have a day in Lihue. *(From Lihue, drive 1 mi. east on Hwy. 56 and turn left at Hwy. 583 or Maalo Rd. The road ends 4 mi. later at the falls.)*

HULEIA NATIONAL WILDLIFE REFUGE. The undeveloped wetlands, fertile hills, and verdant valleys west of the overlook form part of the Huleia National Wildlife Refuge, established in 1973 to protect the habitats of endangered waterbirds—including Hawaii's largest population of *koloa* ducks. The refuge is closed to the public with the exception of a few guided boat and kayak tours up the river. Movie buffs may recognize the valley as the site of Indiana Jones's heart-pounding, rope-swinging escape in an opening scene of *Raiders of the Lost Ark*. If you're at the fishpond, the beautiful scenery along the road makes the short drive worthwhile.

NININI LIGHTHOUSE. A good place to watch for humpback whales in the winter, the 86 ft. Ninini Lighthouse also offers a fantastic and incredibly windy view of the ocean and Nawiliwili Bay. Patches of grass and volcanic rocks can provide the setting for an unforgettable picnic. If you're lucky, an attendant may be around to take visitors to the top of the lighthouse. *(Entrance off Hwy. 51 between the airport and Rice St. About ½ mi. north of Rice St., turn toward the sea at the road with a gatehouse. Drive for ¼ mi. and follow the road as it makes a sharp left at the stop sign. Take the right fork and stay on the paved road. Past a "Shoreline Access-Ninini Point" sign, keep left at the "Running Path" sign; cross the golf cart path. The last stretch of the road is tricky for 2WD and roughly follows the fence of the airport on the left until it comes to a dirt parking lot.)*

ENTERTAINMENT AND NIGHTLIFE

Lihue is the place to be after dark; nightlife here is as thick as it gets on Kauai.

Rob's Good Times Grill (☎246-0311), in Rice Shopping Center. Happy hour draws familiar *pau hana* (literally "quit work time") faces to this casual neighborhood bar. Rob and his wife, Lolly, pour drinks and mingle while customers kick back in booths or battle it out on the foosball table. Pool tables, tons of TVs, and the only dance floor in town keep things going until closing. Enjoy local *pupus* ($5-8), typical bar food ($6), or heartier fare (steak and shrimp, $14.50; mahi mahi, $8) while dancing to Top 40 hits. Happy hour daily 3-7pm; draft and domestic beers $3. Open daily 11am-2am. MC/V.

Duke's Canoe Club Barefoot Bar, 3610 Rice St. (☎246-9599), at the west end of Kalapaki Beach; enter from the beach or the Marriott Courtyard. Only a sidewalk and a neat lawn from the beach, Duke's serves *pupus* ($3-10) and drinks (Mai Tai, $6.75; local beer on tap, $4.50) to tanned beachgoers. The ambience is straight-up tropical: wooden tables are shaded by grass umbrellas, a waterfall cascades through the bar, and servers wear aloha. The stunning view of Kalapaki Beach can't be beat. Patronized by tourists, Duke's prices are a hair higher than other bars', but the setting makes it worth it. Taco Tu (4-6pm) features $2.50 draft beer and $2 fish tacos; Tropical Tu and F (4-6pm) delivers $5.50 tropical drinks. Live music F 4-6pm and 9-11pm. Serves pricey entrees ($18-28) in the restaurant upstairs. Open daily 11am-11:30pm. Restaurant open daily 5-10pm. MC/V.

Nawiliwili Tavern, 3488 Paena Loop (☎245-1781), in the old Hotel Kuboyama next to Kalapaki Beach Hut. Wall-to-wall neon beer signs and bikini girls posters make Nawiliwili Tavern the college fraternity boy fantasy. Darts, billiards, shuffleboard, video games, and beer welcome a diverse crowd; TVs are always tuned to ESPN. Locally brewed Keoki on tap ($3). Practice for the F karaoke contest in the back room with Kauai's largest karaoke collection. Karaoke Tu and Sa 6pm. Happy hour daily 2-6pm; all drinks $0.50 off. Open daily 2pm-2am, food served 6pm-midnight. MC/V.

Lihue Bowling Center (☎245-5263), in the Rice Shopping Center. What could be better than 28 lanes, video games, and cheap food (*pupus* and meals, $2.25-6.25)? A lounge that taps cheap beer (14 oz., $2.25) and offers $5 drink specials. $3.75 per game, seniors and ages 18 and under $2.75; shoe rental $2. "Rock 'n Glow" F-Sa 9-11:30pm, $10 (includes shoe rental). Open M-Th 9am-10pm, F-Sa 9am-11:30pm, Su noon-10pm. Lounge open daily from 4pm to close. MC/V.

Kukui Grove Cinemas, 4368 Kukui Grove Rd. (☎245-5055), across Nawiliwili Rd. from Kukui Grove Shopping Mall. Kukui Grove, Kauai's biggest movie theater has 4 screens of current films. $7, seniors $5.50, ages 12 and under $4. Matinees Sa-Su $4. Shows M-Th 6-9pm, F 4-9pm, Sa-Su 1:30-10pm.

WAILUA

The first Tahitian settlers of Hawaii landed in Wailua (pop. 2,083) where the convergence of the north and south forks of the Wailua River became the center of the Tahitians' new community. Ever since, Wailua, where "two waters become one," has been Kauai's most popular locale. Today, Wailua is characterized by the recreational activities on the Wailua River and the ocean and resorts around town.

ACCOMMODATIONS

Wailua is home to a number of hotels, small B&Bs, and mid-level resorts, most of which advertise on the Internet. A less expensive option is the 200-room **Kauai Sands ❸,** 420 Papaloa Rd., part of a family-owned hotel chain that also operates on Maui and the Big Island. The efficiently run Kauai Sands, bordering the Coconut Marketplace, features immaculate rooms with one king-size bed or two twin beds, a fan, cable TV, mini-fridge, and private lanai. The oceanfront locations boasts two swimming pools, a laundry room, exercise facilities, and a restaurant. (☎822-4951; www.kauaisandshotel.com. Rooms $88-128. AmEx/D/MC/V.) The renovated **ResortQuest Islander on the Beach ❹,** 440 Aleka Pl., behind the Coconut Marketplace, between Wailua and Kapaa, has rooms from $195 and comes with all the standard perks of an oceanfront resort. (☎822-7417; http://RQIslander.com.) More of a true paradise, the much cheaper **Magic Sunrise ❸** is a fantastic B&B set in a tropical garden that ends in a dramatic overlook of the valley and river far below. From Lihue, turn left just past the Wailua River at "Coco Palms"; turn left down Royal Dr. and go to the end of the road. The three rooms each have their own flavor, featuring gorgeous bamboo trimmings and four-poster beds. Guests have access to a kitchen, living room, dining area, outdoor patio, small swimming pool, and an office with Internet access and fax. (☎821-9847; www.magicsunrisehawaii.com. 2-person rooms $55-85; 2-story, 1-bedroom apartment $99-114; 2-bedroom apartment $111-126.)

FOOD

Wailua Shopping Plaza and Kinipopo Shopping Village, across from each other on Kuhio Hwy. north of the Wailua River bridge, both hold a number of restaurants.

Caffe Coco, 4-369 Kuhio Hwy. (☎822-7990), on the *makai* (ocean) side of the highway past Kinipopo Shopping Village. Platters combine salad, rice, and sides with black sesame ahi ($19), Pacific-rim tofu ($18), or slow-roasted pork ($18). BYOB, corking fee $5. Live music nightly: Hawaiian on Th, hula on F, and jazz on Su. The coffee shop is a quiet place to snack on homemade pastries and desserts (samosas, $3.50; mango and raspberry bars, $2-4). Open Tu-F 11am-9pm, Sa-Su 5-9pm. MC/V. ❹

Kintaro, 4370 Kuhio Hwy. (☎822-3341), opposite Caffe Coco. Kintaro's upscale dining room serves Kauai's best Japanese food. Most menu options come with miso soup, rice, and tea (tempura combination of local fish, shrimp, and vegetables; $14). There are also a few Western dishes, such as charbroiled filet mignon with fresh vegetables ($20). Extensive sushi (*make,* $3-14). Hibachi seating or regular tables. Reservations strongly recommended. Open M-Sa 5:30-9:30pm. ❹

The Fish Hut, 4-484 Kuhio Hwy. (☎821-0033), in Coconut Marketplace. This stand prepares fish every way you can imagine: fish tacos, fish burgers, fish wraps, and fish salad are the standard fare ($7-8), or get the plate ($9) and combine oysters, scallops, or shrimp (pick 2), with fries. Freshly baked foccacia bread sandwiches ($7) are a treat. Open M-Sa 11am-9pm, Su 11am-8pm. AmEx/MC/V. ❷

Aloha Kauai Pizza, 4-484 Kuhio Hwy, #29. (☎822-4511), in the Coconut Marketplace. This small stand serves delicious Italian dishes to hungry shoppers. The flavor-filled pizzas come in 7 in., 12 in., and 16 in. pies (cheese, $6/14/17). The house specialty, "Artichoke Eddie," (12in., $18) comes highly recommended. Calzones, lasagna ($6-7.50), and sandwiches ($7), round out the menu. Open daily 11am-9pm. MC/V. ❶

Korean Bar-B-Q Restaurant, 4-356 Kuhio Hwy., Bldg. E. (☎823-6744), in the Kinipopo Shopping Village. A local favorite, this small restaurant also makes lunch to go. The menu's pictures help people unfamiliar with *katsu* (a fried battering) and *bibimbap* (mixed rice). Plate lunches (teriyaki beef and barbecue chicken combo, $8) include rice, miso soup, macaroni salad, *kimchee,* and veggies. Open M-Sa 10am-9pm, Su 10am-8pm. MC/V. ❶

Wailua Family Restaurant, 4361 Kuhio Hwy. (☎822-3325). Their breakfast, lunch, steak, and seafood are good for families and big groups. Customers choose from the menu on the wall on the way in, order and pay, and seat themselves in the dining room or the roomy patio. Steak ranges from 7 oz. sirloin ($10) to the "King Cut" prime rib ($28). Shrimp tempura (with vegetables, rice, and *kimchee;* $12), barbecue (chicken, beef, or pork; $7-8). All-you-can-eat buffet ($13) includes soup, salad, pasta, taco, and dessert bar. Open M-Tu, Th, Su 6:30am-9pm; W and F-Sa 6:30am-10pm. MC/V. ❸

SIGHTS AND ACTIVITIES

WAILUA RIVER STATE PARK. The unifying element of everything in the area is the majestic Wailua River, which flows 21 mi. from Mt. Waialeale to the north end of Lydgate Park, and is known as the only navigable river in Hawaii. Split into two branches for much of its path, the river converges to a single powerful waterway as it descends to sea level, mixing with the ocean in a brackish environment that supports a healthy fish population.

In the time of the *alii* (royalty), the Wailua River basin was the home of royal chiefs, who enjoyed its beaches, easy canoe landing, fertile field, and fresh- and saltwater resources. Known as the King's Highway, in honor of Kauai's last king, Kamehameha, the river is joined by a line of *heiaus* (temples), that parallel the water's path from mountain to ocean. Six of the *heiaus* that form this sacred path are visible today, while the seventh sits atop the wild summit of Waialeale. Nearly all of the sights below fall within the confusing boundaries of the 1000-acre Wailua River State Park, which encompasses the Wailua River, the town of Wailua (p. 370), Opaekaa Falls, Kuamoo Rd., Fern Grotto, and Lydgate Park.

Although tourist-filled riverboats dominate the Wailua River, it is also a favorite of kayakers who launch on the north bank. Turn from Kuhio Hwy. onto Kuamoo Rd. (north of the bridge) and take the second left into Wailua River State Park. A convenient place to rent kayaks is **Wailua Kayak and Canoe,** next to the Smith's Tropical Paradise shack, on the north bank close to Kuhio Hwy. The river is only a short walk from here. All rentals come with a map, dry bag, cooler, and brief orientation for first-time kayakers. Set out early to beat the blustery trade winds. *(☎821-1188. Single $37.50 per day; double $75. Open M-Sa 7am-5:30pm.)* Alternatively, you can rent from **Wailua Kayak Adventures,** just down Kuhio Hwy. Turn *mauka* (toward the mountains) off the highway just past the Lemongrass Grill restaurant; Wailua Kayak Adventures is at the back. Rentals come with dry bags, cooler, map, and a roof rack. They also offer kayak and hiking tours in the Wailua River area. *(☎822-5795 or 639-6332. Open daily 9am-6pm. Singles $25 per day; doubles $50. Tours $50-85.)*

LYDGATE STATE PARK. Picnic tables dot Lydgate's popular long, grassy lawn. A few trees provide shade along the modest beach and the two wonderful saltwater pools. Man-made walls enclose the large pools and shelter swimmers from unpredictable surf, creating a beginning snorkeler's paradise. The larger pool is great for relaxed snorkeling, while the shallower adjoining pool is more appropriate for younger *keiki* (children). Exercise caution when swimming in the ocean outside of the pools. Restrooms, showers, a lifeguard stand (9am-5pm), and a pictorial fish-finder are located at the north end of the park. On the other side of the parking lot, you'll find *keiki*-friendly Kamalani Playground.

Hikina A Ka La Heiau (meaning "rising of the sun"), at the north end of the park, is the first of seven *heiaus*. The stacked-rock walls, built as early as 1300 and originally 11 ft. tall, form a large rectangle, within which the *kahunas* (priests) celebrated dawn with prayer and chant. At one end of the *heiau*, criminals sought sanctuary in **Hauola,** the City of Refuge. Untouchable within its boundaries, the offenders could stay until purified by a *kahuna* and absolved of their crimes. A short nature walk proceeds through a series of four or five informative signs. Behind the sanctuary, near the mouth of the river, the sand hides boulders bearing petroglyphs of human, fish, and geometric images.

KAUAI

Camping is also available at the park; turn off Leho Dr. onto Nehe Rd., before Nalu Rd. The drive-up campsites are right on the ocean and offer a shower, restroom, picnic tables, and grills. *(From Kuhio Hwy., turn toward the ocean onto Leho Dr. at the Lydgate State Park sign just north of mi. marker 5, a few hundred yards south of the bridge over Wailua River. About ½ mi. down, turn right on Nalu Rd. to the parking lot.)*

FERN GROTTO. Once a temple dedicated to Lono, the god of harvest and fertility, the natural amphitheater of the cave now welcomes tourists by the boatload and brides and grooms by the dozens. Although the grotto still retains some of its enchanting natural beauty, it has recently become less than spectacular. In order to facilitate enterprising tourist photographers, the state cut down a number of ancient trees. Unable to adapt to the increased sunlight, the beautiful ferns that cover the entire cave were reduced to sparse, dangling bits. The only way to reach the grotto is by river. **Smith's** (see below) has offered boat rides to the grotto since 1946. *(The marina is on the southern bank of the Wailua River, down a paved road just south of the bridge on Kuhio Hwy. over the river. ☎821-6892. Cruises leave every 30min. 9-11:30am and 12:30-3:30pm. 1½hr. ride $20, ages 2-12 $10. No reservations necessary, just show up 15min. before departure.)*

SMITH'S TROPICAL PARADISE. The Smith family has helped to introduce visitors to the beauty and culture of the island for three generations. The 1½hr. boat tours to Fern Grotto include a 30min. stop at the cave, and an informative guided walk up the trail and some history. Musicians serenade each group from below, taking advantage of the grotto's perfect acoustics. Hula dancers and a Hawaiian band perform on the outbound cruise; local stories and legends are told on the return.

West of the marina, a 30-acre garden, home to over 20 types of fruit and wandering peacocks, is divided into themed areas connected by 1 mi. of pathways. The gardens also host Kauai's most authentic luau (p. 373) three nights a week in winter and five in summer. *(174 Wailua Rd., past the marina. ☎821-6895. Open daily 8:30am-4pm. Self-guided walking tour of gardens $5.25, ages 2-12 $2.50.)*

KUAMOO ROAD (HIGHWAY 580). Running from Coco Palms Resort, where Elvis tied the knot in *Blue Hawaii*, all the way past Opaekaa Falls, the highway runs along the northern bank of the river following the path the *alii* (royalty) walked from one religious site to another. The **Poliahu Heiau** held religious ceremonies here until the abolition of the Hawaiian religion in 1819. The *heiau* (temple) ruin has walls 3 ft. high and thicker than they are tall. A scenic lookout of the Wailua River from the same turnout provides parking for the *heiau* visitors, and signs explain the significance of the river. This site is sacred to Hawaiians: show respect for the *heiau* and avoid touching the rocks. *(On the south side of the road, about 1¼ mi. up Kuamoo Rd. from Kuhio Hwy. ¼ mi. downhill from the Opaekaa Falls overlook.)* **Opaekaa Falls** is a popular scenic viewpoint: a lofty waterfall, surrounded by dense green vegetation, flows in a number of dramatic streams to the pool below. An unofficial trail leads to the top of the falls from a dirt turnout on the north side of the road about 200 yd. past the parking lot, right where the guardrail ends. Keep to the right when you reach the river and follow the steep trail leading to the pool below the falls. *(The viewpoint is located along a sidewalk that runs west from a parking lot 1½ mi. up Kuamoo Rd. on the right.)*

ENTERTAINMENT

Wailua rivals Lihue as the center of Kauai's modest nightlife. The small dance floor at **Tradewinds,** in the Coconut Marketplace, fills with giddy locals and sunburned tourists on weekends. Arcade games, satellite sports, and dart boards entertain the less rhythmically inclined. Although Tradewinds does not have its own kitchen, guests are welcome to order from of any of the restaurants in the shopping center. (☎822-1621. 21+. Happy hour daily 2-7pm; mai tais $4, domestic beers $2.50. Open daily 10am-2am.) The Coconut Marketplace also puts on a free hula show (W 5pm) on the main stage in the middle of the mall. The **Coconut Marketplace Cinema** shows new releases on two screens. (☎821-2324. Shows daily 1:30-9:30pm. $7.25, seniors and under 12 $5.50, matinees $4.25.)

Smith's Tropical Paradise (p. 372) hosts the island's most spectacular luau. Gates open at 5pm, and guests are welcome to take a self-guided tour of the gardens or a guided tram tour ($1). Following the *imu* ceremony (the unearthing of the pig which has been cooking for hours in an underground pit), cocktails and music accompany the buffet dinner, before the party moves to the lagoon amphitheater. Twenty-five dancers and entertainers performs in a fantastic show highlighting the diverse culture of Hawaii. (☎821-6895. In summer M-F 5pm; in winter M, W, and F 5pm, 7:30pm show only. $58, ages 7-13 $29, ages 3-6 $19; show only $15, ages 13 and under $7.50.)

WAIPOULI

The short stretch of highway between Wailua and Kapaa is infamous for its horrendous traffic, though the shopping centers it passes offer some of the island's best prices. Waipouli's many restaurants rival the quality, if not the views, of ritzier North and South Shore establishments.

PRACTICAL INFORMATION. Those with piles of dirty clothes will love the triple-load washers and dryers at the **Kapaa Laundry Center,** 1105J Kuhio Hwy., in Kapaa Shopping Center. (☎823-3113. Wash $1.50, dry $0.25. Open daily 7:30am-9:30pm.) Across from Safeway is **Long's Drugs.** (Open M-Sa 7am-10pm, Su 8am-8pm. Pharmacy open M-Sa 8am-9pm, Su 9am-6pm.) The **Kapaa Post Office,** 1101

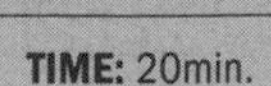

TIME: 20min.

DISTANCE: 13 mi.

SEASON: Any

1 KEALIA BEACH. Just past mi. marker 10, this long, golden-sand beach—a well-known surf spot—is visible from the highway. A dirt parking lot at the northern end, past a lifeguard stand and a port-a-pottie, provides access to the most sheltered part of the beach. Swimmers and less experienced wave-riders are advised to stay within the protective breakwater. Only seasoned boogie boarders and surfers should attempt to battle the giant waves.

2 DONKEY BEACH. One half-mile past mi. marker 11, a short, unmarked driveway leads to a small parking lot. From here, the beach is a 10min. walk down a well-marked path through picturesque privately owned fields. A long crescent of rock-edged golden sand waits at the bottom. Trees provide a bit of shade, and sunbathers will enjoy a pleasant tanning spot in the empty fields behind the secluded beach, surrounded by chirping birds. The waves come f and incredibly strong breaks challenge even experienced surfers.

3 ANAHOLA. A sleepy little community inhabited mostly by Native Hawaiians, Anahola's ma tourist attraction is **Duane's Ono-Char Burger ❶,** on the *makai* (ocean) side of the highway j south of mi. marker 14. Concrete tables topped with umbrellas provide a shady place to eat o endure the sometimes frustratingly long wait. A huge variety of toppings complement the fam ¼ lb. burgers (plain "*ono*" burger, $4.25; "local boy" with teriyaki sauce, cheddar cheese, a pineapple, $6); wash it down with creamy milkshakes for $3.50. (☎822-9181. Open daily 10a 6pm.) Immediately after mi. marker 14, the first Aliomanu Rd. (southern branch) leads to northern half of **Anahola Beach Park.** Most residents favor the more protected waters of southern end, accessible from Anahola Rd. between mi. markers 13 and 14, where uncrowded beach and picnic tables set the stage for a tranquil afternoon. Camping is availa here with a permit ($3) every day except Thursdays.

4 KOOLAU RD. A narrow country road lined with flowering trees and wide green fields, Koo Rd. forms a loop whose ends connect to Hwy. 56; two of the area's prettiest beaches are alo this loop. Crescent-shaped **Moloaa Beach** hides behind a wall of secluded homes and vacat rentals. To get there, turn right on the first Koolau Rd., between mi. marker 16 and 17. Park on side before turning down Moloaa Rd. toward the beach. Walk to the right, to the southern e where the daunting waves that greeted you give way to gentle aquamarine swells. **Larsen's Bea** can be reached from a dirt road branching off about 1 mi. south of the point at which the northe end of Koolau Rd. intersects Hwy. 56, heading *makai* (toward the ocean). A faded white "bea access" post marks the turn onto the dirt road. A short trail leads from a parking area at the e of the dirt road to the beach. Snorkelers will enjoy the exceptionally clear waters during the ca summer months—at other times, a strong rip current can make the waters unsafe.

Kuhio Hwy., is behind the laundry in the back of Kapaa Shopping Center. (Open M-F 8am-4pm, Sa 9am-2pm.) **Postal Code:** 96746.

FOOD. You can buy the most affordable groceries on the island from **Safeway,** 831 Kuhio Hwy. (☎822-2464. Open M-F 8am-8pm, Sa-Su 9am-6pm.) Waipouli's extensive shopping centers contain a wide variety of dining options. **King and I Thai Cuisine ❷,** 901 Kuhio Hwy., in Waipouli Plaza, has a long menu of reasonably priced meals ($7-12) and a section devoted to vegetarian dishes. (☎822-1642. Open daily 4:30-9:30pm. D/MC/V.) North of Waipouli Plaza, on the *mauka* (mountain) side of the road, **Coconuts ❸,** 919 Kuhio Hwy., has a funky, modern dining room with coconut wood furniture, a pleasant patio, and affordable menu. Organic green salads ($8.50), teriyaki-dipped Atlantic salmon ($16.50), coconut shrimp turnover appetizer ($11), and pasta dishes can usually be found on the menu. (☎823-8777. Open M-Sa 4-10pm, Su 4-6pm.) **Papaya's ❶,** 831 Kuhio Hwy., in Kauai Village Shopping Center, sells fresh fruits, veggies, and a host of other organic and vegan food. The popular deli counter caters to a loyal lunchtime clientele. Take your food outside to tables on the grass lawn. (☎823-0190. Veggie stir-fry $6. Sandwiches $6.50. Open M-Sa 9am-8pm; food served until 7pm. AmEx/D/MC/V.)

NIGHTLIFE. Paper-mâché Kahlua bottles and inflatable footballs dangle overhead at **Lizard Lounge Bar and Grill ❸,** in Waipouli Town Center. Talkative regulars down good draft beer ($3) around the pool tables, dart boards, and jukebox. The kitchen cooks a number of entrees like barbecue ribs ($14) and shrimp sauteed in tequila ($16) to satisfy late-night munchies. (☎821-2205. Sandwiches $6.50-8. Happy hour daily 2-6pm. Open daily 11am-1am; food served until 1am. AmEx/D/MC/V.)

KAPAA

Kapaa (pop. 9,472) is the hub of the East Shore, home to a large number of Kauai's residents, and a convenient distance from the shopping centers of Waipouli. Young, independent, and free-spirited travelers support numerous health food stores, and it's no accident that the only two hostels on Kauai are located down the street from each other in Kapaa. In fact, Kapaa is one of few towns where it's easier to find a fresh-fruit smoothie than an ice-cold beer. Affordable restaurants populate the historical wood buildings along Hwy. 56, and unspectacular but family-friendly beaches stretch the length of the town, only blocks east of the highway. Although not home to any amazing surf, Kapaa does have a number of places that rent boards.

ORIENTATION AND PRACTICAL INFORMATION

Downtown Kapaa occupies a few blocks of **Kuhio Highway,** and while tourists tend to hug the coast, most residents of Kauai's most populous town live farther inland.

Bank of Hawaii, 1407 Kuhio Hwy. (☎822-3471), on the *mauka* (mountain) side of the highway at the north end of downtown, and **First Hawaiian Bank,** 1366 Kuhio Hwy. (☎822-4966), on the *makai* (ocean) side in the center of town, each has a **24hr. ATM.** (Both banks open M-Th 8:30am-4pm, F 8:30am-6pm.) A 3-month visitor's card ($10) provides **Internet access** at the **Kapaa Public Library,** 1464 Kuhio Hwy., in the red building on Hwy. 56 south of the stream crossing. (☎821-4422. Open M and W-F 9am-5pm, Tu noon-8pm.) Travelers can also surf the web at **Business Support Services,** on the *mauka* (mountain) of the highway, in the southern part of town. (☎822-5504. Open M-Sa 8am-6pm, Su 10am-4pm. $2.50 per 15min.) Those who prefer chlorine to salt can get wet at **Smokey Louie Gonsalves Jr. Swimming Pool,** a public oceanfront pool at the end of Kou St. (Open in summer Tu-W and Th-Sa 10am-4:30pm, Su 1-4:30pm. Free.)

ACCOMMODATIONS

The lodgings below are within a block of downtown Kapaa and have some of the cheapest rooms on the island.

Kauai Beach House, 4-1552 Kuhio Hwy. (☎822-3313; www.kauai-blue-lagoon.com), on the north side of town, across from Kojima's Supermarket; on the *makai* (ocean) side of the road. There's plenty of parking in back. A relaxed, family-run hostel. Guests of the rambling, 3-story Beach House share an outdoor kitchen, comfortable patio-style common area, a fantastic view of the Pacific from the rooftop shower, and laundry facilities. Spacious dorms with extra-long bunks and mirrored walls open to oceanfront patios. Very friendly management. Linens included. Bunks $25; doubles $40; private rooms $55. Reservations recommended. Cash only. ❶

Kauai International Hostel, 4532 Lehua St. (☎823-6142; www.vrbo.com/861), behind Bubba's Burgers. Steps from downtown Kapaa, the cinder-block International Hostel hosts a diverse clientele of backpackers from around the world. The hostel hosts a televised cooking show (Su 8pm) and a delicious free dinner for guests following. Facilities include laundry, shared kitchen, and lounge with cable TV. Key deposit $10. Lights-out 11pm. Dorms $25; private double $55-75. Reservations recommended. MC/V. ❶

Kakalina's Bed and Breakfast, 6781 Kawaihau Rd. (☎822-2328; www.kakalina.com). Turn toward the mountain on Kawaihau Rd. from Hwy. 58, at the northern end of Kapaa, just before the road leaves town. Kakalina's is 4½ mi. down Kawaihau Rd. on the left side; drive down to the house in the back. Friendly owners give excellent advice on island activities. Rooms overlook a pleasant lake and have coffee makers, microwaves, refrigerators, and access to laundry facilities. Beach towels, mats, and coolers are free for guests to borrow. Continental breakfast included. 2-night min. Studio $85; 1-bedroom $90; 2- to 4-person suites with full kitchen $155-175. ❸

Makaleha Mountain Retreat, 7124A Kahuna Rd. (☎822-3142; www.makaleha.com), toward the mountain on Kawaihau Rd. from Hwy. 58 at the northern end of Kapaa, just before the road leaves town. After about 3 mi., turn right on Kahuna Rd. and drive another 1½ mi.; Makaleha will be on your right. Surrounded by banana trees and ti leaf plants, the Makaleha Mountain Retreat is backed dramatically by the lush green foothills of rainy Mt. Waiaileale. Guests are welcome to use the hammock, pick citrus or papaya in the private garden, or borrow snorkel equipment, body boards, beach chairs, and mountain bikes. 3-night min. Cleaning fee $40. Garden studio with kitchen $60; 2- to 6-person home with wrap-around deck $165; each additional guest $15. Discounts for longer stays available. ❷

FOOD

Small Town Coffee Co., 4-1495 Kuhio Hwy. (☎821-1604), in the bright blue building on the *mauka* (mountain) side, right before the bridge. Filled with shirtless hippies, musicians, care-free wanderers, and even the occasional parrot, Small Town Coffee Co. serves a whole lot of local, friendly atmosphere with every cup of coffee. Popular for its organic coffees and teas, laptop users also flock here for free wireless Internet. Kauai chai ($3-3.65), lemonade topped with real raspberries ($3.50), and macchiatos ($2.25) entice patrons. Live local bands F-Su 7pm; jazz Su noon. Open M-Th 6am-9pm, F-Sa 6am-10pm, Su 6am-6pm. ❶

Olympic Cafe, 1354 Kuhio Hwy. (☎822-5825), in the center of town. Huge windows and open doors welcome the sun into the dining room and provide diners with a great view of the ocean. The extensive menu will please a family of finicky eaters, from meat lovers (chicken fajitas, $15) to fish fans (ahi sandwich, $12), and vegans (tofu salad, $11.25). For breakfast, try the Kalua pig burrito ($11.50) or coconut pineapple pancakes ($7). Open daily 6am-3pm. MC/V. ❷

Java Kai, 1384 Kuhio Hwy. (☎823-6887), in the large green building downtown. Good coffee drinks including cold, blended concoctions of sweet caffeine. Smoothies from $4.50. Big muffins and yummy aloha bars $1-3. Open daily 6:30am-5:30pm, W-Sa also 6:30-9:15pm. MC/V. ❶

Ono Family Restaurant, 1292 Kuhio Hwy. (☎822-1710), on the *makai* (ocean) side at the southern end of downtown. Cozy wooden booths and a great staff welcome diners like family. There's a whole lot of egg for breakfast (omelets, $6-9), as well as fruit smoothies ($4) and tropical pancakes with bananas, macadamia nuts, and coconut ($8). Open daily 7am-2pm. AmEx/D/MC/V. ❷

Blossoming Lotus, 4504 Kukui St. (☎822-7678), in the Historic Dragon Building, just off the main highway through town. The latest in vegetarian cuisine on Kauai, Blossoming Lotus has an amazing menu with a focus on "live" food—vegetables that have not been processed or cooked and nuts and grains that have sprouted. Lunch items include Gaia's Greenwich (pumpkinseed cheese, rainbow chard, zucchini, and avocados on homemade bread, $10), or the Lotus BLT (tofu bacon and veggies, $9). Try Rama's Red Curry (sweet potato in red coconut curry sauce over quinoa or rice, $10). Live entertainment nightly 7-9pm. Gourmet vegan brunch Sa-Su 11am-3pm. Open daily 11am-3pm and 5:30-9:30pm. AmEx/D/MC/V. ❷

KAUAI

BEACHES

If you're tired of fighting traffic on the way to North or South Shore beaches, swim and sunbathe along Kapaa's continuous stretch of sand.

WAIPOULI BEACH PARK (BABY BEACH). *(Open daily sunrise to sunset.)* A long stone jetty runs north from the end of Makaha Rd. and forms a shallow pool perfect for a leisurely dip at the south end of this golden-sand beach. A local *pau-hana* (after work) favorite for a barbecue or fishing, the beach is often lined with pick-up trucks and locals kicking it back in camp chairs. The water can get dirty sometimes, since it's right in town. Better known as Baby Beach, Waipuli Beach Park is on Moana Kai Rd. along the oceanfront south of downtown. A shower and good-sized parking lot lie farther north by the mouth of the river, where the sandy beach all but disappears. Turn down Makaha Rd. off Kuhio Hwy.; turn left on Moana Kai Rd. and continue to the parking area.

KAPAA BEACH PARK. *(Open daily sunrise to sunset.)* On the other side of the canal, Kapaa Beach Park parallels downtown Kapaa. The long, narrow beach is popular with local fishermen and kiteboarders, who usually stick to the south end. Restrooms, a soccer field, and a big parking lot back the sandy shore. Neither Kapaa Beach or Waipouli Beach Park is as rivetingly beautiful or secluded as any of the beaches north of Kapaa but both are family-friendly and very accessible. Turn *makai* (toward the ocean) just before the soccer fields.

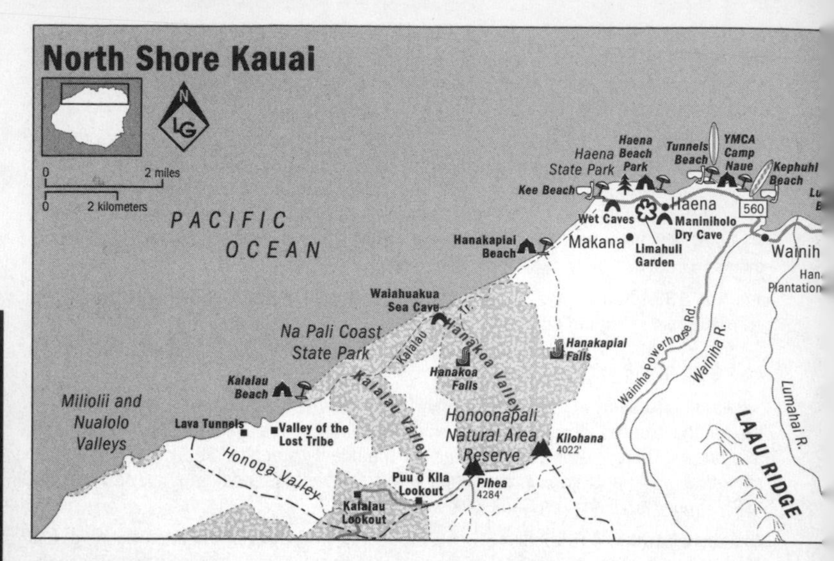

ACTIVITIES

Although the east shore of Kauai isn't as well known for surfing as the north and south shores of the island, Kapaa, Wailua, and Waipouli are all home to a number of shops that rent surfboards, boogie boards, kayaks, and other equipment. **Surfboards** usually rent for $10-20 per day and $50-100 per week, depending on the type of board. Roof racks typically cost an additional $5 per day, or $15 per week. **Boogie boards** and **snorkel gear** are much cheaper, renting at about $5 per day or $15 per week.

Tamba Surf Company, 4-1543 Kuhio Hwy. (☎823-6942), on the west side of Kuhio Hwy., at the northern end of Kapaa, across the street from the Kauai Beach House. The very friendly management sets competitive rates for surfboards and boogie boards that make renting them a solid deal. Longboard rentals $20 per day, $75 per week; includes roof rack. 1½hr. surf lessons $40. Open daily 9am-5pm.

Kauai Water Ski and Surf Company, 4-356 Kuhio Hwy. (☎822-3574), in Wailua, just north of the Kinipopo Shopping Village, has a good selection of snorkel gear, boogie boards, and surfboards at exceptionally low rates. Shortboards $10 per day, $50 per week; long boards $20/75. Roof rack $5 per day. Single kayaks $30, doubles $50. Open daily 8am-6pm.

Activity Warehouse, 788 Kuhio Hwy. (☎822-4000), in Waipouli, across from McDonalds, is a larger rental company that rents surfboards ($25 per day), kayaks ($50 per day), bikes, and golf equipment. They also rent coolers and beach chairs ($4-6 per day) and offer discount Napali and helicopter tours of the island. 2½hr. surfing lessons $65. Open daily 8am-8pm.

NORTH SHORE

The north side of Kauai is the wettest and greenest part of an island known for its heavy rainfall and verdant landscape. The region is remote and life for both locals and wealthy mainlanders is slow and surrounded by beauty. Recent years

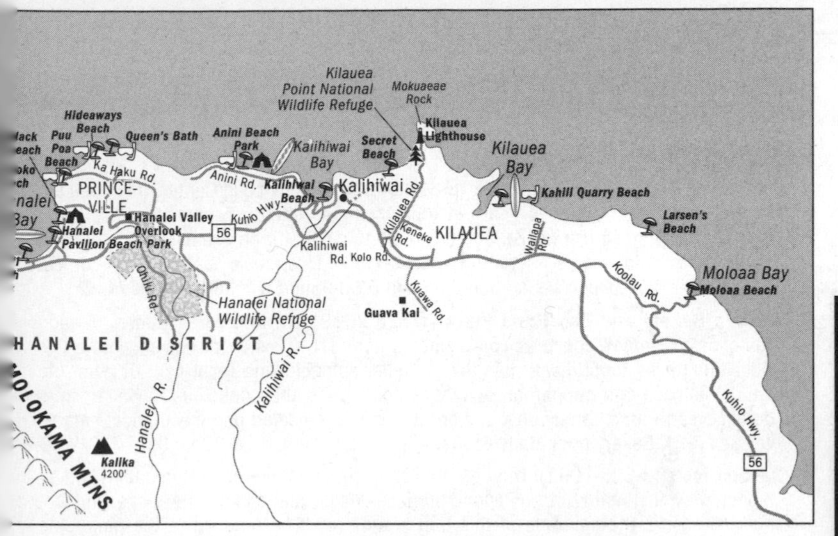

have accelerated development and sent land values skyrocketing. In winter, surf's up on the North Shore, transforming its beaches and bay from swimming and snorkeling coves to the hard-core surfer's paradise. Some of the best surfers in the world spent their childhood enjoying the big wave breaks here.

KILAUEA

Sprawling pastures, organic farms, and grassy bluffs shape Kilauea (pop. 2,002). Many of Hawaii's former plantation towns have embraced tourism after agriculture's decline, but not Kilauea. This eclectic and peaceful North Shore community is home to a motley collection of Hawaiian families, wandering surfers, and dreadlocked hippies, and is best known for its seabird refuge and stirring lighthouse.

ORIENTATION AND PRACTICAL INFORMATION

Kilauea is centered on **Kilauea Road,** which begins 100 yd. down **Kolo Road,** ½ mi. north of mi. marker 23. Kilauea Rd. runs 2-3 mi. northeast to **Kilauea Point,** the northernmost point in the major islands. **The Kong Lung Center,** on Kilauea Rd., at Keneke Rd., has restaurants, shops, and a theater. **Shell,** on the right as you turn off the highway into Kilauea, is the only highway gas station between Kapaa and Princeville. (Open daily 6am-7pm.) Next door, the **Menehune Food Mart** has groceries and an **ATM** inside. (Open M-F 5:30am-7pm, Sa-Su 6am-7pm.)

ACCOMMODATIONS

An old sugar plantation house from the 1920s, **Aloha Plantation ❸,** 4481 Malulani St., is a charming bed and breakfast. Turn onto Kolo Rd. from the highway and turn right onto Malulani after ¼ mi.; Aloha Plantation is the third house on the left. Guests can use the outdoor kitchen, shower, jacuzzi, and communal dining area. (☎877-658-6977 or 828-1693; www.alohaplantation.com. Doubles $69-99; each additional guest $10. Cash or check only.)

FOOD

Kilauea's few restaurants feature fresh ingredients from the surrounding lush valleys. You can buy organic herbs and all sorts of good stuff at the **Sunshine Market** (Th 4:30pm), in the Neighborhood Center parking lot next to **Kilauea Farmers' Market** (p. 380).

Lighthouse Bistro, 2484 Keneke St. (☎828-0480), in Kong Lung Center. This open-air, high-ceilinged bistro serves gourmet food including shrimp parmesan ($27), filet mignon ($34), fresh fish ($26), and salads ($10-15), with an extensive wine list and mixed drinks (Mai Tais, $7; martinis, $6.50-7.50). Live music W-Sa. All-you-can-eat pasta nightly $15. Open M-Sa noon-2pm and 5:30-9pm, Su 5:30-9pm. MC/V. ❹

Kilauea Bakery and Pau Hana Pizza (☎828-2020), in Kong Lung Center. A wide selection of coffees and teas complements gourmet cakes, cookies, and brownies. Delicious pizzas topped with healthy tofurella, spinach, and local fish, or good old Italian sausage and pepperoni, delight customers. Try their delicious Hawaiian sourdough bread with a variety of soups or the Big Kilauea salad made with local organic veggies ($8). Bakery open daily 6:30am-9pm. Pizza served 10:30am-9pm. MC/V. ❸

KAUAI

Banana Joe's (☎828-1092). Look for the yellow sign on the *mauka* (mountain) side of the highway, just north of town. Island produce, locally-made jams, dressings, and granola ($4-5) fill the counters of this fruit stand. You'll be amazed at the pineapple frostie ($3.50), made from freshly frozen fruit. The fruit smoothie ($3-4) hits the spot after a long, hot highway drive. Open M-Sa 9am-6pm, Su 9am-5pm. Cash only. ❶

Kilauea Farmers' Market (☎828-1512), in the Kong Lung Center, next to the movie theater, sells local organic vegetables, gourmet food, wine, and staples. The deli counter throws together hearty sandwiches (apple chutney with cheese, $6.60; ginger teriyaki tofu, $7), homemade soups, and salads. Open daily 8:30am-8:30pm. Deli open M-Sa 10am-2pm. AmEx/MC/V. ❶

BEACHES

Winding mountain roads hide spectacularly secluded beaches and beguiling waterfalls. Most of the best beaches lie west of Kilauea in the town of Kalihiwai. Kalihiwai Rd., once a U-shaped loop bridging the Kalihiwai River, was split when its bridge was destroyed by a tsunami in the 1950s. The split in the road is at the base of Kalihiwai Bay, on the shore of Kalihiwai Beach.

SECRET BEACH. *(Surfing. Open daily 24hr.)* Officially Kauapea Beach, this formerly hidden spot has outgrown its mysterious nickname, and the parking area can barely hold the rows of shiny rental cars. Secret Beach's magnetic appeal is in its irresistible scenery: a vast expanse of super-fine golden sand sprinkled with lava rocks surrounded by bluffs and a fetching view of Kilauea Point. The beach, one of the widest on the island, also features big surfing waves. From the base of the trail, the sands stretch far to the right where a sheltered cove and gently sloping shore provide safer swimming. From Hwy. 56 North, turn right on the first Kalihiwai Rd., just before mi. marker 24; turn right again at the first dirt road. After ¼ mi., the road ends in a parking area. From here, follow a steep, well-marked trail for 5min. to the beach.

KAHILI QUARRY BEACH (ROCK QUARRY BEACH). *(Snorkeling. Surfing. Open daily 24hr.)* Hidden away on a dirt road, Kahili Quarry Beach can be exceptional for swimming, snorkeling, and surfing. The left side of the beach is more protected and safer for swimming, though the mouth of the Kilauea stream can fill the

SPINNING SECRETS. Between 6 and 10am, drive out to Kalihiwai or Secret Beach. There are often spinner dolphins playing in the waters near these beaches during the early morning hours. If you decide to jump in with them, remember to swim at a respectful distance!

water with sediment and create unpredictable currents. In summer, modestly-sized waves and the sandy bottom are ideal for beginning and intermediate surfers. Kahili is accessible from Wailapa Rd., which runs *makai* (toward the ocean) from the highway between mi. markers 21 and 22. After ½ mi., follow a dirt road downhill to the left and park at the end. The beach is a short stroll to the right or left.

KALIHIWAI BEACH AND HANAPAI BEACH. *(Boogie boarding. Surfing. Open daily 24hr.)* Boogie boarders and surfers enjoy the right pointbreak wave, while local families favor the beach for weekend picnics. A wide sandy crescent continues to the west on the other side of the river mouth, which can be a chore to cross in high surf. The smaller, western portion of the beach, known as Hanapai Beach, is also accessible from Anini Rd. The sandy river provides a nice place to splash around, and a short rope swing keeps kids entertained. It is more secluded than the main section of Kalihiwai Beach; a trip to this section is probably not worth the trouble unless you're very curious or in need of quiet. Take the first Kalihiwai Rd. to the end and park under the trees facing the beach, or the second Kalihiwai Rd. and park in the small lot at the end on the left before wading across the shallow river to the beach.

KAUAI

ANINI BEACH PARK. *(Snorkeling. Surfing. Wind sports. Open daily sunrise to sunset.)* The golden sand of Anini Beach covers the coastline for almost 2 mi. around a wide, shallow lagoon of clear, reef-protected water. Swimmers and snorkelers frolic at the east end, while boat owners, surfers, and windsurfers occupy the water to their left. County campgrounds (closed Tu) with spacious beachfront sites, restrooms, and showers, are available. (See **Camping in Hawaii,** p. 75.) The lawn behind the park has pavilions, picnic tables, and grills. The flat shore and incredibly calm summer water make Anini one of Kauai's safest swimming beaches.

Shallow turquoise waters and the warm offshore breeze are so inviting that everyone will want to try his hand at windsurfing. A veteran with 17 years of teaching experience, Celeste at **Windsurf Kauai** takes small groups (up to six) out on the lagoon. A 3hr. introductory lesson, open to competent swimmers ages 5 and up, includes 1hr. on a land simulator before 2hr. on the water. Those who catch the windsurfing bug can take a second lesson that focuses on advanced skills and qualifies students for certification. Rentals ($25 per hr.) and surfing lessons in Hanalei Bay ($75 for 2hr.) are also available. (☎828-6838. 3hr. windsurfing lesson $85, including equipment.) To reach the beach, head toward the ocean on the west Kalihiwai Rd., between mi. markers 25 and 26, and turn left on Anini Rd., which runs north to the shore and then west along the length of the beach.

SIGHTS AND ENTERTAINMENT

Kilauea's green hills shelter a wildlife refuge and secluded beaches. The surrounding land is dotted with farms, and the quiet town is home to one of Kauai's few cinemas. The **Kilauea Theater** (☎828-0438), next to the Kilauea Farmer's Market in the Kong Lung Center, has one screen that plays independent and big-budget films. The funky surfboard-decorated theater shows a mainstream movie at 7:30pm on Wednesdays and a surf movie on Saturdays at 8pm. Call for other showtimes.

KILAUEA POINT NATIONAL WILDLIFE REFUGE. The historic Kilauea Lighthouse and the wild bird population are featured in the Kilauea National Wildlife Refuge. Built in 1913, the Kilauea Lighthouse guided commercial boats on their way to Asia. Although decommissioned in 1976, the 52 ft. tall lighthouse retains its giant clamshell lens, the largest in the world, and an unbeatable view of the frothing blue ocean from 217 ft. above sea level. Today, a small beacon light next to the lighthouse offers guidance to local boaters and aircraft. Though visitors are only allowed into the first floor of the lighthouse, the old communications building has a historical display, a video, reference books, and articles about the lighthouse and refuge.

The various birds that inhabit the refuge include Red-footed Boobies (the most visible species in the refuge; visible year-round), Great Frigatebirds with distinctive red throats (visible year-round), the endangered *nene* (the official state bird; visible year-round), the enormous Laysan Albatross (Dec.-July), Pacific Golden Plovers (Aug.-Apr.), and Wedge-tailed Shearwaters (summer). Humpback whales (Dec.-Apr.), spinner dolphins, endangered monk seals, and sea turtles are commonly seen from shore.

Inaccessible to man and a favorite roosting spot for birds, Mokuaeae Rock forms an island about 100 yd. north of the point. An old story claims that Mokuaeae Rock was the first American possession in Hawaii, lost by King Kalakaua in a poker game to an American ambassador long before Hawaii became the 50th state. The visitor-accessible part of the refuge consists of a Visitors Center and a quarter-mile sidewalk from the parking lot to the lighthouse. *(At the end of Kilauea Rd. ☎828-0168; www.kilaueapoint.org. Refuge open daily 10am-4pm. $3, under 16 free.)*

GUAVA KAI. Fans of the sweet, pink fruit will enjoy a stop at Guava Kai, a plantation and agricultural engineering center dedicated to perfecting guava production. The Visitors Center is a guava gala with guava products, souvenirs, and a video illustrating the life of a plantation-grown guava. A few displays detail the cultivation process next to a table laden with guava-flavored sauces, spreads, and a dispenser of free guava juice samples. Harvested by hand, the plantation's guava trees have been engineered to produce a year-round harvest—as opposed to biannual wild trees—that is maintained by cyclical fertilization, pruning, and simulated seasonal conditions. When guava is harvested, visitors can watch from a viewing area as workers inspect each fruit on the assembly line. A small snack shop adjacent to the Visitors Center serves slices of fresh guava (free), guava floats ($3.50), and other chilly treats (guava ice cream, $3-5; guava smoothie, $4.50), plus heartier burritos ($1.50) and hot dogs ($3). A short nature walk passes tropical flowers such as heliconia and plumeria, a pond, and verdant foliage. Visitors can also wander the orchards and pick one guava from the trees for themselves. *(On Kuawa Rd., toward the mountain off Hwy. 56, just south of mi. marker 23. ☎828-6121; www.guavakai.com. Open daily in summer 9am-6:30pm; in winter 9am-5pm. Free.)*

PRINCEVILLE

Modern Princeville (pop. 1,698) is a meticulously planned resort community where golf courses, condominiums, and the island's most luxurious hotel compensate for the town's lack of personality.

ORIENTATION AND PRACTICAL INFORMATION

Located 28 mi. north of Lihue on Hwy. 56, Princeville is primarily a ritzy resort community. **Ka Haku Road,** the main path through the development, branches off Hwy. 56 north toward the ocean at mi. marker 28 before the Princeville Shopping Center and just past the golf course. It bends left and ends 1-2 mi. farther down at the Princeville Hotel. The only other access to the town from Hwy. 56 is via **Hanalei Plantation Road,** farther down from Ka Haku Rd., just past the Hanalei National Wildlife Refuge overlook on the opposite side of the road.

Princeville Shopping Center, at mi. marker 28, is where the mile markers start at 0 and increase as you head to Haena. Here, a **Chevron gas station** is the last stop for gas until the end of the road. (Open M-Sa 6am-9pm, Su 8am-6pm.) A **Bank of Hawaii** (☎826-6551) is next to the post office, and the **First Hawaiian Bank,** 4280 Kuhio Hwy. (☎826-1560), is in the east end of the shopping center. (Both banks open M-Th 8:30am-4pm, F 8:30am-6pm. Both have **24hr. ATMs.**) The **Princeville Public Library,** 4343 Emmalani Dr., is across the street and has **Internet access** with a 3-month visitor's card ($10) on 3 terminals. (☎826-4310. Open Tu and Th-Sa 10am-5pm, W 1-8pm.) The **Princeville Post Office,** 4280 Kuhio Hwy., will post your letters or coconuts with their Post-a-Nut service. (☎828-0217. Open M-F 10:30am-3:30pm, Sa 10:30am-12:30pm.) **Postal Code:** 96722.

ACCOMMODATIONS

Anyone who's not on a $4800-a-day budget will probably find cheaper B&Bs outside of Hanalei and Kilauea. The crown jewel of the resort community, the **Princeville Hotel ❺**, 5520 Ka Haku Rd., at the end of Ka Haku Rd. has tiered floors with incredible views of Hanalei Bay. The hotel's fantastically posh lobby provides nonguests with an opportunity to enjoy the luxury without the price tag that comes with a room there. (☎826-9644 or 800-325-3589; www.princeville.com. Reserve 3-6 mo. in advance. Rooms $500-5100. AmEx/MC/V.)

The **Hanalei Bay Resort ❺**, 5380 Honoiki Rd., provides a luxurious, slightly less extravagant stay, with tennis courts, pools, and beautiful views. All rooms have lanais, and some have kitchenettes. From westbound Ka Haku Rd., turn left onto Liho Liho Rd. and then immediately right onto Honoiki Rd. Ask about special rates and rooms—you might strike a deal. (☎826-6522 or 800-827-4427; www.hanaleibayresort.com. Rooms $195-400. AmEx/MC/V.)

FOOD

Foodland, in Princeville Shopping Center, contains an extensive deli that sells fried chicken ($1.50), sushi plates ($5-8), and pasta salads, and is the best way to eat on a budge in Princeville. (☎826-9880. Open daily 6am-11pm. AmEx/D/MC/V.)

Paradise Bar and Grill (☎826-1775), across from the post office in the Princeville Shopping Center. Mostly seafood and burgers grace the menu here. Wash everything down with a mai tai ($6) or a beer ($3) at their surfboard table. Fish sandwiches $8.50. Rib-eye steak $18.50. Open daily 11am-10:30pm. MC/V. ❷

CJ's Steak and Seafood (☎826-6211), in the middle of the Princeville Shopping Center. Their most popular dinner entrees include the fresh fish catch of the day ($26) and the teriyaki top sirloin steak ($26.50). Lunch ($7-10) is cheaper. Open M-F 11:30am-2:30pm and 6-9:30pm, Sa-Su 6-9:30pm. AmEx/D/DC/MC/V. Lunch ❷/Dinner ❺

The Beach Restaurant, pool-side, accessible via the 1st fl. of the Princeville Hotel or the path that leads to Puu Poa Beach (p. 384). Serves standard lunchtime fare. Sandwiches with chips (turkey, avocado, and bacon; $16), Kobe beef burger ($17), and salads (grilled chicken Caesar, $15). Food served daily 11am-5:30pm. Bar open 10:30am-sunset. AmEx/MC/V. ❸

ENTERTAINMENT

Paina O Hanalei Luau is the Princeville Hotel's extravagant beachside luau. (☎826-2788. M and Th 6-9pm. Dinner and show $99, seniors and ages 13-19 $90, ages 6-12 $45.) **Happy Talk Lounge,** 5380 Honoiki Rd., offers live entertainment Tuesday through Sunday. Crab cakes ($12.75), pizza ($13.50-16.50), Caesar salad ($8), and fresh fish ($11.50) are all reasonably priced. (☎826-6522. Live local bands Tu-Sa 7-10pm. Jazz Su 4-7pm. Happy hour F-Sa 4-6pm; beer $3.50 and mai tais $4.50. Free pupus F 4:30pm. Food served daily 2-9pm. AmEx/MC/V.)

BEACHES

Princeville's bluff-top location offers excellent views of Hanalei Bay and effusive waterfalls, but makes the descent to the beaches below the resort a challenge.

QUEEN'S BATH. *(Snorkeling. Open daily 24hr.)* A deep lava rock pool filled by aquamarine ocean water, Queen's Bath is a unique swimming and snorkeling spot. Along a half-mile stretch of shoreline in Princeville, waves splash ocean water over black rock walls, and a series of pools and inlets provide swimming holes for visitors, fish, and sea turtles. The largest pool is known as Queen's Bath, but when the surf is down in the summer, other pools and inlets are sometimes swimmable, too. In good weather, visiting the bath is one of the most enjoyable experiences on the whole island. A hike west along the lava rocks yields pool after beautiful pool. The farther you go, the fewer people you see and it isn't hard to find a pool all to yourself. The high tide and heavy surf in the winter can make it too dangerous to swim in the pools; at any time of year, swimming in the open ocean beyond the pools is extremely dangerous. Bring shoes for the walk from your car to the bath, and when hiking around the lava rocks, be mindful of endangered monk seals who doze there. It is illegal to approach them and violators are fined heavily. Arrive early to beat the crowds. *(From Ka Haku Rd., turn toward the ocean on Punahele, which curves to the right to form a loop with Kapiolani. Just past the base of the loop, there is room to park, and a trail leads down toward the ocean. At the end of the trail, turn left and walk across the rocks for another 5min. to Queen's Bath.)*

HIDEAWAYS BEACH (PALI KE KUA BEACH). *(Snorkeling. Open daily 24hr.)* This beautiful, secluded, and short expanse of coarse gold sand has amazingly clear water and exceptional snorkeling. Although swimming is usually safe, be careful in the high surf and unpredictable tides of winter. Park on the right just before you get to the Princeville Hotel, in the tiny public lot between the hotel and Puu Poa condos. From there, Hideaways is 10min. down the narrow, very steep trail between the lot and the tennis court. Wet weather can make the walk dangerous; walk down in something sturdier than sandals.

PUU POA BEACH. *(Snorkeling. Open daily 24hr.)* In front of the Princeville Hotel and south along Hanalei Bay, Puu Poa is the resort's longest and most popular beach. A broad stretch of sand slopes gently to shallow and transparent water, and a long fringe reef protects a wide swath of tranquil water where even the littlest *keiki* (children) can safely swim and snorkel. For shade and a more secluded place to swim, walk left along the shore under the trees; the beach runs all the way to Hanalei Pier at Black Pot Beach. Park in the same public lot as for Hideaways (see above). The beach is accessible from a marked path that begins to the left of the Princeville Hotel's gatehouse and leads down to the beach.

On Kauai, swimmers should always be aware of the ocean's danger. If in doubt about the safety of a beach, do not enter the water. If you are caught in a rip current, swim with the current parallel to the shore. When the current releases you, continue to swim parallel to the shore, then make your way in.

HANALEI

Set in a deep green valley surrounded by sheer cliffs and cascading waterfalls, Hanalei (pop. 278) is marked by natural splendor and a welcoming, relaxed vibe. Within the diverse community, local taro root farmers mingle with affluent mainland tourists in the colorful shopping centers. The name Hanalei can be translated as "lei valley" or "crescent-shaped bay" because rainbows often drape the rain-heavy sky like leis. The pristine bay is the ocean playground of experienced wave riders and a wonderful backdrop for photographs. Its sparkling shore also served as the inspiration for Peter, Paul, and Mary's classic song about **a dragon named Puff.**

ORIENTATION AND PRACTICAL INFORMATION

Hanalei lies a few miles west of Princeville's manicured lawns and condominiums. Two large retail centers, brimming with choice restaurants and shops, face each other across the highway in the center of town. On the *mauka* (mountain) side is the **Hanalei Center,** whose pleasant lawn is dotted with picnic tables. Across the way, the **Ching Young Village** shops line both sides of an outdoor sidewalk where there are restrooms and pay phones.

Internet access is available at **Java Kai** (☎826-6717), in Hanalei Center, for $2.75 per 15min. or $12 for 2hr. over the course of a week. **Discount Activities,** on the corner of Hwy. 56 and Aku St., across from Zelo's, has four computers with DSL and a laptop connection. (☎826-1913. Internet $2 per 10min. Open daily 9am-sunset.) The **Hanalei Post Office,** 5226 Kuhio Hwy., is immediately west of Ching Young Center. (☎826-1290. Open M-F 9am-4pm, Sa 10am-noon.) **Postal Code:** 96714.

ACCOMMODATIONS

Taro Patch Hale ❸, 5475 D-Ojiki Rd., is a fitting name for a peaceful place to sleep in the middle of taro-filled Hanalei Valley. Rooms have kitchenettes, covered lanais, and private outdoor baths. (Turn left after the first bridge upon entering Hanalei and right as the bend in the road straightens out. Go 2 mi. up; Taro Patch Hale is on your left. ☎826-9828; www.hanaleivalley.kauaistyle.com. 3-night min. stay. Cleaning fee $35. Rooms $85.) The **Hanalei Inn ❸❹,** 55468 Kuhio Hwy., has simple but clean studio rooms with full kitchens and private bathrooms ($110-120) and offers a covered lanai, barbecue, hammocks, and a coin-operated washer/dryer. They also own additional rooms (twin bed $49; private rooms $129-169), right across from Hanalei Bay, at 5404 Weke Rd. (☎826-9333. MC/V.)

A PLATE OF LUNCH

If you're looking for a cheap bite to eat in Hawaii, it won't be long before you stumble across that ubiquitous classic, the plate lunch. The plate lunch is personal smorgasbord of meat with a side of carbs and more carbs, in the form of macaroni salad and rice.

Some theories suggest that the plate lunch derives from the Japanese bento, which is a similar single-portion takeout meal consisting of rice, fish, or meat with pickled or cooked vegetables. Others suggest that the plate lunch developed as a literal melting pot of cultural cuisines in the 1800s, when Hawaii's predominantly agricultural economy depended upon workers from Japan, China, Korea, Portugal, and the Philippines.

The plate lunch was made a fast food staple by L&L Drive Inn, founded in 1976. The restaurant earned a reputation for serving fresh plate lunches with generous portions for low prices. They franchised in 1988 and have currently spread to 160 locations, including seven mainland states (New Yorkers, rejoice!). Their entree plate lunch dishes include lau lau (pork chuck wrapped in taro leaves and then steamed), kalua pork (shredded, roasted pork served with cabbage), and chicken katsu (boneless chicken coated with a seasoning and deep fried).

FOOD

Nearly all of the North Shore restaurants take full advantage of the surrounding landscape's dramatic beauty. For a healthy snack or wholesome groceries, visit **Papaya's Natural Foods and Cafe,** 5-5121 Kuhio Hwy. The food window at the back serves salad, soup, and quinoa ($6.50 per lb.), along with strawberry-vanilla muffins ($2.50), and organic smoothies for $5.50. (☎826-0089. Grocery open daily 9am-8pm. Food stand open M-Sa 9am-4pm.) At the west end of Ching Young Village, **Big Save** also sells groceries and has an **ATM.** (☎826-6652. Open daily 7am-9pm.) For fresh fruit and crafts, go to the **Hanalei farmers' market,** on the south side of Hwy. 56, ¼ mi. past the Hanalei Center, at the Neighborhood Center and ballpark (Sa 9:30-11:30am).

Hanalei Dolphin Restaurant and Fish Market (☎826-6113), 5-5016 Kuhio Hwy., in the 1st building past the 1-lane Hanalei Bridge coming from the east. Beautiful woodworking and an airy feel make this restaurant worth the relatively higher cost. Outdoor seating on the grassy banks of the Hanalei River makes for excellent kayak-watching as you dine. Local catches ($23-29) are the signature of this popular seafood restaurant. Salads (fish salad, $11) and burgers (fin burger or charbroiled fresh fish of the day, $10) grace the lunch menu. Open daily 11am-9:30pm. MC/V. ❹

Zelo's Beach House, 5-5156 Kuhio Hwy., Bldg. G4 (☎826-9700), right before Ching Young Village. An extensive beer list (domestic, $3; drafts, $4.50) helps wash down baby back ribs ($20) or beer-battered fish 'n' chips ($14). Try the 52 oz. Party Margarita ($16). Happy hour daily 3:30-5:30pm. Open daily 11:30am-9:30pm. MC/V. ❸

Tropical Taco (☎827-8226), in the long green Halelea building past Kayak Kauai. A Hanalei institution for over 25 years, this former food truck had to move indoors to accommodate the lunchtime demand for its corn tortillas and beer-battered fish burritos ($8). Veggie burrito $7. Beef taco $8. Open M-Sa 11am-5pm. Cash only. ❶

Neide's Salsa and Samba (☎826-1851), in Hanalei Center. Enjoy spicy Mexican *antojitos* or authentic Brazilian cuisine in the sophisticated dining room or on the lanai. Locals rave about the *muqueca* (fresh catch with coconut sauce, shrimp, and Brazilian rice). Fish tacos $13. Nachos grande $9. Huevos rancheros $9. Open daily 11:30am-2:30pm and 5-9pm. MC/V. ❸

Java Kai (☎826-6717), in Hanalei Center. Java Kai's impressive array of coffee drinks is unsurpassed on the North Shore. Savor fabulous aloha bars (shortbread, coconut, macadamia nuts, and chocolate; $3) with your caffeine fix in the comfort of plush armchairs, or start the day with a sweet Kauai Waffle (topped with banana, papaya, macadamia nuts, and whipped cream; $8) on the lanai. Open daily 6:30am-6pm. **Internet access** available (p. 385). AmEx/D/MC/V. ❶

Hanalei Mixed Plate (☎826-7888), in Ching Young Center. Locals and tourists line up for hearty local food. Eat on the small lanai or make a picnic of it. Plate lunch choices include *shoyu* ginger chicken, *kalua* pork, and veggie stir-fry (1 entree, $8.25; 2, $9.25; 3, $10). Less adventurous eaters can nibble on burgers (veggie burger, $7), fresh fish ($12), or sandwiches. Open daily 11am-6pm. Cash only. ❶

Aloha Juice Bar (☎826-6990), on the west side of the Ching Young Center. This mobile juice bar blends smoothies and fresh organic juices (from $5) and sells a variety of local tropical fruit. The Hanalei Passion smoothie (a mix of mango, papaya, banana and passion fruit) is especially yummy. Open daily 9am-5pm. Cash only. ❶

BEACHES

Disarmingly beautiful Hanalei Bay attracts dozens of beachgoers who lie out on its soft, sandy shore; be advised that if you join them, you may never be able to tear yourself away. Swimming is only safe during the summer; currents, large waves, and unpredictable conditions make the water dangerous in winter. Winter surf also draws experienced wave riders who charge the huge peaks breaking inside the bay, while novice surfers attempt the baby swells which gently graze the shallow shoreline from June to August. The beaches below are all on Hanalei Bay.

BLACK POT BEACH. *(Open daily 24hr.)* Black Pot's sturdy pier and picnic tables provide great sunset views and a pleasant place for an evening picnic. Named for the communal cooking pot used by campers, the flat beach blends into the sandy parking lot and slopes gradually into murky water. Camping is only available on weekends and holidays. See **Camping in Hawaii,** p. 75, for information. To get there from the highway, turn *makai* (toward the ocean) on Aku Rd., next to Zelo's. Take a right where Aku ends at Weke Rd. and continue to the end of the road. There are restrooms, picnic tables, and grills.

HANALEI PAVILION BEACH PARK. *(Boogie boarding. Open daily 24hr. Lifeguards 9am-5pm.)* Shady trees and wood benches dot the wide lawn, and a pavilion shelters a few picnic tables at this beach park. In summer, *keiki* (children) play in the gentle waves that break along the sandy shore, and young boogie boarders slide through the water. Winter's larger surf makes swimming unappealing. From Aku Rd., turn right on Weke. The parking area will be on the left. Restrooms and showers are located alongside the pavilion.

WAIOLI BEACH PARK. *(Surfing. Wind sports. Open daily 24hr.)* Nicknamed "Pinetrees" by the local surfers who chill beneath the tall ironwoods, Waioli is a long, wide beach at the base of Hanalei Bay. The east end of Waioli Beach is less crowded than Hanalei Pavilion but sees similar waves. The west half is more exposed to ocean swells and has bigger surf that's more popular with surfing and kiteboard instructors. Summertime waves provide the perfect learning environment, but in winter it's strictly for the experienced. Pinetrees is the training ground of two-time world-champion surfer Andy Irons and his brother Bruce. From Aku Rd., turn left on Weke and then right down Hee Rd., Amaama Rd., or Anae Rd. to small dirt parking areas. Facilities at the east end of the beach.

WAIKOKO BEACH. *(Snorkeling. Open daily 24hr.)* Narrower than other Hanalei Bay beaches, Waikoko is visible from the highway at mi. marker 4. The water is a little too shallow for swimming, but local fishermen and snorkelers find the calm, reef-protected beach perfect. Waikoko's ribbon of fine sand is a nice place to sit and admire the scenery. Pull off the road just after mi. marker 4 to park and walk down to the beach.

ACTIVITIES

Due to high surf, ocean activities on the North Shore do not run during the winter.

Learn to Surf (☎826-7612; www.learntosurfkauai.com). Wanna-be surfers looking for the best value and the most personal attention should call Learn to Surf. Most lessons are taught by the very friendly, knowledgeable, and tall Cliff, who will meet students at whichever beach has that day's best surf. Their flexibility and friendly attitude make a great intro to surfing. 2-person 1½hr. lesson $40 per person; 3 or more $30.

Hawaiian Surfing Adventures (☎482-0749; www.hawaiiansurfingadventures.com), on the far north end of Black Pot Beach, where the Hanalei River enters the bay, offers surfing lessons and rentals. 2hr. lesson $55, private lesson $75. Rentals $5 per hr., $15 per day. 5hr. surfing safari to the best surf spots on the island $150; $50 each additional person.

Kayak Kauai (☎826-9844; www.kayakkauai.com), on the *makai* (ocean) side of the highway on the way into town from the east. Spring through fall, Kayak Kauai offers kayak and hiking tours (including a 17 mi., 13-14hr. kayak trip along the Na Pali Coast; $185). They also offer surfing and kayak lessons and rent out an array of beach and camping equipment. Reserve 24hr. in advance. Surfing and kayak lessons ($50) in Hanalei Bay daily 10am and 2pm. Tent $8 per day, stove $6 per day, snorkel gear $8 per day, surfboards $20 per day, bikes $15 per day, and kayaks for Hanalei and Wailua Rivers $28-75 per day. Rent any equipment for 4 days and get 3 additional days free. Open daily in summer 8am-8pm; in winter 8am-5:30pm.

Hanalei Surf Company Backdoor (☎826-1900, reservations 826-6924), in the Ching Young Village, has surfing lessons with Australian pro Russell Lewis and others. 2hr. lesson daily 10am and 1pm in Hanalei Bay. Private lesson $150, group lesson $65 per person. Open daily 9am-9pm.

Hanalei Surf Company (☎826-9000), in Hanalei Center, across the street from their Backdoor outlet, stocks all kinds of gear. Rents snorkel equipment ($5 per day), boogie boards ($5 per day), and surfboards ($15-20 per day, $65-100 per week). Open daily 9am-9pm.

Snorkel Depot, 5075 Kuhio Hwy. (☎826-9983), across from Kayak Kauai. Rents surfboards ($15-25 per day), boogie boards, snorkel gear, bikes, and even golf clubs.

Pedal 'n Paddle (☎826-9069; www.pedalnpaddle.com), in Ching Young Village. Rents a quality selection of kayaks (single $20, $80 per week; double $35/140), snorkel gear and boogie boards ($5 per day), bikes ($20 per day), and camping equipment (tent $12 per day, sleeping bag $3 per day). Open daily 9am-6pm.

ENTERTAINMENT

The best place to kick back with a drink and enjoy live entertainment is **Sushi and Blues,** in Ching Young Village. A jazz band plays Wednesday and Sunday 8:30-11:30pm, while local slack-key guitar artists perform Thursday and Saturday

8:30-11:30pm. Order fresh sushi (hand rolls, $4.50-6; maki rolls, $9-14), along with entrees such as linguini and scallops ($19) and coconut shrimp ($23). The entrees come with miso soup, vegetables, and a mini-sushi roll. (☎826-9701; www.sushiandblues.com. MC/V.)

SIGHTS

HANALEI NATIONAL WILDLIFE REFUGE. Many years ago, Hawaiians settled Hanalei, cultivating taro root in the fertile wetlands. Today, part of that tradition is preserved in the 917-acre refuge, visible from a highway overlook slightly west and to the *mauka* (mountain) side of the Princeville Shopping Center. The turnout provides a bird's-eye view of the meandering Hanalei River and the patchwork of taro ponds and fields scattered across the valley. The refuge was established in 1972 to protect the endangered native waterbirds, including the gallinule, coot, *koloa* duck, and black-necked stilt, and it also shelters wintering migrant birds. Local Hawaiian farmers work the taro root ponds on a rotating cycle. Less than 5% of the original taro patches remain, as much of the crop has been replaced with sugarcane. While public access to the wildlife refuge is restricted, a tour includes bird-watching, exploring the taro patches, and a stop at the Haraguchi Rice Mill. (☎651-3399; www.haraguchiricemill.org. Tours W at 10am. 3hr. tour $65, includes a picnic lunch.)

HAENA

While Haena has few services or shops, it's home to some of the most beautiful beaches in the state and a handful of intriguing natural sights. Popular activities include fishing, diving, snorkeling, hiking, and surfing. The town is home to a mix of Hawaiian taro root farmers, mainlanders living in fantastic beachfront homes, and visitors intent on exploring the area's unspoiled beauty.

ORIENTATION

Leaving Hanalei, **Route 560** ascends parallel to the western shore of Hanalei Bay before going through the miniscule town of **Wainiha** and following the coast through Haena to **Kee Beach.**

ACCOMMODATIONS AND CAMPING

A number of vacation rentals line the streets of Haena, and those with cash to burn can enjoy their luxury. In summer, staying elsewhere may be your best bet. An online search or a call to a rental agent will turn up many appealing—and certainly pricey—options. Less affluent travelers need not despair, as Haena is also home to one of the North Shore's only budget accommodations, **YMCA Camp Naue ❶**, on Kepuhi beach. Turn towards the ocean onto the west end of Alealea Rd., right before mi. marker 8. The not-for-profit camp, equipped with hot showers, sleeps 56 people in five bunkhouses and can accommodate tents on its lawn. During the summer the camp is typically reserved for large groups from youth organizations and schools and is closed to the public. The best time to find a bunk here is from mid-September to mid-April. Reservations are not accepted; to check availability, visit the campsite—a sign on the front gate will indicate whether or not the camp is open for drop-in travelers. (☎826-6419 or 246-9090. No linens. Tents $3 per person; bunks $12 per person. Arrive before dark. Cash only.)

FOOD

The only convenience store west of Hanalei is the **Wainiha General Store,** at mi. 6.5, on the left after the Wainiha Bridge. In addition to stocking drinks, snacks, and sunblock, it's also the last place to rent snorkel gear ($6 per day) on the way to the beaches. They also store bikes ($5 per day) and bags ($3 per day) for hikers heading to the Kalalau Trail. (☎826-6251. Open daily 10am-dusk.) **Red Hot Mama's ❷,** a food window next to the general store, serves a variety of Mexican-style dishes, including a taco salad ($8.50) and the popular "The Mama," a burrito with rice, lettuce, cheese, corn, beans and choice of protein or veggie for $8. (☎826-7266. Open daily 11am-5pm. Cash only.)

BEACHES

From the stark black lava rocks of Lumahai to the green vegetation on the cliffs at Kee, Haena's beaches are strikingly beautiful. Despite their soft sand and endless winter surf, the beaches of Hanalei Bay pale in comparison to the series of glorious golden beauties that line the shoreline to the west.

LUMAHAI BEACH. *(Boogie boarding. Snorkeling. Open daily 24hr.)* Considered by many to be Kauai's most beautiful beach, a picture of Lumahai sits in every postcard rack on the island. Divided into two stretches of sand by a mass of volcanic rock halfway down the beach, Lumahai is a joy to explore. The west half of the beach, bounded by a stream, is one of the widest beaches on Kauai. Devastating surf and powerful currents make swimming here unsafe year-round; the ocean has claimed more than one life. On the far west side of the beach, there are excellent barrel waves for boogie boarding. Sunbathers and fans of *South Pacific* frequent the captivating beach, and families with children sometimes take a dip in the stream. However, due to the occasional flash flood, swimming is not advised. The east half of Lumahai, also known as **Kahalahala Beach,** is even more exquisite than its western counterpart and a better place to swim and snorkel, but it is consequently more crowded. Powerful winter waves and tides can also make the sometimes placid water quite dangerous; stay away from the lava rocks on either side of the beach—freak waves can be deadly. Both halves of Lumahai are accessible from the other; merely climb over the giant rocks that separate the sands or walk on a path behind them. *(To access the west beach, an opening in the trees leads to a large dirt parking lot ¾ mi. after mi. marker 5. The east end is accessible via a short but steep 100 yd. trail that leads from a highway turnout down to the beach; ignore the misleading "no beach access" signs. Leaving Hanalei, the highway takes a U-curve toward the sea between mi. markers 4 and 5. Long turnouts lined with parked cars hug the base of the curve, and a short marked trail leads down to the beach from the second turnout.)*

KEPUHI BEACH. *(Snorkeling. Surfing. Wind sports. Open daily 24hr.)* This long, narrow ribbon of sand hugs the shoreline, hidden from the highway by a series of residential roads. Few visitors ever come to Kepuhi, and even locals tend to pass it over in favor of Tunnels (p. 391) to the west. The sloping beach provides good snorkeling during calm surf, but beware of occasionally strong currents. During low tide, a long wading pond forms along the rocky shore, which is perfect for small children. Local surfers and kiteboarders also frequent the windier west end of the beach during the summer, where there is a beautiful backdrop of lush green mountains. From the highway, turn right on One-one Rd. between mi. markers 7 and 8 just after Hanalei Colony Resort, left on Alealea, and then right on Alamoo Rd., which curves left to parallel the beach for about ½ mi.

Access is provided by unmarked pathways on both ends of Alamoo Rd., right at the bend in the road where it loops back out to Alealea; park on the grass along the side of the road.

TUNNELS BEACH (MAKUA BEACH). *(Snorkeling. Surfing. Open daily 24hr. Lifeguards daily.)* A wide horseshoe reef encloses the fine, and often hot, sand of the North Shore's premier snorkel and shore dive locale. On calm summer days, Tunnels' crystalline waters and intricate reef are a sight to behold. Despite its fame for complex underwater topography, the beach's name actually describes the hollowness of its winter surf. With the right wind and swell direction, the right-breaking Tunnels is arguably the best surf location on the island. Trees back the long sandy beach, providing much-appreciated shade. The coral reef is close to shore and shallow in parts; take extra care not to touch or step on the coral. There are no facilities, but Haena Beach Park (see below) is only a 10min. stroll along the beach to the west. Two unmarked dirt roads provide access. The first is ½ mi. west of mi. marker 8, just before a "Weight Limit 10 Tons" sign, and the second is ¼ mi. farther. The second dirt road is longer, offers a few more parking spaces, but also ends at a steeper slope to the beach. Due to the popularity of Tunnels, the spots tend to fill up quickly. It may be necessary to park at Haena Beach Park, ½ mi. down the road.

HAENA BEACH PARK. *(Open daily 24hr. Lifeguard 9am-5pm.)* Popular with Kalalau Trail backpackers, Haena boasts a grassy lawn that spawns a multitude of tents. A huge expanse of pleasant sand, picnic, bathroom, camping, and shower facilities, along with the Maniniholo Dry Cave (p. 392) across the street, make the beach park a nexus of North Shore activity. The beach park is closed to camping on Mondays for maintenance. Due to its exposure to ocean currents and the steepness of the beach itself, Haena is dangerous for swimmers, especially in the winter. The surf break, **Cannons,** on the west end of the beach, is exceptionally dangerous due to crazy currents and a sharp, shallow reef. Two parking areas are located on the highway just before mi. marker 9 and across from Maniniholo Dry Cave.

KEE BEACH. *(Snorkeling. Open daily 24hr.)* Kee attracts beachgoers with soft sand, exceptionally clear sapphire-blue water, and towering cliffs. Kalalau day-hikers (Kalalau Trail, p. 393), beachgoers, and cave explorers share the sprawling parking lot, which forks right to restrooms and pay phones. During the summer, experienced snorkelers can explore the area just beyond the reef, where a colorful array of fish swims alongside sea turtles. In winter, rip currents and waves make snorkeling impossible outside the protected reef. The sandy shore stretches east to Haena Beach, but most visitors stick to the area west of the parking lot, where a jumble of lava rocks leads around the bend to stunning views of the Na Pali cliffs—a very popular spot for sunset photographers. The beach is at the end of the highway and additional parking can be found about ½ mi. before the end, on the *makai* (ocean) side of the highway, in a lot marked "Visitor Parking."

SIGHTS

LIMAHULI GARDEN. The final link in the three **National Tropical Botanical Gardens** on Kauai (p. 402), Limahuli Garden features a comprehensive collection of native plants and traditional *lava* rock-wall terraces that date back over 700 years. Nestled in the foothills of the Na Pali cliffs, the garden aims to educate the public and re-establish native plants among more aggressive, introduced flora. Limahuli's focus on conservation complements the art and science themes of its sister gardens, the McBryde and Allerton Gardens, in the Lawai Valley. An uneven ¾ mi. trail meanders through the terraces and climbs up a bluff to a perch with outstanding views of the soft green mountains and bright blue ocean. *(Toward the mountain, between mi. markers 9 and 10, ¼ mi. before Kee Beach. ☎826-1053; www.ntbg.org. Open Tu-F and Su 9:30am-4pm. 2hr. guided tours at 10am by reservation only, $25. Self-guided tours $15, 12 and under free.)*

MANINIHOLO DRY CAVE. More of a landmark than an attraction, Maniniholo Dry Cave is a large crevice carved out of the soaring rock walls. Legend attributes the cave to a *menehune* tribe and a fisherman named Maniniholo who dug into the rock to capture an evil spirit that was stealing their catches. In the 1950s, a tsunami closed much of what was a huge cave. Stop for a quick picture and peak around the cavern. *(Across from Haena Beach Park. Parking available in the beach lot.)*

WET CAVES. Just west of the dry cave lies the boundary of **Haena State Park,** which encompasses Kee Beach and the nearby wet caves. Scientists estimate that the caves were formed 4000 years ago, during an earlier geological period that was marked by a higher sea level. Hawaiian lore offers a different story, crediting the fire goddess Pele with creating the two water-filled caverns. Scouring the islands for a hot, dry home to suit her needs, Pele came across the North Shore of Kauai but quickly left when her subterranean explorations yielded water. Of the two caves, **Waiakapalae,** the eastern cave, is the more impressive one. A short hike from the highway leads to the huge cave, where the water is freezing, though clear. The cave is said to be home to a water-loving lizard goddess, and the graying water of the cavern supposedly reflects her aging hair. The smaller, murkier cave, **Waikanaloa,** is visible from the road, just a few hundred yards west of Waiakapalae. Linked to the ocean below ground, the level of the two freshwater caves fluctuates with the tide, and divers sometimes explore Waikanaloa. Signs request that visitors don't swim and warn of *leptospirosis* and falling rocks, though there are usually people wading around anyway. *(A grassy visitor parking lot on the ocean side of the highway shortly past Limahuli Garden provides access to the trail, which begins a little farther down and across the street. There is also limited parking right at the trailhead. Waikanaloa is farther up the highway, just before the Kee parking lot.)*

NA PALI COAST

The Na Pali Coast refers to 15 rugged miles of jagged cliff and pristine coastline that stretch from **Kee Beach** (p. 391) in the north to **Polihale State Park** (p. 421) in the south. There is no way to drive through this unmarred part of Kauai; visitors can journey either by foot or by boat. Those who do visit the concealed coast will encounter steep lava rock walls, fertile green valleys, secluded sandy beaches, and cascading waterfalls.

The steep *na pali* (cliffs) tower up to 4000 ft. above the ocean. At one time, however, the terrain sloped gradually from the ancient volcanic dome to the sea. Powerful winter surf and constant water flowing from Mt. Waialeale combined to sculpt the coast, eroding its foundations and causing massive landslides. Slowly, the coast's prominent cliffs, narrow canyons, and valleys took shape.

The five large valleys strung between Kalalau and Milolii have rich agricultural lands that once sustained hundreds of inhabitants. Reliable water sources provided easy irrigation for taro root farms where the valley residents cultivated their staple food. Native fishermen reaped abundant catches in the waters offshore, and the moist soil proved perfect for cultivating Polynesian crops such as bananas, sweet potatoes, coconuts, and breadfruit. Today, these trees continue to flourish alongside the more recently introduced mangos, passion fruit, guava, and plums. The simple life of farming and fishing was the standard in the Na Pali valleys for hundreds of years, until the beginning of the 20th century, when many residents began to abandon their remote settlements for the booming towns of Waimea and Hanalei. By the 1920s, the coast's only inhabitants were grazing herds of cattle. When camping hippies took over in the late 1960s, the state worked to control the burgeoning tent cities and protect the wild coast from a sanitation disaster. Beginning with the Kalalau Valley, the establishment of the Na Pali Coast State Park has strictly regulated human access and allowed the coastline to regain most of its original splendor.

KALALAU TRAIL

Long ago, a series of trails stretched all the way from Polihale to Haena, but hundreds of years of wind and waves erased the fragile dirt paths until only the **Kalalau Trail** remained. Originally cleared by Hawaiian traders who traveled the coast by canoe and on foot, the trail was widened in 1860 to allow for the transportation of coffee, oranges, and cattle from Na Pali's valleys to markets in Hanalei.

Today, adventurers from around the globe come to Kauai to experience the Kalalau Trail, traveling 11 mi. southwest along the Na Pali Coast. It crosses five major valleys (from northeast to southwest: Hanakapiai, Hoolulu, Waiahuakua, Hanakoa, and Kalalau) and at least half a dozen streams before it is stopped by the impassable, fluted green cliffs of Kalalau Valley. The trail alternates between exposed oceanside cliffs and ridges with outstanding views of the coastline and sheltered, quiet stretches through shady valleys and streams. Mile markers are posted throughout the trail, though they are difficult to spot. There are three shorter side trails that branch off the Kalalau Trail: the Hanakapiai Falls Trail (2 mi.), the Hanakoa Falls Trail (¼ mi.), and the Kalalau Valley Trail (2 mi.).

The condition of the Kalalau Trail varies greatly with the season and, more importantly, the current weather conditions. The trail is 1 to 2 ft. wide, and rarely flat or very steep. Parts of the trail cross cliff faces where there is poor footing and a dizzying drop to rocks and surf below. Acrophobics or

PASS THE PLACENTA

While the moral status of the human embryo is the centerpiece of many debates in the US, the lowly placenta is usually ignored. However, this changed on April 21, 2006, when Hawaii became the first state to legislate on the tissue, passing a bill allowing hospitals to release placentas to mothers under certain conditions.

Hawaii's interest in placenta is the result of the tissue's historic role in Hawaiian culture. According to ancient Hawaiian folklore, the placenta, or *lewe*, is believed to connect a child to its birthplace. Traditional ceremonies involve burying the placenta under a tree, whose growth then mirrors the spiritual and psychological growth of the child.

With the growing concern over infectious disease and HIV transmission to health care workers, the Hawaii State Department of Health declared the placenta "infectious waste," which should not be returned to the mother. The issue rose to the public spotlight after one couple sued in federal court after being denied the return of the mother's placenta at Kaiser Medical Center in Honolulu.

The state legislature, succumbing under public pressure, passed the bill allowing the release of the placenta under the condition that it test negative for HIV and hepatitis. For now, Hawaiians can have their placenta and bury it too.

anyone with less than sure footing should not attempt the hike to Kalalau Beach. Wet weather makes parts of the trail muddy, and stone stretches can be hazardous, so hiking boots with ankle support are vital. It's wise to wait until high waters recede before attempting to cross streams, since flash floods are common.

In ideal weather, a physically fit hiker can make it from Kee Beach to Kalalau Beach without any stops or side hikes in 7-8hr. Nevertheless, be ready for wet and hot weather, flooded streams, or any number of other obstacles that can slow things down. By leaving early in the morning, you stand a chance of avoiding day-hiker traffic on the first 2 mi., and you can afford to rest more often as you hike the last few dry, exposed miles under the scorching midday sun. The two campsites (Hanakapiai Beach, at mi. marker 2, and the day-use only Hanakoa Stream, at mi. marker 6) are equipped with restrooms and a sheltered picnic table or two. Remember that all water must be treated before drinking. Some hikers cover the entire 22 mi. round-trip in two days, but most people allow up to five days to enjoy the arresting vistas and pristine beaches along the way.

PERMITS. A state park camping permit is required of all campers and dayhikers who go beyond Hanakapiai Beach. Permits cost $10 per night per person, up to 5 people per group, with a 5-day max. stay. Permits can sell out up to a year in advance. During summer, one-third of permits are issued for 1 week periods 4 weeks in advance at the Division of State Parks Office. Pick them up on Wednesdays at 8am. Check with the office (p. 78) for last-minute cancellations even a few days before a potential hike.

HIKING

There are four basic types of hikes on Na Pali Coast: a day hike from Kee Beach to Hanakapiai Beach and back, a multi-day hike to the end of the Kalalau Trail, a hike all the way to Kalalau Beach in one day, and several side hikes.

KEE BEACH TO HANAKAPIAI BEACH. *(2 mi. 1-2hr. Moderate.)* Relatively wide, the hike from the Kee Beach parking lot to Hanakapiai is the part of the trail least likely to induce vertigo. A popular day hike for visitors and locals, traffic on the trail can be congested during the summer, especially along the first mile. The initial part of the trail, laden with rocks, climbs steadily uphill, affording panoramic views of Kee and the green, thickly-vegetated cliffs. Less ambitious hikers can walk a short but strenuous ½ mi. and still enjoy the view. A few hundred yards before reaching Hanakapiai, a striped pole marks the elevation below which hikers would be in danger during a tsunami—it is surprisingly high above sea level. A wide, glorious stretch of sand in summer, Hanakapiai Beach all but disappears during the winter. Totally exposed to the forces of the ocean, it might be Kauai's most dangerous beach, a fact hikers are reminded of by a memorial sign on the side of the trail carved with a tally mark for every recent drowning victim—there are at least 60. Powerful currents moving along the coast to the west and pounding surf make winter swimming here extraordinarily dangerous. Although the beach can be calm and inviting in summer, swimmers are cautioned to evaluate ocean conditions before diving in. Besides swimming in the ocean, Hanakapiai Beach and the surrounding area offer campsites, an outhouse, and plenty of boulders on which to sunbathe. The beach is accessible by bearing right after crossing a stream; the trail continues to the left after the crossing.

HANAKAPIAI FALLS SIDE HIKE. *(4 mi. 2¾-3¼hr. round-trip. Challenging.)* Many day-hikers combine this side trail with the hike from Kee, forming a strenuous 8 mi. round-trip. From Hanakapiai Beach, allow 3hr. to make the 4 mi. round-trip hike to the falls and back, which covers terrain more challenging than most of the Kalalau Trail itself. The side hike splits off from the Kalalau Trail about 30 yd. past the stream crossing; go straight for the campsite and side hike. The Kalalau Trail veers right. The waterfall trail is unmarked until you are past the campsite. There is a sign just beyond a cleared helicopter landing site on the far side of the camping area that reads "trail" with the words "waterfall" etched above. After taro root farms, bamboo groves, the remains of an old coffee mill once operated by *haole* (Caucasian) planters, and three stream crossings, weary hikers are rewarded with an astonishing 250 ft. waterfall. Due to the potential danger of falling rocks, swimming is not recommended, although visitors have been known to take a dip. The trail is not steep, but because it is rocky, uneven, and usually wet, it can be difficult, especially the last mile which is not maintained by the state park.

HANAKAPIAI BEACH TO HANAKOA VALLEY. *(4 mi. 2¾-3¼hr. Challenging.)* An endless series of steep switchbacks that leads 800 ft. uphill, the grueling ascent out of Hanakapiai Valley is arguably the hardest part of the Kalalau trail. About 3½ mi. in from Kee, the trail passes between a cliff on the left and a huge boulder on the right, opening up to a staggering view of Hoolulu Valley, the second of the five major valleys that the Kalalau Trail crosses. Having left behind Hanakapiai Valley and the day-hikers that crowd it, Hoolulu Valley introduces hikers to the real Kalalau Trail: wild, isolated, and awe-inspiring. The trail is gentle as it passes mi. marker 4, proceeding to the other side of Hoolulu and into the next valley, Waiahuakua. Around 5¾ mi., the trail suddenly leaves the ocean behind and takes hikers from windy, exposed cliffs into the quiet, shady, and lush Hanakoa Valley. Mi. marker 6 is about 100 yd. shy of Hanakoa Campground. The outhouse on the far side of the river and sheltered picnic table are a nice convenience, although the area has been semi-permanently closed to camping. The trail then crosses Hanakoa Stream at the point where two branches of the stream meet; the crossing can be tricky when the water level is high. Just across the stream and up the trail to the left are more campsites, another picnic table, and a restroom.

HANAKOA FALLS SIDE HIKE. *(½ mi. 30-40min. round-trip. Easy.)* The Hanakoa Falls Trail branches off the Kalalau Trail near the stream crossing on the Kalalau Beach side, continuing up the left fork of the valley about ½ mi. A small sign on the shelter next to the Kalalau Trail points the way to the trail. The first 100 yd. of the trail are the most difficult to follow, as it crosses back over the right branch of the stream and winds through a few campsites. Bear left, and you will stay roughly on track; eventually all paths lead to the main trail, which is marked by pink and orange ribbons every 50 yd. for most of its length. The trail is not very steep, though it's often wet. You must navigate two side streams to continue onto a ridge that has a stunning view of a larger stream below. Continue along this stream for a few hundred yards to reach the falls. The cliffs surrounding the falls form a 270° arc that puts Hanakoa Falls in the middle of a natural amphitheater, making it one of the most superb, eye-opening views on the entire coast. The remote location means that you'll probably have the place all to yourself. The trip is easily worth the side hike.

HANAKOA VALLEY TO KALALAU BEACH. *(5 mi. 3-3½hr. Challenging.)* After ascending the ridge out of Hanakoa Valley, the lush lowland valleys and flourishing trees are replaced by arid terrain. The dry heat of the West Shore and the lack of shade make this segment of the trail a very sweaty experience, but spectacular views of the surrounding cliffs and coast far outweigh the discomfort. After the trail exits Hanakoa Valley, it winds down a series of steep switchbacks into one of the more nerve-rattling sections of the trail. Narrow and rocky, the trail between mi. markers 7 and 8 traverses a number of cliff edges that require extra concentration to pass safely, as dangerously steep cliffs could cause serious injuries. A glance down to the frothy, churning sea below provides hikers with a peek at gorgeous sea caves and arches. This section of the trail also affords the first, though distant, view of Kalalau Beach during the summer (in winter high surf obscures the beach). Shortly after mi. marker 9, hikers "officially" enter the majestic Kalalau Valley, whose impossibly steep walls and sheer size make other valleys look like the drainage ditches by the roadside. A sign marks the entrance to the valley and sets the tone for the rest of the hike, saying first in Hawaiian, and then in English: "This is sacred land. Give it your utmost care, respect, and leave knowing you have preserved it for future generations." Mi. marker 10 is at the crossing of Kalalau Stream, and the final mile is a nearly flat footpath to the beach.

KALALAU BEACH. Few beaches in Hawaii change as dramatically from season to season as Kalalau. In the summer, the beach spans nearly ½ mi. of the coast; in the winter, the southwestern end is completely overtaken by the surf that pounds the cliff walls. At the northeast end, the waves crash all the way up to the boulders. Swimming is sometimes possible in the summer months, but be cautious—the beach has notoriously vicious currents. The Kalalau Trail finally ends at a small waterfall at the end of the campground where hikers often bathe. There are two outhouses, a sheltered picnic table, a grassy lawn, and dozens of small campsites by the beach. Sand campsites are on the ocean side of the trail, only feet from the water, while dirt campsites lie on the valley side, hidden in the trees that cover most of the land between the trail and looming cliffs. The beach is very windy, so it is best to take a campsite within the protected forest or in one of the sea caves on the far side of the beach in summer.

KALALAU VALLEY SIDE HIKE. *(4 mi. 2-2½hr. round-trip. Easy.)* This spur trail is a pleasant way for multi-day campers to escape the midday sun. The trail begins slightly past mi. marker 10, a few yards up the slope on the southwest bank of the Kalalau Stream, where the Kalalau Trail forms a T. To the right is the ocean and the last mile of the trail that leads to Kalalau Beach; to the left is the valley trail, which gently climbs for 2 mi. until it reaches a series of pools in the stream known as "Big Pools." The valley trail passes through quiet, shady country dotted with guava and mango trees, bamboo, and agricultural terraces originally built by Native Hawaiians. Other, smaller trails branch off the main trail and often lead to campsites of some of the valley's semi-permanent residents, throwbacks to the 1960s when hippies made Kalalau Valley their home. The trail makes two easy stream crossings and offers at least one unforgettable view of the valley from a short stretch of trail that meanders out onto a small, rocky, open field. Here, hikers get the closest and most overwhelming view of the 1000 ft. sheer cliffs that enclose the valley. The trail ends when it runs into the stream at Big Pools. The lower pool is about 6 ft. deep: a wonderful spot for a dip.

WEST OF KALALAU

From Kalalau Valley south to Polihale, the cliffs of the Na Pali Coast are far too steep for hikers. Those who wish to explore this part of the coast must do so by boat or helicopter, and countless companies of both types advertise all over the island. More adventurous travelers can tour the coast by kayak, either alone or with a guided trip; **Kayak Kauai** (p. 388) leads 14hr. sea tours that include transportation back from Polihale. Most kayakers travel only one way—launching at Kee, following the currents from north to south, and finishing at Polihale.

By sea, the 1½hr. hike to **Hanakapiai Beach** from Kee becomes a quick 5min. paddle, but boat landings are prohibited. Cruising past the trail-accessible section of the shoreline, boaters and kayakers pass Kalalau Beach and arrive at Honopu, the second of five major valleys stretching from **Kalalau** in the northeast to **Milolii** in the southwest. Although the verdant valley of Honopu lies far above ocean travelers, its scenic beach, divided by an arch, makes for breathtaking photographs. Continuing west for ¼ mi., **Awaawapuhi Valley** winds through a deep canyon 3000 ft. below sheer, green cliffs. A strenuous trail in **Kokee State Park** (p. 415) ends at a steep ridge overlooking the same valley. Nine miles west of Kee Beach, the beach at **Nualolo** is sheltered by a wide reef, which makes landings much easier than along the exposed coast, and offers some of the best snorkeling on the island. The Nualolo Valley is filled with ancient taro terraces. Another reef provides safe landing at the secluded beach 2 mi. further at Milolii (see **Camping in Hawaii,** p. 75, for more information). A few more miles of plunging cliffs and clear water separate the Na Pali Coast from **Polihale State Park** (p. 421), where kayakers from the North Shore, exhausted and dizzy from resplendent views, can crash on the beach.

Not surprisingly, most visitors to Kauai forego kayaking and skim beside the Na Pali Coast in power **catamarans** that cruise the waters or helicopters that crisscross the Na Pali sky. Countless tour boat operators leave from the West Shore—and a few from the North Shore—most on half-day snorkeling and sightseeing trips. Most of the tours only operate fully in the summer months; in the winter, many companies switch to a limited schedule.

Catamaran Kahanu is a Native Hawaiian-run operation based out of Port Allen that provides a 5hr. morning tour of Na Pali including swimming and snorkeling at Nualolo beach and lunch (M-Sa 8am-1:30pm) and an afternoon tour (M-F 2-7pm) without lunch or swimming. (☎645-6176; www.catamarankahanu.com. $125, ages 4-11 $85.) **Na Pali Riders** offers a full tour of the Na Pali coast in a 30-ft., high speed raft, leaving from Waimea at 6:30, 10:30am, and 2:30pm. (☎742-6331; www.napaliriders.com. $99, ages 5-12 $89; includes snorkeling and snacks.)

SOUTH SHORE

The southern shore of Kauai draws the greatest concentration of tourists, who come for the sun and sand of its unbeatable beaches. The south shoreline encounters the calmest water of the island year-round—it's the only place where swimming is safe in winter. Yet the South Shore is not just a homogeneous region of resorts and beach-bound tourists—Koloa still harbors a small-town ambience.

POIPU

The southernmost town on Kauai, Poipu (pop. 1,075) is known for sunny skies, white-sand beaches, stellar surfing, snorkeling, and huge resorts. Luxurious hotels and expensive restaurants sit mere feet from the water's sandy shore, but budget travelers can find cheaper B&Bs in the area. Sea turtles and colorful fish also favor the warm southern waters, which offer excellent opportuni-

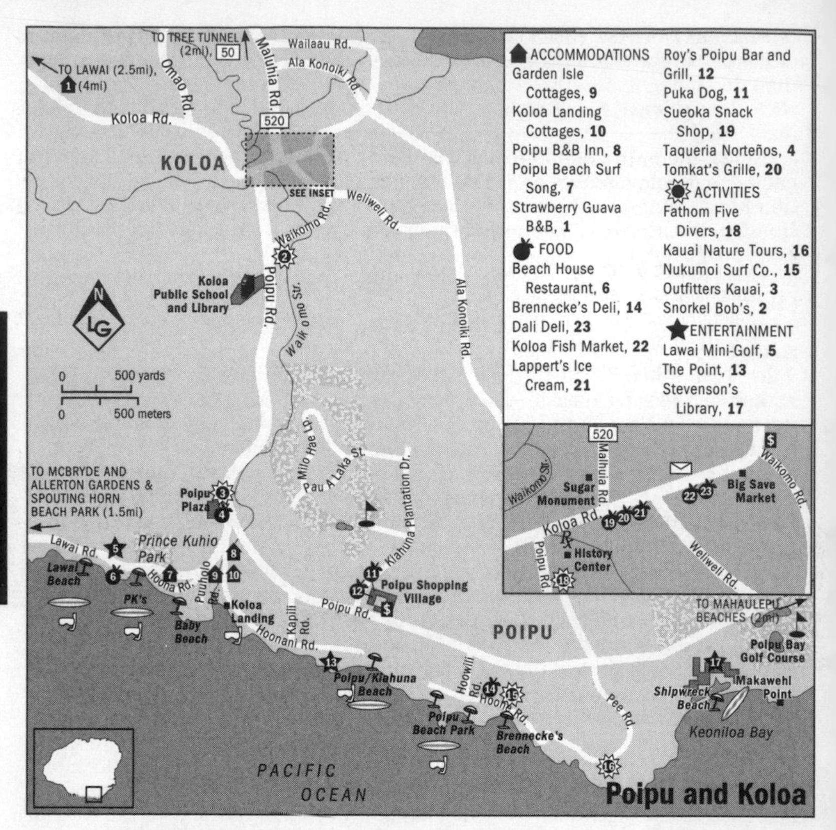

ties for both free diving and scuba diving. The town is overshadowed by the stunning coast; downtown is little more than a shopping center facing a wall of condominiums.

ORIENTATION

From Lihue, **Highway 50** runs 7 mi. until **Highway 520** branches off to the south. The intersection is marked by the Tree Tunnel, made from hundreds of eucalyptus trees donated by Walter Duncan McBryde. The trees shade cars for a full mile along Hwy. 520, which travels south toward Poipu and Koloa. For the sake of simplicity, all the sights and beaches on the ocean will be listed in Poipu. Three miles after leaving Hwy. 50, Hwy. 520 passes through Koloa and continues south on **Poipu Road,** passing Poipu Plaza before forking east where the area's resorts and condominiums are concentrated, and west to **Lawai Road, PK's,** and **Spouting Horn.**

PRACTICAL INFORMATION

Primarily composed of resorts and beaches, Poipu has limited services for non-resort guests. Not to worry—nearby Koloa can supply anything Poipu lacks. A small **Bank of Hawaii,** 2360 Kiahuna Plantation Dr., in Poipu Shopping Village, has a **24hr. ATM.** (☎742-6800. Open M-Th 8:30am-4pm, F 8:30am-6pm.)

ACCOMMODATIONS

Countless condominium developments and a few pricey resort hotels line Lawai and Poipu Rd.; an online search will return many options. To save a few hundred dollars a night, you may want to focus on privately owned and listed condos or vacation homes, or stay in nearby Kalaheo.

Poipu Beach SurfSong, 5135 Hoona Rd. (☎742-2331; www.surfsong.com). The bright salmon-colored building on a peaceful road contains 3 well-furnished studios and a 1-bedroom unit with full kitchen. Right across the street from Baby Beach, but without the steep price tag. The tropical garden has bananas and a gas grill for barbecues. Units $75-135. Discounts for longer stays available. AmEx/MC/V. ❸

Koloa Landing Cottages, 2704B Hoonani Rd. (☎742-1470; www.koloa-landing.com), on Hoonani Rd., about 100 yd. after it branches off Lawai Rd. 4 colorful cottages, from studios to a 2-bedroom house have full kitchens, lanais, and wireless Internet access. Koloa Landing also manages another 2-bedroom "budget" house near the center of Koloa town, and a 3-bedroom house and 1-bedroom cottage near Brennecke's Beach. Units are cheerful, airy, and clean, and the hospitable owners do their best to make you feel at home. Discounts for longer stays available. Cleaning fee $50-75 for stays less than 6 nights. Units $105-200. Cash only. ❸

Garden Isle Cottages, 2658 Puuholo Rd. (☎742-6717; www.oceancottages.com), on the left if you turn south from Lawai Rd. 4 luxurious oceanfront 1-bedroom cottages, each with a private lanai overlooking a rocky cove and the ocean. Laundry, telephone, and kitchenettes. 2-night min. stay. Cleaning fee $50. High season doubles $220; low-season $198; each additional guest $10. Cash only. ❺

FOOD

As grocery prices are high in Poipi, head to the cheap **Sueoka Snack Shop** (p. 405), in Koloa, for basic necessities. (☎742-1601. Open M-F 8am-8:30pm, Sa-Su 8am-6:30pm.) Eating out can be a costly habit in Poipu, but thankfully sandwich shops and burrito stands serve as cheap alternatives.

Beach House Restaurant, 5022 Lawai Rd. (☎742-1424), next to Lawai Beach. Views of surfers and sunsets, and a dazzling oceanfront location keep this casually elegant beachfront restaurant packed. The sophisticated menu blends international flavors with fresh local seafood and vegetables. The fish nacho appetizer with refried black Thai rice, roasted Hawaiian corn and chili salsa, and mango chipotle sauce ($13) is delicious. Entrees include the fire-roasted mahi mahi ($29) and the tasty kiawe grilled filet mignon ($30). Reservations recommended. Open daily 5-10pm. AmEx/MC/V. ❺

Puka Dog, 2360 Kiahuna Plantation Dr. (☎742-6044), in Poipu Shopping Village. The menu is simple, and the food is delicious. A puka dog is a hot dog inserted into a hole cut at the end of a roll, topped with spicy garlic lemon sauce and a range of relishes including Polihale Sunset (papaya relish) and Waimea Canyon (banana relish). Polish or veggie sausage $6.25. Lemonade $2.25. Open M-Sa 11am-6pm. Cash only. ❶

Roy's Poipu Bar and Grill (☎742-5000), in Poipu Shopping Village. The place to see and be seen—Hawaii's celebrity chef, Roy Yamaguchi, has attracted a loyal following with "Hawaiian-fusion" cuisine. For those with the money, there's no better place to go in terms of food quality and **overall bling.** The menu, constantly in flux, features an entire page of nightly specials, including plenty of fresh island fish (gingered tempura mahi mahi, $34), dim sum-style appetizers, fresh local salads, and *imu*-baked pizzas. Reservations recommended. Open daily 5:30-9:30pm. AmEx/MC/V. ❺

Brennecke's Deli, 2100 Hoone Rd. (☎742-1582), across from Poipu Beach Park, serves made-to-order deli sandwiches ($5.25-6.25) to hungry beachgoers, picnickers, and adventurers who take their food to go. Some of the biggest servings of shave ice on the island ($3.50), and a small convenience store with a limited selection of snacks, drinks, and most other beach essentials (including sunscreen). Upstairs is **Brennecke's Beach Broiler** (☎742-7588), a steak and seafood restaurant that offers a beautiful sunset view of Poipu Beach. Happy hour daily 3-5pm; draft beers pitchers $8-11, mai tais and margaritas $4.75. Deli open daily 8am-9pm. Broiler open daily 11am-10pm. MC/V. Deli ❶/Broiler ❹

Taqueria Norteños, 2827A Poipu Rd. (☎742-7222). Ahole-in-the-wall in Poipu Plaza affectionately known as "The Crack," this Mexican food stand serves huge portions for low prices. Huge burritos (meat or veggie), tacos, tostadas, chalupas, and nachos $2-4. Open M-Tu and Th-Su 11am-9pm. Cash only. ❶

BEACHES

Recently recognized as "America's #1 Beach" by Steve "Dr. Beach" Leatherman (see **Dr. Beach on Hawaii's Beaches,** p. 422), sunny Poipu Beach and the neighboring sandy coves that line Kauai's southern coast possess excellent snorkeling sites, safe swimming, crystal-clear waters, and remarkable sea cliffs. Summertime swells are excellent for boogie boarding and surfing, too. The beaches below are listed from west to east, and all lie on or just off Lawai Rd. or Poipu Rd.

LAWAI BEACH (BEACH HOUSE). *(Boogie boarding. Snorkeling. Surfing. Open daily 24hr.)* Close-by condos and the occasional monk seal sighting make this short and narrow stretch of sand and rock a daytime hot spot. Boogie boarders ride the beachbreak, while experienced surfers favor the larger waves behind the Beach House. Swimming is usually safe, and snorkelers enjoy the shallow, clear water just west of the restaurant. High tide covers nearly all of the sand, but the pleasant lawn around the Beach House provides a consistent, comfortable cushion for sunbathers and a great view of Kauai's famous sunsets. The beach is on Lawai Rd., 1 mi. west of the fork, next to the Beach House Restaurant. Public parking is available in a small lot in front of the Lawai Beach Resort.

PK'S. *(Boogie boarding. Snorkeling. Surfing. Open daily 24hr.)* This tiny patch of sand surrounded by rocks is the birthplace of Prince Kuhio ("PK") who witnessed the US overthrow of the Hawaiian monarchy in 1893 and went on to become Hawaii's delegate to Congress for 19 years. Early risers take advantage of relatively calm water to snorkel or spend time with the big sea turtles that frequent often intimidating waves. PK's is also an excellent place for non-snorkelers to watch turtles as they bob in the water. Surfers and boogie boarders revel in the South Shore's best waves, but will have to cope with everyone else who's doing the same. PK's is past Lawai Beach, across from Prince Kuhio Park.

BABY BEACH. *(Open daily 24hr.)* Hidden behind Hoone Rd., a narrow ribbon of fine sand embraces a calm, shallow pool protected by a wall of black lava rocks. As the sand on the bottom of the pool gives way to rock, adults will have to squat rather than swim—this one is definitely for the kids. There are several access points, but the best is a 2min. walk east from PK's to a marked beach access—look for the red handrail just past a brown stone house.

KOLOA LANDING. *(Snorkeling. Open daily 24hr.)* Once the largest port on Kauai, Koloa Landing is now the South Shore's premier scuba diving spot. Local dive shops, including **Fathom Five** (see **Koloa,** p. 404), often bring entry-level shore divers here, and the water can get downright crowded with flopping snorkelers. An old boat ramp provides very easy access to the slightly cloudy near-shore water that clears up farther away from land. A handful of snorkelers can usually be found kicking about the western end of the rocky inlet. From Lawai Rd. eastbound, turn right on Hoonani Rd. and park in the dirt clearing half a block up on the right. More parking is down the driveway to the left, but space is limited. The landing is down a very rough one-lane driveway on the right; it is best to walk rather than drive down.

POIPU/KIAHUNA BEACH. *(Boogie boarding. Snorkeling. Surfing. Open daily 24hr.)* Running from the Sheraton to the Kiahuna Plantation Resort, this long crescent beach is backed by resorts and a neat row of tall, swaying palms along its entire length. Surfers crowd the crisp breaking waves a short paddle offshore. If you thrive on activity, wedge your towel into an available patch of sand or join the throng of boogie boarders or snorkelers. Surfers can use Kiahuna Beach or Poipu Beach Park to paddle out to the waves that break over a shallow reef point between the two beaches. The first of two public parking lots on Hoonani Rd. sits just west of the entrance to the Sheraton, a 5min. walk from the beach. The other, more crowded lot is at the eastern end of the road, directly behind the beach.

POIPU BEACH PARK. *(Snorkeling. Surfing. Open daily 24hr. Lifeguards 9am-5pm.)* Extensive facilities, including picnic tables, grills, showers, restrooms, playgrounds, a large lawn, and a lifeguard station, attract a diverse crowd to Poipu's—and probably Kauai's—most popular beach. At low tide, sunbathers can walk all the way out to the point along a thin sandy peninsula, but high tide submerges the path and turns the tip of the point into an island. Swimming is safe on both sides of the isthmus, but snorkelers prefer the shallow protected area west of the point. Poipu Beach is also home to one of the South Shore's better surf breaks, especially for beginner- and intermediate-level surfers, and it's a cinch to rent a board across the street at the **Nukumoi Surf Company** (p. 402). Sand space is at a premium, and late arrivals will probably be relegated to the western end. Access the beach from Hoowili Rd. From eastbound Poipu Rd., turn right at the sign a few blocks past Poipu Shopping Village. Two large parking lots lie at the end of the road directly across from the beach.

BRENNECKE'S BEACH. *(Boogie boarding. Open daily 24hr.)* A small, semi-protected beach surrounded by rocks, Brennecke's is best known for its tantalizingly large barrel waves perfect for boogie boarding and bodysurfing. The rocky shore on both sides of the narrow beach also attracts a population of sea turtles. From Poipu Beach Park, walk east a couple hundred yards to the end of the grassy area.

SHIPWRECK BEACH (KEONILOA BAY). *(Boogie boarding. Surfing. Open daily 24hr.)* Poipu's widest beach fronts the grand Hyatt Regency. Surprisingly few hotel guests venture onto this beautiful—but slightly windy—beach, preferring the artificial sand-ringed pools and comfy lounge chairs behind the hedge. While mostly populated by locals, the beach is big enough that visitors will not feel like they are intruding. Look out to Makawehi Point, the striking cliff to the east, which made its Hollywood debut as a diving platform for Harrison Ford in

Six Days Seven Nights. Large waves frequently crash here in the summer, making it ideal for boogie boarding and surfing, but beware of the rocky floor. Turn right on Ainako from Poipu Rd. immediately after the Hyatt, at Poipu Bay Golf Course. A parking lot is located right behind the sand.

MAHAULEPU BEACHES. *(Wind sports. Open daily 7:30am-7pm.)* These two pretty, relatively deserted beaches offer great kiteboarding, peaceful sunbathing, limited swimming, plenty of pole-fishing, and a wonderful place for a stroll. From the west section of Mahaulepu to the east, the first stop on the road is long, narrow **Gillin's Beach,** which has little shade and wild waves. The eastern end of Gillin's provides some swimming, and ideal winds for kiteboarders. For slightly calmer waters, either drive or walk along the coast to **Kawailoa Bay,** a pleasant half-crescent of white sand most often visited by picnicking locals. The rocky outcroppings just east of the bay are a popular pole-fishing spot. The area also has a few shady trees and some of Mahaulepu's best swimming. An eastbound stroll from Kawailoa Bay to the fence along the shore rewards walkers with grassy fields, beautiful views, and a very small, secluded stretch of sand where the water is frequently choppy.

Access to the Mahaulepu beaches is over privately owned land, so please respect the surroundings and refrain from giving the owners any reason to suspend access. Continue down Poipu Rd. as it turns into dirt past the Hyatt, and turn right 1½ mi. later at the T; stay right at the second fork for Kawailoa Bay. The parking area for Gillin's Beach is another ½ mi. down. The beach is a short walk down any of the overgrown trails from the lot. To reach Kawailoa Bay, continue down a dirt road until it runs along the ocean. The parking area is on the right.

ACTIVITIES

Kauai Nature Tours, 1770 Pee Rd. (☎742-8305; www.kauainaturetours.com). Geologist Chuck and his son Rob lead small group adventures to most of Kauai's standout natural sites. Tours range from easy coastal walks along Mahaulepu to strenuous day hikes along the Na Pali Coast, Waimea Canyon, and Sleeping Giant. Full-day hikes include lunch, water, snacks, and transportation. $87-97, ages 5-12 $54-64.

Nukumoi Surf Company (☎742-8019; www.nukumoi.com), on Hoone Rd. across from Brennecke's Beach. Good for reasonably priced snorkel and beach gear. Snorkel sets or boogie boards $5 per day, $15 per wk. Surfboards $5-7.50 per hr., $20-30 per day. Open M-Sa 7:45am-7pm, Su 10:45am-6pm. Rentals close half an hour before store.

Outfitters Kauai, 2827A Poipu Rd. (☎742-9667; www.outfitterskauai.com), in Poipu Plaza, rents bikes ($20-45 per day) and offers a selection of tours, including a downhill bicycle ride from the rim of Waimea Canyon ($94, ages 12-14 $75), a 1-day sea kayak along the Na Pali Coast in summer ($200), and a zipline tour of Kapu Falls (3 or 6hr.; $115-155, ages 3-14 $90-115). Open daily 8am-5pm.

SIGHTS

MCBRYDE AND ALLERTON GARDENS. A verdant valley surrounded by steep cliffs, **Lawai Valley** shelters two of the **National Tropical Botanical Garden's** five gardens dedicated to protecting endangered Hawaiian native plants. A tram, the only way to get to the gardens, transports guests from the Visitors Center and parking lot to the valley, winding along a private road and stopping at a high coastal vista of pristine Lawai Kai Beach. Dedicated to science, the

McBryde Garden is divided into four short walking tours, featuring native Hawaiian plants, palm trees, food and spice plants, and canoe plants. Butterflies, wild chickens, and croaking frogs may be your only company on the walk along the 1 mi. loop that links the four areas together. The only way to see the equally beautiful **Allerton Garden** is on a guided walking tour. Volunteer naturalists share their knowledge and admiration of the garden, laid out by Robert Allerton in a series of outdoor "rooms." Fans of *Jurassic Park* will appreciate a stop at the three towering Moreton Bay fig trees that hid a giant cracked eggshell in the movie. The tour ends at the Allerton Family home on Lawai Kai, where a cottage once inhabited by Queen Emma faces a beach now populated by sea turtles. The Visitors Center by the parking lot contains informative displays and a gift shop. *(4425 Lawai Rd., 2 mi. west of the fork, across the street and just before Spouting Horn. ☎ 742-2623; www.ntbg.org. Visitors Center open daily 8:30am-5pm. Trams leave the Visitors Center to the gardens every hr. on the half hour; check-in 15min. in advance. Tours for McBryde Garden daily 9:30am-2:30pm; $15; no reservation required. Allerton Garden 2½hr. guided tours daily M-Sa 9, 10am, 1, 2pm; $30; reservations required.)*

KAUAI

SPOUTING HORN BEACH PARK. Beneath a securely fenced viewing area, a thin shelf of rock extends from the coast. Waves breaking below the shelf move water into the narrow spaces between the rocks, forcing a giant plume of sea spray skyward to the delight and applause of camera-toting tourists. Mini-spouts surround the central plume, while another lava opening contributes the "horn," sounded by a gush of air. High tide or large swells usually causes the most dramatic spouting, when the plume can reach more than 60 ft. high. The overlook provides a pretty view of Kukuiula Harbor to the east, a small lawn dotted with picnic tables, and a row of outdoor gift shops near the restrooms. *(On the makai, or ocean, side of Lawai Rd., immediately west and across the street from the National Tropical Botanical Garden's Visitors Center.)*

ENTERTAINMENT

Pub crawlers and dancing queens may be disappointed with Poipu's mellow evening scene—those looking for a late night should book the next flight to Honolulu. After a long day at the beach, most travelers are simply happy to slather on aloe and crawl into bed. If you've still got energy, **The Point,** at the Sheraton, offers fantastic vistas of Poipu Beach to the east and the setting sun to the west. (☎ 742-1661. Live jazz some nights. DJ Th and Sa 9pm-midnight. Local surf band F until 1am. Open M-Th and Sa-Su 11am-midnight, F 11am-1am. AmEx/D/DC/MC/V.) **Stevenson's Library,** an opulent room at the Hyatt, features a koa wood bar, pool and chess tables, and a pleasant terrace. (☎ 724-1234. Live music nightly 8-11pm. Sushi night M-F 6-9pm. Bar open daily 6-11:30pm.) The **Drums of Paradise Luau,** 1571 Poipu Rd., also hosted by the Hyatt, is one of two luaus on the South Shore. (☎ 742-1234; www.drumsofparadise.com. Open bar. Reservations recommended 1 wk. in advance. Th and Su 5:45-8pm, also Tu in summer. $75, ages 13-20 $65, ages 6-12 $37.50, under 5 free. Show $45/18/18/free.) The Sheraton offers a similar **Surf to Sunset Oceanfront Luau.** (☎ 742-8205; www.sheraton-kauai.com. M and F 5pm. $75, ages 6-12 $37.) Kauai's only **minigolf** course can be found at the Lawai Beach Resort, 5017 Lawai Rd., across the street from Lawai Beach and the Beach House Restaurant. Built as part of the Lawai Beach Resort's recreation center, the 18-hole course sits inside a chain-link fence atop the resort's four-story parking garage, a long way from any natural grass but a little closer to the stars. Use of the tennis facilities is also available to non-guests for the same price. (☎ 240-5350; www.lawai-

SCUBA FOR DUMMIES

Koloa Landing is home to several dive companies, but few cater to first-time divers as well as **Aquatic Adventures.** Beginners start with a 40min. land lesson and a training session in shallow water before embarking on a 1hr. offshore dive. With almost as many instructors as divers, Aquatic Adventures keeps close tabs on every new person—whether checking your air pressure and knowing which buttons to press on your 40 lb. suit and tank, your guides will make your first trip as cushy as possible.

First-time divers are allowed to dive only 40 ft., but that's more than far enough below the surface to experience a completely different underwater world. Before you jump off the boat, the instructors describe the wide variety of Hawaiian sea creatures and the ways to identify them on your dive. During your dive, you may see giant green sea turtles sleeping on the sandy bottom, ink-squirting octopi, snapping dragon moral eels, and whole schools of beautiful striped butterfly fish.

Aquatic Adventures launches most of its dives in southern Kauai at Koloa Landing, the site of some of the best dives in the state. In addition, Aquatic offers dives at Tunnels in the north and Ahukini Beaches in the east.

☎742-4770, www.aas-cuba.com. First dive $100, subsequent dives $70. Certification in 2-5 days $450.

beach.org. Public parking for golfers available on 3rd fl. of garage. Open 9:30am-6pm. $5.)

KOLOA

Hawaii's oldest sugar town (pop. 1,942) has undergone quite a face lift in response to neighboring Poipu's steady stream of tourists. Historic buildings that once housed barbershops and bathhouses have been spruced up and filled with souvenirs and beachwear. A charming raised wooden boardwalk now runs out front along the main street. Underneath its tourism-lacquered facade, however, Koloa retains a comfortable small-town feel and a strong sense of pride in its past.

ORIENTATION AND PRACTICAL INFORMATION

Koloa is about 10 mi. southwest of Lihue—7 mi. west on **Highway 50** and 3 mi. down **Highway 520 (Maluhia Road),** which leads to the center of town. Most of the town's shops and restaurants center around **Old Koloa Town,** at the intersection of Poipu and Koloa Rd., while others lie up the street to the east of Poipu Rd. Koloa ends a few miles north of the coast, where Poipu begins. To bypass Koloa and head straight for the sun and sand of Poipu, turn left on **Ala Konoiki Road** before reaching Koloa. Once in Koloa, head south on **Poipu Road.**

Services include: **First Hawaiian Bank,** 3506 Waikomo Rd. (☎742-1642; open M-Th 8am-4pm, F 8:30am-6pm); **Koloa Public and School Library,** on the west side of Poipu Rd. about ¼ mi. south of the Chevron station, which offers visitor's cardholders high-speed **Internet access** and a huge video and music collection (☎742-8455; open M-Tu and F 8:30am-5pm, W noon-8pm, Th 9am-5pm; 3-month visitor's card $10); the **South Shore Pharmacy,** 5330 Koloa Rd. (☎742-7511; open M-F 9am-5pm); and the **Koloa Post Office,** 5485 Koloa Rd. (☎800-275-8777; open M-F 9am-4pm, Sa 9-11am). **Postal Code:** 96756.

ACCOMMODATIONS

Most of the South Shore's accommodations are found closer to the beaches of Poipu. Near Koloa is the **Strawberry Guava Bed and Breakfast ❸,** 4896 Z Kua Rd., across the highway in Lawai. Turn right on Kua Rd. from Hwy. 50. After ¾ mi., turn right up a steep unmarked hill and continue for ¼ mi. to the

3rd driveway on the right; turn in and bear right at the fork. Small and out-of-the-way, Strawberry Guava's biggest perk is its super-low price tag. Suites are furnished and come with refrigerators but no kitchenettes. Two of the rooms have a gorgeous valley view. (☎332-0385. Breakfast included. Cleaning fee $15. Rooms $60-85. Cash only.)

FOOD

Stock up at the **Big Save Market,** next to First Hawaiian Bank on Koloa Rd. (☎742-1614. Open daily 7am-11pm.) Koloa's weekly **Sunshine Market** is held Mondays at noon at the Koloa Ball Park, north of downtown.

Sueoka Snack Shop, 5392 Koloa Rd. (☎742-1112), behind Sueoka Store. Quick service, rock-bottom prices, and great fries make this place stand out. Hamburgers $1.50. Plate lunches $4.50-4.75. Sueoka Store stocks groceries. Open Tu-Sa 9am-3pm, Su 9:30am-3pm. Cash only. ❶

Dali Deli, 5492 Koloa Rd. (☎742-8824), across from the post office. A comfortable and hip modern cafe, Dali Deli provides a relaxing setting for your morning cappuccino. The limited breakfast menu includes bagelwiches ($6) and a tasty breakfast burrito ($8). Lunch features sandwiches from tuna salad ($6) to portabello mushroom ($8.75) or a spinach wrap ($6). Open M-F 8am-3pm. MC/V. ❷

Lappert's Ice Cream, 5424 Koloa Rd. (☎742-1272), in the middle of downtown. A bright ice cream parlor with a classy coffee shop feel offers 25+ flavors and plenty of frozen treats. Island-inspired flavors such as Kauai pie and Kilauea guava sorbet. A coffee and espresso bar, and good selection of baked goods (macnut shortbread cookies, $2; coconut pineapple muffins, $3.50) make a not-so-healthy but oh-so-good breakfast. Ice cream $3.50. Open daily 6am-10pm. MC/V. ❷

Tomkats Grille, 5404 Koloa Rd. (☎742-8887), near the middle of the downtown storefronts. Sheltered tables surround a sunken outdoor garden, which infuses the place with the soft scent of plumerias. Appetizers include Kalua pig quesadillas ($9) and seared ahi poki ($8). Entrees include fish, steak, and sandwiches ($8-29). Happy hour daily 3-6pm; Mai Tais $4.50, beer $0.50. Open daily 8am-10pm, bar until 12:30am. MC/V. ❸

Koloa Fish Market, 5482 Koloa Rd. (☎742-6199), next door to Dali Deli. A popular local stop for plenty of fresh fish and poke for sale (poke $9.50 per lb., smoked salmon poke $9.60 per lb.). Lunch specials change daily ($6.50-7.25) and frequently include seared ahi and lau lau chicken. Open M-F 10am-6pm, Sa 10am-5pm. MC/V. ❷

ACTIVITIES

The knowledgeable folks at **Fathom Five Divers,** 3450 Poipu Rd., behind the Chevron station, offer scuba diving, snorkel rentals, and a variety of dives. The location of dive meeting points varies seasonally and on request; call for more info. (☎742-6991; www.fathomfive.com. 2-tank shore dive $80; boat dive $115; 3-day certification course for ages 10 and up $395. Boat tours of south side and Niihau $115-325. Snorkel equipment $5 per day. Open daily 7am-5pm.) For high-quality snorkel gear at low prices, head to **Snorkel Bob's,** 3236 Poipu Rd., ¼ mi. south of Koloa Chevron. Rentals have free interisland and 24hr. gear return. (☎742-2206; www.snorkelbob.com. Snorkel sets from $2.50 per day or $9 per week; boogie boards $6.50/26. Open daily 8am-5pm.)

SIGHTS

Koloa (meaning "long cane") was established in 1834 as a commercial center for the plantation community. Home to a sugar plantation and the major Koloa Landing sea port, the town soon became a hub of activity. In the 1850s, Koloa grew oranges, sweet potatoes, and sugar, but one by one these crops fell by the wayside. Ever proud of its key role in Hawaii's history, Koloa has preserved the feel of Old Koloa Town. A **History Center,** at the corner of Koloa Rd. and Hwy. 520, presents a life-size diorama of plantation life with instructional plaques. Across the street, a grassy field immortalizes the plantation tradition. Koloa's **Sugar Monument,** a registered historical landmark, features a white, circular, concrete sculpture that represents a mill stone opened to show seven bronze figures, one for each of the main ethnic groups—Hawaiian, Puerto Rican, Chinese, Korean, Japanese, Filipino, and Portuguese—who played a role in the formation of modern Hawaii. A plaque facing the monument describes an eighth figure as well, a Caucasian overseer on horseback, whose statue was omitted at the last minute in response to heavy criticism. Information on the sugar industry that defined Hawaii in the early 20th century accompanies the monument. Across the field, the crumbling stone tower is all that remains of the first successful sugar mill in Hawaii from the 1830s.

WEST SHORE

The West Shore maintains a sense of small-town community that is more insular than other parts of the island. Its small towns serve mainly as gateways to the parks farther north—Waimea Canyon State Park, Kokee State Park, and Polihale State Park. According to Hawaiian myth, the famed sunsets at Polihale were created when the souls of the dead followed the path of the sun west and departed the world in a blaze of glory.

KALAHEO

If you find yourself in Kalaheo (pop. 3,913), a quiet one-light town, stay in one of its solid accommodations and eat some first-class pizza.

ORIENTATION AND PRACTICAL INFORMATION. Kalaheo is located 11 mi. west of Lihue on **Highway 50** and many establishments line the highway. The **Kalaheo Post Office,** 4489 Papalina Rd. (☎800-275-8777), is behind Kalaheo Company. (☎800-275-8777. Open M-F 8am-4pm, Sa 9-11:30am.) **Postal Code:** 96741.

ACCOMMODATIONS. Kalaheo has a number of excellent accommodations for budget-seekers. To get to **Classic Vacation Cottages ❷**, 2687 Onu Pl., turn right on Puuwai Rd. just after entering Kalaheo, and stay to the right. Follow the winding road until you see the Onu Pl. cul-de-sac on your left; go up the driveway with the "Classic" sign. Tucked away from the main road yet still just a minute or two from the center of Kalaheo, the 12 unique units range from studios (some have kitchenettes, larger units have full kitchens) to a four-bedroom house. The owners have stocked enough picnic gear, beach toys, and sporting equipment (including bikes, tennis racquets, boogie boards, full snorkel gear, and golf clubs) in their garage to make Wal-Mart jealous. Grills, a hot tub, and free use of the Kiahuna Tennis Club facilities are also included. (☎332-9201. Coin-operated laundry on-site. Reserve well in advance with a 50% deposit. Studios from $45; cottages and houses $55-100; Dec. 15-Jan. 15 prices $15-$50 more

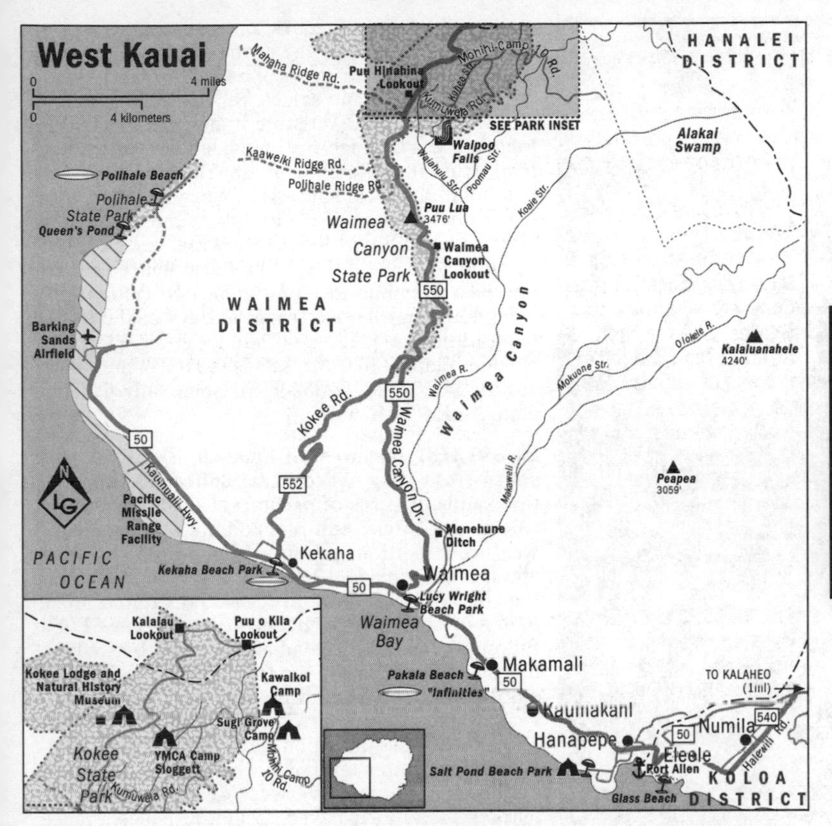

per night. Cash only.) Another good value is the **Kalaheo Inn ❸**, 4444 Papalina Rd. Turn south onto Papalina Rd. at the stoplight where it intersects Hwy. 50; the inn will be one block up on the left. Simple but sparkling clean, the 15 suites with full kitchens or kitchenettes are arranged in tidy rows. There is laundry on-site, a small collection of beach equipment, and free use of the Kiahuna Tennis Club facilities. (☎332-6023; www.kalaheoinn.com. 2-night min. stay. Reserve with $100 deposit; balance due 30 days before arrival. Units $80-120.) Get a lot of bang for your buck at **Aloha Estates ❷**, 4579 Puuwai Rd. Turn right just past the Chevron on Puuwai Rd. and continue ¼ mi. to Aloha Estates on the left. (☎332-7812; www.kalaheo-plantation.com. 2-night min. stay. Reserve with 50% deposit. 2-person rooms $45-69; 4-person $69-75. Cash or check only.)

FOOD. Outstanding Italian food, a friendly coffee shop, juicy hamburgers, and the island's best pizza make Kalaheo the hidden gem of Kauai dining. **Kalaheo Cafe & Coffee Company ❶**, 2-2560 Kaumualii Hwy., on the *makai* (ocean) side of the road just past Papalina Rd., is a popular local meeting spot. Breakfast features egg dishes (from $6) and great burrito ($8). Dinner entrees ($16-23) include a seafood wrap with fish, scallops, and shrimp ($23) and a vegetable sautee ($15). Park in back, off Papalina Rd. (☎332-5858; www.kalaheo.com. Open M-F 6:30am-2:30pm, Sa-Su 6:30am-2pm. Dinner W-Sa 5:30-8:30pm. MC/V.) Locals rave

GOLFING ON A SHOESTRING

If you thought every round of golf in Hawaii would consume a disturbingly large chunk of your wallet, swing by **Kukuiolono Golf Course and Park** (a.k.a. "Kook's"), a quaint nine-hole, par-36 course in Kalaheo that you can play for a shockingly low $8. On an island where a round of golf is often played with a set of clubs worth more than the GDP of a small island nation, where carts have built-in distance-measuring devices, and where grounds are more meticulously manicured than the cuticles of a hand model, Kook's is a refreshing return to rustic simplicity. There are no tee times and no drink cart—just wide lawns, trees, and nine holes of solid golf.

Kook's has a small clubhouse and a few paved cart paths on the top of a hill that affords golfers incredible views of the southern and western shores as well as breakfast and lunch. From the driving range, golfers line up to hit toward Hanapepe, Waimea, and Niihau, all of which are visible on a clear day. The fairways are abnormally wide, forgiving, and hard, lending a tremendous roll to drives. With few hazards, the course is ideal for those prone to slice, pull, and otherwise hack it up.

☎808-332-9151. Head to Kalaheo on Hwy. 50. Turn left on Papalina Rd. The entrance will be on your right; look for the gates and stone pillars.

about **Brick Oven Pizza ❷**, on the *mauka* (mountain) side of the highway at the east end of town. Select from the thin-crust pizza ($21-31), hot sandwiches ($3-7.50), and salads. (☎332-8561. Open Tu-Su 11am-10pm. MC/V.) More Italian cuisine can be found across the highway on the left at **Pomodoro ❹**, on the 2nd fl. of Rainbow Plaza. The house specialties, including veal sauteed in marsala sauce with fresh mushrooms ($24) and eggplant parmesan ($20), have a loyal local following. (☎332-5945. Open M-Sa 5:30-9pm. V.) The **Camp House Grill ❷**, just past Papalina Rd., on the *mauka* (mountain) side, is set in a house from the days of the sugar plantation. Camp House offers fresh fish ($18.50), chicken plates ($6-6.75), salads ($3-8.75), and burgers for $4.25-6.25. (☎332-9755. Open daily 6:30am-9pm. AmEx/D/MC/V.)

SIGHTS. Just west of Kalaheo, Hwy. 540 runs south from Hwy. 50 to **Kauai Coffee.** Though the thousands of acres of oceanfront fields were once filled with sugar and macadamia nuts, adverse weather conditions prompted the switch to coffee about a decade ago. Check out the video highlighting the coffee-making process and sample more than a dozen flavors of freshly-brewed coffee. For a full cup, check out the adjacent coffee bar, which has a window that opens to the lanai. Ice cream, smoothies ($3.25), and pastries ($0.60-2.50) are available. (☎335-0813; www.kauaicoffee.com. Gift shop and museum open daily in summer 9am-5:30pm; in winter until 5pm. Coffee bar open 9am-4:45pm.) A short drive west of Kalaheo, at mi. marker 14, a newly paved turnout provides a place to park for the **Hanapepe Valley Lookout.** High above the valley, the well-maintained vista offers a wide, impressive view of Hanapepe Valley.

KALAHEO TO WAIMEA

ELEELE

A residential community on the west shore of the Hanapepe River, across from mi. marker 16, Eleele (pop. 2,040) affords visitors a surprisingly comprehensive cluster of establishments and a beautiful out-of-the-way beach. The **Eleele Shopping Center** houses a **Big Save** (open M-Sa 6:30am-10pm, Su 6:30am-9pm; AmEx/MC/V), a **First Hawaiian Bank** with a **24hr. ATM** (open M-Th 8:30am-4pm, F 8:30am-6pm), a 24hr. **laundromat** (wash $1.75, dry $1), and a small **post office** (☎335-5338; open M-F 8am-4pm, Sa 9am-11am). **Postal Code:** 96705.

Two popular restaurants cater to locals and Waimea Canyon-bound tourists. **Toi's Thai Kitchen**

❷, in the shopping center, features a huge menu of delicious entrees, all served with papaya salad, a choice of rice, and dessert ($12-17). Diners with a shy palate can order from the "American plate" section, which includes honey-dipped chicken and french fries. (☎335-3111. BYOB. Open M-Sa 10:30am-2pm and 5:30-9pm. Karaoke Sa 9:30pm-1:30am. AmEx/MC/V.) At the far end of the shopping center, **Grinds Cafe and Espresso** ❶ offers a basic menu of baked goods ($1.50-2.50), pizza ($12), and breakfast all day (from $4). Dinner is pricier but still affordable (mahi mahi, $8.25; chili and rice, $5). Cushy seats make a comfy place to sip coffee, while shady outdoor tables are perfect for dinner. (☎335-6027; www.grindscafe.net. Free Wi-Fi. Open daily 6:30am-9pm. AmEx/D/MC/V.)

Farther south from the Eleele Shopping Center, Hwy. 541 (Waialo Rd.) forks right to Port Allen and left to the unique sands of **Glass Beach.** From Waialo, turn left on Aka Ula St. and straight onto the dirt road just past the power plant. Glass Beach is just below, before the road turns left. Without 4WD, it's best to park at the start of the dirt road and walk the rest. If you decide to drive, you can park in a dirt turnout on the right side of the road where it runs into the beach. Once famed for its glistening shore of sea glass, Glass Beach has since lost its treasures to rough surf and greedy visitors. While a decade ago black lava rocks, green cliffs, and blue surf accented the sparkling, multi-hued beach, today an industrial backdrop frames the gray and brown shore. This is a great beach for a leisurely walk, but run-off from nearby factories makes swimming and sunbathing less appealing.

Straight ahead at the fork is **Port Allen,** a favorite local fishing spot where many adventure outfits are located. The tour companies include **HoloHolo Charters,** 4353 Waialo Rd., #5A, which boasts the fastest service on the largest boat to the Na Pali Coast and Niihau. (☎335-0815; www.holoholocharters.com. 7-hr. Na Pali/Niihau tour with snorkeling $175, ages 5-12 $125.) **Captain Andy's,** in the shopping center, offers sailing and snorkeling trips. (☎335-6833; www.napali.com. 5-hr. Na Pali sailing/snorkeling expedition $129, children $89.) **Captain Zodiac** offers rafting and snorkeling excursions. (www.napali.com. 6-hr. Na Pali rafting expedition $149, ages 2-12 $99.) There is a **24hr. ATM** in the Port Allen Marina Center on the right side down Waialo Rd.

HANAPEPE

The self-proclaimed "biggest little town" on Kauai, Hanapepe (pop. 2,153) attracts visitors in search of art galleries and gourmet vegetarian cuisine, and to see the inspiration for Lilo's hometown from Disney's *Lilo and Stitch.* Hanapepe means "crushed bay," perhaps due to the flattened appearance of the surrounding landscape from sea.

ORIENTATION. Less than ¼ mi. past the Eleele Shopping Center, a welcome sign on the right side of the highway marks the turn for **Hanapepe Road.** The road swings north of **Highway 50** and creates a mile-long loop that circles Hanapepe's historic downtown area. In addition to the general stores and banks, the horseshoe-shaped downtown is lined with storefronts featuring the works of local painters, artisans, and designers. In the middle of town, on the corner of Hanapepe Rd. and Kona Rd., is an **American Savings Bank** with a **24hr. ATM.** (Open M-Th 8am-5pm, F 8am-6pm.) Behind the bank is the **Hanapepe Post Office.** (Open M-F 8:30am-4pm, Sa 9:30-11:30am. **Postal Code:** 96716.) **Westside Pharmacy,** 3845 Kamualii Hwy., is well-stocked and has antique decorations inside that certainly evince its claim as Kauai's oldest pharmacy. (Open M-F 8:30am-5:30pm, Sa 8:30am-1pm.) **Internet access** can be found at the **Hanapepe Public Library,** directly across from the pharmacy. (☎335-8418. M-W and F 9am-5pm, Th noon-8pm. 3-month visitor's card $10.) Visitors to Hanapepe can park in the gravel lot on the mountain side of Hanapepe Rd.; turn at the swinging footbridge sign. **Hanapepe**

Park offers additional parking, along with restrooms and picnic tables. Turn off Hanapepe Rd. onto Kona Rd.; the park is immediately on your right.

FOOD. A darling of earth-crunchy food connoisseurs island-wide, the **Hanapepe Cafe ❸**, 3830 Hanapepe Rd., satiates veggie and seafood cravings with healthy lunches (grilled vegetable sandwich, $9), salads ($7-10), and flavorful pastas (southwestern lasagna, $9.75). Dinner is served on Friday nights and the menu changes regularly (entrees, $18-25). For a $5 corkage fee, bring your own bottle of wine. (☎335-5011. Open M-Th 11am-3pm. Dinner F-Sa 6-9pm. Closed the first 2 weeks of June. MC/V.) The **Talk Story Bookstore and Cafe ❶**, 3785 Hanapepe Rd., is a popular local hangout, functioning as a local art gallery, used bookstore, gift shop, and cafe with free wireless Internet. The cafe serves flourless chocolate cake and passion fruit cheesecake for $3.25. (☎335-6469. F live music 6:30-9:30pm. Open M-Th 10:30am-5:30pm, F 10:30am-10pm. AmEx/D/MC/V.) For a delectable dessert, look no further than the **Kauai Kookie Kompany Factory,** 3959 Kaumualii Hwy. (Hwy. 50), on the north side of Hwy. 50, in Hanapepe Place. A small gift shop offers visitors free samples of the cookies, many with Hawaiian-inspired flavors like macadamia nut shortbread. Friends from back home probably wouldn't mind receiving cookies ($2-12) that are famous throughout the islands. On some mornings, a brief tour of the factory is possible; ask for details. (☎800-361-1126; www.kauaikookie.com. Open M-F 8am-4pm, Sa-Su 9am-4pm.) Try **Tahina's Fish and Chips ❷**, 4505 Puolo Rd., on the *mauka* (mountain) side of the hwy., for bubble tea ($4.25), smoothies ($4.75), shave ice ($3.50), seafood and chicken plates ($6.75-8.75) and, of course, fish and chips for $7. (☎335-0260. Open M-F and Su 10:30am-5pm, Sa 11am-4pm. Cash only.)

SIGHTS AND CAMPING. A slightly unsteady but thrilling view of the surrounding hills and fields can be had from the middle of Hanapepe's **swinging footbridge.** The bridge is near the east end of town; turn at the gravel parking lot west of a big green building, about 100 yd. after the road through downtown curves to the left. The footbridge replaces the one that was swept away during Hurricane Iniki in 1992. Heading west of Hanapepe, past mi. marker 17 and left onto Lele Rd., reveals one of Kauai's best-kept secrets. *Kamaaina* (Native Hawaiians) of

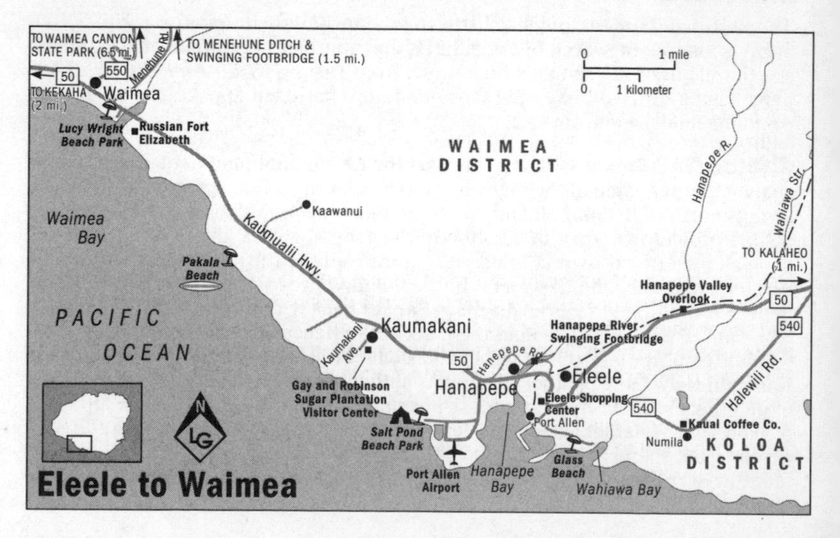

all ages treasure **Salt Pond Beach Park** for its wide, curving bay and soft sand. The park gets its name from the salt flats behind the east end of the beach, where locals still harvest salt from the ocean water. The salt ponds are thought to be among the most ancient in Hawaii; salt has supposedly been harvested here for over 1000 years. Gentle swells make their way over the rocky bar that encloses the uncrowded waters, perfect for swimming but not for snorkeling. The rocky spit creates two protected bays where **monk seals** sometimes bask in the sun. Restrooms, showers, and grills make this a great picnic site. The grassy field by the east end of the beach is one of the best places to camp on the island. For more information, see **Camping in Hawaii,** p. 75. To get to the beach, turn south onto Lele Rd. from Hwy. 50 just west of mi. marker 17, and follow signs to Lolokai Rd.

KAUMAKANI AND MAKAWELI

Most drivers cruise right by the small dirt roads that lead into the sugar plantation towns of Kaumakani (pop. 607) and Makaweli (pop. 635), and the Robinson family probably prefers it that way. The close-knit plantation community of Makaweli, which is home for more than a few immigrants from mysterious Niihau, keeps tourists away with a number of "Private Property" signs. The sugarcane fields that dominate this stretch of highway belong to **Gay and Robinson,** the only family-run sugar plantation still in operation on the islands. The Visitors Center on Kaumakani Ave. has displays about the history of sugar and plantation life, as well as 100-year-old tools and contraptions. The expensive Olokele tour takes visitors north to the Olokele Ditch, the plantation's water source. The Field and Factory Tour includes a walk through the sugar processing factory and sugarcane fields. Wear closed-toed shoes and clothes that can get dirty. (Turn left off westbound Hwy. 50 after mi. marker 19. ☎335-2824. Visitors Center open M-F 8am-4pm, Sa 11am-3pm. Tour reservations recommended. Both tours offered M-F 8:45am and 12:45pm. 2hr. field and factory tour $31, children 7-15 $21; under 7 not allowed on factory portion. 3½hr. Olokele tour $60.)

Also along this stretch of highway is the famous **Pakala Beach,** one of the West Shore's best surf spots. The break has been dubbed **"Infinities,"** because the waves are some of the longest on the island. The muddy water, narrow beach, and nonexistent facilities make this almost exclusively a surfing destination (for the experienced only). Swimmers and sunbathers are uncommon. The murky water and long paddle over a deep bay to the offshore reef (where the waves break) have given Infinities a reputation as a "sharky" spot. Exercise caution and paddle out with a friend. A 5min. walk along a short path leads from Hwy. 50 to the beach. The path is past the west end of the guardrail on the south side of the highway, immediately west of mi. marker 21. There is room to park on both sides of the road. When you get to the beach at the end of the trail, go left to access the best surf spot.

WAIMEA

Once an important agricultural port, Waimea (pop. 1,787) was the first stop for many visitors to Hawaii, including Christian missionaries, Russian emissaries, and the western "discoverer" of Hawaii, Captain Cook (p. 15). The sandalwood trade of the early 1800s, along with the whaling and sugar industries, made Waimea an important port. The historic wooden buildings that line Waimea Rd. downtown evidence the town's colorful past, and Waimea's dusty streets and swinging doors recall the high-noon showdowns of silver screen notoriety. There's no shortage of genuine hospitality; the few tourists who take a picnic to the palm-tree shaded Hofgaard Park or watch a movie at the fabulous Waimea Theater are warmly welcomed.

ORIENTATION AND PRACTICAL INFORMATION

The biggest town on the West Shore, Waimea lies 23 mi. west of Lihue on **Highway 50.** After heading west across the Waimea River and leaving Fort Elizabeth behind, the highway runs through the center of town. Most businesses and restaurants lie along the highway or on the adjacent **Waimea Road.**

The **West Kauai Technology and Visitors Center,** 9565 Kaumaualii Hwy., is a good place to pick up a map or use the free **Internet access** at one of four computers available. The center also offers a 90min. historic walking tour every Monday at 9:30am and a free 90min. walking tour of the old Waimea sugar plantation every Tuesday, Thursday, and Saturday at 9am. (☎338-1338, historic tour reservations 338-1332, sugar plantation tour 335-2824. Open M-F 9:30am-5pm.)

The stately **First Hawaiian Bank,** 4525 Panako Rd., has a **24hr. ATM.** (☎338-1611. Open M-Th 8:30am-4pm, F 8:30am-6pm.) **Waimea Library,** 9750 Kaumualii Hwy., across from the sports field, is a good place to catch up on the news or surf the **Internet.** The library has six computers with speedy cable connections. (☎338-6848. Open M and W noon-8pm, Tu and Th 9am-5pm, F 10am-5pm. 3-month visitor's card $10.) Next door is the **Aloha-n-Paradise Gallery and Espresso Bar,** 9905 Waimea Rd., where **Internet access** costs $4 per 30min. (☎338-1522). Wash the red dirt out of your shorts at **Wishy Washy Laundry Center,** 9889 Waimea Rd., across from the Captain Cook Monument. (Wash $1.25, dry $1.50. Open 24hr.) Other services include: the **Waimea Police Substation** (☎338-1831), on the *mauka* (mountain) side of the highway, across Menehune Rd. from Big Save; the **West Kauai Medical Center,** 4643 Waimea Canyon Dr., located just outside of town on Waimea Canyon Dr. (☎338-9431); and the **Waimea Post Office,** 9911 Waimea Rd., across the street from the bank. (☎800-275-8777. Open M-F 8:30am-4pm, Sa 9-11am.) **Postal Code:** 96796.

ACCOMMODATIONS AND CAMPING

Built to house sugar plantation workers at the beginning of the 20th century, the **Waimea Plantation Cottages ❹,** 9400 Kaumualii Hwy., #367, west of town, have been restored and filled with the modern amenities of a Hawaiian hotel. Each has its own lanai overlooking the spacious palm- and monkeypod-dotted grounds or ocean. The windy dark-sand beach and murky water make for unappealing swimming, but the oceanfront pool is a pleasant place for a dip. Units include the 2-person hotel room ($150-175), cottages with kitchenettes (1-bed/1-bath $210-340, 2-bed/2-bath $260-405, 3-bed/2-bath $300-455), and the luxurious five-bedroom manager's estate for $650-775. (☎338-1625; www.waimeacottages.com. AmEx/D/MC/V.) On the east edge of town, by the mouth of the Waimea River, campsites are available at **Lucy Wright Beach Park ❶,** a small, dusty, and predominantly local park. Traveling west on Kamualii Hwy., take the first left onto Ala Wai Rd. after crossing the Waimea River Bridge. There are restrooms, a pavilion, picnic tables, and a boat launch. You may want to try **Salt Pond Beach Park** (p. 410), which has a better camping beach before settling on this quiet park. For permit information, see **Camping in Hawaii,** p. 75.

FOOD

Waimea offers a plethora of *ono kine grinds* (delicious food) and the largest choice of restaurants on the West Shore. Grab groceries at the **Big Save,** on the corner of Hwy. 50 and Waimea Rd. (Open M-Sa 6am-10pm, Su 6am-9pm.)

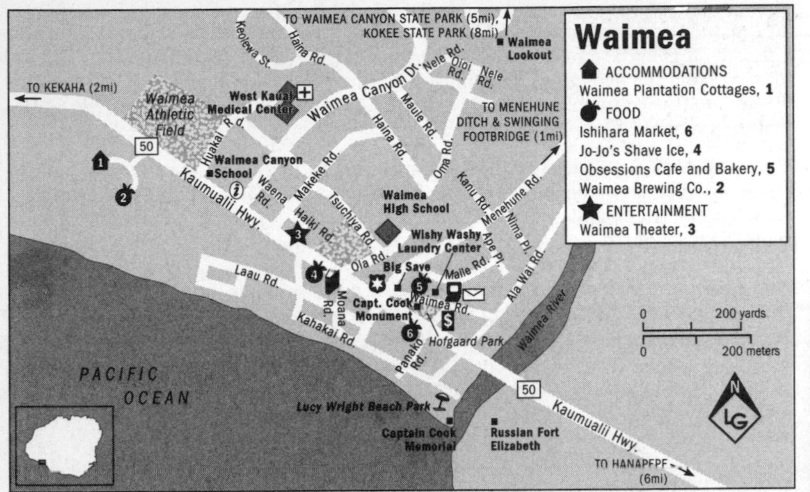

Ishihara Market, 9894 Kaumualii Hwy. (☎338-1751), On the *makai* (ocean) side, across from the Cook Monument. Stock up for a big day of hiking with everything from plate lunches ($4.50-8) to sushi ($3-6), sandwiches ($2-7), and a variety of seafood salads. Ishihara's is also a great place to pick up groceries. No indoor seating. Open M-F 6am-8:30pm, Sa-Su 7am-8:30pm. MC/V. ❶

Obsessions Cafe and Bakery, 9875 Waimea Rd., (☎338-1110), on the left heading up Waimea Rd., just past Big Save. This place has some good vegetarian options and is home to Waimea's only bakery. Order breakfast (asparagus-mushroom omelet, $6.95), salads ($3.50-6.75), a vegetarian wrap ($6.25), or Obsessions Club Sandwich (bacon, turkey, and ham; $7.25. Open daily 6am-4pm. DC/MC/V. ❷

Waimea Brewing Company, 9400 Kaumualii Hwy. (☎338-9733), on the west edge of town. The westernmost brewery in the US serves good food at high prices. Enjoy pupus ($7-14), entrees (Jawaiian Chicken, $16; Grilled Island Ahi, $23), and Kauai mud pie ($8) in the relaxed tropical bar interior or outdoor patio. Especially good is their Kahaoolawe Salad ($11.25) with macadamia nuts, goat cheese, pineapple, guava dressing, and crispy onions. Over 6 locally-brewed beers are named after different parts of the island. Free wireless Internet. Open daily 11am-9pm. AmEx/D/MC/V. ❹

SIGHTS AND ENTERTAINMENT

WAIMEA THEATER. Housed in an Art Deco building that boasted the first electric marquee on Kauai, the restored theater is a local landmark. The large screen and modern sound system don't detract from the charm of the "loge" seating—two rows of roomy, cushioned armchairs that put standard movie theater seats to shame. The theater occasionally shows surfing movies and other cool special-interest films; call in advance to see what's playing. *(9691 Kaumualii Hwy. ☎338-0282, box office 338-0282. Films W-Su 7:30pm and some weekends 2:30 and 5pm. $7; students and over 55 $6; children 4-10 $5.)*

MENEHUNE DITCH. Long before Captain Cook's arrival, the *menehune*, dwarfs of myth, were said to have constructed their own monuments in Waimea. Along the western bank of the Waimea River, 1½ mi. north of the highway, a narrow ditch runs along the left side of Menehune Rd. Supposedly the *menehune* dug this ditch to irrigate taro fields on the flood plains above the river. Though much of the ancient ditch has been obscured by road construction, it still functions to this day. It is hard to make out the sections of the rock wall that are still visible. Across from the swinging footbridge over the river, a plaque honors the *menehune* and their miraculous building skills. About 20 yd. down the road, the ditch enters a tunnel, an impressive display of ancient rock carving.

CAPTAIN JAMES COOK MEMORIALS. Two sites commemorate Captain James Cook, the British explorer who landed at Waimea in 1778 and first "discovered" Hawaii. The triangle of grass that separates Waimea Rd. from the highway is **Hofgaard Park,** home to a sculpture of the captain, a replica of the British original. At the southern end of Ala Wai Rd., a small dirt parking lot faces the mouth of the Waimea River in **Lucy Wright Beach Park.** A small plaque (now decorated with graffiti) is embedded in a rock near the river mouth, memorializing Cook's landing spot. The park also has a baseball field, showers, restrooms, picnic tables, and a pavilion. The beach is small and clouded by the river's sediment. While great boogie boarding waves frequently break, the river mouth is primarily the domain of young, local ocean enthusiasts. The **Waimea Pier** is visible from here. Built in 1865 to transport sugar from Waimea, it was abandoned in the 1930s and is now used recreationally. Turn onto Kahakai Rd. from Alawai Rd. and continue straight until you see the pier on your left.

WAIMEA CANYON STATE PARK

The view from the iron-rich soil of the park's cliffs is one of the most magnificent on the island. Brilliant red cliffs plunge into a valley carved by streams and faults millions of years ago, while birds sweep through the blue sky, flirting with fragrant flowers, impressive waterfalls, meandering streams, and broad green valleys. The red dirt that covers everything is rusted ancient lava and Waimea literally means "reddish water." Though the waterfalls run when it rains, they are often dry since the sugar plantation draws heavily on the water above. Arrive early for a better chance of a cloudless view, and after your visit, you'll see why Waimea Canyon State Park has been nicknamed "The Grand Canyon of Kauai."

LOOKOUTS

From central Waimea, Waimea Canyon Dr. (Hwy. 550) slowly winds up to the rim of the canyon, joining the less windy—but not nearly as scenic—Kokee Rd. after seven glorious miles. Every canyon-facing bend in the road's switchback path has a car-slowing, neck-craning view. About ½ mi. past mi. marker 10, a driveway on the right leads to a huge parking lot that welcomes you to the official **Waimea Canyon Lookout,** the site of a commanding perspective of the colorful canyon below. Back on the road, the next official lookout is **Puu Hinahina,** between mi. markers 13 and 14. Another lookout lies at the end of a short path past the restrooms, where you can see Niihau on clear days. Between these two lookouts a number of smaller lookouts are accessible by numerous dirt turnoffs along the main highway.

HIKING

A way down to the base of Waimea Canyon does exist, despite the seemingly sheer impossibility of it. From the edge of the canyon between mi. markers 8 and 9, the **Kukui Trail** begins a 2000+ ft. descent into the canyon, ending at the Waimea River. The 2½ mi. trail is strenuous because of its steepness, but well defined and marked every ¼ mi. (watch out for markers that have been obscured by plant growth). The trail rapidly descends down the side of the canyon through shrubs and low vegetation for ¾ mi. From mi. marker ¾ to the 1¾, the trail is largely exposed to the sun and traverses a ridge that points into the canyon until the 1¼ mi. marker; at this point it turns left and heads parallel to the river below. The trail becomes less defined here so stick to the wide stretch of red dirt atop the ridge. If you look up here across the canyon to the top of the eastern edge, you can see **Waialae Falls.** After heading straight for about 1¾ mi., the trail turns back down toward the Waimea River and enters a wooded area. As the trail approaches the river, it flattens out and the outhouse and sheltered picnic table of **Wiliwili Campground** appear on the left. The Kukui Trail hits a T here: to the right lies the **Waimea Canyon Trail,** which leads 8 mi. downriver all the way to Waimea town, while to the left a path heads upriver to the start of the **Koaie Canyon Trail.** This trail tiptoes along the western shore of the Waimea River until it crosses the river ½ mi. upstream and passes a picnic table and outhouse marking the Kaluahaulu Camp, 100 yd. from the trail. The 3 mi. Koaie Canyon Trail terminates at Lonomea Camp. Be careful: the Koaie Canyon trail is vulnerable to flash flooding in wet weather. Take a break before you head back up the Kukui Trail; under a scorching sun it seems twice as long on the way up. Bring an adequate supply of water for the steep ascent.

A much less demanding hike that still gives visitors an expansive view of the canyon is the **Iliau Nature Loop.** The loop is ¼ mi. long, and offers great views of Waimea and Waialae Canyons and an introduction to the native flora with a number of small, informational signs.

To get to either trail, park in one of the dirt turnouts ¾ mi. past mi. marker 8 on Waimea Canyon Rd.; the trailhead is at a paved pull-out on the left by an emergency call box. Scramble up the slope on the left for the Iliau Nature Loop. The right path leads to the other side of the loop and, after about 100 yd., to the sign at the trailhead of the Kukui Trail; go straight here for the Kukui Trail, and turn left to continue on the Iliau Nature loop.

KOKEE STATE PARK

Continuing up the road, past mi. marker 14, Waimea Canyon State Park gives way to Kokee State Park. The cool upland forests of Kokee present a marked contrast to the arid climate of Kekaha; temperatures are often 10-15° cooler than at sea level. The sprawling trails of Kokee present accessible and spectacular hiking territory. Most of the trails feature stunning vistas and peaceful forests, but Kokee also has a boardwalk through the muddy, fascinatingly unique Alakai Swamp. Here Kauai's own mokihana berry can be found, along with a host of native birds that are rarely seen elsewhere.

PRACTICAL INFORMATION

For trail information and advice, head first to the **Kokee Natural History Museum,** on the left after mi. marker 15. Comprehensive displays present general information about Kauai's ecology, hunting and fishing opportunities, and the indigenous birds and plants of the park. Historical photographs give a snapshot of the park as it appeared to early explorers, and an absorbing one-room display details the destruction wrought by Hurricane Iniki in 1992 as well as the park's slow but encouraging recovery. The staff at the museum also knows which park roads are closed and can offer hiking advice. Books, short guides to popular trails, maps, and gift items are for sale. The simple Kokee Trails Map ($1.50) will satisfy the needs of most casual hikers, while the amazing **Earthwalk Press Northwestern Kauai Recreation Map** ($8.50), encompassing the coastal region between Hanalei, Polihale State Park, and Mt. Waialeale, including inset maps of the Na Pali Coast

PRESIDENTIAL PROTECTION

After years of conservationists' struggle to preserve an archipelago of 10 islands 1400 mi. northwest of the main chain of Hawaiian islands, President Bush, in an unusual stroke of green consciousness, recently declared the islands a national monument. This act created the world's largest marine reserve, covering a span of 4500 mi. of coral reef and providing an eco system to 7000 species. Some of the protected residents include white-tip reef sharks, green sea turtles, and the 1400 remaining Hawaiian monk seals.

The new reserve is seven times the size of all the 13 marine sanctuaries in the United States combined. Under its new status as a national monument, fishing and oil drilling will be discontinued immediately. Commercial fishing will phase out within the next five years.

This benevolent presidential act highlights the previous failures of legislation in marine conservation, such as the 1972 National Marine Sanctuaries Act, which failed to prevent further pollution of the nation's coasts and harm to its aquatic life. Conservation groups are now looking to reform this act or to lobby for entirely new legislation.

Regardless of past governmental shortcomings, this event is a step in the right direction for endangered marine life.

State Park and detailed descriptions of Kokee State Park trails and the Kalalau Trail, is a worthwhile investment for anyone planning to stay a few days. (☎335-9975; www.kokee.org. Museum open daily 10am-4pm. Donations accepted.)

Next door, the **Kokee Lodge** stocks souvenirs and snacks and maintains public restrooms. The **restaurant ❶**, 3600 Kokee Rd., offers surprisingly good food. Although crowded at lunch time, the lodge's long windows provide a pleasant setting for a meal. The breakfast menu includes quiche ($7), Kokee cornbread ($3.50), and fruit ($3.25). Lunch features sandwiches ($7), hot dogs ($3.50), meat or vegetarian chili ($7), lilikoi or guava chiffon pie ($3.75), and plenty of alcohol for celebrating the completion of a tough hike. (☎335-6061; www.kokee-lodge.com. Lodge restaurant and gift shop open daily 8am-5pm. AmEx/D/MC/V.)

ACCOMMODATIONS AND CAMPING

Kokee Lodge acts as the rental office for the 12 wooden **cabins ❷** scattered along the road to the south. The cabins, ranging from studios to two-bedrooms, some of which can accommodate up to six people, come with kitchens, hot showers, linens, and wood-burning stoves. (☎335-6061. 5-day max. stay. Reservations required 2-4 mo. in advance; 1 yr. for holiday weekends. $35-45. D/MC/V.) Across the meadow from the museum, the beautiful **Kokee campground ❶** is a series of spacious, grassy sites along a dirt road, with restrooms, showers, drinking water, and picnic tables. Three forest reserve campgrounds—Kawaikoi, Sugi Grove, and Camp 10—lie to the east, on the muddy (and 4WD-only) Mohihi-Camp 10 Rd. The campgrounds have pit toilets, picnic shelters, and firepits, but no drinking water. Campers must stay for a minimum of three nights. For permit information, see **Camping in Hawaii**, p. 75.

YWCA Camp Sloggett ❶ has affordable indoor accommodations, although the bunkhouse often fills up with large groups. Two bathrooms are provided for guests; camping facilities are limited to showers. Bring a sleeping bag for the bunkhouse ($20 per person). The 11-person lodge has two bedrooms and a living room and a kitchen (2-night min. stay, $20 per person). The two-person cabin (2-night min. stay, $65) has a kitchen, fireplace, and sheets, but bring your own towels. Tents ($10 per person) are another option. (Down Mohihi-Camp 10 Rd., directly opposite the lodge. Keep left at the first fork and turn right at the second, following the signs to the camp. ☎335-6060, reservations 245-5959; www.campingkauai.com. MC/V.)

SIGHTS

The Kokee lookouts provide expansive views of the wild, untouched **Na Pali Coast** and the endless Pacific Ocean. Across from mi. marker 18, the **Kalalau Lookout,** over 4100 ft. above sea level, presents a mind-blowing view of the verdant cliffs of **Kalalau Valley.** Veterans of the Kalalau Trail will get an extra kick out of seeing the valley they crossed on foot from thousands of feet above.

Many travelers turn around here, but another lesser-known (but equally stunning) vista awaits at the end of the road. Free of tour buses and chatty guides, the **Puu o Kila Lookout** has a magnificent outlook over Kalalau's cliffs and lush river basin. A sign to the east points toward Mt. Waialeale (the rainiest spot on the planet, averaging more than 460 in. per year). Puu o Kila also serves as the trailhead for the Pihea trail into Alakai Swamp.

The road from the Kalalau Lookout to the Puu o Kila Lookout is frequently closed to vehicles, requiring tourists to make the roughly 1 mi. trek from one lookout to the next on foot. Although cool temperatures make hiking more comfortable, the breezy lookouts can be chilly, especially in the winter. Since fog can sometimes roll in, make the lookouts your first stop of the day.

HIKING

The singular network of trails is the highlight of Kokee State Park. About 45 mi. of trails crisscross the park, encompassing everything from short forest walks through groves of Methley plums to heart-pounding balancing acts across narrow, rocky ridges. A few trails begin from Hwy. 550, but the majority of the trailheads are located along the handful of 4WD dirt roads that degenerate quickly from "road" to "mud bog" when it rains. The main dirt roads are the **Mohihi-Camp 10 Road, Kumuwela Road,** and **Halemanu Road.** The longest 4WD dirt road, Mohihi-Camp 10 Rd., contains the most trailheads. It begins across the street from the Kokee Lodge and extends about 4 mi. east of the highway until it reaches its final destination, forestry reserve Camp 10. A sign at the beginning of the road says "Kumuwela Rd." because it leads to Kumuwela Rd. Although Mohihi-Camp 10 Rd. is officially considered a 4WD-only road, the stretch from the highway to about ¼ mi. past the Kumuwela Rd. intersection is frequently passable in 2WD in dry weather. Kumuwela Rd. itself branches to the right about 1½ mi. in and heads south for over 2 mi. Rarely can any part of it be driven in a 2WD car. The third road, Halemanu Rd., branches east of Hwy. 550 near mi. marker 14 and meanders about 1½ mi. into the forest. On dry days, the first mile or so of Halemanu Rd. is passable in 2WD, providing access to a couple popular trailheads. Otherwise, there is room to park on the shoulder of Hwy. 550 where Halemanu Rd. begins.

Another option is to take advantage of the park's **Wonderwalks,** informative and accessible guided hikes led by park employees or local naturalists. State vehicles transport the 4WD-less to otherwise unreachable trailheads, and knowledgeable guides lead hikers through a wide range of hikes. (☎335-9975; www.kokee.org/wonderwalks.html. Reservations recommended. Weekends in summer; most walks leave at 12:30pm and return by 4pm. In winter, call for custom hike for a fee. Donations appreciated.)

Anyone hiking in the park should carry sufficient water; *leptospirosis*, a bacterium that can sneak through most water filters, is a constant concern. Hikers should also avoid attempting the trails during wet and rainy weather; many of the canyon and Na Pali view hikes include extremely steep drops and narrow ledges, and it wouldn't be possible to enjoy the ocean and valley views anyway.

CANYON TRAIL. *(1¾ mi. 2-3hr. round-trip. Moderate.)* The trailhead is ¾ mi. down Halemanu Rd. from Hwy. 550, and then 500 ft. down the dirt road that branches to the right off Halemanu Rd. Kokee Park's most popular hike, and with good reason, the Canyon Trail skirts the edges of the Waimea Canyon and reveals breathtaking views of the forested valley below at every corner. After taking travelers through dense native forest brimming with *koa* trees and blackberry bushes, the trail passes over an old sugar plantation ditch. A quick climb out of the forest leads to a broad ridge with an exhilarating view of the valley below. From here, the trail descends to Waipoo Falls, about 1 mi. from the trailhead. Most hikers turn back at this point, but continue on to escape some of the crowd. To the left, a short spur takes adventurers to a small swimming hole that is only safe when the water is not stagnant. Another magnificent view awaits atop Kumuwela Ridge, before the trail ends at the lower end of Kumuwela Rd.

NUALOLO - NUALOLO CLIFF - AWAAWAPUHI LOOP. *(8¼ mi., 4-7hr. round-trip. Challenging.)* The Nualolo trailhead is 100 yd. south of the lodge road, and the Awaawapuhi trailhead is past mi. marker 17, on the left. The Nualolo-Awaawapuhi Loop is a combination of three relatively strenuous hikes. Together, they form a grueling trek that loops from the highway to and from the majestic Na Pali Coast, and should satisfy any hardcore hiker's hunger for adventure. Start early on a sunny day—wet weather can make a few stretches of trail extremely treacherous. The **Nualolo Trail** gradually descends 3¼ mi. from the highway toward the ocean through dry upland forests dominated by lofty trees, flowering shrubs, and a grassy meadow. Shortly after mi. marker 2¼ comes the first good view of the shimmering Pacific Ocean. After about 3¼ mi., you reach a junction where you can continue on the loop by turning right onto the 2 mi. **Nualolo Cliff Trail,** or hike ½ mi. more toward the ocean to **Lolo Vista,** which is the end of the Nualolo Trail. Lolo Vista is a must-see along the hike, with one of the best views of the Na Pali Coast in an area that is inaccessible except by boat. Do not go beyond the railing at the end of the trail—the ground is unstable and the drop to the valley floor is over 2,000 ft. The Nualolo Cliff Trail tiptoes precariously atop the rim of Nualolo Valley for about 2 mi. and connects the Nualolo Trail and the **Awaawapuhi Trail.** The Nualolo Cliff Trail traverses stretches of bare cliffs with wide-open—and hard-earned—Pacific views and ventures into lush green forest. It reaches an area with picnic tables and a stream near its intersection with Awaawapuhi Trail. The cliff trail crosses another stream and passes by a small, beautiful waterfall ¼ mi. from the intersection of the Nualolo Cliff Trail and the Awaawapuhi Trail. The Awaawapuhi Trail extends 2¾ mi. from the highway to its junction with the Nualolo Cliff Trail, and then an additional ¼ mi. to another lookout on the Na Pali Coast. Awaawapuhi, meaning "valley of ginger," boasts fragrant yellow ginger, blackberries, thimbleberries, guava, and passion fruit. The three-trail loop measures 8¼ mi., but including roundtrips to and from both vistas, and the 1½ mi. hike along Hwy. 550 from one trailhead to the other, hikers could be in for an 11¼ mi. journey. Bring plenty of water on this hike, and no matter which trailhead you start on, be prepared for a 1600 ft. climb from the Nualolo Cliff Trail to Hwy. 550.

CLIFF TRAIL. *(500 ft., 15min. round-trip. Easy.)* This hike has the same trailhead as Canyon Trail. The cliff trail itself is a wide, dirt path that leads to a lookout over Waimea Canyon. The lookout is actually just the last 50 yd. of the trail, which emerges from the forest and heads to the edge of the canyon; hikers can enjoy the expansive view from behind the long guardrail. The lookout is about as close to the headwall of Waimea Canyon as you can get. For those who don't drive down Halemanu Rd. to the trailhead, the hike from Hwy. 550 to the lookout at the end of the trail is about 1 mi. long, and is still a worthwhile and relatively easy hike.

PUU KA OHELO - BERRY FLATS LOOP. *(2 mi., 1hr. round-trip. Easy.)* Take Mohihi-Camp 10 Rd. about 1 mi. and then about ¼ mi. down a dirt trail fork to the left that leads to a small group of private cabins; a sign at the trailhead says "State Park Area." The Berry Flats trailhead is ¾ mi. farther down Mohihi-Camp 10 Rd., past Kumuwela Rd., about 100 yd. before a wide section of the road and a left turn. This pleasant hike wanders through a forest shadowed by tall *koa* trees and lacy ferns. The constant struggle between indigenous and introduced plants is evident—flowering honeysuckle, beautiful but destructively invasive, grows along either side of the path. The Berry Flats part of the loop is dominated by invading Japanese *sugi* pines and California redwoods, which are attractive but have prevented native plants from taking root. Along the loop, two trails branch off to the side. Take a left onto the forested Puu Ka Ohelo Trail. About ½ mi. into the Puu Ka Ohelo Trail, the Water Tank Trail forks to the left and leads about 1 mi. back to Hwy. 550, across the street from the Kokee campground. The loop is a gentle hike that is great for families. If you park your car at one trailhead and plan on hiking the loop, don't forget to factor in the ¾ mi. hike along the road.

KALUAPUHI TRAIL. *(1½ mi., 1hr. round-trip. Easy to moderate.)* Kaluaphui Trail starts a little less than ¼ mi. past the Awaawapuhi trailhead, slightly beyond mi. marker 17; park at the Awaawapuhi lot. The well-maintained trail travels inland, through native upland forest, ending a couple hundred yards past the **Kalalau Lookout.** With a change in elevation of only 120 ft., the peaceful stroll can be enjoyed by all. The trail is particularly susceptible to rain, however. Native Hawaiian flora and fauna prevail here: indigenous birds swoop down from above the forest canopy of *ohia* trees, and strawberry guava grows in abundance. At the T-intersection in the grove, take the left fork—the right fork leads to a dead-end hunting trail. The trail ends in an orchard of Methley plums, harvested by locals in early summer. If you choose to walk back to your car via the highway, it's about 1 mi. to the trailhead.

PIHEA TRAIL TO ALAKAI SWAMP TRAIL. *(3¾ mi., 3-4hr. round-trip. Challenging.)* The Pihea trailhead is to the right of the Puu o Kila Lookout, at the end of Waimea Canyon Dr. The only way to get to the Alakai Swamp without 4WD is via the Pihea Trail, which is memorable in its own right. The first section of the Pihea Trail features sweeping views of the Na Pali cliffs and valleys. Hovering around 4000 ft., this stretch follows the course of an old, abandoned road across the top of Kalalau Valley. The road was intended to link Kokee State Park with the highway at Haena, but failed after 8 months of work, leaving an eroding scar of wind- and rain-sculpted dirt in its place. Parts of this section of trail are shaded by *ohia* trees that form a leafy roof overhead and attract a steady stream of chirping native birds. Bring binoculars if you are an avid bird-watcher—this area of the park is frequented by many different species. The Kauai honey-creeper, Iliwi, and bright-red Apapane are common, while the handful of critically endangered birds in this area, including the beautiful yellow Kauai Akialoa, are rarely seen. After about 1 mi., the trail forks, and a steep offshoot to the left leads to Pihea Vista. The Pihea Vista isn't any more impressive than the half-dozen great vistas that line the first mile of the trail, and it certainly isn't worth the steep scramble up the side trail that leads to it. Meanwhile, the Pihea Trail turns right at the fork and leaves the Na Pali Coast behind, heading to a very steep section where you must grapple up a steep hill with exposed tree roots. After ¼ mi., the trail becomes a narrow boardwalk, descending gradually for another ½ mi. until it reaches a junction with the **Alakai Swamp Trail.** Straight ahead, the Pihea Trail continues for almost 2 mi. until it ends at Kawaikoi Camp, along Mohihi-Camp 10 Rd., 3¾ mi. from Puu o Kila Lookout. To the right are the first 1½ mi. of the Alakai Swamp Trail, which also terminates along Mohihi-Camp 10 Rd. To the left are the last 2 mi. of the Alakai Swamp trail, which ends at the **Kilohana Lookout,** where there is a fantastic view of a few North Shore beaches and 4000 ft. of steep, verdant mountain valleys, including Hanalei and Wainiha Valleys. These last couple miles of the Alakai Swamp trail are a level hike along a boardwalk through havens for endemic birds and short shrubs. The swamp is cool and humid under cloud cover, but can be hot and humid when sunny. Make sure to stay on the boardwalk; the swamp bog is frequently much deeper than it appears.

KEKAHA

Although Kekaha (pop. 3,175) doesn't have much to offer in the way of shopping or nightlife, its miles of remote, uncrowded beaches and spacious public parklands make it a sensational place to relax and get away from the crowds and traffic of other west shore towns. Once a sugar town where life centered around the big—and now rusting—mill, modern-day Kekaha is interesting mainly as a gateway to **Waimea Canyon** (p. 414), **Kokee State Park** (p. 415) to the north, and **Polihale State Park** (p. 421) to the west.

ORIENTATION. The westernmost town in the United States, Kekaha lies 26 mi. west of Lihue on **Highway 50. Kekaha Road** branches right from Hwy. 50 between mi. markers 24 and 25 (follow the "Alternate Kekaha" sign) and runs parallel to the highway for 2 mi. west, past the old sugar mill, to **Waimea Canyon Plaza** at the base of Kokee Rd., which heads north to the canyon. The plaza has a few standard tourist shops with aloha shirts and beach towels, and the last few places to fill your tummy or picnic basket. Take advantage of the "Last Chance Restroom" before heading north to Kokee or west to Polihale.

FOOD. Kekaha doesn't have any restaurants per se, but there are a few nice lunch spots and a convenience store to stock up on snacks. The Menehune Food Mart has a good selection of the basics as well as food to-go: large frozen Icees ($1.50), prepared sandwiches ($3-4), sliced fruit bowls ($3), and manapua ($2). There is also an ATM inside. (☎337-1335. Open daily 5:30am-6pm, Sa until 8pm. AmEx/MC/V.) The Waimea Canyon Snack Shop sells sandwiches ($4.50-5.50), local favorite Lappert's ice cream (2 scoops, $3.50; 3 scoops, $4.50), and wraps. (☎337-9227. Open daily 8am-4:30pm.) A quarter mile before reaching the plaza on the ocean side of Kekaha Rd., is the Thrifty Minimart, 8240 Kekaha Rd., which offers lunch and dinner plates of pork or chicken luau, among other Hawaiian favorites, for around $6. They also sell delicious ahi poke for $9 per lb. or smoked salmon poke for $10 per lb. (☎337-1057. Open daily 8am-9pm. MC/V.)

BEACHES. Across Kekaha Rd. from the Plaza, between the elementary school and ocean, the aging Faye Park—featuring a track, baseball field, tennis courts, basketball court, playground, picnic tables, pavilion, and grills—has hosted many a neighborhood luau. There are restrooms behind the Neighborhood Center and near the baseball field as well as an outdoor shower at the far end of the park (right on the highway facing the beach). Every Saturday at 9am, a modest farmers' market sets up shop next to the tennis courts. Kekaha's main attraction, the glistening white Kekaha Beach Park, runs alongside the highway for 1-2 mi., and offers sunbathers plenty of room to find a secluded stretch of sand. However, like at other West Side beaches, strong rip currents tug the waters of Kekaha, and swimmers should note the surf conditions before entering the water. Locals often use the beach for shore fishing. Families with young *keiki* (children) favor the eastern end of the beach, where a small, reef-fringed pool (just east of the church) creates safer waters, while the western end benefits from being close to a lifeguard tower and an outdoor shower. A little further along, just before mi. marker 29, there is a green lawn with four day-use picnic shelters and grills. Small waves break along the entire length of the beach, making Kekaha Beach Park a decent spot for boogie boarders and surfers.

POLIHALE STATE PARK

Outside of Kekaha, Polihale State Park is well worth at least one trip, if not more. Hwy. 50 ends 5 mi. to the northwest out of Kekaha; follow the signs to Polihale, eventually turning left on a dirt road. While trucks full of local teenagers careen merrily down miles of potholes, bumps, and rocks to the park, visitors in modest rental cars may have a more difficult and bumpy—but definitely worthwhile—ride. Ease off the gas and shift into low gear as you navigate through the dry cane fields. About 3½ mi. later, the road forks to the right at a big monkeypod tree, becomes somewhat narrower, and continues for 1½ mi. to the north end of **Polihale Beach.** Along this road a dirt loop branches off to the left toward the ocean and is the access road for a number of campsites. There are a few more campsites and plenty of beach access points beyond the loop toward the northern end of the road, and the whole area has restrooms, showers, water fountains, grills, and pavilions. Camping permits are required. Permits can be purchased at the Division of Forestry and Wildlife Office, 3060 Elwa Street, #306, in Lihue. (☎274-3444. 5-night max. M-F 8am-3:30pm. $5 per person per night.) For more information, see **Camping in Hawaii,** p. 75. The left fork at the monkeypod tree leads south about ½ mi. to a small parking area on the northern edge of Polihale's famous dunes and provides access to the southern end of Polihale Beach. A relatively calm place to swim is **Queen's Pond,** the only section of Polihale protected by a reef. It is a small bay about 100 yd. north of this parking area. The rest of the beach is usually pounded by surf; swimming is possible (not for children) but requires caution. Polihale is for advanced surfers only. The state has posted almost every caution sign it has at this beach—be aware of dangerous shorebreaks, currents, and high surf. The beach itself is an absolute wonder: up to 50 yd. wide, the white sands stretch for 3 mi. along Kauai's western coast, from the military base on the south to the steeply jutting cliffs of the Na Pali Coast to the north. Powerful waves frequently break against the shoreline along the beach, and the water is crystal clear. On a clear day, Niihau can be seen to the southwest.

STUCK IN THE MUCK. When the Polihale State Park road reaches the beach it quickly becomes less hard-packed dirt, and more loose beach sand. Do not proceed without 4WD; you will get stuck! If you do get stuck, try using a low gear, reverse, and step lightly on the gas. If all else fails, you'll have to get out and push.

Even without entering the water, Polihale will leave a strong impression. At the northern end of the beach, past the campsites, the ruins of an ancient *heiau* (temple) are barely detectable at the base of Polihale Cliff. According to legend, the souls of the dead used the cliff as a departure point, springing away from the earth and into the glorious setting sun. As one stands at Polihale, isolated from the rest of Kauai, gazing out over the unbroken Pacific, it's not hard to imagine why Hawaiians considered this a spiritual place. The incredible Polihale **sunset** is best seen from the northern end, where the blazing orange sun paints the clouds a fiery coral pink as it sinks below crashing waves, a sublime conclusion to a day spent relaxing on the beach.

DR. BEACH ON HAWAII'S BEACHES

The Hawaiian Islands are America's tropical paradise. All the beaches in Hawaii are public, and even the most exclusive resorts must provide public access below the high tide level.

The beaches in Hawaii run the gamut in size, shape, sand color, and wave conditions. The white sand beaches are composed primarily of coral, crushed and ground up by powerful waves. This organically derived sand can range from slightly coarse to super fine. On some islands, especially the Big Island and Maui, volcanic sand varies in color from black to red and even green. These sands are exotic, but can be quite hot to walk on, particularly the heat-absorbing black sand.

Hawaii's climate is perfect for beaching, as average temperatures vary little throughout the year, and even when it is rainy on one side of an island, the other side can be sunny. Summer rains are of short duration, making for terrific single and double rainbows.

Few people seem to watch the weather forecast as it is often the same day after day—gorgeous. The real news is the waves, particularly the huge swells that come rolling in during the winter months. The largest ridable surfing waves in the world are found on the North Shore of Oahu at Waimea Bay (p. 156), where professional surfers ride waves that are several stories high. The good news is that beaches exist at every point on the compass so that you can pick your beach according to your desired activity.

The most visited beach in Hawaii is Waikiki Beach (p. 117) in downtown Honolulu, on Oahu. The water temperature at this world-famous beach is always comfortable, ranging from 77 to 82°, winter to summer. This is where surfing on long boards was invented by Hawaii's kings and first witnessed by European sailors. This may be the best place for a surfing lesson or to ride the waves on an outrigger canoe, as Waikiki Beach is protected by an offshore, fringing coral reef. Breakers on the reef provide good surfing conditions, and at the same time, knock down the big waves, making the nearshore waters safe for year-round swimming. Also on Oahu, Ala Moana Beach (p. 101) was carved out of coral reef rock for a boat basin so that the shallow water drops off to a deep channel; the sand was imported to create the beach. Kailua (p. 143) and Laniki are National Winners in my annual survey of America's Best Beaches (see www.drbeach.org).

On Maui, Kapalua Bay Beach (p. 272) was the first National Winner, and 4 mi. Kaanapali (p. 269) is Maui's best-known beach. The coral sand is divided into sections by points of lava rock, providing varying wave conditions. To the south, Wailea is one of Hawaii's newest luxury beach resort destinations. Adventurous beach enthusiasts will want to visit the Makena area to swim at Big Beach (p. 291) and perhaps to climb over the cinder cone to catch a view at Little Beach (p. 292), known for its nudists.

The Hanalei Bay area (p. 385) on the north coast of Kauai boasts the most famous beach on this island—the classic movie *South Pacific* was filmed here. Nearby Lumahai Beach (p. 390) is one of the most scenic and photographed in Hawaii, but it is better for viewing than swimming due to the dangerous waves and currents. At Po'ipu Beach (p. 397), a sand spit has grown in the protective lee of offshore rocks, forming one of the few tombolo beaches in America, so that the conditions range from flat water, perfect for swimming and snorkeling, to the pounding waves for surfers.

The Big Island is still growing, as witnessed by the frequent volcanic eruptions, tremendous lava flows, and ground-shaking earthquakes. The sand at Hapuna (p. 254) beautifully contrasts with the black lava that bounds this half-mile long pocket beach. Nearby Mauna Kea Beach (p. 254, known to Hawaiians as Kaunaoa Beach) has sparkling clear waters for swimming and snorkeling, except during the winter storm season.

Many Hawaiians choose to vacation in Lanai to "get away from it all" and to enjoy the cooler weather on this high island, while Molokai provides a more rural and native experience. Both islands have beautiful beaches; Hulopoe Beach (p. 353) on Lanai is a past National Winner. So whatever your taste in beaches, you are sure to find one (or more likely, many) to suit your desires in the tropical paradise of the Hawaiian Islands.

Dr. Stephen P. Leatherman, *a.k.a. "Dr. Beach," has written 18 books and more than 200 scientific articles about beaches. He is a professor and Director of the Laboratory for Coastal Research at Florida International University in Miami. See www.DrBeach.org for more information about beaches in Hawaii, and www.nhbc.fiu.edu for information on the National Healthy Beaches Campaign.*

GLOSSARY

COMMON HAWAIIAN WORDS AND PHRASES

WORDS		
aina	eye-nah	land, earth
alelo	ah-lay-low	tongue, language
alii	ah-lee-ee	Hawaiian chiefs, royalty
aloha	ah-low-ha	love, hello, goodbye
aole	ah-oh-lay	no, not, never
halau	hah-lau	a hula school
hale	hah-lay	house, hut
haole	how-lay	Caucasians
hapa	hah-pah	portion, part
hauoli	how-oh-lee	happiness
heiau	hey-ee-au	temple
hui	hoo-ee	club, association, group
hula	hoo-lah	Hawaiian dance
imu	ee-moo	underground oven
kahuna	ka-hoo-na	priest
kalua	kah-loo-ah	baked shredded meat
kane	kah-nay	man, masculine
kapu	kah-poo	taboo, forbidden
keiki	kay-kee	child
koa	ko-ah	valuable endemic Hawaiian lumber tree
kokua	ko-koo-ah	help, aid, relief
koloa	ko-low-ah	a duck native to Hawaii
kumu	koo-moo	teacher, tutor
kupuna	koo-poo-nah	grandparent, ancestor
lanai	lah-nye	porch
lei	lay	necklace of flowers
lomilomi	low-me low-me	massage
luau	loo-ow	Hawaiian feast
mahalo	mah-hah-low	thank you
maikai	mah-ee-kah-ee	good, fine
makaainana	mah-kah-ay-nah-nah	common people
makai	mah-kye	toward the ocean
makua	mah-koo-ah	parent, parent generation
malama	mah-lah-mah	to take care of, attend to
mauka	mah-ow-kah	toward the mountains, inland
mele	meh-leh	a song, chant, or poem
menehune	meh-neh-hoo-neh	legendary race of little people
muumuu	moo-moo	loose gown, dress
nalu	nah-loo	wave, to surf

nani	nah-nee	beautiful
nui	noo-ee	big
ohana	oh-hah-nah	family
okole	oh-ko-lay	buttocks
olelo	oh-lay-low	language, word, quotation
ono	oh-no	delicious
pali	pah-lee	cliff
pakalolo	pah-ka-low-low	marijuana
paniolo	pah-nee-oh-low	Hawaiian cowboy
pau	pow	finished
pule	poo-leh	prayer, incantation
pupu	poo-poo	hors d'oeuvre
pupule	poo-poo-lay	crazy
ukulele	oo-keh-leh-leh	"jumping flea," Hawaiian instrument
wahine	wah-hee-nay	woman, girl, female
wai	why	fresh water, liquid, liquor
wiki wiki	wee-kee wee-kee	very fast, speedy
PHRASES		
aloha aina	ah-low-hah eye-nah	love of the land
aloha ahiahi	ah-low-hah ah-hee-ah-hee	Good evening
aloha kakahiaka	ah-low-hah kah-kah-hee-ah-kah	Good morning
aloha kakou	ah-low-hah kah-koo	Aloha to all, Hello everyone
aole pilikia	ah-o-lay pee-lee-kee-ah	No problem, No trouble
kamaaina	kah-mah-ay-nah	"child of the soil," native-born or long-time resident
kanaka maoli	kah-nah-kah mah-oh-lee	full-blooded Hawaiian person
kipa mai	kee-pah mah-ee	You're welcome
mahalo nui loa	mah-ha-low new-ee low-ah	Thank you very much
mai kai	mah-ee kah-ee	I am fine
okole maluna	oh-ko-lay mah-loo-nah	Bottoms up
owai kau inoa?	oh-why kah-oo ee-no-ah	What is your name?
pau hana	pow hah-nah	end of the work day
pehea oe?	pay-hay-ah oh-ay	How are you?

LOCAL FOODS AND DISHES

adobo: pork or chicken in a vinegar and garlic sauce
ahi: yellowfin tuna, which is frequently eaten raw
arare: crisp rice crackers seasoned with soy sauce
azuki: sweetened red or black beans
crack seed: popular snack of dried fruits mixed with salt, sugar, and seasonings
dim sum: Chinese brunch of appetizer-size food (often dumplings) dispensed from carts
haupia: coconut pudding
huli huli chicken: chicken barbecued on spits over an open grill
laulau: pork, butterfish, beef, or chicken wrapped in taro leaf and then baked or steamed in an imu
li hing mui: preserved plum, a type of crack seed
lilikoi: passion fruit
limu: edible seaweed
loco moco: a fried egg on top of a hamburger, served over rice and smothered in gravy
lomi salmon: cold diced salmon, tomatoes, and onion
kalua pig: barbecued pork, cooked whole in an imu

katsu: pork or chicken dipped in bread crumbs and deep-fried, served with a soy-based dipping sauce
kim chee: spicy pickled cabbage seasoned with garlic, chiles, onions, and other spices
kona coffee: coffee from beans grown in the upcountry Kona District of the Big Island
kulolo: dessert made of baked taro root mixed with coconut milk and honey or sugar
mahi mahi: dolphin fish
malasadas: sweet Portuguese doughnuts without a hole
mochi: sweet or sticky rice, made into rice cakes
musubi: rice ball wrapped in dried seaweed
nori: dried, compressed seaweed
onaga: red snapper
ono: similar to mackerel or tuna
opakapaka: pink snapper
opihi: island limpets (a shellfish delicacy)
plate lunch: two scoops white rice, macaroni salad, and a local-style meat or seafood entree
poi: purple paste-like food made of pounded taro root
poke: appetizer consisting of cubed raw fish, marinated and served with seaweed and sesame oil
puna goat cheese: rich creamy cheese from organically raised goats in the Puna District of the Big Island, used in many regional dishes
saimin: Japanese ramen-like noodle soup
shave ice: shaved ice topped with syrup, lighter and flakier than a snow cone
shoyu: Japanese word for soy sauce
Spam: spiced ham in a can
ulu: breadfruit
wasabi: green, Japanese-style horseradish

INDEX

A

Ahihi-Kinau Natural Area Reserve 292
AIDS/HIV. See health.
airports
- Hana 258
- Hilo International 180
- Honolulu International 88
- Kahului International 258
- Kapalua 258
- Lihue 360
- Molokai 324
- Waimea-Kohala 242

Ala Moana Shopping Center 112
Alekoko Fishpond Overlook 367
Aliolani Hale 108
Aloha Stadium 135
animals
- box jellyfish 81
- Hawaiian monk seal 13
- hoary bat 13
- humpback whale 13
- humuhumunukunukuapuaa 14
- *nene* 13
- Portuguese man-of-war 81
- shark 81

annexation 18
Arizona Memorial 133
ATM cards 41

B

Bailey House Museum 280
Battleship Missouri Memorial 134
beaches
- 20 Mile 342
- 69 254
- Ala Moana 105
- Anaehoomalu 253
- Anahola 374
- Anini 381
- Baby Queen's 128
- Baby, Kauai 400
- Baby, Maui 264
- Bellow Field 143
- Big 292
- Black Rock 270
- Brennecke's 401
- Canoe, Maui 270
- Canoes, Oahu 128
- Charley Young Bridge 288
- Chun's Reef 166
- D. T. Fleming 273
- Dig Me 270
- Dixie Maru 347
- Donkey 374
- Duke Kahanamoku 126
- Ehukai 159
- Fort Derussy 127
- Gillin's 402
- Glass 409
- Gray's 127
- H. A. Baldwin 298
- Haena 391
- Halawa Bay 343
- Hale O Lono Harbor 348
- Haleiwa 165
- Hamoa 305
- Hana 304
- Hanakapiai 394
- Hanakeoo 270
- Hanamaulu 366
- Hanapai 381
- Hanauma Bay 137
- Hapuna 254
- Hauula 152
- Hawaiian Electric 174
- Hideaways 384
- Honokowai 272
- Honolii 228
- Honolua Bay 273
- Hookena 196
- Hookipa 299
- Huluopoe 358
- Infinities 411
- Ka Lae 202
- Kaanapali 270
- Kahaluu 188
- Kahana 272, 279
- Kahe Point 174
- Kahekili 270
- Kahili Quarry 380
- Kaiaka 166
- Kaihalulu Red Sand 305
- Kailua 148
- Kaimana 128
- Kalalau 396
- Kalama 148, 287
- Kalapaki 366
- Kalihiwai 381
- Kamakahonu 188
- Kamaole I, II, III 288
- Kapaa 377
- Kapalua 272
- Kawaaloa Bay 339
- Kawailoa 166
- Kawailoa Bay 402
- Keaau 176
- Kealakekus Bay 196
- Kealia 374
- Keawakapu 288, 291
- Keawaula Bay 176
- Kee 391
- Kekaha 420
- Kekaha Kai 188
- Keomuku 357
- Keoniloa Bay 401
- Kepuhi 348, 390
- Kiahuna 401
- Kiholo Bay 253
- Koki 305
- Koloa Landing 401
- Kua Bay 189
- Kualoa 152
- Kuau Bay 299
- Kuhio 128
- Laniakea 166
- Lanikai 148
- Larsen's 374
- Lauhue 347
- Launiupoko Wayside Park 264
- Laupahoehoe Point 239
- Lawai 400
- Left Overs 166
- Little 292
- Log Cabins 159
- Lopa 358
- Lucy Wright 412
- Lumahai 390
- Maalaea Harbor 282
- Mahaulepu 402
- Maili 175
- Makaha 175
- Makalawena 188
- Makapuu 140
- Make Horse 348
- Makena Landing 291
- Maluaka 292
- Maniniowali 189
- Mauna Kea 254
- Mauu Mae 254
- Milolii 196
- Mokapu 291
- Mokuleia Bay 273
- Moloaa 374
- Murphy's 342
- Nanakuli 175
- Napili Bay 272
- Old Kona Airport Park 188
- One Alii 328
- Onekahakaha 228
- Oneloa 273, 292
- Paia Bay 298
- Pakala 411
- Pali Ke Kua 384
- Papakolea Green Sand 202
- Papapa 347
- Papohaku 347
- Pine Tree 188
- PK's 400
- Poipu 401
- Pokai Bay 175
- Polihale 421
- Polihua 357
- Polo 291
- Poolenalena 291
- Popolana 305

Puamana 264
Punalau 273
Punaluu Black Sand 202
Pupukea 159
Puu Kekaa 270
Puu Poa 384
Queen's Bath 384
Queen's Surf 128
Richardson Ocean Park 228
Right Overs 166
Rock Point 342
Rock Quarry 380
Royal Moana 127
Salt Pond 411
Sandy 139
Sans Souci 128
Secret 380
Shark's Cove 159
Shipwreck, Kauai 401
Shipwreck, Lanai 357
Spouting Horn 403
Sprecklesville Town 298
Sunset 160
Swanzy 152
Three Tables 159
Tracks 174
Tunnels 391
Ulua 291
Waialea 254
Waialua 342
Waikiki 127
Wailea 291
Waimanalo 142
Waimanalo Bay Recreation Area 142
Waimea Bay 159
Waipouli 377
Wawaloli 188
White Sands 188
Yokohama Bay 176
Beyond Tourism 66–73
Big Island 179–255
Hamakua Coast 235–246
Hawaii Volcanoes National Park 203–214
Hilo 221–230
Kailua-Kona 181–192
Kau and Ka Lae 199–203
North Kohala 246–252
Puna 214–221
Saddle Road 230
South Kohala 252–255
South Kona 192–199
Waimea 241
Waipio Valley 239
Bishop Museum 110
bling 400
botanical gardens
Allerton Gardens 402
Amy Greenwell Ethnobotanical 198
Enchanting Floral Gardens 309
Foster Botanical Gardens 109
Hawaii Tropical 235
Hoomaluhia 153
Keanae Arboretum, Maui 295
Koko Crater Botanical Garden 138
Kula Botanical Garden 309
Limahuli Garden 391
Lyon Arboretum 110
Maui Agricultural Research Center 309
McBryde Gardens 402
Smith's Tropical Paradise 372
Tropical Gardens of Maui 280
bowling alleys
Maui Bowling Center 281

C

caldera 204
camping 75
Captain Cook Trail and Monument, the Big Island 198
Captain James Cook Memorial, Kauai 414
car insurance 55
car rental 53
Aloha Rent-a-Car 276
Harper Car and Truck 223
Maui Cruisers 276
Paradise Rent-a-Car 120
Rent-a-Wreck 362
VIP Car Rentals 120
Castle & Cooke 349
Centers for Disease Control (CDC) 47
Charles Lindbergh's grave 307
churches
Kaluaaha, Molokai 341
Kawaiahao, Oahu 108
Keawalai, Maui 291
Liliuokalani Protestant, Oahu 167
Mokuaikaua, the Big Island 190
Our Lady of Sorrows, Molokai 341
St. Andrew's Cathedral, Oahu 106
St. Augustine, Oahu 130
St. Benedict's Painted, the Big Island 198
St. Joseph's, Molokai 340
cinder cone 315
consulates 36
Contemporary Museum 109
Cook, Captain James 15
crack seed 25
currency exchange 39
Curtis Wilson Cost Gallery 310

D

dengue fever. See health.
DFS Galleria 131
Diamond Head 129
dietary concerns. See specific concerns.
disabled travelers. See specific concerns.
Dole Plantation 136
Dole, James D. 16
driving permits 55
Duke Kahanamoku Statue 127

E

earthquakes 83
Eleele 408
email. See Internet access, general.
embassies 36
emergency medical services 49
entrance requirements 36
exchange rates. See currency exchange.
Expeditions Ferry 258, 350

F

Fagan Memorial 306
Fern Grotto 372
Flumin' Da Ditch 250

G

Garden of the Gods 356
Gay and Robinson 411
GLBT travelers. See specific concerns.
Glossary 423
golf courses
Cavendish, Lanai 354
Ironwood Hills, Molokai 337
Mini-Golf, Kauai 403
Grove Farm Homestead Museum 367
Guava Kai 382

H

Haena 389
Haiku 299
Halape Shelter 213
Halaway Valley and Bay 343
Haleakala National Park 311
Haleiwa 161
Halona Blowhole 138
Hana 302
Hana Cultural Center 306
Hanalei 385
Hanalei National Wildlife Refuge 389
Hanapepe 409
Hanapepe Valley Lookout 408
Hanauma Bay 137
haoles 21, 27
Hawaii Maritime Center 105
Hawaii Nature Center
Maui 280
Oahu 110
Hawaii State Art Museum 106
Hawaii State Capitol 107
Hawaii Theatre Center 111
Hawaii Volcanoes National Park 203–214
Hawaii's Plantation Village 135
Hawaiian culture

architecture 27
arts 27
customs and etiquette 26
dress 26
film 29
food 25
holidays and festivals 32
literature 28
music 28
religion 22
health
AIDS/HIV 48
dehydration 47
dengue fever 47
food- and water-borne diseases 48
heatstroke 47
immunizations 46
insect-bourne diseases 47
insurance 46
Lyme disease 48
Medic Alert 49
sexually transmitted infections 48
sunburn 47
tick-borne encephalitis 48
heiaus 22, 27
Ahuena 190
Hale o Kapuni 255
Hikiau 196
Hikina A Ka La 372
Iliiliopae 341
Kahea 358
Kaneki 176
Mailekini 255
Mookini Luakini 250
Puu o Mahuka 161
Puukohola 254
Ulupo 149
Waianapanapa State Park 305
high altitude 82
hiking
Aiea Loop Trail 136
Aihualama Trail 115
Alakai Swamp Trail 419
Boundary-Waiohuli Loop 311
Canyon Trail 418
Cliff Trail 418
Halemaumau Trail 211
Halemauu Trail 315
Honokanenui Valley Trail 251
Honolulu Mauka Trail System 114
Iliau Nature Loop 415
Judd Trail 117
Kaena Point Trail 176
Kaiwa Ridge Trail 149
Kalalau Trail 393
Kaluapuhi Trail 419
Keauhou and Puna Coast Trails 213
Kilauea Iki Trail 211
Koaie Canyon Trail 415
Kolowalu Trail 117
Kukui Trail 414
Lahaina Pali Trail 267
Maiwalu Trail 241
Makiki Valley Loop 116
Manoa Cliff Trail 116
Manoa Falls Trail 114
Mauna Kea Trail 234
Mauna Loa Trail 214
Maunawili Ditch Trail 149
Maunawili Falls Trail 150
Maunawili Trail 149
Moleka Trail 116
Munro Trail 355
Napau Trail 212
Nualolo-Awaawapuhi Loop 418
Nuuanu Trail 117
Observatory Trail 234
Pipiwai Trail 307
Polipoli Loop 311
Pololu Valley Trail 251
Puu Huluhulu Trail 212
Puu Ka Ohelo-Berry Flats Loop 419
Puu Pia Trail 117
Sliding Sands Trail 315
Waahila Ridge Trail 117
Waiakoa Loop 311
Waikama Falls Hike 252
Waimea Canyon Trail 415
Hilo 221–230
hitchhiking 55
Hofgaard Park 414
Holualoa 192
Honokaa 236
Honokowai 270
Honolulu 90–117
accommodations 98
arts and entertainment 111
food 100
hiking 114
local transportation 90
nightlife 113
orientation 92
practical information 95
sights 105
Honolulu Academy of the Arts 105
Honolulu Symphony 111
Honolulu Zoo 129
Hoolehua 338
hula shows
Coconut Marketplace, Kauai 373
Ka Hula Piko 347
Kuhio Beach Torch Lighting and Hula Show, Oahu 130
Polynesian, Maui 267
Smith's Tropical Paradise, Kauai 372
Waikiki hotel shows, Oahu 130
Huleia National Wildlife Refuge 368
Hulihee Palace 190
human sacrifice 22
hurricanes 83
Hyatt Shops 131

I

insurance 46, 54
International Driving Permit (IDP) 55
International Marketplace 131
Internet access, general 56
Iolani Palace 107
Ironman Triathlon 31
Izumo Taisha 109

K

Kaanapali 269
Kahakuloa 274
Kahana 270
Kahanamoku, Duke Paoa 32
Kahoolawe 22
Kahului 274
Kahuna Profile 280
Kailua 143
Kailua-Kona 181–192
accommodations 184
activities 189
beaches 188
food 186
nightlife 191
orientation 182
practical information 182
sights 190
transportation 181
Kakahaia National Wildlife Refuge 340
Kalae and Kualapuu, Molokai 336
Kalaheo 406
Kalakaua Park and East Hawaii Cultural Center 229
Kalaupapa Peninsula 331
Kaluakoi, Molokai 346
Kamakou Preserve 334
Kamalo Wharf 340
Kamehameha I 15
Kamehameha's birthplace 250
Kaneana Cave 177
Kaneohe 150
Kanepuu Preserve 357
Kapaa 375
Kapalua 272
kapu 22
Kapuaiwa Coconut Grove 330
Kau Desert 213
Kauai 360–421
East Shore 360–378
Lihue 362–369
Na Pali Coast 392–397
North Shore 378–392
South Shore 397–406
West Shore 406–421
Kauai Coffee 408
Kauai Museum 368
Kauhola Point Lighthouse 252
Kaumakani and Makaweli 411
Kaumana Caves 229
Kaunakakai Ball Park 331

Kaunakakai Wharf 330
Kealakekua Bay 196
Keanae Congregational Church 295
Kekaha 420
Kennedy Theatre 111
Keokea Gallery 310
Kepaniwai Park 280
Kihei 283–290
Kilauea 379
Kilauea Point National Wildlife Refuge 382
Kilohana 368
Kipahulu Valley 306
Koko Crater 138
Koko Head Regional Park and Environs 137
Koloa 404
Koloa History Center 406
Koloa's Sugar Monument 406
Kona Boys Kayaking 197
kosher. See specific concerns.
Kualoa Ranch 155
Kuan Yin Temple 108
Kula 308
Kula Kai Caverns 203

L

La Pérouse Bay 293
Lahaina 259–269
Lahaina Restoration Foundation 266
Lake Waiau 234
Lanai 349–359
- Central Lanai 355
- Lanai City 351
- North Side 356
- South Side 358

Laupahoehoe 239
Lihue 362–369
luaus
- Drums of Paradise, Kauai 403
- Island Breeze Luau, the Big Island 192
- Kona Village Resort, the Big Island 192
- Old Lahaina Luau, Maui 267

Lyman Museum and Mission House 228

M

Maalaea 282
magic dragons
- Puff 385

Magic Island 105
Magnum, PI 30
Makapuu Point 139
Makaua Valley 177
Makawao 317
Makua Cove 177
Makua Military Reservation 177
Malama Cultural Park 331
Manele Bay 358
Manta Ray's Night Dive 190
Manukua State Natural Area Reserve 203
Matsumoto Shave Ice 165
Maui 256–320
- Central Maui 274–281
- Haleakala National Park 311
- Hana 302
- Kihei 283–290
- Lahaina 259–269
- North Shore 293–307
- South Maui 282–293
- Upcountry Maui 307–320
- West Maui 258–274

Maui Film Festival 281
Maui Nei 267
Maui Ocean Center 283
Mauna Loa, the Big Island 234
Maunaloa, Molokai 345
Menehune Ditch 413
Merrie Monarch Festival 228
Mission Houses Museums 108
Mitchell Pauole Center 327
Mokuleia 168
Molokai 322–348
- Central Molokai 331–339
- East of Kaunakakai 339–345
- Kalaupapa Peninsula 331
- Kaunakakai 325–331
- North Shore Sea Cliffs and Wailau Valley 344
- Western Molokai 345–348

Molokai Ice House 330
Molokai Princess 258, 260
Molokai Ranch 345
Moomomi Preserve 338
Mormon Temple 155
movie theaters
- Aloha Theater, the Big Island 197
- Honokaa People's, the Big Island 239
- Kaahumanu 6 Theaters, Maui 281
- Kahilu, the Big Island 245
- Kilauea Theater, Kauai 381
- Kress Cinemas, the Big Island 230
- Kukui Grove Cinemas, Kauai 369
- Lanai Playhouse, Lanai 354
- Maui Mall Megaplex Cinemas, Maui 281
- Movie Museum, Oahu 111
- Palace Theatre, the Big Island 230
- Prince Kuhio Stadium Cinemas, the Big Island 230
- Varsity Theater, Oahu 112
- Waimea Theater, Kauai 413
- Ward 16, Oahu 112

N

Nahiku 295
Nakalele Blowhole 273
Napili 270
Natatorium 128
National Parks 77
Nature Conservancy 334, 338
Nechung Dorje Drayang Ling 203
Nene O Molokai 340
Niaupala Fishpond 341
Niihau 23
Ninini Lighthouse 369
North Shore Surf and Cultural Museum, Oahu 167
Northwest Hawaiian Islands 24
Nuuanu Pali Lookout 154

O

Oahu 88–177
- Central Oahu 133–137
- Honolulu 90–117
- Leeward Coast 171–177
- North Shore 156–171
- Southeast Oahu 137–143
- Waikiki 117–133
- Windward Coast 143–156

Oheo Gulch 306
Oleo Hawaii 21
Olivine Pools 274
Onizuka Center for International Astronomy 232
Our Lady of Fatima Shrine 295
Outrigger Canoe Club 128

P

Pacific Tsunami Museum 229
Pacific Whale Foundation 282
Pahoa 217
Paia 296
Panaewa Rainforest Zoo 229
Parker Ranch Historic Homes 245
Parker Ranch Visitors Center and Museum 245
passports 37
Pearl Harbor 133
Pelekunu Valley Overlook 336
People's Open Markets 112
petroglyphs
- Luahiwa, Lanai 359
- Lydgate State Park, Kauai 372
- Puu Loa, the Big Island 210
- Shipwreck Beach, Lanai 357

Pidgin 21
pineapple industry 16
plate lunch 25
poi 25
Poipu 397
Pololu Valley Lookout 250
Polynesian Cultural Center 154
Pools of Oheo 307
Post-A-Nut 338
Princeville 382
Puaa Kaa State Park, Maui 295

Puff. See magic dragons.
Pukalani 316
Punchbowl National Memorial Cemetery 110
Pupukea 160
Purdy's Macadamia Nut Farm 337
Puu o Hoku Ranch 342
Puuhonua o Honaunau National Historical Park 198
Puukohola Heiau National Historical Site 254

Q

Queen Emma's Summer Palace 154

R

Red Cross 47
rental cars 53
Road from Hana 307
Royal Hawaiian Free Shows and Lessons 130
Royal Hawaiian Shopping Center 131

S

Saddle Road 230
saimin 25
scenic drives
- Chain of Craters Road, the Big Island 210
- Crater Rim Drive, the Big Island 208
- Kahekili Highway, Maui 273
- Mauna Loa Road, the Big Island 210
- Munro Trail, Lanai 355
- Pepeekeo, the Big Island 235

scenic surroundings 86
Sea Life Park 139
Seven Sacred Pools. See Pools of Oheo.
shaka 26
sharks 81
shave ice 25
slack key guitar 28
Smith-Bronte Landing Site 340
Spam 25
specific concerns
- dietary concerns 63
- disabled travelers 62
- GLBT travelers 61
- kosher 63
- minority travelers 63
- solo travel 61
- women travelers 61

sports and recreation 30
- bodysurfing 85
- boogie boarding 85
- kiteboarding 86
- outrigger canoeing 31
- snorkeling 85
- surfing 31, 84
- windsurfing 86

standby flights 51
State Parks
- Puaa Kaa, Maui 295

state parks 78
- Akaka Falls, the Big Island 236
- Haena, Kauai 392
- Iao Valley, Maui 280
- Kaena Point, Oahu 176
- Keaiwa Heiau State Recreation Area, Oahu 136
- Lapakahi, the Big Island 249
- Lava Tree State Park, the Big Island 221
- Lydgate, Kauai 372
- Polihale, Kauai 421
- Polipoli Spring, Maui 310
- Waianapanapa, Maui 305
- Wailua River, Kauai 371
- Waimea Canyon State Park, Kauai 414

statehood 19
Stones of Life 127
studying
- language schools 70
- universities 70

sugar 16
Sugar Mill and Museum 280
sunsets 86
Surfing Capital of the World 162

T

taxes 42
Tedeschi Vineyards 310
Tennet Foundation Gallery 111
The Real World Hawaii 30
TOEFL 70
transportation
- buses 53
- cars 53
- mopeds 55

travel agencies 50
travel visas 38
traveler's checks 40
Tropical Farms 155
tsunamis 83

U

ukelele 28
Ulupalakua Ranch 310
US customs 39
USS Arizona 133
USS Missouri 134

V

Valley of the Temples 153
Victoria Ward Centers 112
visas. See travel visas.
Volcano Village 214
volcanoes 84
- Kilauea 208
- Mauna Loa 210

Volcanoes National Park. See Hawaii Volcanoes National Park.
volunteering
- community outreach 69
- environmental conservation 67
- wildlife conservation 68

W

Wahiawa 136
Waihee Valley 274
Waikiki 117–133
- accommodations 122
- activities 128
- beaches 126
- entertainment 130
- food 124
- local transportation 119
- nightlife 132
- orientation 120
- practical information 121
- shopping 131
- sights 129

Waikiki Aquarium 129
Waikiki Historic Trail 127
Waikiki Shell 130
Wailea 290
Wailua and Mokuleia 168
Wailuku 274
Waimanu Valley 241
Waimea and Sunset Beach 157
Waimea Valley Audubon Center 160
Waimea, Kauai 411
Waimea, the Big Island 241
Waipahu 135
Waipio Valley 239
Waipouli 373
waterfalls
- Boiling Pots, the Big Island 229
- Hanakapiai, Kauai 395
- Hanakoa, Kauai 395
- Hiilawe, the Big Island 241
- Hipuapua, Molokai 343
- Kalauahine, the Big Island 241
- Maunawili, the Big Island 150
- Moaula, Molokai 343
- Rainbow, the Big Island 229
- Twin, Maui 294
- Waikama, the Big Island 252
- Wailua, Kauai 368

Western Union 41
Wet Caves 392
whale-watching 86
wilderness safety 81
work permits 38, 71
working
- au pair work 71
- long-term work 71
- short-term work 72

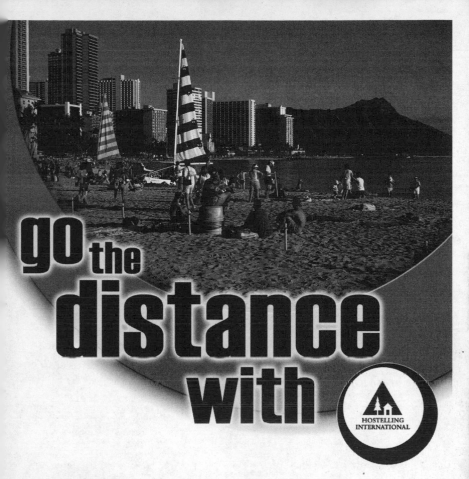

MAP INDEX

Ala Moana 95
Big Island (Hawaii) 180
Eleele to Waimea 410
Haleakala National Park 313
Haleiwa 161
Hamakua Coast 236
Hana 303
Hawaii x-xi
Hawaii Chapters vi
Hawaii Volcanoes National Park 205
Hilo 222
Honolulu and Vicinity 91
  Honolulu, Chinatown and Downtown 99
  Honolulu, Downtown 93
Honolulu Mauka Trails 115
Kaanapali Area Beaches 269
Kahului and Wailuku 275
Kailua 145
Kailua-Kona 183
Kauai 361
Kaunakakai 326
Kihei 283
Kohala Coast 247
Lahaina 259
Lanai 349
Lanai City 351
Leeward Coast, Oahu 172
Lihue, Downtown 365
Lihue Region 363
Maui 257
Molokai 323
North Shore and Upcountry Maui 293
North Shore Kauai 378-379
North Shore Oahu 156
Oahu 89
  Oahu, Central 134
Poipu and Koloa 398
Puna 215
Saddle Road 232-233
South Kona 193
Southern Kau District 199
Waikiki 118-119
Waimea (Big Island) 242
Waimea (Kauai) 413
West Kauai 407
Windward Oahu 142

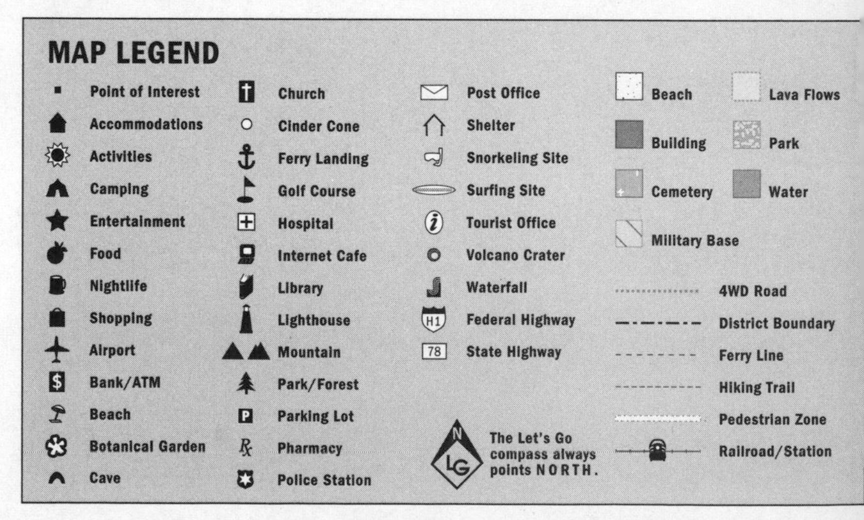